Eastern Europe at the Turn of the Twenty-first Century

> Of the few authors sufficiently knowledgeable to write on all the thirty-plus countries moving from central planning to the market, Ian Jeffries is outstanding … Ranging from front-rank EU candidates to barely changed Cuba and North Korea, this short sequence of books promises to be a 'must buy' for any university library.
>
> Professor Michael Kaser (Universities of Birmingham and Oxford)

Following on from Jeffries' *Economies in Transition: A Guide to China, Cuba, Mongolia, North Korea and Vietnam at the Turn of the Twenty-First Century*, published in June 2001, this comprehensive survey of economic and political developments focuses on the countries of Eastern Europe: Albania, Bulgaria, the Czech Republic, Hungary, Poland, Romania and Slovakia. Analysing major political and economic events in these countries from the mid-1990s onwards, the author presents a detailed, extensive and accessible guide.

Providing a unique level of coverage, this book will be an invaluable source of reference for political and development economists, along with all those interested in Eastern Europe.

This book is the second in a short sequence of volumes. The first book was published in the Routledge Studies in Development Economics series. Forthcoming titles will cover the countries of the former Yugoslavia and of the former Soviet Union.

Ian Jeffries is Member of the Centre of Russian and East European Studies at the University of Wales.

Routledge Studies of Societies in Transition

1 **The Economics of Soviet Break-up**
Bert van Selm

2 **Institutional Barriers to Economic Development**
Poland's Incomplete Transition
Edited by Jan Winiecki

3 **The Polish Solidarity Movement**
Revolution, Democracy and Natural Rights
Arista Maria Cirtautas

4 **Surviving Post-Socialism**
Local Strategies and Regional Response in Eastern Europe and the Former Soviet Union
Edited by Sue Bridger and Frances Pine

5 **Land Reform in the Former Soviet Union and Eastern Europe**
Edited by Stephen Wegren

6 **Financial Reforms in Eastern Europe**
A Policy Model for Poland
Kanhaya L. Gupta and Robert Lensink

7 **The Political Economy of Transition**
Opportunities and Limits of Transformation
Jozef van Brabant

8 **Privatizing the Land**
Rural Political Economy in Post-Communist Socialist Societies
Edited by Ivan Szelenyi

9 **Ukraine**
State and Nation Building
Taras Kuzio

10 **Green Post-Communism?**
Environmental Aid, Innovation and Evolutionary Political Economics
Mikael Sandberg

11 **Organisational Change in Post-Communist Europe**
Management and Transformation in the Czech Republic
Ed Clark and Anna Soulsby

12 **Politics and Society in Poland**
Frances Millard

13 **Experimenting with Democracy**
Regime Change in the Balkans
Geoffrey Pridham and Tom Gallagher

14 **Poverty in Transition Economies**
Edited by Sandra Hutton and Gerry Redmond

15 **Work, Employment and Transition**
Edited by Adrian Smith, Al Rainnie and Adam Swain

16 **Environmental Problems of East Central Europe: 2nd Edition**
Edited by F.W. Carter and David Turnock

17 **Transition Economies and Foreign Trade**
Jan Winiecki

18 **Identity and Freedom**
Mapping Nationalism and Social Criticism in Twentieth Century Lithuania
Leonidas Donskis

19 **Eastern Europe at the Turn of the Twenty-first Century**
A Guide to the Economies in Transition
Ian Jeffries

Eastern Europe at the Turn of the Twenty-first Century

A guide to the economies in transition

Ian Jeffries

ROUTLEDGE
Taylor & Francis Group

London and New York

First published 2002 by Routledge
11 New Fetter Lane, London EC4P 4EE

Simultaneously published in the USA and Canada
by Routledge
29 West 35th Street, New York, NY 10001

Routledge is an imprint of the Taylor & Francis Group

Typeset in Baskerville by Taylor & Francis Books
Printed and bound in Great Britain by TJ International Ltd, Padstow, Cornwall

British Library Cataloguing in Publication Data
A catalogue record for this book is available from the British Library

Library of Congress Cataloging in Publication Data
Jeffries, Ian.
Eastern Europe at the turn of the twenty-first century : a guide to the economies in transition / Ian Jeffries.
p. cm.
Covers Albania, Bulgaria, the Czech Republic, Hungary, Poland, Romania and Slovakia. Simultaneously published in the USA and Canada. Includes bibliographical references and index.
1. Europe, Eastern–Economic conditions–1989– 2. Europe, Eastern–Politics and government–1989– I. Title: Eastern Europe at the turn of the 21st. century. II. Title.

HC244 .J43 2002
330.947 21

2001048493

ISBN 0–415–23671–1

Contents

List of tables xii
Acknowledgements xiii

Introduction and overview **1**

Albania: a summary 4
Bulgaria: a summary 19
The Czech Republic: a summary 30
Hungary: a summary 33
Poland: a summary 36
Romania: a summary 40
Slovakia: a summary 59
Lessons of the first decade of economic transition: a summary 63

PART I
The countries of Eastern Europe **65**

1 Albania **67**

Politics **67**
The political background 67
The Greek minority 68
Political developments from 1 July 1992 until the May–June 1996 general election 70
The May–June 1996 general election 73
Political developments after the May–June 1996 general election 76
And the pyramids came tumbling down 77
The 29 June and 6 July 1997 general election 91
Political developments after the 1997 general election 91

The economy **100**
Alia's economic reforms *100*
Economic policy after mid-1991 *101*
Privatization *104*
Foreign aid and debt *107*
Foreign direct investment *108*
Agriculture *110*
Economic performance *113*

2 Bulgaria **116**

Politics **116**
The general election of 18 December 1994 *116*
Political developments after the 18 December 1994 general election *116*
The general election of 19 April 1997 *121*
Political developments after the April 1997 general election *122*

The economy **133**
The financial crisis *133*
Privatization *142*
Foreign trade *150*
Foreign direct investment *151*
Agriculture *151*
Economic performance *155*

3 The Czech Republic **156**

Politics **156**
The political background *156*
Political developments from January 1993 until the 1996 general election *157*
The general election of 31 May–1 June 1996 *158*
Political developments after the 1996 general election *160*
The general election of 19–20 June 1998 *165*
Political developments after the 1998 general election *166*

The economy **179**
Privatization *188*
Foreign trade *196*
Foreign direct investment *197*
Agriculture *198*
Economic performance *201*

4 Hungary **202**

Politics **202**
The demographic background *202*
Political developments prior to the 1994 general election *202*
The 1994 general election *203*
Political developments after the 1994 general election *205*
The general election of May 1998 *208*
Political developments after the 1998 general election *212*

The economy **222**
Macroeconomic stabilization *222*
Privatization *224*
Foreign trade *230*
Foreign direct investment *232*
Agriculture *235*
Economic performance *238*

5 Poland **240**

Politics **240**
Political developments between the November 1995 presidential election and the general election of September 1997 *240*
The general election of 21 September 1997 *244*
Developments after the 21 September 1997 general election *247*

The economy **268**
'Big bang'/'shock therapy' *268*
Privatization *276*
Foreign trade *293*
Foreign direct investment *295*

6 Romania **297**

Politics **297**
The political background *297*
The Hungarian minority *297*
The German minority *300*
Political developments from May 1993 until the November 1996 presidential and general elections *300*
The 3 November 1996 presidential and parliamentary elections *302*

Political developments after the November 1996 presidential and parliamentary elections 304
The general and presidential elections of 26 November 2000 318

The economy **322**
Privatization 326
Foreign trade 337
Foreign direct investment 338
Agriculture 341
Economic performance 346

7 Slovakia **348**

Politics **348**
The ethnic Hungarian minority and Slovakia's relations with Hungary 348
Gypsies (Roma) 351
The general election of 30 September–1 October 1994 351
Political developments after the 1994 general election 352
The general election of 25–6 September 1998 358
Political developments after the September 1998 general election 359

The economy **365**
Privatization 368
Foreign trade 376
Foreign direct investment 378
Agriculture 379
Economic performance 380

PART II
General issues **381**

8 General issues in the transition from command to market economies **383**

'Big bang'/'shock therapy' versus gradualism **383**
'Big bang'/'shock therapy' 384
Gradualism 388
The quest for compromise 391

The privatization of industrial enterprises **395**
The special problems facing transitional economies in privatizing industrial enterprises 395
The methods of privatization 397

Postscript 408
Bibliography 416
Index 433

Tables

1.1 Albania: selected economic indicators 1990–2000 109
2.1 Bulgaria: the general election of 18 December 1994 117
2.2 Bulgaria: selected economic indicators 1990–2000 134
3.1 The Czech Republic: selected economic indicators 1990–2000 199
4.1 Hungary: the general election of May 1994 204
4.2 Hungary: selected economic indicators 1990–2000 223
5.1 Poland: the general election of 21 September 1997 245
5.2 Poland: selected economic indicators 1990–2000 272
6.1 Romania: the general election of 3 November 1996 303
6.2 Romania: selected economic indicators 1990–2000 340
7.1 Slovakia: the general election of 30 September–1 October 1994 352
7.2 Slovakia: selected economic indicators 1990–2000 366

Acknowledgements

The mammoth task of keeping up to date with rapidly changing economic and political events in thirty-five countries would not have been possible without the help of a magnificent library staff, certain other individuals and the portering/cleaning staff in general. Individuals deserving of particular mention are the following (in alphabetical order): Gwen Bailey (Library); Michele Davies (Library); Dianne Evans (Library); Ray Jones (Library); Nigel O'Leary (Economics); Lis Parcell (Library); Ann Preece (Library); Paul Reynolds (Library); Kathy Sivertsen (Library); Clive Towse (Library); Ray Watts (Library); Chris West (Library).

The earliest possible access to quality newspapers and magazines has, as always, been ensured by the excellent Kays Newsagency, owned and managed by Russell Davies.

Professor Michael Kaser and Professor Paul Hare have continually provided external support and encouragement.

Armenia Economic Trends, *Azerbaijan Economic Trends*, *Belarus Economic Trends*, *Georgia Economic Trends*, *Kazakhstan Economic Trends*, *Moldovan Economic Trends*, *Ukrainian Economic Trends* and *Uzbekistan Economic Trends* are invaluable sources of information which have been provided free of charge. My thanks to all those involved in producing and sending them.

The staff at Routledge have, as always, provided support of the highest degree and professionalism of the highest standard. My thanks in particular (in alphabetical order) go to Yeliz Ali, Oliver Escritt, Tessa Herbert, Alan Jarvis, Liz Jones, Alfred Symons, Annabel Watson, Felicity Watts and James Whiting.

Ian Jeffries
Centre of Russian and East European Studies, University of Wales

Introduction and overview

A Guide to the Socialist Economies was published in 1990. Covering fourteen communist countries (accounting, in mid-1998, for 1.6 billion out of a world population of 5.1 billion), the final amendments to the book had been made in early October 1989. Shortly afterwards communism collapsed in Eastern Europe, followed in late 1991 by the disintegration of the Soviet Union (the largest country in the world by area, covering a sixth of the world's land area excluding Antarctica, and then a 'superpower' able to challenge the USA in terms of military capacity). Yugoslavia also disintegrated, and in a generally very bloody fashion. Academics like myself who had invested a lifetime in studying the communist countries saw their intellectual capital mostly vanish overnight. The effort of trying to comprehend profound changes, in many ways unique events and the multiplication of countries (as well as the disappearance of the GDR into a reunified Germany!) has been staggering.

My first stab at covering what became known as the transitional economies came in 1993 with the publication of *Socialist Economies and the Transition to the Market: A Guide*, which includes analyses of the basic features of command economies and the general issues involved in the transition to a market economy plus chapters on the original fourteen communist countries before 1989 and their individual experiences after 1989 (including the disintegration of the Soviet Union and Yugoslavia). While most countries opted for the market economy and political democracy, Cuba (initially) and North Korea retained the essential features of the traditional communist economic and political system. China, in contrast, adopted gradual and partial economic reform. Vietnam took note of the Chinese model, although there were speedier elements. Both China and Vietnam, however, remained firmly in the grip of the Communist Party.

A Guide to the Economies in Transition was published in 1996. Basically a companion volume to (as opposed to a revised edition of) *Socialist Economies and the Transition to the Market: A Guide*, it covers the period up to the mid-1990s. I am not an economic theorist but the volume includes an overview of the main issues in the transition from command planning to the market (including 'big bang'/'shock therapy' versus gradualism, China as an economic model and privatization). Although I am mostly interested in how economic and political systems actually change, I discuss the basic economic performance of individual countries. Since I am not an econometrician I simply provide readers with an idea both of broad economic magnitudes and of the difficulties of obtaining meaningful data during the transition. The other chapters are devoted to the major political and economic events in thirty-five countries (including the reunification of East and West Germany): the now fifteen independent countries of the former Soviet Union, the countries of Eastern Europe (broadly defined) and the non-European countries (China, Cuba, Mongolia, North Korea and Vietnam).

I am increasing convinced of the artificiality of separating economics and politics. For example, the privatization programmes chosen may be profoundly affected by political factors such as the strength of the central government and whether or not to seek foreign debt forgiveness. I am not a political scientist and I am unable to interrelate the two disciplines to a desirable degree. Instead, I do attempt to do two things: (1) provide a basic guide to understanding how all the 'bits' fit together, and (2) present a richly endowed 'quarry' of up-to-date economic and political information (often presented chronologically where appropriate) to allow the reader to dig out any desired facts and figures.

This is not (and is not meant to be) original research but a broad-brush painting of the overall economic and political picture. I make use of a range of secondary sources in English (necessary given the large number of languages involved). Apart from journals and books, the sources include the following:

1 Reports such as the European Bank for Reconstruction and Development's (EBRD's) *Transition Report*, the United Nations' *World Economic and Social Survey*, the United Nations Economic Commission for Europe's *Economic Survey of Europe*, the United Nations Economic and Social Commission for Asia and the Pacific's *Economic and Social Survey of Asia and the Pacific*, the World Bank's *Transition*, the IMF's *World Economic Survey* and the OECD's *Economic Outlook.*
2 Quality newspapers such as the *International Herald Tribune* (*IHT*), *Financial Times* (*FT*), *The Times*, the *Guardian*, the *Independent*, the *Telegraph* and the *Baltic Times.*
3 Weeklies such as *The Economist* and the *Far Eastern Economic Review* (*FEER*).
4 Quarterlies/monthlies/fortnightlies such as *Business Central Europe*, *Eastern Europe* (*EEN*, formerly *Eastern Europe Newsletter*), *The World Today*, *Asian Survey*, *Current Digest of the Post-Soviet Press* (*CDSP*, before 5 February 1992 known as *Current Digest of the Soviet Press*), *Transition*, *Finance and Development*, *Armenia Economic Trends* (*ARET*), *Azerbaijan Economic Trends* (*AET*), *Belarus Economic Trends* (*BET*), *Georgia Economic Trends* (*GET*), *Kazakhstan Economic Trends* (*KET*), *Moldovan Economic Trends* (*MET*), *Russian Economic Trends* (*RET*), *Ukrainian Economic Trends* (*UET*) and *Uzbekistan Economic Trends* (*UZET*).

A review in the *Times Higher Education Supplement* (29 October 1993) kindly referred to my 'meticulous referencing', even though detailed referencing has the potential to be tiresome to readers. But since this is not original research and I am deeply indebted to many sources, I feel it necessary to make every effort to acknowledge the material used. It is not always feasible to name the correspondents or contributors, but I try, as far as possible, to ensure that credit goes where it is due. Partly for this reason and partly for accuracy I make extensive use of quotations, although where these include commonly quoted sayings or speeches I leave out specific sources.

My task in these four companion volumes is to cover mainly the period from the mid-1990s up to the turn of the century. I once naively thought that things would 'settle down' and that the follow-up volume (in the singular!) would be smaller than the 1996 one. Far from 'settling down', the amount of economic and political material to be processed has expanded almost exponentially! Routledge has kindly supported me in the gargantuan task of writing four separate volumes:

1 *Economies in Transition: A Guide to China, Cuba, Mongolia, North Korea and Vietnam at the Turn of the Twenty-First Century*

This was published in June 2001. The rationale for a separate volume was significantly enhanced by China, North Korea and Cuba on occasion being at the centre of world attention. China's rapid economic progress has aroused considerable interest worldwide in China as an economic model of gradualism. China is increasingly participating in globalization (witness events such as its prospective entry into the WTO). Its economic progress has enormous implications in terms of international affairs. Hong Kong and Macao have been reclaimed but relations with Taiwan remain edgy. China's human rights record is often the cause of friction, especially with the USA. The June 2000 summit between the leaders of North and South Korea turned out to be a dramatic event after decades of bitter division. The Elian Gonzalez case and the actions of his Miami relatives had important implications for US policy towards Cuba. Mongolia continues to provide a fascinating case study of continued commitment to market-orientated economic reform despite political squabbling and changes of government. Vietnam's attitude to economic reform has fluctuated. The Asian financial crisis, for instance, dampened enthusiasm. But in July 2000 the trade agreement with the USA was signed after a year's delay and greater encouragement has been given to the private sector and foreign direct investment.

2 *Eastern Europe at the Turn of the Twenty-First Century: A Guide to the Economies in Transition*

Part I covers Albania, Bulgaria, the Czech Republic, Hungary, Poland, Romania and Slovakia.

Part II deals with general issues, relating to topics such as 'big bang'/'shock therapy' and privatization. These issues are best analysed in this volume, e.g. Poland in 1990 was the first country to adopt 'big bang'/'shock therapy'. The major issues relating to German reunification have already been dealt with in the

1993 and 1996 volumes. The only thing I thought worth including in this volume is privatization in the eastern part of Germany as a revealing case study.

3 *The Former Yugoslavia at the Turn of the Twenty-First Century: A Guide to the Economies in Transition*

The countries covered are Bosnia-Hercegovina, Croatia, the Former Yugoslav Republic of Macedonia, Slovenia and the Federal Republic of Yugoslavia (Serbia and Montenegro).

4 *The Former Soviet Union at the Turn of the Twenty-First Century: A Guide to the Economies in Transition*

The countries covered are Armenia, Azerbaijan, Belarus, Estonia, Georgia, Kazakhstan, Kyrgyzstan, Latvia, Lithuania, Moldova, Russia, Tajikistan, Turkmenistan, Ukraine, Uzbekistan.

Albania: a summary

Albania's transition can be described as a descent into lawlessness. But its support of Nato in the wars in the former Yugoslavia has had a positive effect internally. The Kosovo crisis brought not only Nato troops and increased Western aid into Albania, but also a measure of orderliness.

During the war in Bosnia, Berisha had generally strong support from the Western countries, especially the USA, for keeping Albania out of the limelight. Despite Albania profiting from largely ignoring international sanctions against the Bosnian Serbs and the Federal Republic of Yugoslavia, Berisha was acclaimed for not stirring nationalist passions about the ethnic Albanians in Kosovo and Macedonia in particular. (Albania's population is some 3.5 million. Another 2.5 million ethnic Albanians live in Kosovo, Montenegro, Macedonia and Greece, while an estimated 7 million people of Albanian descent live in Italy, the USA and Turkey: *Punch*, 29 March–4 April 1997, p. 12.) But after the Bosnian war the USA in particular became very critical of Berisha for his increasingly authoritarian behaviour.

It is difficult to know how many ethnic Greeks there were in Albania before the flood of refugees in the 1990s. The Albanian government claimed some 60,000, while the Greek government typically claimed around 300,000. Relations with Greece have improved after a string of incidents. On 25 June 1993, for example, Albania expelled a Greek Orthodox priest, accusing him of stirring up secessionist feeling among the minority Greeks in southern Albania. He allegedly distributed literature claiming that the area was Greek territory (namely North Epirus, the name given by Greek nationalists to southern Albania). The next day, in retaliation, Greece started to expel large numbers (possibly up to 30,000 as of July 1993) of (mostly) illegal Albanian immigrants. *EEN* put the total number eventually deported at over 120,000 (15 March 1995, vol. 9, no. 6, p. 4). (There were originally perhaps up to 300,000 Albanian in total working in Greece. According to *The Economist*, some 400,000 Albanians work abroad, mostly illegally, in Greece and Italy, sending home more than $450 million a year: 18 May 1996, p. 51.) There were also incidents along the border. Greek retaliation took forms such as the expulsion of more Albanians and the blocking of EU financial aid. But the Greek foreign minister visited Albania in March 1995 and this was quickly followed by the signing (on 21 March) of a 'friendship and co-operation' treaty.

The July 1990 'invasion' of various embassies in Tirana was resolved by allowing the 6,000 or so would-be emigrants to leave the country. This proved to be the harbinger of worse to come. Student pro-democracy protests in Tirana began on 9 December 1990. These spread to other towns and other groups such as workers (e.g. the steel centre of Elbasan).

On 11 December 1990 a Central Committee meeting expressed the opinion that 'it is to the benefit of the further democratization of the country's life and of pluralism to create political organizations in accordance with the laws in force'. The next day the Democratic Party was founded by students and by intellectuals such as Gramoz Pashko and Sali Berisha, the first independent party since 1944. Its newspaper, *Democratic Renaissance*, was first published on 5 January 1991, following the formal authorization of opposition newspapers on 28 December 1990. Other parties followed. The decree legalizing independent parties was issued on 17 December 1990 (approved two days later).

Violent protests erupted and were contained by the police and army. A mass exodus started in December 1990, especially members of the Greek minority at first, and there was some loss of life. By mid-April 1991 all 300-plus Jews had left for Israel. (As is often the case, minorities feared discrimination in the new nationalistic environment.) Some Albanians, mainly non-Greeks, returned, but a mass general exodus started again at the end of February 1991. There were further disturbances in the early months of 1991. On 20 February 1991 President Ramiz Alia appointed a new government and took direct presidential control of it. Fatos Nano became prime minister. Another mass exodus started in August due to the dire economic conditions. At the beginning of July 1992 around 6,000 people tried to commandeer ships in two ports and in January 1993 thousands again tried to flee to Italy.

The first free election in the post-war period took place on 31 March and 7 April 1991. The Party of Labour of Albania (PLA) won the election fairly comfortably, although relying on the countryside (where there was a fear of large private landowners returning) and the south. The PLA had held a special conference on 26 December 1990 in order to draw up an election manifesto. The political programme included a promise of 'non-stop' democratic reform and market-orientated economic reforms. At the post-election congress held 10–13 June 1991, the PLA changed its name to 'The Socialist Party' and Fatos Nano was elected president. Its new programme identified itself with the principles advocated by European social democratic parties. It supported the creation of a market economy, although reforms were to be introduced gradually and planning still had an important role to play; privatization received support, but the party favoured preservation of agricultural co-operatives and state control of vital industries.

The Democratic Party's election manifesto pledged a Western-style political democracy. It made no bones about the fact that it favoured the rapid introduction of a market economy based on private ownership. The Democratic Party boycotted the opening of the new parliament in protest at the loss of life during the anti-PLA demonstrations. Its call for a one-day strike, however, met a mixed and rather muted response. But a general strike started on 16 May 1991. About half the urban workforce may have been involved at peak. On 4 June the prime minister Fatos Nano resigned and was replaced by Ylli Bufi (the then minister of food) the next day. There was a return to work on 8 June; a 50 per cent pay increase was conceded as part of a no-strike deal until the new election.

A government of 'national stability' was set up on 12 June 1991. Six political parties were represented, but the individual members of the coalition government were detached from their parties during its temporary period of office. The Socialist Party (the new name for the PLA) was allotted ten of the twenty-two cabinet positions, including interior and foreign affairs. The Democratic Party was given defence and most economic portfolios. Gramoz Pashko became the deputy prime minister and economics minister with overall responsibility for the economy, while Genc Ruli became finance minister. The opposition agreed to participate in order to prevent chaos, which, in turn, could lead to a state of emergency or even a military coup.

As 1991 wore on, the economic situation turned increasingly desperate, with looting, rioting and general lawlessness. On 4 December Sali Berisha pulled the seven Democratic Party members out of the coalition government on the grounds that there was a need to bring forward the date of the next election, that the socialists were destabilizing society in the hope of discrediting democracy and that more should be done to bring former communist officials to book. But the Democratic Party itself started to split, with Gramoz Pashko at loggerheads with Berisha over the wisdom of leaving the coalition and over Berisha's increasingly authoritarian and clannish behaviour. (Berisha is from the north of Albania.) Pashko was actually expelled from the party after the election (on 29 June 1992, to be precise). Pashko and other ex-members of the Democratic Party formed the Democratic Alliance in November 1992.

On 11 December 1991 a new prime minister was appointed. Vilson Ahmeti was a non-partisan technocrat, an engineer and food minister. A new election was arranged.

The Democratic Party convincingly won the general election of 22 and 29 March 1992. The party and its allies, the Social Democratic Party and the Albanian Republican Party, secured between them the two-thirds of seats necessary to change the constitution.

Ramiz Alia resigned as president on 3 April 1992 and he was replaced by Sali Berisha on 9 April. Presidential powers were increased, e.g. the ability to give direct orders to members of the government. Alexander Meksi became prime minister on 14 April 1992 and Eduard Selami became chairman of the Democratic Party. The new premier outlined an economic programme of marketization and privatization on 18 April 1992. Meksi stated that: 'The Albanian economy is going through its worst crisis since the war and there is only one way out – the application of radical reforms in the economy as shown by the experience of former Eastern bloc countries.' What Meksi was referring to was the massive fall in output in 1991, rapidly rising unemployment and galloping inflation.

The Berisha regime became more and more authoritarian and corrupt. The Democratic Party won the May–June 1996 general election amid opposition boycotts and international concerns about the way the election was run.

> Within four years Mr Berisha had created what Human Rights Watch last March [1997] called 'a one-party state based on fear and corruption'. He … turned the justice system into a political instrument. He expanded the National Intelligence Service to a force of 3,000 agents supported by another 3,000 informers which operated as an arm of his party.
>
> (Edward Cody, *IHT*, 5 August 1997, p. 7)

Protests about the failure of pyramid savings schemes started on 15 January 1997. The government was blamed and there were clashes with the police. Pyramid schemes are inherently fraudulent since they can only pay out (high) returns to early investors from fresh funds contributed by later ones. Pure pyramid schemes are backed by nothing but the ability to attract fresh funds until their inevitable demise. What distinguished Albania was the magnitude of the fraud, the seriousness of the consequences and the extent of government involvement:

1 'At their peak the nominal value of the pyramid schemes' liabilities amounted to almost half of the country's GDP. Many Albanians – about two-thirds of the population – invested in them … Albanians sold their houses to invest in the schemes; farmers sold their livestock … The wide appeal of Albania's schemes can be attributed to several factors, including Albanians' unfamiliarity with financial markets; the deficiencies of the country's formal financial system, which encouraged the development of an informal market and, within this market, of the pyramid schemes; and failures of governance … The government was supportive of the companies … During the 1996 elections several of the companies made campaign contributions to the ruling Democratic Party. There were allegations that many government officials benefited personally from the companies … The finance ministry did not warn the public about the schemes until October [1996]' (Jarvis 2000a: 46–7).

   The interim government (set up in March 1997) encountered resistance from both the operators and the outgoing parliamentarians, many of whom were reported to have invested in the schemes. Thus it was not until July that the newly elected parliament passed a law mandating the appointment of foreign administrators from international accounting firms to liquidate the schemes. However, by November 1997, when the administrators took up their duties, the schemes' assets had shrunk considerably. The administrators did not gain full control of all the companies until March 1998. Whatever assets remained were prepared for sale, but much had been lost already (Jarvis 2000a: 46–8).

2 According to some estimates, the savings schemes attracted sums amounting to more than a third of GDP (*FT*, 20 January 1997, p. 2). 'International financial institutions estimate that the funds could have attracted $1 billion, equivalent to more than 30 per cent of the gross domestic product' (*FT*, 27 January 1997, p. 2).

> The absence of a properly functioning banking system has been one of the key institutional deficiencies that has dogged Albania's turbulent emergence from communism. The lack of trust in the state-owned banks and these institutions' inability to develop modern banking services have provided fertile ground for the development of informal financial markets and for the setting up of the string of pyramid schemes, whose progressive collapse has plunged Albania into a political and financial crisis.
>
> (*FT*, Survey, 19 February 1997, p. 14)

> The collapse [took place] three years ago of twenty-four pyramid savings schemes in which savers lost an estimated $1.2 billion … One in three Albanians put their savings into a pyramid scheme … Only the five biggest companies owned assets that could be auctioned to repay creditors … International accounting firms have carried out the liquidation of more than twenty pyramid schemes.
>
> (*FT*, Survey, 23 February 2000, p. 13)

> Investors in Albania's notorious pyramid schemes will get little of their money back, the Albanian government has been told by financial investigators hired to track down $1 billion lost in frauds … PwC, the professional services firm asked by the government to investigate the schemes, has concluded that only $50 million is recoverable … Under pressure from Western lending institutions to adopt credible economic policies, it [the socialist government under prime minister Ilir Mehta] has retracted promises that investors would be compensated in full … At their height they had liabilities equal to half the country's GDP, according to the IMF.
>
> (*FT*, 17 August 2000, p. 6)

3 'Financial pyramid schemes have collapsed with disastrous effects on the social and political texture of the country' (EBRD 1997a: 22). 'These

schemes had attracted funds equivalent to more than half of GDP over the period 1994–96, by exploiting a loophole in the existing legal and regulatory framework' (p. 26).

4 'Losses [have been] incurred by perhaps half of all Albanian families' (*The Economist*, 25 January 1997, p. 43). It is thought that 'more than a third of the population ... have lost their savings in collapsing "pyramid" schemes' (*The Economist*, 1 February 1997, p. 4). 'Berisha ... failed to stop – and his party actually seemed to encourage, in order to raise campaign funds – a proliferation of investment schemes that were bound to collapse' (*The Economist*, 8 March 1997, p. 44).

5 'Fraudulent pyramid schemes in which up to seven Albanian families out of ten have sunk their savings and in many cases their livestock, land and homes ... Because the fraudsters have been visibly on cosy terms with ministers and high-profile contributors to party coffers, the government cannot escape blame' (*The Times*, 27 January 1997, p. 23). Savings lost in the pyramid schemes amount to at least half of GDP (*The Times*, 3 July 1997, p. 25).

6 'Opposition parties have accused the Democrats of using the pyramid schemes to help finance their election campaign, and they have noted that some leaders of the biggest investment schemes have close ties to the government' (*IHT*, 30 January 1997, p. 7). 'Many accuse the government of collusion with those who ran the fraudulent funds, or of failing to take timely action to control the schemes' (*IHT*, 12 February 1997, p. 5).

The human toll involved refugees and loss of life:

1 Nearly 300 people have been killed (*IHT*, 15 April 1997, p. 10). Since the collapse of the pyramid schemes over 700 lives have been lost, many through accidents (*IHT*, 20 May 1997, p. 5). More than 1,500 lives have been lost since March 1997 (*IHT*, 27 June 1997, p. 6; *FT*, 24 June 1997, p. 2; *Guardian*, 26 June 1997, p. 19). 'Some 2,000 people had been killed in the violence that followed the pyramid schemes' collapse' (Jarvis 2000a: 46). 'The violence claimed more than 2,000 lives' (*FT*, 17 August 2000, p. 6).

2 Some 13,000 refugees have fled to Italy (*IHT*, 3 April 1997, p. 5). (More than 40,000 refugees fled to Italy in 1991: *IHT*, 16 April 1997, p. 5.) In the past few weeks over 10,000 Albanians (mostly ethnic Greek women and children) have fled to Greece (*EEN*, 27 April 1997, vol. 11, no. 8, p. 7).

The government banned pyramid savings schemes on 23 January 1997. But violent protests escalated. The first day of large-scale anti-government demonstrations in Vlore occurred on 5 February 1997. Three days later the authorities prevented a demonstration in Tirana. On 9 February clashes occurred between riot police and demonstrators in Vlore. The following day the police lost control of the situation in Vlore. The growing anarchy in Albania was having an inevitably adverse effect on the economy. On 2 March 1997 parliament declared a state of emergency. On 2 March weapons were looted from police and army barracks in towns like Vlore and Sarande (where some 200 prisoners were released by demonstrators). Further pillaging of arms depots took place and Albania became flooded with illegal weapons. Armed gangs were strengthened. Arms amnesties were largely ineffective. Lawlessness spread rapidly. More and more Albanians tried to flee the country, especially to Italy. ('An innovative scheme [has been] started by the United Nations Development Programme [UNDP] to try to mop up some of the half million weapons that fell into civilians' hands when army depots were looted in the 1997 pyramid fund riots. Over the past year the UNDP has been collecting arms and ammunition in return for repairing local roads and utilities in the central Albanian town of Gramsh … Some 6,000 weapons and nearly 140 tonnes of munitions have been turned over to the UNDP, which plans to extend its Gramsh pilot project elsewhere': *FT*, Survey, 23 February 2000, p. 16.)

An EU delegation arrived on 7 March 1997. Berisha appeared on television on 9 March accompanied by opposition leaders. He accepted the need for a transitional government of 'national reconciliation' representing all political parties (and equally split between the Democratic Party and the opposition) and for fresh parliamentary elections within two months. On 11 March 1997 Bashkim Fino of the Socialist Party was named as interim prime minister. The new government was sworn in on 13 March 1997, but prime minister Fino declared that 'We are on the brink of civil war'.

On 16 March 1997 OSCE recommended international military intervention. EU foreign ministers agreed to send a small team of advisers to act in 'civilian as well as police and military fields' to 'help Albania restore civilian structures and law and order'. They also agreed to join OSCE, Greece and Turkey in a delegation whose aim was to be mediation. (Strong advocates of military intervention included France, Italy, the Netherlands, Denmark and Greece, while strong opponents include the UK, Germany and Sweden.)

On 24 March 1997 Albania and Italy agreed on an Italian naval blockade to stem the flood of refugees. (Italian vessels already patrolled Albanian territorial waters, with Albania's permission. But vessels filled with refugees, usually organized by criminal gangs for payment, continued to sail towards Italy.) EU foreign ministers agreed on an Ecu 2 million food and medical aid package (*The Times*, 25 March 1997, p. 12). On 28 March 1997 the UN Security Council approved, for three months, an international force (led by Italy) to protect aid deliveries to Albania.

On 9 April 1997 Socialist Party MPs attended parliament for the first time since the May–June 1996 election (*EEN*, 1997, vol. 11, no. 7, p. 5).

On 9 April 1997, despite political difficulties, the Italian government gained the approval of the Italian parliament to send a 2,500-strong force to Albania. The initial aim was to secure the ports of Durres and Vlore and the airport at Tirana. An advance contingent of Italian troops arrived in Albania on 11 April to prepare for the arrival of the main force. An advance contingent of French troops arrived in Albania on 12 April. The main international force began arriving on 15 April. Named 'Operation Alba' ('Operation Sunrise') by Italy, the 6,000-strong force was made up of troops from Italy (2,500), France (1,000), Greece (800), Turkey (600–800), Spain (450), Romania (400), Austria (120) and Denmark (60).

A general election was held on 29 June and 6 July 1997. On 19 July 1997 the first withdrawal of troops from the international force took place. (The mandate expired on 12 August.) Berisha resigned as president on 23 July 1997 but he remained in parliament as head of the Democratic Party. On 24 July 1997 parliament elected Rexhep Meidani (Socialist Party) as president. Parliament also lifted the state of emergency and the curfew. On 29 July 1997 the new government was approved by parliament. The coalition government comprised the Socialist Party (led by prime minister Fatos Nano), the Democratic Alliance (led by interior minister Neritan Ceka), the Social Democratic Party (led by Skender Gjinushi), the Agrarian Party (led by agriculture minister Lufter Xhuveli) and the Union for the Protection of Human Rights (led by Vasil Melo).

On 11 August 1997 the last troops of the international force left. (Some 600 Italian troops moved in afterwards, e.g. to guard ports and border crossings.)

The Democratic Party has repeatedly boycotted parliament.

On 18 September 1997 a Socialist Party MP shot a Democratic Party MP in parliament and was charged with attempted murder.

On 13 September 1998 about 2,000 supporters of Sali Berisha's Democratic Party set fire to cars outside the interior ministry and stormed and set fire to the prime minister's office in Tirana, claiming that Fatos Nano's Socialist Party had had Azem Hajdari (a leading Democratic Party deputy) assassinated the day before. The prime minister and other cabinet ministers fled. (Both Hajdari and Berisha come from Tropoje in northern Albania, a part of the country that is not under government control and is the centre of arms smuggling to Kosovo. Both have claimed that the Albanian government is not doing enough to support ethnic Albanians in Kosovo.)

On 14 September 1998 the funeral took place in Tirana of Azem Hajdari (and two of his bodyguards). Armed pro-Berisha supporters temporarily took control of the parliament building, the offices of the prime minister and the state television and radio station. Government forces killed three rioters. Fatos Nano believed this was an attempted coup.

On 15 September 1998 about 3,000 pro-Berisha supporters staged an unauthorized but peaceful demonstration in Tirana. The following day about 3,000 pro-Berisha supporters staged another peaceful demonstration in Tirana.

On 18 September 1998 parliament lifted the immunity from prosecution of Sali Berisha, clearing the way for prosecutors to charge him with attempting a coup.

Fatos Nano resigned as prime minister on 28 September 1998.

> In a letter to President Meidani, Mr Nano said on Monday [28 September] he had stepped down because squabbling had made it impossible to form a new cabinet of his five-party coalition government. He told the president he

> had been unable to put together a new cabinet according to his own wishes. He acknowledged his responsibility 'for everything this government has not done' and said that 'the chances of coming out of the crisis are little'.
>
> (*FT*, 30 September 1998, p. 3)

> The demise of premier Fatos Nano had been a virtual certainty since his disappearance in the wake of the mid-September coup attempt by the opposition Democratic Party [DP] led by Sali Berisha … Nano was taken totally by surprise when the DP mob stormed his office, which inexplicably was guarded only by two or three people. Having fled the building and reportedly driven to Macedonia or Greece, he went to ground for a couple of days, leaving [President] Meidani and [Pandeli] Majko to hold the ring. Meidani addressed the nation on television … Meidani, in his capacity as commander-in-chief of the armed forces, and in the absence of the hiding Nano, had called in the special forces and put Berisha's motley army to rout.
>
> (*EEN*, 1998, vol. 12, no. 11, pp. 1–2)

On 29 September 1998 the governing Socialist Party nominated the 30-year-old Pandeli Majko, its secretary-general, to succeed Fatos Nano as Albania's prime minister at the head of a five-party coalition. He was sworn in on 2 October 1998.

On 21 July 1999 the Democratic Party ended its twelve-month boycott of parliament (*EEN*, 1999, vol. 12, no. 19, p. 2).

On 11 October 1999 Fatos Nano narrowly defeated prime minister Pandeli Majko in the contest for chairman of the Socialist Party. The latter resigned as prime minister on 26 October 1999. The following day deputy prime minister Ilir Mehta became prime minister. (He won a vote of confidence in parliament on 5 November.)

On 6 November 1999 a faction within the Democratic Party, led by Genc Pollo, set up the 'Democratic Alternative' to oppose the Berisha wing of the party. On 7 December the Democratic Party suspended the party membership of Genc Pollo after accusations that he had failed to disclose the origin of private funds used to buy real estate in Tirana (*EEN*, 1999, vol. 12, no. 21, p. 4). 'The opposition Democratic Party is split, with the moderates under Genc Pollo forming a "Democratic Alternative" faction that is attending parliament in contrast to the bulk of the Democratic Party under Berisha which continues its parliamentary boycott' (p. 7). On 1 February 2000 the Democratic Party expelled former secretary-general Genc Pollo and three other leading moderates. 'The Democratic Party continues to fragment following a move by a dozen Democratic Party parliamentarians under former Democratic Party secretary Genc Pollo to establish a new anti-Berisha Democratic Party wing. Pollo and his associates were sacked on 1 February' (*EEN*, 2000, vol. 12, no. 22, pp. 2, 4).

The Socialist Party did well in the OSCE-monitored local elections held in October 2000 and was returned to power in the OSCE-monitored June–July

2001 general election. The relatively peaceful election reflected the generally more settled political and economic times.

After mid-1991 post-communist Albania quickly became heavily dependent on Western economic aid. Italy has been the country most directly affected by the flood of refugees and has provided generous assistance, especially food (partly, of course, in order to try to stem the flow). Other important sources of income are remittances from the many Albanians working abroad and profits earned from evading economic sanctions imposed on Serbia. Foreign investment is encouraged, but the response even before the descent into lawlessness was poor. (See Table 1.1, p. 109.) There were signs of recovery as the political situation stabilized somewhat.

The coalition government adopted an essentially 'big bang'/'shock therapy' economic programme in June 1991 (Åslund and Sjöberg 1991: 13–20). The Berisha regime's IMF-inspired economic reform programme was supposed to have been introduced on 1 July 1992, but most of it was postponed because of the imminent 26 July local elections (in which the Democratic Party's share of the vote fell considerably and the Socialist Party came out on top). The programme eventually included austerity measures to reduce the huge budget deficit and a devaluation of the lek. The lek was floated and became convertible on current account (strict controls still existing on the capital account). Foreign trade was liberalized. There is a managed floating exchange rate (EBRD 1999b: 182).

'Full membership of the WTO for Albania was ratified in July 2000, with formal accession taking place in September 2000 … Since October 1999 the EU has granted unilateral trade preferences to Albania' (EBRD 2000b: 126).

> [On 18 September 2000 EU foreign] ministers … approved an EU package granting duty-free access to 95 per cent of imports from Albania, Bosnia, Croatia, Macedonia and Montenegro … The package includes abolition of tariffs on most industrial and farm products to the EU. However, some limits remain on exports of fish products and wine.
>
> (*FT*, 19 September 2000, p. 10)

'The EU in 1999 took some 94 per cent of exports (mainly to Italy, Greece and Germany) and supplied around 80 per cent of imports' (Kaser 2001: 53).

Price liberalization was rapid and the private sector expanded very quickly. The private sector accounted for roughly 5 per cent of GDP in mid-1990. In mid-2000 the figure was 75 per cent (EBRD 1999b: 24, 184; and 2000b: 14, 128).

The GDP growth rate turned positive as early as 1993. Output fell heavily in 1997 (by 7 per cent) as a result of the anarchic conditions (which began in earnest at the start of that year) but there was a strong resurgence thereafter. In 2000 GDP in transitional Albania exceeded its 1989 level for the first time (EBRD 2001: 15). Inflation did not reach hyperinflationary levels in the 1990s, reaching a peak of 226 per cent in 1992. By 1999 consumer prices were more or less stable.

Small privatization proceeded very quickly from 1991 onwards. According to the August 1991 legislation, the sale of state assets would typically proceed by giving the first option to buy to the employees of the enterprise (Blejer *et al.* 1992: 56–7). Thus many entities were taken over by employees (EBRD 1994: 16).

Large privatization, on the other hand, has been very slow, although many enterprises have been broken up and some parts even closed down. A voucher-based mass privatization programme was approved in early 1995, with voucher distribution to start in June 1995. In the programme a total of 400 medium-sized and large enterprises were to be privatized through auctions. As of July 1996 a total of ninety-seven enterprises had been sold under the programme, with the process expected to be completed by the end of 1998 (EBRD 1996b: 11). Emphasis has been put on finding strategic investors for the remaining large enterprises, but so far only one large privatization has been completed (EBRD 1997b: 148).

> The enterprise restructuring agency set up in 1993 to deal with thirty-two problem firms has been relatively successful in restructuring these firms, reducing employment from 50,000 at their peak to 7,000 at the end of 1995. However, only ten have been privatized and only one smaller enterprise liquidated.
>
> (EBRD 1998b: 148)

> Plans for the privatization of strategic utilities are making gradual progress. However, the electricity company is virtually bankrupt … Non-payment for electricity remains rife both among households and state enterprises … The privatization programme is now centred on selling off remaining small and medium-sized enterprises and privatizing public monopolies in strategic sectors. Out of approximately 470 state-owned small and medium-sized enterprises identified in mid-1998 around 300 had been sold or closed by March 1999. Large-scale privatization is focussed first on the telecoms sector and then on copper and chrome.
>
> (EBRD 1999a: 32)

By mid-1998, 469 small and medium-sized enterprises remained in state hands. Of these, more than 300 had been sold, liquidated, leased or closed down by the end of June 1999. The crisis in Kosovo has contributed to delays in the privatization of large strategic enterprises. The government has liquidated two of the three remaining large loss-making enterprises that had been placed under the control of the enterprise restructuring agency. The Kosovo crisis caused the sale of the third to a foreign company to be delayed (EBRD 1999b: 182–3). The privatization of small and medium-sized enterprises was virtually completed in

1999. The privatization of large enterprises is proceeding slowly (EBRD 2000a: 365).

> After successfully concluding the privatization or liquidation of state-owned small and medium-sized enterprises the government is concentrating on larger enterprises and utilities … Five medium-sized state-owned companies (a brewery, winery, dairy factory, pharmaceutical factory and cement factory) were put up for sale in April 2000 … The sale by the government of the second-largest bank … to Kentbank of Turkey was signed in June 2000. Kentbank bought a 60 per cent stake, with the EBRD and IFC each taking 20 per cent.
>
> (EBRD 2000b: 126–7)

> The privatization of large-scale enterprises is proceeding well. The privatization of five targeted medium-sized enterprises was completed by the end of 2000. Privatization is moving ahead in the natural resources sector, but has been delayed in the energy sector due to an ongoing energy crisis … Following the latest energy crisis at the end of 2000 the government has started to implement a comprehensive package of reforms of the state-owned electricity company, Kesh. Quarterly targets for collecting bills and reducing theft have been established. The privatization of telecommunications advanced significantly in 2000 and early 2001 … Plans for the last remaining state-owned bank, the Savings Bank, are proceeding.
>
> (EBRD 2001: 44)

> The Elbasan steel plant has been revived by Turkish managers … Privatization and foreign investment are slowly taking off … As at Elbasan, foreigners still prefer to lease local firms or take over their management rather than buying them. But the country's GSM mobile operator was sold to a Greek–Norwegian consortium in summer [2000] … Italians have taken over the Tirana brewery – one of four medium-sized enterprises privatized this year … The troubled Albanian Commercial Bank has been rescued by Greek investors, allowing it to resume operations.
>
> (Business Central Europe 2000: 35)

On 14 October 1991 it was announced that church land and property confiscated in 1967 were to be returned. On 19 May 1992 it was announced that all buildings belonging to the Socialist Party were to be seized. In May 1993 a restitution law was passed. In 1995, for example, expropriated urban property would be returned to the original owners or their heirs; in the meantime existing domestic or commercial tenants have to pay rent to the former owners (*EEN*, 1993, vol. 7, no. 13, p. 5; vol. 7, no. 15, p. 8; vol. 7, no. 16, p. 3). According to laws passed in 1993, many former owners or their heirs can claim compensation for or restitution of non-agricultural land. In the case of property that has already been privatized there is co-ownership between the new and former owners (EBRD 1994: 16).

'Only in the countries of the former Soviet Union and in Albania was land legally nationalized' (Swinnen 1999: 641). Property rights to collective farmland have been restituted to former owners only in some mountainous regions (p. 639). Albania distributes its collective farmland among rural households (p. 639). State farmland has been distributed to farm workers. Initially, farm workers received privatization vouchers as state farms engaged in joint ventures. As most joint ventures failed, farm workers then received user rights, but ultimately were allocated full property rights (p. 640).

'The continuing disintegration of the agricultural sector resulted in a virtual collapse of the sector during 1990–1' (Cungu and Swinnen 1999: 608).

> The Land Law of July 1991 specified that APC land was to be distributed free of charge and on an equal per capita basis to member families and other rural residents … A number of other decrees on the distribution of other assets and the liquidation of the APCs supplemented the Land Law … Only 50,000 ha of state farms' land were initially distributed among farm workers. Most of the remainder was pooled into joint ventures with foreign capital … When many of these partnerships failed the land was given to workers for cultivation, with the state retaining ownership. In 1995 new legislation stipulated that use rights could be turned into full ownership rights on ex-joint venture land where disputes over the termination of joint venture contracts had been cleared … The Land Law did not recognize prior land ownership or its precollectivization size and boundaries. This caused strong opposition from the pre-1945 owners … In 1993 the government approved a law on the financial compensation of former landowners … In 1995 a new law was passed that provided for former owners to receive physical compensation in seaside and tourist-site properties.
>
> (pp. 610–11)

'The events of 1997 had relatively little effect on agricultural reforms and performance. Agricultural output grew at a rate of almost 2 per cent' (p. 610).

> Albania is the only country that has distributed all collective land among the rural population. Most other Central and Eastern European countries (CEECs), even the Baltic countries that were part of the former Soviet Union, have restituted collective farmland to former owners. Albania has also distributed most of its state farmland to the agricultural workers, although the breakup of the state farms was not as fast and radical as that of the Agricultural Production Co-operatives (APCs). In most other CEECs state farmland is either restituted (e.g. Slovenia and the Baltic countries) or leased in attendance of being sold. Farm restructuring is also more radical in Albania than in other CEECs … Virtually all land is now being used by small individual farms, unlike in other CEECs where large-scale co-operatives,

joint stock companies, limited liability companies and so forth still occupy an important share of the land.

(p. 605)

All APCs and most of the state farms have been completely broken up into individual farms ... More than 95 per cent of land is used by approximately 490,000 individual private farms in at least 1.9 million separate parcels, with an average of about 3.3 separately located parcels for each farm. The average size is 1.0 ha, ranging between 1.3 ha in valley and foothill regions to 0.8 ha in the mountains.

(p. 611)

As in other CEECs the reference date played an important role in Albania's restitution debate. In all CEECs restitution of land under the 1990s reforms is based on the ownership situation just before collectivization but after the communist-inspired land reforms ... In the Albanian land reform debate 1948 owners – those who owned the land after the communist land reform of 1946–48 – were much less vocal than those in many other CEECs and less opposed to distribution than Albania's pre-1948 owners.

(pp. 613–14)

The key piece of legislation was the 22 July 1991 Land Bill. All local co-operative land was to be redistributed by local committees to co-operative farming families free of charge on the basis of 0.1 hectares per family member. Land could be inherited and the intention was to allow land sales after five years. The aim was to have all co-operative land distributed before the end of September 1991 (this would amount to 80 per cent of arable land). A great deal of unofficial land redistribution took place (including that by former owners), however, and uncertainty over land titles adversely affected production.

Most collective farms were abandoned spontaneously in 1991 and their assets (including the land) were taken over by their members. Legal division of land was not supposed to start before June 1992, but by then 77 per cent of cultivated land was already in private hands. By the end of 1992, 90 per cent of land had been disposed of and 80 per cent of peasant families had become landowners (United Nations Economic Commission for Europe 1993: 203). By March 1992 the average amount of land held was 1.2 hectares for highland families and 1.4 for lowland families (*EEN*, 1992, vol. 6, nos 1, 6 and 8). The average farm consists of 1.5 ha split into 3.3 separate parcels of differing quality (*FT*, Survey, 2 October 1995, p. iii).

Former owners are only allowed to reclaim a maximum of 15 ha from their pre-communist holdings. Alternatively they may seek compensation for up to 30 ha. Compensation is in the form of bonds (*EEN*, 21 September 1994, vol. 8, no. 19, p. 6). Most state farms are now partially or wholly farmed by former employees who hope to receive title to their allotted land in three years or so (*EEN*, 21 September 1993, vol. 7, no. 19, p. 8). Though in the case of state farms the law does allow for transfer of ownership to individuals, in practice this category of private farmer is a tenant. Most of the state farms remain intact, although in several cases individuals have been allowed to use state farm land for their own benefit (*EEN*, 21 September 1994, vol. 8, no. 19, p. 6).

A law passed in August 1995 allowed the buying and selling of farmland for the first time. In order to encourage land consolidation a farmer who wishes to sell must offer it to his family and neighbours before putting it on the open market. The government estimates that 96 per cent of agricultural land has been distributed, but only half has been legally titled (*FT*, Survey, 2 October 1995, p. iii). The sale and purchase of land was originally prohibited. In July 1995 a new law allowed the sale and purchase of agricultural land and transformed the titles to usage of land into property titles (EBRD 1996b: 136).

By the end of 1996, 98 per cent of agricultural land had been privatized. But despite the progress made in privatizing land no land market has developed. The main obstacles are the requirement that all land holdings in a village be registered before any can be sold (only 3 per cent of privatized land having been registered) and the absence of clear mechanisms for establishing the legality of land transactions. The law states that land must first be offered for sale to relatives of the current owner, owners of neighbouring properties, other villagers or ex-owners of the land before it can be offered to anyone else. Few informal sales have taken place (EBRD 1997b: 148). By the end of 1993, 92 per cent of agricultural land had been privatized. But land could not be traded effectively, partly due to the fact that only 3 per cent of land had been registered by mid-1997. A new land law was passed by parliament in May 1998. Whereas previously land could not be sold until all plots in a district had been registered, the new law allows for the sale of land on an individual basis (EBRD 1998b: 148). The authorities have made considerable progress in land registration. By March 1999 land registration had been completed in about 40 per cent of the total land by area. This process is enabling a visible market in agricultural land to emerge (EBRD 1999b: 182).

Some 95 per cent of agricultural production is contributed by private farmers (Deutsche Bank, *Focus: Eastern Europe*, 15 February 1995, no. 125, p. 4).

> Private farmers now own 98 per cent of the country's farmland … Sixty per cent of holdings have now been registered … The country's 550 state farms and co-operatives were parcelled up into some 470,000 family farms, with an average of only 1.1 ha each … [But] around 800 'water users' associations' have been set up to rehabilitate and manage irrigation systems and some other associations have been established for the buying and selling of seeds, fertilisers and pesticides … There are also around 200 farming associations with 40 to 50 ha of cereals and vegetables, and some 100 livestock associations with more than 200 sheep each.
>
> (*FT*, Survey, 23 February 2000, p. 14)

> The privatization process has left land ownership highly fragmented. A 1999 survey showed that there were 466,766 holdings with an average area of 4.1 ha, of which 1.8 ha was agricultural land, 2.2 ha forest and 0.1 ha either built on or in other use. The process of registration of title has led to a large number of disputes, especially in the Geg north and central uplands … The IMF's requirement, introduced in February 1998, to facilitate the functioning of a land market by universal land registration, has largely been satisfied, but it has had adverse social consequences because discrimination against 'outsiders', even those settled for two generations, is creating a class of landless peasants … Peasant self-sufficiency, forced on collective farmers by the communist government's prohibition of private marketing, remains very high … [The survey] showed that 42 per cent of farmers still tilled their land with the aid of animal and manpower alone.
>
> (Kaser 2001: 46–7)

Bulgaria: a summary

Bulgaria has had a rough transition. Things in general are now looking up, but problems such as corruption continue to plague the country. President Petar Stoyanov: 'My most intimate fear is corruption. If our reforms are accompanied by corruption, democracy itself will be threatened' (*The Economist*, 17 June 2000, p. 56).

The Berov government survived a series of no-confidence votes tabled by the UDF (e.g. at the end of May 1993, on 9 February 1994 and on 19 May 1994, its sixth). But it resigned on 2 September 1994 and called for an early general election. On 17 October 1994 Reneta Indzhova was named as interim prime minister until the 18 December 1994 general election. She was the first woman to be prime minister, helped the UDF draw up its economic programme and was a former privatization director.

In the general election of 18 December 1994 the Bulgarian Socialist Party, led by Zhan Videnov (who took over in December 1991), did even better than expected, winning an absolute majority of seats in the National Assembly. Filip Dimitrov, the leader of the Union of Democratic Forces, resigned after the election and was replaced by Ivan Kostov.

On 4 June 1996 it was announced that the members of the Union of Democratic Forces had voted against Zhelyu Zhelev as their candidate for president and chose Petar Stoyanov instead. (Zhelyu Zhelev of the Union of Democratic Forces was elected president on 1 August 1990. He became an internationally respected figure and a force for stability in Bulgaria, favouring a strong political centre ground.) On 15 July 1996 President Zhelev warned of possible mass unrest in the autumn because of political and economic chaos (see below). He reiterated his call for strong presidential rule (*IHT*, 16 July 1996, p. 5). Stoyanov won in the second round of the presidential election held on 3 November 1996.

The socialist government eventually collapsed. Politically Bulgaria had become a democratic state in many regards, with impressively free elections and free media. But the extent of corruption in economic life under the Socialist Party reached remarkable proportions. The failure to implement sufficiently bold economic reforms brought Bulgaria to its knees economically (dealt with in detail below). As then-President Zhelev stated:

> We should not forget that the protests in Serbia are based mainly on political demands and the protests here are based on economic factors and social discontent. The difference is clear, as the average salary in Serbia is $200 and in Bulgaria it is $30.
>
> (*IHT*, 13 January 1997, p. 1)

President-elect Stoyanov echoed this: 'The Belgrade slogans are too abstract for the starving Bulgarians. The Serbians are fighting for political and press freedom. Here, the people are fighting for their survival, to be able to buy bread and keep warm.' Monthly wages are 'between $16 and $20 and the price of bread is 50 cents … We must hold elections at the beginning of June. The people are desperate. They cannot survive on a salary of $20 a month' (*IHT*, 13 January 1997, p. 7). On 20 September 1996 Slavi Pashkovski, ambassador to the UN, denounced Bulgaria's government: 'The ghost of communism is looming over Bulgaria, which means also over the Balkans and over Europe … [Bulgaria's economic failings were] a premeditated plot to make certain people richer and to enslave millions of Bulgarian citizens.'

As the economic situation deteriorated the government survived a series of no-confidence votes in parliament (e.g. on 13 June 1996).

On 2 October 1996 Socialist Party MP and former prime minister Andrei Lukanov was murdered outside his home in unclear circumstances. (Andrei Lukanov, who had been minister for foreign economic relations since August 1987, became prime minister on 4 February 1990. Lukanov was arrested on 9 July 1992 on charges which included misappropriating state funds in the communist era, specifically providing aid to left-wing regimes in the third world.)

On 3 January 1997 demonstrators in Sofia called for early parliamentary elections. (A general election did not have to be held until December 1998.) On 10 January parliament voted against an extraordinary debate on an opposition motion calling for an early general election. Opposition MPs walked out. Some of the people who had been protesting daily since 3 January attacked the parliament building. The following day many were injured as riot police cleared crowds from around parliament and escorted Socialist Party MPs from the building. On 13 January 1997 the Socialist Party issued a statement saying that it was ready 'to accept in principle the idea of holding early parliamentary elections in the context of implementing a national anti-crisis programme for the economic and financial stabilization of Bulgaria'. Warning strikes took place in, for example, coal mines, steel works, hospitals, schools and government offices. A one-hour general strike was held across the country on 29 January 1997 and strikes spread thereafter.

Petar Stoyanov was sworn in as president on 19 January 1997: 'I am convinced that the country needs early parliamentary elections and a new agreement between social forces and between the government and the governed … People are demonstrating in the streets because their poverty has reached desperate levels.' (The president is later quoted with respect to economic reforms: 'Although the first UDF government under Filip Dimitrov started serious reform, most of the last seven years we only had the pretence of reform. We deluded ourselves that we could survive without great sacrifices. But things kept getting tougher and we got deeper and deeper into debt. January [1997] marked the turning point when we shed our illusions': *FT*, Survey, 21 October 1997, p. 32.) 'We were never so close to civil war,' said Stoyanov (*FT*, 5 February 1997, p. 2).

On 4 February 1997 a joint statement issued by the Socialist Party and opposition parties said that the president 'should set early general elections in the second ten days of April'.

On 12 February 1997 the president asked Stefan Sofiyansky (the UDF's mayor of Sofia) to head a caretaker government to run the country until the general election on 19 April.

In the general election of 19 April 1997 the United Democratic Forces coalition, comprising the Union of Democratic Forces (led by Ivan Kostov) and the People's Union (comprising Stefan Safov's Democratic Party and Anastasia Moser's Agrarian Party) won 52.26 per cent of the vote and 137 seats in total (123 seats going to the Union of Democratic Forces and fourteen, split equally, going to the People's Union). (The Union of Democratic Forces had changed from an alliance to a party on 16 February 1997.) Ivan Kostov became prime minister. He and President Stoyanov set a firm course for economic reform and membership of the EU and Nato.

On 16 July 1997 the European Commission recommended that Estonia, Cyprus, the Czech Republic, Hungary, Poland and Slovenia open negotiations in early 1998 for entry to the EU. The invitations were formally approved at an EU summit on 13 December 1997, formal negotiations for membership beginning on 31 March 1998. Slovakia, Latvia, Lithuania, Bulgaria and Romania were to be given special EU aid to help them meet the conditions necessary for membership negotiations to begin.

On 13 October 1999 the European Commission recommended that EU leaders at the December 1999 meeting in Helsinki allow Bulgaria, Latvia, Lithuania, Malta, Romania and Slovakia to begin accession negotiations in 2000. The 'principle of differentiation' for entry date would apply to each of the twelve candidates, reflecting differing states of readiness for EU entry. Bulgaria's time horizon for coping with competitive pressures 'stretches beyond the medium term'. In economic terms Bulgaria is making 'substantial' progress although it 'started from a very low level'. In order to begin negotiations Bulgaria must set 'acceptable' closure dates for four units at the Kozloduy nuclear power plant and must make further progress on economic reform. On 8

November 2000 the EU reported that Bulgaria had generally made progress but still lay second from last behind Romania in terms of membership prospects.

'The Bulgarian Socialist Party ... in its May party conference ... for the first time publicly supported eventual membership of Nato after a referendum (in contrast to previous BSP hostility to Nato membership)' (*EEN*, 2000, vol. 12, no. 23, pp. 4, 8).

In the general election held on 17 June 2001, the former king, Simeon II, became the first royal in the former communist countries to successfully enter domestic politics (becoming prime minister). His recently formed National Movement for Simeon II won the largest single number of seats in parliament. He benefited from the economic pain associated with UDF economic reforms (plus the public perception of pervasive corruption) and from the already tarnished reputation of the Socialist Party. Although his platform was to continue with pro-market, pro-EU and pro-Nato policies, he presented a clean image spiced with populist measures promising to quickly improve living standards generally. He was clearly concerned about the extent of poverty in Bulgaria. The results were somewhat better for the National Movement than even opinion polls had predicted.

The transitional era in Bulgaria has never been easy and has on occasion approached catastrophe. The communist economy was heavily dependent on Comecon (especially Soviet) trade and so the collapse of this trade hit Bulgaria particularly hard.

Although GDP growth turned positive in 1994, output plunged in 1996 and 1997. Since then the GDP growth rate has been positive.

> [In 1999] Bulgaria was affected by a disruption to trade links due to the Kosovo conflict and a weakening of its terms of trade when the currencies of many important trading partners depreciated. The currency board arrangement has helped keep the exchange rate and prices stable, but exports have declined.
>
> (EBRD 2000a: 5)

In 2000 GDP was an estimated 70 per cent of the 1989 level (EBRD 2001: 15). Inflation fell in 1992 but there were extraordinary gyrations thereafter. There was hyperinflation in 1997 but consumer prices were more or less stable in 1999 and the inflation rate was still in single figures in 2000.

Debt repayment has been a headache for Bulgaria. On 16 December 1992 the Paris Club of Western creditor nations agreed to reschedule their share of Bulgaria's foreign debt. On 29 June 1994 Bulgaria signed an agreement with the London Club, which provided for a 47.1 per cent reduction in the $8.16 billion debt to commercial banks. Parliament ratified the deal on 27 July 1994.

Prices were largely freed from state control in early 1991, but controls were later reimposed on a substantial scale. After the financial crisis price liberalization resumed.

In March 1994 the government took steps to refinance some of the bad loans arranged in the socialist era by banks to enterprises, issuing bonds to convert enterprise debt into government debt (*FT*, 29 March 1994, p. 3). A programme implemented during 1994 to recapitalize banks provided 'bad loan bonds' (Zunk bonds) to cover non-performing bank assets (which remain on the balance sheets of banks). The low interest rates have created severe liquidity problems for the banks, which the past government addressed by repeated cash recapitalizations during 1994 (partial repurchasing of the 'bad loan bonds') (EBRD 1995a: 54).

'No large state-owned firm was declared bankrupt until the summer of 1996' (United Nations Economic Commission for Europe 1997: 80). 'The Bulgarian crisis has its origins in the inefficient and unviable state-owned sector of the economy, but due to soft budget constraints and repeated bail-outs it spread to the public finances, the banking system and the financial markets' (p. 81).

> The fundamental roots of the crisis are microeconomic in origins ... The primary source of the Bulgarian financial crisis was the large, unstructured, loss-making state-owned industrial sector and the main policy-related problem was the failure by the authorities to address this issue at an early stage by restructuring, privatization, imposing hard budget constraints and a faster rate of liquidation of the biggest loss makers.
>
> (pp. 81–2)

> Bulgaria is in the midst of a major financial crisis caused by increasingly accommodating refinance policies toward distressed commercial banks, along with an attempt by the authorities to decrease interest rates significantly. Downward pressure on the exchange rate depleted foreign exchange reserves in the course of 1996, which, in turn, led to panic and runs on many commercial banks.
>
> (OECD, *Economic Outlook*, December 1996, p. 124)

While direct budgetary subsidies have been largely eliminated, financing of losses through the banking system and suppliers' and tax arrears remained pervasive up to mid-1996. No bankruptcy procedures were recorded against major enterprises before July 1996 (EBRD 1996b: 142–3). 'In 1996 Bulgaria slid into economic crisis, rooted in continued massive bank lending to loss-making state enterprises and a general lack of structural reforms' (EBRD 1997a: 7). 'Much of the banking sector is insolvent, reflecting the banks' funding of state enterprise losses' (p. 22). 'Bulgaria's severe economic crisis was fundamentally the result of years of delays in necessary enterprise restructuring, with mounting losses financed by the largely state-owned banking system (amounting to an estimated 15 per cent of GDP in 1995)' (EBRD 1997b: 159).

Prime minister Videnov, in an address to parliament on 29 May 1996, announced new austerity measures agreed with the IMF. These measures included the following: the introduction of a 5 per cent import levy from 1 July 1996 to 30 June 1997 (except for products such as oil, natural gas, cotton and sugar); the liquidation of sixty-four loss-making enterprises employing 24,000 people (another seventy-one enterprises, employing 230,000, were, as of July 1996, to be cut off from fresh finance from the state budget or the state banking system and given one year to devise restructuring plans, the successful being privatized and the unsuccessful being liquidated); accelerated privatization; consolidation of the banking sector, including the closure of up to five insolvent banks (*FT*, 14 May 1996, p, 2; *FT*, 17 May 1996, p. 2; *Guardian*, 18 May 1996, p. 39; *Business Europa*, June–July 1996, p. 36; *Business Central Europe*, September 1996, p. 24; EBRD 1996b: 143; EBRD 1997a: 27).

The programme of 'isolation' from the financial sector of seventy enterprises covering 230,000 employees (10 per cent of employment) and responsible for 50 per cent of state enterprise losses in 1995 has been largely successful in imposing discipline, forcing the downsizing of enterprises and the preparation of restructuring/privatization plans (yet to be implemented). The 'liquidation programme', which covered some eighty enterprises (25,000 employees) responsible for 25 per cent of state enterprise losses, had been largely completed by July 1997 (with one-third of employees left to wind down operations (EBRD 1997b: 159). A programme of 'isolation' and liquidation targeting the largest loss-making state enterprises was launched in 1996 when thirty state utilities (group A) and forty-eight state commercial enterprises (group B) were cut off from bank credit. All group B enterprises have now exited the programme, with thirty-one privatized and sixteen under liquidation or insolvency proceedings. The financial performance of some of the group A enterprises remains a source of concern and the arrears of a number of these enterprises are increasing (EBRD 1999b: 203).

> All group B [commercial] enterprises ... [in the isolation and liquidation programme] have now exited the programme, with thirteen being privatized, thirteen under liquidation and three under solvency proceedings ... The financial performance of some of the group A enterprises [utilities] remains a source of concern.
>
> (EBRD 2000b: 146)

The IMF has been closely involved in Bulgaria's battle to overcome the financial crisis.

The monthly inflation rate rose from 47 per cent in January 1997 to 243 per cent in February, before falling to 12 per cent in March and an estimated 4.5 per cent in April (*The Economist*, 8 February 1997, p. 45, and 26 April 1997, p. 57). The crisis began in May 1996 and reached its apogee in February 1997 when the monthly inflation rate was 242.7 per cent. The lev fell from 70.4 to the US dollar at the end of 1995 to 487.4 at the end of 1996 to 2,936.7 on 12 February 1997 (Wyzan 1998: 6, 24). 'On an annual basis inflation had soared to almost 500 per cent in January 1997 and surpassed 2,000 per cent in March' (Gulde 1999: 36).

On 17 March 1997 prime minister Sofiyansky announced a stabilization programme, including the liberalization of all prices except for bread, milk, white cheese and chicken which were to benefit from temporary subsidies (*Transition*, 1997, vol. 8, no. 2, p. 24). On 21 April 1997 all remaining price controls were abolished except for bread, milk, cheese and salami (*FT*, 25 April 1997, p. 2).

A currency board was introduced on 1 July 1997, with the lev fixed at 1,000 to the DM. There are only fourteen currency boards in the world, mostly used by small countries.

> After several failed stabilization attempts Bulgaria introduced a currency board on 1 July 1997. Controversial and difficult to implement because of Bulgaria's serious structural problems, the currency board has been a crucial factor in the success of the country's latest stabilization programme. [It combined] a traditional rule-based exchange arrangement with legal and structural measures that addressed pressing banking sector and fiscal issues ... Under the currency board Bulgaria reduced annual inflation to 13 per cent by mid-1998 and to 1 per cent by the end of 1998 while rebuilding foreign exchange reserves from less than $800 million to more than $3 billion – more than six months of imports. The BNB basic interest rate, which had been above 200 per cent at the height of Bulgaria's economic crisis, fell to 5.2 per cent by the end of 1998 ... Bulgaria's stabilization was not disrupted by Russia's crisis of mid-1998, despite close economic ties between Bulgaria and Russia.
>
> (Gulde 1999: 36–9)

> Bulgaria's experience highlights the potential of a currency board to change perceptions and economic behaviour. Yet it also clearly shows a currency board's limitations: if not combined with other policies, most notably structural changes, the stable monetary and financial environment alone could not bring about an instantaneous resumption of growth. While growth turned positive in 1998, after two years of currency stability and moderate inflation output still remains below the pre-crisis level.
>
> (Ghosh *et al.* 2000: 318)

On 5 July 1999 the lev was redenominated to exact parity with the DM. One new lev was made equal to 1,000 old leva. The old and new money were to circulate in parallel until the end of 1999 (*Business Central Europe*, July–August 1999, p. 11).

> Bulgaria's reformist government [was] elected in the winter of 1997. Before this Bulgaria was considered the best example in countries outside the CIS of the capture of policy by strong vested interests. Rapid stabilization and other structural reforms appear to have succeeded not only in turning the economy around after a crisis in 1996 but also in forcing the vested interests to play by the rules.
>
> (Havrylyshyn and Odling-Smee 2000: 9)

The temporary import surcharge introduced in 1996 was abolished ahead of schedule on 1 January 1999. In September 1998 Bulgaria accepted the obligations of the IMF's Article 8 (EBRD 1999b: 202).

The private sector accounted for roughly 10 per cent of GDP in mid-1990. In mid-2000 the figure was 70 per cent (EBRD 1999b: 24, 204, and 2000b: 14, 148).

Rough estimates in mid-year of the private sector as a percentage of GDP are provided by the EBRD: 1990, 10 per cent; 1991, 20 per cent; 1992, 25 per cent; 1993, 35 per cent; 1994, 40 per cent; 1995, 50 per cent; 1996, 55 per cent; 1997, 60 per cent; 1998, 65 per cent; 1999, 70 per cent; 2000, 70 per cent (EBRD 1999b: 24, 204, and 2000b: 14, 148).

By the end of June 1993, 56.5 per cent of small-scale urban properties (83 per cent of shops and restaurants) had been restituted to former owners (Wyzan 1996: 58). The privatization of most small enterprises has taken place through the restitution of some 22,000 municipal entities by mid-September 1996 (EBRD 1996b: 143).

Large privatization has been much delayed because of political wrangling.

A draft privatization law was approved by parliament on 8 May 1992. The government's final privatization scheme (announced on 2 August 1993) was passed by parliament in early June 1994 and came into force on 28 June. Mass privatization based on the free distribution of vouchers was ruled out, but the scheme would enable citizens to buy some vouchers, allow the issuing of vouchers for restitution purposes and permit the participation of foreign investors.

Wyzan (1996: 57) and EBRD (1994: 20) put the number of enterprises on the first wave list at 340. The target was to sell 320 enterprises in 1994 (including seventy large ones) or at least 10 per cent of the state sector ('strategic' sectors such as armaments, transport, oil refining and energy generation being excluded) (*Transition*, 1994, vol. 5, no. 4, p. 9). The privatization of 3,485 enterprises was initiated in 1993 with a programme envisaging individual sales through a variety of mechanisms (direct sales, tenders, auctions, management buy-outs). Management and employees could bid for up to 20 per cent of shares on preferential terms (50 per cent discount). The privatization process was open to foreigners. In November 1994 Brady bonds and Zunks (domestic bad loan bonds) became usable as payment (EBRD 1996a: 142).

By mid-1994 one in sixteen large enterprises had been privatized, while seventeen out of 870 medium-sized enterprises had been privatized (EBRD 1994: 20). By June 1995 only sixty-three large enterprises had been privatized by the privatization agency (EBRD 1996a: 37). By mid-1996 only 6 per cent of total state enterprise assets had been transferred to the private sector (EBRD 1996b: 142).

A programme for the mass privatization of medium-sized enterprises was submitted to parliament on 22 March 1995. This was to involve the privatization of 100 to 150 enterprises between November 1995 and October 1996. (Some 150 enterprises were to be selected for privatization. Those not to be privatized included the Kozloduy nuclear power station, the military–industrial complex, the Bulgarian Telecommunications Company, the Post Office and one or two major banks: *Transition*, 1995, vol. 6, nos 5–6, p. 19.) A further 100 enterprises were to be privatized between February 1996 and January 1998. Payment would be in the form of vouchers (15 to 20 per cent), cash (50 per cent) and 'bad loan bonds' issued by the government as part of the bank recapitalization scheme (30 to 35 per cent). Vouchers would be tradable on the stock market. The first list of enterprises was to be made public in November 1995 (EBRD 1995a: 54). Sectors such as energy and telecommunications were to remain excluded from privatization (1995b: 37). Only in a minority of cases would enterprises' capital be fully privatized. The government would initially retain a majority stake or a blocking minority in most of the partly privatized enterprises. Additional shares were to be offered to investors for cash (EBRD 1996a: 10). The privatization process was to accelerate significantly in the second half of 1996 with the inclusion of a stake in major enterprises such as Bulgarian Telecoms which were previously excluded. The mass privatization programme began in 1996. Some two-thirds of vouchers have been transferred to specialized investment funds (each of which can own up to 34 per cent of the shares of an enterprise). By mid-1998 all state enterprises, except the utilities and a small number of 'strategic' enterprises were to be privatized. The first auction, for shares in over 1,000 enterprises, was scheduled for October 1996 (EBRD 1996b: 142–3). In 1996 509 enterprises were privatized for cash and Brady bonds, the majority in the form of management buy-outs as in previous years. The first auction under a mass privatization scheme took place in October 1996. The funds attracted about two-thirds of the vouchers that had been issued to the population (EBRD 1997a: 27). The first round of mass privatization came to an end in July 1997. Management–employee buy-outs are becoming an increasingly popular means of privatization, as are debt-for-equity swaps (EBRD 1998a: 34).

> Strategic foreign investors are beginning to play a larger role in Bulgaria, producing a pattern of corporate governance that gives a greater role to outside institutions. However, at the same time, management–employee buy-outs are becoming an increasingly popular means of privatization, raising some concerns about future ownership structures.
>
> (p. 28)

'The pace of cash privatization of large-scale enterprises in 1998 has been slower than anticipated' (EBRD 1999a: 35). The second round of mass privatization started in January 1999. Measured by the number of transactions concluded, 1998 saw an acceleration in privatization as management–employee buy-outs proliferated. In mid-1999 significant progress was made in privatization, with several of the largest enterprises being sold (including Balkan Airlines and Kremikovski). A second bank was privatized in late 1998 when 78 per cent of Post Bank (the third largest of the six remaining state banks) was sold to a foreign strategic investor (EBRD 1999b: 202–3).

> Enterprise privatization made remarkable progress in 1999, with more than 1,200 deals completed. By the end of the year over 70 per cent of privatization assets had been sold, compared with 42 per cent a year earlier. Management buy-outs remained the most popular form of privatization in 1999. The state retains shares in some privatized enterprises and the liquidation of remaining state-owned enterprises are priorities … Bank privatization is nearing completion.
>
> (EBRD 2000a: 46)

'While privatization is nearly complete, the restructuring of privatized enterprise, particularly those sold to management, remains a challenge, owing to ineffective corporate governance and bankruptcy procedures … Enterprise restructuring remains sluggish' (EBRD 2000b: 146).

Accusations of corruption were once common:

1 The delay in 'open' privatization has allowed 'hidden' or '*nomenklatura*' privatization to thrive (*Business Central Europe*, February 1994, p. 51).
2 Pomfret makes the point that the *nomenklatura* have exploited business and political connections:

> Many of these people have become fabulously rich running private trading companies that buy from and sell to Bulgaria's state-run factories, creating a bizarre economic subsystem in which production is state-run but profits are private … Essentially, private trading companies control everything sold to the factories and market their production too. Such enterprises can be lucrative through kickbacks or manipulation of antiquated accounting methods. The private trading companies can make windfall profits selling raw materials at market prices, buying finished products at low prices and then selling them at a profit. As the state-run enterprises slip deeply into debt, the private trading companies reap huge profits.
>
> (John Pomfret, *IHT*, 14 May 1994, p. 11)

3 'Diplomats and political observers agree that Bulgaria's state enterprises are being comprehensively asset-stripped by managers and private businessmen with close ties to the former communists' (Julian Borger, *Guardian*, 17 December 1994, p. 9).
4 Although formal privatization has been slow, state and municipal enterprises have been subjected to 'hidden' privatization. This usually involves the formation of private companies to supply state enterprises with inputs at high prices and of other companies to take their subsidized output for resale at market prices. In this way enterprises accumulate inter-enterprises debts and losses while allowing a new class of millionaire to develop. The process of nationalizing losses and privatizing profits is widespread throughout the

former Soviet bloc but has been most blatant in countries such as Bulgaria and Romania (Anthony Robinson, *FT*, Survey, 13 October 1994, p. 14).

5 After 1991, as a general rule, private firms took over distribution, marketing and foreign trade functions. Private wealth has been created through siphoning profits from state enterprises (Zeljko Bogetic and Arye Hillman, *Transition*, 1995, vol. 6, no. 3, pp. 4, 6).

6 The 'Group of 13' is the name given to the business lobby recently founded by the largest private companies. The group controls a large part of the private sector (Virginia Marsh, *FT*, 10 May 1994, p. 3). The 'Group of 13' is 'said to be owned and operated by former communists that are now exerting mafia-like influence in the country's private sector' (*Business Europa*, November–December 1994, p. 35).

> Reforms of the customs service and an overhaul of the tax system have helped to reduce the role in Bulgaria's economy of a half-dozen shadowy conglomerates which dominated business activity in the mid-1990s. Moreover, the withdrawing of the conglomerates from sectors such as banking and energy has contributed to a more level playing field for foreign investors.
>
> (*FT*, Survey, 8 March 1999, p. ii)

More recently privatization has been faster, more transparent and more concerned with corporate governance. For example, on 9 July 1999 a protocol was signed for Dutch and Greek telecommunications operators to buy a 51 per cent stake in BTC, the state telecoms group (*FT*, 12 July 1999, p. 21). On 12 October 1999 the Russian oil company Lukoil was named as the preferred buyer of a majority stake in Neftochim, the biggest oil refinery in the Balkans. Lukoil was to pay $101 million for a 58 per cent stake. The sale followed the acquisition by Western investors of majority stakes in Bulgaria's biggest steelworks, the state-owned telecoms operator and two state banks (*FT*, 13 October 1999, p. 34).

'This autumn [2000] Bulgaria announced a new privatization policy designed to improve transparency and reduce the number of insider sales' (*Business Central Europe*, December 2000 – January 2001, p. 47). 'Barring some big early deals, most privatization sales have gone to managers or second-rate investors' (*Business Central Europe*, June 2001, p. 42).

'The Kostov government … has privatized a lot – but mostly to politically favoured managers and dubious investors, foreign and local' (*The Economist*, 16 June 2001, p. 51).

Foreign direct investment has, not surprisingly, been disappointing. But the volume has increased. (See Table 2.2, p. 134)

Agricultural legislation was relatively quick off the mark. But agriculture has been adversely affected by factors such as the small size of family farms and long delays in granting full titles to restituted property.

The Land Law was adopted in late January 1991, although implementation was to be delayed until the autumn. Provision was made for restitution to former owners or their heirs of land forcibly collectivized. The aim was to restore the land ownership pattern of 1946. Financial compensation was to be available in case physical restitution was not possible. Provision was also made for the auctioning off of about 400,000 ha of state land to those farmers who had never owned land. Land legislation approved in March 1992 allowed restitution of up to 30 ha (74 acres) per person, but there are relatively few claims of this size because of the historical situation (Virginia Marsh, *FT*, 19 November 1992, p. 34).

Although 80 per cent of the farmland available for restitution has been returned to pre-communist owners, full titles have been issued for only 24 per cent. Only about 5 per cent of private farms exceed 2 ha in size, while barely 1 per cent reach the EU average of 20 to 50 ha (*FT*, Survey, 8 March 1999, p. iii).

By the end of 1994, 57.3 per cent of farm land had been restituted (EBRD 1995a: 54). Few land titles have been issued, but 60 per cent of agricultural land has been handed back to the original owners through 'final land decisions' recognized as ownership documents and accepted as collateral (EBRD 1995b: 37). By the end of 1998, 80 per cent of agricultural land had been restituted and over 18 per cent of the land subject to restitution had been titled. More than half of agro-industrial companies (measured by long-term assets) and virtually all grain warehouses have been privatized. A number of steps have been taken to provide a stimulus to a functioning land market, including improvements in the process of land registration (EBRD 1999b: 202). 'By the end of 1999 land restitution was 96 per cent complete, up from 80 per cent at the end of 1998' (EBRD 2000b: 146).

The Czech Republic: a summary

The Czech Republic, under the go-ahead but pragmatic leadership of prime minister Vaclav Klaus, for a while overtook Hungary as the number one economic and political success story in Eastern Europe. (On 28 November 1995 the Czech Republic became the first former communist country to become a member of the OECD.) Despite the later tarnishing of his reputation for political and economic management (e.g. financial scandals and a poor record in industrial restructuring), Klaus achieved a generally rapid economic transition while using subsidies to avoid sudden, large-scale bankruptcies and lay-offs. Klaus also did a good job of 'selling' a consistent policy line to the Czech public. He has made something of a political comeback at a time when the reputation of his arch rival President Vaclav Havel (who has been in poor health) has been damaged somewhat at home by events such as his second marriage. But Klaus himself has been damaged by allegations of using his influence to try to gain favourable coverage on state television (especially since he is interested in the presidency when Havel's term of office ends). (On 28 January 2000 the lower house of parliament passed a constitutional amendment reducing the powers of the president. 'The key part of the amendment is that when a premier resigns the whole government must now step down, and the president must then ask the next largest parliamentary party to try to form a government. When Vaclav Klaus resigned in 1998 Havel put in central bank governor Josef Tosovsky as caretaker premier': *EEN*, 2000, vol. 12, no. 22, p. 2.)

As a result of the general election of 31 May–1 June 1996 the three-party coalition (led by Klaus's Civic Democratic Party) occupied only ninety-nine seats in the 200-seat House of Deputies. Defections later turned this into a slim majority.

Prime minister Klaus resigned on 30 November 1997, although he denied knowledge of dubious party donations allegedly connected with privatization. On 15 January 1998 thirty MPs left the Civic Democratic Party to form a new party called Freedom Union.

The election of 19–20 June 1998 put Milos Zeman's Social Democratic Party in first place, but Klaus's Civic Democratic Party came through very strongly towards the end of the campaign. The former decided to form a minority government with the support of the latter. Klaus became speaker of parliament.

On 20 December 1996 the foreign ministers of the Czech Republic and Germany finally initialled a declaration of reconciliation, including the question of the Sudeten Germans. Klaus and Chancellor Kohl of Germany signed the agreement on 21 January 1997.

On 16 July 1997 the European Commission recommended that the Czech Republic open negotiations for membership of the EU (confirmed at the EU summit on 13 December 1997). But on 13 October 1999 the European Commission put the Czech Republic behind Hungary and Poland in economic terms and talked of uneven and generally sluggish progress in adopting EU laws. Ground had been lost in the last year. It qualified as a functioning market economy, but its 'situation gives rise to concern'. This was confirmed on 10 December 1999 at the EU summit. The EU has also expressed concern at the treatment of Gypsies in the Czech Republic (such as discrimination and the attempts by a number of local authorities to build walls in housing estates). On 8 November 2000 the latest EU report was published. There was recognition of the progress that the Czech Republic had made but familiar criticisms remained.

On 12 March 1999 the Czech Republic became a member of Nato. The Czech nation proved to be by far the least supportive of the three new members over Nato's bombing of Serbia. President Havel was highly embarrassed and critical of his people after his strong personal advocacy of Nato expansion.

Disillusion with the party political scene was illustrated by the holding of a large demonstration (an estimated 50,000) in Prague on 3 December 1999 demanding a new government and fresh elections. The demonstrators called for the resignation of the leaders of the main political parties.

The organizers of the movement, six former student leaders who led the protests against the communist government in 1989, called for new leaders to help prepare the country for EU membership and restore faith in democracy (*IHT*, 4 December 1999, p. 7). The 'Thanks, now leave' movement held nation-wide demonstrations. There was a call for an end to the entente between the Czech Social Democratic Party and the Civic Democratic Party. The former student leaders first issued the appeal ('Thanks, now leave') on 17 November 1999, calling for party political leaders to resign, an appeal subsequently signed by around 100,000 Czech citizens (*EEN*, 2000, vol. 12, no. 21, p. 5). On 14 January 2000 regional activists from the 'Thank you, now leave' movement held an inaugural meeting to form a new right-wing political party, as yet unnamed (*EEN*, 2000, vol. 12, no. 22, p. 5).

The GDP growth rate turned positive as early as 1993, but output declined for three successive years over the period 1997 to 1999. 'The Czech Republic ... [however] seems to have turned the corner ... The recession appears to have ended' (EBRD 2000a: 3, 5). 'The economy began to pull out of recession in spring [1999]' (*FT*, 27 June 2000, p. 10). 'GDP grew moderately in the second half of 1999, reflecting stronger European demand for Czech exports and marking an end to the recession' (OECD, *Economic Outlook*, June 2000, p. 92). In 2000 GDP was an estimated 98 per cent of the 1989 level (EBRD 2001: 15). The inflation record is quite good. The peak year was 1991 (over 50 per cent).

Serious concern has been expressed about things like widening trade deficits, financial scandals, the corporate guidance exercised by investment funds and the regulation of capital markets. The picture has brightened, however.

There have been two rounds of mass (voucher) privatization, the second one being completed on 25 November 1994 (after which sales became the dominant mode of privatization). The bulk of vouchers ended up in investment funds, which were largely owned by banks in which the state retained a controlling or majority stake. Although the evidence is somewhat mixed, the general impression is that the restructuring of Czech industry has been seriously deficient (e.g. banks have given loans to 'their' enterprises to keep them afloat rather than on the basis of profitability). The lack of regulation of financial markets has led to major scandals involving things like the defrauding of shareholders. Legislation has attempted to improve matters. In early 1997 parliament approved the creation of a new securities commission. Since 1 January 1998 the links of banks with non-financial companies have been reduced. In April 1998 legislation on investment funds was approved (e.g. a future reduction in the maximum stake an investment fund can hold in an enterprise). In April 1997 an economic package was approved, involving austerity measures (enhanced in May), faster privatization and improved financial regulation.

The Zeman government was initially cool towards privatization but then gave more of a green light to the process (including banks). In its April 1999 'revitalization' programme a number of struggling private enterprises have been brought under state control with the aim of improving their performance to the extent that they can be sold to strategic investors.

The private sector accounted for roughly 10 per cent of GDP in mid-1990. In mid-2000 the figure was 80 per cent (EBRD 1999b: 24, 212, and 2000b: 14, 156).

There is a relatively liberal foreign trade regime. On 1 October 1995 the Czech Republic formally accepted the conditions of the IMF's Article 8 concerning current account convertibility. Some limited controls still remain on the capital account. The pegged exchange rate regime was changed to a managed floating one on 26 May 1997.

The Czech Republic has reintroduced incentives to attract direct foreign investment. Its positive impact can be best seen in the extraordinary success of the Skoda–Volkswagen company. A record $4.88 billion of direct foreign investment was attracted in 1999, compared with $2.54 billion in 1998 (*FT*, 19 April 2000, p. 12). (See Table 3.1, p. 199, for the volume of net foreign direct investment.)

Hungary: a summary

There has been basic continuity of economic policy despite significant political swings. Although it won a majority of seats in parliament in the May 1994 general election (benefiting from the support of those who particularly felt the pain and uncertainty of economic transition), the Hungarian Socialist Party still decided to form a coalition government with the Alliance of Free Democrats in order to ensure that there would be no slide into inflationary spending increases arising from the more social welfare-orientated elements within the party. There was a swing to the right in the May 1998 general election. Fidesz (the Alliance of Young Democrats) had ended its age maximum and (in April 1995) retitled itself Fidesz–Hungarian Civic Party. Under Viktor Orban it had shifted to the centre-right over time (e.g. assuming a more nationalistic tone), although in the election campaign it adopted a more populist economic policy (e.g. lowering taxes/increasing government spending to stimulate growth and to support the family) than the Hungarian Socialist Party, whose austerity measures had caused considerable and widespread economic pain. Fidesz also played on concerns about crime and corruption. Nevertheless, the coalition government (Fidesz, the Smallholders' Party and Democratic Forum) has basically maintained the traditional economic policy in practice. On 19 March 1995 Hungary and Slovakia signed an agreement guaranteeing borders and minority rights. (In September 1997 the International Court of Justice in The Hague delivered its judgment on the Gabcikovo Dam dispute between the two countries.) On 16 September 1996 Hungary and Romania signed a treaty dealing with minority rights and the inviolability of borders. 'The Hungarian parliament on Tuesday [19 June 2001] adopted a [status] law granting ethnic Hungarians in neighbouring countries special medical, employment and education opportunities in Hungary … The legislation has already triggered international protest, especially in Slovakia and Romania' (*IHT*, 20 June 2001, p. 6).

On 16 July 1997 the European Commission recommended that Hungary open negotiations for membership of the EU (confirmed at the EU summit on 13 December 1997). On 13 October 1999 the European Commission (endorsed by foreign ministers at the EU summit on 10 December 1999) lauded Hungary as a front runner. A generally favourable report was also received on 8 November 2000. (The EU summit held in Sweden that ended on 16 June 2001 issued the following final document after the Irish referendum held on 7 June rejected the December 2000 Nice Treaty: 'The enlargement process is irreversible ... [It should be possible] to complete negotiations by the end of 2002 for those candidates countries that are ready ... The objective is that they should participate in the European parliament elections of 2004 as members.' The Irish government planned to hold another referendum.)

Hungary has not escaped international criticism, however. For example, there is concern about government influence over the media.

On 12 March 1999 Hungary became a member of Nato.

After a good start Hungary lost the image of the 'golden boy' of the transition for a while. Initially Hungary was generally ranked first in terms of overall economic success, but then slipped behind countries like the Czech Republic and Poland. Towards the new millennium Hungary and Poland were generally considered to be transitional leaders. The GDP growth rate turned positive in 1994 but was modest in 1994, 1995 and 1996. Thereafter growth was robust. In 2000 transitional Hungary's GDP exceeded the 1989 level for the first time (EBRD 2001: 15). Inflation has never been out of control, but it took until 2000 for the annual inflation rate to move into single figures.

Hungary has maintained a basic continuity of economic policy in its more gradual approach to transition (as opposed to Poland's 'big bang'/'shock therapy') and has always been among the front runners in terms of economic transition. Hungary became a member of the OECD on 29 March 1996.

Hungary's decision not to seek foreign debt write-offs (as Poland did) has had ramifications in terms of privatization policy. For this and other reasons (such as raising revenue for general budgetary purposes and to improve corporate management) Hungary has placed considerable emphasis on sales in its large privatization policy. (Small privatization has been much more rapid.) This includes a search for strategic foreign investors even in utilities and banking (although the state retains 'golden shares' in sectors such as energy and telecommunications in order to exercise a veto over important decisions affecting companies). Only a modest percentage of shares has been sold at a discount to the employees of enterprises and only partial compensation has been paid to former owners in the form of vouchers exchangeable for shares. Large privatization was very slow at first but has since proceeded gradually and steadily.

The private sector accounted for roughly 25 per cent of GDP in mid-1990. In mid-2000 the figure was 80 per cent (EBRD 1999b: 24, 228, and 2000b: 14, 172).

Hungary is heavily dependent on foreign trade, has a relatively liberal foreign trade regime and rapidly switched trade towards the West (especially the EU). It formally accepted the conditions of the IMF's Article 8 on 1 January 1996 and is gradually liberalizing the capital account. There is a crawling peg exchange rate, with the forint subject to a gradual and controlled monthly devaluation.

> Reflecting the high degree of integration with the EU, the currency composition of the basket to which the currency is pegged was changed in January 2000 to comprise only the Euro. The monthly rate of crawl was reduced to

> 0.3 per cent in April 2000. The government plans to move from the present regime to a fixed exchange rate target with wide intervention bands as soon as inflation falls below 5 per cent and the inflation differential with major trading partners falls below 3 per cent.
>
> (EBRD 2000b: 170)

> Last month [May 2001] … Hungary … widened the band within which the forint trades, allowing the currency to trade more freely. The central bank had long indicated that it wanted to phase out its currency peg, and that first meant loosening it … The forint will continue to be devalued slowly against the euro, with the target peg crawling downwards by 0.2 per cent a month. But from now on the currency will be allowed to fluctuate within a band of 15 per cent either side of the peg, compared to the previous 2.25 per cent.
>
> (*Business Central Europe*, June 2001, p. 13)

'[In June] Hungary floated the forint, abolishing the last currency restrictions. The liberalization means that foreign investors will now be free to buy short-term forint bonds and Hungarians can open foreign bank accounts' (*Business Central Europe*, July–August 2001, pp. 11–12).

Hungary has been outstandingly successful as regards direct foreign investment, helped by the privatization policy outlined above. (See Table 4.2, p. 223.)

> Agriculture was productive enough back in the 1980s. Today, after a decade of botched reform, chaotic restitution and political meddling, it is a mess … Production is still going down … Agricultural production … [is] up to 40 per cent below 1989 levels … Most of the trouble stems from a restitution process that was chaotic even by post-communist standards. Many of Hungary's communist co-operatives ended up being split into tiny plots, many too small even to feed their owners … There are now a staggering 1.2 million smallholders in Hungary. Some of these are owned by absentee landlords who lease out their plots to larger farms. But there are still around 400,000 Hungarian peasant farmers, many of them farming less than a single hectare. While some grumble about the problems faced by big state farms … the real nightmares lie in this sub-culture of subsistence farmers. These farms are too small to buy fertilisers and seed … Farmers cannot afford to buy decent animals … Foreigners are barred from owning farmland in Hungary … There is even a cap set on the amount of land that locals can own … There is no land market … The number of tiny farms is slowly falling, but that just means they are merging to become small farms. And you cannot farm two hectares profitably … Even the biggest farms have not been commercialized yet … [There are] 100-odd big state farms surviving from communist times … There is only one wholesale market in the whole of Hungary.
>
> (*Business Central Europe*, December 2000 – January 2001, pp. 59–60)

'Hungary's 960,000 farms tend to be relatively small; the average farm size … is 163 ha (403 acres)' (*IHT*, Survey, 14 June 2001, p. 19).

Poland: a summary

There has been a basic continuity of economic reform despite the changes of government, squabbling among coalition partners and frequent worker unrest in sectors such as agriculture and coal mining.

The general election of 19 September 1993 was won by the Alliance of the Democratic Left. The ADL formed a coalition government with the Polish Peasant Party. The right-wing parties were divided and minimum thresholds (5 per cent for a party and 8 per cent for an alliance) meant that they were proportionally under-represented relative to the vote they received. The ADL's leader, Alexander Kwasniewski, became president on 19 November 1995 (and becoming increasingly popular thereafter). He beat the increasingly discredited Lech Walesa. Kwasniewski was re-elected on 8 October 2000.

On 23 October 1996 the Sejm voted to abandon proceedings against General Wojciech Jaruzelski for declaring martial law in 1981.

Poland became a member of the OECD on 22 November 1996.

On 16 July 1997 the European Commission recommended (and the EU foreign ministers confirmed on 13 December 1997) that negotiations be started for EU membership.

In the general election of 21 September 1997 the right-wing parties avoided the previous splits. Solidarity Electoral Action (AWS), comprising Solidarity and a large number of other parties of various shades of opinion, formed a coalition government with Freedom Union led by Leszek Balcerowicz (who returned to his old post of finance minister and became deputy prime minister). In June 2000 Freedom Union pulled out of the coalition government largely over the inability of prime minister Jerzy Buzek to control the fissiparous Solidarity bloc. The more populist Solidarity deputies resisted finance minister Balcerowicz's economic policies. The prospects for the disintegrating AWS in the September 2001 general election looked increasingly bleak.

The government itself has also fallen victim to the bill (signed by the president on 22 October 1998) which demands that all judges, ministers, legislators, senior civil servants and other officials of state-owned media declare if they worked or informed for the communist-era security apparatus. A law had taken effect in August 1997 under which candidates for parliament must declare in writing if they were ever secret informers or if they collaborated with the secret police in the communist era. In August 2000 both President Kwasniewski and Lech Walesa were cleared by a screening court of allegations that they had lied about being agents of (informers for) the communist-era secret police. They could thus take part in the 8 October 2000 presidential election.

> In 1997 Poland decide to emulate the Czech Republic and pass a law to keep former secret police agents out of government. In Poland officials must

> declare whether they were informers. Only those found to be lying lose their jobs. Mr Kwasniewski and Mr Walesa said they were not spies and so risked losing the right to run.
>
> (*IHT*, 14 August 2000, p. 8)

> [The] vetting law forces about 22,000 politicians, civil servants and judges to fill out forms denying or admitting collaboration. The declarations were checked out against secret police files and anyone found to be lying by a court was to be banned from public life for ten years.
>
> (p. 7)

'The 1997 legislation imposes no legal penalty for confessing to collaboration as long as the person declares it' (*IHT*, 21 August 2000, p. 7).

On 31 May 1998 the EU's Phare aid was reduced owing to what was considered to be Poland's poor response as regards the preparation of projects. Despite this, on 13 October 1999 the European Commission (endorsed by foreign ministers at the EU summit on 10 December 1999) put Poland in the front ranks of eligible members despite expressing concern at, for example, the progress being made to bring Poland's laws into line with those of the EU. On 8 November 2000 Poland received a more positive EU assessment.

A new system of regional government was introduced on 1 January 1999, a decentralization in line with EU practice (and with that in pre-1939 Poland). The new system has not been without its critics.

The question of antisemitism reared its head in 1998 over the question of crosses erected near the Auschwitz concentration camp. The issue was finally resolved by leaving only one (erected in 1989), namely that used in 1979 at a mass held during the visit of Pope John Paul II.

Poland became a member of Nato on 12 March 1999. The Polish people were the most supportive of those of the three new members of Nato's bombing of Serbia.

In August 2000 both President Kwasniewski and Lech Walesa were cleared by a screening court of allegations that they had lied about being agents of (informers for) the communist-era secret police. The law was passed by parliament in August 1997 and signed by the president on 22 October 1998. (See the respective entries.) They could thus take part in the 8 October 2000 presidential election. Kwasniewski was re-elected in the first round of voting, while Walesa's share of the vote was so derisory that he quickly announced his retirement from politics.

Poland was the scene of the first 'big bang'/'shock therapy' programme (under finance minister Leszek Balcerowicz in 1990). It has always been ranked among the leading transitional economies and its position has strengthened over time. (It is worth recalling, however, that about a half of Poland's foreign debt has been written off, in 1991 as regards debt owed to foreign governments and in 1994 as regards debt owed to foreign commercial banks.) Inflation fell sharply in 1991. The inflation rate reached single figures in 1999, before moving back into double figures the following year. Poland was the first country in Eastern Europe and the former Soviet Union to resume positive GDP growth (in 1992) and the first (in 1996) to recoup the output losses incurred since 1989. (In 2000 it has been estimated that the level of GDP exceeded the 1989 level by 27 per cent: EBRD 2001: 15.) It quickly became a very open economy and Poland still has a relatively liberal foreign trade regime despite increased protectionism stemming from particularly depressed sectors such as coal, steel and agriculture. (Poland, of course, had a largely private sector in agriculture even in the communist era. Problems today revolve around aspects such the typical relatively small farms and the typical technological backwardness of the sector (although there are signs of progress on both fronts). Productivity is such that agriculture accounts for 25 per cent of total employment but only 6 per cent of total output: EBRD 1999b: 250.) In June 1995 Poland formally accepted the conditions of the IMF's Article 8 regarding current account convertibility and aims fully to liberalize the capital account.

Initially the zloty was pegged to the US dollar and used as a monetary anchor as part of macroeconomic stabilization. A crawling peg exchange rate was then used until 12 April 2000 when the zloty was allowed to float.

Poland is often cited as an interesting case study of privatization, where a relatively slow privatization of large enterprises (coupled with a policy of rapid small privatization and of encouraging the growth of new private firms) can still bring benefits when large state industrial enterprises are made to face 'hard budget constraints' (i.e. no automatic bail-outs by the state) and competition from domestic and from foreign companies. 'Investigation shows that Polish managers of state firms performed well because they expected privatization and hoped their achievements would assure their survival when it came' (Havrylyshyn and McGettigan 1999: 5). Large privatization has been slowed up by such factors as changes of government and the power of workers' councils. (The Treasury, which assumed responsibility for privatization in August 1996, has the right to commercialize a state enterprise upon written notification to its management and employees. Their consent is no longer required: EBRD 1987b: 189.) Mass (voucher) large privatization did not even start to get under way until 1995 and is a relatively modest affair. Only something over 500 enterprises are involved. The problem of corporate governance for these enterprises is supposed to be tackled by the creation of fifteen investment funds (National Wealth Management Funds), run by foreign managers, in which Polish citizens exchange their vouchers (purchased for a nominal fee) for shares which account in total for 60 per cent of shares in the funds. Fifteen per cent of shares in the investment funds go to employees of enterprises free of charge, while 25 per cent of shares were allocated to the state (15 percentage points of which are envisaged to go to social funds and other recipients at a later date). To enhance corporate control 33 per cent of the shares of each participating enterprise are owned by a designated lead investment fund. Shares of the investment funds are tradable on the stock exchange.

'The privatization of large-scale enterprises is well-advanced' (EBRD 2000b: 194).

> While progress in large-scale privatization is well advanced, the state still owns a number of large industrial companies, including an oil refinery, major steel mills and coal mines. This slow pace of progress reflects a reluctance to address difficult restructuring issues, including labour market flexibility.
>
> (EBRD 2001: 80)

The emphasis now is on sales, including utilities and banks. Foreign strategic buyers are sought out where deemed appropriate. State policy initially discouraged foreign ownership of banks, but policy has changed. 'Foreign investors control about 70 per cent of Polish banking assets, a level matched in Central Europe only by Hungary' (*FT*, Survey, 17 April 2000, p. ii). According to the IMF, the proportion of total bank assets controlled by foreigners – foreign control being defined as foreigners owning more than 50 per cent of the total equity of a bank – increased from roughly 3 per cent in 1994 to about 53 per cent in 1999. The latter figure for Hungary was around 57 per cent (*The Economist*, 4 November 2000, p. 194).

> More than two-thirds of the banking sector by assets are now in private ownership … The strong presence of foreign strategic investors, including control of about 50 per cent of banking sector assets, and ongoing consolidation contribute to the strengthening of the banking sector.
>
> (EBRD 2000b: 195)

On 14 July 2000 the Sejm narrowly approved the enfranchisement bill.

> The enfranchisement bill … stipulates that every Polish adult receive a share of state assets. Tenants of municipal or co-operation flats will be granted full or part ownership rights to their homes. Others will receive coupons in special funds managing shares in companies undergoing privatization.
>
> (*Transition*, 2000, vol. 11, nos 3–4, p. 39)

'Parliament approved on Thursday [11 January 2001] a long-delayed law compensating Polish citizens whose property was seized between 1944 and 1962 – but only for those who retain Polish citizenship' (*IHT*, 12 January 2001, p. 8).

> Parliament passed a controversial law to compensate former owners for property seized by the communists. The law fulfils the government's election promise, but will only give claimants half the value of their former possessions because of worries about the costs of full restitution.
>
> (*Business Central Europe*, February 2001, p. 11)

> Poland's Senate threw out parts of a bill on restituting property seized by the communists after the war, which would have excluded many Polish émigrés living overseas, many of them Jewish. The bill must now be reconsidered by the lower house.
>
> (*Business Central Europe*, March 2001, p. 9)

President Alexander Kwasniewski vetoed the bill on 22 March 2001 (*FT*, 23 March 2001, p. 10; *Telegraph*, 23 March 2001, p. 20). 'Poland is the only East European government beside Belarus that has not enacted a property restitution programme since the collapse of communist rule in 1989' (*FT*, 23 March 2001, p. 10).

The private sector accounted for roughly 30 per cent of GDP in mid-1990. In mid-1999 the figure was 70 per cent (EBRD 1999b; 24, 252, and 2000b: 14, 196).

Poland has been very successful in attracting foreign investment. (See Table 5.2, p. 272.) 'Foreign direct investment last year [1999] hit a record $8 billion, taking the total to $39 billion, or 40 per cent of the ex-Soviet bloc total' (*FT*, Survey, 17 April 2000, p. i). But Poland is in dispute with the EU as regards the former's special economic zones, the EU wanting them closed.

Romania: a summary

Romania has had a very difficult transition, both economically and politically.

There is still disagreement as to how spontaneous the 1989 revolution was. The general view is that the uprising was a popular one, but soon taken over by the National Salvation Front (apparently formed some six months earlier).

The general election of 20 May 1990 was won by the National Salvation Front (NSF). (On the same day Ion Iliescu won the presidential election.) The platform was seemingly appealing, with a very cautious approach to economic reform. Large-scale unemployment was to be avoided by a relatively slow process of transition to a more mixed economy (the state sector remaining dominant but private activity being encouraged) and to a more market-orientated (though state-regulated) economy. Generous social security was offered to those adversely affected, such as the unemployed. Foreign investment was looked on warily: 'We shall not sell off the country.' Collective farms were to remain the mainstay of agriculture, but farmers were to obtain land which they would be free to manage themselves. But the difficult conditions took their toll. Anti-government demonstrations continued, inspired by deep concern about so many former communists holding power. There were loud domestic and international protests when miners brutally cleared Bucharest of demonstrators on 14–15 June 1990 (although the main Western response was tinged with a general prejudice against a socialist government).

At the NSF's first national convention in March 1991, the reformist prime minister Petre Roman was re-elected party leader. He gained approval for the reshaping of the NSF into a social democratic party committed to a market-based economy. In June of the previous year Roman had given an enthusiastic outline of policy regarding marketization, much to the discomfort of the more traditional elements in the party:

> Our foremost mission is to make a historic transition of an unprecedented scope, namely from a super-centralized to a market economy. The state must abandon to the greatest possible extent its role as proprietor and manager … The present state of the economy can only be overcome by radical reform, carried out in quick steps. Plastic surgery and artificial adjustments cannot but deepen our crisis.

In an October 1990 speech to parliament, he announced a 'leap to a market economy', running until June 1992.

But the Roman government fell in September 1991, the result, ironically, of violent demonstrations in Bucharest by miners (joined by some ordinary citizens) demanding improved pay and working conditions, a price freeze and political changes (including the resignations of Iliescu and Roman). Economic concessions and the use of force by the police restored order. Theodor Stolojan became prime minister on 1 October 1991, a staunch, pro-market technocrat who vowed not to stand in the forthcoming general election (later fixed for 27 September 1992). A coalition government was formed. At the NSF convention held in March 1992 Petre Roman was re-elected party leader, with majority support for his vision of a Western-style social democracy. The split in the party became open when Iliescu later decided to run for president again, but not for Roman's NSF. He became the candidate for Democratic National Salvation Front (DNSF), formed in April 1992. In the late summer of 1993 it became known as the Social Democracy Party of Romania.

Ion Iliescu won 47.34 per cent of the votes in the first round of the presidential election on 27 September 1992 against the 31.24 per cent of Emil Constantinescu (rector of Bucharest University and candidate of the Democratic Convention). (The strongly pro-reform convention comprised seventeen groupings, including the National Peasant Party and Civic Alliance.) In the second round on 11 October Iliescu won 61.4 per cent of the votes on a platform of cautious economic reform. His support lay mainly in the rural areas (where there seemed to be the impression that landlords would otherwise take away peasant land) and among the working class (especially in areas where heavy industry is dominant) fearing unemployment.

In the general election of 27 September 1992 there was no clear-cut result, but the DNSF did surprisingly well, becoming the largest single party in parliament. The Democratic Convention (DC) was very disappointed. The distribution of seats was as follows: DNSF, 166; DC, 116; NSF (led by Petre Roman; it became known as the Democratic Party–National Salvation Front, having merged with the former at the end of May 1993), 61; Romanian National Unity Party (extreme nationalist), 44; Democratic Union of

Hungarians in Romania, 39; Greater Romania Party (extreme nationalist), 22; Socialist Labour Party, 18.

Nicolae Vacaroiu, a senior civil servant in the ministry of finance (head of taxation), was appointed prime minister on 4 November 1992 after Theodor Stolojan declined to stay on. The cabinet mainly comprised other senior civil servants and DNSF members, with no seats for the DC. Deputy prime minister Misu Negritoiu, a reform-minded independent, was put in charge of economic reform. He resigned in late August 1993 and other reformist ministers either resigned or were dismissed amid claims of allegations of corruption against certain remaining government ministers. Vacaroiu himself was seen as cautious about economic reform, stressing the need to take a long-term view and be aware of social costs. He had been dismissed from Petre Roman's government for opposing the lifting of state subsidies and price controls.

The government survived a series of no-confidence votes in 1993 (e.g. December) and in 1994 (e.g. on 1 July, the fifth vote, and on 23 December). In February 1994 negotiations about a possible coalition government began between the Social Democracy Party of Romania (led by Adrian Nastase) and the extreme right-wing nationalist parties. On 19 August 1994 two members of the right-wing National Unity Party (though from the more moderate wing of it) were made ministers (of agriculture and communications).

Presidential and parliamentary elections were held on 3 November 1996. In the first round Ion Iliescu (Social Democracy Party of Romania) came first with 32.25 per cent of the vote, while Emil Constantinescu (Democratic Convention) came second with 28.21 per cent. In the second round of the presidential election, held on 17 November 1996, Emil Constantinescu won with 54.43 per cent of the vote, compared with Iliescu's 45.57 per cent.

Iliescu played on the fears of farmers. On 9 November 1996 he stated:

> The [opposition's] programme makes demagogic promises but what they want to give you is the Romania of 1946, a Romania that was a monarchy. They want to break up the state farms, former royal lands, that now provide most of the country's food. They want to bring back the big landowners.

Some in Romania, says Virginia Marsh, especially the old who form the largest part of the rural population, feared that the opposition might take back land that was handed out under a 1991 restitution law. Exit polls taken on 3 November indicate that Iliescu won more than half the votes of peasant farmers and 42 per cent of the over-65s, while the opposition candidates won the overwhelming support of city dwellers, the young and private businesses (Virginia Marsh, *FT*, 9 November 1996, p. 2). During the campaign Iliescu also claimed that the opposition would close large enterprises and threaten the country's unity by including ethnic Hungarians in the government (Virginia Marsh, *FT*, 19 November 1996, p. 21).

Petre Roman had openly expressed his support for Emil Constantinescu during the campaign. (In March 1996 Petre Roman had formed a new alliance, the Social Democratic Union, comprising his own Democratic Party and the small Social Democratic Party led by Sergiu Cunescu: *EEN*, 1996, vol. 10, no. 9, pp. 6, 8.)

The Democratic Convention, led by Emil Constantinescu, won the parliamentary election. The centre-right coalition comprised, for example, the National Peasant Party/Christian Democrats and the National Liberal Party. On 7 November 1996 the Democratic Convention and the Social Democratic Union (led by Petre Roman) signed a government pact. (They said that 'their priority was to free the exchange rate, tighten monetary policy and overhaul the fiscal system, including a sharp reduction in direct taxes': Virginia Marsh, *FT*, 8 November 1996, p. 2. During the campaign the Democratic Convention advocated faster economic and political reform, a campaign against corruption, removing barriers to private enterprise, improving the welfare system and reducing taxes: Virginia Marsh, *FT*, 19 November 1996, p. 21.) The mayor of Bucharest, Victor Ciorbea, became prime minister. On 17 February 1997 he announced a 'programme of national economic salvation', combining austerity measures with the speeding up of economic reforms.

Eight new cabinet members were announced on 2 December 1997 (*EEN*, 1997, vol. 11, no. 23, p. 8). 'The cabinet reshuffle announced on 2 December was prompted largely by the failure of privatization policy, due partly to wrangling within the governing coalition ... The sense of urgency premier Victor Ciorbea injected into privatization when he took office has evaporated' (p. 4). 'The unimpressive economic performance so far under Ciorbea's government has had little effect on politics – so far' (p. 6).

> The unions have criticized social policies and the way restructuring is being carried out. But demonstrations have for the most part been poorly attended, while golden handshakes have blunted resistance to closures ... Industrial restructuring has usually only happened under multilateral pressure, producing some botched last-minute decisions on closures ... restructuring [is] not far advanced ... The state ownership fund ... is now close to reaching an ambitious target of fifty enterprises a week. In the first nine months of 1997 1,120 firms were privatized ... Restructuring has started ... But problems remain. There has been little progress on broader restructuring – witness the slow rise of unemployment – and less in formulating regional policies. Most of the privatized firms have been small ... Sales of big companies ... are still rare. Few doubt the current government's reform will. But questions are starting to be asked about its competence.
>
> (Business Central Europe 1997: 39–40)

On 14 January 1998 the Social Democrats withdrew their support for prime minister Ciorbea and called for talks to form a new coalition government. But Adrian Severin said that the Social Democrats would remain within the coalition in a 'caretaker capacity'. ('The decision ... amounted to an ultimatum to Mr Ciorbea to step down to pave the way for a government more intent on proceeding with market reforms': *IHT*, 15 January 1998, p. 5. 'The Democratic Party's dissatisfaction with the government's poor record on economic reform is well-founded': *EEN*, 1998, vol. 12, no. 1, p. 5.)

On 15 January 1998 the National Peasants rejected Ciorbea's offer to resign (*FT*, 16 January 1998, p. 2).

> The present clash is not about different approaches to economic reform: it is rather personal rivalries that mean that this basic agreement is being overwhelmed … The political crisis began at the end of last month when the PD [Democratic Party] demanded the replacement of the prime minister, Victor Ciorbea, after the removal of two PD ministers. The foreign minister, Adrian Severin, was forced to resign after failing to substantiate allegations that senior politicians were foreign agents, while the transport minister, Traian Basescu, was sacked for publicly criticizing Mr Ciorbea … Feuding between the parties has helped delay several key reforms, from the restructuring of the oil industry to the redistribution of agricultural land. One reason for this has been the deeply entrenched clientilism of Romanian politics, with politicians acting on behalf of opposing business and industrial interests. But the most important reason for the present split is hostility derived from the past … Reflecting this past is the [Peasants'] Party stand on the restitution of agricultural land to its former owners, something which the PD opposes … The Civic Alliance has been pressing for a much more rigorous approach to the communist past, including the opening of secret police files and the barring from politics of people found to have been Securitate officers or informers – which the PD also opposes. The leadership of the PD, though believers in the free market, is mostly drawn from younger members of the former communist elite … Mr Roman's supporters regard themselves as progressive technocrats, and look down on the Peasants as backward-looking, romantic, inexperienced and incompetent. The peasants for their part see the PD as corrupt former communist apparatchiks who jumped ship from the Ceausescu dictatorship at the last possible moment.
>
> (Anatol Lieven, *FT*, 27 January 1998, p. 3)

'The suspicion is that Mr Roman wants to block reform because it would damage his cronies in business and finance' (*Business Central Europe*, February 1998, p. 7).

> Slow reform, say the Social Democrats. They think themselves superior to the Peasants, and reckon they could run the country better. But the party also has many friends in business and banking whose income streams are threatened by Mr Ciorbea's planned farm reforms and bank privatizations.
>
> (p. 17)

On 29 January 1998 the Democratic Party withdrew its remaining ministers, including the defence minister, from the cabinet (*EEN*, 1998, vol. 12, no. 2, p. 8).

On 6 February 1998 the ruling coalition parties, including the Democratic Party, signed a new co-operation agreement. The Democratic Party no longer insisted on the replacement of prime minister Ciorbea (*EEN*, 1998, vol. 12, no. 2, pp. 1, 8).

Prime minister Ciorbea, however, submitted his resignation to the president on 30 March 1998. Interior minister Gavril Dejeu became acting prime minister. On 15 April 1998 parliament approved a new cabinet under the new prime minister Radu Vasile (deputy chairman of the National Peasants' Party–Christian Democratic Party) (*EEN*, 1998, vol. 12, no. 5, p. 5). He was sworn in by the president the following day. (Former prime minister Victor Ciorbea formed a new party on 19 April 1999, called the National Christian Democratic Alliance, in opposition to the ruling National Peasant Christian Democratic Party: *EEN*, 1999, vol. 12, no. 16, p. 10, and no. 19, p. 3.)

The finance minister was replaced on 23 September 1998.

> At the heart of the coalition's problems has been the ideological conflict between the centre-right National Peasants' Party and the more liberal, technocratic Democratic Party … The Peasants' Party is the largest member of the government and the mainstay of the Democratic Convention … Perhaps the coalition's greatest political problem, however, is the split within the Peasants' Party, which contains paternalistic, conservative and nationalist elements as well as more pragmatic politicians like Radu Vasile, the prime minister. The conservative wing is in large part responsible for the difficult relations with the other governing parties. It is associated with Victor Ciorbea – the former prime minister who was forced out of office in the spring by the Democratic Party. It has uncompromising views on, for example, the need for full property restitution and is also the most resistant to granting ethnic Hungarians all the education rights they demand.
>
> (Virginia Marsh, *FT*, Survey, 28 September 1998, p. ii)

> At issue has been whether to increase the amount of land returned to pre-communist owners to up to 50 ha, as demanded by the National Peasants' Party, the largest member of the coalition, or to stick with the 10 ha granted under previous legislation, the option preferred by the smaller Democratic Party … Midway through their four-year term, the parties have, according to Dinu Gavrilescu, agriculture minister, finally come up with a compromise, allowing for the return of up to 50 ha where possible and providing for financial compensation if not. Mr Gavrilescu says he hopes the government will accept a draft law to this effect shortly … A significant minority is still without full property titles.
>
> (p. iv)

> Sorin Dimitru [privatization minister] quit [on 19 October 1998] following widespread criticism of delays in privatization … Mr Dimitru is leaving office less than a month after the departure of Daniel Daianu, the former finance minister. While the two ministers were criticized by the government for failing to implement reforms, their departures rob Romania of two well-known public advocates of reforms. Both have blamed other ministers and bureaucrats for their lack of progress. Mr Dimitru said yesterday [19 October] he had received no support for privatization from the government, parliament or political parties. His agency privatized 825 companies by the end of August compared with a target for the year of 1,600.
>
> (*FT*, 20 October 1998, p. 3)

> Mr Daianu, who belongs to no political party, was fired as finance minister ostensibly because he failed to increase tax collection … In the end he went primarily because he put too many noses out of joint by refusing to sign off on a $1.5 billion order for ninety-six [US] helicopters. And his call for tax hikes and spending cuts did nothing for his popularity either. Nor was popularity the strong point of privatization minister Sorin Dimitru, who was under pressure to increase the pace of Romania's slow but steady sell-offs. He jumped before he was pushed … In essence Mr Dimitru and the cabinet disagreed over the speed of sell-offs … The government is banking on lucrative telecoms and bank sales to keep the state budget in check.
>
> (*Business Central Europe*, November 1998, pp. 45–6)

The agriculture minister was replaced on 27 November 1998.

According to an opinion poll published in early June 1999, more than 60 per cent of Romanians believed that living standards were better under communism. About 66 per cent were worried that the country was moving in the wrong direction, with three-quarters dissatisfied with living standards. Around 85 per cent were still in favour of a market economy, although 88 per cent believed that the market benefits only high-ranking officials (*Transition*, 1999, vol. 10, no. 3, p. 33). 'In a recent survey 61 per cent said they were better off under the Ceausescu regime. Four-fifths said they were unhappy with their lives' (*Telegraph*, 22 December 1999, p. 11).

On 14 December 1999 prime minister Radu Vasile (of the National Peasants' Party–Christian Democratic Party) was dismissed by the president.

> President Emil Constantinescu dismissed prime minister Radu Vasile early Tuesday [14 December], claiming he was unable to carry out his duties. The move came after seven cabinet ministers from Mr Vasile's own Peasant Party resigned … Alexandru Athanasiu, labour and welfare minister, was named interim prime minister.
>
> (*IHT*, 15 December 1999, p. 4)

'[The prime minister] was charged with incompetence and failing to revive the economy' (*Guardian*, 15 December 1999, p. 17).

> Mr Constantinescu is acting with the support of the Christian Democrats, the dominant partner in the four-party coalition, which yesterday [14 December] suspended Mr Vasile from party offices ... [The party decided] to ban him from running for jobs in the leadership of the party over the next two years. However, Mr Vasile said the president's action was unconstitutional as a prime minister could be sacked only through parliament. 'The presidency has breached the constitution. I consider myself the prime minister' ... Ion Iliescu, leader of the main leftist opposition party, the ex-communist PDSR, also declared the president's move unconstitutional.
>
> (*FT*, 15 December 1999, p. 10)

Radu Vasile went on to establish a 'Popular Group' parliamentary faction within the National Peasants' Party–Christian Democrats with over thirty MPs. He was expelled from the party on 27 December. 'Vasile's demise was probably sealed by the violent demonstration by workers of the Brasov truck plant on 8 November' (*EEN*, 2000, vol. 12, no. 21, p. 8). There was also a violent trade union demonstration in Iasi on 23 November, the start of a national rail strike on 6 December and student unrest (p. 6). On 28 January 2000 ten parliamentary deputies resigned from the ruling National Peasants' Party to join former premier Radu Vasile's new Romanian People's Party (*EEN*, 2000, vol. 12, no. 22, p. 5). 'Radu Vasile, having left the PNT–CD [National Peasants' Party–Christian Democrats], has formed his new Romanian People's Party with the support of at least a dozen PNT–CD MPs' (p. 3).

On 16 December 1999 the president nominated Mugur Isarescu, the governor of the central bank, as prime minister.

> Since then [1989] the West has done little but watch as post-communist Romania stagnated, mired in appalling poverty and systemic corruption. This inaction was possible because, unlike some of its Balkan neighbours, Romania remained basically stable – no civil war or genocide to trigger international concern ... Last month [November 1999] a startling public opinion poll showed that a majority of Romanians believed that 'life was better under Ceausescu' and two-thirds thought the country was 'headed in the wrong direction'. One tangible benefit of life under the dictator had been the guarantee of a job. That is gone. Living standards are falling, unemployment is rampant, and a third of the population lives in poverty ... During their less repressive experience under communism, Poles developed an autonomous civil society and Hungarians a thriving alternative economy. Romanians never had that chance ... Gauged by the sheer amount of social, political and economic change, Romanians have done more, not less, than, say, Czechs ... This month [December 1999] Romania performed what amounts to a miracle in its part of the world: it survived a constitutional

> crisis, salvaged democracy, got an impressive new prime minister, and presented the United States and Western Europe with another chance to do some good … They must not wait. A society can hold on only so long in the grip of misery and isolation … The new prime minister is the perfect candidate to manage Western aid: Mugur Isarescu, head of the Romanian National Bank since 1990. Mr Isarescu … has single-handedly built the credibility of the central bank, kept it out of partisan politics and used its resources to create the building blocks of a market economy while supporting Romanian culture and arts … Without his integrity and expertise at the monetary helm, the country would have defaulted long ago. The fact that he is in office at all is a credit to Romania's political resilience. This month President Emil Constantinescu, confronting popular anger over crime, corruption and deteriorating living standards, fired prime minister Radu Vasile. But someone had apparently forgotten to tell Mr Constantinescu that presidents are not allowed to fire prime ministers under the Romanian constitution. Mr Vasile refused to step down. The opposition walked out of parliament. But the situation never descended into violence. The crisis was defused – with Mr Vasile agreeing to return to a leadership post with the Peasant Party – when Mr Constantinescu named the respected, politically neutral Mr Isarescu as prime minister.
>
> (Daniel Nelson, *IHT*, 28 December 1999, p. 8)

The tenth anniversary of the collapse of the Ceausescu regime on 21 December 1999 was a very quiet affair.

Romania's difficult economic transition has led to much labour unrest. For example, healthcare workers ended a two-week strike on 26 February 1998. They have been awarded a 30 per cent increase in wages (*FT*, 27 February 1998, p. 2). On 10 January 1997 Miron Cozma, the coal miners' leader from the Jiu valley, was arrested. (The charges against him so far have been couched in terms of constitutional infringements rather than the breaking of specific laws: *EEN*, 1997, vol. 11, no. 2, p. 6. He was accused of leading riots in 1991, but the charges against him were dropped in June 1998: *The Economist*, 27 June 1998, p. 51.)

A strike by coal miners in the Jiu valley started on 4 January 1999 over pay and pit closures. On 15 January 1999 a district court ruled the strike to be illegal, but a march on Bucharest started (led by Miron Cozma) and there were violent clashes with police. The prime minister himself negotiated with Cozma and a compromise was reached.

> [On 15 February 1999] Romania's supreme court sentenced Miron Cozma, the militant miners' leader, to eighteen years in jail on Monday [15 February] over offences in 1991 when he spearheaded a march that brought down the government … The union chief … was also convicted of illegal possession of arms and undermining state authority. Mr Cozma had been jailed for eighteen months over leading a miners' march in 1991, which

> turned violent and led to the collapse of the government of then-prime minister Petre Roman. He was released in June 1998.
>
> (*IHT*, 16 February 1999, p. 6)

> Romanian television reported last night that he [Cozma] had gone into hiding ... In reaching its decision the supreme court reversed the ruling of a lower court which last year [1998] reduced the charges against Mr Cozma to public order violations ... Mr Cozma cannot appeal against the supreme court's sentence because of the nature of the charge of undermining the authority of the state ... In 1990 and 1991 he led coal miners on violent rampages through Bucharest which left several people dead. During the events of 1991 ... miners invaded parliament, set government buildings on fire and forced Petre Roman, who was then prime minister, out of office.
>
> (*FT*, 16 February 1999, p. 2)

'[Miron Cozma] was arrested Wednesday [17 February] after clashes between paramilitary police units and miners ... The arrest of Miron Cozma came as he and about 2,000 miners headed towards Bucharest' (*IHT*, 18 February 1999, p. 7).

On 8 November 1999 there was a violent demonstration by workers of the Brasov truck plant (*EEN*, 2000, vol. 12, no. 21, p. 8). There was also a violent trade union demonstration in Iasi on 23 November, the start of a national rail strike on 6 December and student unrest (p. 6).

Nato's secretary-general Javier Solana Madriaga (8 July 1997):

> Today the heads of state and government have agreed to invite the Czech Republic, Hungary and Poland to begin accession talks with Nato ... We affirm that Nato remains open to new members ... We will review the process at our next meeting in 1999. With regard to aspiring members, we recognize with great interest and take account of the positive developments toward democracy and the rule of law in a number of south-eastern European countries, especially Romania and Slovenia.

(A majority of the sixteen Nato countries, led by France, supported the inclusion of Romania and Slovenia in the first wave of invitations. But the USA was adamant that only three countries would be invited to become members of Nato in the first wave.)

President Clinton of the USA visited Bucharest on 11 July 1997 and described Romania as one of the 'strongest candidates' for the second wave of invitations provided it kept to the path of reform. 'The door to Nato is open ... Stay the course and Romania will cross that milestone.' (President Richard Nixon visited Romania in August 1969 and President Gerald Ford visited Romania in August 1975.)

On 16 July 1997 the European Commission recommended that Estonia, Cyprus, the Czech Republic, Hungary, Poland and Slovenia open negotiations in early 1998 for entry to the EU. (The invitations were formally approved at an EU summit on 13 December 1997, formal negotiations for membership beginning on 31 March 1998. Slovakia, Latvia, Lithuania, Bulgaria and Romania were to be given special EU aid to help them meet the conditions necessary for membership negotiations to begin.)

On 13 October 1999 the European Commission recommended that EU leaders at the December 1999 meeting in Helsinki allow Bulgaria, Latvia, Lithuania, Malta, Romania and Slovakia to begin accession negotiations in 2000. The 'principle of differentiation' for entry date will apply to each of the twelve candidates, reflecting differing states of readiness for EU entry. 'Romania has a long way to go' in economic terms. Romania's position is 'very worrying'. In order to begin negotiations Romania must take steps to deal with its weak economic and budgetary position and act to improve the lot of 100,000 children in child-care institutions.

On 8 November 2000 the EU reported that Romania lay last in terms of membership prospects.

The desire for membership of Nato and the EU has helped to produce positive policies with respect to Hungary and to the ethnic Hungarian minority within Romania. According to the *Financial Times* (13 May 1994, p. 2), there are 1.7 million ethnic Hungarians and 2 million Gypsies in Romania. Another source puts the figure for ethnic Hungarians in the range 1.6 million to 2 million (*IHT*, 6 July 1994, pp. 1, 4). There is still widespread discrimination against Gypsies. Gypsies (Roma) account for about 8 per cent of the population (*IHT*, 3 April 2000, p. 6). According to the European Roma Rights Centre, there are more than 1.8 million Gypsies in Romania (*Independent*, 9 August 2000, p. 14).

On 28 May 2000 the National Investment Fund (the largest private investment fund) failed to make payments. Violent protests followed (*EEN*, 2000, vol. 12, no. 23, p. 10). 'Last month [June 2000] the IMF extended a $540 million stand-by loan for Romania until next February [2001]' (*FT*, 17 July 2000, p. 8). 'The IMF has at last signed a delayed loan for about $500 million' (*The Economist*, 10 June 2000, p. 57).

> The IMF has agreed to release $116 million to Romania. The funds represent part of a $535 million stand-by credit originally approved last August [1999]. Romania had drawn only $71 million of the available funds when the funds were halted, following a run on the country's largest bank (Banca Commerciala Romana), the closure of investment fund Fondul National de Investii, and the decision by Banca Populara Romana to suspend payments to depositors. The release of the funds was sanctioned only after the IMF received commitments from the government that state spending would be reduced and salaries pegged and tied to performance.
>
> (*Transition*, 2000, vol. 11, nos 3–4, p. 25)

> Ion Iliescu's Party of Social Democracy was the clear victor in the local elections on 4 June [2000] … even stealing control of right-leaning Bucharest

> for the first time since communism collapsed a decade ago. The results confirm what the opinion polls have been saying: more than half of Romanians think the country is heading in the wrong direction and barely a fifth say life is getting better.
>
> (*The Economist*, 10 June 2000, p. 57)

On 17 July 2000 President Emil Constantinescu announced that he would not run for a second term of office in November 2000. 'In a televised speech Mr Constantinescu said his decision had been prompted by setbacks in his attempts to fight what he called a Mafia-type system of "official corruption, with links to high-ranking state institutions" ' (*IHT*, 18 July 2000, p. 7).

In the general election of 26 November 2000 there was a marked swing to both the left and the right and away from the centre. The Party of Social Democracy made a successful return, as did Ion Iliescu, who comfortably won in the second round of the presidential election held on 10 December 2000 against the candidate of the extreme right-wing Greater Romania Party, Corneliu Vadim Tudor. No radical political or economic policy changes were in the offing, the moderate Adrian Nastase becoming prime minister.

GDP growth turned positive as early as 1993 but output once again fell sharply in three successive years (1997 to 1999). 'Romania remained mired in a recession, with GDP falling by 3.2 per cent in 1999' (EBRD 2000a: 5). Positive growth was recorded in 2000. In 2000 GDP was an estimated 77 per cent of the 1989 level (EBRD 2001: 15). Romania has never experienced anywhere near hyperinflation but progress on the inflation front has nevertheless been slow. In 1997 the rate rose to 154.8 per cent and was not far off 50 per cent even in 2000. Poverty is a serious problem.

It took until the autumn of 1996 for Romania to shake off the dominance of personalities and parties with roots in the communist past. President Iliescu and the Social Democracy Party of Romania (formerly the Democratic National Salvation Front) lost the November 1996 presidential and parliamentary elections respectively largely because of economic factors. (This is not to underestimate the importance of factors such as corruption.) The inconsistency of reform measures can be judged by the fact that on 17 February 1997 prime minister Ciorbea felt obliged to make the following announcement:

> We have prepared a comprehensive programme of economic reforms, with the goal of stabilizing the economy and launching the structural reforms necessary for growth … We inherited a budget deficit (including implicit subsidies) of 13 per cent of gross domestic product from the previous government. Our programmes for 1997 will be to eliminate hidden subsidies and cut the total deficit to roughly one-third last year's level, to 4.5 per cent of GDP. To achieve this we will cut agricultural subsidies, end most price controls, eliminate tax breaks and substantially reduce the public sector …

> At the same time we will put in place programmes of social support to see people through these difficult times.
>
> (*FT*, 18 February 1997, p. 20)

On 17 April 1997 parliament passed an austerity programme (*FT*, 18 April 1997, p. 2). The government planned to put 75 per cent of the economy into private hands within two years and to amend the foreign investment laws by May 1997 (involving tax breaks, the purchase of land and the repatriation of profits) (*Business Central Europe*, April 1997, p. 15). An anti-corruption committee has been set up (*The Economist*, 3 May 1997, p. 36). On 7 August 1997 prime minister Ciorbea announced the immediate closure of seventeen large state enterprises, including engineering enterprises, food-processing enterprises and three (out of eleven) oil refineries. (One enterprise was reprieved when it paid off much of its debt: *The Economist*, 23 August 1997, p. 28. The list has been whittled down from seventeen to twelve: *Business Central Europe*, March 1998, p. 28.)

Romania has had great difficulty meeting conditions laid down for IMF loans. There is a history of delays both in reaching agreement and in the disbursement of tranches.

A floating exchange rate regime was introduced on 8 April 1994, with the exchange rate determined on daily auctions. The leu is virtually fully convertible for the purpose of foreign trade transactions, but there are controls on capital account transactions (EBRD 1994: 33, 109). At the beginning of 1996, in an attempt to control the downward tendency of the leu, the authorities started to impose tight restrictions on enterprises' access to foreign currency and on the foreign currency operations of commercial banks (EBRD 1996b: 168).

The foreign exchange regime was liberalized on 18 February 1997 and both foreign and domestic banks were allowed to operate on the market (*FT*, 18 February 1997, p. 3). In February 1997 prime minister Ciorbea stated that:

> To promote trade and integration with Europe, we have ended controls on the foreign exchange needed for trade purposes, and we have allowed the lei to float freely in the exchange markets. We will also end the cumbersome system of export licensing and import quotas, and we will sharply reduce tariffs and other forms of protection.
>
> (*FT*, 18 February 1997, p. 20)

After unifying the exchange rate in early 1997, Romania introduced full current account convertibility in March 1998. Some restrictions remain on capital account transactions (EBRD 1998b: 184).

The private sector accounted for roughly 15 per cent of GDP in mid-1990. In mid-2000 the figure was 60 per cent (EBRD 1999b: 24, 256, and 2000b: 14, 200).

A privatization bill was passed in late July 1990. This provided for the following:

1 State control of 20 per cent of enterprises (these 'strategic' state-owned so-called 'autonomous entities' included mines, the post, railways, armaments and energy);
2 Eighty per cent state enterprises to be converted into joint stock 'commercial enterprises' before privatization;
3 Thirty per cent of the value of the capital of these joint stock companies to be distributed free to adult residents, in the form of vouchers exchangeable for shares (voucher distribution scheduled to start in the first quarter of 1991 and the sale of shares to begin in the last quarter);
4 A probable 30 per cent of the shares of a particular enterprise to be offered to its employees in exchange for cash or vouchers;
5 A block of shares to be reserved for foreigners.

Further legislation was introduced in August 1991, with the following provisions:

1 Five 'private ownership funds' to be set up and to receive 30 per cent of the shares of each of the commercialized enterprises for free distribution in turn to adult citizens (each citizen to receive a certificate of ownership in each of these funds and the fund shares to be tradable);
2 The remaining 70 per cent of the shares of each of the roughly 6,000 commercialized enterprises to be held in a state ownership fund, with the privatization process supposedly spread over a seven-year period and proceeding via a number of channels (including auctions, direct sell-offs, and sales to foreigners; of the 70 per cent, 10 per cent to be sold to employees of enterprises at a 10 per cent discount).

But implementation of the programme was slow:

1 In 1993 only 250 mainly small enterprises were sold off (management or employee buy-outs being the main methods of privatization during the year) (*FT*, Survey, 3 May 1994, p. 30). Romania has sold off about 900 mainly small state enterprises under the 1991 scheme, with most purchased by management and employee groups (*FT*, 22 March 1995, p. 3).
2 About 270 small enterprises were privatized under the privatization programme in 1993 and another 250 during the first four months of 1994, mostly by management–employee buy-outs (p. 32). By the end of 1994, 891 enterprises had been privatized, primarily through management–employee buy-outs (EBRD 1995a: 62). By mid-1995 more than 1,100 enterprises had been privatized, primarily through management–employee buy-outs (EBRD 1995b: 53). By March 1996 more than 1,500 enterprises had been privatized, primarily through management–employee buy-outs (EBRD 1996b: 167). By the end of 1996 only 45 per cent of all enterprises scheduled for privatization had been privatized. During the first eight months of 1997 privatization accelerated. A further 1,100 enterprises were privatized (140 of

> these being medium-sized or large), bringing the total proportion of enterprises privatized to around 60 per cent (EBRD 1997b: 192).

A new privatization law was passed by parliament on 21 March 1995. Romanians would be able to purchase state assets using 'certificates of ownership' distributed to individuals in 1992 and higher-value coupons which were to be distributed. The new law envisaged the eventual sale through various means of 3,000 enterprises (down from 6,000 in the preceding law). A total of 1,500 enterprises were to be sold in 1995 (EBRD 1995a: 62). The privatization framework foresaw the sale through various means of about 3,900 large and medium-sized enterprises. Up to 60 per cent of the ownership in an individual enterprise might be sold for coupons and certificates of ownership, with the remaining at least 40 per cent to be sold for cash (EBRD 1995b: 53). Between 60 per cent and 70 per cent of the shares in 3,900 enterprises were to be transferred to the population under the scheme (except in selected enterprises in which a majority stake was to be offered to strategic investors). The remaining shares were to be sold for cash (EBRD 1996a: 10). The five ownership funds were converted into private investment funds in November 1996 (EBRD 1997b: 192).

Up to 60 per cent of the equity of most enterprises could be exchanged for coupons, with the remainder to be offered to local or foreign investors for cash, mainly at auctions. The state ownership fund set aside 554 enterprises in which a 51 per cent stake was to be reserved for strategic investors (*FT*, 11 December 1995, p. 27).

Non-residents were to be permitted to acquire up to 51 per cent of the capital of the enterprises on sale. The eighty-four large state enterprises known as 'autonomous bodies of national interest' (*regies autonomes*, operating, for example, in the oil industry, coal mining, power generation, postal services and telecommunications) were to be converted into commercial companies and then partially privatized (Deutsche Bank, *Focus: Eastern Europe*, 1995, no. 141, p. 6).

In February 1997 prime minister Ciorbea was reported as saying that:

> Romania is still burdened with a large state sector which controls three-fifths of the economy and remains inefficient and unreformed. We intend to privatize rapidly as much of this sector as possible, by auctioning enterprises for cash and vouchers. During 1997 we will auction about fifty enterprises a week, liquidate chronic loss-making enterprises and begin restructuring and privatization of leading banks.
>
> (*FT*, 18 February 1997, p. 20)

The government intended to sell 2,750 enterprises by the end of May. Prime minister Ciorbea said that the government would aim to have transferred 69 per cent of enterprises into private hands by the end of 1997 (*FT*, 18 February 1997, p. 20).

In February 1997 the government declared its intention to include seven large *regies autonomes* ('autonomous bodies of national interest') and state farms in the privatization programme (EBRD 1997a: 32). At the start of 1996 over 75 per cent of the total book value of companies allocated to the state ownership fund was still state-owned. The reform programme of early 1997 gave greater decision-making power to the fund, shifting focus to direct sales. More recently increasing emphasis has been placed on IPOs and sales to foreign strategic investors. But 'the pace of privatization remained very slow'. The state ownership fund still maintains a portfolio of 5,500 enterprises to be privatized.

> Little progress has been made in the restructuring of loss-making state-owned enterprises, including the *regies autonomes*. Plans for closing some of the biggest loss-makers – agreed with the IMF and the World Bank in 1997 – have not been realized. However, a rationalization programme was implemented successfully in the mining sector. In addition, the government pressured the *regies autonomes* to develop reorganizational plans. One such plan, for the national oil company Petrom, was submitted in May 1998.
>
> (EBRD 1998b: 184)

> Large-scale privatization has received a new impetus since the last quarter of 1998 … by recent sales to strategic investors of large stakes in the telecommunications operator Romtelecom, the Romanian Development Bank and the oil refinery Petromidia, as well as the agreement to sell the automobile manufacturer Dacia to Renault … The state ownership fund has announced the start of liquidation procedures for forty-nine large loss-making companies. The objective is to reduce overall losses in the economy from these enterprises by 30 per cent.
>
> (EBRD 1999a: 42)

Large privatization has gained pace since the last quarter of 1998 (see below) (EBRD 1999b: 254). Large-scale privatization has been proceeding slowly. Only two large sales involving foreign investors were completed in 1999 – the carmaker Dacia and the Romanian PostaBank. A new privatization law, adopted in June 1999, provides for the sale through investment banks of some of the country's largest assets, including Tarom (the national airline), Sidex (a steel company) and Petrom (an oil company) (EBRD 2000a: 72).

> While there was some progress in privatization in 1999, the pace remains slow … The cumulative total of privatized enterprises at the end of 1999 stood at 35 per cent SOF [state ownership fund] capital … Despite lower enterprise losses, key structural problems remain … The government continues to channel money into some of the largest loss-making firms through the toleration of tax arrears and cross-subsidization by the SOF. Enterprise arrears are growing. Arrears to the government have continued to grow … Domestic arrears to the three major utilities increased by 20 per cent in real terms during the first half of 2000.
>
> (EBRD 2000b: 198–9)

> Large-scale privatization has been slow in Romania and was frozen before the presidential and parliamentary elections of November 2000 … In January 2001 the new government dissolved the state ownership fund, set up a new authority for the privatization and administration of state assets [a restructuring fund that will help enterprises prepare for privatization: p. 28] … The privatization of the energy sector, which includes measures to revitalize the mining sector, is a priority for the new government.
>
> (EBRD 2001: 82)

In November 1998 OTE, the partly privatized Greek telecoms operator, bought 35 per cent of Rom Telecom (*FT*, 13 November 1998, p. 29).

In December 1998 it was announced that 51 per cent of the Romanian Bank for Development (the fourth largest bank) has been sold to a French bank (*IHT*, 15 December 1998, p. 16). This is the first state bank to be privatized (EBRD 1999b: 254).

In early 1999 Automobile Dacia was sold (EBRD 1999b: 254). 'The acquisition of car-maker Dacia by France's Renault was achieved only by granting some unique tax breaks' (Business Central Europe 1999: 36).

On 16 May 1999 the Romanian government announced an accelerated privatization programme. The first wave of sixty-four large and medium-sized state companies represents about 14 per cent of GDP. The list is headed by the national airline Tarom, the giant Sidex steel works of Galati and two aluminium companies (*FT*, 17 May 1999, p. 3).

> The privatization process … has significantly accelerated its pace over the last year … Major deals … include the carmaker Dacia Automobile Pitesti to Renault of France in June … Last year's partial privatization of Rom Telecom, the national phone operator, was the first step in the enormous task of restructuring and privatizing Romania's *regies autonomes*, or public utilities monopolies owned by the state [state-owned monopolies in the public utilities or resources sectors]. Next in line for changes in ownership and administration are the power distribution, oil and gas, transportation, tobacco, postal services and water distribution public utilities … The privatization show will feature the country's biggest companies, all of them operating in the energy sector: the power company Conel; the oil company Petrom; and the natural gas company Romgaz … Petrom is Romania's largest company and accounts for roughly 10 per cent of the economy.
>
> (*IHT*, Survey, 26 October 1999, pp. 18–20)

The new privatization law, approved by parliament in June 1999, provides for the use of investment banks as sales agents, eliminates minimum sales prices linked to book value (thereby allowing sale at market value) and contains provisions for debt workouts. The new law also contains provisions giving minority shareholders the right to more information and control. 'These provisions aim to reduce the power of enterprise insiders, who have gained effective control of privatized enterprises in the majority of cases' (EBRD 1999b: 254–5).

There was controversy in 2000. 'Scandals have accompanied nearly every [privatization] deal, leading to a spate of sales being investigated or cancelled' (Business Central Europe 2000: 40). 'Romania has cancelled several sales' (p. 53).

Foreign direct investment has been disappointing, although the picture improved significantly from 1997 onwards. (See Table 6.2, p. 340.) Western direct investment is now welcomed, but early obstacles included the inability of foreigners to own land (except in the case where Romanian enterprises had majority foreign ownership and where the Romanian partners contributed the land as their share).

> One important hurdle to foreign investment has been removed with the approval recently of a law allowing foreigners to own land. The single clause reads 'Commercial companies with partial or total foreign capital registered as legal Romanian entities may acquire, for their duration, right of ownership and all other title to land necessary for their activities.'
>
> (*EEN*, 27 February 1997, vol. 11, no. 4, p. 4)

A land law was passed in February 1991, some 80 per cent of arable land being eligible for return to former owners or their heirs (*EEN*, 'Romania', 20 August 1991, p. 4). Others eligible for land include members who have worked in co-operatives for at least three years. The land received from the state was limited to a maximum of 10 ha, although up to 100 ha was allowed through purchase or inheritance.

> In Romania, Hungary and former Czechoslovakia current land restitution is (explicitly) not based on the 1945 ownership situation, but the ownership strongly influenced by the post-World War II (between 1945 and 1949) land reforms implemented by a government dominated by the Communist Party ... The Czech government decided to use the February 1948 date as the basis for restitution. Similarly, Hungary took 1948 and Romania took 1947 as their reference dates ... Collective farmland is [thus] restituted to former owners, but state farmland is privatized through different procedures. A reason is the difference in legal ownership: state farms operated mainly on land legally owned by the state. In some cases that farmland was state-owned before 1940; in other cases it was nationalized after the war (taken from foreigners or from the church).
>
> (Swinnen 1999: 642–3)

'Foreign former landowners have not been restituted land' (p. 646).

> In Romania two thirds of the state farmland is in 'new' areas, i.e. land that was created for agricultural use under the communist regime by land

> improvements and drainage investments in the Danube Valley. This land is not privatized yet … in contrast to the rest of Romania's farmland.
>
> (p. 652)

The private sector quickly came to dominate Romanian agriculture. Over 80 per cent of the area farmed had been privatized by the end of 1992 (United Nations Economic Commission for Europe 1993: 223). About 85 per cent of agricultural land is now private, employing 35 per cent of the active workforce and accounting for 25 per cent of GDP. The 700-odd state farms account for about 12 per cent of agricultural land and roughly the same percentage of output (*EEN*, 31 May 1996, vol. 10, no. 11, pp. 4–5). In 1995 the private sector accounted for 89 per cent of the value-added in agriculture. The privatization of state farms has proceeded relatively slowly, especially since the government has decided to preserve them as unified production units (EBRD 1996b: 167).

A number of problems still afflict agriculture. One is the small size of family farms. Most farmland has been returned but the average amount is just 2.2 ha, often split into three or four parcels of land (*FT*, 11 July 1996, p. 31). Private farms are extremely small, with an average size of under 3 ha (*IHT*, Survey, 26 October 1999, p. 21). There have been delays in granting farmers full title to their land. By the end of 1996 only 65 per cent of definitive title deeds had been issued (*EEN*, 1997, vol. 11, no. 16, p. 5).

On 16 September 1997 the Senate amended the 1991 law on land restitution without specifying how much land could be restored to former owners. Parliament would decide the limits on restituted land by 31 March 1998. Under the 1991 law a maximum of 10 ha of farmland and 1 ha of forestland could be restituted per family (*Transition*, 1997, vol. 8, no. 5, p. 24).

> After months of wrangling the Romanian government hopes to agree soon on a new formula for the restitution of agricultural land … The agriculture minister believes the country's multi-party coalition will now accept legislation allowing the return of up to 50 ha of land per former owner and providing for financial compensation where this was not possible.
>
> (*FT*, 9 September 1998, p. 48)

On 9 November 1999 the upper house passed a bill granting the return of some farmland seized during the communist era. The bill provided for the restitution to the original owners of as much as 50 ha of farmland confiscated in the 1950s. A commission of parliament is expected to mediate issues related to the restitution of forest land that was confiscated, which was also voted on (*IHT*, 10 November 1999, p. 6). Families whose land cannot be returned will receive compensation (*The Times*, 10 November 1999, p. 18).

> Almost all 115 large, state-owned pig and poultry farms – most of which were in poor financial shape – have been either privatized or liquidated. The former state monopoly in charge of storing and treating grain was

> dismantled into some sixty regional units; most of them have been privatized. Agricultural service providers and seed farms have also been privatized or liquidated … [The agriculture minister] is bullish about the privatization of the state-owned cereal farms by the end of the year [1999].
>
> (*IHT*, Survey, 26 October 1999, p. 21)

> A radical alteration of the structure of property in Romanian agriculture will begin in the coming weeks, following the passage of two new laws, one concerning the privatization of state-owned farms and another the restitution of land and forests confiscated by the communists. Agricultural land in Romania will be 92 per cent private.
>
> (p. 19)

> [Since 1989] the co-operative farms have been completely transformed into either 'agricultural societies' (ASs), 'farmers' associations' (FAs) or individual farms. 'Agricultural societies' are legal entities that employ both members and non-member workers. 'Farmers' associations' are managed by their members but have no legal status … By 1997 … ASs … occupied 11.8 per cent of total agricultural land. FAs … occupied 8.4 per cent.
>
> (Rizov *et al.* 2001: 1261)

In 1997 individual farms accounted for 58.6 per cent of total agricultural land, commercial companies (former state farms) for 12.0 per cent and other institutions (land belonging to agricultural research networks and local councils being included here) for 9.2 per cent (p. 1260).

Slovakia: a summary

The West's view of Slovakia has been transformed since Vladimir Meciar's fall from high office.

On 8 July 1997 its erstwhile partner the Czech Republic (but not Slovakia) was invited 'to begin accession talks with Nato' (the former becoming a member on 12 March 1999). On 16 July 1997 the European Commission recommended that the Czech Republic, but not Slovakia, open negotiations on membership of the EU (confirmed at the EU summit on 13 December 1997).

> The Commission concludes that Slovakia does not fulfil in a satisfying manner the political conditions set by the European Council in Copenhagen because of the instability of Slovakia's institutions, their lack of rootedness in political life and the shortcomings in the functioning of democracy.

In contrast, on 13 October 1999 the European Commission recommended (and this was confirmed at the EU summit on 10 December 1999) that Slovakia begin accession negotiations and that the 'principle of differentiation' should apply (i.e. the date of EU entry for each and every candidate will be determined by its readiness for EU entry). The Commission noted that Slovakia had made strong progress on political reform since the change of government in September 1998. Slovakia had a good chance of catching up with the group led by Hungary. It should meet the market economy criterion in 2000 and the competitive criterion in the medium term. Slovakia could become a functioning market economy in 2000 if it pushed ahead with promised reform. The 8 November 2000 EU report recognized the progress that Slovakia had made but highlighted the areas still causing concern.

Meciar has been in and out of office. Meciar's government resigned on 14 March 1994, but after the 30 September–1 October 1994 general election he became prime minister for the third time and his Movement for a Democratic Slovakia formed a coalition government with the Association of Slovak Workers and the Slovak National Party. Despite the pronounced nationalistic tone of Meciar's election campaign, Slovakia and Hungary signed an agreement guaranteeing borders and minority rights on 19 March 1995. The International Court of Justice at The Hague delivered its verdict on the Gabcikovo Dam dispute with Hungary on 25 September 1997. A Hungarian consulate opened on 18 August 2000 in Kosice (*EEN*, 2000, vol. 12, no. 24, p. 6). (There is still widespread discrimination against the large Gypsy minority.) Meciar never resolved his bitter clashes with President Roman Kovac. The latter's term of office ended on 2 March 1998. Partly because most of the president's powers devolve to the prime minister in the former's absence, there ensued a long-drawn-out process of finding a replacement. The issue was not resolved until Rudolf Schuster beat Meciar in the second round of a popular presidential election held on 29 May 1999 (parliament having earlier in the year passed a law allowing for direct elections). On 20 April 2000 Meciar was charged with abuse of power and fraud while in office, allegedly paying illegal bonuses to his ministers.

> Slovakia's chief prosecutor dropped charges of fraud against former premier Vladimir Meciar, saying there were no laws against the controversial bonuses Mr Meciar paid to his ministers during his tenure. But Mr Meciar could still face charges of abuse of power.
>
> (*Business Central Europe*, June 2000, pp. 14–15)

In the general election of 25–6 September 1998 a new coalition government was formed, comprising the Slovak Democratic Coalition, the Party of the Democratic Left, the Party of Civic Understanding and the Hungarian Coalition (which won concessions for the Hungarian minority in the regional devolution reforms of February 2001). Mikulas Dzurinda became prime minister, with a far more positive approach to democracy, to economic reform and to the West. The coalition government has survived despite stresses and strains, not least caused by austerity measures to try to overcome the economic legacy left by Meciar. Fear of his return to power has helped maintain a sufficient degree of unity.

Prime minister Mikulas Dzurinda actually left the Slovak Democratic Coalition on 17 January 2000 and set up the Slovak Democratic and Christian Union. Several senior ministers followed him. But the governing coalition survived (*FT*, 18 January 2000, p. 6; *Business Central Europe*, March 2000, p. 44). On 19 February the Democratic Union leader and foreign minister Eduard Kukan switched allegiance to premier Mikulas Dzurinda's new party (*EEN*, 2000, vol. 12, no. 22, p. 6).

Government policy in Slovakia is decidedly pointed to the West. Ivan Miklos (deputy prime minister, 27 March 2000):

> There is broad consensus about this [a policy in favour of joining Nato]. Even Mr Meciar's party … has recently declared it is now in favour. Within the government there is no doubt. A small country like Slovakia cannot be isolated. Nato membership is also crucial to economic recovery, in that it reinforces stability.
>
> (*IHT*, 28 March 2000, p. 2)

'A recent [18 March 2000] HZDS [Movement for a Democratic Slovakia] party congress embraced Nato and the EU much more enthusiastically than ever before' (*FT*, Survey, 25 May 2000, p. 15).

Macroeconomic performance has been relatively good compared with Slovakia's political record. But restructuring was neglected, with substantial state support for ailing enterprises, under the Meciar administrations.

GDP growth turned positive as early as 1994. GDP growth regained its 1989 level in 1999 (EBRD 2000b: 65, and 2001a: 15). The annual inflation rate reached a peak of only 61.2 per cent in 1991. The inflation rate moved into single figures in 1995 but in 1999 and 2000 the rate was in double figures.

The second round of Slovakia's mass (voucher) privatization programme was set to begin in mid-1993 but was delayed. Vouchers were to play only a 'residual' or 'supplementary' role with the bulk of shares sold. On 1 July 1995 the Meciar government introduced a new programme. Vouchers were to be replaced by five-year bonds (although among other things they could be exchanged for shares). The emphasis was to be on sales with preference given to 'insiders' (especially managers) on easy terms. But allegations of corruption abounded as companies were sold cheaply to Meciar supporters. Foreigners played little part in the proceedings and the government resolved to maintain state ownership of strategic enterprises in sectors such as energy, telecommunications and armaments. The new government has reviewed past sales and even renationalized some assets. It is resolved to implement a transparent process of privatization.

> Progress in enterprise restructuring has been hampered by weak corporate governance and by an ineffective bankruptcy system … The September 1999 law on privatization has facilitated the sale of state shares in strategic enterprises. These include majority stakes in the

> dominant telecommunications operator and large banks, and minority stakes in the energy sector companies.
>
> (EBRD 2000a: 76)

'The privatization of large-scale enterprise has been reinvigorated. However, the pace of industrial restructuring and liquidations needs to be accelerated … Despite some recent progress industrial restructuring remains slow' (EBRD 2000b: 206). 'The main focus is now on selling state shares in the banking sector and large infrastructure enterprises, such as those in the telecommunications and energy sectors' (EBRD 2001: 28). 'With progress in privatization well advanced, the remaining state-owned companies are concentrated in the banking and energy sectors … Privatization in the banking sector has proceeded further in recent months' (p. 86).

In July 2000 a 51 per cent stake in the national telephone company was sold to a German company. 'Deutsche Telekom became the new owner of Slovak Telecom, paying Euro 1 billion for a 51 per cent stake. It is the largest Slovak privatization to date' (*Business Central Europe*, September 2000, p. 14).

> Foreign investors are starting to revive some of the companies Mr Meciar's allies destroyed. Take steel-maker VSZ, which was driven to bankruptcy by its Meciar-friendly managers. Revived under the control of its creditors, it was finally sold to US Steel in November 2000 in a $1 billion deal. VSZ was once Slovakia's biggest exporter.
>
> (Business Central Europe 2000: 29)

The private sector accounted for roughly 10 per cent of GDP in mid-1990. In mid-2000 it was 75 per cent (EBRD 1999b: 24, 264, and 2000b: 14, 208).

Slovakia formally adopted the conditions of the IMF's Article 8 relating to current account convertibility on 1 October 1995 and some restrictions remain on the capital account. On 1 October 1998 the pegged exchange rate regime was replaced by a floating one. An import surcharge introduced at the end of May 1999 is destined to be gradually phased out by the end of 2000.

Slovakia has been far less successful than the Czech Republic at attracting direct foreign investment and (like the latter) has reintroduced incentives. (See Table 7.2, p. 366.) 'After years of being a black spot for FDI in Central Europe, Slovakia last year [2000] attracted $2 billion, more than the entire amount received since … 1993' (*FT*, Survey, 4 July 2001, p. iii).

Hungarian oil and gas company Mol has agreed to buy a strategic 36 per cent stake in the Slovak oil company Slovnaft and intends to raise its holding to 50 per cent (*Business Central Europe*, May 2000, p. 15). In April 2000 a significant share in the Slovnaft refinery was sold to Mol. 'This represents the first large acquisition within the region without the direct involvement of investors from a non-transition country' (EBRD 2000a: 76).

> In April 2000 the Hungarian oil and gas company MOL acquired one-third of an oil refinery, Slovnaft, including the right to increase its stake to above 50 per cent after two years. This is the largest single foreign investment in the country to date, as well as the biggest cross-border deal in the region.
>
> (EBRD 2000b: 206)

Lessons of the first decade of economic transition: a summary

There is increasing recognition that the institutional basis of a market economy takes a long time to put in place. Time is required for appropriate (political, legal and economic) institutions, attitudes and behaviour to develop (including informal codes of behaviour such as 'gentlemen's agreements'). There is, for example, a vital need for an efficient and honest legal system to enforce contracts and property rights. 'The evidence now shows clearly that the central lesson of transition is that markets will not function well without supporting institutions, a state that carries through its basic responsibilities and a healthy civil society' (EBRD 1999b: 5).

> Some aspects of a market economy can and have been created quickly, in particular through liberalization and privatization. However, developing the institutions and behaviour required for well-functioning markets and private enterprise takes much longer. The promotion of effective institutions, such as government structures, laws and regulations and the sound behaviour of governments, enterprises and financial institutions, lies at the heart of the challenge of transition as it enters the next decade.
>
> (p. iv)

The Asian financial crisis started in July 1997 with a speculative attack on the currency of Thailand and then spread to other emerging markets. Russia started to be affected in October 1997 and May 1998 was a bad month. But disaster struck on 17 August 1998 when Russia was forced to devalue the rouble and default on its domestic debt. The Asian/Russian financial crisis bolstered the arguments against undue haste in dismantling controls on the capital account.

As regards privatization, the potential for abuse is massive. Thus there is need for an honest, democratic and thus accountable state to control the process of privatization (and, as mentioned above, for an efficient and honest legal system to enforce contracts and property rights). As regards the question of corporate control, the absence of effective regulation of stock markets can lead to the sort of problems experienced by the Czech Republic (such as the defrauding of shareholders). On the other hand, the weaknesses of banking systems have been exposed by the Asian financial crisis which began in July 1997, e.g. banks providing loans on the basis of cronyism and patronage rather than profitability. Poland has shown that a relatively slow process of privatizing large enterprises can still bring benefits when state industrial enterprises are made to face 'hard budget constraints' (i.e. no automatic bail-outs by the state) and competition from domestic and foreign companies. There are a variety of methods of privatization, although in reality privatization programmes are mixtures (packages) of some sort or another. The varying emphases in these mixed programmes reflect political as well as economic circumstances. As is seen below, Russia's weak central (federal) government claimed that it needed to 'buy off' a powerful managerial lobby (in a society sceptical about the value of privatization), while the former Czechoslovakia had a strong central government (which was not faced by severe inflationary pressures, and therefore had less need to raise revenue for budgetary purposes). Although burdened by a large *per capita* foreign debt, Hungary has not sought debt forgiveness. Hence revenue raised from sales has been particularly important. The director of the Slovenian privatization agency has said that 'the political conditions here would make it impossible to do it all through the state like in Germany, because all managers here believe they already own the companies' (*FT*, Survey, 12 April 1994, p. 32).

Part I

The countries of Eastern Europe

1 Albania

POLITICS

The political background

The Democratic Party won 92 out of the 140 seats in the March 1992 general election, the Socialist Party 38, the Social Democratic Party 7, the Union for Human Rights 2 and the Albanian Republican Party 1 seat (Deutsche Bank, *Focus: Eastern Europe*, 1995, no. 125, p. 7).

The Berisha regime showed worrying signs of authoritarianism (see below for details and, for example, *EEN*, 1993, vol. 7, nos 9, 16 and 17; *The Economist*, 9 April 1994, p. 39).

> Within four years Mr Berisha had created what Human Rights Watch last March [1997] called 'a one-party state based on fear and corruption'. He … turned the justice system into a political instrument. He expanded the National Intelligence Service to a force of 3,000 agents supported by another 3,000 informers which operated as an arm of his party.
>
> (Edward Cody, *IHT*, 5 August 1997, p. 7)

Since 1990 there has been a dramatic and uncontrolled exodus from highland villages to the towns. The great majority of migrants in the shanty towns (which are a health hazard) are from the northern and central highlands.

> The ruling Democratic Party (DP), whose president Sali Berisha hails from the north-eastern district of Tropoja, did nothing to prevent the migration – partly because these people came from districts that are identified with the DP establishment, and secondly because it was considered opportune that DP-voting northerners should settle in the opposition's urban strongholds.
>
> (*EEN*, 18 January 1996, vol. 10, no. 2, p. 7)

Government statistics suggest that the urban population has increased from 35 per cent to 44 per cent and may reach over 50 per cent by the end of 1996 (*ibid.*).

The armed forces have been placed under civilian control and their total strength reduced from 90,000 to 35,000. The 600,000-strong reserve force has been disbanded (*FT*, Survey, 19 February 1997, p. 16).

> As the result of waves of emigration in the fifteenth, nineteenth and late twentieth centuries the ethnic diaspora numbers about 1 million in Turkey, nearly 2 million in Greece, 350,000 in the USA, and around 150,000 each in Italy, Germany and Switzerland ... Communities of Albanians in Macedonia, Kosovo and Montenegro ... are not really diaspora, but parts of the ancient Albania Illyria which got folded into Yugoslavia at the end of the Ottoman reign in the Balkans.
>
> (*FT*, Survey, 23 February 2000, p. 13)

The Greek minority

In 1937 the kingdom of Albania had a population of 1,003,097, of whom 92 per cent were Albanians, 4.7 per cent were Greeks and 3.3 per cent were 'others'. Around 71 per cent of the population were Moslems, 19 per cent were Orthodox Christians (mainly in the south) and 10 per cent were Roman Catholics (chiefly in the north). No geological survey had yet taken place. Only about 23 per cent of the land was arable and just 11 per cent was actually cultivated, mostly in the north (*Albanian Life*, 1994, issue 56, no. 1, p. 7).

The population of Albania was 3.4 million at the end of 1998.

Today about 98 per cent of the population are Albanians, 1.7 per cent are Greeks and the rest are mainly Macedonians, Vlachs and Gypsies (*Independent*, 30 June 1993, p. 8).

25 June 1993: Albania expels a Greek Orthodox priest, accusing him of stirring up secessionist feeling among the minority Greeks in southern Albania. (He allegedly distributed literature claiming the area was Greek territory, specifically as northern Epirus.)

The next day, in retaliation, Greece started to expel large numbers (possibly as many as 30,000 up to July) of (mostly) illegal Albanian immigrants. (*EEN* puts the total number deported at over 120,000: 15 March 1995, vol. 9, no. 6, p. 4; in 1994 Greece deported 70,000 Albanians: *The Economist*, 1 April 1995, p. 46.) There were originally perhaps around 300,000 Albanian immigrants in total in Greece. A figure of around 200,000 was later mentioned by *FT* (15 April 1994, p. 3) and *IHT* (23 April 1994, p. 15). There are now 150,000 Albanians working illegally in Greece (*FT*, 6 April 1995, p. 2). Some 400,000 Albanians work (mostly illegally) in Greece and Italy, sending home more than $450 million a year (*The Economist*, 18 May 1996, p. 51).

There were also incidents along the border and among the Greek minority in Albania. *EEN* paints a dismal picture of corruption, thuggery and exploitation in the cross-border movements of Albanians (1993, vol. 7, no. 22, pp. 4–7). In total probably some 500,000 Albanians work abroad (*The Economist*, 1 April 1995, p. 46).

It is difficult to know how many ethnic Greeks there are in Albania. The Greek government, it is typically claimed, says that there are around 300,000 ethnic Greeks in Albania, but most Western estimates are around the 200,000 mark (although *EEN* puts the number at a probable 100,000: 15 March 1995, vol. 9, no. 6, p. 4). The Albanian government puts the number at only 60,000. *IHT* (7 October 1994, p. 4) reports that the Greek government's estimate is 400,000, that of Albania 60,000 and that of the CIA 280,000. (The last population census in the early 1980s put the number at 54,000 and 49,000 voted for the Greek minority party in the March 1992 election: Pavli Qesku, Albania's ambassador to Great Britain, *Independent*, 25 August 1993, p. 35.)

10 April 1994: two Albanian border guards are killed in a raid on a training camp near the border with Greece. Reciprocal expulsions of diplomats follow. (The attack was led by members of the Greek nationalist 'North Epirus Liberation Front', who are demanding the annexation of the area by Greece: Deutsche Bank, *Focus: Eastern Europe*, 1995, no. 125, p. 8. 'North Epirus' is the name given by Greek nationalists to southern Albania.)

30 May 1994: Greece lodges a formal complaint about the arrest of members of the Greek minority in Albania.

7 July 1994: in another border incident a Greek soldier is wounded.

15 August 1994: the trial begins of five ethnic Greeks (members of Omonia: 'Concord' or 'Harmony'). They are charged with (1) treason and spying (military espionage on behalf of the Greek secret service) in an attempt to 'change Albania's frontiers' and (2) illegal possession of weapons. Although the charge of treason is dropped (because it derived from the penal code operating in the communist period), they are still accused of attempting to 'annex southern Albania'. On 7 September they were given prison sentences of six to eight years. They were convicted, among other things, of 'collaborating with Greek secret services to arm the Greek minority in Albania' and informing Greek intelligence of Albanian troop movements. (The appeal produced only a slight reduction in the sentences. But one was pardoned in December 1994 and the other four had their sentences suspended by the Supreme Court on 8 February 1995.)

Greek retaliation took a number of forms: (1) the expulsion of Albanians – perhaps 70,000 by early October; (2) the blocking of EU financial aid worth Ecu 35 million to Albania (the veto was lifted in November 1994); (3) the closing of one of the main crossing points to Albanians and a slowing of commercial traffic.

23 August 1994: a Greek plane (stolen, according to the Greek government) flies into Albanian air space and drops leaflets calling for the removal of the Albanian government.

16 September 1994: Greece accuses Albania of closing its borders to Greek traffic.

13–14 March 1995: the Greek foreign minister Carolos Papoulias visits Albania. The visit is considered a success, e.g. work is to begin on a treaty of peace and friendship. Key issues agreed on were the establishment of private Greek language schools, economic co-operation (such as protection of foreign investment and the creation of a joint Greek–Albanian bank) and the settlement by negotiation of the legal status of Albanian migrant workers in Greece (*EEN*, 1995, vol. 9, no. 6, p. 4).

20 March 1995: Greek security forces arrest several members of the North Epirus Liberation Front as they are preparing to mount a raid across the Albanian border.

21 March 1996: the presidents of Albania and Greece sign a 'friendship and co-operation' treaty during the latter's visit. Albania agrees that schools in southern Albania should provide Greek-language teaching and that visa requirements for Greek businessmen should be lifted. Greece is preparing legislation to allow at least 150,000 Albanians to be issued with temporary work permits (*FT*, 21 March 1996, p. 4).

5 August 1997: Greece agrees to issue temporary work permits to Albanians working illegally in Greece in return for co-operation in combating cross-border crime (*FT*, 6 August 1997, p. 2).

Political developments from 1 July 1992 until the May–June 1996 general election

1 July 1992: around 6,000 people try to commandeer ships in two ports to flee the country.

19 January 1993: thousands again try to flee to Italy.

26 January 1993: Nexhmije Hoxha, the widow of Enver Hoxha, is jailed for nine years for misappropriation of state funds (increased to eleven years on 17 May).

12 February 1993: a friendship and co-operation treaty is signed with Bulgaria.

25 April 1993: the Pope visits Albania.

12 July 1993: the leader of a small opposition party is sentenced to six months in prison for denouncing President Berisha in the party newspaper.

27 July 1993: parliament votes to deprive former prime minister Fatos Nano of his immunity from arrest. Criminal proceedings are started against him for alleged 'abuse of duty and the falsification of official documents in connection with Italian aid' (the single agency he was alleged to have insisted on using overcharged and delivered some foodstuffs which were unfit for human consumption). (He was arrested on 30 July, while other members of the Socialist Party have also been arrested. On 3 April 1994 he was sentenced to twelve years in prison. 'Since Mr Nano's arrest, public political rallies have been banned, except those of the Democratic Party. Indoor meetings organized by the opposition parties are routinely disrupted or banned': *The Economist*, 9 April 1994, p. 39.)

19 August 1993: seven senior communists are placed under arrest, including Ramiz Alia (already under house arrest for abuse of power) and Foto Cami (also already under house arrest). (The trial of Alia and nine others, including former prime minister Adil Carcani, began on 21 May 1994. Alia was charged with misappropriation of state funds and abuse of power, including the policy of shooting Albanians trying to flee the country. On 2 July 1994 he was given a jail sentence of nine years, but he was released from jail on 7 July 1995.)

31 August 1993: former prime minister Vilson Ahmeti is sentenced to two years in prison for alleged abuse of power (for squandering funds in a failed attempt at debt rescheduling; specifically for authorizing a French businessman to negotiate Albania's foreign debt without checking his credentials).

20 September 1993: Momir Bulatovic, the president of Montenegro, visits Albania.

8 and 14 October 1993: the USA and Albania respectively sign an accord on military co-operation. It affirms 'the readiness to broaden and expand defence and military relations between the two countries' with training programmes for Albanian officers and high-level meetings on 'the international security environment'.

Early November 1993: there are protests about a new press law, which gives state institutions the power to withhold information they consider secret or harmful to public or private interests. Newspapers can be confiscated if an article is judged harmful to the public interest (*Albanian Life*, 1994, issue 56, no. 1, p. 33).

9 November 1993: finance minister Genc Ruli resigns (amid allegations of corruption) and trade minister Artan Hoxha is dismissed. (The governor of the central bank was also dismissed.)

20 November 1993: Leka I (proclaimed king by Albanian exiles after the death of King Zog in 1961) visits Albania for the first time since his family fled after the Italian invasion in April 1939. The authorities order him to leave after just a day because his passport is stamped 'Kingdom of Albania'.

3 March 1994: a new right-wing political alliance is formed (the Democratic Party of the Right). One of its main aims is the return of former landowners' property (*EEN*, 13 April 1994, vol. 8, no. 8, p. 8). (It had difficulty getting registered.)

30 October 1994: the Pope announces Albania's first ever cardinal.

6 November 1994: President Berisha holds a referendum on the new constitution after failing to achieve a two-thirds majority in parliament.

Berisha is unsuccessful in the referendum, with only just over 40 per cent voting 'yes' (*Albanian Life*, 1995, issue 57, no. 1, p. 31). According to Deutsche Bank (*Focus: Eastern Europe*, 1995, no. 125, p. 7), the turnout was 84 per cent.

The proposed new constitution separated judicial, executive and legislative powers and granted freedom of religion. But opposition was strong because it granted substantial powers to the president, including the following rights: to nominate the prime minister; appoint or dismiss ministers at the suggestion of the prime minister; preside over the cabinet on special occasions and set the agenda; dismiss or arrest the chairman and members of the supreme court and constitutional court with the approval of parliament.

At the end of December 1994 both coalition partners of the Democratic Party, the Republican Party (one representative) and the Social Democratic Party (seven representatives) announced the end of their co-operation (Deutsche Bank, *Focus: Eastern Europe*, 1995 no. 125, p. 7).

After the failure of the referendum nine out of nineteen cabinet ministers were replaced. Berisha's administration then lost the last of its support as the Republican Party pulled out of the coalition on the grounds that the government was incapable of fighting corruption and inefficiency (*Albanian Life*, 1995, issue 57, no. 1, p. 31).

5 March 1995: Eduard Selami is ousted as chairman of the Democratic Party.

26 March 1995: around a thousand young Albanians storm the United States embassy in Tirana on rumours that visas and work permits are about to be issued. Police open fire and two demonstrators are reportedly injured.

1 May 1995: Amnesty International calls on the government to honour its human rights commitments under national and international law. In its most recent report Amnesty International expresses concern about police behaviour (*Albanian Life*, 1996, issue 59, p. 44).

5 June 1995: the government announces a ban on the street sales of newspapers and magazines in Tirana. Newspapers are to be distributed through state kiosks and bookshops.

17 August 1995: Zef Brozi, chairman of the supreme court, is dismissed. (He had taken steps to review the Fatos Nano case: *FT*, Survey, 2 October 1995, p. ii.)

22 September 1995: the Law on Communist Genocide rules out, until 2002, the participation in national or local elections (and employment in the judiciary or state media) of anyone who was, prior to 31 March 1991, a member of the politburo, central committee or parliament. Those affected include Fatos Nano (leader of the Socialist Party) and Skender Gjinushi (leader of the Social Democratic Party and the communist regime's last education minister).

6 October 1995: a breakaway faction of the monarchist Legality Movement establishes a new party, the National Party of Legality.

30 November 1995: parliament passes the Law on Dossiers. Anyone deemed by a vetting committee to have worked in the past as a Sigurimi (communist security organization) collaborator will be banned from political or state office until the year 2002 (*EEN*, 1995, vol. 9, no. 25, p. 9). The law permits the opening of Sigurimi (communist secret service) files on public figures. A state committee will check the files of all persons who run for parliament, who are appointed to leading local and central government posts, or who are employed by the courts. The files on all other citizens will be closed for thirty years (*Albanian Life*, 1996, issue 60, p. 35).

31 January 1996: the constitutional court rules in favour of the Law on Communist Genocide. The court also supports a law calling for the creation of a nine-member committee with access to former secret police files. The committee will be entitled to issue certificates to politicians stating they did not collaborate with the former communist regime, thus allowing them to stand in elections.

22 February 1996: agreement is announced about the return of 1.5 tonnes of gold ingots and coins (worth an estimated $30 million), held in trust by the Bank of England on behalf of the UK–USA–France commission. (The gold was seized by the Germans during the Second World War and, subsequently, by the Allies.)

26 February 1996: President Berisha blames former communist secret policemen (Sigurimi) for a car bomb explosion in Tirana that kills three people.

24 May 1996: an Albanian court sentences three former senior communist officials found guilty of crimes against humanity and of political persecution (e.g. ordering internal exile for dissidents). The death penalty is ordered for Aranit Cela (former supreme court chairman), Rrapi Mino (former prosecutor general) and Zylyftar Ramizi (former deputy interior minister and head of the Sigurimi secret police). Haxhi Lleshi (president 1953–82) and Manush Myftiu (former deputy prime minister) are sentenced to life in prison.

(On 24 July the death sentences were revoked. Cela and Mino were sentenced to twenty-five years in prison and Ramizi was given a life sentence.)

The May–June 1996 general election

The first round of voting was held on 26 May. The turnout in the first round was over 80 per cent. There was a minimum national turnout of 50 per cent plus one vote in the first round, but there was no minimum in the run-off on 2 June.

In the March 1992 election the 140 parliamentary seats were divided into 100 constituency (first-past-the-post) seats and 40 determined by proportional representation (i.e. by party list). In the 1996 election the respective proportions were 115 and 25 (the 4 per cent threshold for party representation remaining the same).

Opposition parties pulled out of the election on 26 May (polling day), a joint statement issued by six of them talking of 'a climate of terror, psychological pressure and physical violence' (*IHT*, 27 May 1996, p. 6). The Socialist Party alleged 'terror' and poll manipulation, while the Democratic Alliance claimed that the Democratic Party had 'manipulated the polling'. The parties would not take their seats in parliament or contest the run-off on 2 June. ('The presence in parliament of one Republican Party MP and two from the ethnic Greek party [Human Rights Party] … is obviously no substitute for "opposition"': *EEN*, 16 February 1997, vol. 11, no. 3, p. 5.)

After a demonstration in Tirana on 28 May by supporters of opposition parties was broken up by riot police, an unofficial statement was issued by British and Norwegian monitors.

> The elections did not meet international standards for free and fair elections, and they did not conform with the requirements of the election law. The accuracy and proper keeping of the voter registers failed to meet standards prescribed by law. In many cases the number of ballots cast exceeded the number of signatures on the voter lists.
>
> (*IHT*, 29 May 1996, p. 7)

In 'a large number of polling stations' the number of votes declared void was up to 50 per cent (*Telegraph*, 29 May 1996, p. 14).

> In some cases ballots bundled together inside the boxes indicated that the boxes had been tampered with and votes added ... The presence of armed police and unauthorized persons around and inside the polling stations in many cases led to an atmosphere of intimidation and coercion. Observers also witnessed cases of beatings and threats. The general pattern of intimidation had a significant impact on the election process ... It is our conclusion that the will of the Albanian people was not expressed in a free manner in the elections of 26 May 1996.
>
> (*FT*, 29 May 1996, p. 2)

OSCE's preliminary report was published on 29 May 1996 (*IHT*, 30 May 1996, p. 11; *FT*, 30 May 1996, p. 2; *Telegraph*, 30 May 1996, p. 16):

> During the counting process observers noted several instances where the voter register was altered to bring it in line with the number of votes cast. In some polling stations the number of ballots cast exceeded the number of signatures on the voter register. Also, there were widespread reports of the alteration of ballots to make them invalid ... in many instances the implementation of the law failed to meet its own criteria ... The presence of armed individuals and unidentified persons inside polling stations did have an intimidating effect on voters and polling commission officials ... In direct violation of the law, observers noted that decisions of the polling station were not made by majority vote, but by the arbitrary decisions of the government-appointed chairman and secretary.

On 30 May the acting president of OSCE issued a statement in which he called on political parties to 'examine, for the sake of democratic stability, all measures, including the possibility of partial repetition of elections, in order to resolve the dispute ... [The current situation] may jeopardise the country's prospects for democratic development.' The electoral commission has already said that new elections would have to be held in two constituencies owing to 'technical irregularities' (*IHT*, 31 May 1996, p. 6). The official OSCE report came to the conclusion that the conduct of the election violated thirty-two of the seventy-nine articles in Albania's election law. The poll also failed to meet five of the nine election commitments made by OSCE member countries (*FT*, 13 June 1996, p. 2). In July the OSCE parliamentary assembly voted 77 in favour of new elections and 54 against, with 18 abstentions (*EEN*, 18 July 1996, vol. 10, no. 14, p. 3). (On 9 June Berisha said that there would be reruns in seventeen constituencies on 16 June.)

> The way in which the elections were conducted makes a mockery of the Council of Europe's decision last July to admit Albania ... The Democratic

> Party, which Mr Berisha led to a 62 per cent victory in 1992, would probably – and deservedly – have won a comfortable majority had the elections been free and fair ... But Mr Berisha was seeking the two-thirds majority needed to rewrite the revised communist-era constitution in force since 1991. It was such a victory that he sought, and was denied, at a referendum in November 1994.
>
> (Leader comment, *FT*, 31 May 1996, p. 17)

('Albania is the only former communist country where the government controls the airwaves and where private radio and television are not permitted': Jane Perlez, *IHT*, 29 October 1996, p. 2.)

On 31 May 1996 the Italian foreign ministry, on behalf of the EU, advocated 'the repetition, in compliance with current electoral rules in Albania, of elections in constituencies in which grave irregularities were ascertained' (*IHT*, 1 June 1996, p. 2).

The International Helsinki Federation for Human Rights has called for a completely fresh election (*IHT*, 17 June 1996, p. 5).

'Berisha ... used devious tactics to ensure that his Democratic Party won a summer general election that it would probably have won anyway; in the autumn it won local elections by fairer means' (*The Economist*, 8 March 1997, p. 44).

On 16 June 1996 the Democratic Party won all seventeen rerun constituency elections. There were no official OSCE observers, but some foreign observers were present.

The final distribution of the 140 seats was as follows, with the percentage of the votes cast in brackets: Democratic Party, 122 (55.5 per cent); Socialist Party, 10 (20.4 per cent); Republican Party, 3 (5.7 per cent); Human Rights Party, 3 (4.0 per cent); Balli Kombetar, 2 (5.0 per cent) (*FT*, Survey, 19 February 1997, p. 15).

Democratic Party: led de facto by Sali Berisha. When elected president he had formally to resign his post as chairman of the party (Deutsche Bank, *Focus: Eastern Europe*, 1996, no. 166, p. 6). Tritan Shehu is second in command.

Centre Pole: an alliance comprising the Democratic Alliance (chairman Neritan Ceka, with Gramoz Pashko and Arben Imami leading lights) and the Social Democratic Party (chairman Skender Gjinushi and vice-chairman Prec Zogaj).

According to *EEN* (Country Survey, 25 March 1996, p. 6), the Democratic Alliance 'lacks funds and commitment from its members, despite its obvious attraction as a potentially strong centre party that could take in disaffected DP members and MPs'. There was an agreement by which the Socialist Party was to stand down its candidates in the dozen or so constituencies where the Centre Pole alliance was strong (*EEN*, 16 May 1996, vol. 10, no. 10, p. 5).

Socialist Party: chairman Fatos Nano. The three deputy chairmen are Namik Dokle, Ilir Mehta and Servet Pellumbi. According to *EEN* (1996, vol. 10, no. 10, p. 5), Pellumbi 'represents the socialist oldguard, which is competing openly with the "Eurosocialist" wing led by Mehta and others'.

Party of the Democratic Right: led by Petrit Kalakula and Abdi Baleta. Extreme right-wing party. Advocates full restitution of pre-communist property and land (*EEN*, Country Survey, 25 March 1996, p. 6).

Balli Kombetar (National Front): right-wing monarchist party led by Hysen Selfo.

Legaliteti: right-wing monarchist party led by Guro Darollari.

Republican Party: led by Sabri Godo.

Human Rights Party: successor to the banned Omonia ethnic Greek party. Chairman Vasil Melo.

Political developments after the May–June 1996 general election

August 1996: four Albanians are put on trial. They are charged with founding a communist party and conspiring to overthrow the government. In July 1992 the Albanian parliament declared all communist organizations illegal (*Baltic Times*, 8–14 August 1996, p. 7).

4 September 1996: there is an all-party agreement on amendments to the electoral law. The Socialist Party agrees to contest the 20 October local elections. Only the Democratic Alliance is not contesting (*EEN*, 1996, vol. 10, no. 18, p. 11).

12 September 1996: parliament passes the new election law governing local elections. The main elements of the local election law are that the deputy chairmen of the central election commission and all district commissioners will be appointed by the opposition parties, and they will sign the final vote count tally at every polling booth and keep a copy of the document. The 'anti-genocide law', which previously barred from standing anyone deemed to have participated in the communist regime, is amended. Any party official who boycotts the elections or the vote counting can be arrested and imprisoned.

> Since local government has no significant powers, there is little incentive to vote. However, it will be recalled that in July 1992 the Socialist Party severely embarrassed the Democratic Party by winning 52 per cent of the vote only three months after the Democratic Party had won the parliamentary elections. Today the Socialist Party hopes against the odds that it can return the same performance this October. Because of the splits in the party leadership that were so publicized this summer, it is unlikely that the Socialist Party will win more than about 35 per cent of the vote … After a summer of uncertainty within the Socialist Party because of growing rivalry between moderates behind Socialist Party leader Fatos Nano and the conservative wing led by Servet Pellumbi and others, the Socialist Party has a new fifteen-member executive committee, with reformists in all key positions. The Socialist Party congress on 24–5 August brought in a clearer leadership structure.
>
> (*EEN*, 1996, vol. 10, no. 19, p. 2)

16 September 1996: four people are jailed for trying to re-establish a communist party. Five former leading figures in the Albanian Workers' Party (communists) go on trial for genocide (*EEN*, 1996, vol. 10, no. 19, p. 5).

4 October 1996: independent trade unions stage a nationwide one-day strike in protest at poor living conditions (*EEN*, 1996, vol. 10, no. 20, p. 9).

17 October 1996: OSCE announces that it will not monitor the forthcoming local elections because the Albanian government wants to halve the OSCE team of thirty observers. The only intergovernmental organization to monitor the elections will be the Council of Europe (*IHT*, 18 October 1996, p. 10). There are to be over 400 international monitors (*IHT*, 21 October 1996, p. 6).

18 October 1996: the Council of Europe expresses concern at OSCE's withdrawal (*IHT*, 19 October 1996, p. 2).

20 October 1996: in the local elections the Democratic Party wins 52.5 per cent of the vote (Deutsche Bank, *Focus: Eastern Europe*, 1996, no. 166, p. 6). The turnout is 75 per cent.

The Democratic Party claims to have won 37 out of 64 mayorships (compared with the Socialist Party's 4) and 193 out of 309 local councils. (In the run-off on 27 October preliminary results showed that the Democratic Party had won 21 out of 22 city halls and 73 out of 96 districts: *IHT*, 20 October 1996, p. 5.)

Only one large city, Shkoder in northern Albania, elected a mayor who was not from the ruling party (*FT*, Survey, 19 February 1997, p. 15).

22 October 1996: a Council of Europe delegation, which co-ordinated the monitoring by 350 observers from the Council itself, the US Congress and other groups, says it is satisfied with the way the vote was carried out but regretted a few cases of irregularities serious enough to warrant careful examination by the central electoral commission (*IHT*, 23 October 1996, p. 5).

29 October 1996: the Tripartite Gold Commission (the USA, the UK and France), dealing with gold looted by Nazi Germany, returns the gold held in the Bank of England since 1946 (and worth around $20 million). The UK receives around $2 million from Albania as compensation for the two destroyers lost in 1946 when they hit mines in the Corfu channel.

29 December 1996: Balli Kombetar and Legaliteti form a new alliance called the Albanian Joint Rightists Alliance (*EEN*, 1996, vol. 10, no. 25, p. 8).

10 January 1997: Nexhmije Hoxha leaves prison (where she has been detained for misappropriating state funds and for abuse of power).

And the pyramids came tumbling down

Protests about the failure of pyramid savings schemes started on 15 January 1997. The government was blamed and there were clashes with the police.

Pyramid schemes are inherently fraudulent since they can only pay out (high) returns to early investors from fresh funds contributed by later ones. Pure pyramid schemes are backed by nothing but the ability to attract fresh funds until their inevitable demise. Early players in the game, who withdraw their funds and gains in time, benefit, but do so at the expense of the majority of later participants.

> In a typical pyramid scheme a fund or company attracts investors by offering them very high returns; these returns are paid to the first investors out of the funds received from those who invest later. The scheme is insolvent – liabilities exceed assets – from the day it opens for business. However, it flourishes initially as news about the high returns spreads and more investors are drawn in ... The scheme grows until the interest and principal due to the early investors exceeds the money paid in by new investors. To attract new investors a scheme may raise interest rates, but the larger interest payments soon force it to raise rates again. Eventually the high rates begin to arouse suspicion or the scheme finds itself unable to make interest payments. When investors try to get their money out they discover the truth about the scheme, whose demise is swift – and usually accompanied by acts of outright theft by the operators, if they are not caught first. Some of the Albanian companies meet this definition exactly: they were pure pyramid schemes, with no real assets. Other cases are more ambiguous. Some of the largest of the companies – in particular VEFA, Gjallica and Kamberi – had substantial real assets. They were also widely believed to be engaged in criminal activities – including violating United Nations sanctions by smuggling goods into the former Yugoslavia – that were thought to be the source of the high returns they paid ... [At the end of 1995 UN sanctions against the Federal Republic of Yugoslavia were suspended, eliminating an important source of income – smuggling – for the companies] ... However, even if they had not been pyramid schemes from the outset, at some point, probably during early 1996, these companies too became pyramid schemes. When they collapsed it was clear that their liabilities massively exceeded their assets.
>
> (Jarvis 2000a: 47)

> Pyramid schemes work on the principle that money paid in by later investors is used to pay artificially high returns to early investors ... Early investors are drawn in by advertising promising high interest or huge capital gains after a short period ... The final stage is the collapse of the scheme. The interest and principal due to the old investors exceeds the money that the scheme is able to attract from new investors.
>
> (Jarvis 2000b: 7)

> This paper tells the story of the Albanian pyramid scheme crisis of 1996–7 ... The pyramid scheme phenomenon in Albania is important because its scale relative to the size of the economy was unprecedented, and because the political and social consequences of the collapse of the pyramid schemes were profound ... Almost one million weapons were looted.
>
> (pp. 1, 16)

What distinguished Albania was the magnitude of the fraud, the seriousness of the consequences and the extent of government involvement:

1 The magnitude of the fraud

> At their peak the nominal value of the pyramid schemes' liabilities amounted to almost half of the country's GDP. Many Albanians – about two-thirds of the population – invested in them ... Albanians sold their houses to invest in the schemes; farmers sold their livestock ... The wide appeal of Albania's schemes can be attributed to several factors, including Albanians' unfamiliarity with financial markets; the deficiencies of the country's formal financial system, which encouraged the development of an informal market and, within this market, of the pyramid schemes; and failures of governance ... Albania's formal financial system was rudimentary. There were few private banks. The three state banks, which held 90 per cent of deposits, offered real interest rates but had growing portfolios of bad loans, prompting the Bank of Albania to impose tight credit ceilings on them. With the banks unable to satisfy private sector demand for credit, an informal credit market based on family ties and financed by remittances grew ... Operating alongside them, however, were deposit-taking companies that invested on their own account instead of making loans. These companies were the ones that turned into pyramid schemes. There were also governance problems ... the regulatory framework was inadequate, and it was not clear who had responsibility for supervising the informal market. Even after the approval of a banking act in February 1996 that appeared to give the Bank of Albania the power to close illegal deposit-taking institutions, the central bank could not obtain the government's support. Indeed, the government was supportive of the companies ... During the 1996 elections several of the companies made campaign contributions to the ruling Democratic Party. There were allegations that many government officials benefited personally from the companies ... The finance ministry did not warn the public about the schemes until October [1996]. Even then, however, it drew a false and misleading distinction between companies with real investments and 'pure pyramid schemes.
>
> (Jarvis 2001: 46–8).

On 19 November 1996 Sude (which had no real investments) defaulted on its payments and the collapse began. In January 1997 Sude and Gjallica declared bankruptcy. The other schemes soon also ceased to make payments. The government belatedly took some useful steps. First, it refused to compensate depositors for their losses, which made achieving economic stabilization after the crisis much easier than it would otherwise have been. Second, it began to move against some of the companies. In January 1997 it froze the bank accounts of Xhafferi and Populli, two pyramid schemes set up in early 1996. In February parliament passed a law banning pyramid schemes (but not defining them). However, the government continued to differentiate between companies with real investments and pure pyramid schemes and did not move against the largest companies. The major pyramid schemes continued to hang on to their assets, proclaim their solvency and resist closure. Winding up the pyramid schemes proved to be difficult. The interim government (set up in March 1997) encountered resistance from both the operators and the outgoing parliamentarians, many of whom were reported to have invested in the schemes. Thus it was not until July that the newly elected parliament passed a law mandating the appointment of foreign administrators from international accounting firms to liquidate the schemes. However, by November 1997, when the administrators took up their duties, the schemes' assets had shrunk considerably. The administrators did not gain full control of all the companies until March 1998. Whatever assets remained were prepared for sale. But much had been lost already (Jarvis 2000a: 46–8).

> One of the most important causes of the growth of the pyramid scheme phenomenon was the inadequacy of the informal financial system … As a result of these problems [long completion times for transactions] and a general distrust of the banks, the public tended to hold an unusually high proportion of their financial assets in cash.
>
> (Jarvis 2000b: 3)

'Flows of remittances [were] estimated at about $300 million a year (about 12 per cent of GDP)' (p. 6).

> The IMF and the World Bank did give increasingly strident warnings about the schemes in the course of 1996 but these warnings were not heeded and may have been too late to do much good in any case. Both institutions had expressed concern as far back as December 1994 about the dangers of criminal enterprises operating in the informal market, though the concerns were as much about money laundering as about pyramid schemes. However, it was not until August 1996 that a strong warning was given. It was later in the month that the Bank of Albania communicated its concerns to an IMF mission visiting Tirana.
>
> (p. 13)

'In January 1997 both Sude and Gjallica, one of the funds with real investments, declared bankruptcy, triggering riots, especially in the southern city of Vlore, where Gjallica was based. As the riots intensified and spread the remaining schemes ceased payments' (p. 15). 'The sale by the administrators of the remaining assets of the pyramid scheme companies began in mid-1998 … The operators of the schemes are either in jail or out of the country' (p. 25).

> The losses during the period when the operators retained control of the schemes, the difficulty in establishing clear title to some of the schemes' assets, and the further difficulty in selling those assets, especially in busi-

> nesses, in a depressed economy with continuing security problems, have resulted in very limited asset recoveries so far.
>
> (p. 19)

> Although the process of returning money from the realized assets of the schemes is still not complete, and it now appears that the assets of the schemes will be sufficient to cover less than 10 per cent of their nominal liabilities, there have been few complaints or public protests … Parliament has passed legislation designed to prevent a recurrence of the pyramid scheme phenomenon.
>
> (p. 29)

'The paper … concludes that despite the tremendous political effects the economic effects have been surprisingly limited' (p. 2).

> Considering that the face value of their [the pyramid schemes'] liabilities was so large – about half of 1996 GDP – the direct effects of their rise and fall appear to have been limited. They are also extremely difficult to identify, in part because of the limitations of data on the real economy in Albania and in part because their collapse had profound political and social effects, in particular the outbreak of civil disorder, which, in turn, had a powerful effect on the economy.
>
> (pp. 19–20)

> Output is estimated to have fallen by 7 per cent in 1997 … However, it is impossible to separate out the supply-side effects of the civil disorder from the demand-side effects from the loss of savings in the pyramid schemes.
>
> (p. 23)

2 The seriousness of the consequences

According to some estimates, the savings schemes attracted sums amounting to more than a third of GDP (*FT*, 20 January 1997, p. 2). 'International financial institutions estimate that the funds could have attracted $1 billion, equivalent to more than 30 per cent of the gross domestic product' (*FT*, 27 January 1997, p. 2).

> The absence of a properly functioning banking system has been one of the key institutional deficiencies that has dogged Albania's turbulent emergence from communism. The lack of trust in the state-owned banks and these institutions' inability to develop modern banking services have provided fertile ground for the development of informal financial markets and for the setting up of the string of pyramid schemes, whose progressive collapse has plunged Albania into a political and financial crisis.
>
> (*FT*, Survey, 19 February 1997, p. 14)

> The foundations of the first pyramid schemes were laid four to five years ago in a country lacking a functioning banking system and in which the majority of financial transactions were carried on through informal channels, encouraging the use of the schemes for money laundering.
>
> (p. 13)

'The central bank began to alert the government about eighteen months ago to the dangers posed by the growth of the pyramid schemes, but such warnings only started to be echoed in public by government ministers in October [1996]' (p. 14).

> The collapse [took place] three years ago of twenty-four pyramid savings schemes in which savers lost an estimated $1.2 billion … One in three Albanians put their savings into a pyramid scheme … Only the five biggest companies owned assets that could be auctioned to repay creditors … International accounting firms have carried out the liquidation of more than twenty pyramid schemes.
>
> (*FT*, Survey, 23 February 2000, p. 13)

(On 25 April 1997 Berisha dismissed the governor of the central bank, who had been appointed in December 1994. Julian Borger claimed that 'Government ministers specifically exempted the pyramids from a banking law in March last year [1996] which would have otherwise subjected them to regulation': *Guardian*, 26 April 1997, p. 13.)

> Investors in Albania's notorious pyramid schemes will get little of their money back, the Albanian government has been told by financial investigators hired to track down $1 billion lost in frauds … PwC, the professional services firm asked by the government to investigate the schemes, has concluded that only $50 million is recoverable. The PwC report, which is also critical of the help offered by Albanian officials [critical of the help given by some officials – in particular public prosecutors hindered attempts to inspect documents relating to Vefa], has never been published, despite being submitted to the Albanian ministry of finance last January [2000] … Under pressure from Western lending institutions to adopt credible economic policies, it [the socialist government under prime minister Ilir Mehta] has retracted promises that investors would be compensated in full … The PwC report … [concludes] that the seventeen schemes operated until their collapse in early 1997 were 'thoroughly dishonest businesses' … At their height they had liabilities equal to half the country's GDP, according to the IMF … According to the head PwC investigator, the vast bulk of the money was taken out of the country in cash in lorries bound for Greece and other countries. Between $50 million and $100 million has been found in overseas bank accounts, mainly in countries such as Greece, Turkey, Hungary, Macedonia, Germany, the UK and the USA. But Albania

> lacks bilateral agreements to let this money be recovered … Vehbi Almucaj, the principal operator of Vefa, the largest scheme … received a five-year sentence for fraud but the government rejected the sentence as too lenient and has ordered a fresh hearing … [There have also been] investigations into Gjallica, the second largest scheme … [and its operator] Shemsie Kadria … Mrs Kadria's trial on fraud charges continues.
>
> (*FT*, 17 August 2000, p. 6)

'Financial pyramid schemes have collapsed with disastrous effects on the social and political texture of the country' (EBRD 1997a: 22). 'These schemes had attracted funds equivalent to more than half of GDP over the period 1994–96, by exploiting a loophole in the existing legal and regulatory framework' (p. 26).

> The winding up of the pyramid schemes has continued in recent months, with several auctions of the assets of these companies already completed. Revenues from these sales are very small and are unlikely to exceed $10 million in total when they are completed this year [1999].
>
> (EBRD 1999a: 32)

3 The extent of government involvement

'Losses [have been] incurred by perhaps half of all Albanian families' (*The Economist*, 25 January 1997, p. 43). It is thought that 'more than a third of the population … have lost their savings in collapsing "pyramid" schemes' (*The Economist*, 1 February 1997, p. 4). 'Berisha … failed to stop – and his party actually seemed to encourage, in order to raise campaign funds – a proliferation of investment schemes that were bound to collapse' (*The Economist*, 8 March 1997, p. 44).

'Fraudulent pyramid schemes in which up to seven Albanian families out of ten have sunk their savings and in many cases their livestock, land and homes … Because the fraudsters have been visibly on cosy terms with ministers and high-profile contributors to party coffers, the government cannot escape blame' (*The Times*, 27 January 1997, p. 23). Savings lost in the pyramid schemes amount to at least half of GDP (*The Times*, 3 July 1997, p. 25).

'Opposition parties have accused the Democrats of using the pyramid schemes to help finance their election campaign, and they have noted that some leaders of the biggest investment schemes have close ties to the government' (*IHT*, 30 January 1997, p. 7). 'Many accuse the government of collusion with those who ran the fraudulent funds, or of failing to take timely action to control the schemes' (*IHT*, 12 February 1997, p. 5).

Perhaps a third of Albanians have made more from the funds than they lost by investing in the schemes at an early stage (*EEN*, 1997, vol. 11, no. 3, p. 4).

'The upheaval has revived some of the old divisions between north and south. The regions are ethnically divided – Gegs predominate in the north, Tosks and

Greeks in the south – but their rivalry is now primarily political. Enver Hoxha … was from the south, and the region remains a stronghold of the Socialist Party … Berisha, who grew up in the mountainous far north … has surrounded himself with northerners – in particular, bodyguards and secret police. But the north–south divide appears to have little to do with why the south is in flames while the north remains relatively calm. Rather, capitalism – in its legal and illegal forms – had yielded relatively more in the south, giving southerners more money to invest, and lose, in the pyramid schemes' (Christine Spolar, *IHT*, 12 March 1997, p. 2).

(Vefa Holdings was run by Vehbi Almucaj and was Albania's largest private company. It comprised 240 businesses and had 80,000 investors: *FT*, 20 February 1997, p. 2. It had assets but was in part a pyramid scheme. Vefa's monthly deposit rate was cut from 8 per cent to 5 per cent: *EEN*, 30 January 1997, vol. 11, no. 2, p. 9. On 4 February 1997 the monthly deposit rate was again cut, to 3 per cent: *EEN*, 1997, vol. 11, no. 3, p. 8. On 19 February 1997 Vefa announced that it was halting interest payments, having switched from hard currency to lek payments the previous month. There would, however, be full repayment for those who had invested up to $5,000 and gradual repayment for those investing up to $20,000: *Independent*, 20 February 1997, p. 14.)

'The audit of the pyramid schemes has been completed and its findings made public. Liabilities of the schemes exceed their assets sevenfold. The recovery and liquidation of the schemes is likely to be a lengthy process' (EBRD 1998a: 32).

The human toll

The human toll involved refugees and loss of life:

1. Nearly 300 people have been killed (*IHT*, 15 April 1997, p. 10). Since the collapse of the pyramid schemes over 700 lives have been lost, many through accidents (*IHT*, 20 May 1997, p. 5). More than 1,500 lives have been lost since March 1997 (*IHT*, 27 June 1997, p. 6; *FT*, 24 June 1997, p. 2; *Guardian*, 26 June 1997, p. 19). 'Some 2,000 people had been killed in the violence that followed the pyramid schemes' collapse' (Jarvis 2000a: 46). 'The violence claimed more than 2,000 lives' (*FT*, 17 August 2000, p. 6).
2. Some 13,000 refugees have fled to Italy (*IHT*, 3 April 1997, p. 5). (More than 40,000 refugees fled to Italy in 1991: *IHT*, 16 April 1997, p. 5.) In the past few weeks over 10,000 Albanians (mostly ethnic Greek women and children) have fled to Greece (*EEN*, 27 April 1997, vol. 11, no. 8, p. 7).

15 January 1997: the start of protests about the failure of pyramid savings schemes (which pay out high returns to early investors from fresh funds contributed by later ones). The government is blamed and there are clashes with police.

23 January 1997: the government bans pyramid savings schemes. The assets of the two schemes which have failed to date are frozen. (According to *The Times*, the government has banned 'future pyramid schemes; but notably has not dared to close down those that are still in business': 27 January 1997, p. 23.)

25 January 1997: violent protests escalate. The foreign minister (also a deputy prime minister) is attacked by demonstrators.

26 January 1997: parliament authorizes the use of troops to guard roads and government buildings. The prime minister promises to start paying back investors' frozen deposits on 5 February.

Two inmates are killed in prison riots.

28 January 1997: pro-Berisha demonstrators turn out in Tirana.

A high-ranking member of the Socialist Party is attacked and left in a critical condition.

29 January 1997: President Berisha says that only the poorest investors will receive payments immediately from two pyramid schemes whose bank accounts have been frozen. He suggests that a majority of investors in the two schemes will get account statements rather than cash payments (*IHT*, 30 January 1997, p. 7). (Berisha referred to a majority receiving term savings accounts or vouchers to purchase assets, rather than cash. Parliament approved his scheme on 30 January.)

Berisha accuses the Socialist Party of fomenting the protests. The acts of violence 'were performed on the platform of the old secret service' by people who were 'activists and regional leaders of the Socialist Party'. 'They lost the elections and so have chosen the path of burning and destroying.' Police arrest senior opposition officials, including Rexhep Meidani (secretary-general of the Socialist Party, since Fatos Nano is in prison), Skender Gjinushi (chairman of the Social Democratic Party) and Arben Imami (of the Democratic Alliance) (*Telegraph*, 30 January 1997, p. 15).

30 January 1997: opposition parties and organizations (under the chairmanship of a human rights group called the Association of Former Persecuted Prisoners) form an alliance called the Forum for Democracy. In addition, it comprises the Socialist Party, the Democratic Alliance, the Social Democratic Party, the Democratic Party of the Right and the Democratic Ideal (*EEN*, 1997, vol. 11, no. 3, p. 6). The main aims are to persuade the government to set up a caretaker government of technical experts and then to hold fresh elections.

Arrests continue on a substantial scale. (The law banning street protests is still in force.)

5 February 1997: the government starts paying out refunds from the frozen assets of the two pyramid schemes.

(The process could take at least seven to eight months. Savers in one scheme would receive 60 per cent of their deposits, while those in the other would get 52 per cent. There would be a cash ceiling for repayments and sums in excess would be in the form of savings books with time deposits of between three and twelve months: *FT*, 5 February 1997, p. 2; 6 February 1995, p. 2.)

The fourth scheme collapses (*FT*, 6 February 1997, p. 2).

Five investment schemes have collapsed (*IHT*, 5 February 1997, p. 6).

The first day of large-scale anti-government demonstrations in Vlore.

8 February 1997: the authorities prevent a demonstration in Tirana.

9 February 1997: clashes occur between riot police and demonstrators in Vlore. One man dies (seemingly of heart failure after he was beaten up).

10 February 1997: the police lose control of the situation in Vlore. Two more people die, one of heart failure and one of gunshot wounds. The prime minister asks parliament to introduce a state of emergency in Vlore.

12 February 1997: moves to declare a state of emergency in Vlore are called off. President Berisha dismisses the police chief in Vlore and appeals for talks.

19 February 1997: Berisha promises to abolish tax in some areas for the next two years.

28 February 1997: in clashes with the secret police (trying to enter the place where students are on hunger strike) nine are killed, three of them civilians.

'In the past few months the lek has lost a third of its value against the dollar and prices have risen 40 to 50 per cent' (*IHT*, 1 March 1997, p. 2). On 7 March 1997 the lek was valued at 134–7 to the US dollar on the open-air markets, a fall from 104 to the dollar in early January of that year (*The Times*, 8 March 1997, p. 14).

1 March 1997: prime minister Meksi's government is dismissed. The president offers to consult the Forum for Democracy about the formation of the next government.

2 March 1997: parliament declares a state of emergency.

Measures include the following: a dusk-to-dawn curfew; media censorship (the international television satellite link was suspended on 3 March); a ban on more than four people meeting in one place; security personnel are allowed to shoot without warning anyone who defies the emergency regulations; foreigners are ordered out of the southern part of the country.

President Berisha refers to 'a communist rebellion backed by foreign intelligence agencies'. 'Armed communist rebels, helped and financed by foreign espionage services, have started military actions to overthrow the government by force and establish their rule across the country.' He sees the need to 'crush the red terrorist rebellion'.

Weapons are looted from police and army barracks in towns like Vlore and Sarande (where some 200 prisoners are released by demonstrators).

Two people are killed in Vlore.

The headquarters of the main opposition newspaper (*Koha Jone*: 'Our Times') is destroyed by fire.

3 March 1997: parliament re-elects President Berisha by 113 votes to one, with three abstentions.

4 March 1997: Berisha dismisses the army chief of staff.

The international satellite link is restored.

Foreigners are merely advised not to travel to the south of the country.

5 March 1997: there are reports of clashes between the army and armed demonstrators in the south. 'Berisha ... has lost control of the southern, and richest, part of his country' (*IHT*, 6 March 1997, p. 6).

OSCE says that permission to send a mission to Albania has been refused.

But a Council of Europe mission (which does not need permission since Albania is a member) does arrive.

6 March 1997: after talks between Berisha and opposition leaders it is announced that 'offensive military operations' in the south of the country will be suspended for forty-eight hours starting tomorrow. This is to allow time for weapons to be handed in.

It is reported that the authorities have lost control of Tepelene (as is already the case with Vlore, Sarande and Delvina).

7 March 1997: an EU delegation arrives.

8 March 1997: the authorities lose control of Gjirokaster.

9 March 1997: Berisha appears on television with opposition leaders. Berisha accepts the need for a transitional government of 'national reconciliation' representing all political parties (and equally split between the Democratic Party and the opposition) and for fresh parliamentary elections within two months. The arms amnesty is extended for a further week. 'I think the Albanian parliament should declare a general amnesty for all those involved in the revolt, including civilians and army personnel. We should declare a platform of national reconciliation.'

10 March 1997: the Italian ambassador and other Italian diplomats meet with eight Vlore leaders, who agree to try to restore order and encourage civilians to lay down their weapons in return for a swift implementation of the agreement in Tirana. But there is uncertainty about how representative these leaders are of opinion in Vlore and demonstrators elsewhere continue to demand the resignation of Berisha. (The following day the eight Vlore leaders denied that an agreement had been reached.) The authorities lose control of further towns, such as Permet, Berat and Kucove.

11 March 1997: Bashkim Fino of the Socialist Party is named as interim prime minister.

The presidential adviser says that Berisha will resign only if the opposition wins the parliamentary elections.

'About 70 per cent of the army is said to have either deserted or switched support to the rebels' (Helena Smith, *Guardian*, 12 March 1997, p. 11).

12 March 1997: rebel leaders in fourteen southern towns form the National Committee for Public Salvation, based in Gjirokaster. The committee's main aims are the resignation of Berisha and participation in the Tirana talks.

Anti-government rebels pillage an arms depot near Elbasan (55 kilometres from Tirana). In Tirana itself groups of men enter the military academy and remove small arms. 'In some parts of the south the rebellion appeared to have deteriorated into lawlessness, with armed gangs roaming through towns' (*IHT*, 13 March 1997, p. 6). ('In Tirana there was a strong sense that the arming of civilians Thursday [13 March] was organized by Mr Berisha': Jane Perlez, *IHT*, 14 March 1997, p. 7.)

13 March 1997: the new government is sworn in, but prime minister Fino declares that 'We are on the brink of civil war'. Berisha and the opposition parties issue a joint appeal to the WEU (i.e. the European members of Nato) to intervene militarily, admitting that the country is beyond their control.

Lawlessness spreads rapidly throughout the country, including Tirana (despite the presence of army tanks). Berisha sends his wife and children to Italy and the exodus of foreign nationals is speeded up. Prisoners escape from jail, including Ramiz Alia and Fatos Nano. (Other prisoners broke down the door to Nano's cell, but Nano did not leave the prison until its director offered to drive him home.) (In late March 1997 the government approved an amnesty for some 700 of the estimated 1,300 prisoners who had absconded. Others who returned to jail by 5 April 1997 would have their sentences reduced by a third: *The Times*, 29 March 1997, p. 15.)

(More and more Albanians try to flee the country, especially through the port of Durres, where a greater degree of law and order prevails.)

14 March 1997: US, Italian and German rescue helicopters come under fire and operations are suspended. German troops exchange fire with armed attackers.

The head of the OSCE mission, former Austrian chancellor Franz Vranitzky, calls for international military intervention.

An armed Shik (the secret police loyal to Berisha) convoy patrols the centre of Tirana. The head of Shik is reported to have resigned, but this is not the case.

The government triples wages for security personnel.

15 March 1997: a greater degree of law and order is attained in Tirana (helped by the increase in wages for security personnel).

16 March 1997: OSCE recommends international military intervention. (Javier Ruperez, the president of OSCE's parliamentary assembly, believed that 'A modest Nato force could provide security and disarm the population while the EU provides economic assistance, primarily in food and medicine, and the OSCE can prepare for internationally supervised elections': *IHT*, 22 March 1997, p. 6.)

EU foreign ministers agree to send a small team of advisers to help in 'civilian as well as police and military fields' to 'help Albania restore civilian structures and law and order'. They also agree to join OSCE, Greece and Turkey in a delegation whose aim will be mediation. (Strong advocates of military intervention include France, Italy, the Netherlands, Denmark and Greece, while strong opponents include the UK, Germany and Sweden.)

Berisha pardons Fatos Nano, who expresses support for the coalition government and thinks Berisha should resign. Berisha repeats his intention of resigning if the Democratic Party loses the general election.

There is a peace rally in an increasingly calm Tirana.

Government representatives begin talks with rebel leaders in different parts of the country.

17 March 1997: Fatos Nano says that free and fair elections are the ideal way of removing the president. 'I think that he should step aside, not down.' Berisha should 'co-operate, not interfere' with the work of the coalition government.

The domestic political parties can act as 'peacemakers and peacekeepers'. He adds that 'We do not need any [UN] blue helmets and others'.

In Tirana shops reopen and public transport resumes.

19 March 1997: Italy declares a state of emergency until 30 June 1997 to cope with the large influx of Albanian refugees, including a provision for expelling those 'deemed to be a danger to public security'. Italy will send food and medicine to Albania. In contrast, the head of the EU mission says that 'Albania has to solve its own problems before we can help'.

Rebel leaders in Gjirokaster set a deadline of 20 March for Berisha to resign. The prime minister postpones a visit to the south. (Prime minister Fino was formerly the mayor of Gjirokaster, where Agim Gozhita, a retired general, is rebel leader.)

20 March 1997: Tirana airport reopens.

21 March 1997: the National Committee for Public Salvation backs down from its threats to march on Tirana and to form an alternative government. Instead it demands a voice in discussions, supports the coalition government (provided it proves to be independent of Berisha) and demands the resignation of Berisha (to be replaced by a presidential council until the elections).

22 March 1997: the prime minister talks, in Tirana, to rebel leaders from Vlore. He believes that the president should not resign.

23 March 1997: a peace rally is held in Tirana.

24 March 1997: Albania and Italy agree on an Italian naval blockade to stem the flood of refugees. (Italian vessels already patrol Albanian territorial waters, with Albania's permission. But vessels filled with refugees, usually organized by criminal gangs for payment, continued to sail towards Italy.)

EU foreign ministers agree on an Ecu 2 million food and medical aid package (*The Times*, 25 March 1997, p. 12).

28 March 1997: the UN Security Council approves, for three months, an international force (led by Italy) to protect aid deliveries to Albania.

An Albanian vessel carrying refugees sinks after colliding with an Italian warship. (Italy has found four bodies, but the Albanian embassy in Rome drew up a list of those still missing, at first seventy-nine and then eighty-three.)

30 March 1997: the Albanian parliament approves the UN force.

1 April 1997: the prime minister says that he and the president have accepted the resignations of the head and deputy head of Shik. The prime minister also says that Shik has been disbanded.

The prime minister goes to Gjirokaster for talks.

2 April 1997: the Italian prime minister meets the Albanian prime minister in Gjirokaster.

4 April 1997: about twenty MPs from the Democratic Party sign a statement, saying that they will no longer 'accept the diktat of the president' (*Guardian*, 5 April 1997, p. 15).

5 April 1997: prime minister Fino is prevented from visiting Shkoder (in the north of the country) by an armed gang. In consequence, the planned meeting in Vlore (in the south) with the Italian prime minister is postponed.

9 April 1997: despite political difficulties, the Italian government gains the approval of the Italian parliament to send a 2,500-strong force to Albania. (The initial aim is to secure the ports of Durres and Vlore and the airport at Tirana.)

Socialist Party MPs attend parliament for the first time since the May–June 1996 election (*EEN*, 1997, vol. 11, no. 7, p. 5).

11 April 1997: an advance contingent of Italian troops arrives in Albania to prepare for the arrival of the main force.

12 April 1997: King Leka I (son of the late King Zog) arrives in Albania.

13 April 1997: Italian prime minister Romano Prodi is warmly greeted by a large crowd when he arrives in Vlore for talks with Albanian prime minister Bashkim Fino and leader of the National Salvation Committee Albert Shyti.

An advance contingent of French troops arrives in Albania.

15 April 1997: the main international force begins arriving. Named 'Operation Alba' ('Operation Sunrise') by Italy, the 6,000-strong force is made up of troops from Italy (2,500), France (1,000), Greece (800), Turkey (600–800), Spain (450), Romania (400), Austria (120) and Denmark (60).

9 May 1997: the ten main political parties sign an agreement to hold a general election on 29 June 1997. The national salvation committees are to be dissolved at least forty-six days before the election. The Law on Communist Genocide is to be repealed.

13 May 1997: the Democratic Party uses its majority in parliament to vote for an electoral law similar to the previous one. The number of seats will increase from 140 to 155, with 115 seats decided by majority voting and 40 by proportional representation. The electoral threshold will be reduced from 4 per cent to 3 per cent. Opposition parties, led by the Socialist Party, proposed that 40 out of a total of 140 seats should be decided by proportional representation and that the electoral threshold should be 2 per cent (*EEN*, 1997, vol. 11, no. 10, p. 7).

16 May 1997: Berisha dissolves parliament and calls an election for 29 June 1997.

Of the forty seats to be decided by proportional representation ten are to be allocated to the two largest parties and thirty to smaller ones (*EEN*, 1997, vol. 11, no. 10, p. 8).

21 May 1997: the Socialist Party says it will contest the election provided there is full international monitoring.

Berisha says that the caretaker government will be allowed to appoint the members of the central electoral commission (which in turn appoints local electoral officials). Berisha also signs a decree allowing a referendum on the monarchy to be held at the same time as the parliamentary election.

22 May 1997: the Albanian United Right Wing electoral alliance is formed by Balli Kombetar, the Republican Party, the Party of the Democratic Right and the new Movement for Democracy (*EEN*, 1997, vol. 11, no. 11, p. 8).

23 June 1997: an agreement is signed in Rome by the Democratic Party, the Socialist Party and the Social Democratic Party on conducting fair elections (*EEN*, 1997, vol. 11, no. 13, p. 6).

The 29 June and 6 July 1997 general election

There was a two-thirds turnout on 29 June. There were some 500 OSCE observers on 29 June and around 150 on 6 July, although not all polling stations were covered. The international force undertook escort duties.

OSCE concluded that the first round of the election (held on 29 June 1997) was

> adequate and acceptable … despite minor flaws in many areas and some very serious problems in a few areas … Voters were generally able to cast their ballots without fear or intimidation, although there are reports of some serious problems with the counting process in a few zones.

The vote 'can be the basis of a stable democratic system which all Albanians want and deserve'.

> The Socialist leader, Fatos Nano, won popular support with an utterly implausible promise that all savings lost in the pyramid schemes would be refunded. The sum is at least half of Albania's GDP and no reliable record of individual losses exists.
>
> (*The Times*, 3 July 1997, p. 25)

Nano 'has already denied he ever told the voters they would get all their money back from the failed pyramid schemes, and merely talks now of dishing out what is left' (*The Economist*, 5 July 1997, p. 42).

After the first two rounds of voting the Socialist Party was awarded 100 seats and its allies 18. The Democratic Party won 24 seats.

('Within four years Mr Berisha had created what Human Rights Watch last March [1997] called "a one-party state based on fear and corruption". He … turned the justice system into a political instrument. He expanded the National Intelligence Service to a force of 3,000 agents supported by another 3,000 informers which operated as an arm of his party. With the defeat of Mr Berisha's party … the intelligence service has lost its power – officially at least. Its director … fled Albania just before the Socialist victory was confirmed, as did the commander of the presidential guard … and the national police director': Edward Cody, *IHT*, 5 August 1997, p. 7.)

Political developments after the 1997 general election

3 July 1997: one royalist is shot dead and five are wounded in a gunfight after a rally outside the central electoral commission. (A rally the following day was held peacefully.)

7 July 1997: Tritan Shehu (chairman of the Democratic Party) resigns after losing his seat in the second round of the elections.

19 July 1997: the first withdrawal of troops from the international force takes place. (The mandate expires on 12 August.)

21 July 1997: the constitutional court declares that the election should be rerun in an area of the north and that a number of other official results are to be revised (*EEN*, 1997, vol. 11, no. 14, p. 2).

23 July 1997: Berisha resigns as president. But he will be in parliament as head of the Democratic Party.

The opening session of parliament is boycotted by the Democratic Party.

24 July 1997: parliament elects Rexhep Meidani (Socialist Party) as president.

Parliament lifts the state of emergency and the curfew.

29 July 1997: the new government is approved by parliament. The coalition government comprises the Socialist Party (led by prime minister Fatos Nano), the Democratic Alliance (led by interior minister Neritan Ceka), the Social Democratic Party (led by Skender Gjinushi), the Agrarian Party (led by agriculture minister Lufter Xhuveli) and the Union for the Protection of Human Rights (led by Vasil Melo). Other important members of the government include Bashkim Fino (deputy prime minister), Paskal Milo (foreign minister), Sabit Brokaj (defence minister), Arben Malaj (finance minister) and Ylli Bufi (privatization and economics minister).

11 August 1997: the last troops of the international force leave. (Some 600 Italian troops moved in afterwards, e.g. to guard ports and border crossings.)

12 August 1997: the government sends Albanian troops to Vlore, Gjirokaster, Sarande and Tepelene to restore order.

13 August 1997: the Democratic Party ends its boycott of parliament (*EEN*, 1997, vol. 11, no. 16, p. 7).

14 August 1997: the government claims that the police have restored order in Vlore.

17 August 1997: the government gives looters until 30 September 1997 to hand back weapons (*Guardian*, 18 August 1997, p. 12).

18 August 1997: the government orders that all heavy weapons and weapons distributed by the police after the collapse of the state are to be handed in by 31 August 1997. All other light weapons are to be handed in by 30 September 1997 (*EEN*, 1997, vol. 11, no. 16, p. 7). (Very few weapons were actually handed in.)

22 August 1997: the government appoints three administrators to each of the remaining pyramid schemes (*EEN*, 1997, vol. 11, no. 17, p. 6.) (On 17 September Vefa Holdings won its case in the appeals court to stop state administrators from assuming management control: *EEN*, 1997, vol. 11, no. 18, p. 6.)

As of August 1997 four big investment funds were still in operation. They offered lower interest rates than they did during the crisis. But none of the pyramid schemes were taking deposits. In August the new government approved a law that allowed for the auditing of all pyramid schemes along the lines agreed with the IMF and World Bank. Customs duties are being collected on behalf of the government by the customs authorities of Italy and Greece (EBRD 1997b: 149).

18 September 1997: a Socialist Party MP shoots a Democratic Party MP in parliament and is charged with attempted murder.

22 September 1997: the Democratic Party executive decides that the party will again boycott parliamentary proceedings (*EEN*, 1997, vol. 11, no. 19, p. 7).

7 October 1997: the IMF signs a six-month agreement for 'post-conflict' assistance (*EEN*, 1997, vol. 11, no. 20, p. 5).

20 October 1997: Ramiz Alia is acquitted (along with three other senior officials) of charges of 'genocide and crimes against humanity' by a Tirana court. State prosecutors dropped the charges because they were not part of the former communist legislation (Alia was accused of deporting hundreds of his opponents between 1982 and 1986 and of ordering the killing of Albanians seeking to flee Albania between 1986 and 1991. Alia is believed to have fled to France in March 1997: *IHT*, 21 October 1997, p. 5; *The Times*, 21 October 1997, p. 15).

29 January 1998: the Democratic Party announces that it will end its boycott of parliament (*EEN*, 1998, vol. 12, no. 2, p. 7). (But the Democratic Party did not actually end its boycott until 5 March 1998 and that was in order to attend a debate on Kosovo: *EEN*, 1998, vol. 12, no. 4, p. 9.)

22 February 1998: demonstrators in Shkoder demand the release of two senior Berisha supporters. A riot follows.

23 February 1998: interior ministry troops wrest control of Shkoder from armed gangs.

9 April 1998: parliament approves an amendment to allow legalization of the Communist Party (*EEN*, 1998, vol. 12, no. 5, p. 5).

17 April 1998: interior minister Neritan Ceka is dismissed.

14 August 1998: the USA temporarily closes its embassy in Tirana, a week after two US embassies (in Kenya and Tanzania) were bombed with heavy loss of life. An embassy spokesman says:

> Given recent declarations by Islamic extremists against the United States and its citizens and press reports alleging US government participation in the recent apprehension and detention [in Albania] of several Islamic extremists, it is possible that US embassy facilities in Tirana could be among the targets of a terrorist attack.

22 August 1998: former defence minister Safet Zhulali and five other senior officials in the previous Democratic Party government are arrested. They are charged with 'crimes against humanity' before and during the March 1997 uprising (*EEN*, 1998, vol. 12, no. 10, pp. 2, 8).

13 September 1998: about 2,000 supporters of Sali Berisha's Democratic Party set fire to cars outside the interior ministry and storm and set fire to the prime minister's office in Tirana, claiming that Fatos Nano's Socialist Party had Azem Hajdari (a leading Democratic Party deputy) assassinated the day before. The prime minister and other cabinet ministers flee. A protestor is killed and four of the prime minister's guards are wounded. The government offers a $100,000 reward for information leading to the arrest of the assassins.

(Both Hajdari and Berisha come from Tropoje in northern Albania, a part of the country that is not under government control and is the centre of arms smuggling to Kosovo. Both have claimed that the Albanian government is not doing enough to support ethnic Albanians in Kosovo.)

14 September 1998: the funeral takes place in Tirana of Azem Hajdari (and two of his bodyguards). Armed pro-Berisha supporters temporarily take control of the parliament building, the offices of the prime minister and the state television and radio station. Governments forces kill three rioters. Fatos Nano believes this was an attempted coup.

15 September 1998: about 3,000 pro-Berisha supporters stage an unauthorized but peaceful demonstration in Tirana.

The government aims to prosecute Berisha for leading what it considers to be a coup attempt. Parliament is to vote on whether to lift the parliamentary immunity from prosecution enjoyed by Berisha and five other members of the Democratic Party.

> OSCE was trying to persuade the Democratic Party to end its boycott of parliament and renew talks on writing Albania's constitution. 'This was a serious attempt to overthrow the government,' commented Timothy Isles, deputy head of the OSCE mission in Tirana. 'But put in perspective there was a band of no more than 500 militants bent on creating chaos and anarchy. The rest of the country was quiet and they got no widespread support.'
>
> (*FT*, 16 September 1998, p. 2)

16 September 1998: about 3,000 pro-Berisha supporters stage another peaceful demonstration in Tirana.

According to the interior ministry, three days of unrest have left eight dead and eighty injured (*IHT*, 17 September 1998, p. 4).

17 September 1998: a parliamentary committee recommends that Berisha lose his parliamentary immunity against arrest, although it decides against doing so in the case of the other five people pending further evidence (*IHT*, 18 September 1998, p. 5). Parliament has to vote on the issue.

Some 2,000 pro-Berisha supporters stage a peaceful demonstration in Tirana.

18 September 1998: parliament lifts the immunity from prosecution of Sali Berisha, clearing the way for prosecutors to charge him with attempting a coup. Of the 113 members participating in the vote, 108 voted in favour. The Democratic Party has been boycotting the 155-seat parliament since July 1998. Berisha faces the death penalty or life imprisonment if convicted of attempting to overthrow the government. Before the vote Berisha, who blames Nano's government for Azem Hajdari's murder, led a peaceful march of about 3,000 people in Tirana's Skanderbeg Square (*IHT*, 19 September 1998, p. 2).

20 September 1998: pro-Berisha supporters walk from the centre of Tirana to the cemetery on the edge of the capital where Hajdari is buried.

28 September 1998: Fatos Nano resigns as prime minister.

> In a letter to President Meidani, Mr Nano said on Monday [28 September] he had stepped down because squabbling had made it impossible to form a new cabinet of his five-party coalition government. He told the president he had been unable to put together a new cabinet according to his own wishes. He acknowledged his responsibility 'for everything this government has not done' and said that 'the chances of coming out of the crisis are little'.
>
> (*FT*, 30 September 1998, p. 3)

> The demise of premier Fatos Nano had been a virtual certainty since his disappearance in the wake of the mid-September coup attempt by the opposition Democratic Party [DP] led by Sali Berisha … Nano was taken totally by surprise when the DP mob stormed his office, which inexplicably was guarded only by two or three people. Having fled the building and reportedly driven to Macedonia or Greece, he went to ground for a couple of days, leaving [President] Meidani and [Pandeli] Majko to hold the ring. Meidani addressed the nation on television … Meidani, in his capacity as commander-in-chief of the armed forces, and in the absence of the hiding Nano, had called in the special forces and put Berisha's motley army to rout.
>
> (*EEN*, 1998, vol. 12, no. 11, pp. 1–2)

29 September 1998:

> The governing Socialist Party on Tuesday [29 September] nominated Pandeli Majko, its secretary-general, to succeed Fatos Nano as Albania's prime minister at the head of a five-party coalition … If he is approved by President Rexhep Meidani, Mr Majko, thirty, would be the country's youngest leader. He was active in 1990 street protests that helped topple the country's isolationist Stalinist regime … Parliament selects the prime minister but the Socialists hold a comfortable majority in the 155-seat chamber. Although he lacks ministerial experience, Mr Majko has made a name for himself as a mediator in feuds between the government and the opposition leader, Sali Berisha.
>
> (*IHT*, 30 September 1998, p. 5)

Interior minister Perikli Teta resigns (*Telegraph*, 30 September 1998, p. 16).
2 October 1998: Pandeli Majko is sworn in as prime minister.
3 October 1998: the new cabinet is announced.

> A priority was to sack the deputy premier Bashkim Fino, the former mayor of Gjirokaster who took over the premiership after the March 1997 collapse, and whose corruption and patronage is second to none. Former interior minister Neritan Ceka, with the help of less corrupt police generals, had enough information on Fino to do far more than sack him. But Fino, as the

> lynch-pin to Nano's corrupted administration, was too powerful to sack. Majko's new cabinet ... duly excluded him.
>
> (*EEN*, 1998, vol. 12, no. 11, p. 2)

22 November 1998: a referendum results in an overwhelming vote in favour of the new constitution. The turnout was around 50 per cent. OSCE upheld the result. The president gave his approval on 28 November (*EEN*, 1998, vol. 12, no. 13, p. 6).

14 December 1998: President Meidani declines to approve Premier Majko's request that intelligence chief Fatos Klosi be removed from office (*EEN*, 1998, vol. 12, no. 13, p. 6).

13 January 1999: parliament approves legislation aimed at stemming the illegal exodus of people to Italy. It bans boats of less than 70 hp further than two miles from the coast unless they advise the border police first (*The Times*, 14 January 1999, p. 13).

21 July 1999: the Democratic Party ends its twelve-month boycott of parliament (*EEN*, 1999, vol. 12, no. 19, p. 2).

28 September 1999: 'The deputy chairman of the Democratic Party, Genc Pollo, resigns all party positions in protest at party chairman Sali Berisha's dictatorial style. Berisha is reelected chairman in the absence of significant competition' (*EEN*, 1999, vol. 12, no. 20, p. 3).

11 October 1999: Fatos Nano narrowly defeats prime minister Pandeli Majko in the contest for chairman of the Socialist Party (*FT*, 12 October 1999, p. 8).

26 October 1999: prime minister Pandeli Majko resigns.

27 October 1999: deputy prime minister Ilir Mehta becomes prime minister. (He won a vote of confidence in parliament on 5 November.)

6 November 1999: a faction within the Democratic Party, led by Genc Pollo, sets up the 'Democratic Alternative' to oppose the Berisha wing of the party. On 7 December the Democratic Party suspended the party membership of Genc Pollo after accusations that he had failed to disclose the origin of private funds used to buy real estate in Tirana (*EEN*, 1999, vol. 12, no. 21, p. 4). 'The opposition Democratic Party is split, with the moderates under Genc Pollo forming a "Democratic Alternative" faction that is attending parliament in contrast to the bulk of the Democratic Party under Berisha which continues its parliamentary boycott' (p. 7).

February 2000:

> An innovative scheme [has been] started by the United Nations Development Programme (UNDP) to try to mop up some of the half million weapons that fell into civilians' hands when army depots were looted in the 1997 pyramid fund riots. Over the past year the UNDP has been collecting arms and ammunition in return for repairing local roads and utilities in the central Albanian town of Gramsh ... Some 6,000 weapons and

> nearly 140 tonnes of munitions have been turned over to the UNDP, which plans to extend its Gramsh pilot project elsewhere.
>
> (*FT*, Survey, 23 February 2000, p. 16)

1 February 2000: the Democratic Party expels former secretary-general Genc Pollo and three other leading moderates. 'The Democratic Party continues to fragment following a move by a dozen Democratic Party parliamentarians under former Democratic Party secretary Genc Pollo to establish a new anti-Berisha Democratic Party wing. Pollo and his associates were sacked on 1 February' (*EEN*, 2000, vol. 12, no. 22, pp. 2, 4).

1 October 2000: local elections are held.

The elections were monitored by OSCE: '[Voting marked] significant progress toward meeting the standards for democratic elections.' 'The Council of Europe and OSCE said voting had taken place in "a tense but remarkably peaceful atmosphere, with only a few isolated incidents of violence"' (*IHT*, 3 October 2000, p. 5). 'OSCE monitors declared their satisfaction overall with the conduct of the elections' (*EEN*, 2000, vol. 13, no. 1, p. 6).

On 2 October the Socialist Party announced that it had won 52 per cent of the vote.

The second round of voting took place on 15 October, involving those seats where candidates failed to get more than 50 per cent of the vote. 'The opposition Democratic Party declined to participate … [in the] second round of local elections. The ruling Socialist Party won 75 per cent of the seats contested in the second round' (*EEN*, 2000, vol. 13, no. 1, pp. 6, 8).

'This month [October] … [the] Socialists did well in local elections, taking control of Tirana from the right' (*The Economist*, 28 October 2000, p. 48).

> Local elections [in October 2000] give 43 per cent of the vote to the SPA [Socialist Party of Albania] and 34 per cent [33.6 per cent: p. 14] to the DP [Democratic Party]. Irregularities are noted by observers brought in by OSCE, which does not recognize them to be of the scale claimed by the DP.
>
> (Kaser 2001: 10)

'The party's [DP's] massive loss of local authority seats in October 2000 threatened his [Berisha's] dominance' (p. 17).

> In February 2000 Mr Berisha obtained backing to expel the reformist deputies from the parliamentary party. The reformists nevertheless did not oppose official DP candidates in the local elections of the following October and thereby not only gained stature among the DP membership for not splitting the vote but could blame the defeat squarely on Mr Berisha.
>
> (p. 13)

> The October 2000 local elections were conducted on mayoral programmes of municipal improvements: the victory of the parties of the governing

> coalition in 280 of the 378 towns and communes has brought the likelihood of some implementation. The independent mayor of Tirana, who, with government support, defeated the opposition, has begun a major programme of investment in a town swollen from 243,000 in 1990 to some 600,000 today.
>
> (p. 51)

(See the section on Kosovo in the third volume in the series, on the former Yugoslavia, for Albania's role in the Kosovo crisis.)

24 June 2001: a general election is held. The turnout was 60 per cent.

In the 140-seat parliament 100 are elected from single constituencies and 40 from party lists. The first round of election (for the 100 constituency seats) was held on 24 June.

> [It] appeared to be one of the country's most peaceful elections since the end of communism … Gunmen broke into one polling station in the north and burned ballot papers and two men were injured in a shooting outside a polling station in Tirana. But these were insignificant incidents … The ballot is being independently assessed by OSCE … The conflict in neighbouring Macedonia was hardly mentioned.
>
> (*Guardian*, 25 June 2001, p. 10)

> Preliminary results from the first round give the government party a clear lead … The Socialist Party said it had won forty-five of the 100 seats in the first round, putting it in a good position to win an overall majority when voters return to the polls in a fortnight. Mr Berisha's Democratic Party alleged widespread electoral fraud and intimidation of polling station officials by the police … An OSCE preliminary report noted only 'isolated incidents of violence' on election day.
>
> (*Guardian*, 26 June 2001, p. 10)

'Gunfire broke out at one polling station and assailants burned ballots at another' (*IHT*, 25 June 2001, p. 7). 'The election was largely peaceful, with only minor violence reported … The election commission and independent observers said the election had been generally fair' (*IHT*, 26 June 2001, p. 7).

> The 24 June parliamentary elections were won by the ruling Socialist Party, probably with a strong chance of obtaining an absolute majority once all second round elections have been completed in two weeks and the party list seats allocated … Sali Berisha's opposition Democratic Party, running as the 'Union for Victory', remains the only substantial opposition party … Foreign observers declared the elections relatively free and fair.
>
> (*EEN*, 2001, vol. 13, no. 5, p. 3)

'Sali Berisha, the centre-right leader, expressed strong support for ethnic Albanian rebels fighting in Macedonia' (*The Times*, 25 June 2001, p. 10).

The second round of the general election was held on 8 July.

> Albania's Socialist Party last night [8 July] appeared set for reelection by a wide margin after a run-off in almost half the country's 100 constituencies ... The Socialists won thirty-three seats in the first round ... with seventeen going to the right-of-centre Democratic Party ... The polling took place without violent incidents, although both parties reported some irregularities.
>
> (*FT*, 9 July 2001, p. 6)

> Ilir Mehta, Albania's prime minister, said yesterday [9 July] the Socialist Party ... [was] certain of a parliamentary majority after Sunday's [8 July] run-off election, with at least seventy-one seats in the 140-member house. 'We expect to add four more in constituencies where reruns will take place' [said the prime minister]. He said the Socialists had captured about 42 per cent of the vote to about 36 per cent for the right-of-centre Democratic Party. He said the Socialists would resume co-operating with three small centrist parties, which are likely to control another ten seats. 'We intend to form a coalition with our partners in the previous government ... Our priorities are still the same – to become a candidate for EU membership, to go on improving infrastructure and to fight corruption and trafficking,' he said ... OSCE, which monitored both rounds, said Sunday's ballot was 'generally peaceful and there was no serious violence, although there were some irregularities'. But the Democrats, expected to finish with forty-four seats, claimed widespread fraud in both rounds of voting.
>
> (*FT*, 10 July 2001, p. 6)

> After the second round, on 8 July, the Socialists had won seventy out of 140 seats in parliament. They were also ahead in another four constituencies where irregularities had been judged serious enough to warrant a rerun. The right-of-centre Democratic Party captured forty-two seats, the remainder going to four small parties. The Socialists finished with 42 per cent of the vote, to 36 per cent for the Democrats. Observers from OSCE reported some instances of voter intimidation and ballot-stuffing, but the violence ... [of past elections] was noticeably absent ... Sali Berisha ... refused to accept defeat, alleging fraud had been widespread. But this time, instead of urging his supporters to demonstrate in the streets of Tirana, Mr Berisha said he would take his case to the European Court ... Ilir Mehta says he wants to team up again with smaller pro-EU parties like the Democratic Alliance and the Social Democrats that were part of the Socialist-led coalition last time. This would give the Socialists the eighty-four parliamentary votes needed to elect a new president next year [2002] ...

> Talks are to start later this year on a stabilization and association pact with the EU.
>
> (*The Economist*, 14 July 2001, p. 45)

27 June 2001:

> Seven governments … yesterday signed an agreement aimed at liberalizing trade in at least 90 per cent of goods trade between them. The move by Albania, Bosnia-Hercegovina, Bulgaria, Croatia, Romania, Macedonia and Yugoslavia marks the latest stage in efforts, under the EU's Stability Pact for South-Eastern Europe, to enhance stability in the region through economic growth. Moldova is expected to join the arrangement shortly.
>
> (*FT*, 28 June 2001, p. 8)

THE ECONOMY

Alia's economic reforms

In September 1989 President Ramiz Alia accepted the need for unemployment in the case of 'idlers' and the 'irresponsible'. The following month it was accepted that indirect rather than direct steering would characterize the new economic system. In January 1990 Alia proposed the election of enterprise managers by workers, a decentralization of decision-making, wages linked to performance and market prices for some non-essential goods. In April he advocated greater self-financing for enterprises (long-term bank credits, as opposed to grants, being the rule rather than the exception), and concessions to the private sector. In July craftsmen and traders were allowed, although only family labour was to be employed (a restriction subsequently removed), and direct foreign investment permitted. The 28 February 1991 decree allowed individual ownership of cars.

In May 1990 the then prime minister Adil Carcani outlined the new economic system, to take effect on 1 January 1991. Enterprises were to be placed in three categories: those subject to physical output planning (e.g. oil and sugar); those allowed to determine above-plan output deliveries within their own districts in conjunction with the local authorities; and those free to determine their own output and prices. Certain enterprises were to be permitted to use up 20 per cent of their capacities for self-determined above-plan output sold at market prices. Foreign trade still had to be conducted through state foreign trade corporations, although some foreign exchange could be used by the enterprises themselves for imports such as machinery. Wholesale prices were to be based on the highest cost producers in order to reduce planned losses and thus subsidies. Enterprises were to be self-financing as far as possible and 90 per cent of planned profit could be retained (85 percentage points for investment and 5 percentage points for bonuses). If an enterprise (or sub-unit) planned and succeeded in reaching targets for above-plan profits, one half would go to bonuses and the other half to investment. Penalties for a poorer-than-planned performance (not due to extraneous circumstances) included high interest rates, the sacking of managers and even plant closure. Workers could receive up to a quarter of pay in bonuses, but unplanned losses would result in a pay reduction of 10 per cent. Only the total wage bill was to be planned, with the enterprise deciding on the distribution among workers. The total wage bill could be exceeded if the plan was overfulfilled. New workers could be taken on, but new jobs would have to be found for those dismissed. Workers laid off through circumstances beyond their control would receive 80 per cent of their normal wages, but those responsible for shortages would receive only half their normal wages. Independent trade unions were formally legalized on 18 February 1991. Schnytzer (1992) interprets these proposals as a pragmatic response of a regime willing to sacrifice ideology in order to stay in power.

In mid-1990 free markets were allowed for the sale of agricultural products from private plots. Other changes included the enlargement of private plots and the end of restrictions on the number of private livestock.

Economic policy after mid-1991

The main planks of the coalition government's 'big bang'/'shock therapy' economic programme of June 1991 comprised the following (Åslund and Sjöberg 1991: 13–20):

1. Macroeconomic stabilization was to be achieved as soon as possible. The three key aims were a balanced budget, price liberalization and currency convertibility.
2. Rapid and extensive privatization. A rapid auctioning of small enterprises such as shops was envisaged, current occupants would be given their housing and the privatization of much of large-scale industry was to proceed by means of free distribution via investment funds.

The Berisha regime's IMF-inspired economic reform programme was supposed to have been introduced on 1 July 1992, but most of it was postponed because of the imminent 26 July local elections (in which the Democratic Party's share of the vote fell considerably and the Socialist Party came out on top). The programme eventually included the following elements.

1 Austerity measures to reduce the huge budget deficit

These measures included the phasing out of the generous unemployment compensation scheme. The law on social assistance did not become fully operational until July 1992. Unemployment pay was to be limited to one year, 70 per cent of the previous year's average wage for the first six months and 60 per cent for the next six months. A wage inflation tax is in operation (Pashko 1993:

912–15). A nominal wage ceiling was introduced in September 1992, which may be exceeded only by certain relatively successful enterprises (Deutsche Bank, *Focus: Eastern Europe*, 1995, no. 125, p. 3). There are no longer any wage ceilings for state or private enterprises. An agreement is in place between the government and the largest trade union to index government wages to the prices of twenty-four basic consumer goods (EBRD 1996b: 136). Defence did not escape the axe. The armed forces were placed under civilian control and their total strength reduced from 90,000 to 35,000. The 600,000-strong reserve force was disbanded (*FT*, Survey, 19 February 1997, p. 16).

Tax revenues remain very low, at around 13 per cent of GDP. In an effort to boost them the government introduced a new tax law in January 1999. The law raised the top rate of income tax to 30 per cent and also set the profit tax at that rate. Strict limits on exemptions from profit tax have been introduced and tax holidays have been abolished (EBRD 1999b: 182).

The banking law, which separated the functions of the central bank and the commercial banks, was not implemented until June 1992 (Pashko 1996: 81). The National Bank of Albania enjoys formal independence modelled on the German Bundesbank. The central bank has been radically restructured to concentrate on credits to small businesses, while the bulk of state industry has effectively closed down (*Guardian*, 24 July 1993, p. 35). A bankruptcy law was adopted in 1992, but no bankruptcies have yet taken place. A rapid accumulation of inter-enterprise arrears in 1991–2 was halted in early 1993 by a settlement system relying on payment before delivery. Arrears were netted out and a strictly limited number of financially viable enterprises were granted the means to write off their claims on non-viable enterprises (EBRD 1994: 16). Plans to initiate the liquidation or privatization of several large problem enterprises were scrapped and these enterprises were included in the mass privatization programme approved in early 1995 (EBRD 1995b: 33). A new bankruptcy law was passed in October 1995. It defined bankruptcy procedures for all enterprises (the previous one covering only state enterprises), but no bankruptcies have actually taken place (EBRD 1996b: 136).

2 A devaluation of the lek

The lek was floated and became convertible on current account (strict controls still existing on the capital account). Foreign trade was liberalized. On 11 May 1992 Albania and the EU signed a ten-year trade and co-operation agreement. A free trade agreement was signed with EFTA in December 1992.

Excise taxes on imported and domestically produced goods were harmonized as of 1 January 1999 and the maximum tariff was to be reduced from 30 per cent to 20 per cent as of 1 April 1999 (EBRD 1999a: 32). There is a managed floating exchange rate. In January 1999 a new maximum tariff rate of 20 per cent was introduced, with about two-thirds of all goods rated at 10 per cent or less. Since April 1999 there have been only three non-zero tariffs. The unweighted average tariff is now about 14 per cent. The government has also taken steps to improve customs collection (EBRD 1999b: 182).

> Full membership of the WTO for Albania was ratified in July 2000, with formal accession taking place in September 2000. Albania has also made progress in lowering tariff barriers to imports. In December 1999 it reduced the maximum tariff rate on goods from 20 per cent to 18 per cent, with the unweighted average tariff rate declining to 13 per cent ... Since October 1999 the EU has granted unilateral trade preferences to Albania, including exemptions from duties and abolition of quantitative restrictions for industrial goods, special concessions for selected agricultural and fishery products, and provision of specific ceilings for textiles. About 90 per cent of all exports from Albania to the EU are now duty-free. However, customs duty continues to be an important element of the Albanian government's revenues and about 90 per cent of imports are from the EU ... Training courses for tax inspectors are being conducted with the assistance of the IMF and World Bank. A EU Customs Assistance Mission is also helping in a number of areas.
>
> (EBRD 2000b: 126)

> [On 18 September 2000 EU foreign] ministers ... approved an EU package granting duty-free access to 95 per cent of imports from Albania, Bosnia, Croatia, Macedonia and Montenegro ... The package includes abolition of tariffs on most industrial and farm products to the EU. However, some limits remain on exports of fish products and wine.
>
> (*FT*, 19 September 2000, p. 10)

'The EU in 1999 took some 94 per cent of exports (mainly to Italy, Greece and Germany) and supplied around 80 per cent of imports' (Kaser 2001: 53).

3 Price liberalization

In August 1992 almost all prices were freed and the few controlled prices of basic food products were raised by 300 to 400 per cent (United Nations Economic Commission for Europe 1993: 221). Price liberalization has been comprehensive, although twenty-five items remain subject to administrative price-setting (EBRD 1994: 17). The prices of bread, gas and kerosene were liberalized in July 1996. Price controls and subsidies (amounting to less than 1 per cent of GDP) still apply for public transport, rail fares, postal tariffs, electricity and rural water supply (EBRD 1996b: 136). All price controls on food items that were reimposed during the state of emergency have now been removed (EBRD 1997b: 148).

4 The expansion of the private sector

The private sector has expanded very rapidly in importance. Rough estimates in mid-year of the private sector as a percentage of GDP are provided by the EBRD: 1990, 5 per cent; 1991, 5 per cent; 1992, 10 per cent; 1993, 40 per cent; 1994, 50 per cent; 1995, 60 per cent; 1996, 75 per cent; 1997, 75 per cent; 1998, 75 per cent; 1999, 75 per cent; 2000, 75 per cent (EBRD 2000b: 14, 128).

The informal sector accounts for about half of GDP (EBRD 2000a: 36).

'It has been extremely hard for any businessman in Albania to succeed independently of the mafia or of government corruption' (*EEN*, 12 October 1996, vol. 10, no. 20, p. 4).

Privatization

Small privatization proceeded very quickly from 1991 onwards. Even as early as January 1992 almost 75 per cent of retail trade and small services was in private hands (Pashko 1996: 69). According to the August 1991 legislation, the sale of state assets would typically proceed by giving the first option to buy to the employees of the enterprise (Blejer *et al.* 1992: 56–7). Thus many entities were taken over by employees (EBRD 1994: 16).

Large privatization, on the other hand, has been very slow, although many enterprises have been broken up and some parts even closed down. A voucher-based mass privatization programme was approved in early 1995, with voucher distribution to start in June 1995. In the programme a total of 400 medium-sized and large enterprises were to be privatized through auctions. As of July 1996 a total of ninety-seven enterprises had been sold under the programme, with the process expected to be completed by the end of 1998 (EBRD 1996b: 11). Emphasis has been put on finding strategic investors for the remaining large enterprises, but so far only one large privatization has been completed (EBRD 1997b: 148).

> The enterprise restructuring agency set up in 1993 to deal with thirty-two problem firms has been relatively successful in restructuring these firms, reducing employment from 50,000 at their peak to 7,000 at the end of 1995. However, only ten have been privatized and only one smaller enterprise liquidated.
>
> (EBRD 1998b: 148)

> Plans for the privatization of strategic utilities are making gradual progress. However, the electricity company is virtually bankrupt ... Non-payment for electricity remains rife both among households and state enterprises ... The privatization programme is now centred on selling off remaining small and medium-sized enterprises and privatizing public monopolies in strategic sectors. Out of approximately 470 state-owned small and medium-sized enterprises identified in mid-1998 around 300 had been sold or closed by

> March 1999. Large-scale privatization is focussed first on the telecoms sector and then on copper and chrome.
>
> (EBRD 1999a: 32)

Small privatization proceeded rapidly in the early stages of transition. By mid-1998, 469 small and medium-sized enterprises remained in state hands. Of these, more than 300 had been sold, liquidated, leased or closed down by the end of June 1999. The divestment by the state of the remainder is expected before the end of 1999. The crisis in Kosovo has contributed to delays in the privatization of large, strategic enterprises. The government has liquidated two of the three remaining large, loss-making enterprises that had been placed under the control of the enterprise restructuring agency. The Kosovo crisis caused the sale of the third to a foreign company to be delayed. Albania's banking sector remains dominated by the state-owned National Commercial Bank and the Savings Bank, which together account for over 70 per cent of total banking assets. A strategic investor for the former was selected through a competitive tender in May 1999. The energy sector is dominated by the state-owned Albanian Energy Corporation. It is on the verge of bankruptcy because of non-payment and theft of electricity. A pilot privatization programme for regional distribution companies is under way in Shkoder, Elbasan and Vlora (EBRD 1999b: 182–3). Some progress has occurred in restructuring the virtually insolvent state-owned electricity company. The privatization of small and medium-sized enterprises was virtually completed in 1999. The privatization of large enterprises is proceeding slowly (EBRD 2000a: 365).

> After successfully concluding the privatization or liquidation of state-owned small and medium-sized enterprises the government is concentrating on larger enterprises and utilities. In October 1999 parliament passed a law that defines tendering as the privatization method for packages of shares of the commercial companies that operate in non-strategic sectors. Five medium-sized state-owned companies (a brewery, winery, dairy factory, pharmaceutical factory and cement factory) were put up for sale in April 2000 … The government is also planning to privatize or liquidate all copper and chrome mines during 2000, including 80 per cent of Albchrom … Parts of the oil sector are also to be prepared for sales before the end of the year … An 85 per cent stake of the state-owned mobile phone company, Albanian Mobile Communications, was sold in July 2000 to a [foreign] consortium … 15 per cent will remain for the company employees and for the owner of the land where its headquarters is located … The sale by the government of the second-largest bank, the National Commercial Bank, to Kentbank of Turkey, was signed in June 2000. Kentbank bought a 60 per cent stake, with the EBRD and IFC each taking 20 per cent. This leaves only the Savings Bank, the largest bank … in state hands. It too is being prepared for privatization … The state-owned Power Generation and Distribution Company, KESH, remains in serious financial difficulties …

> An eighteen-month contract to manage KESH was awarded in May 2000 to the Italian Company ENEL, with the objectives of cutting technical losses and theft … The enterprise sector remains dominated by very small businesses (about 98 per cent of enterprises have ten employees or fewer), many of which operate in the informal economy.
>
> (EBRD 2000b: 126–7)

> The privatization of large-scale enterprises is proceeding well. The privatization of five targeted medium-sized enterprises was completed by the end of 2000. Privatization is moving ahead in the natural resources sector, but has been delayed in the energy sector due to an ongoing energy crisis … Following the latest energy crisis at the end of 2000 the government has started to implement a comprehensive package of reforms of the state-owned electricity company, Kesh. Quarterly targets for collecting bills and reducing theft have been established. The privatization of telecommunications advanced significantly in 2000 and early 2001 … Plans for the last remaining state-owned bank, the Savings Bank, are proceeding.
>
> (EBRD 2001: 44)

Strategic industries such as telecommunications were to be handled separately (*FT*, Survey, 2 October 1995, p. iv).

On 14 October 1991 it was announced that church land and property confiscated in 1967 were to be returned. After the March 1992 election, on 19 May to be precise, an announcement was made that all buildings belonging to the Socialist Party were to be seized. In May 1993 a restitution law was passed. In 1995, for example, expropriated urban property would be returned to the original owners or their heirs; in the meantime existing domestic or commercial tenants have to pay rent to the former owners. But the law provides only for compensation of up to 10 per cent for country owners (mostly land) and even then only in the form of bank guarantees (*EEN*, 1993, vol. 7, no. 13, p. 5; vol. 7, no. 15, p. 8; vol. 7, no. 16, p. 3). The purchase of land is currently forbidden in order to prevent 'tenants' selling the pre-1946 landowners' land (*EEN*, 21 September 1993, vol. 7, no. 19, p. 8). 'Families which want to repossess land that was expropriated by the communists in the 1940s have to pay vast bribes to acquire title' (*EEN*, 16 February 1997, vol. 11, no. 3, p. 3). According to laws passed in 1993, many former owners or their heirs can claim compensation for or restitution of non-agricultural land. In the case of property that has already been privatized there is co-ownership between the new and former owners (EBRD 1994: 16).

The stock exchange was opened on 2 May 1996, initially dealing only in Treasury bills and privatization vouchers.

Further developments in privatization

> The Elbasan steel plant has been revived by Turkish managers ... Privatization and foreign investment are slowly taking off ... As at Elbasan, foreigners still prefer to lease local firms or take over their management rather than buying them. But the country's GSM mobile operator was sold to a Greek–Norwegian consortium in summer [2000] ... Italians have taken over the Tirana brewery – one of four medium-sized enterprises privatized this year ... The troubled Albanian Commercial Bank has been rescued by Greek investors, allowing it to resume operations.
>
> (Business Central Europe 2000: 35)

Foreign aid and debt

Post-communist Albania quickly became heavily dependent on Western economic aid. Italy has been the country most directly affected by the flood of refugees and has provided generous assistance, especially food (partly, of course, in order to try to stem the flow). According to Pashko (1996: 70), food aid amounted to more than $600 million in the period 1991–2, a sum equivalent to 63 per cent of GDP. Pashko is cited as saying that 'Foreign aid, remittances from Albanians working abroad and embargo-breaking now account for three-quarters of national income' (*IHT*, 1 April 1995, p. 11). (According to Raymond Bonner, Albania was the biggest embargo-breaker for fuel delivered to the Federal Republic of Yugoslavia: *IHT*, 3 April 1995, p. 1.) In the period 1991–6 total committed or promised aid amounted to £2.02 billion, compared with $1.07 billion actually disbursed (*FT*, Survey, 19 February 1997, p. 18). (Remittances sent by more than 300,000 Albanians working abroad rose from virtually zero in 1991 to $334 million in 1993: *FT*, 29 June 1994, p. 3. Other estimates put the figure as high as $500 million: *Business Central Europe*, May 1994, p. 80; Deutsche Bank, *Focus: Eastern Europe*, 22 March 1994, no. 100, p. 35. The Deutsche Bank later talked of a conservative estimate of $200 million to $250 million transferred annually: *Focus: Eastern Europe*, 15 February 1995, no. 125, p. 5. Some $400 million annually is remitted: *Guardian*, 13 March 1995, p. 9; *EEN*, 15 March 1995, vol. 9, no. 6, p. 4. According to *The Economist*, some 400,000 Albanians work abroad, mostly illegally, in Greece and Italy, sending home more than $450 million a year: 18 May 1996, p. 51. Emigrant workers abroad accounted for an estimated 18 per cent of the labour force in 1995: EBRD 2000a: 37.)

Gross foreign debt was around $900 million at the end of 1994. Albania, whose payments problems started in 1990, barely serviced its outstanding foreign debt. It sought to negotiate a debt agreement with foreign commercial banks to which it owed around $400 million. In July 1993 the IMF approved a loan of $60 million, while by mid-1994 the World Bank had approved project financing of over $120 million (Deutsche Bank, *Focus: Eastern Europe*, 1995, no. 125, pp. 5–6).

> [Some] $300 million in grants and soft loans [has flowed in yearly] from international donors ... Even though the international community has committed aid worth $600 million a year, this has only been disbursed at the rate of $300 million a year.
>
> (*FT*, Survey, 23 February 2000, p. 13)

Foreign direct investment

Foreign investment is encouraged, but the response even before the descent into lawlessness was poor. (See Table 1.1.) Net foreign direct investment was $20 million in 1992, $58 million in 1993, $53 million in 1994 and $70 million in 1995 (United Nations Economic Commission for Europe 1996: 149). Direct foreign investment amounted to only $39 million in the period 1990–3 (EBRD 1994: 123). Attempts have been made to improve the economic environment. In July 1995, for example, a law was passed which allowed foreign individuals or companies to buy land if they combine the purchase with a three times as large investment in the usage of land (EBRD 1995b: 33). On 15 May 1996 it was announced that a German company had been allowed to take an 80 per cent stake in the chromium mining and processing industry, the first foreign investor in the sector. The other 20 per cent was to be owned by Albanian shareholders via the voucher scheme. A law on mine privatization passed in 1995 allows foreigners to own up to 80 per cent of mines (*FT*, 16 May 1996, p. 33). A Western consortium is to invest $250 million to develop the largest onshore oil field, the largest single foreign investment in Albania (*FT*, 17 December 1997, p. 2). 'Inflows of foreign direct investment have dwindled to about $45 million yearly over the past three years' (*FT*, Survey, 23 February 2000, p. 13).

> Albania's new-found if precarious stability has brought back Greek and Italian investors who shut up shop after the pyramid schemes collapsed three years ago ... A Turkish bank has taken over one of the two state-controlled banks. A copper mining concession has been bought by an American group.
>
> (*The Economist*, 29 April 2000, p. 49)

> An Italian–British consortium has taken over some of the chrome industry; Canadian and prospectively Turkish firms are investing in the copper deposits; and a British company is reopening a cobalt and nickel mine ... Onshore [oil] extraction is expected to increase ... as a result of a $250 million investment programme by Premier Oil (UK) and Preussag (Germany) in a joint venture with Albpetrol [the petroleum corporation].
>
> (Kaser 2001: 48)

'Kent Bank of Turkey has bought 60 per cent of the National Commercial Bank' (p. 51). 'In 2000 the Albanian government sold its mobile operator, Albanian Mobile Communications, to a Greek–Norwegian consortium' (p. 30).

Table 1.1 Albania: selected economic indicators 1990–2000

Economic indicator	*1990*	*1991*	*1992*	*1993*	*1994*	*1995*	*1996*	*1997*	*1998*	*1999*	*2000 (estimate)*
Rate of growth of GDP (%)	-10.0	-27.7	-7.2	9.6	8.3	13.3	9.1	-7.0	8.0	7.3	6.0
Rate of growth of industrial output (%)	-7.6	-36.9	-51.2	-10.0	-2.0	6.0	13.6	-5.6	4.1	6.4	
Rate of growth of agricultural output (%)	-6.9	-24.0	18.5	10.4	8.3	13.2	3.0	1.0	5.0	3.7	6.8
Inflation rate (consumer, %)	0.0	35.5	226.0	85.0	22.6	7.8	12.7	33.2	20.6	0.4	0.4
Budget surplus or deficit (% GDP)[a]	-3.7	-44.0	-23.1	-15.5	-12.6	-10.1	-12.1	-12.6	-10.4	-11.3	-8.8
Unemployment rate (annual average, %)	9.5	9.2	27.9	28.9	19.6	16.9	12.4	14.9	17.8	18.0	17.1
Balance of payments (current account, $ billion)	-0.122	-0.293	-0.427	-0.357	-0.279	-0.177	-0.245	-0.276	-0.186	-0.293	-0.332
Foreign direct investment (net, $ million)			20	45	65	89	97	42	45	51	92
Population (million)			3.2	3.2	3.2	3.2	3.3	3.3	3.4	3.4	3.4

Sources: Various issues of European Bank for Reconstruction and Development, *Transition Report*; United Nations Economic Commission for Europe, *Economic Survey of Europe*; United Nations, *World Economic and Social Survey*; IMF, *World Economic Outlook*.

Note:

[a] General government balance: includes the state, municipalities and extrabudgetary funds (EBRD)

'Foreigners … may purchase land only if combined with an investment at least three times as large as the cost of the land' (p. 43).

Agriculture

'Only in the countries of the former Soviet Union and in Albania was land legally nationalized' (Swinnen 1999: 641). Property rights to collective farmland have been restituted to former owners only in some mountainous regions (p. 639). Albania distributes its collective farmland among rural households (p. 639). State farmland has been distributed to farm workers. Initially, farm workers received privatization vouchers as state farms engaged in joint ventures. As most joint ventures failed, farm workers then received user rights, but ultimately were allocated full property rights (p. 640).

'The continuing disintegration of the agricultural sector resulted in a virtual collapse of the sector during 1990–1' (Cungu and Swinnen 1999: 608).

> The Land Law of July 1991 specified that APC land was to be distributed free of charge and on an equal per capita basis to member families and other rural residents … A number of other decrees on the distribution of other assets and the liquidation of the APCs supplemented the Land Law … Only 50,000 ha of state farms' land were initially distributed among farm workers. Most of the remainder was pooled into joint ventures with foreign capital … When many of these partnerships failed the land was given to workers for cultivation, with the state retaining ownership. In 1995 new legislation stipulated that use rights could be turned into full ownership rights on ex-joint venture land where disputes over the termination of joint venture contracts had been cleared … The Land Law did not recognize prior land ownership or its precollectivization size and boundaries. This caused strong opposition from the pre-1945 owners … In 1993 the government approved a law on the financial compensation of former landowners … In 1995 a new law was passed that provided for former owners to receive physical compensation in seaside and tourist-site properties.
>
> (pp. 610–11)

'The events of 1997 had relatively little effect on agricultural reforms and performance. Agricultural output grew at a rate of almost 2 per cent' (p. 610).

> Albania is the only country that has distributed all collective land among the rural population. Most other Central and Eastern European countries (CEECs), even the Baltic countries that were part of the former Soviet Union, have restituted collective farmland to former owners. Albania has also distributed most of its state farmland to the agricultural workers, although the breakup of the state farms was not as fast and radical as that of the Agricultural Production Co-operatives (APCs). In most other CEECs state farmland is either restituted (e.g. Slovenia and the Baltic countries) or

> leased in attendance of being sold. Farm restructuring is also more radical in Albania than in other CEECs … Virtually all land is now being used by small individual farms, unlike in other CEECs where large-scale co-operatives, joint stock companies, limited liability companies and so forth still occupy an important share of the land.
>
> (p. 605)

> All APCs and most of the state farms have been completely broken up into individual farms … More than 95 per cent of land is used by approximately 490,000 individual private farms in at least 1.9 million separate parcels, with an average of about 3.3 separately located parcels for each farm. The average size is 1.0 ha, ranging between 1.3 ha in valley and foothill regions to 0.8 ha in the mountains.
>
> (p. 611)

> As in other CEECs the reference date played an important role in Albania's restitution debate. In all CEECs restitution of land under the 1990s reforms is based on the ownership situation just before collectivization but after the communist-inspired land reforms … In the Albanian land reform debate 1948 owners – those who owned the land after the communist land reform of 1946–48 – were much less vocal than those in many other CEECs and less opposed to distribution than Albania's pre-1948 owners.
>
> (pp. 613–14)

The key piece of legislation was the 22 July 1991 Land Bill. All local co-operative land was to be redistributed by local committees to co-operative farming families free of charge on the basis of 0.1 hectares per family member. Land could be inherited and the intention was to allow land sales after five years. The aim was to have all co-operative land distributed before the end of September 1991 (this would amount to 80 per cent of arable land). A great deal of unofficial land redistribution took place (including that by former owners), however, and uncertainty over land titles adversely affected production.

Most collective farms were abandoned spontaneously in 1991 and their assets (including the land) were taken over by their members. Legal division of land was not supposed to start before June 1992, but by then 77 per cent of cultivated land was already in private hands. By the end of 1992, 90 per cent of land had been disposed of and 80 per cent of peasant families had become land owners (United Nations Economic Commission for Europe 1993: 203). By March 1992 the average amount of land held was 1.2 ha for highland families and 1.4 for lowland families (*EEN*, 1992, vol. 6, nos 1, 6 and 8). The average farm consists of 1.5 ha split into 3.3 separate parcels of differing quality (*FT*, Survey, 2 October 1995, p. iii).

Former owners are only allowed to reclaim a maximum of 15 ha from their pre-communist holdings. Alternatively they may seek compensation for up to 30 ha. Compensation is in the form of bonds (*EEN*, 21 September 1994, vol. 8, no.

19, p. 6). Most state farms are now partially or wholly farmed by former employees who hope to receive title to their allotted land in three years or so (*EEN*, 21 September 1993, vol. 7, no. 19, p. 8). Though in the case of state farms the law does allow for transfer of ownership to individuals, in practice this category of private farmer is a tenant. Most of the state farms remain intact, although in several cases individuals have been allowed to use state farmland for their own benefit (*EEN*, 21 September 1994, vol. 8, no. 19, p. 6).

A law passed in August 1995 allowed the buying and selling of farmland for the first time. In order to encourage land consolidation a farmer who wishes to sell must offer it to his family and neighbours before putting it on the open market. The government estimates that 96 per cent of agricultural land has been distributed, but only half has been legally titled (*FT*, Survey, 2 October 1995, p. iii). The sale and purchase of land was originally prohibited. In July 1995 a new law allowed the sale and purchase of agricultural land and transformed the titles to usage of land into property titles (EBRD 1996b: 136).

By the end of 1996, 98 per cent of agricultural land had been privatized. But despite the progress made in privatizing land no land market has developed. The main obstacles are the requirement that all land holdings in a village be registered before any can be sold (only 3 per cent of privatized land having been registered) and the absence of clear mechanisms for establishing the legality of land transactions. The law states that land must first be offered for sale to relatives of the current owner, owners of neighbouring properties, other villagers or ex-owners of the land before it can be offered to anyone else. Few informal sales have taken place (EBRD 1997b: 148). By the end of 1993, 92 per cent of agricultural land had been privatized. But land could not be traded effectively, partly due to the fact that only 3 per cent of land had been registered by mid-1997. A new land law was passed by parliament in May 1998. Whereas previously land could not be sold until all plots in a district had been registered, the new law allows for the sale of land on an individual basis (EBRD 1998b: 148). The authorities have made considerable progress in land registration. By March 1999 land registration had been completed in about 40 per cent of the total land by area. This process is enabling a visible market in agricultural land to emerge (EBRD 1999b: 182).

> The programme of registration of private property … begun in 1998 is proceeding, but is likely to take longer than originally expected. By the middle of 2000 the project … was completed in about 40 per cent of all cadastral zones … Completion will probably be in 2002.
>
> (EBRD 2000b: 126)

Whereas in 1990 50 per cent of agricultural production came from cooperatives, today 95 per cent is contributed by private farmers (Deutsche Bank, *Focus: Eastern Europe*, 15 February 1995, no. 125, p. 4).

Private farmers now own 98 per cent of the country's farmland … Sixty per cent of holdings have now been registered … The country's 550 state farms and co-operatives were parcelled up into some 470,000 family farms, with an average of only 1.1 ha each … [But] around 800 'water users' associations' have been set up to rehabilitate and manage irrigation systems and some other associations have been established for the buying and selling of seeds, fertilisers and pesticides … There are also around 200 farming associations with 40 to 50 ha of cereals and vegetables, and some 100 livestock associations with more than 200 sheep each.

(*FT*, Survey, 23 February 2000, p. 14)

The privatization process has left land ownership highly fragmented. A 1999 survey showed that there were 466,766 holdings with an average area of 4.1 ha, of which 1.8 ha was agricultural land, 2.2 ha forest and 0.1 ha either built on or in other use. The process of registration of title has led to a large number of disputes, especially in the Geg north and central uplands because of conflicting claims over assets previously held on quasi-feudal terms. Fewer registration problems have arisen in the south and the littoral plain, where ownership had been decided before the Second World War and much land had been reclaimed in the communist period, having had no owner before collectivization. The IMF's requirement, introduced in February 1998, to facilitate the functioning of a land market by universal land registration, has largely been satisfied, but it has had adverse social consequences because discrimination against 'outsiders', even those settled for two generations, is creating a class of landless peasants … Peasant self-sufficiency, forced on collective farmers by the communist government's prohibition of private marketing, remains very high: the 1999 survey indicated that 48.5 per cent of farm households never bought arable or animal produce from outside … [The survey] showed that 42 per cent of farmers still tilled their land with the aid of animal and manpower alone.

(Kaser 2001: 46–7)

Economic performance

The GDP growth rate turned positive as early as 1993. Output fell heavily in 1997 (by 7 per cent) as a result of the anarchic conditions (which began in earnest at the start of that year) but there was a strong resurgence thereafter. (See Table 1.1.) In 2000 GDP in transitional Albania exceeded its 1989 level for the first time (EBRD 2001: 15). Inflation did not reach hyperinflationary levels in the 1990s, reaching a peak of 226 per cent in 1992. By 1999 consumer prices were more or less stable.

The influx of more than 400,000 refugees from Kosovo during the first half of 1999 imposed an enormous strain on social services and the budget. But the end of the conflict in June 1999 was quickly followed by the return of most of the refugees. The vast majority were back in Kosovo by the end of July 1999 (EBRD 1999b: 183).

The United Nations classified Albania as a 'least-developed nation', the only one ever in Europe (Henry Kamm, *IHT*, 4 August 1993, p. 5). By the end of the 1980s Albania was still the poorest country in Europe. The World Bank's estimate for *per capita* income (for June 1991) was $600. By way of comparison, the 1989 figure for Portugal (the poorest country in Western Europe) was $4,250 and for Turkey $1,370 (Åslund and Sjöberg 1991: 6, 8). James Hansen cited a World Bank estimate of *per capita* income at just below $300 a year (*IHT*, 1 April 1995, p. 9).

Unemployment is very high, although the estimates vary. According to official data, unemployment reached 26.3 per cent at the end of 1992 and fell to 19.6 per cent at the end of 1993. But real unemployment (i.e. including those seeking work but excluded from the statistics) was at least 30 per cent at the end of 1993 (Deutsche Bank, *Focus: Eastern Europe*, no. 125, p. 3). Unemployment as a percentage of the non-agricultural labour force was 37 per cent at the end of 1992 and 44 per cent by mid-1993. Some 200,000 to 300,000 have left to work elsewhere (Sjöberg 1996: 91–2). The (end of year) unemployment rate was 9.8 per cent in 1990, 9.4 per cent in 1991, 24.2 per cent in 1992, 22.0 per cent in 1993 and 19.0 per cent in 1994 (United Nations Economic Commission for Europe 1994: 86, and 1995: 111).

> After successfully concluding the privatization or liquidation of state-owned small and medium-sized enterprises the government is concentrating on larger enterprises and utilities. In October 1999 parliament passed a law that defines tendering as the privatization method for packages of shares of the commercial companies that operate in non-strategic sectors. Five medium-sized state-owned companies (a brewery, winery, dairy factory, pharmaceutical factory and cement factory) were put up for sale in April 2000 … The government is also planning to privatize or liquidate all copper and chrome mines during 2000, including 80 per cent of Albchrom … Parts of the oil sector are also to be prepared for sales before the end of the year … An 85 per cent stake of the state-owned mobile phone company, Albanian Mobile Communications, was sold in July 2000 to a [foreign] consortium … 15 per cent will remain for the company employees and for the owner of the land where its headquarters is located … The sale by the government of the second-largest bank, the National Commercial Bank, to Kentbank of Turkey, was signed in June 2000. Kentbank bought a 60 per cent stake, with the EBRD and IFC each taking 20 per cent. This leaves only the Savings Bank, the largest bank … in state hands. It too is being prepared for privatization … The state-owned Power Generation and Distribution Company, KESH, remains in serious financial difficulties … An eighteen-month contract to manage KESH was awarded in May 2000 to the Italian Company ENEL, with the objectives of cutting technical losses and theft … The enterprise sector remains dominated by very small

businesses (about 98 per cent of enterprises have ten employees or fewer), many of which operate in the informal economy.

(EBRD 2000b: 126–7)

Full membership of the WTO for Albania was ratified in July 2000, with formal accession taking place in September 2000 … Since October 1999 the EU has granted unilateral trade preferences to Albania, including exemptions from duties and abolition of quantitative restrictions for industrial goods, special concessions for selected agricultural and fishery products, and provision of specific ceilings for textiles. About 90 per cent of all exports from Albania to the EU are now duty-free. However, customs duty continues to be an important element of the Albanian government's revenues and about 90 per cent of imports are from the EU … Training courses for tax inspectors are being conducted with the assistance of the IMF and World Bank. A EU Customs Assistance Mission is also helping in a number of areas.

(EBRD 2000b: 126)

[On 18 September 2000 EU foreign] ministers … approved an EU package granting duty-free access to 95 per cent of imports from Albania, Bosnia, Croatia, Macedonia and Montenegro … The package includes abolition of tariffs on most industrial and farm products to the EU. However, some limits remain on exports of fish products and wine.

(*FT*, 19 September 2000, p. 10)

The programme of registration of private property … begun in 1998 is proceeding, but is likely to take longer than originally expected. By the middle of 2000 the project … was completed in about 40 per cent of all cadastral zones … Completion will probably be in 2002.

(EBRD 2000b: 126)

2 Bulgaria

POLITICS

Earlier developments are dealt with in the Introduction and Overview.

The general election of 18 December 1994

The turnout was over 75 per cent. There was a 4 per cent threshold for parliamentary representation. The Bulgarian Socialist Party did even better than expected, winning an absolute majority of seats in the National Assembly (see Table 2.1). Only five parties won seats in the National Assembly. Smaller ones failed to do so, e.g. the Democratic Alternative for the Republic (a centre-left coalition). The parties with seats in the National Assembly were as follows:

Bulgarian Socialist Party: leader Zhan Videnov. (The Bulgarian Socialist Party was joined in an election pact by the Bulgarian Agrarian Party 'Alexander Stamboliski' and the Political Club 'Ecoglasnost': Deutsche Bank, *Focus: Eastern Europe*, 1995, no. 130, p. 3.)

Union of Democratic Forces: leader Filip Dimitrov. (He resigned after the election and was replaced by Ivan Kostov.)

People's Union: a coalition of the Democratic Party (which split from the UDF) and the Agrarian Party.

Movement for Rights and Freedoms: leader Ahmed Dogan.

Bulgarian Business Bloc: leader Georgi Ganchev (a former émigré). (The bloc became part of the coalition government, but Ganchev was later disqualified as an MP because he held a US passport at the time of the election: *EEN*, 14 April 1995, vol. 9, no. 8, p. 1, and 28 April 1995, vol. 9, no. 9, p. 8.)

Political developments after the 18 December 1994 general election

24 January 1995: the new government is announced. Membership includes Roumen Getchev (vice-premier in charge of the economy and privatization; he

Table 2.1 Bulgaria: the general election of 18 December 1994

Party	*Seats in the National Assembly*	*% vote*[a]
Bulgarian Socialist Party	125	43.5
Union of Democratic Forces	69	24.23
People's Union	18	6.15
Movement for Rights and Freedoms	15	5.44
Bulgarian Business Bloc	13	4.72
Total	240	

Note:
[a] There is a 4 per cent threshold for parliamentary representation

favours growth over a lower rate of inflation), Dimitar Kostov (finance), Kyril Tsochev (trade), Georgi Pirinski (foreign affairs) and Dimitar Pavlov (defence).

1 February 1995: the EU association agreement comes fully into effect.

25 May–17 June 1996: King Simeon II visits Bulgaria (the first time he has been in the country since 1946). A large number of people turn out to see him.

4 June 1996: it is announced that the members of the Union of Democratic Forces have voted against Zhelyu Zhelev as their candidate for president. He received 34 per cent of the vote compared with 66 per cent for Petar Stoyanov.

13 June 1996: the government survives a no-confidence vote in parliament.

15 July 1996: President Zhelev warns of possible mass unrest in the autumn because of political and economic chaos. He reiterates his call for strong presidential rule (*IHT*, 16 July 1996, p. 5).

23 July 1996: the constitutional court rules that the Socialist Party's candidate, Georgi Pirinski, is ineligible to run in the 27 October 1996 presidential election on the grounds that the president 'must be a Bulgarian citizen and to be such by birth'. (Nevertheless, Pirinski, born in New York of a Bulgarian émigré father and a Slovak–American mother, said that he intended to run for the presidency. If he is elected and a formal complaint is lodged, the constitutional court may rule his election invalid: *FT*, 25 July 1996, p. 2.)

27 August 1996: the electoral commission refuses to register Georgi Pirinski and Petar Stoyanov on the grounds that their papers are incomplete and contain irregularities. They have three days to appeal to the supreme court.

4 September 1996: the Bulgarian Socialist Party replaces Georgi Pirinski as its presidential candidate with Ivan Marazov (the culture minister).

6 September 1996: Petar Stoyanov is registered by the electoral commission.

12 September 1996: New Liberal Alliance is finalized, composed of New Choice Union, New Democracy Party and the Radical Democratic Party, with President Zhelev as an honorary member (*EEN*, 1996, vol. 10, no. 19, p. 6).

20 September 1996: Slavi Pashkovski, ambassador to the UN, denounces Bulgaria's government. 'The ghost of communism is looming over Bulgaria, which means also over the Balkans and over Europe.' Bulgaria's economic failings are 'a premeditated plot to make certain people richer and to enslave millions of Bulgarian citizens'. Pashkovski claims that someone tampered with his car by cutting the connectors to the steering wheel and recalls the assassination of Georgi Markov in 1978. (Pashkovski was appointed in 1992. The present government has twice omitted him from its list of official delegates for the UN General Assembly but has been unable to gain the approval of President Zhelev to remove him as ambassador.)

2 October 1996: Socialist Party MP and former prime minister Andrei Lukanov is murdered outside his home in unclear circumstances.

> The view in Sofia was that the assassination mainly reflected conflict between powerful economic interests, but would have inevitable political repercussions on an unpopular government presiding over a deep financial crisis and facing presidential elections later this month.
>
> (Anthony Robinson, *FT*, 3 October 1996, p. 2)

'As yet no one has claimed responsibility for the killing, but it is likely to be part of the increasingly lethal mafia and politics mixture in Sofia' (James Pettifer, *The Times*, 3 October 1996, p. 17). 'Lukanov ... was gunned down outside his house, apparently in connection with disputes over corruption in the Socialist Party' (Jane Perlez, *IHT*, 29 October 1996, p. 8). 'His colleagues said the killing was linked to his plans to publicize corruption at the party's top level' (*IHT*, 24 December 1996, p. 5).

Parliament unanimously passes a resolution: 'We will not allow this terrorist act to lead to the declaring of a state of emergency in Bulgaria.'

(Lukanov was prime minister from 4 February to 29 November 1990 and was arrested on 9 July 1992. According to the *FT*, he was jailed without trial for six months: 3 October 1996, p. 2.)

27 October 1996: the first round of the presidential election is held. The turnout is 60 per cent. There are thirteen candidates, but the top three poll as follows: Petar Stoyanov (Union of Democratic Forces), 44.9 per cent; Ivan Marazov (Bulgarian Socialist Party), 26.98 per cent; Georgi Ganchev (Bulgarian Business Bloc), 21.86 per cent.

3 November 1996: the second round of the presidential election is held. The turnout is 61 per cent. Stoyanov wins with 59.73 per cent of the vote, compared with Marazov's 40.27 per cent.

13 November 1996: Georgi Pirinski resigns as foreign minister the day after prime minister Zhan Videnov survived a vote of no confidence at a plenum of the Socialist Party (by 87 to 69, with 2 abstentions). Pirinski resigns on the grounds that the government no longer has public confidence (*EEN*, 1996, vol. 10, no. 23, p. 8).

24 November 1996: Stoyanov promises an enquiry into the death of Georgi Markov in 1978.

21 December 1996: prime minister Zhan Videnov announces the resignation of himself (as prime minister and party chief) and of the entire cabinet.

24 December 1996: Georgi Parvanov accepts the leadership of the Socialist Party but not the premiership.

3 January 1997: demonstrators in Sofia call for early parliamentary elections. (A general election does not have to be held until December 1998.)

The government agrees that in mid-February 1997 it will introduce a currency board system (which will tie the money supply to the level of hard currency reserves) (*FT*, 4 January 1997, p. 2).

6 January 1997: the Socialist Party nominates interior minister Nikolai Dobrev as prime minister.

10 January 1997: parliament votes against holding an extraordinary debate on an opposition motion calling for an early general election. Opposition MPs walk out. Some of the people who have been protesting daily since 3 January attack the parliament building.

11 January 1997: many are injured as riot police clear crowds from around parliament and escort Socialist Party MPs from the building.

12 January 1997: Georgi Parvanov agrees to talks with the opposition about holding an early general election, but before one can be held he wishes to form a new government (lasting at least a year) to deal with the deepening economic crisis.

President Zhelev: 'We should not forget that the protests in Serbia are based mainly on political demands, and the protests here are based on economic factors and social discontent. The difference is clear, as the average salary in Serbia is $200 and in Bulgaria it is $30' (*IHT*, 13 January 1997, p. 1).

President-elect Stoyanov: 'The Belgrade slogans are too abstract for the starving Bulgarians. The Serbians are fighting for political and press freedom. Here, the people are fighting for their survival, to be able to buy bread and keep warm.' Monthly wages are 'between $16 and $20 and the price of bread is 50 cents ... We must hold elections at the beginning of June. The people are desperate. They cannot survive on a salary of $20 a month' (*IHT*, 13 January 1997, p. 7).

13 January 1997: the Socialist Party issues a statement saying that it is ready 'to accept in principle the idea of holding early parliamentary elections in the context of implementing a national anti-crisis programme for the economic and financial stabilization of Bulgaria'.

14 January 1997: the government thinks the new government should last 500 days before elections are held.

15 January 1997: Socialist Party MPs return to parliament and agree to hold elections at the end of 1997. (The trade unions Promyana, Podkrepa and KNSB promise to hold nationwide strikes after giving the legally required week's notice: *EEN*, 1997, vol. 11, no. 2, p. 3.)

Warning strikes take place, for example in coal mines, steel works, hospitals, schools and government offices.

19 January 1997: Petar Stoyanov is sworn in as president (although he formally assumes power on 22 January):

> I am convinced that the country needs early parliamentary elections and a new agreement between social forces and between the government and the governed ... People are demonstrating in the streets because their poverty has reached desperate levels.

(The president is later quoted with respect to economic reforms:

> Although the first UDF government under Filip Dimitrov started serious reform, most of the last seven years we only had the pretence of reform. We deluded ourselves that we could survive without great sacrifices. But things kept getting tougher and we got deeper and deeper into debt. January [1997] marked the turning point when we shed our illusions.
>
> (*FT*, Survey, 21 October 1997, p. 32)

27 January 1997: President Stoyanov announces that he is to give a mandate to the Socialist Party to form a new government. But he appeals to the Socialist Party to return the mandate and allow the formation of 'an efficient caretaker cabinet supported by all political forces and institutions'. He also calls for an election in May.

28 January 1997: Nikolai Dobrev accepts the mandate to form a new government.

The three main trade unions (Promyana, Podkrepa and KNSB) say that a general strike will start the following day.

29 January 1997: Nikolai Dobrev talks of 'an explosive situation' and suggests that the new government should serve for only three to five months. 'The chaos and power vacuum may cause a threat to civil peace. The deadlock is so complicated and the confidence in the government so low that the only alternative is new elections.'

A one-hour general strike is held across the country (*EEN*, 1997, vol. 11, no. 2, p. 4).

30 January 1997: Nikolai Dobrev says that he is willing to give up the mandate and allow the president to form a coalition government.

Strikes spread.

31 January 1997: parliament passes a bill permitting a doubling of state salaries (*IHT*, 1 February 1997, p. 4).

2 February 1997: the Union of Democratic Forces declines the Socialist Party's offer of more talks on a coalition, insisting that the Socialist Party first hands back its mandate. Under the constitution the Socialist Party's offer would have paved the way for elections two months after a coalition government was formed. 'The opposition's rejection of the proposal seems designed to force earlier elections' (*IHT*, 4 February 1997, p. 5).

4 February 1997: a joint statement issued by the Socialist Party and opposition parties says that the president 'should set early general elections in the second ten days of April'.

Earlier the Socialist Party named a new cabinet after the opposition had rejected the offer of a coalition government. A single-party government is not what is needed right now, but 'It is better than having no government at all,' says Dobrev (*IHT*, 5 February 1997, p. 6). The attempt to form a new government is abandoned.

'We were never so close to civil war,' says Stoyanov (*FT*, 5 February 1997, p. 2).

5 February 1997: the Union of Democratic Forces ends its boycott of parliament.

6 February 1997: the majority of Socialist Party members boycott parliament as a protest against the agreement to hold an early general election (*IHT*, 7 February 1997, p. 5).

7 February 1997: the Union of Democratic Forces declines the president's invitation to form a government.

10 February 1997: the Popular Union also declines. It being the third to be asked, the president is now constitutionally free to appoint a caretaker government and to call an early election.

12 February 1997: the president asks Stefan Sofiyansky (the UDF's mayor of Sofia) to head a caretaker government to run the country until the general election on 19 April.

14 February 1997: the government bans the export of food and fuels (*EEN*, 1997, vol. 11, no. 4, p. 9).

16 February 1997: the Union of Democratic Forces changes from an alliance to a party (*EEN*, 1997, vol. 11, no. 4, p. 7).

17 February 1997: the caretaker government announces that it will seek full membership of Nato (*IHT*, 18 February 1997, p. 5).

22 February 1997: former Bulgarian Socialist Party members set up the Bulgarian Euro-Left movement, chaired by Alexander Tomov (*EEN*, 1997, vol. 11, no. 4, pp. 6, 9).

11 March 1997: the UDF and the small Bulgarian Social Democratic Party sign an electoral agreement for joint lists. The Movement for Rights and Freedom, the Democratic Centre Party, the Green Party and the Liberal Forum agree on an electoral alliance, though not on joint lists (*EEN*, 1997, vol. 11, no. 5, p. 6).

6 April 1997: the Bulgarian Socialist Party, led by Georgi Parvanov, withdraws its support from the caretaker government 'ostensibly because of the sacking of a disproportionate number of BSP officials from government posts, but in reality as part of a last-ditch election campaign ruse' (*EEN*, 1997, vol. 11, no. 7, p. 7).

16 April 1997: King Simeon II visits Bulgaria for the second time.

The general election of 19 April 1997

The turnout was 60 per cent. There was a 4 per cent threshold for the 240 seats in the National Assembly. The United Democratic Forces coalition, comprising the Union of Democratic Forces (led by Ivan Kostov) and the People's Union (comprising Stefan Safov's Democratic Party and Anastasia Moser's Agrarian

Party), won 52.26 per cent of the vote and 137 seats in total (123 seats going to the Union of Democratic Forces and 14, split equally, going to the People's Union). The Bulgarian Socialist Party (led by Georgi Parvanov) won 22.07 per cent of the vote and 58 seats (relying mainly on support in the countryside and among the elderly). The Alliance for National Salvation (a coalition of ethnic Turks, monarchists, republicans and environmentalists) won 7.6 per cent of the vote and 19 seats. Euro-Left won 5.5 per cent of the vote and 14 seats. The Bulgarian Business Bloc (led by Georgi Ganchev) won 4.93 per cent of the vote and 12 seats.

Political developments after the April 1997 general election

21 May 1997: parliament approves the appointment of Ivan Kostov as prime minister. His cabinet is also approved.

16 July 1997: the European Commission recommends that Estonia, Cyprus, the Czech Republic, Hungary, Poland and Slovenia open negotiations in early 1998 for entry to the EU. (The invitations were formally approved at an EU summit on 13 December 1997, formal negotiations for membership beginning on 31 March 1998. Slovakia, Latvia, Lithuania, Bulgaria and Romania were to be given special EU aid to help them meet the conditions necessary for membership negotiations to begin.)

22 October 1997: the interior minister informs parliament of the names of twenty-three leading public figures who served in the intelligence services during the communist era. Among them are fourteen members of parliament (including four from the Socialist Party and Ahmed Dogan, leader of the mainly ethnic Turkish Movement for Rights and Freedom), four magistrates and a banker. Only a few are accused of informing on compatriots. The prime minister has said that government officials who worked for the communist state security services will be dismissed. Under a recent law 600 leading officials were screened to determine whether they had collaborated during the communist era (*IHT*, 23 October 1997, p. 5; *FT*, 23 October 1997, p. 3; *Telegraph*, 23 October 1997, p. 19).

4 June 1998: the high court hands back to exiled King Simeon II the former dynasty's property which had been confiscated in 1947 (*IHT*, 5 June 1998, p. 7; *Independent*, 5 June 1998, p. 16).

5 August 1998: Todor Zhivkov dies.

After the collapse of communism Zhivkov was arrested and charged with misappropriating state funds. He was tried, found guilty and sentenced to seven years' imprisonment. Saved from jail by poor health, he spent several years under house arrest. His sentence was eventually overturned on appeal, although he remained under further investigation for past crimes. After his release in September 1997 he found a new platform as a member of the Socialist Party (*The Times*, 7 August 1998, p. 23).

In 1992 he was convicted of embezzlement and sentenced to seven years in prison, although he was allowed to serve his time under house arrest. In February 1996 Bulgaria's highest court acquitted him of the embezzlement charges, although he remained under indictment on charges of human rights abuses (*IHT*, 7 August 1998, p. 5).

4 November 1998: a law comes into force barring former senior communist officials from holding public office for five years (*EEN*, 1998, vol. 12, no. 12, p. 7).

In 1998 the constitutional court revoked a controversial clause on 'lustration' included in legislation passed by parliament. The clause would have banned former communist officials from working in the public administration, even in junior posts (*FT*, Survey, 8 March 1999, p. ii).

29 November 1998: the ethnic Turkish based Movement for Rights and Freedoms sets up the new Liberal Democratic Union party by merging with three small liberal parties (*EEN*, 1998, vol. 12, no. 13, p. 6).

23 December 1998: King Simeon II starts his first Christmas in Bulgaria since he left in 1946 (*IHT*, 24 December 1998, p. 18).

13 October 1999: the European Commission recommends that EU leaders at the December 1999 meeting in Helsinki allow Bulgaria, Latvia, Lithuania, Malta, Romania and Slovakia to begin accession negotiations in 2000.

The 'principle of differentiation' for entry date will apply to each of the twelve candidates, reflecting differing states of readiness for EU entry. A 'fully flexible, multi-speed accession process' is envisaged. 'Each country will be able to proceed on merit, including the possibility for those which join the negotiations from 2000 to catch up with the others.' The European Commission thinks that existing EU members should undertake internal reforms by the end of 2002: 'Whether the first accessions can take place as from 1 January 2003 will then depend entirely on the speed with which the applicant countries can make progress on meeting the criteria.'

Bulgaria's time horizon for coping with competitive pressures 'stretches beyond the medium term'. In economic terms Bulgaria is making 'substantial' progress although it 'started from a very low level'. In order to begin negotiations Bulgaria must set 'acceptable' closure dates for four units at the Kozloduy nuclear power plant and must make further progress on economic reform.

(*FT*, 14 October 1999, pp. 1, 10; *IHT*, 14 October 1999, p. 5; *Guardian*, 14 October 1999, p. 14; *Independent*, 14 October 1999, p. 18; *The Times*, 14 October 1999, p. 21; *Telegraph*, 14 October 1999, p. 20.)

(For further details, see the Hungary entry for 10 December 1999, p. 214–15.)

22 November 1999: Bill Clinton visits Bulgaria, the first US president to do so.

20 December 1999: prime minister Kostov announces a major government reshuffle, dropping ten ministers in the sixteen-member cabinet and creating an economics super-ministry. Three deputy prime ministers are dismissed. Petar Jotev, the new economics minister and deputy prime minister, will also have responsibility for the industry, commerce and tourism ministries. Prime minister Kostov takes over the portfolio for state administration.

7 May 2000: Georgi Parvanov is re-elected chairman of the Bulgarian Socialist Party at the party congress. 'The Bulgarian Socialist Party … in its May party conference … for the first time publicly supported eventual membership of Nato after a referendum (in contrast to previous BSP hostility to Nato membership)' (*EEN*, 2000, vol. 12, no. 23, pp. 4, 8). (On 31 May Ecoglasnost withdrew from the alliance with the BSP after the decision to support Nato membership: p. 8.)

18 May 2000: an opposition-proposed vote of no confidence in the government fails by a wide margin.

'The elite around Kostov is seen as self-serving, corrupt and arrogant … Ivan Kostov's Union of Democratic Forces government [has been] seriously rocked by public allegations of high-level corruption and nepotism, particularly around Kostov's own family' (*EEN*, 2000, vol. 12, no. 23, pp. 3, 5).

'Corruption is widespread' (*The Economist*, 17 June 2000, p. 56). President Petar Stoyanov: 'My most intimate fear is corruption. If our reforms are accompanied by corruption, democracy itself will be threatened' (p. 56).

26 October 2000: the secretary of the ruling Union of Democratic Forces (Khristo Biserov) and executive committee member Yordan Tsonev resign after calling for premier Ivan Kostov to resign. 'Division within the ruling Union of Democratic Forces continues to grow in the wake of secretary Khristo Biserov's resignation and criticisms of Kostov, whose reputation for presiding over a corrupt regime is growing' (*EEN*, 2000, vol. 13, no. 1, pp. 6, 8).

'[Earlier] the Internal Macedonian Revolutionary Organization … [left the] ruling Union of Democratic Forces alliance in protest at the lack of consultation by premier Ivan Kostov's cabinet' (*EEN*, 2000, vol. 13, no. 1, p. 6).

8 November 2000: the EU reports that Bulgaria has made progress but still lies second from last behind Romania in terms of membership prospects. The EU's report on Bulgaria (*Progress Towards Accession*, 8 November 2000, p. 87):

> Bulgaria has clearly made further progress towards becoming a functioning market economy. It is not yet able to cope with competitive pressure and market forces within the Union in the medium term. Bulgaria is establishing a satisfactory track record of macroeconomic stabilization and performance. Good progress has been made in privatization, especially as regards banks … However, structural reforms still need to be taken further and enterprise restructuring needs to be advanced … Major efforts are needed to develop a strong, independent, effective and professional judicial system. The fight against corruption needs to be strengthened … [As regards the Roma] further concrete actions and adequate financial resources are still required.

(For further details, see the entry for Hungary.)

'The decision [has been made] by EU ministers to lift visa requirements for Bulgarian nationals … but to keep visa requirements for Romanians' (*Independent*, 25 November 2000, p. 14).

> This month the EU took Bulgaria off its list of countries whose citizens need visas to enter. Now Bulgarians can come in freely again – but not to

> get jobs. In return, Bulgaria agreed to restrict the entry of people from farther east, such as Moldovans and Ukrainians.
>
> (*The Economist*, 9 December 2000, p. 54)

January–February 2001: 'The Bulgarian Socialist Party … joined forces with fourteen other groupings and civil movements to form a Coalition for Bulgaria to fight this year's election' (*Business Central Europe*, February 2001, p. 13).

8 February 2001: 'The constitutional court rules that King Simeon II cannot stand in the presidential elections in the autumn of 2001 because he has not been resident in Bulgaria for the minimum required six months per year over the previous five years' (*EEN*, 2001, vol. 13, no. 2, p. 4).

12 March 2001: 'The Sofia City court … declared Balkan Airlines insolvent' (*Business Central Europe*, April 2001, p. 32).

14 March 2001: 'The "Dialogue and Partnership" parliamentary group is established by ten MPs as potential vehicle for King Simeon II' (*EEN*, 2001, vol. 13, no. 4, p. 6).

> Ivan Kostov's ruling Union of Democratic Forces (SDS) faces the possibility of widespread defections to former SDS members, led by Khristo Biserov and Dimitur Ivanov, who are now floating the possibility of King Simeon II standing as a new party political leader and potential premier in the run-up to this June's parliamentary elections. The new party ('For Dialogue and Partnership') so far has around a dozen MPs, including seven from the SDS.
>
> (p. 5)

15 March 2001:

> The EU agreed Thursday [15 March] to lift visa requirements for Bulgaria … EU justice and interior ministers also agreed conditionally to lift the visa requirements for Romania … pending further progress on tackling the problem of illegal immigration. Bulgarians will no longer need a visa to visit one or more EU member nations for a period of up to three months.
>
> (*IHT*, 16 March 2001, p. 4)

21 March 2001: 'The Ruling Union of Democratic Forces signs an electoral alliance with the ethnic Turk splinter movement the National Movement for Rights and Freedom' (*EEN*, 2001, vol. 13, no. 4, p. 6).

6 April 2001:

> Simeon Saxe-Coburg, formerly King Simeon II of Bulgaria, yesterday [6 April] launched a movement to take part in the country's general election in June, and became the first royal heir in the former communist bloc to enter politics. 'Today I announce my intention to found and lead a new public movement, the National Movement for King Simeon II,' he said, reading a statement outside his residence in Sofia. Mr Saxe-Coburg, who has no

> constitutional role, fled the country as a child in 1946 to escape communist rule and settled in Spain. The communists abolished the monarchy but Saxe-Coburg never abdicated.
>
> (*FT*, 7 April 2001, p. 6)

> Former King Simeon II of Bulgaria announced yesterday that he is to head a new political party that he hopes will win enough votes … in the general election of 17 June … to bring about the restoration of the monarchy … He made his live television announcement from the symbolic setting of his former royal palace in Vrania, which was returned to his family only in 1998 … 'By European standards most of our people live in misery, while some politicians bathe in inexplicable luxury,' he said … King Simeon and King Michael of Romania are the only two members of East European royal families to have reigned … He [Simeon] became king at the age of six after the death of his father Boris III in 1943, but was expelled three years later when Bulgaria became a republic after a referendum.
>
> (*The Times*, 7 April 2001, p. 19)

'Simeon, while not ruling out a restoration of the monarchy, has said the country must concentrate its energies on building the economy' (*IHT*, 18 June 2001, p. 4).

'According to opinion polls, there is only about 15 per cent support for restoring the monarchy' (*Independent*, 19 June 2001, p. 11).

23 April 2001:

> The attempted political comeback of the former Bulgarian king Simeon II received a potentially fatal blow yesterday [23 April] when a court rejected his movement's application to take part in elections in June. The Sofia city court cited nine 'substantial violations' of political party law … His legal team will appeal, but the deadline for party registration is 2 May.
>
> (*Telegraph*, 24 April 2001, p. 16)

28–9 April 2001:

> King Simeon II … has circumvented a court ruling barring his party's entry into politics … The supreme court at the weekend upheld a ruling rejecting the registration of his National Movement to contest parliamentary elections in June … He will nominally form a coalition with two tiny parties that offered him unconditional support and legally registered names: the Party of Bulgarian Women and the Oborishte Party for National Revival. In effect the two parties will merge and, once unified, change their name to the National Movement … The election commission is expected to issue a ruling on the move today [30 April]. A commission official was quoted as saying the tactic was legally acceptable.
>
> (*Telegraph*, 30 April 2001, p. 10)

'King Simeon II confirms [28 April] that his Simeon II National Movement will make an electoral alliance with the Oborishte Movement for National Alliance and the Party of Bulgarian Women' (*EEN*, 2001, vol. 13, no. 5, p. 5).

> Last week … the electoral commission ruled that he [Simeon II] could use two small parties as a flag of convenience. Earlier the country's legal system had ruled that his own party, the National Movement for Simeon II, had failed to meet the registration requirement … Simeon rose to the Bulgarian throne at the age of six in 1943 after the death of his father, Boris III, but was forced out in 1946 … Simeon never abdicated after the Communists held a rigged referendum abolishing the monarchy.
>
> (*IHT*, 7 May 2001, p. 5)

'"Give me 800 days and I'll improve your life," he said in April when he launched his National Movement' (*IHT*,16 June 2001, p. 2).

> Mr Saxe-Coburgotski … promises that in 800 days all will be well. He suggests that the first year is for 'damage control or assessment', the second is to 'start building and put in place the trend', and the third year sees 'an opportunity for dividends'.
>
> (*Independent*, 16 June 2001, p. 18)

Simeon II: 'The 800 days is simply a normal economic parameter: one year to see what has to be done; the second year to implement it; and the third year hopefully the shareholders see some dividends' (*The Times*, 18 June 2001, p. 15).

17 June 2001: a general election is held for the 240 seats in parliament. There is a 4 per cent threshold.

The turnout was 67 per cent (*EEN*, 2001, vol. 13, no. 5, p. 4).

The results were somewhat better for the National Movement for Simeon II than even opinion polls had predicted. (Simeon II himself was not running as a candidate.)

'The head of the election observers mission for OSCE said the election had gone "extremely well"' (*IHT*, 19 June 2001, p. 5).

The results were as follows:

National Movement for Simeon II: 43.4 per cent of the vote and 120 seats (one short of an absolute majority in parliament).

Union of Democratic Forces (UDF): 18.3 per cent of the vote and 51 seats.

Bulgarian Socialist Party's Coalition for Bulgaria: 17.4 per cent of the vote and 48 seats.

Movement for Rights and Freedoms: 6.7 per cent of the vote and 21 seats. 'The Movement for Rights and Freedoms represents mainly the Turkish and Roma minorities' (*Guardian*, 18 June 2001, p. 2).

'A new party led by Bulgaria's ex-king, Simeon II, has a comfortable lead in the opinion polls … He is promising to create jobs and spur investment in a country where living standards are plummeting' (*IHT*, 16 June 2001, p. 2).

> Part of Mr Saxe-Coburgotski's … appeal is simply that the other parties are so unloved and distrusted. Some nine out of ten voters think that the UDF is corrupt. The Socialists have also lost any credit that they might once have enjoyed.
>
> (*Independent*, 16 June 2001, p. 18)

> Mr Saxe-Coburg-Gotha … [has benefited from] disillusionment with the political elite … Prime minister Ivan Kostov … has accused the former king of 'wild populism' for promising to increase the average salary to 400 levs a month within 800 days. Mr Saxe-Coburg-Gotha has built up a team of young, Western-educated economists who have worked for British and American banks. He pledges to introduce incentives for small and medium-sized enterprises and to fight corruption and organized crime.
>
> (*The Times*, 16 June 2001, p. 20)

> In the past four years … Ivan Kostov, the prime minister and head of the ruling centre-right UDF party … has pulled Bulgaria out of an economic crisis and put it on track for eventual Nato and EU membership. But, like many economic reformers, he is being punished for being too slow in delivering the fruits of reform. Even though the economy grew at an annual rate of growth of more than 5 per cent last year [2000], ordinary Bulgarians feel disappointed with rising unemployment, low pay and pensions and miserable living standards. They are also furious about widespread corruption … Simeon's … economic specialists have devised a radical liberal reform programme, including tax cuts, public spending cuts and a target of zero public borrowing. They intend to follow a similar road to the UDF but faster, more efficiently and with less corruption … But … Simeon has [promised] … early increases in public pay, pensions and, most controversially, interest-free loans of 5,000 levs available to all.
>
> (*FT*, 16 June 2001, p. 15)

> The sixty-four-year-old Simeon Borisov Saxe-Coburgotski … has promised to accelerate the present government's reform process, including privatizations, assuring Bulgarians that they will notice a change for the better within 800 days of his administration taking over … The governing centre-right Union for Democratic Forces (UDF), which pursued a reformist programme for the past four years, appears to have suffered because it failed to translate the reforms into a better standard of living for the country's 8 million people.
>
> (*FT*, 18 June 2001, p. 1)

> Simeon has promised prosperity within 800 days, but economists say his financial programme is unrealistic. Drawn up by a team of Bulgarian expat bankers from the City of London, it promises zero-rate corporate tax to attract foreign investment, and lower personal income tax – but also a balanced budget.
>
> (*Independent*, 18 June 2001, p. 11)

'Simeon personally promised low interest loans for every citizen of Bulgaria during the election, only for his economic team to backtrack rapidly' (*Independent*, 19 June 2001, p. 11). 'The vote was not a public endorsement for reinstating the monarchy – there is little support for that. It was a massive protest against existing political parties from a nation tired of living in poverty' (*Independent*, 13 July 2001, p. 13).

> The core of Simeon's economic team is made up of Bulgarians in their early thirties who have prospered abroad. They include Nikolai Vasilev, vice-president of Lazards in London, and Milen Velchev, vice-president of Merrill Lynch … They will reduce licensing requirements to cut the notorious paperwork … exempt reinvested profits and capital gains from tax, and cut taxes in general while reducing the budget deficit to zero … provide zero-interest micro-credits to aspiring entrepreneurs … [and] maintain the currency board … [But] voter expectations are sky-high, encouraged by Simeon's populist campaign promises.
>
> (*Business Central Europe*, July–August 2001, pp. 39–40)

'During his exile, in Spain, he [Simeon II] spent thirteen years as chairman of the Spanish subsidiary of Thomson CSF, the French defence and electronics group recently renamed Thales SA' (*IHT*, 13 July 2001, p. 5).

> The central electoral commission had registered no less than three movements that had Simeon II in their name. Two of these movements were false ones created to divert votes from NDS [Simeon II National Movement]. If these false movements had not been there, NDS would have won 134 seats out of the 240 in parliament. Nearly 5 per cent of the NDS vote was lost thanks to the [false movements].
>
> (*EEN*, 2001, vol. 13, no. 5, p. 2)

'President Petar Stoyanov has been especially critical of the king, accusing him of dealing in fairy tales at a time when the country needs firm stewardship' (*Telegraph*, 18 June 2001, p. 11).

Ivan Kostov: 'We have taken a lot of unpopular decisions and also made mistakes. We wanted the voter to pay a higher price than he was prepared to pay' (*Independent*, 19 June 2001, p. 11).

26 June 2001: 'The Union of Democratic Forces chairman and outgoing premier Ivan Kostov resigns the party chairmanship. Ekaterina Mikhailova is elected chairwoman' (*EEN*, 2001, vol. 13, no. 5, p. 6).

27 June 2001:

> Seven governments … yesterday signed an agreement aimed at liberalizing trade in at least 90 per cent of goods trade between them. The move by Albania, Bosnia-Hercegovina, Bulgaria, Croatia, Romania, Macedonia and Yugoslavia marks the latest stage in efforts, under the EU's Stability Pact for South-Eastern Europe, to enhance stability in the region through economic growth. Moldova is expected to join the arrangement shortly.
>
> (*FT*, 28 June 2001, p. 8)

5 July 2001:

> Parliament met yesterday [5 July] for the first time since last month's general election … Ahmed Dogan, leader of the … Movement for Rights and Freedoms … said the MRF … was ready for a coalition with … the National Movement for Simeon II.
>
> (*FT*, 6 July 2001, p. 6)

12 July 2001:

> Former King Simeon II was named Bulgaria's next prime minister on Thursday [12 July]. He thus becomes the first Eastern European king to attain political power after exile … He is to form a new government within ten days … The chairman of parliament … said he would call an extraordinary session on 24 July to vote in the new cabinet.
>
> (*IHT*, 13 July 2001, p. 5)

> The president will give Simeon the mandate to form the next government this Sunday [15 July], after which he has seven days to submit a list of names for approval by parliament … His National Movement … plans to form a coalition government and one ally is all but certain … [the] Movement for Rights and Freedoms.
>
> (*Telegraph*, 13 July 2001, p. 22)

> Although he [Simeon II] never abdicated, he will have to make a pledge of loyalty to Bulgaria's republican constitution when he is sworn in on 24 July … The centre-right National Movement is expected to form a coalition with two smaller parties.
>
> (*The Times*, 13 July 2001, p. 17)

'Becoming prime minister means … swearing allegiance to Bulgaria's republican constitution' (*Guardian*, 13 July 2001, p. 21). 'His first task will be to form a coalition government. The candidates include the former government party, the

Union of Democratic Forces, and … [the] Movement for Rights and Freedoms' (p. 13).

15 July 2001:

> Simeon Saxe-Coburg yesterday [15 July] became the first monarch in modern Europe to be nominated as prime minister. President Petar Stoyanov officially handed him the mandate to form a cabinet … Simeon said he hoped the outgoing United Democratic Forces (UDF) would participate in the new government. But the … Movement for Rights and Freedoms is emerging as a more likely ally. Parliament is scheduled to vote on Simeon's nomination on 24 July.
>
> (*FT*, 16 July 2001, p. 6)

22 July 2001:

> Simeon II … on Sunday [22 July] submitted to President Petar Stoyanov the list of his future cabinet, which includes two ministers with professional experience in the West and two ethnic Turks. Parliament is scheduled to vote on the new government on Tuesday [24 July]. A coalition between Simeon's National Movement and the predominantly ethnic Turkish Movement for Rights and Freedoms holds 141 seats in the 240-seat chamber … Simeon has said he would try to include as many experts as possible in the new government, ignoring political affiliations … Simeon's deputy prime ministers include a thirty-two-year-old financial analyst, Nikolai Vasilev, who worked for Lazard Capital Markets in London. He will also be economics minister. Milen Velchev, thirty-five, who was vice-president of the emerging markets unit of Merrill Lynch in London, was named finance minister. Other deputy prime ministers included Kostadin Paskalev, forty, the Socialist former mayor of the city of Balgoevgrad, who will also hold the regional development and urbanization portfolio, and Lydia Shuleva, forty-four, who will head the ministry of labour and social affairs.
>
> (*IHT*, 23 July 2001, p. 4)

> Simeon Saxe-Coburg … presented President Petar Stoyanov with a draft list of a coalition cabinet that includes the National Movement for Simeon II … the Movement for Rights and Freedoms and experts from the Bulgarian Socialist Party … The outgoing centre-right United Democratic Forces (UDF) refused to take part in the coalition.
>
> (*FT*, 23 July 2001, p. 9)

'Both Mr Vasilev and Mr Velchev went to university in the USA before ending up in the Square Mile [in London] covering emerging markets' (*Independent*, 23 July 2001, p. 12). 'Milen Velchev is a specialist in debt restructuring' (*Telegraph*, 23 July 2001, p. 11). 'Nikolai Vasilev … was until February an emerging markets analyst … Milen Velchev … was an emerging markets specialist' (*FT*, 25 July 2001, p. 6).

> The main opposition United Democratic Forces, a right-wing coalition whose biggest component is (confusingly) the Union of Democratic Forces (UDF), says it will not contest his [Simeon's] nomination … Milen Velchev … says: 'Our economic philosophy is much the same [as the UDF's], but our policy [for implementing it] will be more radical' … He reels off a list of measures he hopes to enact: abolishing taxes on profits reinvested in the company; lowering income tax gradually from a top rate of 38 per cent to 29 per cent; removing capital gains taxes; letting foreigners buy land; and rapidly privatizing the big companies that Mr Kostov funked selling off, notably telecoms, the tobacco monopoly, gas distribution, energy utilities and two big banks.
>
> (*The Economist*, 21 July 2001, p. 39)

24 July 2001:

> Former King Simeon II … was approved as prime minister … The former king … took an oath of loyalty to the constitution after parliament backed him, 141 to fifty, with forty-six abstentions. Lawmakers also approved his sixteen-member coalition government, which is mostly composed of technocrats.
>
> (*IHT*, 25 July 2001, p. 1)

> Simeon Saxe-Coburg … was yesterday [24 July] sworn in as the country's prime minister, becoming the first former monarch to return to power in post-communist Eastern Europe … Mr Saxe-Coburg took the oath of loyalty to the republican constitution in the presence of Patriarch Maxim of the Bulgarian Orthodox Church … Mr Saxe-Coburg's National Movement for Simeon II … will govern in coalition with the Movement for Rights and Freedoms … The outgoing centre-right United Democratic Forces (UDF) voted against the new government, and criticized Mr Saxe-Coburg … for nominating as ministers two members of the Socialist Party … However, UDF leaders said they would co-operate with the new government on issues that would continue the reformist programme of the past four years … Mr Saxe-Coburg … [among other things] said his coalition would fight corruption by introducing strict procedures and introducing 'one-stop-shops' for processing new investment. While the economy will be in new hands, the appointment of Solomon Passy as foreign minister underscored Mr Saxe-Coburg's desire for continuity in Bulgaria's drive to join Nato and the EU. Mr Passy is founder and head of the Atlantic Club, a non-governmental organization that has spearheaded Bulgaria's drive to become a member of Nato.
>
> (*FT*, 25 July 2001, p. 6)

> Over the past three years ... [a London pub] has been home to a political movement in exile which helped to see the former king elected prime minister of Bulgaria. The Bulgarian City Club, a group of expatriate professionals ... largely drafted the former king's economic strategy and some of its members now hold positions in his government ... Members are being approached for other important positions, such as the privatization agency ... Mr Vasilev and Mr Velchev have been putting the finishing touches on a strategy first mooted in [the London pub] ... The plan includes allowing profits that are reinvested to be free of tax, to reduce income tax, to negotiate a new deal with the IMF ... and to draw up a balanced budget.
>
> (*FT*, 26 July 2001, p. 6)

20 August 2001:

> Simeon II has unveiled his economic programme, cutting taxes and increasing the minimum wage ... [The] package includes doubling child welfare payments, while cutting state jobs by 10 per cent and raising electricity prices ... Finance ministry officials said increased spending would be funded by more efficient revenue collection and by fighting corruption.
>
> (*Telegraph*, 21 August 2001, p. 12)

THE ECONOMY

The transitional era in Bulgaria has never been easy and has on occasion approached catastrophe. (See Table 2.2.) The communist economy was heavily dependent on Comecon (especially Soviet) trade and so the collapse of this trade hit Bulgaria particularly hard. Exports to the former Comecon countries may have fallen by about 66 per cent in 1991 and by a further 15 to 25 per cent in 1992 (Borensztein *et al.* 1993: 6). In 1992 the EU accounted for 31 per cent of Bulgaria's foreign trade compared with only 28 per cent for the countries of the former Soviet Union (*FT Survey*, 5 May 1993, p. 31).

The financial crisis

Debt repayment has been another headache for Bulgaria and creditor governments had to agree to a rescheduling in April 1991. The West penalized Bulgaria for choosing a socialist government in its first free elections by, for example, delaying aid (despite qualified approval of the election by international observers). The Popov programme gained IMF approval and credits in February 1991. In April 1992 the IMF commented favourably on the first year of economic reform, especially with respect to macroeconomic stabilization and a stand-by loan was approved. In October 1992 Bulgaria resumed interest payments on its foreign debt and on 16 December the Paris Club of Western creditor nations agreed to reschedule their share of Bulgaria's foreign debt. In

Table 2.2 Bulgaria: selected economic indicators 1990–2000

Economic indicator	*1990*	*1991*	*1992*	*1993*	*1994*	*1995*	*1996*	*1997*	*1998*	*1999*	*2000 (estimate)*
Rate of growth of GDP (%)	-9.1	-11.7	-7.3	-1.5	1.8	2.9	-10.9	-6.9	3.5	2.4	5.0
Rate of growth of industrial output (%)	-16.5	-27.3	-6.4	-6.2	5.9	-5.4	-11.8	-11.3	4.3	-12.5	12.0
Rate of growth of agricultural output (%)	-6.0	-0.3	-14.8	-30.2	9.4	14.5	-7.4	32.9	1.4	0.6	-15.5
Inflation rate (consumer, %)	26.3	333.5	82.0	73.0	96.3	62.0	123.0	1,082.0	22.2	0.7	9.9
Budget surplus or deficit (% GDP)[a]	-12.8	-14.7	-2.9	-8.7	-3.9	-5.7	-10.4	-2.1	0.9	-0.9	-1.0
Unemployment rate (end of year, %)	1.8	10.5	15.3	16.4	12.8	11.1	12.5	13.7	12.2	16.0	17.9
Balance of payments (current account, $ billion)	-1.200	-0.800	-0.360	-1.099	-0.031	-0.026	0.016	0.428	-0.062	-0.681	-0.696
Foreign direct investment (net, $ billion)	0.004	0.056	0.042	0.040	0.105	0.098	0.138	0.507	0.537	0.806	0.975
Population (million)			8.48	8.46	8.43	8.38	8.34	8.28	8.23	8.20	8.12

Sources: Various issues of European Bank for Reconstruction and Development, *Transition Report*; United Nations Economic Commission for Europe, *Economic Survey of Europe*; United Nations, *World Economic and Social Survey*; IMF, *World Economic Outlook*.

Note:

[a] General government balance: includes the state, municipalities and extrabudgetary funds (EBRD)

1993 there were some delays in payment of interest on the debt owed to Western creditor banks, but a debt reduction and rescheduling agreement in principle was reached with them on 25 November (with detailed negotiations due to be completed by the 30 June 1994 deadline). On 15 April 1994 the Paris Club of creditor governments agreed to reschedule $200 million in debt repayments due in the year to March 1995. Bulgaria owed the banks $9.25 billion out of a total foreign debt of $12.95 billion (*EEN*, 1994, vol. 8, no. 1, p. 4). On 29 June 1994 Bulgaria signed an agreement with the London Club, which provided for a 47.1 per cent reduction in the $8.16 billion debt to commercial banks. Parliament ratified the deal on 27 July 1994.

IMF-inspired austerity measures have been implemented to try to reduce the budget deficit (see Table 2.2). Prices were substantially freed from state control on 1 February 1991, accounting for over 70 per cent of retail turnover according to Borensztein *et al.* (1993: 6). Even those prices remaining controlled were raised substantially as subsidies were reduced, e.g. milk 500 per cent and public transport 1,100 per cent. For all practical purposes prices were set free except for energy and public utilities (OECD 1992: 32). Price controls have been maintained on a number of products and services, e.g. energy, telecommunications, water supply and transport (*Transition*, April 1994, vol. 5, no. 4, p. 9). VAT was introduced (after some delay) on 1 April 1994. But although in February 1991 about 90 per cent of prices in the consumer basket were liberalized (excluding primary energy and public transport), new controls were subsequently introduced in the form of ceiling prices for petrol (1992) and for other fuels (1993) and controls on tobacco and certain other products (March 1994). Since mid-1994 government 'monitoring' of basic food prices and restrictions on profit margins have strongly expanded, reducing the share of genuinely free prices to 54 per cent (EBRD 1995b: 37). The share of unrestricted prices was reduced from 90 per cent of the basket of goods in the consumer price index in 1991 to 69 per cent in mid-1994 (p. 18). Since January 1995 prices covering only 54 per cent of the consumer basket have been free of administrative controls. Fixed prices apply to energy products, post and telecoms and tobacco products. Ceiling prices apply to most fuels. During 1996 there was significant progress in adjusting administered prices, including fuels, electricity, heating, urban transport, railways and telecoms, to cost recovery levels (EBRD 1996b: 143). By 1996 controls affected more than half the consumer basket as well as key agricultural producer prices. Minimum farm-gate prices were established for the 1997 wheat crop that were well above prices in neighbouring countries (EBRD 1997b: 159). According to *The Economist* (19 October 1996, p. 55), 'The market sets prices for less than half the goods sold.' Whereas in 1991–2 18 per cent of all prices were subject to some form of government regulation, in 1996 the share was 45 per cent (Wyzan 1998: 24). The law on prices, which formed the legal basis for state intervention in price setting, was abolished in July 1999. The liberalization has left only the prices of coal, electricity, central heating, telephone calls, postal services, gas and cigarettes administered. The prices of energy, central heating and household electricity have been significantly increased since September

1998. Energy subsidies were to be phased out over a three-year period beginning in September 1998 (EBRD 1999b: 202–3).

Tripartite corporatist structures have emerged, such as the National Council for Social Co-operation. For example, in January 1991 a 200-day 'social pact' was reached between the government, trade unions and employers. This included a ban on strikes until July 1991 and partial (70 per cent) wage compensation for price rises. Wage increases have also been curbed by a wage inflation tax. Unemployment compensation lasts for a year at most and then social assistance is available. Wages continue to be set in principle by a trilateral commission, which includes unions, employers and government. The degree of unionization in the state sector is high. But the private sector has remained largely outside this scheme (EBRD 1997b: 160).

Provisions for bankruptcy were included in a 1989 law, but the environment is very protective of debtor enterprises and allows infinite deferral of creditor claims (EBRD 1994: 20). A bankruptcy law was passed by parliament in July 1994, but banks were not covered (EBRD 1995a: 54). No bankruptcy procedures were taken against major enterprises before July 1996 (EBRD 1996b: 143). Bankruptcy legislation has been little used until recently (EBRD 1997b: 159). Although legislation on bankruptcy and insolvency has improved, its application remains largely ineffective (EBRD 1999b: 203). Only a few (mainly small) enterprises have been closed down (*FT*, 29 March 1994, p. 3). Of the 3,500 state enterprises scheduled for privatization two-thirds are operating at a loss. But there have been no closures, a bankruptcy act passed in July 1994 existing only on paper (Deutsche Bank, *Focus: Eastern Europe*, 1995, no. 130, p. 5). Parliament approved a bank bankruptcy law on 14 May 1996. Government officials said that bank deposits would be protected, but no guarantee scheme has yet been implemented. As banks imposed strict limits on the amounts they were prepared to pay out each day, many depositors were keeping cash at home (*FT*, 17 May 1996, p. 2). A bank deposit guarantee scheme, designed to protect certain deposits in banks declared bankrupt, was passed by parliament on 23 May 1996 (*FT*, 24 May 1996, p. 2; 29 May 1996, p. 2).

In March 1994 the government took steps to refinance some of the bad loans arranged in the socialist era by banks to enterprises, issuing bonds to convert enterprise debt into government debt (*FT*, 29 March 1994, p. 3). A programme implemented during 1994 to recapitalize banks provided 'bad loan bonds' (Zunk bonds) to cover non-performing bank assets (which remain on the balance sheets of banks). The bonds have a twenty-five-year maturity and a five-year grace period, and pay a fraction of market interest rates for seven years. The low interest rates have created severe liquidity problems for the banks, which the past government addressed by repeated cash recapitalizations during 1994 (partial repurchasing of the 'bad loan bonds') (EBRD 1995a: 54). Legislation to allow the liquidation of insolvent banks was passed in May 1996 (EBRD 1996b: 143).

'No large state-owned firm was declared bankrupt until the summer of 1996' (United Nations Economic Commission for Europe 1997: 80). 'The Bulgarian crisis has its origins in the inefficient and unviable state-owned sector of the economy, but due to soft budget constraints and repeated bail-outs it spread to the public finances, the banking system and the financial markets' (p. 81).

> The fundamental roots of the crisis are microeconomic in origins ... The primary source of the Bulgarian financial crisis was the large, unstructured, loss-making state-owned industrial sector and the main policy related problem was the failure by the authorities to address this issue at an early stage by restructuring, privatization, imposing hard budget constraints and a faster rate of liquidation of the biggest loss makers. A policy of 'muddling through' and expensive, unconditional bail-outs not only failed to resolve the problems, but, on the contrary, aggravated them considerably.
>
> (pp. 81–2)

> The key to successful transformation in the lagging transition countries may therefore lie in a new symbiosis of a more generous and long-term programme of international assistance coupled with a coherent and well-defined long-term policy commitment by the national authorities.
>
> (p. 84)

> Bulgaria is in the midst of a major financial crisis caused by increasingly accommodating refinance policies toward distressed commercial banks, along with an attempt by the authorities to decrease interest rates significantly. Downward pressure on the exchange rate depleted foreign exchange reserves in the course of 1996, which, in turn, led to panic and runs on many commercial banks.
>
> (OECD, *Economic Outlook*, December 1996, p. 124)

> Its banks have indulged in a mixture of ill-judged lending, over-expansion and corruption ... Mixed with lax supervision, inadequate regulation and industrial chaos (most large companies do not bother to service their debts), this cocktail has put the country's banking sector on its back ... The Bulgarian National Bank is finally getting its act together. It recently stopped granting new banking licences, introduced a deposit-insurance scheme and drafted a bankruptcy law for banks ... it also plans to toughen its supervision of the banking system, to raise capital requirements to encourage mergers, and to recapitalize banks ... Talk of recapitalization unnerves some ... In 1993 the country's banks were recapitalized with $2.7 billion of so-called 'zunk' bonds. That money has since disappeared down Bulgaria's black hole.
>
> (*The Economist*, 20 April 1996, p. 90)

While direct budgetary subsidies have been largely eliminated, financing of losses through the banking system and suppliers' and tax arrears remained pervasive up to mid-1996. No bankruptcy procedures were recorded against major enterprises before July 1996 (EBRD 1996b: 142–3). 'In 1996 Bulgaria slid into economic crisis, rooted in continued massive bank lending to loss-making state enterprises and a general lack of structural reforms' (EBRD 1997a: 7). 'Much of the banking sector is insolvent, reflecting the banks' funding of state enterprise losses' (p. 22). 'Bulgaria's severe economic crisis was fundamentally the result of years of delays in necessary enterprise restructuring, with mounting losses financed by the largely state-owned banking system (amounting to an estimated 15 per cent of GDP in 1995)' (EBRD 1997b: 159).

According to diplomats and political analysts,

> Bulgaria is teetering on the brink of economic disaster that could usher in hyperinflation and tear apart the governing Socialist Party … the national currency, the lev, plunged to fresh lows … Bulgarians rushed to withdraw their savings Thursday [9 May] and many banks were unable to meet demand. Shopkeepers were refusing to take leva for goods other than food … An IMF mission arrived in Sofia on Wednesday [8 May] for another round of talks on the country's delayed plans to overhaul its heavily indebted banking system and to close unprofitable state companies.
>
> (*IHT*, 10 May 1996, p. 15)

Prime minister Videnov, in an address to parliament on 29 May 1996, announced new austerity measures agreed with the IMF. These measures included the following: increased petrol prices; an increase in the rate of VAT from 18 per cent to 22 per cent; the introduction of a 5 per cent import levy from 1 July 1996 to 30 June 1997 (except for products such as oil, natural gas, cotton and sugar); the liquidation of sixty-four loss-making enterprises employing 24,000 people (another seventy-one enterprises, employing 230,000, were, as of July 1996, to be cut off from fresh finance from the state budget or the state banking system and given one year to devise restructuring plans, the successful being privatized and the unsuccessful being liquidated); accelerated privatization (42 per cent of all state enterprises were to be sold for cash or privatization vouchers); consolidation of the banking sector, including the closure of up to five insolvent banks (*FT*, 14 May 1996, p. 2; *FT*, 17 May 1996, p. 2; *Guardian*, 18 May 1996, p. 39; *Business Europa*, June–July 1996, p. 36; *Business Central Europe*, September 1996, p. 24; EBRD 1996b: 143; EBRD 1997a: 27).

The programme of 'isolation' from the financial sector of seventy enterprises covering 230,000 employees (10 per cent of employment) and responsible for 50 per cent of state enterprise losses in 1995 has been largely successful in imposing discipline, forcing the downsizing of enterprises and the preparation of restructuring/privatization plans (yet to be implemented). The 'liquidation programme', which covered some eighty enterprises (25,000 employees) responsible for 25 per cent of state enterprise losses, had been largely completed by July 1997, with one-third of employees left to wind down operations (EBRD 1997b: 159). A programme of 'isolation' and liquidation targeting the largest loss-making state enterprises was launched in 1996 when thirty state utilities (group A) and forty-eight state commercial enterprises (group B) were cut off from bank credit. All group B enterprises have now exited the programme, with thirty-one privatized and sixteen under liquidation or insolvency proceedings. The financial performance of some of the group A enterprises remains a source of concern and the arrears of a number of these enterprises are increasing (EBRD 1999b: 203).

> All group B [commercial] enterprises ... [in the isolation and liquidation programme] have now exited the programme, with thirteen being privatized, thirteen under liquidation and three under solvency proceedings ... The financial performance of some of the group A enterprises [utilities] remains a source of concern.
>
> (EBRD 2000b: 146)

On 27 May 1996 a preliminary agreement had been reached with the IMF on a stand-by loan (*Transition*, 1996, vol. 7, nos 4–5, p. 21). A continuation of the restrictive incomes policy has been agreed between the government and the IMF (EBRD 1996b: 143). On 24 September 1996 the central bank raised its base interest rate to 300 per cent (from the 108 per cent set in May 1996) and put nine private and state banks under special supervision (*FT*, 25 September 1996, p. 2; *IHT*, 25 September 1996, p. 15). Interest rates subsequently fell. But on 15 November 1996 there began a run on the State Savings Bank on rumours that the government was using its deposits to repay government debt.

The monthly inflation rate rose from 47 per cent in January 1997 to 243 per cent in February, before falling to 12 per cent in March and an estimated 4.5 per cent in April (*The Economist*, 8 February 1997, p. 45, and 26 April 1997, p. 57). At the beginning of 1997 the lev was 600 to the US dollar. On 5 February 1997 the rate of exchange was 3,000 (*IHT*, 6 February 1997, p. 5). The lev fell from 70 to the US dollar at the start of 1996 to 3,000 at the turn of the year, stabilizing at around 1,500 to the US dollar in February 1997 (*FT*, 5 May 1997, p. 2, and Survey, 21 October 1997, p. 31). The crisis began in May 1996 and reached its apogee in February 1997 when the monthly inflation rate was 242.7 per cent. The lev fell from 70.4 to the US dollar at the end of 1995 to 487.4 at the end of 1996 to 2,936.7 on 12 February 1997 (Wyzan 1998: 6, 24).

> On an annual basis inflation had soared to almost 500 per cent in January 1997 and surpassed 2,000 per cent in March. The causes of the rapid acceleration of inflation included liquidity injections to support the country's weakening banking system, continued central bank financing of the budget deficit, and – increasingly important – faltering confidence in the Bulgarian lev, which reduced domestic money demand ... Real output, which had grown in 1994 and 1995, contracted by more than 10 per cent during 1996.
>
> (Gulde 1999: 36)

On 17 March 1997 prime minister Sofiyansky announced a stabilization programme, including the liberalization of all prices except for bread, milk, white cheese and chicken, which were to benefit from temporary subsidies. The government had earlier announced a 257 per cent increase in the prices of heating, electricity and coal. Services offered by the Bulgarian Telecommunications Company were to be increased eight-fold (*Transition*, 1997, vol. 8, no. 2, p. 24). On 21 April 1997 all remaining price controls were abolished except for bread, milk, cheese and salami (*FT*, 25 April 1997, p. 2).

On 17 March 1997 an IMF mission agreed to a $657 million conditional loan package. The IMF board approved the package on 11 April 1997 (divided into a stand-by loan of $510 million and the remainder for grain imports). A further $400 million in loans was to come from the G24 countries and negotiations were in progress for World Bank loans worth some $290 million. The IMF and the government agreed a budget deficit of 6.2 per cent of GDP for 1997 and this was approved by parliament at the end of June 1997. A currency board was introduced on 1 July 1997, with the lev fixed at 1,000 to the DM.

> After several failed stabilization attempts Bulgaria introduced a currency board on 1 July 1997. Controversial and difficult to implement because of Bulgaria's serious structural problems the currency board has been a crucial factor in the success of the country's latest stabilization programme. [It combined] a traditional rule-based exchange arrangement with legal and structural measures that addressed pressing banking sector and fiscal issues … The exchange rate [was] 1,000 lev to 1 DM … The issue department holds all of the BNB's [central bank's] monetary liabilities – banknotes and coins, and deposits from banks and other non-governmental parties, and the banking department. The BNB is required to have sufficient foreign exchange and gold reserves at all times to cover these liabilities in full. The issue department is required to issue and redeem monetary liabilities for the peg currency [DM] at the official rate on demand and without limit … Because of the problems facing Bulgaria's financial sector, a separate banking sector was established, and the currency board has 'excess coverage' – that is, more foreign exchange than needed to cover the central bank's monetary liabilities. The banking department deposits these supplemental funds, which can be used to make collateralized loans to commercial banks in the event of an acute liquidity crisis, in the issue department. The banking department also holds all other assets and claims on the central bank, including outstanding long-term loans to the government and long-term deposits by commercial banks, and acts as the fiscal agent for Bulgaria's relations with the IMF … Under the currency board Bulgaria reduced annual inflation to 13 per cent by mid-1998 and to 1 per cent by the end of 1998 while rebuilding foreign exchange reserves from less than $800 million to more than $3 billion – more than six months of imports. The BNB basic interest rate, which had been above 200 per cent at the height of Bulgaria's economic crisis, fell to 5.2 per cent by the end of 1998

> ... Bulgaria's stabilization was not disrupted by Russia's crisis of mid-1998, despite close economic ties between Bulgaria and Russia.
>
> (Gulde 1999: 36–9)

> Following the introduction of the currency board annual inflation fell to 13 per cent by mid-1998, to 1 per cent by the end of 1998 and is estimated at 1.8 per cent for 1999. The BNB basic interest rate has fallen from more than 200 per cent at the height of the crisis to 4.5 per cent by mid-1999. Retail interest rates moved close to German levels as soon as the currency board was introduced. Neither the Russian crisis of August 1998 nor the Kosovo crisis of spring 1999 have resulted in a serious decline in reserves. In fact foreign exchange reserves increased from less than $800 million in late 1996 to about $2.7 billion in mid-1999. While several smaller banks had to be closed – a process that went smoothly and without spillover effects to other institutions – the health of the banking system as a whole has improved significantly, with all but two major banks privatized during the period. No support has yet been provided through funds from the banking department. Bulgaria's experience highlights the potential of a currency board to change perceptions and economic behaviour. Yet it also clearly shows a currency board's limitations: if not combined with other policies, most notably structural changes, the stable monetary and financial environment alone could not bring about an instantaneous resumption of growth. While growth turned positive in 1998, after two years of currency stability and moderate inflation output still remains below the pre-crisis level.
>
> (Ghosh *et al.* 2000: 318)

On 15 May 1998 the IMF decided to release the final tranche of the stand-by loan (*EEN*, 1998, vol. 12, no. 6, p. 6).

In July 1998 the IMF released $500 million (*IHT*, 11 August 1998, p. 13). On 28 September 1998 it was announced that the IMF had approved a $840 million three-year loan (*IHT*, 29 September 1998, p. 15).

On 17 February 1999 the IMF approved the disbursement of the third tranche of the three-year loan (*EEN*, 1999, vol. 12, no. 15, p. 8).

On 5 July 1999 the lev was redenominated to exact parity with the DM. One new lev was made equal to 1,000 old leva. The old and new money were to circulate in parallel until the end of 1999 (*Business Central Europe*, July–August 1999, p. 11).

> Bulgaria's reformist government [was] elected in the winter of 1997. Before this Bulgaria was considered the best example in countries outside the CIS of the capture of policy by strong vested interests. Rapid stabilization and other structural reforms appear to have succeeded not only in turning the economy around after a crisis in 1996 but also in forcing the vested interests to play by the rules.
>
> (Havrylyshyn and Odling-Smee 2000: 9)

Privatization

In order to stimulate the growth of the private sector, the ceiling placed on the number of people that a private enterprise could employ was lifted in March 1990. The sale of small businesses started on a limited scale in March–June 1991 (e.g. some petrol stations were sold), but small privatization only picked up pace later on under the 1992 restitution law. For example, by June 1992, 65 per cent of shops had been returned to former owners or their heirs (*Employment Observatory*, 1992, no. 3, p. 2). By the end of June 1993, 56.5 per cent of small-scale urban properties (83 per cent of shops and restaurants) had been restituted to former owners (Wyzan 1996: 58). The privatization of most small enterprises has taken place through the restitution of some 22,000 municipal entities by mid-September 1996 (EBRD 1996b: 143).

It is not easy to trace the growth of the private sector and there are varying estimates of its importance. According to official figures, the private sector as a whole accounted for 5 per cent of GDP in 1991, 10 per cent of GDP in 1992 and 12 to 13 per cent in 1993 (United Nations Economic Commission for Europe 1993: 215; 1994: 57). Wyzan (1996: 47) cites figures of 9.1 per cent of GDP in 1990, 11.8 per cent in 1991, 15.3 per cent in 1992 and 19.4 per cent in 1993. In mid-1994 the private sector accounted for roughly 40 per cent of GDP (EBRD 1994: 10). Between 30 per cent and 50 per cent of GDP was generated in the private sector, mostly in the trade/retail and service sectors (p. 20). In 1994 the private sector accounted for 80 per cent of agricultural output, 50 per cent of services and only 18 per cent of industrial output (EBRD 1995b: 37). In mid-1995 and mid-1996 the private sector accounted for roughly 45 per cent of GDP (EBRD 1995b: 11, and 1996b: 11). It accounted for 90 per cent of value-added in agriculture but less than 15 per cent in industry (p. 142). In mid-1997 the private sector accounted for roughly 50 per cent of GDP (EBRD 1997b: 14).

Rough estimates in mid-year of the private sector as a percentage of GDP are provided by the EBRD: 1990, 10 per cent; 1991, 20 per cent; 1992, 25 per cent; 1993, 35 per cent; 1994, 40 per cent; 1995, 50 per cent; 1996, 55 per cent; 1997, 60 per cent; 1998, 65 per cent; 1999, 70 per cent; 2000, 70 per cent (EBRD 1999b: 24, 204, and 2000b: 14, 148).

Large privatization has been much delayed because of political wrangling. A draft privatization law was approved by parliament on 8 May 1992. At least 20 per cent of the shares of privatized companies were to be retained by the government and used to finance social security funds and limited compensation for former owners. Up to 20 per cent of the shares of privatized enterprises could be offered to employees at a substantial discount, and if more than 30 per cent of employees voted to endeavour to buy their enterprise at auction the price was to be reduced by 30 per cent. The government's final privatization scheme (announced on 2 August 1993) was passed by parliament in early June 1994 and came into force on 28 June. Mass privatization based on the free distribution of vouchers was ruled out, but the scheme would enable citizens to buy some vouchers, allow the issuing of vouchers for restitution purposes and permit the participation of foreign investors.

Bulgarians aged 20 or more would be eligible (between 1 September and 14 October 1994) to buy vouchers worth 30,000 lev. (They would have to pay 1,500 lev, two weeks' average wages, and the rest between 1999 and 2005.) Some 150,000 vouchers worth 100,000 lev each would be issued to cover restitution claims. Vouchers would be eligible for placement in special investment funds. The first wave was to include some 500 medium-sized and large (but non-strategic) enterprises valued at 180 billion lev (to be followed, if successful, by a second wave of up to 700 enterprises) (*Business Central Europe*, October 1993, p. 62). Wyzan (1996: 57) and EBRD (1994: 20) put the number of enterprises on the first wave list at 340. The target was to sell 320 enterprises in 1994 (including seventy large ones) or at least 10 per cent of the state sector ('strategic' sectors such as armaments, transport, oil refining and energy generation being excluded) (*Transition*, 1994, vol. 5, no. 4, p. 9). The privatization of 3,485 enterprises was initiated in 1993 with a programme envisaging individual sales through a variety of mechanisms (direct sales, tenders, auctions, management buy-outs). Management and employees could bid for up to 20 per cent of shares on preferential terms (50 per cent discount). The privatization process was open to foreigners. In November 1994 Brady bonds and Zunks (domestic bad-loan bonds) became usable as payment (EBRD 1996a: 142).

Political factors have delayed large privatization. Only two large enterprises have been privatized, the first being in May 1993 (*IHT*, 1 December 1993, p. 14). Two years after the passing of a privatization law which envisaged the sale of more than 3,000 enterprises the agency responsible for selling medium-sized and large enterprises has completed less than twenty transactions (*FT*, 29 March 1994, p. 3). By mid-1994 one in sixteen large enterprises had been privatized, while seventeen out of 870 medium-sized enterprises had been privatized (EBRD 1994: 20). Thirty-four medium-sized and large enterprises have been privatized (*IHT*, 19 December 1994, p. 5; *The Economist*, 7 January 1995, p. 33). So far only around 275 enterprises have been privatized out of a scheduled total of some 3,500 enterprises (Deutsche Bank, *Focus: Eastern Europe*, 31 May 1995, no. 130, pp. 4–5). By June 1995 only sixty-three large enterprises had been privatized by the privatization agency (EBRD 1996a: 37). By mid-1996 only 6 per cent of total state enterprise assets had been transferred to the private sector (EBRD 1996b: 142).

Legislation to set up a mass privatization programme was approved just before the Berov government resigned on 2 September 1994. In late November 1995 the final list for mass privatization was approved, consisting of 1,227 enterprises (*Business Central Europe*, December 1995 to January 1996, p. 27).

A programme for the mass privatization of medium-sized enterprises was submitted to parliament on 22 March 1995. This was to involve the privatization of 100 to 150 enterprises between November 1995 and October 1996. (Some 150 enterprises were to be selected for privatization. Those not to be privatized included the Kozloduy nuclear power station, the military–industrial complex, the Bulgarian Telecommunications Company, the Post Office and one or two major banks: *Transition*, 1995, vol. 6, nos 5–6, p. 19. Instead of shutting down the two oldest units at the Kozloduy nuclear plant at the end of 1998 as agreed, the government has decided to extend their lifespan until 2005, when the modernization of units five and six is due to be completed (*FT*, Survey, 8 March 1999, p. iii). A further hundred enterprises were to be privatized between February 1996 and January 1998. Payment would be in the form of vouchers (15 to 20 per cent), cash (50 per cent) and 'bad loan bonds' issued by the government as part of the bank recapitalization scheme (30 to 35 per cent). Vouchers would be tradable on the stock market. The first list of enterprises was to be made public in November 1995 (EBRD 1995a: 54). Sectors such as energy and telecommunications were to remain excluded from privatization (1995b: 37). Vouchers began to be distributed to the population in early 1996 but the take-up was low. The end of the registration period was set for 8 April 1996 and it was planned that vouchers could start being exchanged for shares in 1,063 enterprises (about a third of all state enterprises) in June 1996. Only in a minority of cases would enterprises' capital be fully privatized. The government would initially retain a majority stake or a blocking minority in most of the partly privatized enterprises. Additional shares were to be offered to investors for cash (EBRD 1996a: 10). The privatization process was to accelerate significantly in the second half of 1996 with the inclusion of a stake in major enterprises such as Bulgarian Telecoms which were previously excluded. The mass privatization programme began in 1996. Some two-thirds of vouchers have been transferred to specialized investment funds (each of which can own up to 34 per cent of the shares of an enterprise). By mid-1998 all state enterprises, except the utilities and a small number of 'strategic' enterprises, were to be privatized. The first auction, for shares in over a thousand enterprises, was scheduled for October 1996 (EBRD 1996b: 142–3). In 1996, 509 enterprises were privatized for cash and Brady bonds, the majority in the form of management buy-outs as in previous years. The first auction under a mass privatization scheme took place in October 1996. Shares in 968 enterprises (with a book value of assets equivalent to 11 per cent of GDP) were offered to the public and eighty-one specialized investment funds against payment in vouchers. (The funds attracted about two-thirds of the vouchers that had been issued to the population.) Under a cash and mass privatization programme agreed with the IMF, all state enterprises except the utilities and a small number of 'strategic' enterprises were to be transferred into private hands by mid-1998 (EBRD 1997a: 27). During August–September 1997 there was a tender to foreign consulting firms of contracts to privatize twenty-seven large enterprises (EBRD 1997b: 158). The first round of mass privatization came to an end in July 1997. Vouchers became tradable on the stock exchange on 3 March 1998. The second and final round was expected to start in late summer 1998, foreign investors being eligible this time. Management–employee buy-outs are becoming an increasingly popular means of privatization, as are debt-for-equity swaps (EBRD 1998a: 34).

> Strategic foreign investors are beginning to play a larger role in Bulgaria, producing a pattern of corporate governance that gives a greater role to

outside institutions. However, at the same time, management–employee buy-outs are becoming an increasingly popular means of privatization, raising some concerns about future ownership structures.

(p. 28)

'The pace of cash privatization of large-scale enterprises in 1998 has been slower than anticipated' (EBRD 1999a: 35). The second round of mass privatization started in January 1999. Measured by the number of transactions concluded, 1998 saw an acceleration in privatization as management–employee buy-outs proliferated. In mid-1999 significant progress was made in privatization, with several of the largest enterprises being sold (including Balkan Airlines and Kremikovski). A second bank was privatized in late 1998 when 78 per cent of Post Bank (the third largest of the six remaining state banks) was sold to a foreign strategic investor (EBRD 1999b: 202–3). 'Enterprise privatization made remarkable progress in 1999, with more than 1,200 deals completed. By the end of the year over 70 per cent of privatizable assets had been sold, compared with 42 per cent a year earlier. Management buy-outs remained the most popular form of privatization in 1999. The state retains shares in some privatized enterprises and the liquidation of remaining state-owned enterprises are priorities … Bank privatization is nearing completion' (EBRD 2000a: 46).

Major sales … included the oil refinery Neftochim, the steel giant Kremikovski, the fertilizer producer Agropolychim and Balkan Airlines … [But 1999] saw several privatizations of majority stakes of large enterprises annulled because of purchaser non-payments … The government announced in August 2000 that the negotiations to sell 51 per cent of … Bulgarian Telecommunications Company … had failed … A new tender for the sale will be held … While privatization is nearly complete, the restructuring of privatized enterprise, particularly those sold to management, remains a challenge, owing to ineffective corporate governance and bankruptcy procedures … Enterprise restructuring remains sluggish.

(EBRD 2000b: 146)

The privatization of enterprises is nearing completion. As of December 2000 the privatization agency had only 400 companies left in its portfolio, excluding the large utilities … But enterprise restructuring remains sluggish due to weak corporate governance and ineffective bankruptcy procedures … Financial restructuring has been slow, particularly in companies with insider ownership. Weak bankruptcy procedures and limited access to new commercial credit delayed the imposition of hard budget constraints on existing firms … In August 2000 negotiations to sell 51 per cent of the state-owned telecommunications operator, BTC, to a consortium of KPN Telecom of the Netherlands and QTE of Greece failed … The slow pace of energy reform is a source of concern. Privatization of the National Electricity Company (NEK) has not yet taken place and tariffs are still

> heavily regulated … Foreign-owned banks hold more than 70 per cent of total bank assets.
>
> (EBRD 2001: 54)

Long-delayed mass privatization began on 7 October 1996. Some 3 million Bulgarians were expected to bid for shares in 986 of the 1,063 enterprises up for sale. The state would continue to control 'strategic' enterprises, such as oil refineries and tourist offices (only 25 per cent of their shares would be offered to investors). Banks, armament factories, railways, power plants and service enterprises would not be privatized. About 65 per cent of shares in medium-sized and large enterprises and 90 per cent in small enterprises were to be privatized. Results of the bids were supposed to be announced by the end of November 1996 (*Transition*, September–October 1996, vol. 7, nos 9–10, p. 23).

Accusations of corruption were common:

1. The delay in 'open' privatization has allowed 'hidden' or '*nomenklatura*' privatization to thrive (*Business Central Europe*, February 1994, p. 51).
2. Pomfret makes the point that the *nomenklatura* have exploited business and political connections: 'Many of these people have become fabulously rich running private trading companies that buy from and sell to Bulgaria's state-run factories, creating a bizarre economic subsystem in which production is state-run but profits are private … Essentially, private trading companies control everything sold to the factories and market their production too. Such enterprises can be lucrative through kickbacks or manipulation of antiquated accounting methods. The private trading companies can make windfall profits selling raw materials at market prices, buying finished products at low prices and then selling them at a profit. As the state-run enterprises slip deeply into debt, the private trading companies reap huge profits. (John Pomfret, *IHT*, 14 May 1994, p. 11)
3. 'Diplomats and political observers agree that Bulgaria's state enterprises are being comprehensively asset-stripped by managers and private businessmen with close ties to the former communists' (Julian Borger, *Guardian*, 17 December 1994, p. 9).
4. The economic power of the *nomenklatura* is particularly strong in Bulgaria.

> By supplying raw materials at market prices to state firms run by friends, and then buying back the finished products cheaply, companies can make money twice, first on the raw materials and then by selling the finished goods. The state firm then makes a thumping loss – but that is passed on to the government … What the Bulgarians call the 'mafiaisation' of the economy.
>
> (*The Economist*, 7 January 1995, p. 33)

> Business, of a sort, is thriving, but it is mostly crooked: members of the old *nomenklatura* control much of the economy through shadowy

'economic groups' tied to the state. Corruption and incompetence are spectacular. The Russian mafia is prominent … A good quarter of the economy is probably 'grey'.

(*The Economist*, 19 October 1996, p. 55)

5 Although formal privatization has been slow, state and municipal enterprises have been subjected to 'hidden' privatization. This usually involves the formation of private companies to supply state enterprises with inputs at high prices and of other companies to take their subsidized output for resale at market prices. In this way enterprises accumulate inter-enterprise debts and losses while allowing a new class of millionaire to develop. The process of nationalizing losses and privatizing profits is widespread throughout the former Soviet bloc but has been most blatant in countries such as Bulgaria and Romania (Anthony Robinson, *FT*, Survey, 13 October 1994, p. 14).

6 According to official figures, the private sector contributed 22 per cent of GDP in 1994. But a World Bank estimate, which encompasses illegal and quasi-legal activities as well as legal activities outside the government tax base, puts the figure at 50 per cent. The World Bank also suggests that at least 90 per cent of profits in the economy may accrue to the informal private sector. Since the private sector accounts for only 5 per cent of long-term assets, less than 10 per cent of total credits, 22 to 26 per cent of employment and 10 to 12 per cent of labour income, this suggests that private-sector profits are somehow channelled from the state enterprise sector. After 1991, as a general rule, private firms took over distribution, marketing and foreign trade functions. Private wealth has been created through siphoning profits from state enterprises (Zeljko Bogetic and Arye Hillman, *Transition*, 1995, vol. 6, no. 3, pp. 4, 6).

7 'Western bankers say businessmen from the former communist party have stripped state enterprises of their assets, with the connivance of state officials, and sent the money abroad … Western bankers estimate that $3 billion to $5 billion has been bled out of the economy and squirreled abroad' (Jane Perlez, *IHT*, 29 October 1996, p. 8).

8 The 'Group of 13' is the name given to the business lobby recently founded by the largest private companies. The group controls a large part of the private sector (Virginia Marsh, *FT*, 10 May 1994, p. 3). The 'Group of 13' is 'said to be owned and operated by former communists that are now exerting mafia-like influence in the country's private sector' (*Business Europa*, November–December 1994, p. 35). Until mid-1995 the most important of the groups were united in the so-called 'Group of 13'; seven now remain in the group (*Transition*, 1995, vol. 6, no. 3, p. 5).

Reforms of the customs service and an overhaul of the tax system have helped to reduce the role in Bulgaria's economy of a half-dozen shadowy conglomerates which dominated business activity in the mid-1990s. Moreover, the withdrawing of the conglomerates from sectors

> such as banking and energy has contributed to a more level playing field for foreign investors.
>
> (*FT*, Survey, 8 March 1999, p. ii)

Further developments in privatization

The purchase has been finalized by a Bulgarian chemical company of 60 per cent of a major chemical company, the first big sell-off (*FT*, 20 December 1996, p. 3).

On 7 October 1997 the UDF announced a new privatization programme envisaging the privatization of 80 per cent of state enterprises by the end of 1998 (*EEN*, 1997, vol. 11, no. 20, p. 5).

In October 1997 an agreement was reached between Gazprom (the Russian gas monopoly) and Bulgargas (the state gas company) which guaranteed Russian gas supplies to Bulgaria for the next ten to fifteen years. It cleared the way for the construction of a new transit gas pipeline between Russia and western Turkey before the year 2000.

> The deal also leaves a question hanging over the future of Topenergy, the energy company set up three years ago as a joint venture between Gazprom and Bulgargas. Gazprom subsequently changed the ground rules by gaining an effective majority stake through its links with Bulgarian subsidiaries of Multigroup ... The new UDF government ... insisted that any deal should be done directly between Gazprom and Bulgargas, cutting out Topenergy.
>
> (Anthony Robinson, *FT*, Survey, 21 October 1997, pp. 31–2)

The government is now forcing Multigroup and other Bulgarian investors in Topenergy to sell their shares to Bulgargas (*EEN*, 1997, vol. 11, no. 20, p. 4).

> The coalition government under the premiership of Ivan Kostov [was] elected in April 1997 on a law-and-order platform ... Part of this effort has been directed at the business empires. Multigroup, the biggest conglomerate, has become Mr Kostov's main target. In April [1998] it was squeezed out of a joint venture in natural gas with Gazprom, the Russian energy giant, when its stake was taken over by Bulgargas, the state gas company. Last month [September 1998], after an official investigation, its sugar-trading subsidiary, Bartex, was accused of involvement in a smuggling racket.
>
> (*The Economist*, 17 October 1998, p. 50)

(On 20 March 1998 the government signed an agreement with Gazprom for delivery of Russian gas in return for Gazprom's acquisition of 100 per cent of Topenergy, the Bulgarian distribution company: *EEN*, 1998, vol. 12, no. 5, p. 5.)

Several industrial behemoths have been sold. Privatization is moving on a three-track process: some companies are to be sold in a voucher plan linked to pension funds; some are to be sold directly by the government; and a third group are to be sold by outside advisers. The government wants to privatize 1,500 small and medium-sized enterprises by the end of 1999 and giants like the telecommunications companies and oil refineries by the end of 2001. The government has recently said that it would sell its 78.23 per cent stake in the postal savings bank to US and Greek companies. A shipyard has been sold to a Slovak company (*IHT*, 11 August 1998, p. 13).

The privatization agency estimates that Bulgaria sold about 29 per cent of state assets between the start of privatization in 1993 and the end of September 1998. The plan is to privatize about 50 per cent of remaining long-term assets by the end of March 1999 and a cumulative 70 per cent is scheduled to be in private hands by the end of 1999. Enterprises included among expected sales of major assets to strategic investors include the largest oil refinery (Neftochim), Balkan Airlines, Bulgartabak, the telecommunications company BTC and four pharmaceutical manufacturers. About 30 per cent of assets, including the one nuclear power plant, coal mines, postal services, ports, water supply and sewage systems, roads and railways and the electricity grid, are not to be privatized (*IHT*, 22 October 1998, p. 19).

Bulgaria has agreed to sell the Kremikovski steelworks to a local metals trading company for one US dollar in an attempt to meet a privatization deadline agreed with the IMF. The enterprise is among a group of about twenty loss-making enterprises due to be sold or placed in liquidation by 30 June 1999. Daru Metals offered to take over $200 million of debts owed to the government and an Austrian bank. It plans to set up a joint venture with an Italian steelmaker (*FT*, 28 May 1999, p. 3).

> Come 1997 and the post-collapse government decided to speed things up a bit. In the next two years it privatized many of the small companies still in state hands. Most were sold by direct sale, often through tenders. And that is where the problems start to show. There is little foreign interest in Bulgaria and most companies are too wobbly to excite much interest anyway. As a result the bulk of sales have been management buy-outs. Predictably, there are some outrageous examples of cronyism and more than a whiff of corruption. But in the end the biggest problem is that companies have no access to outside knowledge or cash, essential for restructuring.
>
> (*Business Central Europe*, July–August 1999, pp. 42, 44)

'In its efforts to stop big companies from being a drain on the economy the government imposed a "privatize or close" order on the biggest loss-makers ... [There is an] end of June [1999] deadline for sixteen of them' (p. 40).

On 9 July 1999 a protocol was signed for Dutch and Greek telecommunications operators to buy a 51 per cent stake in BTC, the state telecoms group (*FT*, 12 July 1999, p. 21). 'However, delays have been encountered due to concerns over regulatory and pricing issues' (EBRD 2000a: 46). 'A $600 million deal to sell Bulgarian telecoms monopoly BTC to a consortium of Greece's OTE and Holland's KPN fell through after a year of negotiations. Bulgarian privatization officials said the consortium's conditions would have violated EU telecoms regulations' (*Business Central Europe*, September 2000, p. 16).

On 12 October 1999 the Russian oil company Lukoil was named as the preferred buyer of a majority stake in Neftochim, the biggest oil refinery in the Balkans. Lukoil was to pay $101 million for a 58 per cent stake. The sale followed the acquisition by Western investors of majority stakes in Bulgaria's biggest steelworks, the state-owned telecoms operator and two state banks (*FT*, 13 October 1999, p. 34).

On 21 June 2000 it was announced that Bulgaria's largest state-owned bank, Bulbank AD, was to be sold to an Italian–German group (*IHT*, 22 June 2000, p. 13).

'This autumn [2000] Bulgaria announced a new privatization policy designed to improve transparency and reduce the number of insider sales' (*Business Central Europe*, December 2000–January 2001, p. 47). 'Barring some big early deals, most privatization sales have gone to managers or second-rate investors' (*Business Central Europe*, June 2001, p. 42).

'The Kostov government … has privatized a lot – but mostly to politically favoured managers and dubious investors, foreign and local' (*The Economist*, 16 June 2001, p. 51).

Foreign trade

The foreign trade regime has been liberalized. The state trade monopoly was abolished in 1990, import quotas were largely removed in February 1991 and trade protection now mainly takes the form of tariffs (which have tended to increase of late). On 1 February 1991 the lev was floated at a unified rate. There are few restrictions on current account transactions, but heavy ones on the capital account. In 1996, however, a foreign exchange crisis led to *de facto* restrictions on drawdowns from foreign currency deposits (EBRD 1996b: 143). A currency board was introduced on 1 July 1997, with the lev fixed at 1,000 to the DM. A trade agreement with EFTA went into effect on 1 July 1993 with EFTA countries dismantling barriers more quickly (there would be restrictions mainly on steel and textiles during the interim period). An association agreement with the EU was announced on 8 March 1993 covering a ten-year period (although EU restrictions on agricultural imports from Bulgaria will remain). The agreement went into effect on 1 February 1995. Bulgaria became a member of the WTO in December 1996. In July 1998 Bulgaria signed an accession agreement with the Central European Free Trade Association, with full membership occurring in January 1999 (EBRD 1998b: 158). The tariff regime has been simplified, with reductions in the number of tariff bands, in the dispersion of rates and in the level of certain tariffs. Most export tariffs have been eliminated and the number of products subject to licensing requirements has been greatly reduced. The temporary import surcharge introduced in 1996 was abolished ahead of schedule on 1 January 1999. In September 1998 Bulgaria accepted the obligations of the IMF's Article 8 (EBRD 1999b: 202).

Foreign direct investment

Foreign direct investment has, not surprisingly, been disappointing. But the volume has increased. (See Table 2.2.)

Legislation intended to encourage and attract foreign investment was passed in February 1992, but the holding up of much economic legislation and specific factors (such as the ban on purchases of land by foreign citizens and legal entities) have resulted in a poor response to date. As of 1 July 1996 foreign investors were exempted from paying profit tax for three years, with a 50 per cent reduction for the next two years, as long as the joint venture is at least 50 per cent foreign owned, has fixed capital assets of over $5 million and invests at least 50 per cent of the retained tax in tangible assets (*Business Europa*, September–October 1996, p. 42). The United Nations Economic Commission for Europe (1996: 149) puts net direct foreign investment at $4 million in 1990, $56 million in 1991, $42 million in 1992, $40 million in 1993, $105 million in 1994 and $82 million in 1995. Foreign direct investment amounted to $164 million in the period 1990–3 (EBRD 1994: 123). Although ownership of land by foreigners is not permitted, foreign-owned local companies may own land (except land intended for agricultural use) (EBRD 1996b: 144). On 15 October 1997 an amendment to the land tenure act was passed, allowing foreigners to own agricultural land provided they are in a partnership (joint venture) with Bulgarian entities (*EEN*, 1997, vol. 11, no. 20, p. 5). In 1998 restrictions on amounts of farmland purchased by foreign investors were lifted (*FT*, Survey, 8 March 1999, p. iii).

Agriculture

Agricultural legislation was relatively quick off the mark. At the beginning of 1990 the government abolished state orders and in February restrictions were lifted on the size of private farms. The Land Law was adopted in late January 1991, although implementation was to be delayed until the autumn. Provision was made for restitution to former owners or their heirs of land forcibly collectivized. The aim was to restore the land ownership pattern of 1946. (Before 1946, 63.1 per cent of farms were 5 ha or less in size: Frydman *et al.* 1993: 33.) Financial compensation was to be available in case physical restitution was not possible. Provision was also made for the auctioning off of about 400,000 ha of state land to those farmers who never owned land. Land legislation approved in March 1992 allowed restitution of up to 30 ha (74 acres) per person, but there are relatively few claims of this size because of the historical situation (Virginia Marsh, *FT*, 19 November 1992, p. 34).

> In Bulgaria most land was still formally privately owned and was restituted to the former owners. An important consequence of this policy was a rather egalitarian distribution of land, except to the Turkish minority. This Turkish minority represents almost 10 per cent of the population and was mainly employed in agriculture. They owned less land and therefore received less

> land under the restitution programme … [But] the allocation of 50 per cent of non-land assets to labour contributors … benefited Turkish agricultural workers.
>
> (Swinnen 1999: 645)

By the end of 1992 about 6 per cent of farmland had been returned to private ownership. This figure rose to 23 per cent (*EEN*, 20 July 1993, vol. 7, no. 15, p. 3) and then 35 per cent at most (*EEN*, 10 August 1993, vol. 7, no. 16, p. 4). By the end of 1992 only 10 per cent of arable land had been restored to the original owners (United Nations Economic Commission for Europe 1993: 203). Around 30 per cent of the land is now worked by farmers who own it (*Employment Observatory*, December 1993, no. 5, p. 4).

There are more than 1.7 million conflicting restitution claims. More than 90 per cent of the land that has passed into private hands is in tiny plots of less than 1 ha. Because much of the land has been transferred on a temporary basis pending final decisions on claims, the land cannot yet be used as collateral or sold (*The Economist*, 7 August 1993, p. 63). The average plot size is 0.16 ha (Mark Milner, *Guardian*, 4 September 1993, p. 35). Around 50 per cent of farmland is now in private hands, most of it outside the highly productive regions. About 25 per cent of land has been returned to former owners (42 per cent of agricultural land reserved for restitution has been distributed so far). To help farmers obtain bank credit, land protocols or temporary land titles can be used as collateral under the amended law (*Transition*, April 1994, vol. 5, no. 4, pp. 9–10).

Virginia Marsh and Anthony Robinson (*FT*, Survey, 5 May 1993, p. 32) reported that the policy of the Berov government was to try to avoid breaking up all the large farms (especially those with long-maturity crops, such as vineyards and orchards) and to encourage voluntary co-operatives. In the earlier phases many animals were slaughtered because of factors such as livestock being given to farmers who did not have land and the selling off of co-operatives' fodder before returning animals to individual farmers. *EEN* (18 August 1994, vol. 8, no. 17, p. 5) referred to

> the parlous state of agriculture generally – endless derelict collective farms and acres of fertile but abandoned land. The vaunted privatization of land is a fiction: about half the land has been privatized, but the poor security of ownership and the extreme difficulty of getting credit or vital agricultural inputs makes farming a nightmare.

Theodor Troev is not so pessimistic (*FT*, Survey, 13 October 1994, p. 14). But he notes that about 60 per cent of the new landowners now live in cities or towns and many are unable or unwilling to return to farming. Some work their newly returned plots of land only at weekends and with simple implements. The average size of newly returned plots is only 1.6 ha. Some new co-operatives have been formed. Only 50 per cent of farmland had been returned with full titles by the end of September 1994. The privatization of state agricultural enterprises is now slowly moving ahead (e.g. pig farms, poultry farms, mills, machine repair works and fisheries) (p. 14). 'Livestock belonging to collective farms was distributed indiscriminately to householders, who often lacked cash to feed their newly acquired animals and experience of looking after them. The result was widespread slaughtering of cows, including breeding stock, for food.' The number of cattle fell from 648,000 in 1989 to 358,000 at the end of 1996. About 70 per cent of the 5.8 million ha included in the privatization programme has been returned to former owners or their heirs, but titles have been issued for only 5 per cent of holdings. 'Although another 30 per cent of privatized land is registered under a temporary arrangement intended to make it possible to rent or lease landholdings, large tracts of arable land remain uncultivated.' Private producers account for over 70 per cent of farm output on holdings averaging less than 1 ha (Kerin Hope and Theodor Troev, *FT*, 15 July 1997, p. 33). Some 18 per cent of owners have received official titles. The rest have been given temporary titles which may be contested in the courts (Kerin Hope and Theodor Troev, *FT*, Survey, 21 October 1997, p. 33). The wheat harvest is a healthy 3.7 million tonnes, compared with only 1.8 million tonnes last year (and an average of 5 million tonnes in the communist era). The average farmer owns less than 2.5 ha of land, although several big farming groups in north-eastern Bulgaria have increased their holdings to more than 1,000 ha by leasing land from relatives and neighbours. In early November 1997 parliament passed land reform legislation providing for the leasing of unlimited amounts of land and by permitting foreigners to buy agricultural land in joint ventures with Bulgarian partners (Kerin Hope and Theodor Troev, *FT*, 4 November 1997, p. 31). Although 80 per cent of the farmland available for restitution has been returned to precommunist owners, full titles have been issued for only 24 per cent. Only about 5 per cent of private farms exceed 2 ha in size, while barely 1 per cent reach the EU average of 20 to 50 ha (*FT*, Survey, 8 March 1999, p. iii).

By the end of 1994, 57.3 per cent of farm land had been restituted (EBRD 1995a: 54). Few land titles have been issued, but 60 per cent of agricultural land has been handed back to the original owners through 'final land decisions' recognized as ownership documents and accepted as collateral (EBRD 1995b: 37). Titles to less than 20 per cent of land have been issued. 'Uniquely in Central Europe, agriculture is effectively taxed through the price and export regime … Export restrictions on agricultural and certain other commodities (taxes and selective bans) … have significantly increased in scope' (EBRD 1996b: 143). By the end of 1998, 80 per cent of agricultural land had been restituted and over 18 per cent of the land subject to restitution had been titled. More than half of agro-industrial companies (measured by long-term assets) and virtually all grain warehouses have been privatized. A number of steps have been taken to provide a stimulus to a functioning land market, including improvements in the process of land registration (EBRD 1999b: 202). 'By the end of 1999 land restitution was 96 per cent complete, up from 80 per cent at the end of 1998' (EBRD 2000b: 146).

On 27 April 1995 President Zhelev vetoed the changes in the Land Act which had been passed by parliament on 14 April (*EEN*, 1995, vol. 9, no. 9, p. 6). (The amended Land Act has now passed into law: *EEN*, 25 May 1995, vol. 9, no. 11, p. 7.) The amendments specified the following:

1 Only the amount of land declared on entering the collective farm would be returned to the claimant. Opponents argued that peasants had routinely declared less land in order to avoid the heavy taxes imposed on private farmers.
2 The owner's original land would remain part of the co-operative. Opponents argued that this could mean a claimant receiving inferior land as compensation.
3 A seller of land could resort to the free market only if the offer were to be successively rejected by owners of neighbouring plots, by relatives and by the municipal authorities. Moreover, the sale price would be fixed by the state.
4 People who received land from the communist regime would receive full title and pay prices set by the state, while former owners would receive compensation.

(*EEN*, 25 May 1995, vol. 9, no. 11, p. 7)

Parliament passed the controversial amendment on 14 April 1995. Owners wishing to sell their land have to offer it in the first place to the state, which has two months to decide whether to buy it. The amendment also restricts the right to sell small plots that are part of larger land blocks or to plant crops different from those in the rest of the block. The opposition vowed to refer the matter to the constitutional court (*Transition*, 1995, vol. 6, no. 4, p. 19). The court rejected some of the provisions of the amended Land Act.

> Problems have been caused by restitution … Instead of insisting on people producing title deeds to their land, Bulgaria said it would also accept the testimony of friends and neighbours … Not surprisingly, claims were filed for a far higher amount of land than actually existed. There then followed a hideously complex restitution process involving not just verification of claims but the grading of land and so on … In theory 80 per cent of land has been restituted. In fact just 17 per cent of restituted land has registered owners. The bulk of farmers work on tiny plots, good for nothing but subsistence … Most farmers have no official title to their land, so they cannot sell it. Nor can they borrow any money because they have no collateral. So bad is the situation that spending on fertiliser and seed, let alone on equipment, has all but dried up … There aren't any [subsidies].
>
> (*Business Central Europe*, July–August 1999, p. 48)

Economic performance

Although GDP growth turned positive in 1994, output plunged in 1996 and 1997. Since then the GDP growth rate has been positive. (See Table 2.2.)

> [In 1999] Bulgaria was affected by a disruption to trade links due to the Kosovo conflict and a weakening of its terms of trade when the currencies of many important trading partners depreciated. The currency board arrangement has helped keep the exchange rate and prices stable, but exports have declined.
>
> (EBRD 2000a: 5)

In 2000 GDP was an estimated 70 per cent of the 1989 level (EBRD 2001: 15). Inflation fell in 1992 but there were extraordinary gyrations thereafter. There was hyperinflation in 1997 but consumer prices were more or less stable in 1999 and the inflation rate was still in single figures in 2000.

3 The Czech Republic

POLITICS

The political background

The Czech Republic, under the go-ahead but pragmatic leadership of prime minister Vaclav Klaus, for a while overtook Hungary as the number one economic and political success story in Eastern Europe. (On 28 November 1995 the Czech Republic became the first former communist country to become a member of the OECD.) Despite the later tarnishing of his reputation for political and economic management (e.g. financial scandals and a poor record in industrial restructuring), Klaus achieved a generally rapid economic transition while using subsidies to avoid sudden large-scale bankruptcies and lay-offs. Klaus also did a good job of 'selling' a consistent policy line to the Czech public. He has made something of a political comeback at a time when the reputation of his arch rival President Vaclav Havel (who has been in poor health) has been damaged somewhat at home by events such as his second marriage.

Communist or socialist parties appear to have little chance of making a comeback. David Ottaway (*IHT*, 28 May 1994, p. 5) suggests two possible reasons: (1) the 'velvet revolution' was so rapid that little real reform took place within the Communist Party; (2) in reality prime minister Klaus has followed a highly statist approach to economic reform, carefully incorporating trade unions as partners and allowing heavy state spending on social welfare measures and subsidies to hold down unemployment.

The Economist (22 October 1994, p. 26) talks of a tacit social contract in which workers accept low wages in exchange for high employment and a low cost of living. (Note that housing rents and most utility prices are controlled.)

> From now on the main thrust of government and business policy will shift increasingly from the macro to the micro level, concentrating above all on the restructuring of the industrial sector. Here, Premier Klaus appears to have been right. His view has been that the process of restructuring, which will take a very heavy toll, can be more easily weathered, at a more bearable

social cost, in a period of economic growth than during the adjustment recession.

(Deutsche Bank, *Focus: Eastern Europe*, 22 December 1994, no. 123, p. 3)

Political developments from January 1993 until the 1996 general election

26 January 1993: Vaclav Havel is elected president by parliament.

30 June 1993: the Czech Republic is admitted to the Council of Europe.

26 August 1993: during a visit by Yeltsin a friendship and co-operation treaty with Russia is signed.

24 October 1993: Jiri Hajek, one of the founders of Charter 77, dies.

11–12 January 1994: President Clinton visits Prague. (On the second day he met the leaders of the Czech Republic, Slovakia, Hungary and Poland mainly to discuss the Partnership for Peace policy.)

1 July 1994: over a thousand Gypsies become non-citizens when the deadline passes for Slovak citizens wishing to claim Czech citizenship. Citizenship requires proof of two years' fixed residence and a five-year trouble-free police record (*EEN*, 1994, vol. 8, no. 25, p. 4). Almost all the 250,000 Gypsies were classified as Slovaks even though two-thirds were born on Czech territory, and the rest were (usually forcibly) moved from Slovakia by the communists (to replace the Sudeten Germans, for example) (*FT*, Survey, 19 December 1994, p. vi). The law, which came into effect on 1 January 1993, states that anyone under 40 whose parents were registered as Slovaks in Czechoslovakia is classified as Slovak and has to apply for Czech citizenship.

6 July 1994: it is announced that Radio Free Europe/Radio Liberty will move to Prague.

29 October 1994: the Pope announces that a Czech has been made a cardinal.

2 November 1994: Jaroslav Lizner, director of the Centre for Coupon Privatization (which processes applications from would-be investors), is arrested on charges of taking bribes.

18–19 November 1994: in local elections the Civic Democratic Party wins over 32 per cent of the vote.

1 February 1995: the EU association agreement comes fully into effect.

22–3 April 1995: a new communist party is established. The Party of Czechoslovak Communists is led by Miroslav Stepan.

20–2 May 1995: the Pope visits the Czech Republic. The Pope canonizes the seventeenth-century priest Jan Sarkander, amid considerable controversy over his role in the Counter-Reformation.

28 November 1995: the Czech Republic becomes a member (the twenty-sixth) of the OECD, the first former communist country to achieve this distinction. (*Per capita* GDP, about $8,850 at purchasing power parity exchange rates in 1994, is almost half the OECD average: OECD, *Economic Outlook*, June 1996, p. 104. Hungary joined on 29 May 1996 and its figure is $6,300: p. 111.)

November 1995: overriding a presidential veto, the Czech parliament has passed an extension to a law prohibiting top communists from holding high-level political, judicial and academic posts. The law, originally passed in 1991 and scheduled to expire at the end of 1996, will now remain in effect until 2000 (*Business Central Europe*, December 1995–January 1996, p. 27).

4 January 1996: the Czech Republic and Slovakia sign a treaty defining their new common border. Over 400 ha are to be exchanged to satisfy claims on both sides (*IHT*, 5 January 1996, p. 5).

The general election of 31 May–1 June 1996

The turnout was 76.29 per cent. Sixteen parties competed for the 200 seats in the House of Deputies on the same basis as before: 100 per cent proportional representation, no minimum national turnout and a 5 per cent threshold for individual parties (7 per cent for alliances). The results of the June 1992 election are to be found in Jeffries (1993: 504).

The governing coalition, consisting of three parties, lost their parliamentary majority. The parties won only 99 seats despite a rise in their combined share of the vote from 42 per cent to 44.1 per cent:

Civic Democratic Party: (29.62 per cent of the vote and 68 seats). Led by Vaclav Klaus, with Jan Vlach second in command. Centre right.

Christian Democratic Alliance/Czech People's Party: (8.08 per cent of the vote and 18 seats). Led by Josef Lux. Roman Catholic constituency. Advocated a social market economy (a more equitable society), more powerful local government and the restitution of property to the Roman Catholic Church.

Civic Democratic Alliance: (6.36 per cent of the vote and 13 seats). Led by Jan Kalvoda. Vladimir Dlouhy is a member. A centre-right party with a pro-economic reform and decentralization stance.

The other parties were as follows:

Social Democratic Party: (26.44 per cent of the vote and 61 seats). Led by Milos Zeman, with Petra Buzkova second in command. Its increased support had seemed to slip of late so its strong showing came as a surprise to most observers. It advocated a 'socially and ecologically orientated market economy', with increased spending on health and education, increased pensions (and a separation of pension funds from the state budget), subsidies for industry and the maintenance of the generous subsidies on rents, transport and utilities. It also stressed the need for regional decentralization, an attack on tax dodging and for more transparent capital markets and privatization (being against further privatization of transport and energy and in favour of a bill requiring individuals to prove ownership of private property worth over 5 million crowns).

In an interview after the election Milos Zeman (who became speaker of parliament) commented:

> We are going toward the classic European political model, a model with very strong social and ecological aspects, from a Thatcherite model, which to my mind is one-sided ... We have no objection to privatization but rather toward the method of privatization ... Millions of small shareholders have no voice in the whole procedure. Companies and enterprises are owned by the so-called investment funds. The investment funds are owned mainly by banks and the banks in the majority of cases are state-owned ... We would actually suggest another form of privatization for the remaining assets, something that is called management buy-out. We are opposed to privatization only in the areas of medical service, health service and education. And ... we are against privatizing the rail network ... As for public spending, we would like to increase our budget not by increasing taxes but by trying to combat tax evasion ... Our legislation is insufficient particularly in combating crime and conflict of interest ... In privatizing some of our large companies attempts have been made to gain illegal money and illegally to enrich oneself.
>
> (*IHT*, 15 July 1996, p. 6)

Communist Party of Bohemia and Moravia: (10.33 per cent of the vote and 22 seats). It is a far left (unreformed communist) party led by Miroslav Grebenicek. It advocated collectivization and a powerful state. It lost out to the Social Democratic Party but appealed to pensioners and those who had done badly in the transition.

Republican Party: (8.01 per cent of the vote and 18 seats). Led by Miroslav Sladek, it is a far right (neo-fascist) party which presented an anti-Gypsy and anti-German platform.

Comment

> Czechs did not follow the lead of other former Soviet bloc countries in returning former communists to power, but the vote signalled an apparent desire to slow the quick pace of reform pursued by Mr Klaus ... While this signalled that Czech politics are becoming more like those of Western Europe, with classic left and right blocs, it makes for immediate uncertainty.
>
> (*IHT*, 4 June 1996, p. 5)

> If the electorate had voted for the CSSD [Social Democratic Party] in protest at the speed of economic reform, the ODS [Civic Democratic Party] would have been in trouble. This did not in fact happen. The impact of economic transformation has been well cushioned, with rates of inflation and unemployment still comfortably below the tolerance threshold. Klaus's undoing was caused by an inept election campaign which over-emphasized past successes without offering a vision for the future.
>
> (*EEN*, 1996, vol. 10, no. 12, p. 6)

Political developments after the 1996 general election

27 June 1996: the existing coalition partners agree on the division of cabinet posts: Civic Democratic Party, eight posts (including finance, foreign affairs and interior); Christian Democratic Alliance/Czech People's Party, four posts; Civic Democratic Alliance, four posts.

25 July 1996: the Klaus coalition government wins a (delayed) vote of confidence in parliament by 98 to 40. (Sixty-two MPs were not present when the vote was taken.)

17 September 1996: Klaus concedes to demands by the Social Democratic Party for a parliamentary investigation into banking failures (*IHT*, 18 September 1996, p. 19).

9 October 1996: parliament passes the first reading of the 1997 budget bill.

> Four of the opposition Czech Social Democratic Party (CSSD) MPs voted with the government and two MPs abstained – despite strong pressure from the CSSD leader Milos Zeman to vote against the budget, possibly forcing Klaus's resignation. The CSSD is now embroiled in a potentially debilitating internal row, with Zeman portrayed as an authoritarian leader who is rapidly alienating CSSD MPs ... Zeman's personality is the main cause of the conflict. He is authoritarian, arrogant and habitually abrasive with his colleagues.
>
> (*EEN*, 1996, vol. 10, no. 21, p. 5)

15–16 November 1996: the first round of elections to the new, 81-member Senate takes place. A majority system in single-member constituencies is used to elect members for six years (with one third of members being re-elected every two years). The turnout is 35.5 per cent. The Senate will normally have no legislative powers, only the power to approve or reject bills already passed by the lower house. The Senate will assume interim legislative functions only when the lower house has been dissolved by the president prior to new elections (*EEN*, 1996, vol. 10, no. 22, p. 4). The Senate can draft and submit bills and it can return legislation to the lower house. But the lower house has the power to veto the Senate (*Business Central Europe*, December 1996–January 1997, p. 19).

The Social Democratic Party believes that the Senate should be abolished (*FT*, Survey, 6 December 1996, p. iii).

Only four candidates receive the required 50 per cent plus one vote of the registered voters, leaving seventy-seven to be decided in the second round to be held on 22–3 November. The Civic Democratic Party gains 36.5 per cent of the vote and three of their candidates win at the first attempt, compared with the Social Democratic Party's 20.3 per cent and one candidate respectively.

22–3 November 1996: in the second round of the Senate elections the turnout is only 30.5 per cent. The government coalition parties bring their total number of seats to fifty-two, compared with the Social Democratic Party's twenty-five.

The distribution of the 81 seats was as follows: Civic Democratic Party, 32; Social Democratic Party, 25; Christian Democratic Alliance/Czech People's

Party, 13; Civic Democratic Alliance, 7; Communist Party of Bohemia and Moravia, 2; Democratic Union (extreme right-wing), 1; Independents, 1.

9 December 1996: the parliamentary budget committee votes to reduce the 1997 defence budget.

13 December 1996: the House of Deputies approves the 1997 draft budget by one vote.

17 December 1996: Jan Kalvoda resigns as chairman of the Civic Democratic Alliance, as deputy premier/minister of justice and as an MP after admitting that he had lied about having a Doctor of Law title. (A Christian Democrat MP also resigns for the same reason. The governing coalition now has ninety-seven MPs: *EEN*, 1996, vol. 10, no. 25, p. 8.)

The Social Democratic Party vice-chairman Jozef Wagner (who is also chairman of the parliamentary budget committee) and another vice-chairman are sacked as deputies by the party executive for voting with the government in the 9 October budget debate (*EEN*, 1996, vol. 10, no. 25, p. 8).

18 December 1996: the Senate holds its first meeting and Petr Pithart is elected chairman.

A Social Democrat MP resigns because of the fraudulent use of a Doctor of Law title (*EEN*, 1996, vol. 10, no. 25, p. 8).

20 December 1996: the foreign ministers of the Czech Republic and Germany initial a declaration of reconciliation:

> The German side recognizes the responsibility of Germany for its role in a historical process that led to the Munich Agreement of 1938, the flight and expulsion of people from the Czechoslovakian border area and to the dismemberment and occupation of the Republic of Czechoslovakia. It deplores the suffering and injustice Germans inflicted on the Czech people by National-Socialist crimes. The German side is also aware that the National-Socialist policy of violence against the Czech people helped to create the basis for the post-war flight, expulsion and forced resettlement.
>
> The Czech side deplores the fact that the expulsion that followed the end of the war and the forced resettlement of Sudeten Germans from the former Czechoslovakia inflicted great suffering and injustice on innocent people, as was also true of the collective nature of the ascribing of guilt. It especially deplores the excesses that took place in contradiction of elementary humanitarian principles and the legal norms in effect at the time.

(After the Second World War 2.5 million ethnic Germans were expelled from the Sudetenland and their property was confiscated. In the declaration of 20 December 1996 there was no provision by the Czech Republic for a restitution of property or financial compensation for the Sudeten Germans. A DM 160 million fund for social and cultural initiatives, mainly financed by Germany, was to be set up to help victims of the war. The joint fund to help both sets of victims was set up on 3 October 1997.)

Agreement on the Czech–German Fund for the Future to aid Czech victims of Nazism was reached on 29 December 1997, although the question of who was to manage the fund was left unresolved because of a dispute over the number of Sudeten Germans to be included in management. The DM 165 million fund, set to begin functioning on 1 January 1998, was to provide for the building and operation of pensioners' homes and sanatoriums for about 8,000–8,500 Czech survivors of Nazism (about a quarter of whom are Jewish, the others including Gypsies, Catholics, Jehovah's Witnesses, homosexuals and political prisoners). The fund would also be used for joint projects such as youth conferences, the care of memorials, and joint scientific and ecological projects to foster better understanding between the Czech and German peoples. Germany was to release DM 20 million in 1998 and DM 40 million in each of the following three years. The Czech Republic was to contribute DM 20–25 million to the fund (*IHT*, 30 December 1997, p. 5; *FT*, 30 December 1997, p. 2).

('Chancellor Gerhard Schröder … used the occasion of the visit this month [March 1999] by the Czech prime minister, Milos Zeman, to announce that Germany would never seek compensation on behalf of more than 2 million Sudeten Germans … Mr Zeman, in turn, said that the 1945 laws that led to that expulsion were defunct, although he stopped short of questioning the legitimacy of the decrees': Roger Cohen, *IHT*, 15 March 1999, p. 4.)

21 January 1997: prime minister Klaus and Chancellor Kohl sign the declaration of reconciliation. (President Havel missed the signing because he was recuperating from lung cancer surgery.)

30 January 1997: the German Bundestag approves the declaration of reconciliation.

14–16 March 1997: the Social Democratic Party's congress 'was dominated by the longstanding clash between the radical and pragmatic wings of the party' (*EEN*, 1997, vol. 11, no. 6, p. 5).

19 March 1997: the Czech Republic and Norwegian companies sign a twenty-year agreement to supply annually about 3 billion cubic metres of natural gas. This will diversify the Czech Republic's supply, since at present Russia's Gazprom (which considers the Norwegian deal to be incorrect and economically unjustified) supplies annually all 9 billion cubic metres (*IHT*, 22 March 1997, p. 11).

22–3 March 1997: Michael Zantovsky is elected chairman of the Civic Democratic Alliance.

25 March 1997: Tomas Teplik, a Social Democratic Party MP, defects to the Civic Democratic Party, giving the coalition government a parliamentary majority of one (*EEN*, 1997, vol. 11, no. 6, p. 8).

> Tomas Teplik … has been expelled [from the Social Democratic Party] as has … Jozef Wagner … [who] though he would be independent, would in future vote with the government. As a result of these two expulsions the government coalition has 101 votes, the opposition only ninety-nine.
>
> (p. 5)

16 April 1997: an economic reform package is introduced. (See below.)

20–1 April 1997: Russian prime minister Chernomyrdin visits the Czech Republic.

24 April 1997: President Havel addresses the German parliament.

25–7 April 1997: the Pope visits the Czech Republic.

24 May 1997: three ministers resign, namely the finance, interior, and trade and industry ministers. (Economic problems provided the backdrop, including balance of payments difficulties, speculation against the crown, bank collapses and corruption.)

10 June 1997: Klaus wins a vote of confidence in the (200-seat) House of Deputies by 101 votes to 99. ('The vote was won thanks to the support of former Czech Social Democratic Party MP Jozef Wagner, who … extracted from Klaus a commitment to set in motion the privatization of the state banks which still control much of the industrial economy': *EEN*, 1997, vol. 11, no. 12, p. 5.)

8 July 1997: the Czech Republic (but not Slovakia) is invited 'to begin accession talks with Nato'. (The foreign ministers of the sixteen Nato countries signed the protocol of accession on 16 December 1997.)

16 July 1997: the European Commission recommends that the Czech Republic (but not Slovakia) open negotiations in early 1998 for entry to the EU. (The invitation was formally approved at an EU summit on 13 December 1997, formal negotiations for membership beginning on 31 March 1998. Slovakia, Latvia, Lithuania, Bulgaria and Romania were to be given special EU aid to help them meet the conditions necessary for membership negotiations to begin.)

21 October 1997: interior minister Jan Ruml announces his resignation.

23 October 1997: foreign minister Jozef Zieleniec resigns, citing turmoil in his Civic Democratic Party (*IHT*, 24 October 1997, p. 5). He also steps down as deputy leader of the party. Zieleniec criticized Klaus 'for bypassing him when making important cabinet and party policy decisions' (*EEN*, 1997, vol. 11, no. 21, p. 5). Zieleniec also cited a lack of transparency in party financing (*IHT*, 28 November 1997, p. 7).

29 November 1997: Jiri Skalicky replaces Michael Zantovsky as chairman of Civic Democratic Alliance (*EEN*, 1997, vol. 11, no. 23, p. 7).

30 November 1997: prime minister Klaus resigns, although he denies knowledge of party donations which were the immediate cause of the crisis. (A large contributor to the Civic Democratic Party's funds was only recently discovered after the original donor names proved to be incorrect. The actual contributor, who had been successful in the privatization of a steel enterprise in October 1995, denoted a large sum in November 1995. There were also allegations that there was a party bank account in Switzerland containing corporate donations from successful participants in privatization. Prime movers against Klaus included finance minister Ivan Pilip and former interior minister Jan Ruml.) (On 6 December a small bomb exploded outside the home of Ivan Pilip: *EEN*, 1997, vol. 11, no. 23, p. 2.)

A subsequent independent audit by an international accounting firm concluded that the Civic Democratic Party had 'systematically misrepresented' its political donations. The party failed to record certain donations and recorded false names for other sums (*Business Central Europe*, June 1998, p. 13). The party violated tax, accounting, political party and campaign finance laws (p. 18).

14 December 1997: Klaus is re-elected as chairman of the Civic Democratic Party with 72 per cent of the vote. He thus easily defeats Jan Ruml.

17 December 1997: central bank governor Josef Tosovsky is appointed prime minister.

30 December 1997: the new prime minister nominates his seventeen-strong cabinet, a combination of former ministers and six non-partisan experts. Four members are from the Civic Democratic Party, including Ivan Pilip (who remains finance minister). Josef Lux (head of Christian Democratic Alliance/Czech People's Party) retains agriculture and Jiri Skalicky (head of the Civic Democratic Alliance) retains environment. Jaroslav Sedivy (non-party) remains foreign minister. The defence portfolio goes to a former diplomat, Michal Lobkowicz. (Vaclav Klaus has already ruled himself out.) (*IHT*, 31 December 1997, p. 7; *FT*, 31 December 1997, p. 2.)

'The four Civic Democrats nominated for the new government are anti-Klaus rebels' (*The Economist*, 3 January 1998, p. 33).

'The appointments of Mr Pilip and Mr Lobkowicz were considered most controversial since both had opposed Mr Klaus publicly and inspired the party rebellion against him' (*IHT*, 31 December 1997, p. 7).

After a meeting with the new prime minister the previous day, Klaus said that his party would neither support nor participate in the new government (*FT*, 31 December 1997, p. 2).

2 January 1998: President Havel formally appoints the new government.

5 January 1998: Klaus: 'They [the four Civic Democrats] should either stop using the abbreviation of our party behind their names or quit the government' (*FT*, 6 January 1998, p. 3).

8 January 1998: Ivan Pilip resigns from the Civic Democratic Party (ODS): 'Because the ODS has decided not to clarify its financial scandals ... I have decided to end my membership.'

12 January 1998: the caretaker government announces that an early general election will be held on 19 June 1998.

15 January 1998: thirty MPs leave the Civic Democratic Party and form a new party called Freedom Union.

20 January 1998: Vaclav Havel is re-elected president, although by a surprisingly narrow margin. This is his second and final (five-year) term of office.

In the first round of voting an absolute majority was required in each house but Havel won only 91 (of the 200) votes in the lower house and 39 (of the 81) votes in the Senate. Miroslav Sladek (leader of the Republican Party who is currently in jail charged with inciting racial hatred) and Stanislav Fischer (supported by the Communist Party) won a total of 31 and 23 votes respectively Only Havel entered the second round of voting where an absolute majority of those parliamentarians present was needed. He secured 99 votes in the lower house, a majority of only 1 among the 197 deputies present. (Miroslav Sladek was not allowed to vote as he was in jail.) He secures 47 votes in the Senate. (*FT*, 21 January 1998, p. 2; *IHT*, 20 January 1998, p. 5, and 3 February 1998, p. 4.)

23 January 1998: Miroslav Sladek is acquitted by a judge of having incited national hatred (*EEN*, 1998, vol. 12, no. 2, p. 8).

20 February 1998: Jiri Skalicky resigns as deputy prime minister, environment minister and leader of the Civic Democratic Alliance after admitting that the party had accepted donations from three businesses (*FT*, 21 February 1998, p. 2).

14 April 1998: Vaclav Havel has an emergency operation in Austria to remove part of the large intestine. (Three more operations followed and he did not return to Prague until 6 May 1998.)

15 April 1998: the Chamber of Deputies approve Nato membership by 154 votes to 38. (The Senate gave its approval on 30 April.)

The general election of 19–20 June 1998

The Civic Democratic Alliance decided not to run. Its popular support fell below 1 per cent after campaign funding scandals (*Business Central Europe*, June 1998, p. 13).

The turnout was 74 per cent. The parties competed for the 200 seats in the House of Deputies on the same basis as before: 100 per cent proportional representation, no minimum national turnout and a 5 per cent threshold for individual parties (7 per cent for alliances).

Although the Social Democratic Party gained the expected first place, the election threw up a number of surprises:

1 Vaclav Klaus's Civic Democratic Party came through very strongly towards the end.

> Klaus ... staged a remarkable political recovery, increasing his support from only 10 per cent in opinion polls three months ago to 27.7 per cent in this weekend's vote, mainly by playing on fears of communism ... The Social Democrats increased their vote from 26.4 per cent in 1996 to 32.3 per cent. However, they failed to convince middle-class urban voters, the core of Mr Klaus's constituency, they had nothing to fear from a left-wing government.
>
> (Robert Anderson and Stefan Wagstyl, *FT*, 22 June 1998, p. 26)

> The Czech Republic is the only country in post-communist Europe where the right has ruled without a break since the fall of communism nearly a decade ago. But despite widespread popular discontent with the Thatcher-like economic policies of Mr Klaus, falling living standards and the corruption and mismanagement that marred his rule, the Czechs apparently decided not to take a chance.
>
> (Peter Green, *IHT*, 22 June 1998, p. 4)

2 Both Miroslav Sladek's Radical Party (whose share of the vote fell from 8.01 per cent in the 1996 election to 3.9 per cent) and the Pensioners for a Secure Life failed to reach the 5 per cent threshold. The latter had polled nearly 10 per cent in pre-election voter surveys (*IHT*, 22 June 1998, p. 4). 'Sladek and his colleagues' vicious and well-publicized election campaign evidently pushed voters into Klaus's arms. As for the pensioners, they had little organization and no follow-up, instead coming across as tongue-tied, even faintly idiotic' (*EEN*, 1998, vol. 12, no. 7, p. 2).

The results were as follows:

Social Democratic Party: (32.31 per cent of the vote and 74 seats). Led by Milos Zeman. The deputy leader, Mr Svoboda, has suggested that the budget deficit could exceed 3 per cent of GDP to finance housing and infrastructure investment. It remains to be seen whether the party intends to implement these measures after the election (Deutsche Bank Research, *Emerging Europe Weekly*, 12 June 1998, p. 2). Policies include a budget deficit of 3 per cent of GDP to kick start growth, active industrial and export policies, a slowdown in price deregulation and a slowdown in privatization (especially of big banks) (*FT*, 15 June 1998, pp. 3, 29).

> Zeman has pledged to slow down privatization, regulate the markets, keep key utilities under state control, and engage in deficit spending. He has also toyed with the idea of a swingeing millionaire's tax and scrutinizing the books of those boasting fortunes of more than £2 million and requiring them to prove that their wealth was acquired cleanly.
>
> (Ian Traynor, *Guardian*, 22 June 1998, p. 12)

Civic Democratic Party: (27.74 per cent of the vote and 63 seats). Led by Vaclav Klaus.

Communist Party of Bohemia and Moravia: (11.03 per cent of the vote and 24 seats). Led by Miroslav Grebenicek.

Christian Democratic Alliance/Czech People's Party: (9.0 per cent of the vote and 20 seats). Largely backed by farmers and devout Roman Catholics (*IHT*, 22 June 1998, p. 4).

Freedom Union: (8.6 per cent of the vote and 19 seats). Formed on 15 January 1998. Led by Jan Ruml.

Political developments after the 1998 general election

22 June 1998: President Havel asks Milos Zeman to try to form a government.

8 July 1998: the Social Democratic Party announces (to general surprise and after failure to form a coalition government) that it will form a minority government with the support of the Civic Democratic Party. Vaclav Klaus will become speaker of the House of Deputies. The need for political stability is stressed.

> They [Zeman and Klaus] have apparently worked out a compromise. It has been agreed, it seems, that utility prices and household rents will be liberalized more slowly. The sale of utilities will also be gradual. State-owned banks will not now be sold off until 2000 or so. And Mr Klaus's people, overturning past policy, say they will now stomach a budget deficit.
>
> (*The Economist*, 11 July 1998, p. 48)

Under the agreement the Civic Democratic Party will permit the formation of a minority government by leaving parliament during the vote on approval. In exchange the Civic Democratic Party will be allowed to appoint the speakers of both chambers of parliament and the chairmen of key parliamentary committees. Both parties agreed not to initiate a no-confidence vote during the lower chamber's four-year term and not to push to dissolve the chamber before the term's end. Each side promised not to form a coalition or an alliance with a third party to the detriment of the other (*IHT*, 11 July 1998, p. 10).

10 July 1998: Zeman announces the end of further restitution of church property and that state banks (the 'big four') will be sold off to finance primarily new housing (*EEN*, 1998, vol. 12, no. 9, p. 4).

17 July 1998: Milos Zeman is formally appointed prime minister by President Havel.

22 July 1998: President Havel appoints a minority Social Democrat Party cabinet. The cabinet includes the following: Milos Zeman (prime minister); Egon Lansky (deputy prime minister and foreign affairs and security – defence minister Vladimir Vetchy reports to Lansky); Pavel Mertlik (deputy prime minister and economic policy); Ivo Svoboda (finance); Jan Kavan (foreign affairs); Vaclav Grulich (interior); Miroslav Gregr (industry and trade).

(In his regular radio address, a few days after the appointments ceremony, Havel described the agreement between the Social Democratic Party and the Civic Democratic Party as contrary to the principles of democracy. He vowed to step in if the parties used the agreement to 'abuse power': *EEN*, 1998, vol. 12, no. 9, pp. 1–2.)

Josef Tosovsky is reappointed to the governorship of the central bank.

26 July 1998: Havel has a successful stomach operation to restore the digestive tract.

3 August 1998: Havel undergoes a (fourth) tracheotomy to aid his breathing amid concern that he may develop pneumonia.

4 August 1998: Havel is 'temporarily' in a critical condition owing to heart problems.

19 August 1998: the government wins a vote of confidence in parliament. As arranged, the Civic Democratic Party left before the vote was taken.

20 August 1998: the Russian president, Boris Yeltsin, comments on the thirtieth anniversary of the Warsaw Pact invasion of Czechoslovakia: '[The Prague

Spring was] an attempt to escape from ideological dogmatism and lies. Even shy attempts at reform called down terror from those who wanted to preserve the totalitarian system.'

28 August 1998: Havel leaves hospital.

24 September 1998: Christian Democrat leader Josef Lux resigns on health grounds. He is replaced by party deputy chairman Jan Kasal (*EEN*, 1998, vol. 12, no. 11, p. 5).

November 1998:

> Czech voters delivered a rebuff to the ruling Social Democrats in the country's local and Senate elections. In the local elections the Social Democrats gathered only 17.5 per cent of the vote, against 24.3 per cent for the ODS, party of former premier Vaclav Klaus. In the Senate elections [eighty-one seats] the Social Democrats won only twenty-three seats, compared with the ODS's twenty-six. But the big winner was the four-party centre-right coalition dominated by the Christian Democrats, which won twenty-eight seats.
>
> (*Business Central Europe*, December 1998–January 1999, p. 110)

15 January 1999: parliament approves the 1999 budget.

> The budget was passed at third reading by 114 votes to 83 with the help of Communist and Christian Democrat deputies. The Christian Democrats' vote has added to speculation that the party may soon enter the cabinet and caused a rift with their allies, the centre-right Freedom Union … The new budget envisions a deficit of … about 1.6 per cent of GDP and no longer includes a rise in pension contributions. The budget is the first to plan a deficit … The 1998 balanced budget ended in deficit.
>
> (*FT*, 16 January 1999, p. 4)

12 March 1999: the Czech Republic, Hungary and Poland become members of Nato at a signing ceremony in Independence, Missouri, USA (where Nato was founded on 4 April 1949 during the presidency of Harry Truman), raising membership from sixteen to nineteen. It was in Missouri, at Westminster College in Fulton on 5 March 1946, that Winston Churchill delivered his famous speech: 'From Stettin in the Baltic to Trieste in the Adriatic an iron curtain has descended across the Continent.'

'Mikhail Gorbachev … said that he felt "betrayed" by Nato's expansion, adding that the West was taking advantage of Russia's weakness and humiliating Russians in ways like the Allies' treatment of defeated Germany after World War I' (*IHT*, 13 March 1999, p. 4).

20 July 1999: 'Prime minister Milos Zeman dismissed [finance minister] Ivo Svoboda, who has been attacked for his business dealings, the widening budget deficit and a bungled bond sale. Deputy prime minister Pavel Mertlik was named to the post' (*IHT*, 21 July 1999, p. 15).

> Milos Zeman … yesterday sacked his finance minister, Ivo Svoboda, after he was charged with defrauding creditors of a company he had once managed. The dismissal was widely expected … His reform-minded replacement, Pavel Mertlik, will continue as deputy prime minister for economic affairs.
>
> (*FT*, 21 July 1999, p. 2)

13 October 1999: the European Commission recommends that EU leaders at the December 1999 meeting in Helsinki allow Bulgaria, Latvia, Lithuania, Malta, Romania and Slovakia to begin accession negotiations in 2000.

The 'principle of differentiation' for entry date will apply to each of the twelve candidates, reflecting differing states of readiness for EU entry. A 'fully flexible, multi-speed accession process' is envisaged. 'Each country will be able to proceed on merit, including the possibility for those which join the negotiations from 2000 to catch up with the others.' The European Commission thinks that existing EU members should undertake internal reforms by the end of 2002: 'Whether the first accessions can take place as from 1 January 2003 will then depend entirely on the speed with which the applicant countries can make progress on meeting the criteria.'

Malta and Cyprus have already met the economic terms set by the EU, being able to cope with competitive pressures and market forces in the EU. Hungary and Poland come next in economic terms, followed by Slovenia, Estonia and then the Czech Republic. Hungary, Poland, Estonia and Slovenia have improved their ability to cope with competitive pressures and market forces 'in the medium term' (meaning more than one year from 2000). Hungary is the closest of the Eastern European countries to meeting the criteria on a market economy with the capacity to withstand competition within the EU.

The Czech Republic is making uneven and generally sluggish progress in adopting EU laws. The Czech Republic has lost ground in the past twelve months. It qualifies as a functioning market economy, but its 'situation gives rise to concern'.

(*FT*, 14 October 1999, pp. 1, 10; *IHT*, 14 October 1999, p. 5; *Guardian*, 14 October 1999, p. 14; *Independent*, 14 October 1999, p. 18; *The Times*, 14 October 1999, p. 21; *Telegraph*, 14 October 1999, p. 20.)

'The Commission still sees a Kafkaesque shadow of impenetrable bureaucracy. Public administration is badly managed, the government's economic policies incoherent, and there is widespread discrimination against the country's 250,000-strong Roma minority' (*Business Central Europe*, November 1999, p. 40).

(For further details, see the Hungary entry for 10 December 1999.)

The authorities in Usti nad Labem build a concrete wall to separate Gypsy council housing from private homes.

24 November 1999: the authorities in Usti nad Labem pull down the concrete wall built on 13 October 1999 to separate Gypsy council housing from private homes. The authorities have decided to buy the homes of three families who complained most about the noise from the Gypsy area. The central government and the president have criticized the action of the local authority.

'The wall had become a focus of international criticism over the treatment of the 300,000 Gypsies in the Czech Republic' (*IHT*, 25 November 1999, p. 7).

> A wall built to segregate Romany council tenants from their neighbours was pulled down yesterday [24 November] after it threatened the Czech Republic's hopes of joining the EU. Usti nad Labem council in north Bohemia agreed to demolish the two-metre high wall it built last month [October] and to buy three houses beyond the wall whose owners had complained about the behaviour of their Romany neighbours. The government, which had demanded the wall be demolished, will provide a ... subsidy.
>
> (*FT*, 25 November 1999, p. 11)

> The central government has started to take measures to improve the lot of the impoverished Roma community. There are new committees and Gypsy advisors, and new schools. And the thousands of Roma who had Czech citizenship removed by the government of Vaclav Klaus are now having it returned. But tackling decades of Roma exclusion is an awesome task.
>
> (*Business Central Europe*, December 1999–January 2000, p. 56)

1 December 1999: Freedom Union chairman Jan Ruml resigns (*EEN*, 2000, vol. 12, no. 21, p. 5).

2 December 1999: parliament votes to lift the statute of limitations for crimes committed by former communist officials between 1948 and 1989. The law applies to crimes committed by public officials or crimes committed during persecution of individuals and groups of citizens. The law needs Senate approval (*IHT*, 3 December 1999, p. 5).

3 December 1999: an estimated 50,000 people demonstrate in Prague demanding a new government and fresh elections. They call for the resignation of Milos Zeman and Vaclav Klaus. The organizers of the movement, six former student leaders who led the protests against the communist government in 1989, call for new leaders to help prepare the country for EU membership and restore faith in democracy. The movement started in November (*IHT*, 4 December 1999, p. 7).

The 'Thanks, now leave' movement holds nationwide demonstrations calling for the resignation of main party political leaders. Nearly 50,000 people attend the rally in Prague. There is a call for an end to the entente between the Czech Social Democratic Party and the Civic Democratic Party. The former student leaders first issued the appeal ('Thanks, now leave') on 17 November 1999, calling for party political leaders to resign, an appeal subsequently signed by around 100,000 Czech citizens (*EEN*, 2000, vol. 12, no. 21, p. 5).

14 January 2000: regional activists from the 'Thank you, now leave' movement hold an inaugural meeting to form a new right-wing political party, as yet unnamed (*EEN*, 2000, vol. 12, no. 22, p. 5).

28 January 2000: the lower house of parliament passes a constitutional amendment reducing the powers of the president.

> The key part of the amendment is that when a premier resigns the whole government must now step down, and the president must then ask the next largest parliamentary party to try to form a government. When Vaclav Klaus resigned in 1998 Havel put in central bank governor Josef Tosovsky as caretaker premier.
>
> (*EEN*, 2000, vol. 12, no. 22, p. 2)

22 May 2000: Slovakia and the Czech Republic announce a formal end to their property dispute. (The Czech Republic and Slovakia reached agreement on 24 November 1999 on long-standing property disputes, including cross-border stakes in major banks: *IHT*, 25 November 1999, p. 7.)

26 May 2000: parliament passes an election law amendment providing for an increase in the number of constituency seats from eight to thirty-five (the remainder being proportional representation) (*EEN*, 2000, vol. 12, no. 23, p. 9).

The lower house of parliament passes an amendment to the election law. The amendment increases the number of constituencies from eight to thirty-five, introduces the d'Honte method of allocating seats and requires that coalitions of four or more parties win at least 20 per cent of the vote in order to be represented in the lower house. The amendment is to be challenged in the constitutional court (*FT*, 29 May 2000, p. 8).

23 June 2000: on 23 June the Senate passed a controversial amendment to the electoral law, giving dominance to majority seats rather than proportionally elected ones. President Havel vetoed the amendments and returned to the lower house, which overturned the veto on 10 July. On 17 July President Havel requested the constitutional court to rule against implementation of parts of the new electoral law passed by parliament (*EEN*, 2000, vol. 12, no. 24, p. 5).

14 July 2000:

> The Czech parliament yesterday [14 July] approved amendments restricting central bank independence that the European Central Bank believes are incompatible with EU rules. The lower house voted by 121 votes to 32 to force the central bank to consult the government before setting its inflation target or changing the exchange rate regime, and to report to the parliament at least twice a year on monetary development … Other changes give the government, rather than the bank governor, the power to nominate the bank's board.
>
> (*FT*, 15 July 2000, p. 5)

6 August 2000:

> The Czech Senate has rejected a new central bank bill on the grounds that it compromises the bank's independence and violates the constitution. The

> bill, which has been criticised by the European Central Bank, must now be approved again by the lower house but is likely to face further obstruction from President Vaclav Havel and the constitutional court before it takes effect in January [2001].
>
> (*FT*, 7 August 2000, p. 6)

> On Friday [27 October] the lower house voted to overrule a Senate veto. President Vaclav Havel yesterday [30 October] vetoed proposed legislation which he said compromised the independence of the Czech National Bank … Mr Havel's veto means the bill will have to be approved for a third time.
>
> (*FT*, 31 October 2000, p. 10)

> Mr Havel has returned the bill to the lower house and he is expected to refer it to the constitutional court when it is passed again … Josef Tosovsky, governor of the Czech National Bank, yesterday [31 October] resigned … effective from 1 December.
>
> (*FT*, 1 November 2000, p. 9)

26 September 2000: there takes place the official opening in Prague of the annual meeting of the IMF and the World Bank.

10 October 2000: the Temelin nuclear power station is started up despite strong objections from Austria in particular.

8 November 2000: the latest EU report is published. There is recognition of the progress that the Czech Republic has made but familiar criticisms remain.

The EU's report on the Czech Republic (*Progress Towards Accession*, 8 November 2000, p. 103):

> The reform of public administration has not advanced significantly … The reform of the judiciary is equally a short-term priority … The fight against corruption and economic crime has so far been insufficient … A lasting improvement in the situation of the Roma requires sustained effort over time … The Czech Republic can be regarded as a functioning market economy and should be able to cope with competitive pressure and market forces within the Union in the near term, provided that it keeps up and completes the implementation of structural reforms … The strengthening of competition and of supervision in the financial sector is crucial in order to reinforce macroeconomic policies and to foster economic activity … The efforts to privatize and restructure the state-owned enterprises must continue and corporate governance must improve.

(For further details, see the entry for Hungary.)

November 2000:

> [In] elections for a third of senatorial seats … the ruling Social Democrats took a trouncing … The turnout was very low indeed at 34 per cent … The

> losses suffered by the Social Democrats have benefited a fistful of minority parties in the Senate … Those minority parties are precisely those that dominate the lower house.
>
> (*Business Central Europe*, December 2000–January 2001, p. 42)

'The Social Democrats now have just fifteen seats in the Senate, while the "Quad Coalition" of four smaller parties have thirty-nine between them' (Business Central Europe 2000: 23).

Regional and Senate elections were held on 12 November 2000.

> The ruling Czech Social Democracy Party fails to win any seats. The turnout is little over 30 per cent. The 'Quad' coalition leads in the Senate elections. Vaclav Klaus's ODS wins in regional elections. The second round of Senate elections [held on 19 November] produces a turnout of only 20 per cent. The 'Quad' coalition wins sixteen out of nineteen second round contests.
>
> (*EEN*, 2001, vol. 13, no. 2, p. 4)

The Quad coalition comprises the Christian Democrats, Freedom Union, the Democratic Union and the Civic Democratic Alliance. The Quad is now led by Jiri Svoboda of the Christian Democrats. He was elected on 28 January 2001. In the 80-member Senate the Social Democratic Party has 15 seats, the ODS 22, Quad 39 and the KSCM communists 3. 'A majority of local councils are now run by Quad and the ODS' (*EEN*, 2001, vol. 13, no. 2, p. 2).

24 November 2000: President Havel names Zdenek Tuma as governor of the central bank despite criticism by Zeman and Klaus (*FT*, 24 November 2000, p. 12). 'Zdenek Tuma became the new head of the Czech National Bank after the resignation of Josef Tosovsky. The government challenged the decision' (Business Central Europe, 2000: 11). (Tuma was previously deputy governor of the central bank.)

> Late last year [2000] parliament amended the 1992 banking law, in order to give parliamentarians more control over the bank … Starting this year [2001] parliament will take over control of the bank's budget for policy-making and overheads, including salaries … Another amendment requires the finance ministry to work with the central bank on setting exchange rates and inflation targets … Finally, members of parliament gave themselves a voice in picking board members and the governor – a task previously reserved for the president. But that change remains frozen by a legal challenge, led by President Vaclav Havel, for which the constitutional court has yet to schedule a hearing.
>
> (*Business Central Europe*, February 2001, p. 41)

20 December 2000: 'Public television news … journalists are refusing to accept the appointment last week [on 20 December] of Jiri Hodac as station director.

They contend that he has connections to politicians and would seek to increase political control over the service' (*IHT*, 26 December 2000, p. 4).

> Staffers at the [state-run Czech television] station's news department have refused to recognize new management appointed on 20 December and blocked the newsroom to editors named by the managers ... Jiri Hodac ... was elected to run the station by the country's nine-member broadcasting council. The council is nominated by parliament.
>
> (*IHT*, 27 December 2000, p. 5)

> President Vaclav Havel voiced support Wednesday [27 December] for news staff members at Czech Television ... Mr Havel said ... that Mr Hodac's appointment might have followed the letter of the law but was 'against its sense, its spirit. And that is immensely dangerous' ... Journalists, backed by other employees, unions and a large section of the management, refuse to recognize the selection of Jiri Hodac as director-general by the Czech Television Council.
>
> (*IHT*, 28 December 2000, p. 7)

> In a statement the journalists said: 'All of us face a danger that before elections [due in 2002] Czech TV will become an obedient instrument of the people in power' ... Mr Havel is widely known to despise Mr Klaus and the two men have been trying to undercut each other for years ... Mr Klaus would like to succeed Mr Havel as president in 2002 and has worked with prime minister Milos Zeman ... to cut back on Mr Havel's powers ... Mr Zeman and Mr Klaus have tried to change the electoral law to make it harder for small parties to get into parliament and to prevent Mr Havel from naming the new director of the central bank without reference to parliament. But Mr Zeman's party [the Social Democratic Party] did not do well in this year's Senate elections, and this strange coalition of convenience lost its majority in the upper house, making Mr Klaus's selection as the next president, who is elected by parliament, more dicey. In return ... Jiri Pehe, an adviser to President Vaclav Havel ... suggests [that] ... Mr Zeman agreed to let Mr Klaus and his allies take control of the television.
>
> (Steven Erlanger, *IHT*, 29 December 2000, pp. 1, 4)

'The fight between Mr Havel and Mr Klaus, known here as "the battle of the two Vaclavs", has defined recent politics, with Mr Klaus opposing the rapid entry into the EU that Mr Havel favours' (Steven Erlanger, *IHT*, 4 January 2001, p. 5).

> Yesterday [27 December] Mr Havel ... compared Mr Hodac's appointment to the communist takeover of Czechoslovakia in 1948, which was done 'in an absolutely legal way and in accordance with the wording of the law, but against the spirit of the ... constitution' ... The journalists say the appoint-

> ment was forced through by … Vaclav Klaus and Mr Hodac is there to bias the news in Mr Klaus's favour.
>
> (*Independent*, 28 December 2000, p. 12)

'Vaclav Klaus … is known to favour privatization of state television' (*The Times*, 29 December 2000, p. 19).

1 January 2001:

> On Monday [1 January] Czech television staff began warning strikes … The crisis is the culmination of two years of interference by the Czech Television board into the station's management which has led to the departure of two director generals … Seven of the board's nine members were nominated by the two big parties.
>
> (*FT*, 3 January 2001, p. 7)

3 January 2001:

> At least 50,000 Czechs came out into the cold Wednesday night [3 January] to give their support for striking television journalists … Some fifty television journalists have barricaded themselves in their newsrooms since 23 December [2000] … and have tried to put out rival newscasts. Mr Hodac had a troubled four months last year [2000] as news director before resigning … The journalists say Mr Hodac once applied to be Mr Klaus's spokesman. They also oppose his appointment of Jana Bobosikova, a former Klaus adviser, as news director. Mr Hodac denies political bias and has tried to fire thirty of the dissident journalists, who have tried to protect themselves legally by declaring a strike … According to the journalists, more than 330,000 people have signed a petition in their support … In a emergency session Wednesday [3 January] the relatively powerless Czech Senate called for Mr Hodac to resign.
>
> (*IHT*, 4 January 2001, p. 5)

'More than 120,000 people have signed a petition in support of the strikers' (*FT*, 3 January 2001, p. 7). 'The huge demonstration in Wenceslas Square was a triumph for Czech Television staff who have occupied the station's newsroom for two weeks … Seven of the nine-member board that named Mr Hodac last month were chosen by the two dominant parties' (*FT*, 4 January 2001, p. 6).

'Almost 200,000 Czechs have signed a petition protesting at Mr Hodac's appointment' (*Guardian*, 13 January 2001, p. 17).

At least 50,000 demonstrated (*The Economist*, 6 January 2001, p. 34). Other reports put the number of demonstrators in Prague at about 90,000 (*The Times*, 4 January 2001, p. 15; *Telegraph*, 4 January 2001, p. 18) and around 100,000 (*Independent*, 4 January 2001, p. 11; *Guardian*, 4 January 2001, p. 12; *IHT*, 7 January 2001, p. 6, and 9 January 2001, p. 5).

4 January 2001:

> Jiri Hodac was taken to hospital after what appeared to be a breakdown from exhaustion ... The feud has inspired the Social Democratic cabinet to speed up a legal amendment that would dismiss the council that chose Mr Hodac and replace it with a body elected from candidates proposed by professional and civic groups, not by politicians.
>
> (*IHT*, 5 January 2001, p. 2)

'A Czech Television spokesman said Jiri Hodac had suffered a heart attack. Other reports hinted at a nervous breakdown' (*Telegraph*, 5 January 2001, p. 19).

> [On 8 January] Mr Hodac ... left the hospital where he was admitted after suffering what was suspected to be a heart attack ... A resolution [was] approved on Saturday [6 January] by the lower house of parliament urging that Mr Hodac step down ... In its resolution parliament urged the supervisory panel – the Czech Television Council – to dismiss Mr Hodac if he refused to quit ... The public broadcaster has been in disarray since staff journalists holed up in the newsroom beginning 20 December [2000] to demand Mr Hodac's resignation.
>
> (*IHT*, 9 January 2001, p. 5)

On 11 January 2001 Jiri Hodac resigned, the announcement coming before large-scale demonstrations took place across the country. The reason given for his resignation was ill health.

> But tens of thousands of demonstrators still gathered here [in Prague] to back journalists' demands that those supporting Mr Hodac also quit and cleanse the network of what they call political appointees. More than 50,000 ... flooded Wenceslas Square ... Journalists at the network who refused to work under Mr Hodac announced that they would continue their strike until his supporters were also dismissed and other demands were met ... Mr Hodac's announcement came only hours after two members of the panel resigned to protest its failure to dismiss him earlier this week.
>
> (*IHT*, 12 January 2001, p. 4)

'[On 17 January] journalists took over the station's headquarters ... [and] appointed their own director ... Later the police asked the journalists to leave the premises, which they did without incident' (*IHT*, 18 January 2001, p. 7).

24 January 2001: a constitutional court ruling cancels several key parts of the new electoral law (that favour the larger parties) (*EEN*, 2001, vol. 13, no. 2, p. 2). 'The constitutional court upholds President Havel's objections to various key parts of the proposed new election law, including the increase in the number of electoral regions from eight to thirty-five' (p. 5).

28 January 2001:

> The Quad Coalition of four small centre-right parties surprisingly elected Cyril [Jiri] Svoboda as their nominee for prime minister at the weekend, despite the fact that he was not one of the three proposed candidates. Mr Svoboda, a former chief negotiator with the EU and interior minister, is on the left wing of the Christian Democrats … Mr Svoboda, forty-four, was a compromise choice after the two dominant parties in the coalition – the Christian Democrats and the Freedom Union – rejected each other's proposed candidates.
>
> (*FT*, 30 January 2001, p. 10)

10 February 2001: 'Striking journalists signed a deal with their new interim director, Jiri Balvin … Saturday after he met most of the strikers' demands, including the firing of several unpopular figures' (*IHT*, 12 February 2001, p. 4).

'The Czech constitutional court struck down parts of a controversial new election law that would have split the country into thirty-five electoral districts, favouring the ruling Social Democrats and the opposition ODS' (*Business Central Europe*, February 2001, p. 12).

10 April 2001:

> Pavel Mertlik, the Czech finance minister, resigned yesterday [10 April] after being repeatedly defeated in cabinet by Miroslav Gregr, the interventionist industry minister. The resignation of the Social Democrats' leading economic reformer will increase worries that the minority government will ignore the country's yawning budget deficit and gamble on a pre-election boom.
>
> (*FT*, 11 April 2001, p. 11)

'Pavel Mertlik … resigned to protest his lack of influence over key government decisions, raising fears of delays in privatizations and other fiscal changes' (*IHT*, 11 April 2001, p. 18).

> The country's finance minister has resigned after losing numerous political battles over plans to privatize and clean up state companies … Pavel Mertlik, who pushed through the privatization of major Czech banks and who fought demands to pump money into virtually bankrupt industrial conglomerates, said he was quitting because he could no longer influence government policy … His biggest battles have been with the minister of trade and industry, Miroslav Gregr, who has repeatedly pushed for big, new government spending to shore up Czech industry and who opposed Mr Mertlik's efforts to rapidly privatize the state-owned power and gas companies. Mr Mertlik adamantly opposed most efforts to spend government money on troubled industrial conglomerates like Skoda … and Tatra … Earlier this year … the government closed down an unusual agency he supported to clean up and then sell off the country's biggest and most troubled companies. Known as the revitalization

> agency, it was run by Western investment bankers who were given the responsibility for reorganizing the companies without additional government money. But the agency came under repeated attack from Mr Gregr and government officials ultimately refused to let the investment bankers plan to acquire control of the conglomerates' bad loans. The revitalization office ceased operations last month [March] and its activities were taken over by a new government agency … Mr Mertlik resigned after losing another battle Monday [9 April] over privatizing the state-owned gas and electric companies … The government rejected his calls for accelerated privatization and cancelled a decision on hiring advisers for the deal. Several other senior government officials resigned Tuesday [10 April] along with Mr Mertlik. One was the deputy finance minister, Jan Mladek. Another was Jiri Havel, head of the national property fund, which oversees the privatization of state-owned property.
>
> (*IHT*, 12 April 2001, p. 6)

> Finance minister Pavel Mertlik resigned amid rows over energy privatization and the large budget deficit. His deputy, Jan Mladek, and privatization chief Jiri Havel also resigned. New finance chief Jiri Rusnok promised more fiscal prudence, but the cabinet also approved a controversial $7 billion spending plan … Cyril Svoboda, leader of the opposition Quad Coalition, resigned just two months after he was elected. A row over its shadow cabinet has undermined attempts to consolidate the four-party grouping.
>
> (*Business Central Europe*, May 2001, p. 12)

> [In April] premier Milos Zeman stepped down as chairman of the Social Democrats … [He was replaced by the] labour and social affairs minister Vladimir Spidla … Two weeks earlier Karel Kuehnl replaced Cyril Svoboda as head of the Quad Coalition … Two members of the Quad Coalition's shadow cabinet quit.
>
> (*Business Central Europe*, May 2001, pp. 43–4)

25 May 2001: 'Czech legislators voted Friday [25 May] to compensate people who were members of the resistance against the Nazis during World War II and victims of persecution under the country's former communist regime' (*IHT*, 26 May 2001, p. i, supplementary page).

May–June 2001:

> The Quad's recent fall in popularity reflects concern over Freedom Union rather than doubts about the KDU–CSL [Christian Democrats] … At the end of May the KDU–CSL party congress elected a new chairman, Cyril Svoboda … [who has] a reputation for impeccable moral character. Svoboda earlier this year resigned as Quad chairman … On 23 June Freedom Union chairman Karel Kuehnl stood down and was replaced by Hana Marvanova.
>
> (*EEN*, 2001, vol. 13, no. 5, p. 3)

THE ECONOMY

The Czech Republic has never had a serious inflation problem by the standards of transitional countries. The inflation rate peak was a relatively modest 56.7 per cent in 1991. The unemployment has been remarkably low. There was a tax on excessive wage increases until mid-July 1995. Price liberalization has been extensive. (The only remaining significant price controls pertain to utility charges, rents and public services. In addition mark-ups are closely regulated in the energy sector: EBRD 1994: 23. The government established after the June 1998 elections has not continued with energy price deregulation: EBRD 1999b: 2111. Energy prices were scheduled to be fully adjusted to cost-recovery levels by the end of 2002: EBRD 2000a: 50. 'Significant [energy] tariff increases have occurred recently ... with a commitment ... that household electricity and gas prices will be raised to cost-recovery levels by the end of 2002': EBRD 2001: 29.) But not everything in the Czech garden has been lovely by any stretch of the imagination. GDP did not start to grow again until 1994 and concern has been expressed about things like widening trade deficits, financial scandals (and bank failures), the corporate guidance exercised by investment funds, and the regulation of capital markets. Some of the problems are as follows:

1 Otto Pick argues that

> The Czech Republic is one of the most heavily taxed countries in Europe, with the top rate of income tax running at 42 per cent and the [top] rate of VAT at 23 per cent. As a result, large-scale tax evasion and tax avoidance are the order of the day. At the same time the heavy tax burden discourages investment, especially as the government is adamant in its refusal to grant any tax privileges to domestic or foreign investors.
>
> (*The World Today*, November 1994, p. 208)

2 Much restructuring of industry remains to be done. The 1991 bankruptcy law did not go into effect until 22 April 1993 and actual bankruptcies, although increasing in number, have been relatively few. (Creditors are not keen and the government has, for example, deferred tax bills in order to avoid large-scale unemployment.) In fact, debtor companies whose shares are at least 50 per cent voucher-privatized are protected from bankruptcy during privatization, specifically until two months after the shares have been transferred to new owners. The law also provides a three-month protection period (which may be extended to six months with court approval) to allow firms to come to an agreement with creditors (Brom and Orenstein 1994: 898). Private farmers were to be protected from bankruptcy until December 1994 (EBRD 1994: 22). 'In the Czech Republic there has not been a single major bankruptcy since the collapse of communism' (*The Economist*, 31 May 1997, p. 87).

3 Much has been made of the important role played by banks in investment funds and the degree to which the banks remain owned by the state. (Most investment funds are owned by the large banks, of which the state still owns, on average, 40 per cent and to which former state enterprises are heavily indebted. The banks are naturally reluctant to call in their loans: Portes 1994: 1186–7. In mass privatization the large banks have become, through their investment funds, the most significant owners of the privatized sector: Brom and Orenstein 1994: 893. The government still owns approximately 40 per cent of each of the largest banks: p. 895.)

> Since the funds [in the first wave of privatization] collected investment points only, most Czech funds were strapped for cash. Consequently, some funds were known to make claims on newly privatized firms, such as demanding excessive dividends, that could have a questionable effect of firm values.
>
> (Hingorani *et al.*: 1997: 393)

> The Czech Republic has got it badly wrong, because it is insulating industrial owners, and therefore management, from the very market forces which must be allowed to shape industry ... The Czechs ... have still failed to impose any form of market governance on industry, let alone provide a framework for direct restructuring ... The country has yet to have a major bankruptcy ... The bulk of the voucher funds are controlled by domestic banks, and this combined with appallingly lax capital market regulation in allowing Czech industry to stagnate – there are at most four funds in the country interested in hands-on restructuring or even active trading ... Control of the bulk of industry is ... concentrated in the hands of banks using their influence to grab banking business – which in the Czech Republic means loan financing.
>
> (*Business Central Europe*, May 1996, pp. 11–13)

> The crisis in the Czech banking sector stems from two widely acknowledged problems: continuing political control and the disgraceful state of the Czech stock exchange. State meddling makes banks more concerned with preserving Czech industry than with commercialism. Inadequate bourse regulation allows corporate drift, with companies treating minority shareholders with contempt, while compliant banks which should be controlling them let managers do as they like. The result is rudderless Czech industry, and the danger of companies becoming uncompetitive. And if that happens, then bad debts will bring down the banks ... State control of Czech banks is grotesquely blatant. Not only does it retain a chunk of each of the four banks, but their supervisory boards are crammed with representatives of the National Bank and the Ministry of Finance. So the Czechs must make true bank privatization a priority. This means involving international investors ... The only way to deal with the corporate governance

> problem is a complete ban on banks owning non-financial companies. Similarly, the use of investment funds to build up industrial empires must be stopped. Chinese walls to prevent insider dealing between investment and commercial banking arms are non-existent. The Czechs must therefore pass strict legislation to separate the two. This would prevent investment funds (and their managers) owning controlling stakes in companies, and banks lending money to companies in which they hold direct or indirect stakes. Only then will companies be forced to restructure in order to compete for scarce finance.
>
> (*Business Central Europe*, October 1996, p. 7)

> The Czech market is suffering one of its worst slumps since the fall of communism in 1989 ... The problem with Prague, according to fund managers, is the prevalence of foul play in the market and the unwillingness of Czech regulators to enforce even the modest rules enacted by the legislature.
>
> (Peter Green, *IHT*, 9 November 1996, p. 17)

Hewer (1997) concludes that only the largest Investment Privatization Funds, those holding significant stakes in a few enterprises in selected sectors, met expectations as regards enterprise governance and restructuring (p. 17).

> Most funds are passive investors and have not bothered to replace the managers of the companies they control ... Commercial banks find it more attractive to extend loans to their traditional clients, rather than get involved in debt restructuring or reorganizing production, including bankrupting unviable enterprises ... Apart from in foreign-owned enterprises, few managers seem to have been replaced.
>
> (p. 18)

> There is plenty of evidence that the structure of the Czech economy has undergone substantial change over a brief period of time: more than a million jobs have been created in the service sector, exports have been reorientated dramatically, and purchase of capital and equipment goods represents an important share in total imports ... At the enterprise level considerable 'passive' restructuring of assets and liabilities has taken place initially ... But evidence of successful physical restructuring is less compelling. Except in sectors representing traditional strongholds of the Czech economy, such as glass and ceramics production, most products have not yet reached world class levels. There are, however, examples of significant improvements in enterprise performance, especially when they involve strategic partnerships with foreign investors, such as the Skoda–Volkswagen enterprise.
>
> (p. 18)

An Organization for Economic Co-operation and Development (1998) report states that the Czech voucher approach to privatization produced ownership structures that 'impeded efficient corporate governance and restructuring'. The problem was that insufficiently regulated privatization investment funds ended up owning large or controlling stakes in many firms privatized through vouchers, as citizens sought to limit their risk by transferring their vouchers into these funds in exchange for shares in the latter. But many of the largest funds were owned by major domestic banks, in which the Czech state retained a controlling or majority stake. The results, say critics, were predictable:

1 Investment funds did not pull the plug on poorly performing firms, because that would have forced the funds' bank owners to write down the loans they had made to these firms. The state-influenced, weakly managed and inexperienced banks tended to extend credit to high-risk, unpromising privatized firms (whether or not they were owned by subsidiary funds) and to persistently roll over credits rather than push firms into bankruptcy.
2 The bankruptcy framework was weak and the process lengthy, further diminishing financial market discipline.
3 The lack of prudential regulation and enforcement mechanisms in the capital markets opened the door to a variety of highly dubious and some overtly illegal actions that enriched fund managers at the expense of minority shareholders and harmed firms' financial health.

(Nellis 1999: 17)

There is an urgent need for some more effective bankruptcy legislation. At the moment creditors have few rights, because bankruptcy laws are based on nineteenth-century German and Austrian ones designed to prevent company collapses, and it is next to impossible for creditors to get their money back until then – debtors must agree to their assets being seized ... There are plans to amend the bankruptcy act.

(*Business Central Europe*, December 1999–January 2000, pp. 50, 52)

I do not share the opinion held by some that the entire transformation process was misconceived, badly thought out and poorly directed. I would say rather that our problem is precisely the opposite. The transformation stopped half way, which may well be the worst thing that could have happened to it. Yes, all manner of enterprises have been formally privatized, but which of them have clear and specific owners who are fully committed to enhancing their productivity and their long-range prospects? ... How, then, can we expect the desired restructuring of companies and entire branches of industry when there are so few transparent owners and when so many managers see their jobs, their missions, their commitments as no more than opportunities to cream off the money entrusted to them by someone

> else and then walk off the job? The role our banks often play in this seems very strange to me. They indirectly own companies that lose money, and the more those companies lose, the more the banks lend them. A small businessman is unable to borrow half a million crowns for a sensible and specific investment, while some shady pseudo-entrepreneur can easily borrow half a billion without anyone taking a hard look at what he actually needs it for … Do we really have to pay for the rapidity of our privatization process – a rapidity that was welcome and proper – with stolen billions, even tens of billions of crowns?
>
> (Vaclav Havel, *The New York Review of Books*, vol. XLV, no. 4, 5 March 1998, p. 44)

> Especially in the Czech Republic … [there are] scams such as 'tunnelling'. In one guise, this involves powerful shareholders inducing the company management to make loans to shell companies which then disappear; in others, it means buying assets at inflated prices and selling them very cheaply. The insiders sell their shares before news leaks out.
>
> (*The Economist*, Survey, 22 November 1997, p. 15)

> It has been revealed that investment fund managers were able to sell controlling shares of smaller firms through shady 'bypass enterprises' to investors who were ready to pay – not over the counter but under the table – fat premiums above the shares' market price. This 'tunnelling' of assets clearly undermines trust and makes a mockery of fair business practices.
>
> (Joseph Stiglitz, *Transition*, 1997, vol. 8, no. 6, p. 1)

> The investment fund managers sell company shares in the portfolio to dummy companies at absurdly cheap prices. The dummy companies sell the shares on the market. The dummy companies deposit the ensuing profits into overseas bank accounts. The fund investors (the trusting public) are left with nothing. But that's the least of it. The Czech public is now learning that dishonest operators have systematically squeezed the assets from many of the country's best companies, its municipalities, and its banks (private and state-owned). The locals have coined a charming euphemism for the criminals – tunnellers. The tunnellers have achieved their wealth primarily through the corrupt collusion or, at the very least, the benign neglect of the state.
>
> (Andrew Schwartz, *Transition*, 1997, vol. 8, no. 6, p. 4)

'[Tunnelling is] the widespread practice whereby managers or controlling shareholders secretly raid a healthy firm's cash flow for personal gain, or to cross subsidize unprofitable subsidiaries' (*Business Central Europe*, April 1999, p. 26).

> The adverse effects of privatizations leading to asset stripping, rather than wealth creation in the presence of inadequate corporate governance (in the

> context of the Czech Republic often referred to as 'tunnelling'), is corroborated in research showing that privatizations in those economies in transition and without strong corporate governance do not lead to faster growth.
>
> (James Wolfensohn and Joseph Stiglitz, *FT*, 22 September 1999, p. 22; James Wolfensohn is president of the World Bank and Joseph Stiglitz is the World Bank's chief economist and senior vice-president)

The lack of regulation has led to phenomena such as stock manipulation, including the bidding up of shares and insider trading. There have been cases where investment funds have indulged in asset-stripping. A Czech finance ministry report lists fifteen ways that investment funds and their managers have used to enrich themselves at the expense of enterprises and the capital markets. Because minority shareholders had no protection under the law the corporate raiders discovered, the report says, 'a risk-free method of removing money from companies' (Jane Perlez, *IHT*, 3 December 1997, p. 17).

> We use the term 'tunnelling', coined originally to characterize the expropriation of minority shareholders in the Czech Republic (as in removing assets through an underground tunnel), to describe the transfer of assets and profits out of firms for the benefit of those who control them.
>
> (Johnson *et al.* 2000: 22)

But others are not so pessimistic as regards restructuring.

> Czech manufacturers have been cutting up to 30,000 jobs a month in the period since 1990 as part of their restructuring efforts. Because these workers have subsequently found employment elsewhere, our rate of unemployment has stayed very low. Coupled with our surge in industrial output … this 'leaning down' has been behind the jumps in industrial productivity … These rises indicate the basic fallacy in the conventional wisdom analysis. It is these very same companies, allegedly about to undergo urgently needed restructurings, that have manufactured the modern, competitively priced products selling so well on domestic and foreign markets … Rather than a single wave now breaking over all our companies, each of our companies has been engaged in its own highly individual process of restructuring since the beginning of the revolution … Of course, this process is not fully completed, and restructuring will take place in the future. The [conventional wisdom] analysis also fails to take account of the prime product of our country's economic transformation: our newly founded, small-scale manufacturers … which now account for 20 per cent of our total industrial revenues.
>
> (Vladimir Dlouhy, minister of industry and trade, quoted by Terry Swartzberg, *IHT*, Survey, 25 April 1996, p. 13)

Since 1995 there has been a consolidation of ownership among many enterprises, commonly known as the 'third wave' of privatization. An active role has been played by investment funds, some of which have converted into holding companies (see below). 'Some unofficial estimates suggest that by mid-1996 many companies included in the mass privatization programme had either dominant or majority owners. These trends, combined with the increase in fixed investment, are an indication that further restructuring is underway' (EBRD 1996b: 147). Despite a variety of concerns expressed during the implementation of mass privatization, the investment funds 'have maintained liquidity, have taken a long-term and active role in enterprise management and are acting like "real" owners' (Brom and Orenstein 1994: 917). Kenway and Klvacova (1996: 806) draw a number of interim conclusions about cross-ownership in the privatized financial sector:

> That it exists, and on quite a substantial scale; that it masks the extent of continuing state ownership, although while the Fund of National Property remains passive that is of little significance; and that, by providing incentives for co-operation between funds, it helps to strengthen the intermediaries as a whole when individually they are weak.

Up to the end of 1992 the former large state industrial enterprises were broken up on average into three independent enterprises either prior to or during the privatization process (United Nations Economic Commission for Europe 1994: 167). The average number of employees per industrial enterprise has fallen from 1,665 in 1990 to 360 (*Transition*, July–August 1994, vol. 5, no. 6, p. 21). Pohl *et al.* (1997) analysed data for more than 6,000 industrial enterprises in seven countries (Bulgaria, the Czech Republic, Hungary, Poland, Romania, Slovakia and Slovenia).

> Our comprehensive analysis shows that privatization has been the single most important determinant of success. Privatized firms have increased productivity three to five times more than similar state-owned firms. The method of privatization has been less important. Massive giveaways of firms through voucher privatization or management buy-outs have had results similar to case-by-case sales to foreign or domestic investors.
>
> (p. 15)

> Initially it was believed that mass privatization and management–employee buy-outs would not lead to much restructuring. Our results do not confirm these fears. One indicator is productivity growth. It is slightly higher in the Czech and Slovak Republics, which implemented mass privatization programmes, than in Hungary and Poland, which relied more on case-by-case privatization. The results are similar for profitability: the Czech

> Republic now has the highest percentage of profitable firms and the lowest percentage of financially distressed firms in the region.
>
> (pp. 16–17)

> We analyze worker mobility during the period from 1994 to 1998 in the Czech Republic ... Many researchers have argued that the low unemployment in the Czech Republic during most of the 1990s reflected a lack of restructuring of the economy ... Counter to this view we show that the Czech labour market achieved greater shifts in the structure of sectoral employment than the other transition economies and that it did so at a lower cost in terms of incidence and duration of unemployment.
>
> (Sorm and Terrell 2000: 432, 451)

> We conclude that the Czech labour market has demonstrated considerable flexibility when compared to other transition economies; hence the low unemployment rate was not a sign of a lack of sectoral restructuring. There has been a significant shift in the structure of employment away from the traditional sectors to the new ones needed in a market economy.
>
> (p. 452)

'We show that there has been significant movement into the finance, trade and tourism sectors and out of the agricultural and industrial sectors' (p. 431).

A bold package of economic reforms was introduced on 16 April 1997 (*Business Central Europe*, May 1997, p. 19; *FT*, 17 April 1997, p. 3; *IHT*, 29 April 1997, p. 13). The package included the following measures:

1 Reductions in government spending. Excise taxes to be increased, but corporate tax to be cut from 39 per cent to 35 per cent from the beginning of 1998. (Bank reserve obligations were to be reduced, however.)
2 A 7.3 per cent limit to the growth of wages in the public sector, with pressure on the private sector to follow suit.
3 The accelerated restructuring or liquidation of remaining state enterprises. Strengthened bankruptcy legislation and procedures to investigate delays in bankruptcies. An independent securities commission to supervise capital markets. Regulations to limit the connections between banks, investment funds and enterprises (e.g. the separation of banks' lending and portfolio management functions) and to tackle fraud in investment funds. Faster privatization and improvement of corporate governance through sales to foreign strategic partners or managerial groups.
4 As of 21 April 1997 importers to deposit 20 per cent of the value of foodstuffs and consumer goods in non-interest-bearing accounts for 180 days. Exporters to be helped through loans and guarantees. (In May 1997 parliament passed an anti-dumping law to protect Czech producers. The April 1997 import deposit scheme, designed to halt the deterioration in the trade balance, was abolished in August 1997: EBRD 1997b: 165.)

Further austerity measures were announced on 28 May 1997, including expenditure cuts, tightened monetary policy and a freeze on wages in the government and in state enterprises (*IHT*, 30 May 1997, p. 18).

Severe flooding affected much of the eastern part of the country in July 1997. In July and August 1997 the government commenced the issue of five-year 'flood bonds' to help meet the costs (EBRD 1997b: 166). A 'flood tax' was considered but then rejected. Estimates of the flood damage vary: the government said it amounted to more than $1.8 billion (with fifty lives lost in the Czech Republic and fifty-five in Poland) (*FT*, Survey, 1 December 1997, p. iii); $2–3 billion or at least $1.75 billion (*Business Central Europe*, September 1997, pp. 17, 24); $2 billion (5 per cent of GDP) (Deutsche Morgan Grenfell, *Focus: Eastern Europe*, 5 September 1997, p. 22). Severe flooding in July 1997 caused damage equivalent to 3.5 to 4 per cent of GDP and accounted for about a half of 1 percentage point of the decline in GDP growth in 1997 (IMF, *World Economic Outlook*, May 1998, p. 54).

In early November 1997 the lower house of parliament passed an amendment to the Banking Act (Robert Anderson, *FT*, 10 November 1997, p. 2). As of 1 January 1998 the following were to apply:

1. Banks would not be allowed to control more than 50 per cent of the shares of non-financial companies.
2. Banks would have to limit their exposure to any one non-financial company to 15 per cent of a bank's capital and, in addition, limit the total value of all stakes of 10 per cent or more held by a bank in non-financial companies to 60 per cent of its capital.
3. Banks would not be allowed to appoint their employees to the boards of non-financial companies.
4. Banks would be forced to set up Chinese walls between investment and commercial banking activities (i.e. segregated activities) and to separate proprietary and non-proprietary trading.

In early November 1997 parliament approved the creation of a new securities commission (called the Commission for Securities Trading) to oversee the operations of the Prague stock exchange. It was to be answerable (controversially) to the finance ministry. The aim was to make it operational by February 1998 (*FT*, Survey, 1 December 1997, p. iv). Parliament insisted that the commission be funded by the state rather than stock exchange members. Parliament also deprived it of rule-making powers, which will remain with the finance ministry. Moreover, the commission's top people will be government-appointed and not subject to parliamentary approval (*Business Central Europe*, December 1997–January 1998, p. 55). The new securities commission started work on 1 April 1998.

On 17 April 1998 the lower house of parliament approved new legislation on investment funds.

> After numerous frauds and incidents when stakes were traded with little concern for fundholders' interests, fund shares now trade at a discount of about 30 per cent to the net asset value per share (NAV) of their investments. After the amendment passes the Senate later this summer all funds will be forced to become open-ended by the end of 2002, allowing shareholders to redeem their shares at their NAV rather than the stock exchange trading price. Funds which are trading at a 40 per cent discount to NAV will be forced to become open-ended in the first year after the amendment is passed. The amendment also cuts the maximum stake a fund can hold from 20 per cent to 11 per cent by the end of 2000. Together with the need to raise cash to pay shareholders, this will compel funds to sell the large shareholdings they built up using the vouchers.
>
> (Robert Anderson, *FT*, 20 April 1998, p. 2)

> The chaos of recent years is subsiding … The surviving privatization funds – those that were not gutted by thieves – are gradually transforming themselves into reputable mutual funds … Some of the crooks used a regulatory loophole to create holding companies, beyond the reach of the securities commission. They transformed privatization funds into holding companies in order to grab the coupon money or strip company assets before they closed up shop. That loophole was belatedly closed in 1998 … Some [fund managers, however] saw opportunities to make an honest profit as well as contribute to the Czech transition. Since 1999 they have co-operated with a securities commission order to transform the two kinds of voucher-holding mechanisms – so-called investment funds and closed-end funds – into private, closely regulated, open-end mutual funds. The securities commission's goal is to stop the funds being strategic investors in Czech companies and turn them into global portfolio investors … As early as 1996, when it was clear that the securities commission had lost control over the coupon system, some of the funds began regulating themselves. They did so by forming UNIS [the Union of Investment Companies].
>
> (*Business Central Europe*, June 2001, pp. 36–7)

Privatization

Adrian Bridge (*Independent*, 20 January 1994, p. 12) reported a draft law returning properties expropriated from Jews during the period of Nazi rule. The Jewish community, which now numbers only 3,000, compared with 120,000 before the Second World War, will be handed back synagogues, cemeteries, libraries and other community buildings that were confiscated by the Nazis and are still in state hands. The law was passed on 2 May 1994. In July 1994 the constitutional court ruled as follows: (1) the residence clause (claims could be made only by permanent residents) had to be removed; (2) the six-month deadline set in 1991 for claims to property by those living in exile was too short and November 1994 should be the new deadline (Deutsche Bank, *Focus: Eastern Europe*, 1994, no. 112,

p. 7). On 8 March 1995 the constitutional court upheld a 1945 decree issued by President Eduard Benes stripping ethnic Germans of their property (*IHT*, 9 March 1995, p. 2). On 10 July 1998 prime minister Milos Zeman announced the end of further restitution of church property (*EEN*, 1998, vol. 12, no. 9, p. 4).

There are varying estimates of the importance of the private sector, but some idea can be given from the following. The private sector's share of GDP rose from close to zero in 1989 to about 18 per cent in 1992 and some 50 per cent in 1993 (United Nations Economic Commission for Europe 1994: 168). Three 1994 sources said that the private sector accounted for around 60 per cent of GNP (Deutsche Bank, *Focus: Eastern Europe*, 22 March 1994, no. 100, p. 16; *EEN*, 4 January 1994, vol. 8, no. 1, p. 3; *Guardian*, 26 February 1994, p. 33).

Rough estimates in mid-year of the private sector as a percentage of GDP are provided by the EBRD: 1990, 10 per cent; 1991, 15 per cent; 1992, 30 per cent; 1993, 45 per cent; 1994, 65 per cent; 1995, 70 per cent; 1996, 75 per cent; 1997, 75 per cent; 1998, 75 per cent; 1999, 80 per cent; 2000, 80 per cent (EBRD 1999b: 24, 212, and 2000b: 14, 156).

The second and final round of large (voucher) privatization was set to involve around 861 enterprises and take place in the second half of 1993 (the starting date for voucher sales later being fixed for 30 September). The first of the auction rounds was subsequently fixed for 11 April–12 May 1994. The second round was completed on 25 November 1994 (EBRD 1995a: 55). Following the completion of mass privatization, sales of state enterprises have continued through standard methods (direct sales, public auctions and public tenders). By the first quarter of 1996 over 90 per cent of all the property originally designated for inclusion in the large privatization programme had been transferred into private ownership. In addition, the national property fund retains shareholdings either as residual holdings in partly privatized enterprises or through its holdings in designated 'strategic' enterprises. The national property fund is currently selling its residual holdings. Before the (1996) general election the government indicated its intention of privatizing the strategic enterprises by direct sales, including sales to foreign strategic partners. Towards the end of 1995 the sale of 49 per cent of the state petrochemical company and 27 per cent of SPT Telecom to two consortia of Western companies were finalized. The new government has yet to announce its decision on the privatization of other 'strategic' entities, such as the railways and the utilities. Investment funds are restricted to holding no more than 20 per cent of the shares of any one enterprise, while the holding in any one enterprise cannot represent more than 10 per cent of the investment fund's portfolio. Some funds have converted themselves into holding companies (EBRD 1996b: 146–8). A recent amendment to the investment law has permitted investment funds to transform themselves into holding companies and thus take majority stakes in the enterprises (p. 16). Mass voucher privatization, the dominant method of privatization, was undertaken in two waves. It has been estimated that 58 per cent of large companies were privatized via vouchers, while 14 per cent were privatized via direct sales (EBRD 1998b: 162). The state has retained significant ownership stakes in mines, steel mills, chemical companies, oil refineries, regional energy distribution companies and other large enterprises such as Ceske Energeticke Zavody (CEZ), SPT Telecom and the two largest banks (Komercni Banka and Ceske Sporitelna). While the pace of privatization has been slow in the last twelve months, with only bank privatization advancing, private investors have gained substantial shares in the mining and energy distribution companies through consolidation of publicly traded shares and acquisition of shares held by municipalities. However, in the case of regional distribution companies the state's ownership has risen above 50 per cent following share purchases in the market by CEZ and Transgas, two state enterprises. In response to significant problems in the industrial sector (such as declaring the bankruptcy in early 1999 of Chemapol, a holding company controlling most of the chemical industry), the government set up a restructuring agency in May 1999. It was envisaged that the agency would target a limited number of large companies to safeguard employment and industrial capacity (EBRD 1999b: 210–11).

> Although privatization is well advanced, the state retains significant ownership stakes in enterprises such as telecommunications, steel mills, chemical companies, oil refineries and energy sector companies. The government has announced an acceleration of the privatization process.
>
> (EBRD 2000a: 50)

'The government reinvigorated the privatization process in 2000 ... The remaining 30 per cent share in Skoda Auto was sold to Volkswagen in June 2000' (EBRD 2000b: 154). 'The main focus is now on selling state shares in the banking sector and large infrastructure enterprises, such as those in the telecommunications and energy sectors' (EBRD 2001: 28). 'The government plans to proceed quickly with large-scale privatization this year [2001] ... The revitalization agency ... set up in May 1999 ... merged with Konsolidacni Banka in February 2001 to streamline revitalization efforts' (EBRD 2001: 58).

According to Deutsche Bank (*Focus: Eastern Europe*, 31 March 1993, no. 72, p. 7), only 30 per cent of the book value of enterprises was to be accounted for by vouchers as opposed to 60 per cent in the first round. Investors gave 72 per cent of their points to investment funds in the first round but only 64 per cent in the second round (Brada 1996: 73). Only 65 per cent of people entrusted their vouchers to investment funds, compared with 72 per cent in the first round (*Business Central Europe*, April 1994, p. 58). According to *Prague News* (7–21 April 1994, p. 1), the 353 investment funds will have some 60 per cent of registered vouchers at their disposal, ten percentage points less than in the first wave.

The National Property Fund still has a stake of more than 20 per cent in 400 enterprises (*The Economist*, 20 May 1995, p. 93). Investment funds control about 29 per cent of all outstanding shares, while the National Property Fund holds 40 per cent and industrial and portfolio investors own 25 per cent. The top twenty or so investment funds obtained 90 per cent of those vouchers entrusted (*FT*, Survey, 2 June 1995, p. vi).

After the second round of privatization the state retained a significant stake in only a few large utilities such as the national power utility CEZ and the petrochemical conglomerate Chemapol. Chemapol was the subject of much indecision about whether to involve foreign companies and only at the 13 July 1994 cabinet meeting was it decided to allow an international oil consortium to take a large minority stake (*EEN*, 1994, vol. 8, no. 4; *EEN*, Czech Republic Country Briefing, 21 July 1994, p. 3).

At the peak, 60 per cent of the population owned shares in privatized enterprises, a proportion now thought to have fallen to about 40 per cent (OECD, *Economic Outlook*, June 1996, p. 104). The Prague stock exchange opened on 6 April 1993.

> The Czech government yesterday [14 April 1999] agreed a plan to take several struggling private companies back under state control before selling them on to strategic investors ... Within a month the Social Democrat government will establish a development agency, led by a foreign adviser, which will take charge of loans made to up to thirty selected companies by state-controlled banks. The agency will take control of the indebted companies, typically through a debt–equity swap, then extend or guarantee new working capital and install professional managers who will prepare for the entry of a strategic investor.
>
> (*FT*, 15 April 1999, p. 3)

'The Czech government came up with a new version of its long-awaited "revitalization" plan. The plan envisages an agency, owned jointly by the state and banks, which will temporarily take control of problem companies' (*Business Central Europe*, May 1999, p. 9).

> A revitalization agency will be set up, with half or more of its shares held by local banks and by its management company – a foreign investment bank to be chosen by tender. The agency will take controlling stakes via debt–equity swaps in less than ten companies, chosen on the basis of their strategic importance to the economy and their future liability ... The agency will replace the existing management and dilute shareholdings. Once the firms are 'revitalized' – planned for around 2002 – the agency will look for new buyers. The scheme could cost as much as $1 billion.
>
> (p. 24)

> Industry minister Miroslav Gregr ... wanted to bail out a pile of companies and leave them under the same management. Fortunately he lost out to more reformist voices, led by finance minister Pavel Mertlik ... [The companies to be revitalized are the chemical companies Aliachem and Spolana; the engineering companies CKD and Skoda Plzen; the truck company Tatra; the textile company Tiba; the steel company Vitkovice; and the tractor company Zetor] ... The present revitalization scheme [is] run by

hospital bank Konsolidacni ... Under it the UK investment bank Lazard will try to sell seven struggling companies to foreigners. That will almost certainly mean splitting them up ... In the meantime the companies are back in state hands, and will probably stay there for the next few years ... But for revitalization to succeed there is an urgent need for some more effective bankruptcy legislation. At the moment creditors have few rights, because bankruptcy laws are based on nineteenth-century German and Austrian ones designed to prevent company collapses, and it is next to impossible for creditors to get their money back until then – debtors must agree to their assets being seized ... There are plans to amend the bankruptcy act ... [There are] thousands of companies reentering state control as Konsolidacni buys bad debts from the big privatizing banks ... There are no concrete plans to deal with them.

(*Business Central Europe*, December 1999–January 2000, pp. 50, 52)

One year on the sceptics have still to be proven wrong about the Revitalization Agency, the government's ambitious programme for industrial restructuring. Last October [1999] Latona Associates of Europe and Lazard Frères signed up to manage the agency, a subsidiary of Konsolidacni Banka (KOB), the state bank for working out bad debts. They were handed out a list of eight of the country's biggest and most troubled enterprises and instructed to prepare restructuring plans and search for foreign investors ... The government has carried out several massive carve-outs from the big state-owned banks which have concentrated bad loans in KOB. It now has 197.5 billion crowns of loans on its books, of which 62 per cent are non-performing. This has meant that the state is now directly the biggest creditor of the target companies and, if it is not already, can become the main shareholder too through debt for equity swaps or buying out owners. Skoda Plzen [the engineering group], CKD [the engineering group], the Tatra truck-maker, and Zetor [the tractor producer] have effectively been renationalized. But this highlights a weakness of the agency. Political interests, notably the interventionist industry ministry, are keen to get involved ... The agency has started to financially restructure Skoda Plzen, Tatra and Vitkovice, the state-owned steel group. KOB has sold CKD's freight car division and the CHZ Sokolov chemical company, while Latona and Lazards managed the sale of ZPS [ZPS Zlin, the machine tool manufacturer] on behalf of its administrator. Yet even at Vitkovice and Skoda Plzen, which are making huge job cuts, real operational restructuring is still in its early stages.

(Robert Anderson, *FT*, Survey, 26 September 2000, p. v)

Miroslav Gregr ... the minister for trade and industry ... [is] notorious for his Revitalization Act of 1999, which saw the state renationalizing several troubled firms ... [He] now wants to throw 265 billion crowns ($7 billion) at reviving the economy in general and industry in particular ... [including]

> bailing out the old industrial zombies … Even as Mr Gregr announced his latest plans in mid-February [2001], the revitalization agency created to carry out the first scheme shut. It has been folded into the state bail-out bank Konsolidacni … Western advisers … will be retained to sort out the four companies [out of seven] left in the scheme. Of the others chemicals-makers Spolan and Aliachem have already been sold to Western firms, while tram-maker CKD was already being handled directly by Konsolidacni, rather than the agency.
>
> (*Business Central Europe*, March 2001, p. 19)

> [Gregr's] revitalization plan [was] unveiled in March [2001] … The Strategy for Promotion of National Economic Growth … calls for the government to steer privatization proceeds, local government funds and private money into projects to benefit key industries and create jobs in depressed regions, such as North Bohemia. The support could include subsidies for e-commerce projects and export promotion … Despite Mr Gregr's clout, the cabinet has been debating the strategy for months.
>
> (*Business Central Europe*, June 2001, p. 47)

Further developments in privatization

On 10 July 1998 prime minister Milos Zeman announced that state banks (the 'big four') would be sold off to finance primarily new housing (*EEN*, 1998, vol. 12, no. 9, p. 4).

On 21 January 1998 agreement in principle was announced of the sale of the state's 36 per cent stake in Investicni a Postovni Banka (the country's third largest bank by assets) to Nomura International, a Japanese investment bank. This was approved by parliament on 5 March 1998. Agrobanka, which is under central bank administration, is in the process of being sold to General Electric Capital of the USA (*FT*, Survey, 8 May 1998, p. iv, and Survey, 14 May 1998, p. iii; *IHT*, 23 January 1998, p. 13).

('Masked police armed with machine guns occupied the headquarters of the Czech Republic's third largest bank Friday [16 June 2000] as regulators wrested Investicni a Postovni Banka from its largest shareholder, Nomura International PLC, after a rush by retail customers to withdraw deposits from the troubled bank … Analysts said Nomura did little more than pump some fresh capital into the bank and arrange for other Nomura subsidiaries to buy attractive industrial assets held by an investment bank that Nomura controlled': *IHT*, 17 June 2000, p. 11. 'Investicni a Postovni Banka [IPB], the Czech bank put into forced administration last week, is to be taken over by Ceskoslovenska Obchodni Banka [CSOB, the former trade finance bank], owned by KBC of Belgium … The takeover of the third biggest bank by the fourth will transform the Czech banking sector … Three of the four big banks are now foreign owned … Nomura Securities indirectly held 46 per cent of IPB's shares': *FT*, Tuesday 20 June 2000, p. 38. 'The deputy finance minister said yesterday [22 June] that the bank's shareholders – the largest of whom was Nomura Securities of Japan – had failed to strengthen the bank's capital when requested and would lose their entire investment': *FT*, 23 June 2000, p. 10. 'On 16 June the central bank put Investicni a Postovni Banka (IPB), the third-largest Czech bank, into forced administration. By 19 June it had found a buyer ... Ceskoslovenska Obchodni Banka ... The merger will create the Czech Republic's largest retail bank ... Analysts were widely scathing of Nomura's involvement, noting that its losses were more than offset by the sale of some juicy industrial assets held by IPB – such as some Czech breweries': *The Economist*, 24 June 2000, p. 124.)

Privatization is also to involve other banks. State-owned shares amount to 48.7 per cent in Komercni Banka (the country's largest commercial bank), 45 per cent in Ceska Sporitelna (the former state savings bank and the largest retail bank) and 65.6 per cent of CSOB (Ceskoslovenska Obchodni Banka, mainly involved in financing foreign trade). Parliament approved the government's banking privatization plans on 4 September 1997. But the sale of Komercni Banka and CSOB is complicated by the Slovak government's claimed stakes of 16 per cent (13 per cent, according to the Czech government) of the former and of 24.1 per cent of the latter. (*IHT*, Survey, 23 September 1997, p. 13; *FT*, 22 September 1997, p. 3, 22 September 1997, p. 3, and Survey, 14 May 1998, p. iii.)

On 22 June 1998 it was announced that GE Capital, the financial services arm of the US conglomerate General Electric, had bought Agrobanka, a retail bank under forced administration (*FT*, 23 June 1998, p. 34).

On 31 May 1999 it was announced that a Belgian bank (KBC) had been chosen to buy a 66 per cent stake in Ceskoslovenska Obchodni Banka, the former state trade bank and the country's fourth largest bank (*FT*, 1 June 1999, p. 26).

On 5 January 2000 it was announced that Komercni Banka (the largest Czech bank) had sold new shares in the first round of its equity increase, an increase that granted the Czech government a majority stake before its planned sale (*IHT*, 6 January 2000, p. 13).

On 2 February 2000 the cabinet agreed to sell a 52 per cent stake in Ceska Sporitelna, the second largest bank, to Erste Bank of Austria for $521 million. It is the largest retail bank with about a third of deposits (*FT*, 3 February 2000, p. 28).

> In June 2000 the Investment and Post Bank (IPB) was put into forced administration after its largest investor, Nomura, failed to improve its bad loan portfolio and did not increase capital to meet capital adequacy requirements. IPB's assets and liabilities were sold immediately to CSOB, the former trade bank majority owned by Belgian KBC Bank, with full state guarantees. The combined banking entity will control 46 per cent of the local market.
>
> (EBRD 2000b: 155)

(IPB was placed under forced administration on 16 June and CSOB took over IPB on 19 June: *EEN*, 2000, vol. 12, no. 24, p. 5.)

> Konsolidacni Banka, the government-owned bail-out agency … thanks to an ambitious effort to clean up and sell off the country's bankrupt state-owned banks … sits on a mountain of more than $8 billion in nearly worthless loans. The 'assets' … will soon include more than $1 billion in bad loans from a bank that was raided and seized last June [2000] by government anti-terrorist squads. Little of this stems from the communist era. Most flows from the mistakes made in the first heady wave of Czech capitalism … State-owned banks lent freely to well-connected industrial companies, only to discover years later that about half their money had been wasted … Czech bankruptcy laws made it almost impossible for banks to seize property that had been used as collateral for loans … Today almost all the big Czech banks have been taken over by foreign institutions … But the mess left behind remains in Czech hands – specifically on the books of Konsolidacni Banka … [which] is now the biggest creditor and often a major shareholder in some of the Czech Republic's largest conglomerates. Beyond that it holds thousands of small loans … Many of the biggest debtors are also among the country's biggest employers making it politically difficult to force much-needed restructuring. Selling the loans to outside investors has been painfully slow … Thus far Konsolidacni Banka has sold off only a sliver of its loans … Government officials say they will be happy to recover just 10 per cent of the missing money. But … the bailout bank paid about 60 per cent of face value for many of its loans … The worst case may well be Investicni a Postovni Banka, or IPB. Nomura International … acquired 49 per cent of IPB in February 1998, with much of the balance apparently held by people linked to IPB's Czech management. Czech officials allege that the bank's top management systematically looted the bank … by making dubious loans and transferring more than $1 billion of assets to shell companies around the world. Last June [2000] rumours about IPB's precarious position caused a panic among depositors, who lined up by the thousands to withdraw their money. On 17 June anti-terrorist police surrounded the bank headquarters as government officials seized control. A few days later the Czech National Bank and the ministry of finance transferred all of IPB's assets to Ceskoslovenska Obchodni Banka, which is controlled by KBC Bancassurance Holding NV of Belgium … Bad loans will be transferred to Konsolidacni Banka … [As regards the forthcoming] privatization of Komercni Banka … the government has already bought about $2 billion of the bank's bad loans and recently agreed to guarantee a further $500 million. Four European banks … are now bidding for the government's 60 per cent in the cleaned-up bank.
>
> (Edmund Andrews, *IHT*, 17 January 2001, p. 14)

'[On 28 June 2001] Societé Generale of France won the tender for a 60 per cent stake in Komercni Banka, the third-largest Czech bank and the last big government-owned bank in Eastern Europe to be sold off' (*IHT*, 29 June 2001, p. 21).

Foreign trade

The aim is membership of the EU as soon as possible and the Czech Republic will certainly be in the first wave of countries to join. In an interview early in 1993 prime minister Klaus thought that the Czech Republic would be ready to join the EU in two or three years in political, economic and social terms (as opposed to living standards). By then the Czech Republic would, in all important respects, be a standard, normal European country (*IHT*, 1 February 1993, p. 2). The EU initialled separate bilateral association agreements with the Czech Republic and Slovakia on 23 June 1993; these replaced the one with Czechoslovakia. On 4 October separate trade and co-operation agreements were signed, which needed to be ratified by the Czech and Slovak governments. In 1994, 46 per cent of Czech trade was with the EU (*The Times*, Survey, 2 May 1995, p. 11). The association agreement with the EU went fully into effect on 1 February 1995.

Full convertibility on the trade account was introduced in 1991 and full current account convertibility was achieved on 1 October 1995. A high degree of capital account liberalization was already in place by 1993 as far as foreigners were concerned, and this was extended to Czech residents on 1 October 1995, with remaining restrictions limited to certain short-term transactions (OECD, *Economic Outlook*, June 1996, p. 104). On 1 October 1995 a new foreign exchange law came into operation which conformed to Article 8 of the IMF's guidelines on convertibility, i.e. full convertibility for current account transactions and partial liberalization for capital account transactions (*FT*, 28 September 1995, p. 3; EBRD, 1995b: 40). Czech citizens have the right to convert crowns into hard currency to buy foreign real estate and Czech companies have the right to buy foreign currency to make investments abroad. The exchange rate is pegged to a basket comprising the DM and the US dollar, with approximate weights of 65 per cent and 35 per cent respectively. At the end of February 1996, as a result of substantial capital inflows during 1995, the central bank widened the fluctuation band around the central parity from plus or minus 0.5 per cent to plus or minus 7.5 per cent (EBRD 1996b: 147).

> GDP growth slowed in 1996, due to the deterioration of the foreign balance caused by disappointing export growth and continuing strong import demand. Unemployment is low and real wages are increasing substantially faster than productivity, hampering the process of disinflation and external adjustment. With the Czech crown pegged to a currency basket, there was a

> sharp real exchange rate appreciation, leading during May [1997] to significant pressure to devalue.
>
> (OECD, *Economic Outlook*, June 1997, p. 83)

On 26 May 1997, after a sustained bout of speculation against the crown which had started in early May and which the central bank tried to resist, the exchange rate regime was changed to what was officially described as a 'managed float'. The crown was allowed to depreciate, with the aim of reaching what was officially described as a sustainable level against the DM.

The foreign exchange regime was liberalized very quickly. The Czech economy is very open. The sum of imports and exports is about equal to GDP. Average tariffs were reduced to low levels in the early stages of liberalization and there is no special protection for agriculture (OECD, *Economic Outlook*, June 1996, p. 104). A very liberal trade regime has been maintained (EBRD 1996b: 147). But as of 21 April 1997 importers were required to deposit 20 per cent of the value of foodstuffs and consumer goods in non-interest-bearing accounts for 180 days. Exporters were to be helped through loans and guarantees (*Business Central Europe*, May 1997, p. 19; *FT*, 17 April 1997, p. 3). On 21 August 1997 the government lifted the requirement for cash deposits against imports (*EEN*, 1997, vol. 11, no. 16, p. 8).

Foreign direct investment

Concessions formerly granted to foreign investors have been virtually ended so as not to disadvantage domestic businessmen. In the Czech Republic most tax exemptions for foreign investors were abolished in 1993, although negotiable tax contracts remain available in certain priority sectors such as electricity plants and consulting services (Lansbury *et al.* 1996: 107). The authors undertook an econometric analysis of the factors affecting OECD investment in Hungary, the Czech Republic, Poland and Slovakia during the period 1991–3. (See the chapter on Hungary.) The Czech Republic eliminated nearly all special incentives in 1993 (EBRD 1994: 125). The government has offered a package of incentives to induce Intel of the USA to build a computer chip plant in the Czech Republic (*Business Central Europe*, November 1997, p. 26). The government has approved a generous package in an effort to encourage General Motors to build an engine plant in the Czech Republic. The package is thought to include a five-year tax holiday, a duty-free zone and infrastructural investments (*Business Central Europe*, December 1997–January 1998, p. 29). The government approved a package of incentives on 29 April 1998. It included a five-year deferment of corporation tax, with a waiver and tax credit for the entire amount if investment conditions are fulfilled. The package also amended the customs system by waiving duty on imported high technology equipment, remitting VAT deposits and permitting zones with customers' facilities on site (*FT*, 30 April 1998, p. 3).

There are free economic zones. Enterprises which are more than 30 per cent foreign-owned are exempt from customs duties for one year (p. 127). Direct foreign ownership of land is not allowed, but ownership through a Czech legal entity wholly owned by foreigners is permitted (EBRD 1996b: 146).

According to the Deutsche Bank (*Focus: Eastern Europe*, 1993, no. 94, p. 9), Germany accounted for one-third of total direct foreign investment as of mid-1993, the USA for 28 per cent and France for 13 per cent. By the end of 1994 direct foreign investment amounted to $3.1 billion, of which Germany accounted for 36.2 per cent and the USA 21.2 per cent (*FT*, Survey, 2 June 1995, p. i).

Net direct foreign investment was $120 million in 1990, $511 million in 1991, $947 million in 1992, $517 million in 1993, $842 million in 1994 and $2.526 billion in 1995 (the 1993 and 1994 figures excluding flows between the Czech Republic and Slovakia) (United Nations Economic Commission for Europe 1996: 149). Foreign direct investment was $983 million in 1992 and $606 million in 1993 (EBRD 1994: 123).

'Volkswagen–Skoda alone accounts for a staggering 8 per cent of Czech exports' (*Business Central Europe*, November 1998, p. 52). ('The government has agreed to sell its remaining 30 per cent stake in Skoda Auto to German car maker Volkswagen for $315 million. Volkswagen already owns the rest of the company, which it bought in 1991': *Business Central Europe*, June 2000, p. 14.) 'Almost 60 per cent of all Czech manufactured exports originate in foreign-owned plants ... in a country where foreign direct investors account for only 18 per cent of the manufacturing workforce' (p. 56). Car-maker Volkswagen–Skoda now accounts for 10 per cent of total Czech exports (*Business Central Europe*, December 1999–January 2000, p. 46). Foreign-owned companies as a whole account for nearly half of Czech exports (p. 48).

A record $4.88 billion of direct foreign investment was attracted in 1999, compared with $2.54 billion in 1998 (*FT*, 19 April 2000, p. 12).

(See Table 3.1 for the volume of net foreign direct investment.)

Agriculture

The majority of restitution claims are for less than 2 ha and less than a third of farmland is in private hands. The former collectives are now co-operatives and associations, which dominate the scene. (They were to be included in the second wave of voucher privatization.) (*Business Central Europe*, September 1993, p. 25.)

'Gone are the former agricultural co-operatives. In their place stand more than 600 share-owning co-operatives and some 1,500 commercial co-operatives' (*The Times*, Survey, 10 July 1995, p. 10).

The former co-operatives were converted into around 600 new, mostly share-owning co-operatives and some 1,500 commercial companies. At the end of 1994 there were some 91,000 independent farmers. Privatization projects have been prepared for nearly all state farms, usually involving some kind of subdivision. The average size of farm is around 140 ha, ten times that of the average EU farm (*Observer*, 15 September 1996, p. 14).

By 1993 the co-operatives had been transformed into either share-owning co-

Table 3.1 The Czech Republic: selected economic indicators 1990–2000

Economic indicator	*1990*	*1991*	*1992*	*1993*	*1994*	*1995*	*1996*	*1997*	*1998*	*1999*	*2000 (estimate)*
Rate of growth of GDP (%)	-1.2	-11.6	-0.5	0.1	2.2	5.9	4.8	-1.0	-2.2	-0.8	3.1
Rate of growth of industrial output (%)	-3.5	-22.3	-7.9	-5.8	2.9	11.8	11.1	0.1	2.8	-0.4	5.8
Rate of growth of agricultural output (%)	-2.3	-8.9	-12.1	-3.8	-6.6	3.2	2.5	-1,5	-1.8	2.3	-2.0
Inflation rate (consumer, %)	9.7	52.0	11.1	20.8	9.9	9.1	8.8	8.5	10.7	2.1	3.9
Budget surplus or deficit (% GDP)[a]	0.1	-2.0	-3.1	0.5	-1.1	-1.4	-0.9	-1.7	-2.0	-3.3	-4.9
Unemployment rate (end of year, %)	0.7	4.1	2.6	3.5	3.2	2.9	3.5	5.2	7.5	9.4	8.8
Balance of payments (current account, $ billion)				0.456	-0.787	-1.369	-4.292	-3.211	-1.336	-1.567	-2.369
Foreign direct investment (net, $ billion)	0.180	0.511	0.983	0.563	0.749	2.526	1.276	1.275	3.591	6.234	4.477
Population (million)			10.3	10.3	10.3	10.3	10.3	10.3	10.3	10.3	10.3

Sources: Various issues of European Bank for Reconstruction and Development, *Transition Report*; United Nations Economic Commission for Europe, *Economic Survey of Europe*; United Nations, *World Economic and Social Survey*; IMF, *World Economic Outlook*.

Note:

[a] General government balance: includes the state, municipalities and extrabudgetary funds; excludes privatization revenues and bank restructuring costs (EBRD)

operatives or commercial companies. By mid-1995 almost 250 of the 316 state farms had been privatized. At the time it was estimated that 40 per cent of agricultural land had been privatized (EBRD 1996b: 146).

'In … the Czech Republic … many of the large [communist-era] farms have been transformed into market-driven corporations' (Lerman 1999: 273).

'In formerly collectivized Central Europe … the majority response of landowners [after restitution] was to rent their land to the larger units that emerged from the transformation process, whether it was the transformed co-operative or a new successor company' (Swain 1999: 1205). 'Most people … rejected the idea of farming their newly acquired land themselves and rented it back to either the co-operative or one of its successor companies' (p. 1216).

> The structure of agricultural holdings in the Czech Republic continued to be one in which co-operatives featured strongly. By 1994 co-operatives farmed 47.7 per cent of agricultural land, other corporate bodies (successor companies to collective farms) farmed 25.7 per cent, and private individual farms accounted for 23.2 per cent. Over 80 per cent of private individual farms were of less than 10 ha, and around 2 per cent of individual private farms were over 100 ha.
>
> (p. 1210)

> In Romania, Hungary and former Czechoslovakia current land restitution is (explicitly) not based on the 1945 ownership situation, but the ownership strongly influenced by the post-World War II (between 1945 and 1949) land reforms implemented by a government dominated by the Communist Party … The Czech government decided to use the February 1948 date as the basis for restitution. Similarly, Hungary took 1948 and Romania took 1947 as their reference dates … Collective farmland is [thus] restituted to former owners, but state farmland is privatized through different procedures. A reason is the difference in legal ownership: state farms operated mainly on land legally owned by the state. In some cases that farmland was state-owned before 1940; in other cases it was nationalized after the war (taken from foreigners or from the church).
>
> (Swinnen 1999: 642–3)

'Foreign former landowners have not been restituted land' (p. 646).

> Shifting the reference date for land restitution from 1948 to 1945 … would allow land confiscated from the Catholic Church between 1945 and 1948 to be restituted. However, there was little support for this proposal, because it would also imply restituting land to two to three million heirs of Sudeten Germans … and also to Czechs and Slovaks who had collaborated with the Nazis during the war.
>
> (p. 647)

'After Klaus lost his majority in the 1996 election the Christian Democratic parties used their increased bargaining power to force Klaus's minority government into concessions on their demands for church land restitution' (p. 651).

Economic performance

The GDP growth rate turned positive as early as 1993, but output declined for three successive years over the period 1997 to 1999. (See Table 3.1.) 'The Czech Republic ... [however] seems to have turned the corner ... The recession appears to have ended' (EBRD 2000a: 3, 5). 'The economy began to pull out of recession in spring [1999]' (*FT*, 27 June 2000, p. 10). 'GDP grew moderately in the second half of 1999, reflecting stronger European demand for Czech exports and marking an end to the recession' (OECD, *Economic Outlook*, June 2000, p. 92). In 2000 GDP was an estimated 98 per cent of the 1989 level (EBRD 2001: 15). The inflation record is quite good. The peak year was 1991 (over 50 per cent).

(It is interesting to note that the Czech Republic, in the early years after the split from Slovakia, was generally considered to be transitional front runner.)

Prime minister Klaus thought that the 'bottom of the valley' had been reached in the second quarter of 1992; GNP started to improve in the third quarter and again in the fourth quarter of 1992 (*IHT*, 1 February 1993, p. 2).

The unemployment rate was amazingly low for a long time but rose sharply as the recession began to bite later in the decade. (See Table 3.1).

According to *The Economist* (18 February 1995, p. 90), there are a number of factors explaining the low rate of unemployment. For example, an incomes policy ensuring low real wages, special public works programmes, the separation from Slovakia (where a lot of moribund industry was situated) and a tourist boom centred on Prague.

The low overall unemployment masks a massive sectoral reallocation of labour. Employment in manufacturing fell by almost 30 per cent between 1989 and 1994, compared with an aggregate employment decline of about 16 per cent. Employment also fell precipitously in agriculture, but picked up sharply in trade, financial services and tourism (EBRD 1995a: 4–5).

4 Hungary

POLITICS

The demographic background

The population of Hungary is markedly homogeneous. Hungarians constitute 92 per cent of the population, Gypsies 5 per cent, Germans 2 per cent and South Slavs 1 per cent (*Independent*, 7 May 1994, p. 11).

Political developments prior to the 1994 general election

16–18 April 1993: at its fifth congress the Federation of Young Democrats permits those over 35 years of age to join the party. Viktor Orban is re-elected president. The party is pro-market and pro-democracy.

30 April 1993: a treaty is signed by Hungary and Ukraine which states that 'neither country has, nor will have, any territorial claims on the other'. Ukraine gives guarantees about the treatment of its Hungarian minority (*EEN*, 1993, vol. 7, no. 10, p. 2).

1 June 1993: Istvan Csurka and three other members on the extreme right wing of the Hungarian Democratic Forum are expelled from the parliamentary party. A nationwide party meeting on 5 June confirmed the decision, saying that Csurka's movement Hungarian Way was incompatible with membership of the party. He then formed the Hungarian Justice Party on 22 June 1993 (later called Hungarian Justice and Life after its 1930s namesake).

22 August 1993: the electoral deal agreed in July between the Alliance of Free Democrats and the Federation of Young Democrats is widened to include the Entrepreneurs' Party (led by Peter Zwack) and the Agrarian Alliance. For example, joint candidates may be put up in the second round of voting (*EEN*, 25 August 1993, vol. 7, no. 17, p. 3, and 29 March 1994, vol. 8, no. 7, p. 4).

4 September 1993: Admiral Miklos Horthy (the 'Regent' of Hungary, pending a Habsburg 'restoration', from March 1920 to October 1944, who died in Portugal in 1957) is reburied in Hungary amid controversy.

12 December 1993: prime minister Jozsef Antall dies at the age of 61 (of heart trouble after battling against cancer for a number of years). Peter Boross, the interior minister, is asked to carry on as acting prime minister (parliament electing him prime minister on 21 December).

February 1994: the dismissal or forced retirement of 129 journalists from the state-owned radio is seen by opposition parties as another example of government interference in the media.

1 April 1994: Hungary formally applies to join the EU (the first ex-socialist country to do so).

Agreement in principle is reached that Russia will pay off its remaining debt to Hungary of $900 million by the deadline in 1996 through means such as debt–equity swaps and arms deliveries. In 1993 Hungary acquired armaments worth $800 million in part payment of the total debt of $1.7 billion (*FT*, 2 April 1994, p. 2).

The 1994 general election

There were two rounds, on 8 and 29 May 1994. The 386 seats were contested on (1) a proportional basis (5 per cent threshold), in which 152 candidates were elected via regional party lists (Budapest was counted as one of the twenty 'counties' for the purpose) and 58 were allocated to the highest-scoring runners-up; (2) a first-past-the-post basis, involving 176 individual constituencies. A second round of voting was held when no candidate won 50 per cent of the vote and/or the turnout was less than 50 per cent.

Before the election result was known Nicholas Denton and Edward Mortimer (*FT*, 5 May 1994, p. 25) observed:

> Economic policy as such has been almost absent from the Hungarian election campaign … Economic policy is not what divides the parties. Voters' feelings about the economy may be the decisive factor in the election, but the political class reserves its passion for the 'national question'. This is, in essence, a question about what makes a Hungarian: ethnicity or citizenship? … Hungarians are being asked to choose between left and right, not in the sense of socialism versus capitalism, but in the much older sense of 'cosmopolitan' freethinkers versus Christian nationalists.

The main parties

Hungarian Democratic Forum: led by Peter Boross. Conservative.

Christian Democratic People's Party: led by Laszlo Surjan. Conservative. Opposes the sale of land to foreigners.

Independent Smallholders' Party: led by Jozsef Torgyan. Pro-farming.

Hungarian Justice and Life Party: led by Istvan Csurka. Neo-fascist.

Alliance of Free Democrats: the parliamentary group is led by Gabor Kuncze. The party president is Ivan Peto. Liberal, but seen as perhaps having moved somewhat to the left. Still to the right on economic policy.

Federation of Young Democrats (Fidesz): led by Viktor Orban. Liberal, strongly pro-market (e.g. advocates a more investment-friendly corporate tax regime). Economic growth should have a higher priority than reducing inflation. Weakened by criticism about some dubious business deals and the defection to the Alliance of Free Democrats of Gabor Fodor.

Hungarian Socialist Party: led by Gyula Horn. Generally pro-market and offers no dramatic change in economic policy. But the party does contain diverse elements as regards economic policy. Finance supremo Laszlo Bekesi is very much to the right, while Sandor Nagy (head of the National Association of Trade Unions, which claims around 1 million members) was second only to Gyula Horn on the party list. The party advocates a 'social pact' between government, employers and trade unions. Greater social protection for the most disadvantaged would be one element of the pact. Although privatization was supported, the process would be brought under parliamentary control in order to stop abuses. (Bekesi was reported not to be keen on the small shareholder programme.)

Workers' Party: led by Gyula Thurmer. Communist.

The result (see Table 4.1)

Table 4.1 Hungary: the general election of May 1994

Party	*Seats*	*% vote*
Hungarian Socialist Party	209	53.9
Alliance of Free Democrats	70	18.1
Hungarian Democratic Forum	37	9.6
Independent Smallholders' Party	26	6.8
Christian Democratic People's Party	22	5.8
Federation of Young Democrats	20	5.3
Others	2	0.5
Total	386	100

The first round There was a 68.9 per cent turnout in the first round, although only 127 parliamentary seats were decided (only two of the 176 constituency seats, both won by the Hungarian Socialist Party). Overall the vote was for the centre (especially the centre-left) and against extremism. Headlines included one which said, 'Socialists first, liberals second'.

1 The Hungarian Socialist Party, as predicted, came out well in front with 32.5 per cent of the vote (55 seats). Although it had promised no radical shift in policy, it benefited from the support of those who most felt the pain and uncertainty of economic transition (aggravated by the increasing disparities in income and wealth) and of those who perceived a seemingly relatively united, competent, experienced and tolerant team. Thus the

support was widespread, from pensioners and the unemployed to managers and university graduates in general.

2 The Alliance of Free Democrats did even better than expected, winning 19.8 per cent of the vote (20 seats).

3 The Hungarian Democratic Forum won 11.8 per cent of the vote (18 seats).

4 The Christian Democratic People's Party won 7 per cent of the vote.

5 The Independent Smallholders' Party won 8.5 per cent of the vote.

6 Fidesz won 7 per cent. (At a post-election conference the party changed its name to the Federation of Young Democrats–Hungarian Civic Party and confirmed the move to the right: *EEN*, 12 May 1995, vol. 9, no. 10, p. 10.)

7 Hungarian Justice and Life won 1.43 per cent.

The second round The Hungarian Socialist Party did even better in the second round than had been generally forecast. Despite winning a surprising overall majority of seats, a coalition government with the Alliance of Free Democrats was still sought by the party leaders in order to ensure that there would be no slide into inflationary spending increases arising from pressure from the more social welfare-orientated elements within the party.

The coalition government

An agreement was signed on 24 June 1994. The Alliance of Free Democrats were awarded three of the twelve ministerial posts, namely interior and deputy prime minister (Gabor Kuncze), culture and education (Gabor Fodor) and 'infrastructure', combining transport, telecommunications and water (Karoly Lotz). But there would be joint decision-making at the cabinet level between the two coalition partners over policy and personnel, the so-called 'guarantee of joint government'. Among the posts occupied by members of the Hungarian Socialist Party were those of prime minister (Gyula Horn), finance and the economy (Laszlo Bekesi), foreign affairs (Laszlo Kovacs), defence (Gyorgy Keleti) and industry and trade (Laszlo Pal).

Political developments after the 1994 general election

14 July 1994: the prime minister says he is ready to sign new bilateral agreements with Romania and Slovakia on the inviolability of borders, provided the rights of the Hungarian minorities are guaranteed.

15 July 1994: the new session of parliament begins.

28 July 1994: Expo '96, the world fair planned to take place in 1996, is cancelled by parliament on the grounds of cost. (The project was conceived in the late 1980s as a joint project with Austria, but Austria pulled out because of the expense. It was meant to celebrate the 1,100th anniversary of the founding of the state. Seven Magyar – nomadic – tribes from east of the Urals arrived in the Carpathian basin in 896.)

5 September 1994: the Romanian foreign minister, Teodor Melescanu, visits Hungary.

11 December 1994: in the local elections the ruling coalition parties do well, although not quite as well as in the general election.

28 January 1995: finance minister Laszlo Bekesi resigns (effective 1 March). The main reason is the prime minister's decision to take responsibility for privatization away from the finance ministry and put it in the hands of a new privatization minister. (The previous privatization commissioner, Ferenc Bartha, was effectively dismissed on 12 January; the government said he had agreed to leave 'by mutual consent'. The governor of the central bank, Peter Akos Bod, was forced to resign in December 1994.)

31 January 1995: the prime minister says that 'It is of strategic importance that the country should not be dependent either on foreigners or on domestic private businesses in terms of its power supply'. He also says that the central bank should co-ordinate its policies more with the government.

Two former militiamen are sentenced to five years in prison for crimes against humanity, specifically for taking part in the firing on unarmed civilians demonstrating on 8 December 1956 (forty-six died, but there was no proof that the two militiamen were directly responsible).

1 March 1995: the West approves of the new appointments to the presidency of the central bank (Georgyi Suranyi, a banker and former president of the central bank 1990–1) and to the finance ministry (Lajos Bokros, a banker and former chairman of the Budapest stock exchange). (They were recommended by the prime minister on 7 February, but formally took up their duties on 1 March. Tamas Suchman was nominated as privatization minister on 21 February.)

13 March 1995: the ministers of welfare and national security offer to resign when the government's package of austerity measures is announced (see below).

15 March 1995: the education minister offers his resignation.

19 March 1995: Hungary and Slovakia sign, as part of the European Stability Pact, an agreement guaranteeing borders and minority rights.

19 June 1995: parliament re-elects Arpad Goncz as president.

22 June 1995: industry and trade minister Laszlo Pal is dismissed (effective 15 July) for his resistance to gas and electricity privatization. He is replaced by Imre Dunai.

6 October 1995: labour minister Magda Kovacs resigns (effective 30 November) over changes in sick pay provision. She says the austerity package takes into consideration neither the social cost nor the constitution.

7 January 1996: Karoly Grosz dies (see index to Jeffries 1993).

18 February 1996: finance minister Lajos Bokros resigns, effective 29 February. (The issue was his proposals to meet the social security deficit, including raising the retirement age and restructuring the pension system. According to *EEN*, 'The cabinet under Horn did not back Bokros – preferring to use privatization income to cover the deficit rather than accept Bokros' proposal of a new tax': 1996, vol. 10, no. 5, p. 5. Although the cabinet agreed to raise the retirement age to 62, up from 55 for women and 60 for men, it failed to support changes to the

1996 social security budget. Over the past decade welfare's share of government spending has risen from 39 per cent to 55 per cent. Around a third of annual state spending is channelled through the heavily indebted national health and pension funds, which are subordinate to parliament. 'Central government has no direct control over them but must finance any deficit they incur': Virginia Marsh, *FT*, 12 March 1996, p. 2.)

26 February 1996: Peter Medgyessy is proposed as the new finance minister.

3 March 1996: the nationalist candidate Sandor Leszek is elected leader of Democratic Forum (DF), defeating the more moderate Ivan Szabo.

6 March 1996: Democratic Forum splits. Ivan Szabo leads a new breakaway party called the Hungarian Democratic People's Party, with sixteen former DF MPs. According to *EEN* (1996, vol. 10, no. 7, p. 7), no fundamental differences exist between the two groups. The *FT* (Survey, 16 December 1996, p. iii) talks of 'the more moderate, intellectual wing' forming the new party.

29 March 1996: Hungary becomes the twenty-seventh country to join the OECD.

3 July 1996: the government announces that it has agreed to compensate survivors of the Holocaust. (About 600,000 of the 800,000 Jews in Hungary died in the Holocaust. There are 100,000 Jews in Hungary today, including 20,000 survivors: *IHT*, 4 July 1996, p. 7.)

16 September 1996: the prime ministers of Hungary and Romania sign a 'basic treaty' (treaty of 'reconciliation and friendship'). Country borders are deemed inviolable. Although ethnic Hungarians in Romania are granted human rights, the treaty does not recognize their 'collective rights' or grant territorial autonomy along ethnic lines. (For details, see Romania.)

6 October 1996: Tamas Suchman, the industry and trade minister, is dismissed (effective 15 October). Although the prime minister does not question Suchman's personal integrity, on 4 October the government sacked the supervisory and management boards of the privatization agency over irregular payments to a lawyer negotiating with municipalities on the agency's behalf (*FT*, 7 October 1996, p. 2). 'The coalition government … has been badly shaken by the "Toscik" affair involving the alleged transfer of funds to the ruling parties during the privatization process' (*EEN*, 1997, vol. 11, no. 4, p. 5). (Tamas Suchman replaced Imre Dunai as industry and trade minister in August 1996. The official reason given was Dunai's health but there was speculation that he was unhappy with the decision to delay the rise in energy prices.)

17 February 1997: the defence ministers of Hungary and Romania sign an accord on the protection and exchange of military secrets and agree to set up a joint peace-keeping battalion for use with Nato, the UN and OSCE (*Independent*, 18 February 1997, p. 10).

24 February 1997: farmers begin strikes and road blocks in protest at new tax arrangements (*EEN*, 1997, vol. 11, no. 4, p. 9).

14 April 1997: the president of the Alliance of Free Democrats, Ivan Peto, resigns. (Possible reasons are said to include the Toscik affair.)

24 May 1997: Gabor Kuncze is elected president of the Alliance of Free Democrats.

8 July 1997: Hungary is invited 'to begin accession talks with Nato'. (The foreign ministers of the sixteen Nato countries signed the protocol of accession on 16 December 1997.)

16 July 1997: the European Commission recommends that Hungary opens negotiations in early 1998 for entry to the EU. (The invitation was formally approved at an EU summit on 13 December 1997.)

25 September 1997: the International Court of Justice at The Hague delivers its verdict on the Gabcikovo Dam. (See Slovakia.)

16 November 1997: the referendum on Nato membership asks: 'Do you agree that Hungary should ensure the defence of the country by joining the North Atlantic Treaty Organization?'

The referendum is non-binding. To be valid at least a quarter of the total electorate must say 'yes' or there must be a majority vote in favour with a turnout of over 50 per cent.

Although the turnout is slightly below 50 per cent, there is an unexpectedly high (85.33 per cent) 'yes' vote.

The general election of May 1998

There were two rounds, on 10 May and 24 May 1998. The arrangements for contesting the 386 seats were as in the 1994 election.

In the first round the turnout was 56.26 per cent. Overall there was a swing to the right. Fidesz as a party had shifted to the centre-right. The government coalition of the Hungarian Socialist Party and the Alliance of Free Democrats (which ran lacklustre campaigns) had achieved an impressive economic turnaround and success on both the Nato and EU fronts. But the former had been achieved at considerable economic pain and there was concern at corruption and growing economic inequalities between people and regions. Appeals to economic populism and to nationalism proved successful.

'Half the population are now calculated to be living on or below subsistence level, after the Socialist-led government abolished many automatic welfare payments in 1995' (*Guardian*, 11 May 1998, p. 10). Viktor Orban has promised to reintroduce automatic child benefit (*Guardian*, 26 May 1998, p. 11).

'The have-nots' sense of grievance is sharpened by the whiff of corruption that surrounds both government and the economy … Budapest and western parts of the country have had the lion's share of foreign investment' (*The Economist*, 16 May 1998, p. 46).

> Fidesz [was] once a dissident student group but [is] now part of the conservative mainstream … Viktor Orban, who seemed a thorough-going liberal until he took on a populist tinge in order to broaden his party's appeal, has promised to slash taxes, bolster welfare and make the economy grow by 7

per cent, all without upsetting the trade balance: his figures baffle many economists.

(*The Economist*, 16 May 1998, pp. 46–7)

'The Smallholders' fiery leader, Jozsef Torgyan is ... stridently nationalist – and still viscerally hostile to the Socialists because of their communist past. For instance, he opposes land sales to foreigners' (*The Economist*, 16 May 1998, p. 47).

Hungary may be over the toughest days of market reform, but voters appeared poised to register healthy complaints about the downside of economic transition. Concerns about crime, corruption and the struggle to make ends meet top voters' interests, polls show. Several high profile crimes since January ... have increased jitters and resentments perceptibly.

(Christine Spolar, *IHT*, 25 May 1998, p. 6)

After the first round of balloting, Mr Orban was quick to allay fears that Hungary could jump from the track of reform. He assured investors that Hungary would rearrange some social priorities but would not veer from larger economic goals. But Mr Orban made many promises during the campaign, some of which appear nearly impossible to implement. He presented an economic programme that envisioned a hefty 7 per cent growth in GDP – compared with a current 4 per cent – that was criticized by some Western analysts as unrealistic. He also promised reviews of privatization contracts and increases in social benefits that prompted speculation about his sincerity.

(Christine Spolar, *IHT*, 26 May 1998, p. 10)

Fidesz has campaigned on a platform of law and order, anti-corruption and measures to support the family. He [Viktor Orban] has also called for moves to accelerate economic growth to 7 per cent a year in order to double GDP in a decade through a programme of cuts in taxes and social welfare contributions ... Beyond the economy there are concerns that a Fidesz–Smallholders coalition and the shift to the right in Hungarian politics could lead to much louder nationalist rhetoric ... Orban hardly stilled fears about a rising nationalist mood when he observed ... that the boundaries of the Hungarian state and those of the Hungarian nation did not coincide.

(*FT*, 26 May 1998, p. 3)

In search of faster growth and lower unemployment, Fidesz has promised to cut taxes, increase consumption and even abolish the crawling peg devaluation of the forint, which had been the centrepiece of the outgoing government's anti-inflation policy ... Some of the Smallholders' policies seem even more dubious. They have proposed to scrap university tuition

> fees, build low-cost housing projects and spend money on regional development, but have little to say about how they would fund such initiatives.
>
> (p. 23)

Fidesz promised improvements in health provision and assured teachers that their wages would catch up with the national average within two years. Other promises included scrapping tuition fees for university students (university fees hit higher-income families), reintroducing family allowances regardless of income levels (the top 10 per cent of the population having been excluded) and cutting employer social security contributions from 39 per cent of wages to 34 per cent (*Business Central Europe*, July–August 1998, pp. 11, 18).

The Socialist vote held up extremely well, with 1.9 million votes (32.92 per cent) compared with 1.7 million (29.48 per cent) for Fidesz. But Hungary's complicated electoral system, combining first-past-the-post with proportional representation, gave Fidesz its narrow victory. During the campaign Fidesz said that it would support small and medium-sized businesses by, for example, drastically cutting the national insurance payments payable by companies for each employee. It rejected the Smallholders' Party's idea of a complete return of all lands nationalized by the communists, arguing that land should be owned by those now working it. Fidesz was founded in March 1988 as what was described as 'a new, autonomous and independent youth organization that unites politically radical and reform-minded youth groups and individuals'. It was a rival to the Young Communist League. In 1989 Fidesz played a prominent role in the opposition roundtable which negotiated with the Hungarian Socialist Workers' Party a peaceful handover of power. Fidesz joined the Liberal International. In 1993 it kept the title Fidesz but replaced 'Young Democrats' with 'Hungarian Civic Party' (*EEN*, 1998, vol. 12, no. 7, pp. 3–4). Viktor Orban founded the Federation of Young Democrats in 1988 with fellow students in the Budapest law faculty. It started out as a staunchly anti-communist liberal party, equally hostile to both the old regime and the nationalist right. But its disastrous showing in the 1994 elections persuaded Orban that the party's future lay in occupying the centre-right ground.

> Orban borrowed the nationalist right's vocabulary in his criticisms of the Socialist–Free Democratic coalition government, accusing it of weakening the nation and its communities with its cultural policies, and of being 'alien in style'. For the nationalist right, this is a thinly disguised attack on communist, and by implication Jewish, influence. The pitch worked magnificently in the May elections.
>
> (p. 5)

> The centre-right Civic Party emerged at the weekend [24 May] as the winner of general elections on a slogan of 'Hungary First'. It may be depen-

dent in government on the support of the far-right Justice and Life Party, which has stirred up antisemitism and anti-foreigner sentiment.

(Roger Boyes, *The Times*, 26 May 1998, p. 12)

On 30 March 1988 thirty-seven students announced the formation of an independent Alliance of Young Democrats (popularly known, from its Hungarian initials, as Fidesz) … The Alliance of Young Democrats has been transformed almost beyond recognition … In the new party statutes adopted at the [fifth party] congress [held in the spring of 1993 at Debrecen] the upper age limit of thirty-five was abolished and a centralized hierarchical structure established for the party in place of the earlier decentralized association that had been based on local autonomy and collective leadership. Viktor Orban was elected to the newly created post of party leader … The Debrecen congress also saw a distinct shift away from the previous radical and alternative policies to more conservative and nationalist ones … In the aftermath of Debrecen the more radical, alternative wing of Fidesz gradually departed from the party, led by Gabor Fodor. Fodor and many of his supporters would eventually join the Alliance of Free Democrats … [After the 1994 election] Fidesz was to be transformed into a centre-right 'catch-all' party espousing conservative and nationalist values at least as much as liberal ones. At the same time the party would abandon its previously strict monetarist approach and adopt more populist economic policies [Fidesz promised to reduce both income tax and national insurance contributions, restore the universal principle for social benefits such as child benefit and abolish tuition fees in higher education: p. 121] … In April 1995 they renamed their party the Fidesz–Hungarian Civic Party.

(Lomax 1999: 112–15)

[In the second round of voting in the 1998 election] the Socialists' vote held up well … [But] it was the enterprising and successful, the reasonably well-off members of society who had previously voted for the Free Democrats who deserted the government. This was particularly in the more prosperous counties of western Hungary … This time it was in these counties that Fidesz secured its highest vote … The Socialist Party had few potential supporters among the parties forced to drop out. Also the Socialist Party's support was more evenly spread throughout the country than that of Fidesz, giving it a built-in advantage for polling based on individual constituencies [there were also regional lists and a national list] … The issues that most concerned the voters were those of rising crime levels, safety on the streets and continuing suspicions of corruption in public life in the wake of the Toscik affair. The inability of the police to put a stop to a series of terrorist bombings, some directed at political targets, also increased disaffection from the government … Fidesz promised a government of law and order that would act immediately to reverse the rising crime wave. In foreign affairs they would give greater support to the Hungarian minorities in neighbouring

> countries and put more emphasis on Hungarian national interests in negotiating with Nato and the EU … Hardly was the election over [however] when Viktor Orban made a lightning visit to Bonn … to make it clear that the catchword of his government would be stability and continuity, particularly in the fields of economic and foreign policy. Within days he let it be known that his choices for the key ministries of foreign affairs, economics and finance were to be moderate and respected experts … Almost half of cabinet ministers, including those holding the key economic, foreign and interior posts, are not elected members of parliament … It is a government of technocrats and specialists … some of whom have previous government experience.
>
> (pp. 120–4)

The results of the first round were as follows:

1 The Hungarian Socialist Party won 32.25 per cent of the vote in the first round, very slightly down on 1994.
2 Its coalition partner, the Alliance of Free Democrats, did very badly, winning only 7.9 per cent of the vote.
3 The big winner was Fidesz, with 28.2 per cent of the vote.
4 The United Historic Smallholders' Party saw a substantial increase in its vote, to 13.8 per cent.
5 The far-right Hungarian Justice and Life Party, led by Istvan Csurka, won 5.6 per cent of the vote and thus seats for the first time.
6 The far-left Workers' Party won 4.1 per cent of the vote.
7 The centre-right Hungarian Democratic Forum won 3.4 per cent of the vote.
8 The Christian Democrats won 2.1 per cent of the vote.

In the second round of the general election, held on 24 May 1998, the swing to the right was confirmed. The turnout was 57.01 per cent. The final distribution of seats was as follows: Fidesz, 148; Hungarian Socialist Party, 134; United Historic Smallholders' Party, 48; Alliance of Free Democrats, 24; Democratic Forum, 17; Hungarian Justice and Life Party, 14; independents, 1.

Political developments after the 1998 general election

6 July 1998: parliament approves Viktor Orban as prime minister.

8 July 1998: the new government is sworn into office. The coalition government comprises Fidesz, the United Historic Smallholders' Party and Democratic Forum. Key ministers include the following: Janos Martonyi (foreign affairs); Sandor Pinter (interior); Janos Szabo (defence); Zsigmond Jarai (formerly president of the Budapest stock exchange: finance); Attila Chikan (economics); Jozsef Torgyan (agriculture and regional development).

5 September 1998: Laszlo Kovacs is elected president of the Socialist Party, succeeding Gyula Horn who announced his resignation after the May 1998 general election (*FT*, 7 September 1998, p. 2).

October 1998:

> Local elections in Hungary are politically very useful. The process is so complicated that every party worth its salt can claim to have won ... The Socialists won in terms of individual seats, but the ruling centre-right Fidesz–Smallholders–MDF bloc won in terms of votes cast for party lists.
>
> (*Business Central Europe*, December 1998–January 1999, p. 44)

12 March 1999: the Czech Republic, Hungary and Poland become members of Nato at a signing ceremony in Independence, Missouri, USA (where Nato was founded on 4 April 1949 during the presidency of Harry Truman), raising membership from sixteen to nineteen. It was in Missouri, at Westminster College in Fulton on 5 March 1946, that Winston Churchill delivered his famous speech: 'From Stettin in the Baltic to Trieste in the Adriatic an iron curtain has descended across the Continent.'

'Mikhail Gorbachev ... said that he felt "betrayed" by Nato's expansion, adding that the West was taking advantage of Russia's weakness and humiliating Russians in ways like the Allies' treatment of defeated Germany after World War I' (*IHT*, 13 March 1999, p. 4).

13 October 1999: the European Commission recommends that EU leaders at the December 1999 meeting in Helsinki allow Bulgaria, Latvia, Lithuania, Malta, Romania and Slovakia to begin accession negotiations in 2000.

The 'principle of differentiation' for entry date will apply to each of the twelve candidates, reflecting differing states of readiness for EU entry. A 'fully flexible, multi-speed accession process' is envisaged. 'Each country will be able to proceed on merit, including the possibility for those which join the negotiations from 2000 to catch up with the others.' The European Commission thinks that existing EU members should undertake internal reforms by the end of 2002: 'Whether the first accessions can take place as from 1 January 2003 will then depend entirely on the speed with which the applicant countries can make progress on meeting the criteria.'

Latvia has made good political progress but falls short of international standards on the protection of the linguistic rights of minorities. (Estonia is also criticized as regards linguistic rights.) Latvia has made 'significant and sustained progress' towards meeting market economy criteria and in regards to its ability to withstand competitive pressures. Latvia has a good chance of catching up with the group led by Hungary, with Lithuania not far behind. Latvia joins Malta and Cyprus, Hungary, Poland, Estonia and Slovenia in having functioning market economies. Lithuania could become a functioning market economy in 2000 if it pushes ahead with promised reforms.

Malta and Cyprus have already met the economic terms set by the EU, being able to cope with competitive pressures and market forces in the EU. Hungary and Poland come next in economic terms, followed by Slovenia, Estonia and then the Czech Republic. Hungary, Poland, Estonia and Slovenia have improved their ability to cope with competitive pressures and market forces 'in the medium term' (meaning more than one year from 2000). Hungary is the closest of the Eastern European countries to meeting the criteria on a market economy with the capacity to withstand competition within the EU.

(*FT*, 14 October 1999, pp. 1, 10; *IHT*, 14 October 1999, p. 5; *Guardian*, 14 October 1999, p. 14; *Independent*, 14 October 1999, p. 18; *The Times*, 14 October 1999, p. 21; *Telegraph*, 14 October 1999, p. 20.)

7 December 1999: a cabinet reshuffle includes the replacement of economics minister Attila Chikan by Gyeorgy Matolcsi (*EEN*, 2000, vol. 12, no. 21, p. 5).

10 December 1999:

> The EU agreed yesterday [10 December] to launch accession negotiations with five East European countries and Malta early next year [2000] ... Government heads also decided that the EU would be ready by the end of 2002 'to welcome' new members from the six countries already negotiating and potentially the six it agreed to talk with yesterday ... [But] diplomats acknowledged that, in spite of the optimistic gloss put on the accession schedule by heads of government, it was likely to be 2004 at the earliest before any country could join the fifteen already in the EU ... Günter Verheugen, EU enlargement commissioner ... [said] that member states' ratification of new entrants would start after they had approved reform of the EU treaties. Reform ratification must be completed by the end of 2002, government heads decided yesterday. Ratification of individual countries' accession to the EU will take at least another year. Mr Verheugen insisted the unanimous decision by member states to start talks in January or February [2000] with six more states would not slow down existing negotiations with the other six.
>
> (*FT*, 11 December 1999, p. 6)

'Although government heads agreed the EU should be "in a position to welcome new members by the end of 2002", diplomats said ratification of accession treaties was unlikely to be completed for at least another year after that' (*FT*, 13 December 1999, p. 10).

Günter Verheugen (European commissioner for enlargement since August 1999):

> We must balance two contradictory objectives, the speed and quality of enlargement ... The EU must bring the candidates into line with the EU as quickly as possible. And the enlargement process must stick to the Copenhagen criteria. Which means candidates must respect democracy and human rights, create a functioning market economy so that they can compete in the EU, and implement the whole *acquis communautaire* (the EU treaty and legislation). Accession is only for those who are properly prepared and can meet all the rules applying to any member state ... From now on

> negotiations will be carried out on a country-by-country basis, taking account of each country's state of preparations. Therefore negotiations will progress according to merit, and progress largely depends on the candidates' own efforts. Which is why a target date for accession cannot be set yet. All we can do is name a target date for the EU to be ready to take the first accession decisions. This date will be 2002, as long as the EU carries out the institutional reforms necessary to ensure a proper functioning of a Union of twenty-seven or twenty-eight members – and providing that negotiations with candidate countries have reached a conclusion. I firmly believe that negotiations with the most advanced candidate could be concluded in 2002.
>
> (Business Central Europe 1999: 17)

On 11 December Turkey was added to the list of candidate members, albeit with especially strict conditions as regards areas such as human rights and relations with Greece. Formal negotiations were not even to begin until 2004.

1 January 2000: the crown of St Stephen, given to the founder of Hungary, King Stephen (Istvan, Hungary's first Christian king) by Pope Sylvester II in 1000 AD, is controversially moved from the national museum to the national parliament. It was returned by the USA in 1978, having been sent there in 1945.

'Hungary marked 1,000 years of statehood and Christianity on Sunday [20 August 2000] with a series of events culminating in the Eastern Orthodox Church's canonization of King Stephen, who ruled from 1000 to 1038 and was credited with introducing Christianity' (*IHT*, 21 August 2000, p. 5).

'To mark the occasion the Orthodox Church recognized the sainthood of Hungary's founder Saint Stephen I. It is the first time the Orthodox Church has recognized a Catholic saint since the churches split in 1054' (*Business Central Europe*, September 2000, pp. 13–14).

1 March 2000:

> Hungary's media policies have been criticized … by the United States, the EU and press freedom organizations … The state's media law requires that three eight-member boards for two public television stations and national radio have equal representation from the government and the opposition. But it requires the opposition parties … to agree on candidate slates … When the law was written in 1996, under the previous government, it required the opposition to field joint delegates if there were fewer than four opposition parties … With the opposition hopelessly divided the government, as it did last year, appointed four-member boards with its own supporters on 1 March … State television and radio have been accused of tilting news coverage … The government has also been criticized for awarding radio broadcast frequencies to rightist supporters, for excluding more established but independent broadcasters, and for police searches of the homes and offices of journalists who wrote reports the government objected to … An independent media analyst [from Hungary argues that] … Hungarian governments, including the previous Socialist–liberal alliance,

> have repeatedly viewed public broadcasting as one of the spoils of electoral victory and all three governments since the collapse of communist rule in 1989 have installed their own supporters in key management and editorial positions.
>
> (Peter Finn, *IHT*, 16 March 2000, p. 4)

> Public television should be overseen by a board of eight people, four of them government appointees and four of them chosen by opposition parties. In fact, though, the board has had no opposition members since prime minister Viktor Orban came to power in 1998. As a result, Hungarian Television (MTV) has become a government mouthpiece … The problem is that opposition parties have to agree between themselves on how to share out the seats on the television council – there is no arrangement for the larger parties to be guaranteed more seats. And they failed to strike a deal … But the government could have ensured that MTV's board remained balanced.
>
> (*Business Central Europe*, February 2001, pp. 16–17)

6 June 2000: it takes three rounds of voting to elect Ference Madl as the new president, even though he ran unopposed. He will take over from Arpad Goncz in August 2000.

8 November 2000: the EU publishes its report on enlargement.

The report on Hungary is generally favourable (*Progress Towards Accession*, 8 November 2000, pp. 81–3):

> Hungary is a functioning market economy and should be able to cope with competitive pressure and market forces within the Union in the near term, provided that it stays with its present reform path … However, the slow progress towards price stability is a cause for concern … The intermediation role of the financial sector needs to improve the delivery of service to domestic small and medium enterprises … The situation in respect of the restructuring of the Hungarian steel industry is still unsatisfactory … Despite a number of important measures taken to fight corruption, this remains a problem … Hungary started to implement the medium-term Roma action programme … Sustained implementation of this programme is needed.

The report does not specify an exact entry date for the first of the new members:

> Transitional measures and all outstanding issues will be addressed by the Union with the most advanced countries by June 2002 at the latest … [The EU should be able] to conclude negotiations in the course of 2002 with those candidate countries who fulfil all the criteria for membership, thus allowing [the EU] to welcome new members from the end of 2002.

'The legal ratification process cannot be done in much less than eighteen months after the end of negotiations. So 1 January 2004 looks like the earliest possible prospect for formal accession' (*FT*, 9 November 2000, p. 30). 'January 2005 is the most likely date' (*FT*, 8 November 2000, p. 10). 'Every country's accession will have to be approved by every existing [EU] member ... Since ratification is expected to take at least eighteen months ... The speediest timetable, therefore, has the first entrant joining in 2004 ... But 2005 may be more realistic' (*The Economist*, 11 November 2000, p. 73).

The report makes general comments:

> Corruption, fraud and economic crime are widespread in most candidate countries, leading to a lack of confidence by the citizens and discrediting the reforms ... Trafficking in women and children [is a growing problem in some countries] ... [Roma] continue to face widespread discrimination in social and economic life.

Cyprus and Malta are the leading candidates in terms of the two economic criteria. Both have 'functioning market economies' and should be able to cope with the 'capacity to withstand competitive pressure and market forces with the Union'.

Estonia, Hungary, Poland, the Czech Republic and Slovenia are functioning market economies and 'should be able to meet the second criterion in the near term'. Latvia, Lithuania and Slovakia should be ready in the 'medium term'.

> The Czech Republic welcomed the Commission's recognition of its much improved economic performance and the acceleration in its rate of legislative alignment but questioned why it had been placed in the third group of countries for its capacity to withstand competitive pressure and market forces within the EU.
>
> (*FT*, 9 November 2000, p. 22)

'Good progress [has been made in the Czech Republic] in adapting legislation to meet EU standards. Problems remain with reform of administration and [the] judiciary. Anti-corruption efforts have been insufficient' (*FT*, 8 November 2000, p. 10).

Poland was given a much more positive assessment than in the previous year. But further progress was needed in, for example, the judiciary, customs, home affairs, anti-corruption measures and state aid. Continuing economic problems include inflation, a high current account deficit and inadequate restructuring of sectors such as agriculture and steel.

'[Poland has promised] to speed up legislation previously planned for 2002 to meet the timetable for early membership' (*The Economist*, 11 November 2000, p. 73).

Bulgaria has made progress but still lies well behind the other Eastern European countries, second from last behind Romania.

The report says that Romania has made 'too limited progress towards meeting the [economic] criteria'. Romania was criticized for continuing discrimination against Roma and for the slow pace of 'demilitarizing' its police. There has been little improvement in corruption. Progress has been made in conditions in orphanages.

> Slovakia has made progress on meeting short-term priorities but it varies widely from sector to sector. Privatizations are under way and good progress has been made on restructuring state-owned banks. Progress [has been] made in the fight against crime and corruption and in efforts to end discrimination against minorities. But problems remain with environmental measures, border controls, agricultural reforms, and efforts to improve administration and the judiciary.
>
> (*FT*, 8 November 2000, p. 10)

> Slovenia was criticized over a number of issues that have been long-running concerns of the Union, including the continued slow pace of the denationalization process – the Slovenes' name for the restitution process for communist-era confiscation. The country also needs to work at its public administration. There was also criticism of the slow pace of economic reform, in particular of the slowness of removing state influences over significant financial institutions such as two of the largest banks.
>
> (*FT*, 9 November 2000, p. 22)

(*FT*, 8 November 2000, p. 10, and 9 November 2000, p. 22; *The Economist*, 12 November 2000, p. 73; *Guardian*, 9 November 2000, p. 13; *Independent*, 9 November 2000, p. 14; *Telegraph*, 9 November 2000, p. 22: *IHT*, 9 November 2000, p. 5.)

> A generally positive assessment of …[Estonia's] readiness for EU membership [is] contained in a report published by the European Commission … Latvian and Lithuanian leaders acknowledged the need for more work in preparation for accession … [There was] a less-than-glowing assessment of Lithuania's readiness … The Latvia report reflected the country's 'satisfactory' progress on accession preparation, said … the head of the European Commission's delegation to Latvia … Within two to four years Latvia should be able to cope with competitive pressure in the EU provided the pace of structural reform is maintained, [he] said … The European Commission's report on Lithuania is a 'touch more positive' than last year said … the head of the commission's delegation to Lithuania. It nonetheless contained many reservations.
>
> (*Baltic Times*, 16–22 November 2000, pp. 1, 8)

3 December 2000: the mayor of Budapest Gabor Demsky is elected chairman of the Alliance of Free Democrats (*EEN*, 2001, vol. 13, no. 2, p. 5).

7–11 December 2000: an EU summit is held in Nice.

A longer-than-anticipated summit finally saw agreement reached on various changes designed to accommodate new members and make decision-making more feasible in a much-expanded EU. New voting weights in the Council of Ministers were assigned to existing and prospective members and the range of areas subject to qualified majority voting was expanded.

> EU leaders yesterday [9 December] pledged to speed the entry of the former Soviet bloc countries of Eastern and Central Europe … EU leaders said that some could become members by mid-1994 … Their original draft text repeated the Union's long-standing aim of completing reforms to be ready for new members that meet its conditions from the end of 2002. Yesterday the leaders added that this would be carried 'in the hope that they [new members] participate in the new European Parliament elections' – due in June 2004.
>
> (*FT*, 9 December 2000, p. 5)

The 60,000-strong Rapid Reaction Force was approved.

January–February 2001:

> Five members of the Smallholders left the party. The move follows a party row over the autocratic style of its leader, agriculture minister Jozsef Torgyan … The government announced that finance minister Zsigmond Jarai will replace central bank governor Georgyi Suranyi in March. The new finance minister will be Laszlo Varga.
>
> (*Business Central Europe*, February 2001, pp. 11–12, 42)

(Varga became finance minister on 1 January.)

8 February 2001: Jozsef Torgyan resigns as agriculture minister (*EEN*, 2001, vol. 13, no. 2, p. 5).

> Within the Smallholders there is widespread and growing opposition to Torgyan's autocratic and demagogic style … Six leading Smallholders' Party deputies [have resigned] so far … The anti-Torgyan deputies [are] now grouped informally into the 'Reform Smallholders'.
>
> (p. 2)

11 February 2001:

> The first independent Roma radio station in Central Europe, Radio C can reach most of Budapest's 150,000 Roma, or Gypsies, who make up between 6 per cent and 8 per cent of Hungary's population of some 10 million … Radio C is on a temporary lease – it started broadcasting on 11 February and its licence is good only until 21 March. The national radio and television board, beholden to parliament, is supposed to decide soon whether to award the rare vacant frequency to Radio C or another applicant … Hungarian state television and radio have hourlong programmes aimed at

> the Roma, but Radio C ... is broadcasting twenty-four hours a day ... Radio C has had considerable support from EU diplomats and aid funds, as well as from the American embassy here [in Budapest]. Private groups, like the Soros Foundation, Levi Strauss and a local mobile telephone network, Pannon GSM, have also contributed, helping the station buy its equipment ... There are more than 10 million [Roma] spread over Europe, but they are politically and tribally divided, often hold themselves aloof from the dominant culture and suffer considerable racial discrimination.
>
> (Steven Erlanger, *IHT*, 6 March 2001, p. 6)

27 April 2001: 'Beginning on 3 June Russians will require a visa ... the first EU candidate to adopt EU standards on the matter ... The visa obligations will be reciprocal and will concern not only Russia, but also Bosnia-Hercegovina, Belarus and Moldova' (*IHT*, 28 April 2001, p. 2).

1 May 2001: 'The Smallholders' Party reelects Jozsef Torgyan as party chairman after the party splits between anti- and pro-Torgyan factions' (*EEN*, 2001, vol. 13, no. 5, p. 6).

14 June 2001: 'The Alliance of Free Democrats chairman Gabor Demsky resigns in protest at moves to form an electoral alliance with the Hungarian Socialist Party' (*EEN*, 2001, vol. 13, no. 5, p. 6).

June 2001:

> Some 3 million ethnic Hungarians live in countries that neighbour Hungary ... This month [June] parliament will vote on a bill giving up to 6 billion forints ($20 million) a year to improve their lot ... It has caused consternation among its neighbours. The so-called 'Status Law' would support ethnic Hungarians in their home countries, by giving them scholarships to study Hungarian or 20,000 forint grants for medical care. It would also allow them to work in Hungary for up to three months a year, granting them full health benefits and discounts on train and bus fares ... Slovakia and Romania are up in arms about it, accusing Hungary of meddling in their internal affairs ... According to surveys, almost half of Hungarians have contacts with their ethnic cousins abroad, either as relatives, friends or business partners.
>
> (*Business Central Europe*, June 2001, p. 46)

> The Hungarian parliament on Tuesday [19 June] adopted a law granting ethnic Hungarians in neighbouring countries special medical, employment and education opportunities in Hungary. Deputies approved the so-called status law by an overwhelming 306 to seventeen, with eight abstentions. The law is scheduled to enter into force on 1 January 2002 ... Ethnic Hungarians in six neighbouring countries will be entitled to a series of privileges inside Hungary ... The status law will allow those eligible a three-month work permit in Hungary and educational and cultural benefits. In its first year it will cost Hungary 9 billion forints ($31.3 million). An esti-

mated 800,000 Hungarians outside the country are expected to take advantage of the law by applying for identity cards ... The legislation has already triggered international protest, especially in Slovakia and Romania, where government officials criticize what they see as a move to extend Hungarian jurisdiction to citizens of another country. The critics also see it as an apparent attempt to revive nationalist sentiment ... Hungarian government officials say the law is intended to avert mass immigration once Hungary joins the EU ... A recent poll showed that 25 per cent of Hungarians abroad were considering returning to the country. Government officials say this number would halve under the status law ... Austria ... was dropped from the law because of objections from the EU ... The EU was against any regulation favouring one population over another.

(*IHT*, 20 June 2001, p. 6)

The law ... will give ethnic Hungarians a special identity document allowing them to work and study temporarily in Hungary, to pay tax and national insurance, and to be entitled to welfare payments ... Ethnic Hungarians will also be able to study more easily in Hungary and use libraries and other facilities ... At the moment tens of thousands work illegally in Hungary ... The leaders of Romania and Slovakia have reacted furiously ... Neighbouring governments have accused Hungary of interfering in their internal affairs, and have said they will prevent ethnic Hungarians from taking advantage of the new legislation ... The Hungarian prime minister, Viktor Orban ... [said that] 'We are not pioneers in this issue; on the contrary, we have adopted certain elements from the Slovak and Romanian status laws.'

(*Guardian*, 21 June 2001, p. 14)

16 June 2001:

The notable achievement of the EU summit meeting that concluded here [Gothenburg, Sweden, on 16 June] ... was an agreement by leaders of the fifteen member states on a firm timetable to admit new members from Eastern Europe by 2004 ... 'The enlargement process is irreversible,' it [the final document] said, adding that it should be possible 'to complete negotiations by the end of 2002 for those candidate countries that are ready' ... The objective is that they should participate in the European parliament elections of 2004 as members ... An Irish referendum [albeit with a low turnout] on 7 June rejected the [December 2000] Treaty of Nice, the accord that would reform the EU's decision-making structure and make possible a new round of enlargement ... The treaty must be ratified by all member countries ... Irish voters [are] the only people in the EU [who are] given the right to vote on it.

(*IHT*, 18 June 2001, p. 6)

> The EU will open its doors to enlargement in early 2004, paving the way for some East European countries to participate as members in the European parliament elections that June ... Under the terms of the deal, best prepared countries should be able to 'complete negotiations by the end of 2002. The objective is that they should participate in the European parliament elections of 2004 as members' ... It gives some countries the prospect of full membership by early 2004. It makes the enlargement process 'irreversible'. It gives negotiations more momentum.
>
> (*FT*, 18 June 2001, p. 6)

(The Irish government plans to hold another referendum.)

THE ECONOMY

Hungary adopted a more gradual approach to economic transition, eased by the earlier acquaintance with market-type reforms.

Macroeconomic stabilization

Austerity measures were soon introduced in line with IMF guidelines, e.g. reducing the budget deficit. The Horn government was to gain the confidence of the West for its macroeconomic policy. For example, in 1995 the West approved of the new appointments to the presidency of the central bank (Georgyi Suranyi, a banker and former president of the central bank 1990–1) and to the finance ministry (Lajos Bokros, a banker and former chairman of the Budapest stock exchange). They had been recommended by the prime minister on 7 February, but formally took up their duties on 1 March 1995. (See above in the political section for changes in the cabinet.) On 29 March 1996 Hungary became the twenty-seventh country to join the OECD. Horn's government eventually introduced an unexpectedly tough package of austerity measures on 13 March 1995. The package included the following: (1) expenditure cuts, including social welfare; (2) increases in wages in the public sector to be limited to 3 per cent; (3) a 9 per cent devaluation of the forint against the US dollar (followed by small weekly devaluations for the rest of the year); and (4) an 8 per cent increase in import duties, with the exception of machinery/equipment, energy and components for exportables (the surcharge was to be phased out during the first half of 1997). (On 24 February 1997 farmers began strikes and road blocks in protest at new tax arrangements: *EEN*, 1997, vol. 11, no. 4, p. 9.) A measure of the success of the austerity measures came on 16 February 1998. The IMF announced the end of its stand-by arrangement, agreed in 1996, owing to the strength of the Hungarian economy. The $264 million had never been used by Hungary (*IHT*, 17 February 1998, p. 13; *FT*, 17 February 1998, p. 2). (See Table 4.2.)

Table 4.2 Hungary: selected economic indicators 1990–2000

Economic indicator	*1990*	*1991*	*1992*	*1993*	*1994*	*1995*	*1996*	*1997*	*1998*	*1999*	*2000 (estimate)*
Rate of growth of GDP (%)	-3.5	-11.9	-3.1	-0.6	2.9	1.5	1.3	4.6	4.9	4.5	5.2
Rate of growth of industrial output (%)	-9.6	-18.2	-9.7	4.0	9.6	4.6	3.4	11.1	12.4	10.4	18.0
Rate of growth of agricultural output (%)	-4.7	-6.2	-20.0	-9.7	3.2	2.6	7.0	-1.8	-0.3	-2.8	
Inflation rate (consumer, %)	28.9	35.0	23.0	22.5	18.8	28.2	23.6	18.3	14.3	10.1	9.8
Budget surplus or deficit (% GDP)[a]	0.5	-2.2	-7.2	-6.6	-8.4	-6.7	-5.0	-6.6	-5.6	-5.6	-3.3
Unemployment rate (end of year, %)[b]	1.7	7.5	9.3	14.5	12.4	12.1	11.8	11.6	10.1	9.9	
Balance of payments (current account, $ billion)	0.127	0.267	0.324	-3.453	-3.912	-2.480	-1.678	-0.982	-2.298	-2.076	-1.648
Foreign direct investment (net, $ billion)	0.311	1.460	1.471	2.328	1.097	4.410	1.987	1.653	1.453	1.414	
Population (million)			10.3	10.3	10.2	10.2	10.2	10.1	10.1	10.1	10.0

Sources: Various issues of European Bank for Reconstruction and Development, *Transition Report*; United Nations Economic Commission for Europe, *Economic Survey of Europe*; United Nations, *World Economic and Social Survey*; IMF, *World Economic Outlook*.

Notes:

[a] General government balance (EBRD)

[b] Registered unemployed: data from the labour force survey for 1992 to 2000 indicate lower rates of, respectively, 9.7, 10.9, 9.7, 9.9, 9.2, 7.7, 7.0, 6.5 and 6.0 per cent.

A new multi-pillar pension system was implemented in January 1998. Hungary thus became the first country in Eastern Europe to adopt such a scheme. Since July 1998 all new labour force entrants (and, optionally, existing workers) have made mandatory contributions to both the existing pay-as-you-go arrangement (the first pillar) and to a fully funded second pillar, based on a system of personal savings accounts held in privately managed pension funds. A voluntary third pillar is also available for top-up contributions. The pension reform also includes an increase in the retirement age (EBRD 1998b: 171).

By the start of 1991 about 90 per cent of prices had been deregulated. Hungary has not benefited from foreign debt reductions and repayments have continued. A tough-sounding bankruptcy law was approved on 8 April 1992. Many enterprises filed for bankruptcy. The law was substantially amended in September 1993 because of the danger of forcing potentially profitable enterprises into liquidation (EBRD 1994: 26). A new unemployment benefit scheme came into effect in March 1991 (the first was introduced as early as 1986). The period of benefit ranged from six months to two years (depending on the previous length of employment), but this was reduced by 25 per cent at the start of 1992. An excess wage tax was introduced in 1991, exceptions including joint ventures where the foreign stake was over 20 per cent; the scheme was modified in 1992 (Frydman *et al.* 1993: 100). The taxing of wage increases above a defined limit was abolished in 1993 (EBRD 1994: 27). Following large increases in the prices of electricity and gas during the course of 1995, prices were again raised in March 1996. The intention was to raise them again in October 1996 to levels that would ensure cost recovery to producers. But in late August 1996 the government took the controversial decision to postpone the increases until January 1997 (EBRD 1996b: 154). In January 1997 domestic prices for electricity were increased by 24.9 per cent and for gas by 18.8 per cent. At the same time producer prices were increased by an estimated 18.3 per cent and 16.9 per cent respectively (EBRD 1997a: 29). About 84 per cent of consumer prices, weighted by their share in the consumer price index, are free of administrative controls (EBRD 1997b: 174). 'Administered prices were increased by up to 6 per cent in early 2000 for electricity, gas, phone, post, water, sewerage services, radio and television broadcasting, rail passenger transport, bus transport and local public transport … Oil product prices … are not administered' (EBRD 2000b: 170). 'Energy prices continue to be capped at low rates' (EBRD 2001: 68).

Privatization

The employment limit on private enterprises was removed in 1990. The keynote of Hungarian privatization has been on sales in order to raise revenue (for the Treasury and to help pay off the substantial foreign debt) and to improve management.

The size of the private sector is difficult to estimate, but official estimates put the figure in 1992 at about one-third of GDP (Bartholdy 1993: 124). The Deutsche Bank (*Focus: Eastern Europe*, 1 July 1993, no. 82, p. 4) merely gave a range of 33–45 per cent of GDP, but later gave a more definite figure of around 50 per cent (22 March 1994, no. 100, p. 16). The United Nations Economic Commission for Europe (1993: 215) opted for ranges: the officially estimated ones for the entire private sector as a percentage of GDP are 10.0–15.8 per cent in 1990, 18.2–41.0 per cent in 1991 and 25–45 per cent in 1992. In March 1994 it was announced that the government had reached its target of 50 per cent of GDP contributed by the private sector eight months ahead of schedule (*IHT*, Survey, 19 April 1994, p. 17). In mid-1994 the private sector accounted for roughly 55 per cent of GDP, in mid-1995 for roughly 60 per cent of GDP, in mid-1996 for roughly 70 per cent of GDP and in mid-1997 for roughly 75 per cent of GDP (EBRD 1994: 10; 1995b: 11; 1996b: 11; and 1997b: 14). The private sector's share of GDP is 55 per cent (*The Economist*, 29 October 1994, p. 56). If the black economy is included, the private sector accounts for 60 per cent of GDP (*The Economist*, 7 May 1994, p. 45). Up to two-fifths of the 500,000 officially unemployed people probably live off a black economy whose value may amount to nearly a third of GDP (*The Economist*, 11 March 1995, p. 50). The president of Hungary's central bank puts the share of the black economy at 30 per cent of national output (*The Economist*, 18 November 1995, p. 27). Estimates put the grey economy as large as one-third of official GDP (*Business Central Europe*, May 1995, p. 59). The World Bank puts the black economy at 30 per cent of GDP (*IHT*, 26 December 1996, p. 1).

Rough estimates in mid-year of the private sector as a percentage of GDP are provided by the EBRD: 1990, 25 per cent; 1991, 30 per cent; 1992, 40 per cent; 1993, 50 per cent; 1994, 55 per cent; 1995, 60 per cent; 1996, 70 per cent; 1997, 75 per cent; 1998, 80 per cent; 1999, 80 per cent; 2000, 80 per cent (EBRD 1999b: 24, 228, and 2000b: 14, 172).

The privatization programme has certainly not been without problems. Early abuses were associated with 'spontaneous' privatization, in which managers benefited in the form of shares or well-paid positions in the new private firms as assets were sold off cheaply. State controls were consequently introduced. (But there was an enquiry into the activities, including alleged corruption, of the State Property Agency itself, which was set up to take control of the programme. An enquiry was ordered in October 1994 into the State Holding Company. On 12 January 1995 the privatization commissioner, Ferenc Bartha, was dismissed. See also the autumn 1996 'Toscik' affair discussed above in the section on politics.) After considerable delay a three-year privatization programme was announced at the end of September 1990. This envisaged half the state sector being affected, including all small businesses. Policy was to avoid a large 'give-away' of shares, although some modest percentage of shares could be sold at a discount to an enterprise's workers. Policy was also to compensate former owners only partially, in the form of vouchers exchangeable for shares.

Small privatization went ahead, e.g. over 30 per cent of shops had been privatized by the end of April 1992 (Frydman *et al.* 1993: 136). Small privatization has been basically completed (*IHT*, 11 December 1995, p. 11). The privatization of small enterprises is virtually complete (EBRD 1996b: 154). The pace of large privatization was very slow at first but then proceeded steadily. The following facts and figures show the progress of privatization:

1. By the end of April 1992 only about 10–13 per cent of state assets had been privatized (Kiss 1992: 1015, 1033).
2. According to the OECD, around 18 per cent of state enterprise assets had been privatized by the end of 1992. This was well short of the government's target of privatizing half the state sector by the end of its term in 1994 (*FT*, 1 November 1993, p. 17; *FT Survey*, 17 November 1993, p. 47).
3. In 1989 Hungary had about 2,000 state enterprises. By September 1993 the State Property Agency had sold 273 enterprises outright, disposed of majority shareholdings in 144 others and minority shareholdings in 71. A further 370 enterprises were 'liquidated' (p. 47). (Note that 'liquidated' enterprises were not necessarily unprofitable, the assets simply being sold off.) The State Property Agency said that in 1993 404 companies passed from state ownership to the private sector and some portion of a further 185 companies was sold (*FT*, 2 March 1994, p. 22).
4. Up to July 1994 the State Property Agency and the State Holding Company had sold 47 per cent of the former state-owned stock. The remaining 720 enterprises that comprised the former's portfolio were still to be sold, while most of the 166 enterprises in the latter's portfolio were to be privatized completely and the remaining forty-five or so only partially (Helgard Wienert, *The OECD Observer*, April–May 1995, no. 193, p. 38).
5. The State Property Agency estimates that 47 per cent of state property has been privatized (*FT*, Survey, 11 November 1994, p. 29).
6. By the end of 1994 Hungary had sold off about 40 per cent of state enterprises by book value (*The Economist*, 20 May 1995, p. 93).
7. Large privatization has been gradual but steady (EBRD 1994: 26). When it started operations in 1990, the State Property Agency had 1,848 large enterprises. By the end of 1994, 653 were fully privately owned and state ownership in a further 204 had been reduced to less than 50 per cent. Of the original 1,848 enterprises, 437 were in liquidation by December 1994. The state retained on average 53 per cent of the shares in the remaining 1,411 enterprises (EBRD 1995a: 57).

In mid-1991 great hope was placed in 'self-privatization' in which companies choose consultants (ultimately responsible, for a fee, for privatization) from a list drawn up by the State Property Agency. In March 1993 the government announced plans to encourage the general public to participate more by means of interest-free, long-term loans. The Small Investor Shareholder Programme, involving around seventy enterprises, was set to begin in January 1994, but the start was delayed somewhat (beginning with one enterprise on 18 April 1994). On 28 February 1994 it was announced that four public offerings were to be made in April. The Horn government's privatization programme was announced on 3 November 1994, but not approved by parliament until 9 May

1995 (see, for example, *FT*, 20 September 1994, p. 3; 4 November 1994, p. 2; Survey, 11 November 1994, pp. 29–31). The emphasis was to be on sales in order to raise revenue, majority or full state ownership was to be restricted to fewer enterprises (161, e.g. the electricity grid, would have majority state ownership and 46, e.g. the railways, would be kept in full state ownership: EBRD 1995a: 57). The privatization programme was to be largely completed by the end of the government's term of office in 1998. (Horn expects the share of private property in the economy to reach two-thirds by then: *Transition*, January–February 1995, p. 19. Horn said that 'We want to finish privatization by the end of 1997. The dominance of private property in the economy should reach 80–85 per cent by then. Today it is 55 per cent': cited in *FT*, Survey, 21 November 1995, p. iii. The privatization process is drawing to a close in 1998: EBRD 1998a: 36.) The electricity and gas industries were to be demonopolized and substantially privatized. The State Property Agency and the State Holding Company were to be merged into the Hungarian Privatization and Holding Company (this actually taking place on 19 June 1995).

An amendment to the privatization law in July 1997 identified privatized enterprises in which the state was to maintain a significant ownership stake. In twenty-seven enterprises, ranging from energy and telecoms to agribusiness, the state was to retain a golden share, which entitles it to such wide powers as the right to veto changes in product lines and to approve mergers, share conversions and divestments. In 116 enterprises the state would retain a long-term ownership stake. But the amendment also included plans for a further divestment of state shares in blue-chip companies through public share offerings. Shares in 158 companies were sold in 1997. Among the most important privatizations in 1997–8 were the international public offerings of minority stakes in the telecommunications company Matav, OTP bank and the oil and gas company MOL (reducing the government's share from 59 per cent to 42 per cent). Matav was privatized in 1993 and 1995, with 67 per cent sold to a German–American consortium of strategic investors; a further 19 per cent was sold in November 1997. The privatization process was scheduled to be completed by the end of 1998 (EBRD 1998b: 170–1).

The new act took effect on 16 June 1995. The government was to retain majority ownership in 134 enterprises, primarily providing such 'public goods' as bus services in rural areas, the conservation of forests and postal services. The government was also to take a 'golden share' in a number of other enterprises. The privatization of some 150–200 small and medium-sized enterprises was to be carried out via the so-called 'simplified privatization' (by tender) over the following two years. Since the beginning of 1990, 749 enterprises have been sold by the privatization agencies, with investors having taken golden stakes in many of the 700 enterprises remaining in the portfolio (*IHT*, 11 December 1995, p. 11).

A number of large privatization deals were completed in November and December 1996. In the largest individual deal Magyarcom (the 50:50 joint venture between Ameritech and Deutsche Telekom) acquired 37 per cent of the shares of Matav (the main Hungarian telecommunications company). This raised Magyarcom's total ownership in Matav to 67 per cent. In addition, the government (and the municipality of Budapest) sold majority stakes in six regional gas distributors, large minority stakes in six regional electricity distributors, and large minority stakes in two power generating companies. A majority stake in Budapest Bank was sold in December 1995. According to the intentions of the privatization law passed on 9 May 1995, forty-six enterprises would remain fully state-owned, including postal services and the railways. The state would maintain majority stakes in MVM which holds the electrical grid and the only nuclear power plant. (The state attempted to sell 24 per cent of MVM in December 1995 but failed.) The state would also maintain 25 per cent in some of the largest banks. (Two of the five largest banks remain state-owned. There is a substantial presence of smaller private banks, most of them with foreign participation: p. 155.) The bulk of the 'old' industrial enterprises have been privatized, mainly in sales undertaken between 1991 and 1995. By the end of March 1996 state ownership had been reduced to less than 50 per cent in 1,109 of these enterprises (up from 902 in April 1995). About 190 of the original 1,676 enterprises were in liquidation or actually liquidated (as of March 1996) and another 62 had been transferred to other institutions (such as municipalities and ministries), leaving 316 joint stock companies with majority state ownership in the hands of the state privatization agency (EBRD 1996b: 153–4). After the sale of the Hungarian Credit Bank in December 1996 only one of the former five large state banks remained to be privatized. Some 85 per cent of the banking sector is now in private hands (EBRD 1997a: 29). More than 50 per cent of assets in the banking sector are in foreign hands (EBRD 1998a: 26). Under the 1997 amendments to the privatization act, the state property agency will retain a permanent stake in ninety-eight companies. This provision includes eight companies, primarily in the energy, telecommunications and agribusiness sectors, in which the state will retain a golden share. This share provides the government with a wide range of powers, such as the right to veto changes in product lines and to approve mergers, share conversions and divestments. The state will also permanently retain a residual ownership stake in twenty-six agricultural companies that account for more than a quarter of total agricultural sale revenues. So far the state property agency has acted as a passive shareholder in those companies where it is a minority investor. A notable exception is the oil and gas company MOL, where it initiated significant board changes in February 1999, including the removal of the chairman appointed prior to privatization under the previous government. Privatization efforts over the past year have concentrated on the sale of residual stakes, notably the sale of the remaining 5.75 per cent stake in telecommunications company Matav in June 1999 (although the privatization agency retains a single golden share in the company). The government announced in February 1999 that up to 15 per cent of the electric generation market will be opened to new producers in January 2001. If this reform is successful there will be further liberalization in 2001. The aim is full liberalization in advance of EU accession. Postabank, the second largest domestic bank by deposits, has been progressively recapitalized, with the state now holding 100 per cent of the bank. The local corporate sector, consisting largely of small and medium-sized enterprises, has lagged behind foreign-owned enterprises in terms of restructuring and modernization. The main constraints affecting domestic enterprises are the lack of medium- and long-term finance, poor business infrastructure, training and red tape (EBRD 1999b: 226–7). 'The state retains shares in some privatized companies, but remains a largely passive shareholder.' The privatization of Matav, the telecommunications company, is complete. It retains a monopoly over long-distance calls within Hungary until the end of 2001, although the monopoly may be ended earlier than scheduled (EBRD 2000a: 58).

> As prescribed by law, the state property agency will retain a permanent stake in ninety-three companies. This provision includes eight companies, primarily in the energy, telecommunications and agribusiness sectors, in which the state will retain a golden share. So far the state property agency has acted as a passive shareholder in almost all those companies where it is a minority investor. The state-owned oil and gas company, MOL, is a notable exception … The sale of the remaining state assets continues … The local corporate sector has lagged behind foreign-owned enterprises in terms of restructuring and modernization.
>
> (EBRD 2000b: 170)

(Around 60 per cent of banking assets are now in foreign hands: *Business Central Europe*, October 1999, p. 47. Between 1994 and 1998 foreign ownership in the banking sector increased from 15 per cent to 60 per cent, while direct state ownership of the sector fell from 67 per cent to 20 per cent: World Bank (2000), *World Development Report 1999/2000*, p. 162. According to the IMF, the proportion of total bank assets controlled by foreigners – foreign control being defined as foreigners owning more than 50 per cent of the total equity of a bank – increased from about 20 per cent in 1994 to about 57 per cent in 1999: *The Economist*, 4 November 2000, p. 194.)

In November 1997, 25 per cent of the shares in Matav (the telecommunications company which has a dual monopoly over international and domestic trunk calls until 2002) were sold to foreign and domestic investors in a public offering. Some 17 per cent of the shares were sold by the state privatization agency and a further 8 per cent by the Magyarcom partners. The Magyarcom stake thus fell from 67 per cent to 59 per cent. The consortium, formed by Ameritech of the USA and Deutsche Telekom of Germany, had acquired a 30 per cent stake in December 1993 and increased this to 67 per cent in 1995 (*FT*, Survey, 9 December 1997, p. iv). Matav is currently 59.53 per cent owned by Magyarcom, a 50:50 joint venture between Deutsche Telekom and Ameritech, while the remaining 40.47 per cent is publicly traded following the sale of the state's residual 6 per cent holding in May 1999. The state has retained a golden share.

> The government has maintained a stake of 25 per cent and one share in MOL, which has allowed it considerable scope for intervention in the group's affairs, including the ability to orchestrate a complete change of the board and of top management this year [1999].
>
> (*FT*, 9 December 1999, pp. ii, iv)

As regards Matav, Deutsche Telekom bought out its US partner, Ameritech, in early July 2000 (*IHT*, 8 July 2000, p. 11).

Total proceeds realized through privatization totalled around $7 billion as of 30 June 1997. Of that, six-sevenths was from non-Hungarian investors (*IHT*, Survey, 12 December 1997, p. ii).

'Hungary postponed the privatization of its national airline on Monday [8 January 2001], saying it had received no bids for a 47 per cent stake in Malev' (*IHT*, 9 January 2001, p. 12). 'Although seven airlines acquired the tender documents for the carrier ... not one followed through with a concrete bid' (*FT*, 9 January 2001, p. 10). 'The Hungarian government cancelled a tender to sell 10 per cent of national airline Malev after receiving no bids. The loss-making airline now plans to speed up restructuring before attempting another sale' (*Business Central Europe*, February 2001, pp. 12, 23).

> The key to Hungary's economic renaissance has been its structural transformation. Over the 1990s whole new industries grew up from greenfield foreign investment – notably cars, where Hungary had no manufacturing tradition – while the consumer sector exploded ... Privatization is all but complete and restructuring of former state-owned industries has advanced.
>
> (Justin Keay, *IHT*, 3 May 2001, p. 16)

Foreign trade

'Around 40 per cent of the country's GDP now goes through the channels of foreign trade, and one in every three jobs is export-related' (Attila Chikan, minister of economic affairs in Hungary, *IHT*, 25 November 1999, p. 4).

A liberal foreign trade system has gradually been established. The aim was to make the forint fully convertible as soon as possible. The forint is generally convertible for current account transactions (there are restrictions as regards tourism by Hungarian citizens), while capital account transactions are gradually being liberalized (EBRD 1994: 27). The import of energy products, cars and many agricultural products still requires a licence, as does the export of energy products, pharmaceuticals and some agricultural products. A number of industrial and 'sensitive' products (such as textiles and agricultural products) remain substantially protected by import tariffs. Some of these tariffs are being phased out for trade with the EU in accordance with the Europe agreement and in trade with the other members of CEFTA. On 20 March 1995 an 8 per cent import surcharge was imposed on all goods except primary energy carriers and machinery for investment. The government has announced a schedule for the phase-out of the surcharge, with removal altogether by June 1997. (Hungary still applies an annual global quota on imported consumer goods, the level fluctuating between $400 million and $600 million over the period 1994 to 1998. Around 6 per cent of exports are still subject to non-automatic licence requirements: *Transition*, December 1998, vol. 9, no. 6, p. 25.) The forint was declared convertible for current account transactions from 1 January 1996 by pledging compliance with Article 8 of the IMF agreements. The exchange rate is pegged to a basket of currencies. The central rate against the basket is devalued daily at a pre-announced rate. The cumulative monthly rate of devaluation was reduced from 1.3 per cent to 1.2 per cent on 1 January 1996 (to 1.1 per cent on 1 April 1997 and to 1 per cent on 15 August 1997). The spot rate may fluctuate within a band of plus or minus 2.25 per cent of the central rate. The basket was changed in May 1994 from 50 per cent US dollar and 50 per cent DM to 30 per cent US dollar and 70 per cent Ecu. As of 1 January 1997 the DM was to replace the Ecu. Capital account transactions have been gradually liberalized during the 1990s. A number of measures were taken in mid-1996 to liberalize capital transactions so as to pave the way for Hungary's membership of the OECD, which became effective on 7 May 1996 (EBRD 1996b: 154–5). A package of measures was introduced in January 1998 to liberalize international capital flows (EBRD 1998b: 170). In January 1997 the DM replaced the Ecu in the currency basket against which the forint is pegged. The weights of the DM and the US dollar are 70 per cent and 30 per cent respectively (EBRD 1997a: 29). The exchange rate regime is a crawling peg with band (EBRD 1999b: 228).

> Reflecting the high degree of integration with the EU, the currency composition of the basket to which the currency is pegged was changed in January 2000 to comprise only the Euro. The monthly rate of crawl was reduced to 0.3 per cent in April 2000. The government plans to move from the present regime to a fixed exchange rate target with wide intervention bands as soon as inflation falls below 5 per cent and the inflation differential with major trading partners falls below 3 per cent.
>
> (EBRD 2000b: 170)

> Last month [4 May 2001] ... Hungary ... widened the band within which the forint trades, allowing the currency to trade more freely. The central bank had long indicated that it wanted to phase out its currency peg, and that first meant loosening it ... The forint will continue to be devalued slowly against the euro, with the target peg crawling downwards by 0.2 per cent a month. But from now on the currency will be allowed to fluctuate within a band of 15 per cent either side of the peg, compared to the previous 2.25 per cent.
>
> (*Business Central Europe*, June 2001, p. 13)

'[In June] Hungary floated the forint, abolishing the last currency restrictions. The liberalization means that foreign investors will now be free to buy short-term forint bonds and Hungarians can open foreign bank accounts' (*Business Central Europe*, July–August 2001, pp. 11–12).

There has been a relatively successful switch from Comecon to Western trade. For example, in September 1992 Hungarian exports to the EU exceeded 50 per cent of the total for the first time; by way of comparison the figure was 14 per cent in the 1970s and 25 per cent in the 1980s (*FT*, Survey, 29 October 1992, p. 33). In 1992, 75 per cent of exports went to OECD countries (*Employment Observatory*, 1993, no. 4, p. 2). Another source puts the figure at 70.5 per cent (Deutsche Bank, *Focus: Eastern Europe*, 1993, no. 85, p. 6). In 1995 the former Eastern bloc countries accounted for 24 per cent of foreign trade. The EU accounted for 63 per cent of exports and 61.5 per cent of imports (*FT*, 13 February 1996, p. 2). A trade agreement with EFTA was due to have come into force on 1 July 1993, but the date was put back to 1 October 1993. An association agreement with the EU came into force on 1 February 1994. On 1 April 1994 Hungary became the first ex-socialist country to apply formally for EU membership. '[In 1997] In a first for the entire Central and East European region, advanced industrial products accounted for more than 50 per cent of Hungary's exports to the EU' (*IHT*, Survey, 4 June 1998, p. 20). Some 75 per cent of foreign trade is now conducted with the EU (*IHT*, 29 June 2000, p. 15).

In 1994 exports of goods and services represented around a quarter of GDP (compared with over a third in 1991). But customs-free zones are playing a rapidly increasing role in foreign trade and this may distort the comparison. Trade with developed market economies now accounts for 70 to 75 per cent of foreign trade (OECD, *Economic Outlook*, June 1996, p. 111).

Foreign direct investment

Hungary has been outstandingly successful as regards direct foreign investment. (See Table 4.2 for annual net volumes.) Estimates are as follows:

1 The *FT* (6 October 1993, p. 8) reported an accumulated total of more than $5.5 billion since 1988, more than half the aggregate for Eastern Europe, according to the government.
2 By the start of 1994 Eastern Europe had attracted $18.3 billion (actually paid up), of which Hungary accounted for a third. More than $10 billion (over 55 per cent) of the total went to Hungary, the Czech Republic and Poland (*FT*, 10 May 1994, p. 6).
3 In 1993 only $5 billion flowed into the former Soviet bloc countries (excluding East Germany), representing just 3 per cent of all foreign direct investment. Within Central and Eastern Europe Hungary accounted for 25.9 per cent, the former Czechoslovakia for 26.4 per cent, Poland 15.7 per cent, Romania 1.4 per cent and Bulgaria 1.2 per cent (*Guardian*, 3 September 1994, p. 35).
4 Net direct foreign investment in Hungary was $311 million in 1990, $1.46 billion in 1991 and $1.47 billion in 1992. The respective total figures for

Bulgaria, the former Czechoslovakia, Hungary, Poland and Romania combined were $573 million, $2.261 billion and $2.825 billion. Hungary and Czechoslovakia together accounted for some 90 per cent of the total (United Nations Economic Commission for Europe 1993: 19, 239). In 1993 the net flow into Hungary was $2.328 billion, in 1994 it was $1.097 billion and in 1995 it was $4.4 billion (United Nations Economic Commission for Europe 1996: 149).

5 Foreign direct investment in Hungary amounted to $5.441 billion in the period 1990–3 (EBRD 1994: 123). The total for Eastern Europe and the former Soviet Union amounted to $12.417 billion, of which Hungary, the Czech Republic and Slovakia alone accounted for two-thirds.

'Annual measured FDI inflows into Eastern Europe and the former Soviet Union rose ten-fold between 1990 and 1993. Even so, however, they represented only approximately 10 per cent of total FDI flows into developing countries in 1993' (EBRD 1994: 122). (In 1994 direct foreign investment in the countries of the former Soviet Union and Central and Eastern Europe was only $6.5 billion, equivalent to the total received by Malaysia and Thailand: World Bank 1996: 136. In 1995 Central and Eastern Europe, with a population of 125 million, attracted $10.5 billion in direct investment. This was about the same as Singapore and Malaysia with a combined population of 22 million: *Business Central Europe*, June 1996, p. 11. Over a third of all direct foreign investment inflows into Central and Eastern European transition countries since 1990 has been absorbed by Hungary: OECD, *Economic Outlook*, June 1996, p. 111. The net flow of direct foreign investment into the East European, European CIS and Baltic states reached a record $10.6 billion in 1995, compared with only $4.3 billion in 1994. Of the 1995 total, Hungary accounted for $4.4 billion and the Czech Republic $2.5 billion: United Nations Economic Commission for Europe 1996: 148. According to official figures, total foreign direct investment amounted to $23 billion as of 31 March 2000: *IHT*, 29 June 2000, p. 15.)

Companies with foreign ownership, most of them manufacturers, account for 25 per cent of GDP. Since 1990 foreign companies have invested nearly $9 billion. To date privatizations have brought in about $3 billion from foreign investors. According to the OECD, companies with at least 10 per cent foreign ownership accounted for 50 per cent of exports in 1993. Some studies suggest that the proportion reached nearly 60 per cent in 1994 (*IHT*, 9 December 1995, p. 9). In 1995 about 70 per cent of industrial exports came from foreign-invested enterprises (*FT*, 13 February 1996, p. 2). Foreign-owned companies produce about one-third of GDP and account for about 25 per cent of private sector employment (EBRD 1999b: 226).

Since the beginning of 1994 Hungary has ceased to offer incentives to new foreign investors (*FT*, 28 September 1994, p. 6). Hungary has abandoned its general incentive scheme (*Business Central Europe*, April 1994, p. 37). Hungary has abolished tax holidays for enterprises with foreign participation, but the Horn government has promised to reinstate broader incentives (EBRD 1994: 125).

> Despite the phasing out of most foreign investment incentives, a stable and favourable business environment and a large pool of skilled and adaptable workers continues to attract a robust flow of foreign direct investment, increasingly into capital and skill intensive sectors.
>
> (EBRD 2000b: 170)

Total direct foreign investment inflows in the period 1991–3 were equivalent to 25 per cent of total fixed domestic capital formation (Lansbury *et al.* 1996: 104). In Hungary preference was given to a programme of privatization for cash through auctions or direct tender. Although there was a voucher scheme it affected only about 10 per cent of the population. Consequently, foreign investors could bid directly for a relatively large portion of state property (p. 106). Some tax holidays were abolished in 1994, but certain priority investments (both domestic and foreign) may be entitled to preferential treatment and fully foreign-owned offshore companies can, under certain conditions, obtain an 85 per cent tax holiday for a limited period of time (p. 107). The authors undertake an econometric analysis of the factors affecting the pattern of OECD investment in Hungary, the Czech Republic, Poland and Slovakia during the period 1991–3.

> Our empirical results support and extend the findings from earlier surveys of investment in Central Europe. Whilst it is clear that the timing and form of privatization programmes had a marked influence on the pattern of inward investment, we also find a significant effect from relative labour costs and an indicator of research intensity. The latter findings are consistent with those from many other studies of investment in developing countries. This evidence is consistent with the notion that some investors have been attracted to Central Europe by a combination of relatively low labour costs and the availability of skilled workers in particular sectors and countries. In the short term the continued strength of inward investment in these economies is likely to depend heavily on the continuation and expansion of privatization programmes. Post-privatization investments, which have already begun in some economies … are more likely to depend on market growth and costs relative to those elsewhere in Europe.
>
> (p. 112)

A new land law was passed by parliament on 6 April 1994. Although existing holdings were not affected, new purchases of land by foreign individuals and companies would be banned. Non-Hungarians would be allowed to lease no more than 500 ha and then only for ten years as a rule. The measures would apply only in the interim period leading up to EU accession and until land prices reached 'realistic' levels (Nicholas Denton, *FT*, 7 April 1994, p. 28).

(See agriculture, below, for later developments.)

Agriculture

In 1992, 34 per cent of the population was rural and agriculture accounted for 15 per cent of employment in the period 1990–2 (industry 31 per cent and services 54 per cent) (*The Economist*, Survey, 8 April 1995, p. 4).

There is only an element of restitution in the form of land or limited financial compensation as far as agriculture is concerned. Agricultural privatization started off slowly. Anthony Robinson (*FT Survey*, 29 October 1992, p. 32) reported that the aim was to place nearly 80 per cent of cropland in private hands by the end of 1994. But there was, he argued, little desire or ability to return to small-scale peasant farming. There would be a mixture of private and family farms, farming associations and voluntary co-operatives.

The basic aim of legislation reforming the collective farms was to force them to transform themselves into new business organizations (such as private or public companies) or, if they so wished, into new, free co-operatives. Although the deadline has technically gone by (the end of 1992) many issues remain unresolved. Few members of the former co-operatives who had re-established as new co-operatives opted to take their land and other assets out in order to farm independently. The privatization of state farms has also been slow (Matthew Harley, *OECD Observer*, 1994, no. 186, p. 33).

Only 119 co-operatives have been liquidated so far and only 10 per cent of the membership has opted for individual farming (United Nations Economic Commission for Europe 1993: 204).

Restitution has produced 2 million owners of small plots, most of whom lease their land to private farmers. The average size of private farms is only 6 ha (*Business Central Europe*, September 1993, p. 25).

All the collective farms have been privatized, but many cannot be broken up because of legal conflicts about land ownership (*The Economist*, 7 August 1993, p. 63).

Co-operatives have been broken up, but the new owners often lack the knowledge (or willingness) to work the land (*Business Central Europe*, December 1993–January 1994, pp. 14–15).

> The splintering of hundreds of enormous state farms and co-operatives into private plots did not produce the unworkable operational patchwork many feared. On the other hand, the transformation of socialist co-operatives into slightly smaller ones based on nominal private ownership has not been as disastrously ineffective as others prophesied … With privatization more or less complete, the average size of commercial farms is now around 800 ha.
>
> (*Business Central Europe*, December 1995–January 1996, p. 45)

The major problem is the structure of the co-operatives, which still account for half of production.

> The problem is that co-operative managers tend to have a hard time persuading members (who each have a vote) to act as shareholders rather

> than employees – they prefer to invest profits in higher wages rather than in new machinery ... The thousands of full-time family-owned farms that have emerged over the past few years face the opposite problem. Even where they have managed to lease 100 ha, they are too small to make investments in machinery investments pay off or to overcome the limitations of rural infrastructure.
>
> (p. 46)

According to the land law, which went into effect in January 1995, only Hungarian individuals (not legal entities) can own agricultural land (p. 46).

An OECD report found that Hungary had a lower level of agricultural subsidy than any OECD country except New Zealand. But 1993 did see some retrogression towards protectionism and in 1994 the proportion of all imports subject to licensing was to rise from 10 per cent to 12 per cent with the inclusion of certain agricultural products in the controls (Nicholas Denton, *FT*, 15 December 1993, p. 28).

'In formerly collectivized Central Europe ... the majority response of landowners [after restitution] was to rent their land to the larger units that emerged from the transformation process, whether it was the transformed co-operative or a new successor company' (Swain 1999: 1205). 'Most people ... rejected the idea of farming their newly acquired land themselves and rented it back to either the co-operative or one of its successor companies' (p. 1216).

> The initial response ... was to stay with the co-operatives and keep them together ... However ... there were both political pressures (government campaigns against co-operatives and their managers) and economic pressures (assiduous enforcement of bankruptcy legislation ...) to enforce change ... Hence, to a greater degree than in the Czech and Slovak Republics, the co-operative transformation process became one of co-operative breakup. But assets were not destroyed or abandoned as was so often the case in Bulgaria and Romania. They were used rather by management as stepping stones in the creation of private large-scale successor farms. At the same time, some who had already established significant private farms on the basis of 'second economy' household plot farming in the socialist years expanded further. Nationally, by the end of 1994 31.7 per cent of land was farmed by co-operatives, 35.9 per cent by private corporate farms and 32.4 per cent by individual farmers. Of individual farms larger than one hectare, however, 90.6 per cent were smaller than 10 ha.
>
> (pp. 1213–14)

> Restitution of farmland to former owners is the most significant land reform procedure in terms of total agricultural land ... Typically [in Central European countries – CECs – which are defined to include Albania, Bulgaria, Romania and Slovenia], the reform laws specify that former owners be restituted land in historical boundaries, if possible. Otherwise,

they receive property rights to a plot of land of comparable size and quality. With the exception of Poland and Albania, most farmland is restituted to former owners … Land reform procedures for collective farmland and state farmland differ … CECs most often restituted collective farmland to former owners. The main exceptions are in Hungary and in Albania. In Hungary one-third of collective farmland is restituted; another third is auctioned for compensation bonds and another third is distributed among farm workers … In the majority of CECs state farmland is leased, pending sale of the land.

(Swinnen 1999: 638–9)

Non-land assets have been restituted in some countries, but in most cases were privatized using vouchers … During collectivization private farmers and landowners were forced to bring their assets into collectively organized production units. Most non-land assets … gradually became collective property as the original assets were replaced … In many [countries] … collectivized land remained legally privately owned throughout the communist regime. Only in the countries of the former Soviet Union and in Albania was land legally nationalized.

(pp. 640–1)

Hungary, where only part of the collective land is restituted, is a special case. After 1968 owners who were no longer active in the collective farms were forced to sell their land to the collective farms … By the end of the 1980s most of the land was owned by the collective farms, with approximately one-third of the land still formally privately owned. This privately owned land has been restituted to its owners, while land owned by the collective farm is used partly for compensation through a voucher privatization scheme and partly for distribution among collective farm employees. Former owners who were forced to sell land (at artificially low prices) are not restituted their land, but are compensated with vouchers, which can be used, among other things, to purchase land set aside for this purpose … In Romania, Hungary and former Czechoslovakia current land restitution is (explicitly) not based on the 1945 ownership situation, but the ownership strongly influenced by the post-World War II (between 1945 and 1949) land reforms implemented by a government dominated by the Communist Party … The Czech government decided to use the February 1948 date as the basis for restitution. Similarly, Hungary took 1948 and Romania took 1947 as their reference dates … Collective farmland is [thus] restituted to former owners, but state farmland is privatized through different procedures. A reason is the difference in legal ownership: state farms operated mainly on land legally owned by the state. In some cases that farmland was state-owned before 1940; in other cases it was nationalized after the war (taken from foreigners or from the church).

(pp. 642–3)

'Foreign former landowners have not been restituted land' (p. 646). 'In Hungary the government has agreed to partially compensate owners who lost their land between 1939 and 1948' (p. 650).

> The Hungarians are seeking the right to keep temporarily their rules against foreign and corporate buying of agricultural land … The Smallholders are among the most stubborn supporters of Hungary's policy of barring agricultural land sales to companies or foreign individuals. Corporately-owned land … was all either purchased through state farm privatization or bought between 1990 and July 1994, when the ban was introduced. Much land worked by companies is leased from small farmers … Hungary is seeking to continue the ban for ten years after EU membership, in breach of rules requiring free movement of capital.
>
> (*FT*, Survey, 9 December 1999, p. iii)

> Agriculture was productive enough back in the 1980s. Today, after a decade of botched reform, chaotic restitution and political meddling, it is a mess … Production is still going down … Agricultural production … [is] up to 40 per cent below 1989 levels … Most of the trouble stems from a restitution process that was chaotic even by post-communist standards. Many of Hungary's communist co-operatives ended up being split into tiny plots, many too small even to feed their owners … There are now a staggering 1.2 million smallholders in Hungary. Some of these are owned by absentee landlords who lease out their plots to larger farms. But there are still around 400,000 Hungarian peasant farmers, many of them farming less than a single hectare. While some grumble about the problems faced by big state farms … the real nightmares lie in this sub-culture of subsistence farmers. These farms are too small to buy fertilizers and seed … Farmers cannot afford to buy decent animals … Foreigners are barred from owning farmland in Hungary … There is even a cap set on the amount of land that locals can own … There is no land market … The number of tiny farms is slowly falling, but that just means they are merging to become small farms. And you cannot farm two hectares profitably … Even the biggest farms have not been commercialized yet … [There are a] 100-odd big state farms surviving from communist times … There is only one wholesale market in the whole of Hungary.
>
> (*Business Central Europe*, December 2000–January 2001, pp. 59–60)

'Hungary's 960,000 farms tend to be relatively small; the average farm size is 163 ha (403 acres)' (*IHT*, Survey, 14 June 2001, p. 19).

Economic performance

After a good start Hungary lost the image of the 'golden boy' of the transition for a while. Initially Hungary was generally ranked first in terms of overall economic success, but then slipped behind countries like the Czech Republic and Poland. Towards the new millennium Hungary and Poland were generally considered to be transitional leaders. The GDP growth rate turned positive in 1994 but was modest in 1994, 1995 and 1996. Thereafter growth was robust. (See Table 4.2.) In 2000 transitional Hungary's GDP exceeded the 1989 level for the first time (EBRD 2001: 15). Inflation has never been out of control, but it took until 2000 for the annual inflation rate to move into single figures.

5 Poland

POLITICS

Political developments between the November 1995 presidential election and the general election of September 1997

5 November 1995: there is a 64.7 per cent turnout for the first round of the presidential election (the second being fixed for 19 November). Thirteen candidates actually take part, four having dropped out. Alexander Kwasniewski comes first with 35.11 per cent of the vote. Lech Walesa's continuing resurgence takes him into second place with 33.11 per cent. (Walesa continually plugged his theme that former communists would control the presidency as well as the government and parliament if Kwasniewski won.) Jacek Koron won 9 per cent of the vote, Waldemar Pawlak 4.3 per cent and Hanna Gronkiewicz-Waltz 2.8 per cent.

19 November 1995: Kwasniewski wins the presidency with 51.72 per cent of the vote in a 68 per cent turnout. Walesa receives 48.28 per cent of the vote. (Soon afterwards the defence, foreign and interior ministers announced their intention to resign.)

26 November 1995: Kwasniewski resigns from the Alliance of the Democratic Left.

9 December 1995: the Supreme Court rules that the presidential result stands despite the fact that Kwasniewski broke the electoral law by falsely claiming that he had an economics degree. The court feels that it is impossible to determine the effect it had on preferences. (Some 600,000 people signed an application to annul the result.)

19 December 1995: Walesa, backed by the outgoing interior minister Andrzej Milczanowski, convenes a meeting of selected parliamentary and legal personalities to discuss an alleged 'grave threat to state security'. It is claimed that prime minister Jozef Oleksy spied for the Soviet Union and Russia during the period 1982 to 1995.

23 December 1995: Alexander Kwasniewski is sworn in as president.

9 January 1996: Walesa says that he is thinking of applying for his old job as an electrician in the Gdansk shipyard. (On 2 April 1996 he returned to his job as an electrician in the Gdansk shipyard, but was allowed time off for political activities and lectures. He was to remain until parliament agreed to give former presidents a pension. The Sejm did so on 12 April 1996.)

15 January 1996: Walesa accepts the position of a consultant to the Solidarity trade union.

24 January 1996: prime minister Oleksy resigns after the military prosecutor announces that there is sufficient evidence to start a formal investigation into the question of whether the prime minister provided 'information to foreign intelligence and participated in foreign intelligence'. Oleksy maintains his innocence but accepts that he befriended the Russian diplomat now accused of being a spy. (The military prosecutor announced on 22 April 1996 that he would not be proceeding with the case because of lack of evidence.)

28 January 1996: Oleksy is elected leader of Social Democracy of the Polish Republic (the leading party within the Alliance of the Democratic Left). He succeeds Kwasniewski.

1 February 1996: Wlodzimierz Cimoszewicz, deputy speaker of the Sejm and deputy president of the Alliance of the Democratic Left, is appointed prime minister by President Kwasniewski.

7 February 1996: The new cabinet is sworn in. It includes replacement interior and justice ministers.

15 February 1996: parliament approves the new government.

18 February 1996: a referendum is held on privatization, called by Lech Walesa when he was still president. The main question is 'Are you for carrying out a general transfer of [state] property to the citizen?' Another question asks whether a more flexible type of privatization voucher (able to be used for the purchase of property) should be introduced. There are also questions on whether more enterprises should take part in mass privatization and on whether privatization proceeds should be used to pay state debts to pensioners and civil servants and to finance new pension funds. But the turnout was only 32.4 per cent (instead of the minimum 50 per cent). Of those who voted, 94.5 per cent approved the main question. (Walesa took the low turnout as a personal defeat.)

6 April 1996: 'About a hundred nationalists carrying antisemitic and anti-Western banners demonstrate outside the Auschwitz memorial to protest efforts to block construction of a shopping centre nearby' (*IHT*, 8 April 1996, p. 5). ('A gaggle of pathetic skinheads they may have been, but that parade of Polish anti-semites through the arch into Auschwitz was deeply repugnant ... It was not just the evidence offered of the virulence of contemporary antisemitism. There was a worrying absence of Polish response': *Independent*, editorial, 8 April 1996, p. 14.) (On 10 April both the government and the Roman Catholic Church condemned the march.)

8–10 April 1996: Kwasniewski visits Russia.

25 April 1996: a Gdansk court drops proceedings against General Wojciech Jaruzelski over the shooting of forty-four protesters in 1970 when he was defence minister. The judge rules that as the general has been charged among other things with infringing the constitution, the court has no authority in the case and that he can be tried only by Poland's special State Tribunal (*IHT*, 26 April 1996, p. 6).

7 July 1996: prime minister Cimoszewicz expresses 'deep regret' for past atrocities against the Jews. (On 4 July 1946 forty-two Jews were killed in Kielce. 'As many as 2,000 to 3,000 Jews are believed to have been killed by Poles in the following months, a demonstration of antisemitism that thrived even after almost all of Poland's 3 million Jews were murdered by the Nazis. After the pogrom here, most of the remaining 300,000 Polish Jews emigrated': Jane Perlez, *IHT*, 8 July 1996, p. 6.)

8 August 1996: a court declares the Gdansk shipyard to be bankrupt.

The Sejm approves a reorganization of government structures, to be implemented on 1 October 1996 (*EEN*, 14 August 1996, vol. 10, no. 16, p. 3; *FT*, 15 August 1996, p. 2; *IHT*, 9 August 1996, p. 15).

1 October 1996: seven ministries are abolished and four new ones created. The principal changes are as follows:

1. A new Treasury ministry, which takes over some of the functions of the finance and other ministries. For example, it oversees both state sector holdings and the new privatization agency (which is a replacement for the privatization ministry). (The finance ministry will only be responsible for drawing up and implementing the budget: Deutsche Bank, *Focus: Eastern Europe*, 1996, no. 162, p. 7.) (Control over most of the 3,700 enterprises still in state hands will pass from ministers to provincial governors: *IHT*, 9 August 1996, p. 15. The Treasury ministry has begun to take control of 204 of the largest strategic state enterprises – power plants, coal mines and vodka distilleries – while ownership of 1,168 enterprises is being transferred to local governments: *Transition*, September–October 1996, vol. 7, nos 9–10, p. 25.)

   Miroslaw Pietrewicz (Polish Peasant Party) is appointed Treasury minister.
2. The trade and industry ministry is merged with the foreign trade ministry to form a new ministry of the economy. 'The reshuffle leaves Mr Grzegorz Kolodko, deputy premier responsible for the economy and the finance minister, in place' (*FT*, 2 October 1996, p. 2).
3. The central planning office is incorporated into one large ministry of industry.
4. The construction ministry is transformed into a housing and development office.
5. The cabinet office is to be replaced by a smaller prime minister's chancery.
6. The cabinet office's role in overseeing local administration is transferred to the interior ministry, which changes its name to the ministry of internal affairs and administration.
7. The European Union affairs office, currently with the cabinet office, is upgraded to a separate committee for European integration.

8 The government has a new strategic studies centre. Overall the prime minister's powers are to be strengthened in relation to the cabinet (*EEN*, 14 August 1996, vol. 10, no. 16, p. 3).

30 August 1996: the Sejm approves a new abortion law by 208 votes to 61, with 15 abstentions. (Other deputies walked out.) Women will be able to have abortions up to the twelfth week of pregnancy 'in difficult personal and economic circumstances' in state hospitals or private clinics.

3 October 1996: the Senate rejects the new abortion law by 52 votes to 40. (The Sejm can overrule the Senate's decision with at least a 50 per cent plus one vote. The Sejm narrowly did so on 24 October 1996, by 228 votes to 195. But on 28 May 1997 the constitutional court ruled that the abortion law was at variance with the constitutional right of life – interpreted as from conception rather than birth. Parliament had six months to amend the abortion law in line with the court's ruling or to overturn the ruling by at least a two-thirds majority.)

23 October 1996: the Sejm votes by 211 to 146, with 60 abstentions, to abandon proceedings against General Wojciech Jaruzelski for declaring martial law in 1981. (A parliamentary commission found that he had taken action out of a sense of the 'higher necessity' of warding off Soviet intervention.)

22 November 1996: Poland becomes the twenty-eighth member of the OECD.

20 December 1996: it is announced that Wieslaw Kacmarek is to head the new ministry of the economy.

4 February 1997: Grzegorz Kolodko, the finance minister, resigns. The president's economic adviser, Marek Belka, is named as replacement.

20 February 1997: the Sejm approves a law returning cemeteries, synagogues and religious buildings to Jewish communities in Poland. Restitution of Jewish private property confiscated during the Second World War will be subject to separate legislation (*IHT*, 21 February 1997, p. 5).

26 February 1997: there is an arson attack on the only synagogue in use in Warsaw (*IHT*, 27 February 1997, p. 5).

6 March 1997: it is announced that the Gdansk shipyard is to be closed, although it is hoped that a buyer can still be found. (Demonstrations, sometimes violent, followed. On 20 March 1997 the government announced that about 2,000 people would be employed in the period 1998–2000 building five ships for the state-owned Szczecin yard.)

10 March 1997: the chief of staff of the armed forces is replaced for resisting the strengthening of civilian control over the armed forces, one of the conditions laid down by Nato for entry into the organization.

2 April 1997: both houses of parliament approve the draft of the new constitution, by 451 votes to 40 with 6 abstentions. There will be a referendum on 25 May and, if approved, the new constitution will take effect by the end of 1997. It includes the following: the separation of church and state; guarantees of civil and economic liberties; executive powers to be shared between the prime minister and the president (with the president continuing to have special responsibility for defence and security policy, but whose veto can now be overturned by a three-fifths majority in the Sejm instead of one of two-thirds); a 'social market economy'; free basic health care and education; abortion is permitted under defined circumstances; a minimum wage and a commitment to combating unemployment; the national debt is to be capped at 60 per cent of GDP and the central bank is forbidden to finance the budget deficit; an independent monetary council, headed by the central bank governor, has responsibility for monetary policy (*FT*, 3 April 1997, p. 2 and 4 April 1997, p. 2; *IHT*, 3 April 1997, p. 5; *The Economist*, 5 April 1997, p. 46).

7 April 1997: President Kwasniewski visits the Pope in the Vatican.

10 April 1997: the agriculture minister, Roman Jagielinski, is dismissed. He is replaced by Jaroslaw Kalinowski.

25 May 1997: the turnout is less than 42 per cent for the referendum on the constitution. The 'yes' vote is 52.71 per cent and the 'no' vote is 45.89 per cent.

31 May–10 June 1997: the Pope pays his seventh visit to his homeland since he became Pope in 1978.

8 July 1997: Poland is invited 'to begin accession talks with Nato'. (The foreign ministers of the sixteen Nato countries signed the protocol of accession on 16 December 1997.)

10 July 1997: President Clinton visits Poland.

16 July 1997: the European Commission recommends that Poland opens negotiations in early 1998 for entry to the EU. (The invitation was formally approved at an EU summit on 13 December 1997.)

The floods of July 1997 cause $4 billion to $5 billion worth of damage (*Business Central Europe*, September 1997, p. 17).

August 1997: a law took effect in August 1997 under which candidates for parliament must declare in writing if they were ever secret informers or if they collaborated with the secret police in the communist era. The electorate will be handed ballots noting admissions of collaboration. Those elected after the 21 September election and incumbents such as the president face a judicial evaluation of their statements by a special commission of judges. Proven liars will be banned from elected and appointed office for ten years (Christine Spolar, *IHT*, 28 August 1997, p. 5).

19 August 1997: the Polish Peasant Party submits a motion asking parliament to dismiss prime minister Cimoszewicz for blocking advance payments to farmers for this year's grain harvest (*IHT*, 21 August 1997, p. 5).

27 August 1997: the Polish Peasant Party withdraws its support for the motion of no confidence after reaching agreement that the government will purchase an extra 300,000 tonnes of grain (*FT*, 28 August 1997, p. 2).

The general election of 21 September 1997

There was a 5 per cent threshold. The turnout was 48 per cent. The result was not as close as expected, as Table 5.1 shows. Although the Alliance of the Democratic Left won a higher percentage of the vote than the previous time, it still lost power. The right-wing parties avoided the splits which had caused them to be underrepresented in the last parliament.

Table 5.1 Poland: the general election of 21 September 1997

Party	*Seats in Sejm*	*% seats*	*% vote*[a]
Solidarity Electoral Action	201	43.7	33.83
Alliance of the Democratic Left	164	35.6	27.13
Freedom Union	60	13.0	13.37
Polish Peasant Party	27	5.9	7.31
Movement for the Reconstruction of Poland	6	1.3	5.56
German minority	2	0.4	
Total	460		

Note:
[a] There is a 5 per cent threshold for parliamentary representation

The parties and their platforms were as follows:

Alliance of the Democratic Left: led by Jerzy Szmajdzinski. The party's slogan was 'A good today, a better tomorrow'.

Solidarity Electoral Action: led by Marian Krzaklewski. The alliance's slogan was 'Poland, Freedom, Family' and it espoused 'patriotic and Christian values'.

Krzaklewski formed Solidarity Electoral Action in October 1996, comprising Solidarity plus thirty-seven small and medium-sized right-wing parties (*EEN*, 24 October 1996, vol. 10, no. 21, p. 3). Solidarity Electoral Action has been weakened by the departure of the small National Democratic Party in order to join the Polish Peasant Party (*EEN*, 3 July 1997, vol. 11, no. 13, p. 8). On 4 July 1997 the Confederation for an Independent Poland withdrew from Solidarity Electoral Action (*EEN*, 1997, vol. 11, no. 14, p. 7).

'A disparate group of thirty-six parties united mainly by anti-communism' (*FT*, 23 September 1997, p. 22). Solidarity Electoral Action was a coalition of anti-communist parties. Support was concentrated among the unionized workers of state enterprises and public sector workers (*FT*, Survey, 26 March 1997, p. i). Solidarity Electoral Action and the Movement for the Reconstruction of Europe

> tend to varying degrees of xenophobia and are less than enthusiastic believers in privatization and the kind of market-orientated reforms needed to make Poland eligible for EU membership. But this can also be said of the Polish Peasant Party, the junior member of the present coalition.
>
> (*FT*, Survey , 26 March 1997, p. i)

Solidarity Electoral Action 'is torn between a liberal conservative wing and a populist wing inspired by the movement's trade union membership … In the West … there are some concerns about the populist and anti-reform elements' (*FT*, 9 September 1997, p. 2).

'The economic programme it [Solidarity Electoral Action] unveiled in May [1997] was more centrist than expected in macro-policy, though it contained worrying talk of keeping industry in Polish hands' (*Business Central Europe*, July–August 1997, p. 24).

Freedom Union: led by Leszek Balcerowicz.

> Mr Balcerowicz admits that the Alliance of the Democratic Left's economic policies and goals as expressed by Mr Marek Belka, the new finance minister, are virtually indistinguishable from those of Freedom Union, and certainly closer than to any of the parties who define themselves as 'right-wing' in terms of their historical anti-communism.
> (*FT*, Survey, 26 March 1997, p. i)

Polish Peasant Party: led by Waldemar Pawlak.
Movement for the Reconstruction of Poland: led by Jan Olszewski. Its members are nationalists, including an antisemitic fringe. The party tries to appeal to small shopkeepers who feel threatened by foreign supermarket chains (*FT*, Survey, 26 March 1997, p. ii).

Some of the parties not winning enough votes to enter the Sejm included the following:

Polish Socialist Party: led by Jan Mulak.
Social Democracy of the Polish Republic: led by Jozef Oleksy.
Non-Party Bloc in Support of Reform: led by Stanislaw Kowolok.
Confederation for an Independent Poland: led by Adam Slomka.
Labour Union: led by Ryszard Bugaj.
Democratic Christian National Bloc for Poland: led by Leszek Zielinski.
Pensioners' Party: led by Zenon Ruminski.
Pensioners' Coalition of the Republic of Poland: led by Marek Albiniak.
Polish Republic's Right-Wing Union: led by Janusz Korwin Mikke.

Comments after the election

> Four years ago these right of centre voters spread their votes over a group of small parties, which because they failed to reach more than 5 per cent of the overall vote, were not represented in the last parliament. By bringing more than thirty small parties and union groupings under the umbrella of Solidarity Electoral Action Mr Krzaklewski was able to unite into one party the anti-communist feelings across Poland.
> (*IHT*, 23 September 1997, p. 10)

> In power the SLD [Alliance of the Democratic Left] … largely continued the reforms originally mapped out in 1989 by Leszek Balcerowicz … But the SLD was less ready to jettison the bad old political habit of packing the media, bureaucracy and state industries with party loyalists.
>
> (*The Times*, 23 September 1997, p. 19)

> They have packed Poland's state-owned companies with *nomenklatura* cronies. State broadcasting is firmly under Warsaw politicians' thumbs. So is regional government: the forty-nine voivodships, the tier between local and central administration, are in the gift of central government.
>
> (*The Economist*, 27 September 1997, p. 18)

'The outgoing coalition may have been accused of cronyism and corruption, but it proved itself capable of delivering stability, growth and cautious reform' (*FT*, 23 September 1997, p. 22).

Developments after the 21 September 1997 general election

9 October 1997: Ryszard Bugaj, chairman of the Labour Union, resigns.

11 October 1997: Waldemar Pawlak is voted out of office as leader of the Polish Peasant Party. Jaroslaw Kalinowski is elected party chairman (*EEN*, 1997, vol. 11, no. 20, p. 6).

15 October 1997: Solidarity Electoral Action and Freedom Union agree to nominate Jerzy Buzek as prime minister.

17 October 1997: the president approves the nomination of Jerzy Buzek as prime minister.

20 October 1997: the opening day of the new parliament.

31 October 1997: the new cabinet is sworn in. There are fifteen ministers and five ministers without portfolio.

Among the posts allocated to Solidarity Electoral Action are the following: Jerzy Buzek, prime minister; Janusz Tomaszewski, interior minister and one of two deputy prime ministers; Janusz Steinhoff, economy minister responsible for trade and industrial policy as well as arms procurement; Emil Wasacz, Treasury and privatization; Longin Komolowski, labour and social affairs (includes pension reform; supported by Teresa Kaminska who is responsible for social service reforms); Ryszard Czarnecki, European Integration Committee (EU entry negotiations); Jacek Janiszewski, agriculture.

Among the posts allocated to Freedom Union are the following: Leszek Balcerowicz, finance minister and deputy prime minister (also head of the top economic decision-making body); Janusz Onyszkiewicz, defence; Bronislaw Geremek, foreign affairs (excluding EU entry negotiations); Hanna Suchocka, justice.

10 November 1997: the new government is endorsed by the Sejm.

7 December 1997: Leszek Miller replaces Jozef Oleksy as leader of Social Democracy of the Polish Republic.

8 December 1997: Marian Krzaklewski launches a new party, Solidarity Electoral Action Social Movement, to propagate 'basic Christian principles in education, the economy and public life'. The registration of the new party comes soon after Lech Walesa registered his own political party called Christian Democracy of the Third Polish Republic (*FT*, 9 December 1997, p. 2).

17 December 1997: the Sejm endorses (by 268 votes to 160, with 11 abstentions) the constitutional court's decision of 28 May 1997 which ruled the 1996 abortion law unconstitutional. Abortion will now be allowed only in cases of irreparable damage to the foetus, pregnancy resulting from crime (such as rape and incest) or serious danger to the life or health of the mother. (The government has already banned separate sex education classes in schools and has plans to stop state subsidies on certain contraceptives: *Telegraph*, 19 December 1997, p. 15.)

26 December 1997: President Kwasniewski returns the bill on the amendment of the abortion law (*EEN*, 1998, vol. 11, no. 25, p. 8).

30 December 1997: the government fails to overrule two presidential vetoes. The first vetoed law would have linked increases in pensions to some 300,000 retired military and police personnel to inflation (as is already the case with non-military pensioners) as opposed to increases in the average industrial wage. The second vetoed law would have ended a plan to train teachers to conduct sex education classes in schools. The government fell eight and seven votes short, respectively, of the 267 votes needed in the Sejm to overrule a presidential veto (*FT*, 31 December 1997, p. 2).

Parliament fails to overturn the presidential veto on the abortion law and on the law on pensions for servicemen (*EEN*, 1998, vol. 11, no. 25, p. 8).

8 January 1998: the Sejm ratifies a treaty with the Vatican. The concordat, passed by 274 votes to 160 with 2 abstentions, governs relations between the state and the Roman Catholic Church. Among other provisions, the treaty makes church marriages legally binding and provides for religious classes starting from kindergarten (*IHT*, 9 January 1998, p. 5; *FT*, 26 March 1998, p. 3). (The concordat was formalized during a ceremony at the Vatican on 25 March 1998.)

31 May 1998: the EU's Phare aid for 1998 is reduced by 16 per cent owing to Poland's poor response. This is the first time that a Phare programme for any country has been cut (*The Economist*, 6 June 1998, p. 51).

The EU cancelled Ecu 35 million of Phare aid on the grounds that the projects co-ordinated by Poland's European Integration Committee were poorly prepared. In July 1998 prime minister Buzek took direct control of the committee, although he did not actually dismiss its head, Ryszard Czarnecki (*FT*, 28 July 1998, p. 2). 'Czarnecki ... was one of a dozen voices claiming to speak for Poland on European matters, creating confusion in EU capitals about who was calling the tune' (Lionel Barber, *FT*, 30 July 1998, p. 24).

Czarnecki was kept in the government as a minister without portfolio (*Business Central Europe*, September 1998, p. 19).

5 June 1998: the Sejm passes a law creating twelve new provinces to replace the previous forty-nine districts (*EEN*, 1998, vol. 12, no. 7, p. 8).

Poland has forty-nine 'voivodships'.

> Voivods (governors) serve at the whim of the central government. This is about to change … Poland is poised to create two new tiers of elected government, giving them many functions of central government and half its tax revenues … These plans to decentralize government and make it more democratic … still face big obstacles … And the details of the reform are still so hazy that it is unclear how much power will really flow from Warsaw to the provinces.
>
> (*The Economist*, 7 February 1998, p. 45)

But the changes look radical. The number of regions will be far less than forty-nine. Governors will 'supervise' regional government. Real power will belong to elected assemblies and to their chairmen, who will act as the new regions' chief executives. They will control 30 per cent of the income tax and 15 per cent of the VAT raised within their regions. Although the assemblies may not pass laws, they will oversee large swathes of government, including economic development and the police. A new level of government, 320 elected counties (*powiaty*) will administer much state welfare, including health and education beyond primary level, although government will continue to set basic policy. Primary schools will remain the responsibility of the 2,489 municipalities (*The Economist*, 7 February 1998, p. 45).

14 June 1998: President Kwasniewski reiterates his support for the creation of seventeen new provinces rather than twelve (*EEN*, 1998, vol. 12, no. 7, p. 8).

1 July 1998: the Sejm votes in favour of the creation of fifteen new regions (*EEN*, 1998, vol. 12, no. 8, p. 6).

2 July 1998: President Kwasniewski vetoes the bill (*EEN*, 1998, vol. 12, no. 8, p. 6).

19 July 1998: the Sejm approves a compromise plan to revamp the provincial system by dividing the country into sixteen provinces. The government originally wanted to create twelve regions to replace the forty-nine provinces created in 1975 (*IHT*, 20 July 1998, p. 5).

24 July 1998: Solidarity Electoral Action is known as AWS in Poland.

> The AWS alliance … is beginning to fall apart. Since last September's election, defections have eroded AWS's representation in the Sejm … from 201 seats to 187; the majority of the governing coalition (AWS and the liberal Freedom Union) has dropped from thirty-one to seventeen. Most of these defectors have joined the Patriotic Movement for the Fatherland, an embryonic party formed by seven ex-AWSers and four other right-wing MPs led by Jan Olszewski, a former prime minister. On 24 July six more members of the alliance defected, possibly to join the new party … The six most recent defectors belong to the 'Radio Maryja gang' of MPs, who take their cue

> from a fervently Catholic, rabidly nationalist radio station ... No one knows how many more of the Radio Maryja crew of as many as thirty-five MPs could jump ship ... The new party ... would halt the sale to foreign investors of land and 'national treasures' like the telephone monopoly and it would protect farmers from foreign competition.
>
> (*The Economist*, 8 August 1998, p. 34)

> Those who have already quit voice similar grievances: the AWS is ignoring its populist campaign manifesto, dumping its pro-family tax policies and its plans to distribute free shares to the population at large – all to appease the monetarist sensibilities of its coalition partner, the Freedom Union ... The final straw for the latest six AWS defectors was the declaration by a Polish court that the bankrupt Gdansk Shipyard, birthplace of Solidarity, was to be abandoned to the neighbouring Gdynia Shipyard.
>
> (*Business Central Europe*, September 1998, p. 19)

> In July an independent Polish court decided that a consortium comprising the Gdynia Shipyard and consultant group Evip Progress was the only realistic offer on the table for the bankrupt Gdansk Shipyard. Right-wing MPs promptly quit the government ranks ... The government's response was to backtrack, saying it would push for an illusory deal between Gdansk and its creditors.
>
> (p. 28)

> The main AWS rebels have been the KPN–OP [Confederation for an Independent Poland–Patriotic Camp] led by Adam Slomka, who took six deputies with him when he was expelled from the AWS in June for opposing local government reform. In July six deputies linked with Radio Maryja also left. A seventh Maryja supporter, Jan Lopuszanski, was expelled at the same time as Slomka, and for the same reason.
>
> (*EEN*, 1998, vol. 12, no. 10, p. 6)

On 29 July 1998 AWS expelled KPN–OP (p. 9).

11 August 1998: the head of the Polish Catholic Church, Cardinal Jozef Glemp, calls for an end to the setting up of more crosses near the perimeter of the Auschwitz concentration camp. Dozens of crosses have been placed outside the camp in the last three weeks by a group pledged to defend a wooden cross used during a 1979 papal mass and brought ten years later to its present location (the spot where the Pope prayed in 1979). The group is led by Kazimierz Switon, an anti-communist veteran known for his antisemitic views, whose aim is to set up 152 crosses, one for each Polish victim of a wartime (1941) execution at the site (*Guardian*, 12 August 1998, p. 13; *IHT*, 12 August 1998, p. 4, and 15 August 1998, p. 4; *Telegraph*, 20 August 1998, p. 18). (A 1978 UNESCO agreement bans all religious symbolism at Auschwitz: *The Economist*, 22 August 1998, p. 31.)

Outside the Auschwitz death camp … 240 crosses have been placed by Roman Catholic zealots over the last five months … The crosses have a self-styled guard, Kazimierz Switon. A former member of Poland's Solidarity Union, he arrived here on 14 June … He took up residence, declared he had come to defend Polish soil against the Jews, planted a cross and, with conspicuous success, invited sympathizers to follow suit … The adjacent camps of Auschwitz and Birkenau have been at the centre of repeated conflict in recent years as divergent Polish and Jewish views of World War II have clashed, envenomed by each people's sense of enormous loss. But the forthright anti-Jewish oratory of Mr Switon and his vociferous followers appears to mark an escalation in an atmosphere clouded by new Polish fears of Jewish claims for restitution of property lost during the war. At the same time, the inability of the centre-right Polish government of prime minister Jerzy Buzek to remove the crosses, or even stop their proliferation, has illustrated the enduring sensitivity of religious and nationalist issues in a deeply Catholic country still grappling with the divisive legacy of more than forty years of communist rule … So far, as legal battles boil, no attempt has been made to take the crosses down or even to evict Mr Switon. Even the Polish episcopate's formal condemnation of the new crosses in August has failed to break the deadlock … There have been repeated provocative issues in recent years. An eight-metre-high (twenty-six-foot) so-called 'papal cross' erected in 1989 and still standing at the centre of the new crosses, a Catholic convent that abutted the camp until its Carmelite nuns left in 1993, and the presence until their removal last year of crosses and Stars of David near the Birkenau gas chambers have all caused bitter exchanges between Polish authorities and Jewish groups. At the root of the friction lie starkly divergent senses of history. Many people in Poland have the sense that the 3 million non-Jewish Poles who died during the Nazi occupation, of whom close to 100,000 were killed at Auschwitz, are somehow invisible to the Jews because of the scale of the Holocaust. Jews, by contrast, see an unspeakable affront in the placing of Christian symbols at the place that stood at the heart of the Nazi extermination programme. They are troubled by enduring expressions of antisemitism in Poland and point to the fact that more than 1 million of the victims of the Auschwitz–Birkenau complex were Jews … Mr Switon has found critical local support from a wealthy real-estate dealer and former communist security services agent, Zbigniew Janosz, who has veered from communism to nationalism since 1989. Mr Janosz heads an association of Polish war victims and leased the land on which the crosses now stand from the departing Carmelite nuns in 1993. His lease runs until 2033. The Polish government has now drafted a law to be submitted to parliament in the next few weeks that would put all former concentration and death camps and the land around them in the control of the state. The law would override all previous property claims; land would be bought out at market prices.

(Roger Cohen, *IHT*, 21 December 1998, p. 4)

19 August 1998: the government announces that it has terminated a lease for land on which the original cross stands. The thirty-year lease was held by the Association of War Victims.

19 September 1998: Lech Walesa is elected chairman of the new Christian Democracy of the Third Republic (*EEN*, 1998, vol. 12, no. 11, p. 5).

20 September 1998: four more crosses are erected, bringing the total to around 200 (*IHT*, 21 September 1998, p. 5).

22 September 1998: the Sejm approves a bill allowing people to view files on themselves gathered by the security police in the communist era. The bill now goes to the Senate and the president for approval. If the president refuses to sign the bill a three-fifths majority is needed to overturn the veto (*FT*, 23 September 1998, p. 3).

11 October 1998: the Alliance of the Democratic Left (led by Leszek Miller) won 32 per cent of the vote for the sixteen new regional assemblies and more assembly seats than any other grouping. The AWS, with 33 per cent, actually won the largest share of the vote. Smaller right-wing groupings were routed. The far-right Fatherland movement (led by former prime minister Jan Olszewski) and the Polish Family (an extreme Catholic party) managed to win just one seat between them. 'The most striking thing about these elections, therefore, is the extent to which the big parties now dominate the middle ground.' There was, however, a comeback for the Polish Peasants' Party. It entered the vote in coalition with two small left-wing parties and garnered a respectable eighty-nine seats and 12 per cent of the vote. Freedom Union saw its vote fall to 11.7 per cent from its 13.4 per cent showing in 1997. 'This led to recriminations within the party over Mr Balcerowicz's decision to launch a flat-rate income tax initiative in the middle of campaigning' (*Business Central Europe*, November 1998, p. 45).

The Alliance of the Democratic Left gains control of nine of the sixteen new powiats (regions), with the AWS successful in the traditional Solidarity strongholds in the south and south-east. Freedom Union did poorly, coming fourth after the Social Alliance (consisting of the Polish Peasants' Party, the Labour Union and the Polish Pensioners' Party) (*EEN*, 1998, vol. 12, no. 12, p. 10).

22 October 1998: the president signs the bill, which demands that all judges, ministers, legislators, senior civil servants and other officials of state-owned media declare if they worked or informed for the communist-era security apparatus (*FT*, 23 October 1998, p. 2). The penalty for lying is a fine and a ten-year ban from public office (*Business Central Europe*, November 1998, p. 14).

10 November 1998: the only surviving synagogue near Auschwitz (Oswiecim) is rededicated. It will become the centre of a Jewish religious and cultural institute. The synagogue was confiscated by the Nazis in 1939, seized by the communists after the Second World War and was until recently used as a carpet store. The building was returned to the local Jewish community in March 1998 and is the first building to be returned under a programme to provide restitution of seized Jewish religious property.

18 December 1998: the Sejm overrides the president's veto on a bill that will allow victims of communist-era repression to see secret police files. The president signs the bill.

1 January 1999: a new system of local government is introduced. The existing forty-nine regions are replaced by sixteen larger ones, while 308 new administrative units are introduced at the local level (*Business Central Europe*, February 1999, p. 12; supplement; see also October 1998, p. 50). ('The new scheme brings back 308 county-level units that existed in Poland decades ago … The makeover … replaces the communist-era division into forty-nine regions with sixteen larger ones, which designers say are more in line with existing administrative regions in EU countries': *Transition*, 1998, vol. 9, no. 6, p. 27.)

The country is now divided into sixteen regions (voivodships), each of which is split into borough counties (powiats, a new tier of government), which in turn are split into local councils (gminas, set up in 1990). All three layers of government have their own independent budgets and elected officials.

The sixteen voivodship parliaments (sejmiks) are elected locally and appoint their own governments. These governments are responsible for regional development and also oversee public services like higher education, specialized health services, sustainable environmental development, road and transport management and public security. The national government appoints a voivod for each region, he or she ensuring coherence between national and regional programmes.

The 373 powiats are responsible for maintaining daily public services like secondary schools, general hospitals, police, fire and tax offices. The sixty-five urban powiats consist of one town or city and also perform gmina functions. (This explains the figure of 308 new units above.)

The 2,489 gminas are responsible for basic community services like kindergartens, primary schools, libraries and local roads.

'All in all some 60 per cent of public money will be spent at the local level, compared with just 20 per cent before' (*Business Central Europe*, October 1998, p. 50).

> The new structure is important historically because it recreates Poland's pre-1939 local government structure. It is significant for the future because it will help prepare the country for entry into the EU, which places a big emphasis on regional self-government … The community council, or gmina, was restored in 1990 … The secretary of state for regional reform says that the key purposes are to 'decentralize power, create local identity, prepare for the EU and promote economic development' … Unlike voivodships and districts [powiats], which are responsible for the tasks they are assigned, community councils can tackle any local issues as long as they have the financial resources. Under the reform the proportion of public money administered locally has increased from about 15 per cent to 40 per cent. But this exaggerates the amount of local discretion, since the great bulk will

> be spent on essential services such as schools, where levels of provisions are set nationally.
>
> (Stefan Wagstyl, *FT*, Survey, 30 March 1999, p. 4)

> Eighteen months on, a dispute over Warsaw's city council shows up the limitations of local power. Last month [May 2000] prime minister Jerzy Buzek suspended the Warsaw city council's government, replacing it with an administrator. He claimed that the council had ceased to function. But critics – including President Alexander Kwasniewski – argue that the conflict had more to do with party politics … All the dispute really shows is that local government is still tightly controlled by the centre … Local authorities remain near powerless because they still rely on central government for their cash … The district and regional levels live off lump transfers from the central budget, while councils keep just a tiny share of the taxes collected in their region … And the government limited the local authorities' powers as well as their funding. The regions were not given control over policing and environmental funds, for example, while most state agencies failed to open provincial offices. In fact the only big concession to local governments was that they are now allowed to open employment centres … Far from becoming more accountable, the different parts of local government still tend to pass the buck when it comes to providing everyday services. There is also a good deal of corruption, according to a recent World Bank report … Public tenders are regularly rigged in favour of companies who bankroll parties' election campaigns.
>
> (*Business Central Europe*, June 2000, p. 45)

(On 18 May 2000 the government appointed a commissioner to run central Warsaw after a prolonged deadlock between the local government and the provincial government: *EEN*, 2000, vol. 12, no. 23, p. 10.)

12 March 1999: the Czech Republic, Hungary and Poland become members of Nato at a signing ceremony in Independence, Missouri, USA (where Nato was founded on 4 April 1949 during the presidency of Harry Truman), raising membership from sixteen to nineteen. It was in Missouri, at Westminster College in Fulton on 5 March 1946, that Winston Churchill delivered his famous speech: 'From Stettin in the Baltic to Trieste in the Adriatic an iron curtain has descended across the Continent.'

'Mikhail Gorbachev … said that he felt "betrayed" by Nato's expansion, adding that the West was taking advantage of Russia's weakness and humiliating Russians in ways like the Allies' treatment of defeated Germany after World War I' (*IHT*, 13 March 1999, p. 4).

10 May 1999: it is announced that President Kwasniewski has signed into law a bill allowing the government to remove crosses erected by Roman Catholics near Auschwitz. The government plans to remove all but one cross but needs to consult with Roman Catholic authorities before any action is taken (*IHT*, 11 May 1999, p. 6).

28 May 1999:

> Army troops removed about 300 crosses and a wooden hut that had been erected by radical Catholics at a lot bordering Auschwitz … The government received new authority over the property adjoining Auschwitz under a new law that took effect Tuesday [25 May] that created protected zones 100 metres wide around former Nazi camps in Poland. A radical Catholic activist said Thursday [28 May] he put explosive devices on the site to protect it. The police detained the activist, Kazimierz Switon, and detonated the explosives … A larger cross on the property, erected more than a decade ago to commemorate 152 Polish Catholics killed there by the Nazis, was left standing … The eight-metre wooden cross was used in a 1979 mass by Pope John Paul II. Jewish groups have called for its removal, saying it can be seen from inside Auschwitz and insults the memory of more than 1 million Jews killed at Auschwitz and the nearby facility of Birkenau during World War II. But conservative Catholics led by Mr Switon began a campaign last year [1998] to protect the papal cross, saying Poland had the right to honour its Holocaust victims with a cross. The campaign had anti-semitic tones, with Mr Switon complaining that Jews had too much influence in Poland … Mr Switon had rallied people to erect the 300 smaller crosses next to the papal cross and oversaw construction of a wooden hut on the property that was consecrated by a retired priest on 16 May. The Roman Catholic Church rejected the ceremony and joined the government in calling for the smaller crosses to be removed.
>
> (*IHT*, 29 May 1999, p. 2)

5–17 June 1999: the eighth papal visit to Poland by Pope John Paul II.

> Pope John Paul II made an unprecedented speech to the Polish parliament … on Friday [11 June] … the first by a Roman Catholic pontiff to a national parliament … He echoed his prayer from his first pilgrimage home twenty years earlier, when he asked the Holy Spirit to 'renew the face' of Poland. Those words are credited with helping spark the birth of Solidarity a year later, leading to the end of communism in 1989 … Later Friday, flanked by Jews … the Pope prayed at the site from where the Jews of the Warsaw Ghetto were sent to the gas chambers in World War II … The Pope paid tribute to Jewish victims of the Holocaust at Umschlagplatz monument in Warsaw.
>
> (*IHT*, 12 June 1999, p. 2)

1 July 1999: Leszek Miller is elected chairman of the Democratic Left Alliance Party (*EEN*, 1999, vol. 12, no. 19, p. 3).

9 August 1999: Poland requests the extradition from Britain of Helena Wolinska-Brus. Now a British citizen, she is accused of signing illegal arrest warrants that allowed the communist authorities to imprison and later execute

August Fieldorf, a general in the Polish Home Army that resisted the Nazi occupation from 1939 to 1945. She is also accused of the wrongful arrest of fourteen other people. She is a survivor of the Warsaw ghetto and the Polish underground during the Nazi occupation. She left Poland after the 1968 antisemitic campaign (*IHT*, 10 August 1999, p. 5; *Guardian*, 10 August 1999, p. 10).

10 August 1999: it is announced by the recently established Institute of National Remembrance (IPN) that communist-era secret police files are to be opened to the public in about six months. The IPN holds secret police files covering the period 1944 to 1990. It is responsible for showing them to those who came under secret police surveillance in that period. Public access will be limited to the individuals concerned who will only be allowed to see their own files. The IPN will also prosecute Nazi war criminals and those responsible for crimes committed under the communist regime. The issue of opening police files has been controversial (*FT*, 11 August 1999, p. 2).

1 September 1999: the presidents of Poland and Germany meet in Gdansk (formerly Danzig) to commemorate the sixtieth anniversary of the outbreak of the Second World War. On 1 September 1939 the German battleship *Schleswig-Holstein* fired a salvo at Polish fortifications.

'The neighbouring countries commemorated the beginnings of the Second World War jointly for the first time' (*Guardian*, 2 September 1999, p. 12).

2 September 1999: interior minister and deputy prime minister Janusz Tomaszewski is dismissed over suspected links with the communist-era secret police. 'Mr Tomaszewski ... joined a list of politicians who have left the government over similar charges' (*IHT*, 3 September 1999, p. 5).

> Janusz Tomaszewski ... had been accused of failing to admit contacts with the secret police in the late 1980s ... There are also suspicions that what was at stake was not so much Mr Tomaszewski's past but his increasingly powerful position as interior minister and his political ambitions, which threatened those of his colleagues. The administration has now lost some of its most competent figures to *lustracja*. Janusz Kaczurba, one of Poland's top negotiators involved in membership talks with the EU, resigned after stating that he had contacts with the security services when he was a Communist Party member in the 1980s. Most recently Robert Mroziewicz, the deputy defence minister responsible for relations with Nato, resigned after officials involved in the *lustracja* process found discrepancies in his papers and passed his case to the court ... Poland's decision earlier this year [1999] to weed out former collaborators with communist secret police from public positions has [thus] rebounded against the policy's architects ... [Under] *lustracja* ... government officials, parliamentary deputies and 'persons of public trust', such as lawyers, have to declare if they had dealings before 1989 with the secret police. These declarations are then checked against police files. Cases are considered by a special court.
>
> (*FT*, 6 September 1999, p. 2)

> Just months after the Solidarity-led government pushed through a law to drive collaborators with the former communist secret police from public life in the new Poland, heads are rolling. Solidarity heads … Mr Tomaszewski is the third government minister to be forced out since the spring for alleged collaboration … Eight members of parliament are also under investigation … The opposition Democratic Left Alliance … has emerged unscathed … Unlike other countries in Eastern Europe Poland came late to what is called 'lustration', from the Latin word for purification … The law forces more than 22,000 officeholders, including the president, cabinet ministers, members of parliament, judges and senior civil servants, to declare whether they ever helped the communist security services. Collaboration is defined as the secret passing of information or documents to someone the informant knew to be a member of the secret police. Anyone who admitted collaboration could be punished, but anyone found to be lying would be banned from public life for ten years … [Critics of lustration say] it is unclear whether those currently accused of collaboration were threatened or bribed by the police or whether they were, in fact, committed to the old regime … [There is also the problem of] a vetting system that relies on communist documents and testimony, and can ruin careers before the accused has a day in court.
>
> (*IHT*, 10 September 1999, p. 7)

24 September 1999: 'Poland saw one of its largest demonstrations since the fall of communism yesterday [24 September] when 50,000 farmers, miners and other industrial workers marched through Warsaw to demand an easing of the tight economic policies of the centre-right coalition government' (*FT*, 25 September 1999, p. 3). The demonstrators were demanding government subsidies and pay increases (*IHT*, 25 September 1999, p. 2). (The number of people demonstrating was significantly lower than expected.)

13 October 1999: the European Commission recommends that EU leaders at the December 1999 meeting in Helsinki allow Bulgaria, Latvia, Lithuania, Malta, Romania and Slovakia to begin accession negotiations in 2000.

The 'principle of differentiation' for entry date will apply to each of the twelve candidates, reflecting differing states of readiness for EU entry. A 'fully flexible, multi-speed accession process' is envisaged. 'Each country will be able to proceed on merit, including the possibility for those which join the negotiations from 2000 to catch up with the others.' The European Commission thinks that existing EU members should undertake internal reforms by the end of 2002: 'Whether the first accessions can take place as from 1 January 2003 will then depend entirely on the speed with which the applicant countries can make progress on meeting the criteria.'

Latvia has made good political progress but falls short of international standards on the protection of the linguistic rights of minorities. (Estonia is also criticized as regards linguistic rights.) Latvia has made 'significant and sustained progress' towards meeting market economy criteria and in regards to its ability to withstand competitive pressures. Latvia has a good chance of catching up with the group led by Hungary, with Lithuania not far behind. Latvia joins Malta and Cyprus, Hungary, Poland, Estonia and Slovenia in having functioning market economies. Lithuania could become a functioning market economy in 2000 if it pushes ahead with promised reforms.

Malta and Cyprus have already met the economic terms set by the EU, being able to cope with competitive pressures and market forces in the EU. Hungary and Poland come next in economic terms, followed by Slovenia, Estonia and then the Czech Republic. Hungary, Poland, Estonia and Slovenia have improved their ability to cope with competitive pressures and market forces 'in the medium term' (meaning more than one year from 2000). Hungary is the closest of the Eastern European countries to meeting the criteria on a market economy with the capacity to withstand competition within the EU.

Concern was expressed about Poland's progress in bringing its laws into line with those of the EU.

(*FT*, 14 October 1999, pp. 1, 10; *IHT*, 14 October 1999, p. 5; *Guardian*, 14 October 1999, p. 14; *Independent*, 14 October 1999, p. 18; *The Times*, 14 October 1999, p. 21; *Telegraph*, 14 October 1999, p. 20.)

> When it comes to adapting its laws and structures to EU needs Poland 'has not progressed significantly', says the Commission. There has been 'a notable lack of progress' on critical issues like state aid, steel restructuring, and on everything from fisheries to regional policy. And Poland's infrastructure needs urgent improvements – especially its roads … Poland … cannot join until it launches 'substantial transformation' of its agricultural and fisheries sectors, says the Commission.
>
> (*Business Central Europe*, November 1999, p. 40)

(For further details, see the Hungary entry for 10 December 1999.)

20 January 2000: it is announced that nine Russian diplomats are to be expelled for spying. The following day Russia expels nine from the Polish embassy in Moscow.

28 May 2000:

> The Freedom Union voted Sunday [28 May] for its five government ministers, including the party leader, finance minister [and deputy prime minister] Leszek Balcerowicz … [and foreign minister Bronislaw Geremek], to submit their resignations Monday [29 May]. The ministers will remain in office in a caretaker capacity until a new government is formed. The Freedom Union is ruling out rejoining a new government led by Solidarity, but it is insisting that prime minister Jerzy Buzek resign … A new government could be patched together if Solidarity dumps Mr Buzek and agrees to Mr Balcerowicz's belt-tightening 2001 budget. The coalition government has repeatedly teetered on the brink of collapse over clashes on economic reforms sponsored by the fiscally conservative Mr Balcerowicz and rejected by populist elements within the Solidarity bloc. Solidarity, although it takes

its name from the independent trade union that broke the back of communism, is now a collection of thirty different political groupings under one umbrella. And party discipline … has proven very difficult to obtain … The finance minister has been frustrated by Mr Buzek's inability to control maverick members of parliament within Solidarity's ranks who have repeatedly voted against his economic proposals. This month [May] Solidarity members of parliament helped vote down an increase in value-added tax on farm products that was designed to bring Poland into line with the EU … Solidarity members have already proposed that he [Buzek] be replaced with a central bank economist, Boguslaw Grabowski, whose economic views mirror those of Mr Balcerowicz. Some Solidarity members of parliament, however, are insisting that if Mr Buzek departs, Mr Balcerowicz should also go … If Solidarity cannot entice Freedom Union back into government it will be forced to rule as a minority government. And if it cannot pass a budget parliament will have to be dissolved … According to opinion polls, the Democratic Left Alliance, which governed from 1993 to 1997, would again emerge as the largest party … [It] is considered certain to continue the process of economic reform essential for EU accession. In the days leading up to the Freedom Union vote, the markets shrugged off the impending crisis – a clear endorsement of the country's economic fundamentals whatever the makeup of the government.

(Peter Finn, *IHT*, 29 May 2000, p. 4)

29 May 2000:

Prime minister Jerzy Buzek rejected Monday [29 May] the resignations … Finance minister Leszek Balcerowicz had called on Mr Buzek to defer accepting his notice to quit in order to give coalition leaders room to negotiate … Other Freedom Union leaders said that Mr Balcerowicz had been wrong to suggest that the resignations were just a gesture. Financial markets proved resilient to the political storm … Mr Balcerowicz and eight other senior and junior ministers from the liberal Freedom Union handed in resignation letters after the party decided Sunday [28 May] to abandon its partnership to protest Solidarity's failure to back reforms. Mr Balcerowicz … said Mr Buzek's decision to reject the resignations would open the way to fresh coalition talks. Ministers from Freedom Union would continue to run their departments but would not make any major political decisions while talks went on, Mr Balcerowicz said. The Freedom Union vote to leave the government stemmed from its despair at the inability of Solidarity leaders to control rebel deputies, who have voted against free-market reforms and spending cuts agreed on by the cabinet.

(*IHT*, 30 May 2000, p. 4)

6 June 2000: Freedom Union abandons the talks. The prime minister says that there will be a minority government.

8 June 2000: Jaroslaw Bauc, previously a deputy finance minister, is named as finance minister to replace Balcerowicz (*FT*, 9 June 2000, p. 10).

Three ministerial appointments are made to replace outgoing Freedom Union ministers. But Freedom Union ministers of defence and foreign affairs are to remain in office for three months (*EEN*, 2000, vol. 12, no. 23, p. 10).

14 July 2000: the Sejm narrowly approves the enfranchisement bill by 222 votes to 213 with 2 abstentions. The bill now goes to the Senate for scrutiny. A three-fifths majority in the Sejm is needed to overturn a presidential veto. (See the section on the economy, below.)

10 August 2000: President Kwasniewski is cleared by a screening court of allegations that he had lied in 1998 when he denied being an agent of the communist-era secret police.

The law was passed by parliament in August 1997 and signed by the president on 22 October 1998. (See the respective entries.)

> In 1997 Poland decide to emulate the Czech Republic and pass a law to keep former secret police agents out of government. In Poland officials must declare whether they were informers. Only those found to be lying lose their jobs. Mr Kwasniewski and Mr Walesa said they were not spies and so risked losing the right to run.
>
> (*IHT*, 14 August 2000, p. 8)

> [The] vetting law forces about 22,000 politicians, civil servants and judges to fill out forms denying or admitting collaboration. The declarations were checked out against secret police files and anyone found to be lying by a court was to be banned from public life for ten years.
>
> (p. 7)

'The 1997 legislation imposes no legal penalty for confessing to collaboration as long as the person declares it' (*IHT*, 21 August 2000, p. 7).

11 August 2000: Lech Walesa is also cleared by the screening court.

> Lech Walesa … was yesterday [11 August] acquitted on charges of collaborating with communist-era secret police after it emerged that key documents used against him in a Warsaw court were forgeries made by a special unit set up to discredit him … If found guilty Mr Walesa … faced being banned from holding public office for ten years. [He would also have been] forbidden from voting … [He] is one of eighteen candidates running for president in October [8 October] … The trials of Mr Walesa and Mr Kwasniewski resulted from a law passed in 1997 which requires top officials, including presidential candidates, to declare past links to the secret police and forces the vetting of those applying for top posts … [In 2000] former secret police files will be open to the public for the first time.
>
> (*Guardian*, 12 August 2000, p. 2)

> Documents presented to the tribunal suggest that the secret police fabricated an elaborate file aimed at discrediting the Solidarity leader … The tribunal brief under the 1997 vetting law is to establish whether a candidate for high office has lied about secret police contacts … If the evidence against Mr Walesa [had been accepted] he would have been banned from political office for ten years.
>
> (*The Times*, 12 August 2000, p. 10)

> Poland's newly created National Remembrance Institute … [is] modelled in part on Germany's Gauck Commission … [The institute's] brief is to investigate crimes and prosecute perpetrators and to educate the public on communist- and Nazi-era crimes against the Polish nation … between September 1939 and the collapse of communism in December 1989. A network of regional offices of the institute, with their headquarters in Warsaw, will begin opening secret police files to the public next year [2001] … As in Germany, access to files will be limited to people designated as victims of the secret police … Leon Kieres [head of the institute] and others have questioned whether that definition should exclude former agents who later became police victims or people who collaborated with the police under duress.
>
> (*FT*, 23 August 2000, p. 6)

30 August 2000: the twentieth anniversary of the foundation of Solidarity is celebrated.

'Whereas twenty years ago Solidarity had 10 million members – a quarter of the population – today it claims just 1.2 million' (*FT*, 28 August 2000, p. 15).

11 September 2000: President Kwasniewski vetoes legislation on mass property privatization (*EEN*, 2000, vol. 12, no. 25, p. 4).

12 September 2000:

> In this small Polish town [Oswiecim], whose German name – Auschwitz – became the synonym for the genocidal policies of the Nazis, a fragment of Jewish life returned on Tuesday [12 September] with the reopening of a synagogue, the first such place of worship here since World War II. The restored early twentieth century synagogue, which the Nazis used as a munitions dump and the communists used as a carpet showroom, will offer a place to retreat for those visiting the Auschwitz–Birkenau death complex and site of the extermination of more than 1 million people … The last Jew in Oswiecim died in May [2000] … Of the [former] 14,000 residents 8,000 were Jewish and their presence in the town as doctors, merchants and artisans dated back to the fifteenth century … All vestiges of Jewish life in the town were expunged, murdered and dispersed by the Nazis. Eleven synagogues were destroyed … Poles and Jews have struggled, often bitterly, over

> the spiritual ownership of Auschwitz–Birkenau where both communities suffered enormously.
>
> (Peter Finn, *IHT*, 13 September 2000, p. 8)

8 October 2000: President Kwasniewski is re-elected in the first round of voting, with around 54 per cent of the vote.

There were thirteen candidates. Andrzej Olechowski was second (with about 17 per cent) and Marian Krzaklewski was third (with over 15 per cent).

Lech Walesa, who gathered less than 1 per cent of the vote, announced on 15 October that he was retiring from politics.

(On 10 October Andrzej Olechowski announced 'the establishment of a new right-wing party to be called New Centre': *EEN*, 2000, vol. 13, no. 1, p. 7.)

25 October 2000:

> A special court ruled Wednesday [25 October] that former prime minister Jozef Oleksy, who resigned in 1996 amid allegations he had spied for Moscow, once worked as a military intelligence agent in communist Poland. The decision means that, unless he wins an appeal, Mr Oleksy, a former communist, must forfeit his seat in parliament.
>
> (*IHT*, 26 October 2000, p. 11)

8 November 2000: Poland received a more positive EU assessment than in the previous year.

The EU's report on Poland (*Progress Towards Accession*, 8 November 2000, pp. 87–8):

> The need for further effort applies ... to strengthening of administrative capacity ... With regard to the fight against corruption ... further efforts are needed ... Considerable improvement is required in law enforcement bodies dealing with the fight against organized crime, in particular the police services ... Poland is a functioning market economy and should be able to cope with competitive pressure and market forces within the Union in the near term, provided it continues and completes its present reform efforts. It has maintained adequate macroeconomic stability and its growth performance has again been impressive. The pace of privatization has been encouraging and there has also been further restructuring in sensitive sectors such as the coal and defence industries. However, a number of economic imbalances have emerged: inflation is high and the current account deficit has widened to a level that raises the issue of sustainability. Ensuring medium-term fiscal sustainability remains a challenge. There are delays in privatization in the steel sector and the restructuring of agriculture. Large parts of the state-owned enterprise sector still need to be restructured ...

> The lack of concrete progress in steel restructuring remains a cause for concern.

(For further details, see the entry for Hungary.)

16 December 2000: Bronislaw Geremek is appointed leader of Freedom Union.

17 December 2000: the Alliance of the Democratic Left and the Labour Union agree to form an electoral alliance.

10 January 2001: prime minister Jerzy Buzek replaces Marian Krzaklewski as chairman of Solidarity Electoral Action.

11 January 2001:

> Andrzej Olechowski, a former finance and foreign minister, Maciej Plazynski, speaker of Poland's lower house, and Donald Tusk of the liberal Freedom Union … announced a new conservative–liberal grouping to run in this year's parliamentary election … scheduled for September.
>
> (*FT*, 12 January 2001, p. 10)

> Several members of … Poland's ruling Solidarity Electoral Action (AWS) and its former coalition partner, the Freedom Union, quit to form a new centrist movement called the Citizens' Platform … [Later] former finance minister Leszek Balcerowicz began a six-year stint as head of Poland's central bank. He replaces Hanna Gronkiewicz-Waltz, who has become deputy head of the EBRD.
>
> (*Business Central Europe*, February 2001, p. 11)

> There is an air of optimism surrounding the new Citizens' Platform, a centre-right grouping set up in the middle of January by a former presidential candidate, Andrzej Olechowski … It will only become a party after this October's parliamentary elections … The three founders [Olechowski, Tusk and Plazynski] share the same liberal views. And they are positioning themselves as anti-establishment heroes who will stamp out corruption, cut red tape and liberalize Poland's restrictive labour laws. They also want to improve the country's dismal education system and to help out beleaguered farmers. It all adds up to a pro-business agenda with a populist touch … Maybe the Platform will have enough popular appeal to push through the kind of reforms – notably a flat-rate income tax – that the Freedom Union failed to push through.
>
> (*Business Central Europe*, March 2001, pp. 38–9)

> [In mid-January] several leading Freedom Union members … [defected] to a tentative new group to be called 'Civic Platform' … Civic Platform's four leading figures are Maciej Plazynski (chairman of parliament and hitherto AWS member), former foreign minister Andrzej Olechowski, Donald Tusk (Freedom Union) and Freedom Union mayor of Warsaw Pawel Piskovski.
>
> (*EEN*, 2001, vol. 13, no. 2, p. 2)

> In late January … Andrzej Olechowski … teamed up with … Donald Tusk, a rising star in the Freedom Union, who had lost a bitter battle for that party's leadership, and parliament's popular speaker, Maciej Plazynski, who had left Solidarity after trying and failing to supplant its leader. Mr Olechowski will not compete in this year's election and will let Mr Plazynski head Platform … a new liberal conservative party … in parliament … Many followers of Mr Tusk who were shoved aside after his leadership bid failed have already defected to the new party … [The] campaign manager [is] Pawel Piskovski, the mayor of Warsaw.
>
> (*The Economist*, 10 March 2001, pp. 46, 49)

'Parliament approved on Thursday [11 January 2001] a long-delayed law compensating Polish citizens whose property was seized between 1944 and 1962 – but only for those who retain Polish citizenship' (*IHT*, 12 January 2001, p. 8).

> Parliament passed a controversial law to compensate former owners for property seized by the communists. The law fulfils the government's election promise, but will only give claimants half the value of their former possessions because of worries about the costs of full restitution.
>
> (*Business Central Europe*, February 2001, p. 11)

> Poland's Senate threw out parts of a bill on restituting property seized by the communists after the war, which would have excluded many Polish émigrés living overseas, many of them Jewish. The bill must now be reconsidered by the lower house.
>
> (*Business Central Europe*, March 2001, p. 9)

18 March 2001: 'The Conservative Peasant Party resolves to leave the ruling Solidarity Electoral Action [AWS] coalition in favour of an alliance with the new Civic Alliance movement' (*EEN*, 2001, vol. 13, no. 4, p. 7).

'The Conservative People's Party, one of the four main groups in the AWS, said it joined the Citizens' [Civic] Platform to stop the … SLD from regaining power' (*Business Central Europe*, April 2001, p. 15).

22 March 2001:

> President Kwasniewski has vetoed a reprivatization bill that would have returned 50 per cent of the property seized from private owners by the country's former rulers … Mr Kwasniewski … said the bill was too expensive for the budget and excluded former owners or their heirs who did not have Polish citizenship, including many Jews. He argued that the restoration of confiscated property seized at the end of the Second World War, for which most owners received no compensation, would 'create social divisions'. Poland is the only East European country beside Belarus that has not

> enacted a property restitution programme since the collapse of communist rule in 1989.
>
> (*FT*, 23 March 2001, p. 10)

> President Alexander Kwasniewski yesterday [22 March] vetoed a … compensation payment to hundreds of thousands of people whose property was seized by the government in the communist era … [opposing] the measure on the grounds that the economy could not afford it and it would undermine public service reforms. The bill passed by … the Sejm allowed victims to receive 50 per cent of the value of their property as compensation. It would have denied compensation to anyone who was not a Polish citizen in 1999 … There is little chance that the issue will be readdressed before parliamentary elections in September.
>
> (*Telegraph*, 23 March 2001, p. 20)

'The bill he turned down might have cost the government $11.75 billion, compensating successful claimants to the tune of half the property's present value – provided they held a Polish passport' (*The Economist*, 9 June 2001, p. 54).

29 April 2001: 'The Conservative Peasant Party approves an electoral alliance with the new Civic Platform' (*EEN*, 2001, vol. 13, no. 5, p. 7).

15 May 2001:

> Wojciech Jaruzelski … is charged with manslaughter … Specifically the allegation is that as minister of defence in December 1970 … [he] ordered army troops to shoot demonstrating workers in the port cities of Gdansk, Gdynia and Szczecin. Several days of rioting over price hikes, food shortages and abysmal living conditions left forty-four workers dead … The session Tuesday [15 May] was adjourned until Thursday [17 May] … Eight other senior military, police and communist officials [are] on trial with him.
>
> (*IHT*, 16 May 2001, p. 4)

'The trial against the general and ten other senior functionaries opened in 1998 but had to be abandoned after he was taken ill' (*The Times*, 16 May 2001, p. 10).

'[Former interior minister] Czeslaw Kiszczak … goes on trial today [16 May] in connection with the shooting of nine miners shortly after the imposition of martial law [in December 1981]' (*Independent*, 16 May 2001, p. 15).

18 May 2001: 'A Polish court in Warsaw gave … General Wojciech Jaruzelski one week on Friday to find a new legal team to defend him in a trial over his role in the 1970 massacre of striking workers. His previous lawyers quit on Thursday [17 May]' (*IHT*, 19 May 2001, p. 8).

May 2001: 'The Solidarity trade union, from which the AWS emerged, has announced its withdrawal from party politics, following a change in the law … Some 40 per cent of Polish parliamentarians have trade union links' (*Business Central Europe*, June 2001, p. 55).

May–June 2001:

> Last month [May] Lech Kaczynski, the AWS justice minister, set out a new stall by launching Law and Justice, a party committed to tougher penalties against criminals, including capital punishment … The minority Solidarity government, facing certain defeat [in the September 2001 general election], is fragmenting into new political groupings as its members seek to shore up their positions for the next four years. Opinion polls show the opposition Democratic Left Alliance or SLD will win, barring a huge political upset … Many Poles are gloomy about their prospects. They point to an economic slowdown, rising unemployment, widespread corruption, social distress and a growing gap between a few wealthy cities and the rest of the country … [The reforms of] Poland's right-wing leaders … included a quadruple overhaul of state-run health care, education, the pension system and local government … The reforms have met their goals in some areas, but foundered on design flaws, poor preparation, venality and incompetence in many others.
>
> (*FT*, Survey, 25 June 2001, pp. i–ii)

18 June 2001: 'Leading Solidarity Electoral Action politician Janusz Tomaszewski forms a new breakaway parliamentary faction with a view to establishing a new right-wing party' (*EEN*, 2001, vol. 13, no. 5, p. 7).

6 July 2001:

> A Polish regional court on Friday [6 July] convicted a seventy-eight-year-old Polish man … Henryk Mania … of helping Nazis kill Jews in a World War II death camp and sentenced him to eight years in prison. It was the first case brought by the government's Institute of National Remembrance, which in June of last year [2000] began investigating archives and documents relating to communist- and Nazi-era crimes.
>
> (*IHT*, 7 July 2001, p. 5)

10 July 2001: President Alexander Kwasniewski (on the massacre of up to 1,600 Jews in the village of Jedwabne on 10 July 1941, two weeks after German troops took over the area from Russian troops):

> This was a particularly cruel crime. It was justified by nothing. The victims were helpless and defenceless … The authors and instigators of this crime bear sole responsibility for it … For this crime we should beg the souls of the dead and their families for forgiveness … [Although German occupiers] incited [locals] we know with all certainty that Poles were among the oppressors and assassins … We can have no doubt that here in Jedwabne Polish citizens were killed at the hands of fellow citizens … This is why today, as a man, citizen and president of the Polish Republic, I beg pardon in my own

name and in the name of those Polish people whose consciences are shocked by this crime.

> Many villagers, including the parish priest, boycotted the ceremony … The [original] plaque, officially replaced on Tuesday, blamed 'Nazi Germans' … The [new] inscription does not explicitly blame the Polish townspeople … A new book [*Neighbours*, published in 2000] by a Polish-American scholar, Jan Gross, and a documentary on the killings allege that, while Nazi soldiers were in Jedwabne and encouraged the massacre, it was the townspeople who planned and carried it out … After the speeches from the president and others, the crowd walked silently from the village square to the former site of the barn where most of the victims died, burned alive … In May leaders of the Roman Catholic Church in Poland expressed sorrow at the killings in Jedwabne.
>
> (*IHT*, 11 July 2001, p. 4)

> In a poll by agency CBOS in April 48 per cent of respondents felt Poland should not apologize for Jedwabne … The National Remembrance Institute, set up to prosecute Nazi- and Soviet-era crimes, has launched its own investigation into the massacre and another one nearby.
>
> (*FT*, 11 July 2001, p. 10)

'The Polish Catholic Church refused invitations to attend, after … Cardinal Jozef Glemp said that Poles were being "constantly vilified" ' (*Guardian*, 11 July 2001, p. 14).

> In 1949 twenty-three residents of Jedwabne were charged. Twelve were found guilty of aiding and abetting the crime and were sent to prison. One Pole was sentenced to death but the sentence was not carried out … Since the [Gross] book was published the Institute for National Remembrance in Poland has found that about forty Poles were involved.
>
> (*Telegraph*, 11 July 2001, p. 15)

24 July 2001: 'Poland's ministry of telecommunications is to be absorbed into the country's economics ministry, after state auditors identified systemic corruption there and its chief was dismissed … last week … for insufficient supervision over the ministry' (*FT*, 25 July 2001, p. 6).

> Jerzy Buzek's minority cabinet has disintegrated to a remarkable degree. Three ministers and one deputy in Poland's conservative government have resigned or been dismissed this month [July] amid allegations of corruption and abuse of power … This month Mr Buzek sacked … [the] deputy defence minister responsible for tenders after a newspaper report that an aide solicited a bribe in exchange for a contract … Police detained and released on bail … [the] ex-head of PZU's life insurance unit, amid allega-

> tions that the state-controlled company's former managers used company money to benefit themselves and political allies ... Corruption is prevalent in Polish public life.
>
> (*FT*, 27 July 2001, p. 7)

29 July 2001: Eduard Gierek dies. He was First Secretary of the Communist Party from 20 December 1970 to September 1980.

28 August 2001:

> [Prime minister] Jerzy Busek yesterday [28 August] sacked his finance minister ... Jaroslaw Bauc ... His replacement is Halina Wasilewska-Trenkner, a deputy minister for budgetary affairs. Mr Busek ... said he dismissed Mr Bauc not for raising the alarm on Poland's worsening fiscal problems but for failing to do so sooner ... [The prime minister] upheld a pledge to limit next year's budget to ... 5 per cent of GDP. Ms Wasilewska-Trenkner said she planned to send a draft budget to parliament by 30 September ... Mr Bauc ... two weeks ago ... warned that without radical spending cuts and revenue-generating measures Poland would run a deficit next year [2002] of ... more than 11 per cent of GDP. The warning caused an uproar in a country experiencing its worst economic downturn in a decade ... Mr Bauc had previously faced criticism for drafting overly optimistic growth and other assumptions on this year's budget ... Worries over loose fiscal policy have prompted Poland's main banks to maintain painfully high interest rates.
>
> (*FT*, 29 August 2001, p. 7)

Jerzy Buzek: '[I have dismissed Jaroslaw Bauc] not because he presented a dramatic situation of the state finances and an austerity plan, but because he has done that so late and not in line with principles of co-operation within the government' (*IHT*, 29 August 2001, p. 5).

THE ECONOMY

'Big bang'/'shock therapy'

> In 1989 we had but one asset. That was the enthusiasm born of the newly-won freedom. And we invested that asset in economic reform. We succeeded in securing such an emotional upswing that the fall of 30 per cent in living standards in the first two years of reform caused neither strikes nor uprisings.
>
> (Bronislaw Geremek of Democratic Union, *Moscow News*, 15–21 April 1994, p. 4)

In 1990 Poland became the transitional 'guinea-pig' for 'big bang'/'shock therapy', adopting rapid and comprehensive change on the advice of Western advisers like Jeffrey Sachs and international organizations like the IMF. Finance minister Leszek Balcerowicz was in no doubt that what Poland needed was a 'normal Western market economy'. (Balcerowicz lost this position when the new Olszewski government was approved by the Sejm on 23 December 1991. In January 1993 he joined the president's Council of Economic Advisers. On 2 April 1995 he was elected leader of Freedom Union. He became finance minister and deputy prime minister after the September 1997 general election.)

Macroeconomic stabilization aimed to tackle the near hyperinflation. The inflation rate reached 640 per cent for the year to December 1989 and 244 per cent on average for the whole year. In the month of October 1989 inflation was 54 per cent, equivalent to an annual rate of more than 17,000 per cent (Sachs 1994: 40). Macroeconomic stabilization involved the following:

1 A strict fiscal policy. For example, there were drastic reductions in subsidies. A near balanced budget was the aim for 1990, after a deficit of around 8 per cent of GDP in 1989.
2 A tight monetary policy.

> The confidence of the financial markets has been reinforced by … the recent confirmation of a second term for Hanna Gronkiewicz-Waltz as governor of the National Bank of Poland. The interest rate regime has been set, since early this year [1998], by a newly-formed monetary policy council chaired by the central bank governor. Ms Gronkiewicz-Waltz has traded some of her individual influence for greater independence for the bank with parliament giving up its previous power to approve the guidelines of monetary policy.
>
> (*FT*, Survey, 25 March 1998, p. 1)

3 An incomes policy. At the end of 1989 general wage indexation in the state enterprise sector, which had been introduced in July 1989, was eliminated (Balcerowicz *et al.* 1997: 138). Money wage increases over a centrally fixed norm were subject to a high and sharply progressive tax. This was called the *popiwek*, which initially applied to state and private sector firms alike but later on applied only to the former. The excess wage tax was suspended in August 1994 and replaced for the remainder of the year with regulations linking wages to increases in the relevant enterprise's profitability (EBRD 1995b: 52). The *popiwek* system was formally abolished at the start of 1995. The 1994 'Strategy for Poland' sought to find a means of reaching agreement on wage settlements in the public sector through the 'tripartite commission' representing trade unions, employers and government. For 1995 it was agreed that average wages in state enterprises could increase by up to 23.5 per cent, with a renegotiation on offer if inflation turned out to

be greater than the expected 22.7 per cent (Blazyca and Rapacki 1996: 90–1).

(A multi-pillar pension system was to begin operation in 1999. The three pillars are as follows: a reformed pay-as-you-go social insurance fund; mandatory pension funds; and additional voluntary insurance. The pensionable age was to be set at 62 for both men and women: EBRD 1998b: 183.)

4 The exchange rate was initially used as a monetary anchor.

The zloty was reduced to a single rate in line with the free market rate. The zloty became internally convertible for current account transactions and was backed by a $1 billion 'stabilization fund' provided by the West. (The fund in fact did not have to be used for this purpose.) The rate of 9,500 zlotys to the US dollar held until 17 May 1991, when the zloty was devalued to 11,100 in order to make exports more competitive.

In January 1990 the zloty was pegged against the US dollar (after a 31.6 per cent devaluation on 1 January 1990).

> Initially (starting on 1 January 1990) a fixed exchange rate was selected, pegged to the US dollar at the then-prevailing free-market rate; it was backed by a $1 billion stabilization fund provided by the G24 which was not used but enhanced regime credibility … Government preferences for disinflation assigned to the exchange rate the role of nominal anchor for the entire stabilization programme.
>
> (Nuti 2000: 53–4)

In May 1991 the zloty was pegged to a basket of five currencies (after a 17 per cent devaluation): 45 per cent US$; 35 per cent DM; 10 per cent GBP; 5 per cent FRF; 5 per cent CHF.

> Subsequently, concerns about external balance and the maintenance of trade competitiveness led to a crawling peg regime, with intermittent additional devaluations, then to an increasingly broader band around a central parity crawling at rates progressively decreasing over time … Poland has gradually been able to consolidate the exchange rate, stabilize the crawling regime and even experience occasional nominal revaluations.
>
> (Nuti 2000: 53–4)

The details are as follows: October 1991, crawling peg (pre-announced crawling devaluation at a rate of 1.8 per cent); February 1992, 10.7 per cent devaluation; August 1993, 7.4 per cent devaluation (monthly crawling rate of 1.6 per cent); September 1994, monthly crawling rate of 1.5 per cent; November 1994, monthly crawling rate of 1.4 per cent; February 1995, monthly crawling rate of 1.2 per cent; May 1995, crawling band, band plus or minus 7 per cent, same crawling rate; December 1995, 6 per cent revaluation; January 1996, monthly crawling rate of 1.0 per cent; February 1998, band plus or minus 10 per cent, monthly crawl of 0.8 per cent; July 1998, monthly crawling rate of 0.65 per cent; September 1998, monthly crawling rate of 0.5 per cent; October 1998, band plus or minus 12.5 per cent; January 1999, new basket (55 per cent Euro and 45 per cent US dollar); March 1999, band plus or minus 15 per cent, monthly crawling rate of 0.3 per cent (Nuti 2000: 53–4).

The zloty is pegged to a basket of five currencies (the US dollar, the Deutschmark, the pound sterling, the French franc and the Swiss franc) under a crawling peg mechanism. The central bank pre-announces the exchange rate and commercial banks can buy and sell currency within two percentage points above and below the central rate (*The Economist*, 15 April 1995, p. 99).

As of 16 May 1995 the central bank was able to set daily rates within a band 7 per cent either side of a fixed mid-rate and to intervene in the interbank foreign exchange market. The policy under which the zloty is devalued by 1.2 per cent a month to match domestic inflation was maintained (*FT*, 12 May 1995, p. 2). The crawling peg monthly devaluation of the zloty against a basket of currencies was reduced from 1.2 per cent to 1 per cent as of 8 January 1996 (*FT*, 8 January 1996, p. 2; Deutsche Bank, *Focus: Eastern Europe*, 1996, no. 150, p. 9). On 25 February 1998 the rate of crawl was reduced to 0.8 per month (Deutsche Bank, *Global Emerging Markets*, June 1998, p. 59). At the end of February 1998 the rate of the exchange rate crawl was cut to 0.8 per cent per month and the width of the band enlarged to plus or minus 10 per cent (OECD, *Economic Outlook*, June 1998, p. 123). On 9 September 1998 there was a reduction from 0.65 per cent to 0.5 per cent in the amount by which the zloty was permitted to fall each month against a basket of currencies (*FT*, 10 September 1998, p. 2).

The exchange rate regime is a crawling peg with band (EBRD 1999b: 252).

'Poland's central bank said Tuesday [11 April 2000] that it would let the zloty's rate be set solely by market demand starting Wednesday [12 April] … The central bank also abolished the monthly devaluation, the so-called crawling peg' (*IHT*, 12 April 2000, p. 14).

> [This makes the zloty] only the second central European currency after the Czech koruna to float freely. The monetary policy council, the arm of the National Bank of Poland responsible for co-ordinating monetary policy, said it was freeing the currency from its central-bank-set trading band of plus or minus 15 per cent against a fixed rate. The body also said it would scrap the 0.3 per cent monthly gradual devaluation of the zloty beginning today [12 April].
>
> (*FT*, 12 April 2000, p. 10)

> The Polish central bank allowed the zloty to float on 12 April. Until this week it had traded in a wide band around a central parity, fixed against the euro and the dollar, which was devalued by 0.3 per cent a month.
>
> (*The Economist*, 14 April 2000, p. 146)

Table 5.2 Poland: selected economic indicators 1990–2000

Economic indicator	*1990*	*1991*	*1992*	*1993*	*1994*	*1995*	*1996*	*1997*	*1998*	*1999*	*2000 (estimate)*
Rate of growth of GDP (%)	-11.6	-7.0	2.6	3.8	5.2	7.0	6.1	6.9	4.8	4.1	4.1
Rate of growth of industrial output (%)	-26.1	-11.9	2.8	6.4	12.0	9.6	8.3	11.5	4.8	4.4	7.1
Rate of growth of agricultural output (%)	-2.2	-1.6	-12.7	6.8	-9.3	10.7	0.7	1.0	1.0	-2.0	0.0
Inflation rate (consumer, %)	585.8	70.3	43.0	35.3	32.2	27.8	19.9	14.9	11.8	7.3	10.1
Budget surplus or deficit (% GDP)[a]	3.1	-6.5	-4.9	-2.4	-2.2	-3.1	-3.3	-3.1	-3.2	-3.3	-3.0
Unemployment rate (end of year, %)	6.1	11.8	14.3	16.4	16.0	14.9	13.2	8.6	10.4	13.0	15.0
Balance of payments (current account, $ billion)	0.700	-2.200	0.900	-0.600	0.677	5.310	-1.371	-4.312	-6.858	-11.569	-9.892
Foreign direct investment (net, $ billion)	0.088	0.117	0.284	0.580	0.542	1.134	2.741	3.041	4.966	6.348	9.299
Population (million)			38.4	38.5	38.6	38.6	38.6	38.7	38.7	38.7	38.7

Sources: Various issues of European Bank for Reconstruction and Development, *Transition Report*; United Nations Economic Commission for Europe, *Economic Survey of Europe*; United Nations, *World Economic and Social Survey*; IMF, *World Economic Outlook*.

Note:

[a] General government balance: includes the state, municipalities and extrabudgetary funds; excludes privatization receipts (EBRD)

On 1 January 1990 most prices were liberalized. After 1990, 90 per cent of prices were determined by the market and there have been significant increases in controlled prices as well (Balcerowicz *et al.* 1997: 138). Prices are market-determined except those of electricity, gas, central heating, hot water, basic medicines, rents in housing belonging to local authorities, television fees and spirits (EBRD 1994: 33). In February 1997 the government abolished the requirement that liquid fuel and gasoline price changes receive its approval (EBRD 1997b: 190). The price of domestically produced fuels was freed in February 1997 (OECD, *Economic Outlook*, June 1997, p. 106).

Industrial enterprises were expected to fend for themselves in the new harsh financial environment, free now to make most of their own production decisions. But there were actually very few bankruptcies, a number of factors explaining this. There was, for example, the growth of inter-firm credit/debt. (This started to fall by the end of 1991 and is no longer a financing option for loss-making enterprises: Blanchard 1994: 1170.) Other factors included the laying-off of workers, lower real wages and, initially, the support provided by Comecon trading links (though adversely affected by the switch to convertible currency trading in January 1991 and the general disruption of trade after 1989). There was an encouraging surge in hard currency exports (a surplus on the convertible currency current account of the balance of payments being achieved in 1990).

Poland is generally regarded as proof of the virtues of rapid and comprehensive change. (On 22 November 1996 Poland even became a member of the OECD.) But substantial Western aid has also been an important factor. For example, in March 1991 Western governments agreed to forgive about half the $33 billion owed to them, albeit conditionally. The unused $1 billion stabilization fund has been allowed to be used for financial restructuring of enterprises and banks. But there has been concern about backsliding on the reform programme at times.

> The first stage of stabilization effort in the beginning of 1990 was quite successful in bringing monthly inflation of 30 to 50 per cent down to 3 to 5 per cent. Unfortunately, due to the political instability and premature loosening of monetary and fiscal policies, the disinflation process in subsequent years was rather slow.
>
> (Balcerowicz *et al.* 1997: 142)

The IMF suspended the programme in September 1991 and it was only in November of the following year that terms were agreed. An IMF stand-by credit of $655 million was approved in March 1993. On 11 March 1994 Poland and the London Club of commercial banks signed an agreement in principle to reduce (by 42.5 per cent) and reschedule the $13.2 billion debt over a thirty-year period. (The formal signing took place on 14 September 1994. Some put the final percentage reduction at over 49 per cent.)

> Poland has bought back $750 million of its outstanding Brady bonds, for the second time since the bonds were launched in 1994 … The finance ministry said yesterday [18 December] that it had begun buying back long-dated bonds as emerging debt prices crashed in the aftermath of Russia's debt default in August … The bonds were bought with foreign currency reserves held at the National Bank of Poland … The ministry issued bonds to the central bank in exchange, which will be redeemed in zlotys in 2024, when the Brady bonds it bought were due to mature. The move reduces the country's outstanding debt owed to international commercial creditors to about $5.3 billion from $6.05 billion … Last year [1998] the government bought back about $1.7 billion of its outstanding Brady bonds, coinciding with another tumble in emerging bond markets during Asia's financial crisis.
> (*FT*, 19 December 1998, p. 3)

Inflation tumbled in 1991 after the high rate of 1990. It reached single figures in 1999, before moving back into double figures the following year. But output fell sharply in 1990–1 and unemployment rose. (See Table 5.2.) (Note that there is now normally a twelve-month limit on unemployment benefit.) The recorded fall in real incomes in 1990 was around 30 per cent, but this is an exaggeration to some degree because of factors such as the increasing availability of goods in the shops. There is a general problem in measuring output growth when shortages are reduced, quality increases and private sector activity, rapidly increasing, is inadequately measured. There is, in fact, considerable debate about the figures for Poland. Sachs, for example, paints a very rosy picture of events: 'There has been no significant fall in living standards. Unemployment, while high, is not soaring to the levels that were feared.' Moreover, 'the lost production reflects the cutbacks in production of enterprises that lack customers, mainly the cutback of Poland's excessively heavy industry' (Sachs 1994: 67). The actual level of unemployment is probably closer to two-thirds of the measured rate (p. 73). Ellman (1993: 30), on the other hand, makes the point that the distribution of the falls in industrial output in 1990 was perverse, with the biggest falls in the consumer goods sector (such as textiles), hit by the decline in demand, rather than in the capital and intermediate goods sectors (where most of the wasteful production was probably situated).

Polish agriculture (already largely private, as we have seen) was badly affected by the depressed state of the economy, the more open economy and the decline in subsidies. Farm incomes have fallen by a half since 1988 (*FT*, Survey, 17 June 1993, p. x). Around 40 per cent of Poles still live in rural areas and 17 per cent continue to depend exclusively on agriculture for their livelihood, while farm incomes have fallen by more than 50 per cent (*FT*, Survey, 28 March 1995, p. v). In 1992, 37 per cent of the population was rural and agriculture accounted for 27 per cent of employment in the period 1990–2 (industry 37 per cent and services 36 per cent) (*The Economist*, Survey, 8 April 1995, p. 4). As a result of these problems Poland adopted a more protectionist attitude towards agriculture. There is now extensive intervention in the markets for farm products. There are price supports, export subsidies, credit guarantees and management of state reserves (EBRD 1996b: 166).

But despite the poor performance of agriculture and niggling inflation there have been encouraging signs of change in the economy as a whole (see Table 5.2). Poland achieved a positive rate of growth as early as 1992, the first in Eastern Europe. In 1996 Poland became the first East European country to recoup the output losses since 1989. (In 2000 it has been estimated that the level of GDP exceeded the 1989 level by 27 per cent: EBRD 2001: 15.) General shortages were quickly eliminated and the variety and quality of goods have been much improved. The private sector has expanded rapidly (see below). Output stabilized in mid-1992, while unemployment steadily increased until mid-1993 (Blanchard 1994: 1169). The World Bank, however, has calculated that 14 to 15 per cent of the population live in poverty (*Transition*, 1994, vol. 5, no. 6, p. 18; Deutsche Bank, *Focus: Eastern Europe*, 1994, no. 112, p. 8).

There has been labour unrest, however, as the following events show:

6 October 1993: the coal miners' strike ends (generous redundancy payments are awarded).

7 March 1994: the Solidarity trade union begins a series of strikes to protest at the austerity measures.

21 April 1994: strikes begin in four open-cast lignite mines in protest at government restructuring plans.

27 April 1994: some (hard coal) miners go on strike.

28 April 1994: Solidarity calls a national strike in protest at government wage controls in state enterprises. (It proposed a tripartite commission of government, trade unions and employers to deal with wage policy.) (More than 10 per cent of industries take part in the eight-hour strike: *IHT*, 29 April 1994, p. 2.)

26 May 1995: in Warsaw police clash with protesters who are supporters of the Solidarity trade union.

8 August 1996: a court declares the Gdansk shipyard to be bankrupt.

6 March 1997: it is announced that the Gdansk shipyard is to be closed, although it is hoped that a buyer can still be found. (Demonstrations, sometimes violent, followed. On 20 March 1997 the government announced that about 2,000 people would be employed in the period 1998–2000 building five ships for the state-owned Szczecin yard.)

Unrest continued after this date. Sectors such as coal mining and agriculture have been particularly badly hit.

> Poland is on course to have one of Europe's lowest personal and corporate tax regimes within five years, following parliament's approval of a controversial tax-cuts package. The reform, which has still to be approved by President Alexander Kwasniewski, would cut the existing 34 per cent corporate tax rate in stages to 22 per cent in 2004 … Income tax would also be cut by stages from brackets of 19 per cent, 30 per cent and 40 per cent to just two rates of 18 per cent and 28 per cent in 2002. The reforms had a stormy passage through parliament and had threatened to undermine the

> government when Leszek Balcerowicz … threatened to resign over the issue. Mr Balcerowicz … sees the tax cuts as a crucial element in stimulating economic growth.
>
> (*FT*, 22 November 1999, p. 7)

On 29 November 1999 President Kwasniewski vetoed part of the tax bill dealing with the reduction of top rates of income tax (*EEN*, 2000, vol. 12, no. 21, pp. 6, 8).

> Labour market reform … Mr Balcerowicz says, is 'the reform which has not happened in Poland'. The minimum wage is high at 40 per cent of average wages, automatic wage indexation is rife in the public sector, adding relentlessly to costs, and rules governing hiring and firing are too restrictive. Employers' social security payments, helping to finance one of the world's most flexible (and easily abused) disability pension schemes, add nearly 100 per cent to basic wage costs … If the hidden unemployment in over-manned state industry and agriculture is taken into account, the real unemployment rate is about 20 per cent, not 13 per cent as shown in the official data.
>
> (Stefan Wagstyl, *FT*, Survey, 17 April 2000, p. ii)

'In a recent report, the OECD estimates the real current rate of unemployment is not the official figure of 13 per cent but 20 per cent, once over-manning in bloated public sector enterprises is taken into account' (p. i).

Privatization

The formal privatization of large enterprises has been slow and contentious, owing to factors such as political wrangling, powerful workers' councils and the desire to link privatization with pension reform. But Balcerowicz points out that privatization in the broad sense has been quite rapid by comparison with other countries, thanks mostly to the rapid growth of the private sector and the related privatization of the assets of state enterprises (1994: 29). Bankruptcies of large enterprises have been rare, but many of them have undertaken radical divestitures by selling off or leasing out substantial parts of their assets. The growth of the private sector as a whole has indeed been rapid when the contribution of newly established firms is taken into account. (As already indicated, the definition of the private sector is now broader, e.g. co-operatives are now included.) The following figures indicate the dimensions:

1 Rough estimates of the size of the private sector in 1992 are to be found in a number of sources (OECD, *Economic Outlook*, June 1993, p. 121 and December 1993, p. 113; Deutsche Bank, *Focus: Eastern Europe*, 1992, no. 55, p. 4 and no. 65, p. 4; *The Economist*, 23 January 1993, p. 24; *FT*, 1 May 1993, p. 2; Blaszczyk and Dabrowski 1993: 9, 32–3, 65; United Nations Economic

Commission for Europe 1993: 215, 220). The figures were as follows: the private sector as a whole (i.e. including agriculture) contributed 45 to 50 per cent of GDP and employed 58.4 per cent of the workforce at the end of the year; the private sector accounted for 31 per cent of industrial output (33 per cent in the first half of 1993).

2 The private sector accounted for 28.6 per cent of GDP in 1989, 30.9 per cent in 1990, 42.1 per cent in 1991, 47.2 per cent in 1992 and probably over 50 per cent in 1993. (United Nations Economic Commission for Europe 1994: 205, 207).

3 The private sector now accounts for more than 60 per cent of the economy and around 60 per cent of total employment (*FT*, Survey, 18 March 1994, p. ii).

4 *The Economist* (Survey, 16 April 1994, p. 16) informs us that the 1.8 million or so private non-agricultural firms now employ 30 per cent of the workforce and produce about 40 per cent of GDP. (Their output rose by more than 40 per cent in 1993. Most employed five or fewer people.) The private sector accounts for 37 per cent of industrial output (p. 19). The private sector's share of GDP is about 55 per cent (*The Economist*, 29 October 1994, p. 56). Agriculture produces 8 per cent of GDP and accounts for 30 per cent of employment (p. 5). (Agriculture accounts for 25 per cent of total employment but only 6 per cent of total output: EBRD 1999b: 250. Agriculture now accounts for only 5 per cent of GDP. Two million families live on farms smaller than 1 ha. An average farm is just 8 ha, although this is an increase from 7 ha 'a few years ago'. A growing number of those 2 million families now farm only part-time, taking other jobs to supplement their income. Only 3 per cent of soil ranks as good by international standards. 'Two-thirds of farmland might be hogged by subsistence farmers, but the larger, commercial farms that use the remaining third are becoming increasingly competitive … Already they account for three-quarters of output and they are working closely with the country's shops and food processors to increase efficiency': *Business Central Europe*, February 2000, pp. 50–1. 'Much [of agriculture] is at subsistence level: 1.4 million of the country's estimated 2 million farms do not produce for the market': *IHT*, 24 March 2000, p. 19. 'Of Poland's 2 million farms, about 200,000 efficient operations are taking an ever-bigger share of the market': *FT*, Survey, 25 June 2001, p. iv.)

The privatization of state farms has been very slow. By the end of March 1993 less than 1 per cent of state arable land had been sold and 7 per cent leased (*Business Central Europe*, September 1993, p. 25).

> Slovenia has based its restitution policy on the citizenship of the land's owner in 1945. If this person was Slovenian and the heirs have a different citizenship, they are still restituted the land … [Slovenia and Poland] have transferred the state farmland into a state fund responsible for privatizing the land and managing its use during transition.

> However, while Poland is selling most of this land, Slovenia is restituting most of its farmland to former owners.
>
> (Swinnen 1999: 647)

5 Rough estimates in mid-year of the private sector as a percentage of GDP are provided by the EBRD: 1990, 30 per cent; 1991, 40 per cent; 1992, 45 per cent; 1993, 50 per cent; 1994, 55 per cent; 1995, 60 per cent; 1996, 60 per cent; 1997, 65 per cent; 1998, 65 per cent; 1999, 65 per cent; 2000, 70 per cent (EBRD 1999b: 24, 252, and 2000b: 14, 196).

6 In 1994 the private sector accounted for 38 per cent of industrial sales (23.4 per cent in 1992) and 38.6 per cent of industrial employment. Some 60 per cent of GDP is now generated in the private sector (Deutsche Bank, *Focus: Eastern Europe*, 4 July 1995, no. 133, pp. 2–3).

7 Some 40 per cent of industrial workers are still employed by state firms (*Business Central Europe* 1999: 24). 'At least 35 per cent of industrial production still languishes in state hands' (*Business Central Europe*, February 2000, p. 39). '[About] 30 per cent of industrial workers still work for state firms' (*Business Central Europe*, May 2001, p. 42). 'While a healthy 70 per cent of Poland's GDP is generated by the private sector, an alarming three-quarters of total assets still languish in state hands' (*Business Central Europe*, June 2001, p. 50).

8 'The state still owns 3,000 companies, including more than 120 employing 500-plus. Whole sectors such as energy are still only half-reformed' (*FT*, Survey, 17 April 2000, p. ii).

The Mazowiecki government had planned to privatize 50 per cent of state assets in three years, while in January 1991 the Bielecki government spoke of this being achieved in two years (Blazyca 1991: 15). Early problems involved, for example, the so-called 'emancipation of the *nomenklatura*', where managers converted state enterprises into companies in which they held a controlling interest and where the shares were undervalued. A significant form of privatization, especially for smaller enterprises, has been 'liquidation'. Here the assets of not necessarily insolvent enterprises are sold, mainly to managers and workers. Under the first privatization bill, eventually passed in July 1990, enterprises were to be transformed into joint stock companies (i.e. 'commercialized' or 'corporatized'). The shares were to be held at first by the Treasury, which would then sell them on the open market within two years. The normal limit for foreign investors was fixed at 10 per cent and workers would get 20 per cent of the shares in their enterprise at a discount. Originally some 20 per cent of shares were seen as likely to be distributed free to the general public. Only a limited amount of partial compensation was to be available to certain former owners. (A draft law was to be submitted to the Sejm in May 1995. Only property confiscated between 1944 and 1962 in violation of the law at the time would be covered. Compensation would be in the form of 'privatization coupons', with no restitution in kind: *Transition*, 1995, vol. 6, no. 3, p. 18. Restitution may only be enforced if the original nationalization law provided for compensation and none was paid: EBRD 1995b: 52.)

The Bielecki privatization programme was unveiled on 27 June 1991. Some 400 large enterprises were listed, accounting for a quarter of industrial sales and employing 1.6 million people (12 per cent of the industrial workforce). Between five and twenty National Wealth Management Funds (NWMFs) were to be set up, which would be endowed with 60 per cent of the shares. Ten per cent of shares were to be given free to the workers in their own enterprises and 30 per cent were to be retained by the state. Each adult Polish citizen was to receive vouchers worth one share in each of the funds. (The Bielecki government then began to take a sectoral – industrial – approach to privatization, asking Western advisory companies to look at whole industries and their prospects.) But in mid-October 1991 a drastic scaling back of the programme was announced, due to fear of the social consequences (such as unemployment). The number of enterprises was reduced from 400 to 204 (representing only 7 per cent of industrial sales). The Olszewski programme for 1992 listed 200 enterprises for mass privatization in the first round set to begin in the second half of 1992 and there was to be a nominal charge for vouchers instead of being totally free. A more interventionist policy to state industry could be detected in government, aspects of this emerging 'industrial policy' including advice on restructuring.

The privatization of large enterprises continued to be stalled by political uncertainty and changes of government. On 18 March 1993 the Sejm rejected the privatization programme involving around 600 medium-sized and large enterprises. The government then decided to submit a revised programme (passed by the Sejm on 30 April) in which only 200 enterprises would be involved in the first stage. These would be transferred to five NWMFs (still managed by Western agents but with their rights and duties strictly defined), whose shares would be distributed free to pensioners and public sector workers as compensation for a (subsequently deemed illegal) failure to index pensions and state employees' pay in 1991. The privatization of the remaining 400 enterprises would take place more slowly via another fifteen or so funds. Each of the roughly twenty funds would have a lead shareholding of 33 per cent in twenty to thirty enterprises, with 27 per cent of the shares being split evenly between the other funds, 25 per cent going to the state and 15 per cent going to employees free of charge. Another concession was that enterprises on the list would be able to opt out. After ten years the shareholders would decide what to do with the funds.

After the September 1993 general election prime minister Pawlak displayed considerable reluctance to approve the remaining enterprises in the programme involving the NWMFs (some one hundred enterprises). In fact he only signed on 19 October 1994 after he had excluded from the list twenty enterprises of interest to the rural sector. His reluctance stemmed from suspicion of the role of both foreign managers and big business in general, a feeling that the enterprises were being undervalued and an inclination to think that restructuring ought to precede privatization (Christopher Bobinski, *FT*, 20 October 1994, p. 3). The prime minister approved board members for the fifteen funds on 7 December 1994. The law was approved by the Sejm on 30 June 1995 and a presidential veto was overridden on 21 July. On 31 July Walesa sent the bill to the constitutional court.

The actual number of enterprises on the mass privatization list has fluctuated. The mass privatization list settled at 413 enterprises (with additional enterprises to be added later in 1995). The managements of fifteen National Wealth Management Funds (National Investment Funds) were to receive (over a ten-year period) fees, a share of the value of the assets of their funds and longer-term bonuses. Starting in November 1995 the privatization units purchased by Poles (for a nominal fee) were to be converted into fifteen shares (one for each NWMF) and these were to be tradable on the Warsaw stock exchange (possibly starting in early 1997). The shares of the enterprises were to be allocated in a complex system of lottery rounds beginning on 17 July 1995. This was to be followed by a trading process.

In each participating enterprise 33 per cent of the shares are owned by a designated 'lead National Investment Fund', about 2 per cent by each of the remaining fourteen NIFs, 25 per cent by the Treasury and 15 per cent by employees who receive their shares free of charge: EBRD 1996a: 17). This has been put another way. Initially the government was to transfer 60 per cent of its holdings in the 413 enterprises to the NWMFs. Each of the NWMFs were to take a 33 per cent 'lead shareholding' in twenty-eight of the 413 enterprises. (The 33 per cent block of shares can only be sold or traded in its entirety: Brada 1996: 73.) The NWMFs were also to take 'minority holdings' of 27 per cent in other enterprises. At a later stage the government was to allocate, free of charge, 15 per cent of the shares to employees of the participating enterprises. A further 15 per cent were to be allocated to social funds and other recipients. By then 90 per cent of the shares of the 413 enterprises would be in the hands of funds, workers or institutions, leaving a balance of 10 per cent with the Treasury (Anthony Robinson, *FT*, 14 July 1995, p. 2; *IHT*, 18 July 1995, p. 13).

The new privatization law was designed to speed privatization by cutting back the powers of employees and management to delay sales. Individual sales of state-sector enterprises would henceforth have to be approved by the entire cabinet (rather than by the privatization minister) (Christopher Bobinski, *FT*, 22 July 1995, p. 2). In the version supported by parliament the privatization of enterprises in banking, insurance, crude oil, gas supply, coal, defence, power generation, telecommunications, ports, airports and alcoholic drinks would depend on a decision in parliament (Deutsche Bank, *Focus: Eastern Europe*, 1995, no. 135, p. 9). A new law was adopted by parliament in July 1995, making privatization in a number of areas (including telecommunications, energy and banking) subject to parliamentary approval. This was overturned by the constitutional court in November 1995 and a revised version was to be submitted to parliament in early 1996 (EBRD 1996a: 10).

Thus in 1995 the long-delayed voucher-based mass privatization programme at last got under way. The management for fifteen National Investment Funds was selected in February and the allocation of 413 enterprises to the funds took place in July–October. An additional 106 enterprises were to be allocated later in 1995 (EBRD 1995b: 52). At the end of September 1995 another 101 enterprises were added to the list, making 514 in total (*Business Europa*, November–December 1995, p. 41). The sale of vouchers began on 22 November 1995 (and ended exactly a year later) and the first public offerings for NIFs were to take place towards the end of 1996 (EBRD 1996a: 10). Although Poland's long-delayed mass privatization scheme has now reached the implementation stage, the scale of the programme is modest, with shares in only 512 enterprises distributed to the so-called National Investment Funds out of a total of about 4,500 enterprises that remain in state ownership. There is tension between the government-appointed supervisory boards and the private fund managers, owing both to performance failures by management teams and ambiguity in the respective roles of the boards and fund managers. The 1996 privatization guidelines called for the commercialization and sale of ninety (medium-sized and large: *FT*, 4 October 1996, p. 2) enterprises, but only eleven were sold in the first half of the year (EBRD 1996b: 165). The exchange of certificates for shares in the NIFs began with the listing of these funds on the Warsaw stock exchange in June 1997. A law of August 1996 reshaped the framework for future privatizations with effect from January 1997. The state Treasury (which assumed responsibility for privatization in August 1996) has the right to commercialize a state enterprise upon written notification to its management and employees. Their consent is no longer necessary. Employees of an enterprise gained the right to acquire 15 per cent of that enterprise's shares held by the Treasury free of charge. The 1997 guidelines called for the sale of 120 state enterprises, as well as shares in fifty enterprises of which the state is a partial owner. But in the first half of 1997 the Treasury privatized only fifteen enterprises through equity sales (EBRD 1997b: 189).

The government approved the privatization plan for 1997 on 30 September 1996. Some 120 medium-sized and large enterprises, together with about 300 smaller enterprises, were to be sold. Most state assets would be privatized by the year 2000 (*Transition*, September–October 1996, vol. 7, nos 9–10, pp. 24–5).

The pace of large privatization has thus been much less rapid than intended, while that of small privatization has been fast:

1 Only seven large enterprises were privatized between the end of November 1990 and October 1991.
2 By the end of September 1992 forty-three large enterprises had been privatized through 'capital privatization' (public tender or direct offer to a potential investor), 349 enterprises had been taken over by their employees or management (leasing of property) and 100 enterprises had been 'liquidated' and sold (Mullineux and Belka 1993: 11).
3 By July 1994 there had been only twenty-four public offerings on the Warsaw stock exchange and about sixty sales to foreign investors. There had been, however, about a thousand privatizations by means of the 'liquidation'

of medium-sized enterprises via employee ownership or leases (Lucja Swiatkowski Cannon, *FT*, 9 September 1994, p. 17).

4 By the end of 1993:

(a) 'capital privatization' (the sale of enterprises to outsiders through sales or auctions) accounted for only about 100 out of 8,000 state enterprises (under this arrangement workers get 20 per cent of the shares at a discount but lose control of the enterprise);

(b) 'liquidation' accounted for 850 enterprises (this allows workers and managers to buy their enterprise by paying 20 per cent of the estimated value of the enterprises and making lease payments, at attractive terms, for the remainder over a period of five to ten years; these have typically been small to medium-sized enterprises with under 200 enterprises);

(c) even if sales of insolvent enterprises ('asset sales') are added, amounting to an additional 1,010, the total number came to about 2,000 enterprises or 25 per cent of state enterprises. The private sector accounted for 84 per cent of employment in trade (Blanchard 1994: 1172; Aghion and Blanchard 1994: 6–7). By the end of 1995, 160 enterprises had been privatized via 'capital privatization' (*IHT*, Survey, 17 October 1996, p. 14).

5 The 1990 large privatization programme envisaged a multi-track approach. At the end of 1993, 12 per cent of the 8,772 enterprises owned by central government agencies at the outset of the reforms had been privatized (EBRD 1994: 32). Around 93 per cent of trading activity is now in private hands (p. 13). By the end of 1994, 32 per cent of the 8,772 larger enterprises owned by the central government and about 20 per cent of the 4,500 enterprises owned by regional governments had been privatized (EBRD 1995a: 61). By the end of June 1996, 2,624 of the 8,853 enterprises that were owned by the state in July 1990 had been liquidated or privatized through asset sales and 284 had been sold in cash privatizations. In addition, 1,049 had been commercialized, of which 512 were included in the National Investment Funds programme (EBRD 1996a: 165). About 1,470 enterprises have been privatized through the use of other methods, namely cash sales to outside investors or management buy-outs (p. 17). By the end of 1996, 3,937 of the 8,853 medium-sized and large enterprises which were state-owned in July 1990 had entered into the privatization process. Direct privatizations totalled 1,712, while commercialized enterprises numbered 1,226, of which 183 were privatized through equity sales. The commercialization included 512 enterprises included in the NIF programme (EBRD 1997b: 189). In May 1998 the government unveiled its draft privatization guidelines through 2001, calling for the sale of most remaining state assets. It placed particular emphasis on large enterprises in infrastructure, heavy industry, mining and finance. There remain about 2,863 state enterprises, with an estimated book value equivalent to 30 to 35 per cent of GDP. About three-quarters of the top Polish companies by turnover are still state-owned.

In July 1998 the transport ministry awarded the first licences for nationwide railway services to independent operators (EBRD 1998b: 182–3).

> The projected revenues in the 1998 privatization guidelines were exceeded, due to a number of big-ticket privatizations in late 1998 (BHP, Pekao SA, TPSA). Nevertheless, only seventeen of the intended fifty enterprises were sold … Poland went ahead with the initial public offering of around 15 per cent of the telecoms company (TPSA) in November 1998.
>
> (EBRD 1999a: 41)

The government planned to privatize fifty enterprises in 1998, but only seventeen sales took place. The authorities aim to finish the privatization of all major industries by 2001, with the exception of certain coal mines, the railways and the postal service. 'Employment in the state-owned enterprise sector remains large compared with that in the other first-wave accession countries at 33 per cent of total employment in 1998' (EBRD 1999b: 250). The privatization of energy sector companies, steel mills and other industrial enterprises is proceeding slowly and with mixed results. However, the largest oil refinery, PKN, was successfully floated on the stock market in November 1999 and several energy sector companies were sold to strategic investors. Restructuring is urgently required in the coal sector (EBRD 2000a: 70).

> The privatization of large-scale enterprises is well-advanced … The government is implementing a coal restructuring plan … Although restructuring in the steel sector was launched in 1999 … strong union resistance to restructuring plans and the limited interest of strategic investors may delay the process … The authorities plan to implement radical reform of the railway … There has been little progress in restructuring of the gas sector.
>
> (EBRD 2000b: 194–5)

> While progress in large-scale privatization is well advanced, the state still owns a number of large industrial companies, including an oil refinery, major steel mills and coal mines. This slow pace of progress reflects a reluctance to address difficult restructuring issues, including labour market flexibility … Plans for infrastructure privatization in 2001 include the sale of a further 35 per cent of the dominant fixed line telecommunications provider, TPSA, and a number of power generating companies, combined power and heating plants, and energy distribution companies … Foreign investors now control the majority of assets. However, a recent controversy over management control between the Treasury and the strategic investor in PZU, the dominant insurance provider, has highlighted the risks of government

> interference on corporate governance through remaining share holdings in partly privatized companies.
>
> (EBRD 2001: 80)

6 As of 28 November 1994, 5,096 of the 8,441 medium-sized and large enterprises were still owned by the state (Deutsche Bank, *Focus: Eastern Europe*, 1994, no. 123, p. 10).
7 By the autumn of 1991, 80 per cent of retail trade was in private hands. Shops and wholesalers are now more than 90 per cent private. Some 900 larger companies have been privatized through 'liquidation', which usually entails the sale or lease of a company's assets to its employees. By early February 1994, 100 companies had been sold to investors or privatized through the stock market (*The Economist*, Survey, 16 April 1994, p. 15). By early 1995, 200 had been sold to strategic investors or through the stock market (*The Economist*, 20 January 1995, p. 75).

Despite the delays encountered in large privatization, a feature of Poland's relative success has been the way in which state enterprises have generally been forced to become more efficient by the imposition of 'hard budget constraints' and the competition provided by private Polish firms and by foreign companies at home and abroad.

Demonopolization was initiated in the period 1989–90 with the break-up of large state enterprises (United Nations Economic Commission for Europe 1994: 205). But the inherited structure of industry was still highly monopolistic and, according to Blazyca (1992), the initial reaction of state enterprises was disappointing in the sense that there tended to be a greater stress on raising prices and reducing output rather than searching for new products and markets. There have, in fact, been a number of somewhat contradictory empirical studies on the issue:

1 A World Bank survey revealed that even the state manufacturing sector has shown encouraging signs of adaptation in areas such as increasing profitable sales and cost reduction. Managers stressed the need for restructuring before privatization (which is still the known ultimate aim, it should be stressed).

> Poland's experience shows that shock therapy can have valuable effects by giving an unambiguous signal, changing relative prices, and indicating the government's commitment to hard budgets. But Poland's experience also shows that rapid changes in ownership may be unnecessary, and that restructuring before privatization may be desirable.
>
> (Pinto *et al.* 1993: 255)

The encouraging signs of adaptation are due to a hardening of budget constraints, competition from imports (and the resulting improvement in relative price determination) and managers' expectations of personal benefit when privatization takes place. (See also Hume and Pinto 1993: 18–20.)

The hardening of budget constraints and market competition (in part the result of liberalized trade) have initiated significant enterprise restructuring and large productivity gains (EBRD 1996b: 165). Government-led restructuring efforts are highly visible, state enterprises leading the process of consolidation in the oil and chemical industries. Coal and steel are next in line for restructuring (EBRD 1997a: 21). Many of remaining large state enterprises are in problem sectors, such as defence, hard-coal mining, steel, chemicals and shipbuilding. The government has made the restructuring and privatization of these difficult sectors a major priority (EBRD 1998b: 182).

'Poland has demonstrated good overall economic performance, led by hard budgets and a good competition framework, despite the fact that the long-delayed privatization programme has taken off only recently' (John Nellis, *Transition*, November–December 1996, p. 7).

'Investigation shows that Polish managers of state firms performed well because they expected privatization and hoped their achievements would assure their survival when it came' (Havrylyshyn and McGettigan 1999: 5).

'Poland ... forced state industry to focus on long-term profits rather than short-term growth ... by whacking hard budget constraints on companies, which forced them to sell off non-core assets to private entrepreneurs in order to survive' (*Business Central Europe*, November 1999, p. 19).

2 Estrin and Richet (1993) painted a more gloomy picture, based on a sample of three state enterprises in the period 1989–92. Enterprises made relatively positive adjustments in product differentiation and marketing, but overall changes were relatively modest and the governance of enterprises hardly changed. The magnitude of the fall in demand 'has left all three firms with excess capacity, large wage bills and rising debt. The demand shock was clearly associated with the Polish "big bang" transition policy, and appears to have weakened the ability of firms to respond' (p. 17).

3 Blanchard (1994: 1171) saw little evidence of restructuring beyond labour shedding.

4 Kennedy (1997) examines the transformation path of various sectors during the period 1989–93 (p. 842). He finds striking variation as regards restructuring between two groups, group A accounting (in 1993) for 53 per cent of GDP and 59 per cent of employees and group B accounting for 41 per cent of GDP and 22 per cent of employees (p. 842). Group A comprised wood and paper, light manufacturing, food processing, construction and trade, while group B comprised forestry, mining, fuel and power, metallurgy, electro-engineering, chemicals, minerals, transport, communications, and banking, securities and finance (p. 846). (Note that agriculture is excluded from these groupings.) Kennedy concludes that sectors in group A experienced a large shift of activity from the state to the private sector, high rates of new firm entry, falling concentration ratios, rapidly rising output (following a short-term decline) and significant foreign investment. Sectors

> in group B were dominated by large state enterprises which were slow to restructure, high concentration ratios, poor economic performance, and more selective foreign investment (pp. 841, 842, 845, 853, 859).

Banks

The National Bank is still not fully independent of the Sejm. The Sejm must approve the monetary programme each year and may set an upper or lower limit on central bank financing of the budget deficit (Balcerowicz *et al.* 1997: 145).

Private banks were allowed in 1989 and by the end of 1991 they appear to have accounted for about 13 per cent of all deposits. Some 10 per cent of the private banks are foreign-owned. Commercial banks in general are allowed to take equity stakes in enterprises, but central bank approval is needed if an individual stake exceeds 25 per cent. Likewise, lending to any one enterprise needs approval if the figure is greater than 15 per cent of the bank's capital. Commercial banks were converted into joint stock companies in October 1991 as a prelude to privatization (Eastwood and Durski 1993: 3–7).

The National Bank has said that it will stop issuing licences to foreign banks. But foreigners will still be able to buy a majority stake in existing banks (*Business Central Europe*, September 1993, p. 51).

A law to deal with bad debt came into effect in March 1993 as an incentive to restructure insolvent enterprises. A bank holding 30 per cent of the debt can apply for a debt–equity swap (*Business Central Europe*, June 1993, p. 9).

Bonin and Leven (1996) make an economic case for creating larger domestic banking groups and combining this with greater foreign competition. 'With three large domestic banking groups, the Polish government should be comfortable opening up the banking sector to reap the benefits of foreign competition' (p. 71).

> The structure of the banking sector in Poland is significantly different from that in either Hungary or the Czech Republic. The two most striking differences are the high participation of foreign banks both as partners and as foreign-owned, fully licensed banks in Hungary and the high degree of concentration in the Czech Republic ... Poland has significantly restricted foreign bank competition. The structure of the Czech banking sector is highly concentrated, with the big four domestic banks dominating a large number of very small, fringe banks [foreign banks accounted for only 3.2 per cent of total credits in 1993: p. 59] ... Poland's basic strategy has been to strengthen domestic banks through recapitalization, privatization and, most recently, consolidation before opening up the banking sector to significant foreign competition.
>
> (p. 58)

The finance ministry reckons that the state accounts for 68 per cent of the banking system. The government's original plan was rapidly to privatize all nine regional banks, but difficulties arose. To speed up the process the government has persuaded three of the regional banks to join forces with Pekao Bank to create the largest banking group. The hope is that it will be easier to privatize the new group, which accounts for 23 per cent of the assets of the entire banking system (*FT*, Survey, 30 October 1996, p. ii).

Four of the nine regional banks have merged (*IHT*, Survey, 16 September 1996, p. 14).

On 23 June 1998 it was announced that an Italian bank and a German insurance company had bought a majority stake in Pekao, the biggest bank in Poland (*IHT*, 25 June 1999, p. 15). Pekao was floated on the stock exchange in 1998 (*FT*, Survey, 27 October 1998, p. iv).

On 24 June 1999 it was announced that Allied Irish Banks was to take an 80 per cent stake in Bank Zachodni. Bank Zachodni aimed to double its share of the domestic market to 7 per cent. The sale of Zachodni made it the last of the nine banks carved out of the National Bank of Poland in 1989 to pass into private hands. Zachodni was the twelfth biggest Polish bank by assets. Allied Irish Banks bought 60 per cent of the regional bank Wielkopolski Bank Kredytowy in 1991. Combined, the two Polish banks constitute the fifth biggest bank in Poland (*IHT*, 25 June 1999, p. 15). The acquisition of Zachodni gave Allied Irish Banks 6 per cent of the Polish market. Foreign banks now control almost two-thirds of the Polish banking system. Only one bank remains to be privatized: PKO, the second largest, with a dominant position in domestic retail lending and deposits and the largest branch network (*FT*, 25 June 1999, p. 28).

The following are estimates of the changing ownership structure of the Polish banking system:

The finance ministry reckons that the state accounts for 68 per cent of the banking system (*FT*, Survey, 30 October 1996, p. ii).

By the end of 1996 there were twenty-four banks with majority foreign ownership. Their share of total bank loans was 15.3 per cent (EBRD 1997b: 191). Foreign banks have been required, in most cases, to take over existing troubled Polish banks in order to obtain licences. But remaining restrictions on the entry of foreign banks will be lifted in 1999 (EBRD 1998b: 183). Significant stakes in banks have been sold: 37 per cent of Bank Przemyslovo Handlowy was sold to Bayerische Hypo and Vereinsbank AG in October 1998; 52.1 per cent of Pekao (one of two large savings banks) was sold to Unicredito Italiano and Allianz in June 1999; and 80 per cent of Bank Zachodni was sold to Allied Irish in June 1999 (EBRD 1999b: 251).

The state's share of the banking system is 55 per cent (*FT*, 27 August 1997, p. 2).

More than half of bank assets are in state hands (*Business Central Europe*, September 1997, p. 14).

'With Pekao now in the private sector more than half the industry is outside state control' (*FT*, Survey, 27 October 1998, p. iv).

Foreign banks have a 25 per cent share of the banking system (Business Central Europe 1998: 18).

Foreign banks now control almost two-thirds of the Polish banking system (*FT*, 25 June 1999, p. 28).

Some 63 per cent of bank capital is now in foreign hands (*FT*, 25 August 1999, p. 2).

Foreigners now control nearly 60 per cent of the banking industry measured by capital (*The Economist*, 28 August 1999, p. 64).

'Foreign investors control about 70 per cent of Polish banking assets, a level matched in Central Europe only by Hungary' (*FT*, Survey, 17 April 2000, p. ii).

According to the IMF, the proportion of total bank assets controlled by foreigners (foreign control being defined as foreigners owning more than 50 per cent of the total equity of a bank) increased from roughly 3 per cent in 1994 to about 53 per cent in 1999. The latter figure for Hungary was around 57 per cent (*The Economist*, 4 November 2000, p. 194).

> More than two-thirds of the banking sector by assets are now in private ownership ... The strong presence of foreign strategic investors, including control of about 50 per cent of banking sector assets, and ongoing consolidation contribute to the strengthening of the banking sector.
>
> (EBRD 2000b: 195)

'Some 70 per cent of Polish banking assets are foreign owned' (*Business Central Europe*, 'Polish financial review', May 2001, p. 5).

Further developments in privatization

8 November 1998:

> Poland has completed one of the largest stock offerings with the sale of a stake in Telekommunikacja Polska, the national telecommunications operator. Domestic and foreign demand was more than twice subscribed for the 15 per cent of the company's equity on offer, despite the adverse market conditions ... Next year the Treasury will be looking for a strategic investor, which will be offered between 25 per cent and 35 per cent of the equity in the company.
>
> (*FT*, 9 November 1998, p. 26)

The government sold the 15 per cent stake through an initial public offering (IPO) (*IHT*, 26 July 2000, p. 15).

An additional 15 per cent was distributed to present and former employees (EBRD 1999b: 251).

On 25 July 2000 it was announced that France Telecom and a Polish investment company (Kulczyk Holdings) had agreed to buy a 35 per cent stake (25 per cent and 10 per cent, respectively) in Telekommunikacja Polska for $4.3 billion 'in what would be the biggest sale of state assets in Eastern Europe since the collapse of communism'. The government plans to sell a further 30 per cent stake in 2001. France Telecom and Kulczyk Holdings have an option to acquire an additional 16 per cent of this 30 per cent by the end of September 2001 (*IHT*, 26 July 2000, p. 15). '[The agreement represents] post-communist Eastern Europe's largest privatization' (*FT*, 26 July 2000, p. 29).

February 1999:

> Poland's bickering politicians have failed to privatize much of the country's industry. Poland's industrial base is crumbling. State-owned firms account for a third of industrial sales and employ more than 40 per cent of industrial workers, but produce only 5 per cent of profits. Because they cannot afford essential investment they are growing ever less competitive ... Polish food-processing is still largely state-owned ... Under pressure from the EU ... Poland has started to sell some companies. In the past year it has sold part of its telecom monopoly, TPSA, and several big banks ... [But there was a] failure to sell thirty-five of the fifty firms that were due to be privatized ... Plans to extend the successful mass privatization of 1995 never got off the ground ... Its National Investment Fund scheme of 1995 placed 414 state companies in the hands of Western-managed funds that were subsequently listed on the stock exchange. To increase the value of their holdings the fund managers restructured the companies. Some were shut, others merged and the rest sold. But none was left to stagnate, as the companies remaining in state hands have been.
>
> (*The Economist*, 20 February 1999, p. 87)

March 1999: a 20 per cent stake in PAK (a group of power plants) is sold to a large Polish conglomerate after negotiations with a British company are broken off (EBRD 1999b: 251).

November 1999: 'Following the initial public offering of a 30 per cent share in the dominant oil refinery, PKN Orlen, in November 1999, a further 26 per cent was floated on the stock market in June 2000' (EBRD 2000b: 194).

7 January 2000:

> Poland, alone among Central European countries, has passed no law on the return of property that was summarily nationalized after 1945. Restitution bills failed in parliament in 1991 and 1993. Late last year [1999] the Solidarity-led coalition proposed a law that would compensate those people who were Polish citizens at the time their property was seized, a group that would include tens of thousands of Polish Jews and Roman Catholics who fled to the United States, Canada, Western Europe and Israel after the war ... The government had proposed a broad, complicated package that would return property or partly compensate claimants with government bonds or shares in privatized enterprises ... The government's original proposal would have allowed the heirs of Polish citizens to file claims, but only in

> Polish courts … The law … would only compensate individuals if they can prove that the communist regime violated its own nationalization laws in postwar Poland when it seized property, a provision that is more liberal than it might appear because the communists paid little attention to their own laws … But a parliamentary committee, including Solidarity members, this week amended the proposed law, limiting the right to recover nationalized property or obtain any financial compensation only to current Polish citizens who have lived in the country for the last five years … The EU says that international law requires Poland to recognize the property rights of former citizens and those Poles living outside the country.
>
> (Peter Finn, *IHT*, 8 January 2000, pp. 1, 5)

('A Polish government plan to return property seized under communism to former owners is hanging in the balance after the upper house of parliament on Friday [26 January 2001] made big changes to a bill passed earlier by the lower house. The Senate threw out clauses which would have excluded from the law most claimants living overseas, including many Jews and other émigrés. The government had originally intended to include these overseas claimants … However, the lower house earlier this month would have excluded most overseas claimants unless they were the original pre-Second World War owners. Heirs would have qualified only if they held Polish citizenship at the end of 1999 … The Senate voted forty-four to thirty-six in favour of widening eligibility. The bill must now pass through the lower house again … Any bill must be signed by President Alexander Kwasniewski … before it becomes law. He has yet to declare his hand … The opposition SLD … opposes the restitution plan … Under the plan claimants would win back 50 per cent of their property or receive financial compensation where the physical return is not possible … The government estimates there could be about 170,000 claims … Most of the affected properties are now in the hands of local authorities. Poland is the last ex-communist state to pass a restitution law': *FT*, 29 January 2001, p. 10.)

'Several electricity generating companies were sold to foreign strategic investors in early 2000 and privatization of other electricity generating and distribution companies is well advanced' (EBRD 2000b: 195).

April 2000: 'Poland has modified its privatization process. Under the mass enfranchisement programme up to 7 per cent of privatized companies will be distributed to ordinary Poles' (*Business Central Europe*, April 2000, p. 13).

The modification involves setting aside 5 per cent of the revenue from forthcoming privatizations for an 'enrichment' fund, which would distribute the proceeds to the population at large (*FT*, Survey, 17 April 2000, p. iv).

30 June 2000: it is announced that $422 million has been raised from selling shares in PKN Orlen SA, the country's largest refinery and fuel distributor (*IHT*, 1 July 2000, p. 11).

14 July 2000: the Sejm narrowly approves the enfranchisement bill by 222 votes to 213 with two abstentions. The bill now goes to the Senate for scrutiny. A three-fifths majority in the Sejm is needed to overturn a presidential veto.

Under the plan tenants of municipal or co-operative flats will be granted full or partial ownership rights to their homes. Those who lease small plots of land from the state will become their owners. Other beneficiaries will receive coupons in special funds – like units in mutual trust funds – to which some shares in companies undergoing privatization are to be allotted.

(*IHT*, 15 July 2000, p. 5)

The enfranchisement bill … stipulates that every Polish adult receive a share of state assets. Tenants of municipal or co-operation flats will be granted full or part ownership rights to their homes. Others will receive coupons in special funds managing shares in companies undergoing privatization. The ruling Solidarity Electoral Action sees the enfranchisement bill as an act of historical justice for those who did not benefit from earlier legislative provisions granting free shares to workers of privatized companies. The Democratic Left Alliance and the liberal Freedom Union opposed the bill, claiming it would hurt public finances.

(*Transition*, 2000, vol. 11, nos 3–4, p. 39)

The bill … would distribute state property – mainly municipal housing – directly to its current tenants. It would also hand out vouchers to those Poles who have missed out during privatization, such as pensioners and public sector employers. They can sell the vouchers to the National Enfranchisement Fund, which will hold shares in companies being privatized. The Senate went a step further by including garden allotments in the bill's provisions … The bill has been criticized for being socially unfair, economically pernicious and legally flawed. Many perceive it as a crude attempt by the AWS [Solidarity party] to boost the electoral appeal of its unpopular leader Marian Krzaklewski … But it is the bill's impact on the property market that has many up in arms. Take garden plots. These are managed by associations who charge membership fees for their upkeep and many are on prime urban real estate. Opponents say it is foolish to dole them out to individual owners with neither the money nor the incentive to maintain them. The same goes for city-owned flats, which could be sold for a song if poor residents acquire them.

(*Business Central Europe*, September 2000, pp. 45–6)

Poland's Treasury minister yesterday [14 November] ended months of boardroom wrangling, accusations and alleged threats at Poland's largest insurer, PZU, when he replaced its managers. He did so after asking a court on Monday [13 November] to annul the Treasury's sale of 30 per cent of PZU to Netherlands-based Eureko and Poland's BIG Bank Gdanski and removing their representatives from PZU's board. The Treasury claimed that Eureko and BIG violated PZU's 1999 privatization agreement, which bound the investors to develop the insurance company. The ministry says the partners … in fact needed PZU to protect BIG in a separate shareholder

> battle with Deutsche Bank. The companies say the claims have no merit and that they are considering legal action.
>
> (*FT*, 15 November 2000, p. 12)

'Eureko claims the Treasury did not respect the rules for conflict resolution and pledges to split PZU's board seats evenly between itself and the consortium' (*FT*, 16 November 2000, p. 14).

'Poland's Treasury called for the renationalization of a 30 per cent stake in insurer PZU, sold a year earlier to a consortium including pan-European insurer Eureko. The step sparked concerns about the country's foreign investment climate' (Business Central Europe 2000: 11). 'In November [2000] the Treasury annulled the 1999 sale of a 30 per cent stake in PZU to pan-European insurer Eureko. A compromise may be in the offing, but Poland's investor-friendly reputation has taken a battering' (p. 27).

11 January 2001: 'Parliament approved on Thursday [11 January 2001] a long-delayed law compensating Polish citizens whose property was seized between 1944 and 1962 – but only for those who retain Polish citizenship' (*IHT*, 12 January 2001, p. 8).

> Parliament passed a controversial law to compensate former owners for property seized by the communists. The law fulfils the government's election promise, but will only give claimants half the value of their former possessions because of worries about the costs of full restitution.
>
> (*Business Central Europe*, February 2001, p. 11)

> Poland's Senate threw out parts of a bill on restituting property seized by the communists after the war, which would have excluded many Polish émigrés living overseas, many of them Jewish. The bill must now be reconsidered by the lower house.
>
> (*Business Central Europe*, March 2001, p. 9)

22 March 2001:

> President Kwasniewski has vetoed a reprivatization bill that would have returned 50 per cent of the property seized from private owners by the country's former rulers ... Mr Kwasniewski ... said the bill was too expensive for the budget and excluded former owners or their heirs who did not have Polish citizenship, including many Jews. He argued that the restoration of confiscated property seized at the end of the Second World War, for which most owners received no compensation, would 'create social divisions'. Poland is the only East European country beside Belarus that has not enacted a property restitution programme since the collapse of communist rule in 1989.
>
> (*FT*, 23 March 2001, p. 10)

> President Alexander Kwasniewski yesterday [22 March] vetoed a … compensation payment to hundreds of thousands of people whose property was seized by the government in the communist era … [opposing] the measure on the grounds that the economy could not afford it and it would undermine public service reforms. The bill passed by … the Sejm allowed victims to receive 50 per cent of the value of their property as compensation. It would have denied compensation to anyone who was not a Polish citizen in 1999 … There is little chance that the issue will be readdressed before parliamentary elections in September.
>
> (*Telegraph*, 23 March 2001, p. 20)

May 2001:

> Treasury chief Aldona Kamela-Sowinska … seems close to ending a simmering dispute that has sullied Poland's image among foreign investors … [She has agreed] to mend fences with pan-European insurer Eureko over control of Poland's biggest insurer PZU … The PZU saga … started last November [2000] when [the] former Treasury minister … stripped Eureko and its Polish partner BIG Bank Gdanski of their 30 per cent stake in PZU … By early April [2001] she [the new Treasury minister] had reinstated the privatization agreement and promised Eureko a further 21 per cent stake in PZU when the insurer is floated. In return Eureko is calling off its legal battle and the Treasury will retain management control.
>
> (*Business Central Europe*, June 2001, p. 34)

Foreign trade

Tariffs largely replaced quotas and the former were generally relatively low. (But pressures from the agricultural and industrial lobbies led to tariff increases in spring 1991 and in August 1991: Balcerowicz *et al.* 1997: 138.)

Most quantitative trade restrictions and export subsidies were eliminated in 1990. But in sectors such as automobiles, import barriers can be substantial. There have been several upward revisions in import tariffs after the sharp reductions in 1990 (EBRD 1994: 33). Largely current account convertibility exists, with limits on residents' capital account transactions. There is a pre-announced crawling peg regime (p. 109). The regime was adjusted in September 1994 and in February 1995, the combined effect of which was to slow the monthly rate of currency depreciation from 1.5 per cent to 1.2 per cent (EBRD 1995a: 61). In June 1995 Poland accepted the obligations of Article 8 of the IMF on current account convertibility (EBRD 1995b: 52). In June 1993 a 6 per cent import surcharge was imposed. In May 1995 quantitative restrictions on agricultural imports were converted into tariffs. The import surcharge, which was cut to 3 per cent at the beginning of 1996, was to be eliminated by the end of that year. There is extensive intervention in the markets for farm products. There are price supports, export subsidies, credit guarantees and management of state reserves

(EBRD 1996b: 166). 'It is striking that Poland, with the strongest overall growth of any country in the region and a sound transition, has maintained some restrictions on short-term portfolio flows (such as those on capital and money market instruments)' (EBRD 1998b: 9). In September 1998 a new foreign exchange bill came into effect, radically liberalizing the foreign exchange regime and setting the groundwork for full capital account liberalization by 2000 (p. 182). When Poland joined the OECD in November 1996 it committed itself to full liberalization of the capital account by 1 January 2000. A significant step in this direction was taken in January 1999 when a new foreign exchange law took effect, eliminating all restrictions on internal foreign exchange transactions between banks and non-banking entities. The central bank retains the authority to impose extraordinary restrictions in case of threats to the stability and integrity of the financial system. Some restrictions on short-term capital flows remain (EBRD 1999b: 250).

> Despite an agreement with the OECD to abolish the requirement to obtain central bank approval for non-bank short-term capital flows by the end of 1999, the authorities postponed this step owing to concerns about currency volatility. However, the controls constitute little impediment to capital flows due to the existence of large offshore zloty markets.
>
> (EBRD 2000b: 194)

There has been a major switch towards trade with the West. For example, the EU accounted for 28 per cent of Poland's foreign trade in 1988. In 1991, however, the EU took 54 per cent of exports and provided 48 per cent of imports (*FT*, 11 May 1992, p. 4). The EU took 44 per cent of exports in 1990 and 63 per cent in 1993 (the respective figures for Eastern Europe and the countries of the former Soviet Union were 21.5 per cent and 12.9 per cent respectively). Average tariffs were cut to 5.5 per cent in the early days of the reform, but have crept back to over 18 per cent. Products such as food, textiles and clothing are the most heavily protected (*The Economist*, Survey, 16 April 1994, pp. 15, 21). In 1992, 72.2 per cent of exports went to OECD countries, 57.9 percentage points of which went to the EU (Deutsche Bank, *Focus: Eastern Europe*, 1993, no. 85, p. 6). The EU and other developed markets account for more than 70 per cent of foreign trade (*FT*, Survey, 28 March 1995, p. ii). Some 63 per cent of exports go to the EU, from which Poland takes 57 per cent of imports (p. ix). A surplus of $557 million in 1989 in agricultural trade with the EU turned into a deficit of $333 million by 1993 (p. v).

> Last month's breakthrough on liberalizing farm trade ... covers trade worth over $1 billion a year, slashing import tariffs and export refunds on 75 per cent of Polish agricultural exports to the EU ... It also means the EU will have to scrap its export subsidies, and can no longer offload so much of its surplus production in Poland ... [the Polish] consumer will have greater access to foreign produce – particularly citrus fruits, vanilla and olives ...

> The two sides have been struggling to reach a deal ever since last year [1999], when Warsaw slapped tariffs on a range of EU goods following a wave of protests from Polish farmers railing at cheap EU imports … The [agricultural sector in Poland] is increasingly polarized between efficient, larger producers and the tiny, inefficient ones that sell little on the market.
>
> (*Business Central Europe*, November 2000, p. 49)

Foreign direct investment

The amount of foreign investment was at first relatively disappointing but then made encouraging progress:

1. Net direct foreign investment was $10 million in 1990, $117 million in 1991, $284 million in 1992, $580 million in 1993, $580 million in 1994 and $1.134 billion in 1995 (United Nations Economic Commission for Europe 1996: 149).
2. Direct foreign investment amounted to $839 million in the period 1990–3 (EBRD 1994: 123).

'Foreign direct investment last year [1999] hit a record $8 billion, taking the total to $39 billion, or 40 per cent of the ex-Soviet bloc total' (*FT*, Survey, 17 April 2000, p. i).

Poland has phased out almost all tax advantages for foreign investments (*FT*, 6 October 1993, p. 8).

In Poland a three- to six-year tax exemption was granted in priority sectors for large investments made before December 1993 (Lansbury *et al.* 1996: 107). The authors undertook an econometric analysis of the factors affecting the pattern of OECD investment in Hungary, the Czech Republic, Poland and Slovakia during the period 1991–3. (See the chapter on Hungary.)

On 15 March 1996 the Sejm approved a bill liberalizing investment rules. Joint ventures would no longer have to secure special licences to operate in certain sensitive economic sectors, including financial services, wholesale trade in imported consumer goods, real estate and the production of armaments (*IHT*, 16 March 1996, p. 11).

(See Table 5.2 for the increasing volumes of net foreign direct investment.)

Poland has opened its first free enterprise zone. Euro Park Mielec is to have a twenty-year life span, with participants enjoying ten years of corporate tax relief (dependent on investment and exports) and a 50 per cent cut in corporate tax for the second decade (*FT*, 11 October 1995, p. 3). On 19 June 1996 the government approved the setting up of a special enterprise zone in Katowicze (*FT*, 20 June 1996, p. 5). Three special economic zones have been set up (*IHT*, Survey, 17 October 1996, p. 17). Apart from the three special economic zones already in existence (Mielec, Katowicze and Suwalki), the government has recently decreed the creation of three more (Lodz, Legnica and Walbrzych) and another four are planned by the end of 1997 (*IHT*, Survey, 13 June 1997, p. 23). On 26 May

1999 Poland announced a temporary ban on issuing new permits after pressure from the EU, which says that the (seventeen) special investment zones break competition rules (*FT*, 27 May 1999, p. 3). Poland ordered each of its seventeen special economic zones to stop issuing permits to new investors. The order was prompted by EU pressure to scrap the zones altogether (*Business Central Europe*, June 1999, p. 10). 'The government will limit tax breaks for new investors in Poland's special economic zones after EU complaints that the old incentives were too generous. Existing investors in the zones will keep their privileges' (*Business Central Europe*, March 2000, p. 11).

> The main issue with the EU is Polish policy on special enterprise zones which give investors relief on corporate tax for twenty years. The EU wants these closed. The ministry of the economy is proposing that from next year [2001] access to the zones will be limited for new investors and no new investment permits will be issued from 2002 onwards. Those, like GM which has located a car plant in the Gliwice zone, will be allowed to stay on present terms.
>
> (*FT*, Survey, 17 April 2000, p. iv)

6 Romania

POLITICS

The political background

There is still disagreement as to how spontaneous the 1989 revolution was. The general view is that the uprising was a popular one, but soon taken over by the National Salvation Front (apparently formed some six months earlier).

Caritas ('Charity') was a pyramid scheme started by Ion Stoica in June 1992 (the claim was that profits were to go to 'good works', hence the name). Cluj became the main centre (Stoica enjoying the support of the extreme right-wing nationalist leader Gheorghe Funar, the mayor of Cluj). Pyramid schemes promise large returns, but are bound to fail in the long run because out-payments rely on ever-increasing new donations. Regular payments began to be missed in autumn 1993, but it was not until February 1994 that the local authorities closed down a recently opened branch in Snagov. Action was then taken against other schemes. On 19 May Stoica announced that he was to close the scheme down. He was arrested on 24 August 1994 and in mid-June 1995 he was sentenced to six years in jail. (In October 1995 the court of appeal knocked four years off the sentence: *Independent*, 23 October 1995, p. 12.)

The government survived a series of no-confidence votes in 1993, e.g. one in December. In February 1994 negotiations about a possible coalition government began between the Social Democracy Party of Romania (see below) and the extreme right-wing nationalist parties.

Gypsies (Roma) account for about 8 per cent of the population (*IHT*, 3 April 2000, p. 6). According to the European Roma Rights Centre, there are more than 1.8 million Gypsies in Romania (*Independent*, 9 August 2000, p. 14). There is still widespread discrimination against Gypsies.

The Hungarian minority

There are 1.7 million ethnic Hungarians and 2 million Gypsies (*FT*, 13 May 1994, p. 2). Another source puts the figure in the range 1.6 million to 2 million Hungarians (*IHT*, 6 July 1994, pp. 1, 4).

20 July 1993: an accord is signed aimed at improving the rights of the ethnic minorities, e.g. more elementary school lessons in history and geography taught in minority languages, multilingual street signs in areas where a minority represents at least 30 per cent of the population, and more university places for Hungarian teachers.

4 October 1993: the Council of Europe votes to admit Romania as the thirty-second member (Hungary abstained in the vote). The formal admission ceremony was held on 7 October.

10 August 1994: the government rejects calls for 'special status' from the Hungarian minority (e.g. greater control over education and cultural matters) and for this special status to be included in the treaty currently under discussion between Romania and Hungary (*Independent*, 11 August 1994, p. 10).

On 10 December 1994 the Democratic Union of Hungarians in Romania (DUHR) declared that it wanted the right to autonomous self-determination (*Business Europa*, February–March 1995, p. 44.) In mid-January 1995 the DUHR resolved to form special 'councils of local government' in anticipation of an ethnic Hungarian autonomous region. Both it and the Romanian Social Democratic Party have now left the Democratic Convention (*EEN*, 2 March 1995, vol. 9, no. 5, p. 6).

The education law passed by parliament at the end of June 1995 established Romanian as the national language and the main language of education. The new law met resistance from ethnic Hungarians.

9 November 1994: the Chamber of Deputies approves legislation which specifies that the punishment for flying foreign flags or singing foreign anthems may be up to three years in jail.

2 September 1996: the Romanian National Union Party is removed from the coalition government after cabinet members did not distance themselves from the comments made by the party's president, Gheorghe Funar. (Funar called the proposed signing of the treaty with Hungary 'an act of treason' and demanded the impeachment of President Iliescu for supporting it: *FT*, 3 September 1996, p. 2.) The ministers of justice, agriculture and communications are dismissed, while the minister of transport retains his position after he announced his resignation from the party.

16 September 1996: the prime ministers of Romania and Hungary sign a 'basic treaty' (treaty of 'reconciliation and friendship'). Country borders are deemed inviolable. Although ethnic Hungarians in Romania are granted human rights, the treaty does not recognize their 'collective rights' or grant territorial autonomy along ethnic lines.

The treaty requires both countries to protect the civil liberties and cultural identity of national minorities. Education at all levels is guaranteed by the state in the minority's native tongue, as is the right to use one's historic language in administrative and judicial proceedings in areas of minority concentration. The same goes for road signs, print and broadcast media and virtually every other aspect of communal life. Each country commits itself in the treaty to support Nato and EU membership for the other (Donald M. Blinken and Alfred H.

Moses, US ambassadors to Hungary and Romania respectively, *IHT*, 19 September 1996, p. 8).

17 February 1997: the defence ministers of Romania and Hungary sign an accord on the protection and exchange of military secrets and agree to set up a joint peace-keeping battalion for use with Nato, the UN and OSCE (*Independent*, 18 February 1997, p. 10).

(The Democratic Union of Hungarians in Romania became a member of the coalition government. See politics section, below, for developments after the entry for 10 December 1996.)

22 February 1997: Valeriu Tabara ('a relative moderate') becomes acting leader of the Romanian National Unity Party, replacing Gheorghe Funar (*EEN*, 1997, vol. 11, no. 4, p. 4).

> There is no doubt that the moderate wing of UDMR [Democratic Union of Hungarians in Romania] is firmly in control. As the Hungarian and Romanian governments continue to establish closer ties – such as by opening Hungarian consulates in Cluj and Constanta, and Romanian consulates in Szeged and Gyor – the stock of moderate Hungarians will continue to rise, for they will be seen to have delivered a satisfactory modus vivendi for the first time since 1920. The harnessing of rabid nationalism by Hungarians and Romanians has removed a major political risk from Romania.
>
> (*EEN*, 27 February 1997, vol. 11, no. 4, p. 5)

May 1997: a government decree refers to towns where members of an ethnic minority make up at least a fifth of the population. They should be able to deal with local elections in their own language and the signs on streets and public buildings should be bilingual (*The Economist*, 20 December 1997, pp. 39, 42).

July 1997: a decree guarantees minority-language schooling wherever fifteen or more children can be found to make up a class (*The Economist*, 20 December 1997, p. 42).

22 October 1997: during a visit to Romania by Hungarian prime minister Gyula Horn the Romanian government announces that a Hungarian-language university will be created (*FT*, 23 October 1997, p. 3).

9 December 1997: the Senate (upper house of parliament) rejects a personal appeal by President Constantinescu and votes to ban separate university education in minority languages. It also votes that even in minority-language schools history and geography must be in Romanian. The law must be debated in the lower house (*FT*, 24 December 1997, p. 2).

16 December 1997: the upper house of parliament votes to restrict the Hungarians' new education rights, forbidding them to form Hungarian-speaking faculties at universities and obliging them to learn Romania's history and language in Romanian (*The Economist*, 20 December 1997, p. 42).

29 June 1998: Laszlo Toekes, an ethnic Hungarian bishop of the Reformed Church whose opposition to Ceausescu sparked the 1989 revolution, admits that he collaborated with the Securitate (secret police) after years of harassment. About a quarter of the adult population is believed to have collaborated with the Securitate (*FT*, 30 June 1998, p. 2; *The Times*, 30 June 1998, p. 13).

30 June 1999: parliament endorses key minority rights elements of the proposed new education bill to the satisfaction of ethnic Hungarians (*EEN*, 1999, vol. 12, no. 19, p. 3). The new education law provides for the limited use of the Hungarian language (p. 6).

The German minority

> Transylvania … [in] north-western … Romania, has been a haven for ethnic Germans for some eight centuries … [But] the Germans are withdrawing from the mess that is today's Romania … Some 250,000-strong in 1939, a good tenth of the Germans who survived the Second World War were carted off – once the communists took over – to Russian labour camps: almost none returned. Around 180,000 Germans sat tight until the mid-1970s, when Nicolae Ceausescu … began to let a steady trickle go – at a hefty price in DMs. Communism's fall in 1989 prompted a huge outward spurt. From 110,000 the number of Germans plummeted to 41,000 in less than two years. Now the figure has shrivelled again – to less than 17,000.
>
> (*The Economist*, 2 January 1999, p. 35)

Political developments from May 1993 until the November 1996 presidential and general elections

8 May 1993: the Romanian Communist Party has been resurrected (*EEN*, 1993, vol. 7, no. 10, p. 8).

30 May 1993: Petre Roman announces that the National Salvation Front is to merge with the former Democratic Party to form the Democratic Party–National Salvation Front (DP–NSF).

28 August 1993: four ministers leave the cabinet, including Misu Negritoiu (the reform-minded independent deputy prime minister in charge of economic policy, who resigns). Emilian Ijdelea, the president of the Romanian Development Agency responsible for foreign investment and the development of small and medium-sized enterprises, was dismissed (there have been allegations about corruption in government; Ijdelea accused certain government ministers of personally intervening in state contracts: *EEN*, 7 September 1993, vol. 7, no. 18, p. 4). Aurelian Dochia, the head of the privatization agency, resigned later on; he was in favour of bringing the state ownership fund under government control to prevent its board, dominated by members of the Social Democracy Party of Romania (leader Adrian Nastase; formed in late summer 1993; formerly the Democratic National Salvation Front), from stressing management or employee buy-outs (*FT*, 9 September 1993, p. 3).

29 December 1993: parliament agrees (with many members choosing not to vote) that the government should be able to rule by decree during the recess in January 1994.

26 January 1994: Romania becomes the first country to sign a Partnership for Peace agreement with Nato.

30 January 1994: a military agreement is signed with Russia.

21 June 1994: the Democratic Agrarian Party says it will withdraw its support from the ruling Social Democracy Party of Romania.

1 July 1994: the government survives its fifth vote of no confidence.

19 August 1994: two members of the right-wing Romanian National Unity Party (though from the more moderate wing of it) are made ministers (of agriculture and of communications).

7 October 1994: former King Michael is denied entry to the country.

14 October 1994: a British couple who bought a baby and then attempted to smuggle it out of the country are given jail sentences of twenty-eight months each. The three men convicted of arranging the sale are given thirty-two months and the teenage parents will serve a year in jail when they are eighteen.

2–4 November 1994: President Iliescu visits the UK. He is to pardon the British couple if their appeal fails.

16 November 1994: the court of appeal reduces the prison sentence on the British couple to two years, suspends the sentence and orders the couple to leave the country.

23 December 1994: the Vacaroiu government survives another vote of no confidence.

1 February 1995: the EU association agreement comes fully into effect.

19 October 1995: Romania Mare is expelled from the coalition government (*EEN*, 1995, vol. 9, no. 23, p. 9).

11 November 1995: Corneliu Coposcu, leader of the National Peasants' Party, dies. (He was replaced by Ion Dianconescu.)

March 1996: Petre Roman forms a new alliance, the Social Democratic Union, comprising his own Democratic Party and the small Social Democratic Party led by Sergiu Cunescu. There is also a tactical alliance with the Civic Alliance Party (led by Nicolae Manulescu), and Liberal Party '93 is expected to join the new alliance soon (*EEN*, 1996, vol. 10, no. 9, pp. 6, 8).

22 April 1996: a friendship and co-operation treaty is signed with the Federal Republic of Yugoslavia (*EEN*, 1996, vol. 10, no. 9, p. 8).

2 June, 16 June and 30 June 1996: local elections are held. The turnout was 56.5 per cent in the first round, held on 2 June, and 54.7 per cent in the second round, held on 30 June. A handful of third-round elections was held on 30 June. The ruling Social Democracy Party of Romania did relatively poorly. It lost in most large towns and cities (including Bucharest, where the former tennis star Ilie Nastase failed to win). It did better in the countryside but even there lost votes.

(Prime minister Nicolae Vacaroiu recently joined the Social Democracy Party of Romania: *FT*, Survey, 9 July 1996, p. i.)

2 September 1996: the Romanian National Union Party is removed from the coalition government after cabinet members do not distance themselves from the comments made by the party's president, Gheorghe Funar. (Funar called the proposed signing of the treaty with Hungary 'an act of treason' and demanded the impeachment of President Iliescu for supporting it: *FT*, 3 September 1996, p. 2.) The ministers of justice, agriculture and communications are dismissed, while the minister of transport retains his position after announcing his resignation from the party.

26 September 1996: Nicu Ceausescu dies at the age of forty-five awaiting a liver transplant.

The 3 November 1996 presidential and parliamentary elections

The presidential election

The president has the power to veto legislation unless parliament upholds it by a two-thirds majority (*FT*, 16 November 1996, p. 2; *The Economist*, 23 November 1996, p. 61). There were sixteen candidates. In the first round the results were as follows:

Ion Iliescu (Social Democracy Party of Romania): 32.25 per cent;
Emil Constantinescu (Democratic Convention): 28.21 per cent;
Petre Roman (Union of Social Democrats): 20.54 per cent;
Gyorgy Frunda (Democratic Union of Hungarians in Romania): 6.02 per cent. 'A moderate when it comes to demands for ethnic Hungarian autonomy' (*EEN*, 1996, vol. 10, no. 15, p. 4);
Corneliu Vadim Tudor (Romania Mare): 4.72 per cent;
Gheorghe Funar (Party of Romanian National Unity): 3.22 per cent;
Tudor Mohora (Socialist Party): 1.27 per cent;
Adrian Paunescu (Socialist Workers' Party): 0.69 per cent.

The parliamentary election

The parliamentary election results are shown in Table 6.1. There was a 3 per cent threshold.

The parties/alliances and their platforms are as follows:

Social Democracy Party of Romania: led by Adrian Nastase.
Social Democratic Union: led by Petre Roman. Dominated by the Democratic Party (led by Roman), with the Romanian Social Democratic Party (led by Sergiu Cunescu) and the Romanian Ecological Convention (led by Dan Hazaparu).
Democratic Convention: led by Emil Constantinescu. Centre-right coalition comprising, for example, the National Peasant Party/Christian Democrats and the National Liberal Party.

Table 6.1 Romania: the general election of 3 November 1996

	Chamber of Deputies		*Senate*	
	Seats	% vote[a]	Seats	% vote
Democratic Convention	122	30.17	53	30.70
Social Democracy Party of Romania	91	21.53	41	23.08
Social Democratic Union	53	12.93	23	13.16
Democratic Union of Hungarians in Romania	25	6.64	11	6.81
Romania Mare	19	4.46	8	4.54
Party of Romanian National Unity	18	4.36	7	4.22
Ethinic minority organizations	15		0	
Total	343		143	

Note:
[a] There is a 3 per cent threshold for parliamentary representation

National Liberal Alliance: formed by Liberal Party '93 (led by Dinu Patriciu) and the Civic Alliance Party (led by Nicolae Manulescu). A small group of parties that broke away from Democratic Convention (*Business Central Europe*, October 1996, p. 21).

National Union of the Centre: led by Ioan Pop de Popa. Formed by the Democratic Agrarian Party (led by Victor Surdu, who left the Party of Romanian National Unity and formed the DAP), the Humanist Party of Romania (led by Dan Voiculescu) and the Romanian Ecological Movement.

Democratic Union of Hungarians in Romania: led by Gyorgy Frunda.

Romania Mare (Greater Romania): led by Corneliu Vadim Tudor. Ultra-nationalist.

Party of Romanian National Unity: led by Gheorghe Funar. Extreme nationalist.

Socialist Workers' Party: led by Ilie Verdet and Adrian Paunescu. Neo-communists (*Business Central Europe*, October 1996, p. 21).

Socialist Party: led by Tudor Mohora. Reformed communists (*Business Central Europe*, October 1996, p. 21). Quasi-communist (*EEN*, 1996, vol. 10, no. 23, p. 2).

National Liberal Ecological Alliance: led by Radu Campeanescu. Dominated by the National Liberal Party.

7 November 1996: the Democratic Convention and the Social Democratic Union sign a government pact. (They said that 'their priority was to free the exchange rate, tighten monetary policy and overhaul the fiscal system, including a sharp reduction in direct taxes': *FT*, 8 November 1996, p. 2. During the campaign the Democratic Convention advocated faster economic and political reform, a campaign against corruption, removing barriers to private enterprise, improving the welfare system and reducing taxes: *FT*, 19 November 1996, p. 21.) Petre

Roman expresses his support for Emil Constantinescu in the second round of the presidential election.

9 November 1996: Iliescu:

> The [opposition's] programme makes demagogic promises but what they want to give you is the Romania of 1946, a Romania that was a monarchy. They want to break up the state farms, former royal lands, that now provide most of the country's food. They want to bring back the big landowners.

Some in Romania, says Virginia Marsh, especially the old who form the largest part of the rural population, fear the opposition might take back land that was handed out under a 1991 restitution law. Exit polls taken on 3 November indicate that Iliescu won more than half the votes of peasant farmers and 42 per cent of the over 65s, while the opposition candidates won the overwhelming support of city dwellers, the young and private businesses (Virginia Marsh, *FT*, 9 November 1996, p. 2). During the campaign Iliescu also claimed that the opposition would close large enterprises and threaten the country's unity by including ethnic Hungarians in the government (Virginia Marsh, *FT*, 19 November 1996, p. 21).

17 November 1996: there is a 75.9 per cent turnout for the second round of the presidential election. Emil Constantinescu wins with 54.43 per cent of the vote, compared with Iliescu's 45.57 per cent.

19 November 1996: the mayor of Bucharest, Victor Ciorbea, is nominated as prime minister. (He won 56.7 per cent of the vote in Bucharest on 2 June 1996, compared with Ilie Nastase's 43.3 per cent.)

27 November 1996: Petre Roman is elected president of the Senate by 87 votes to 52.

29 November 1996: Constantinescu is sworn in as president, with the Patriarch of the Romanian Orthodox Church in attendance. (A religious service is held on 1 December.)

10 December 1996: the new coalition government is approved by parliament: prime minister, Victor Ciorbea; foreign minister, Adrian Severin; defence minister, Victor Babiuc; interior minister, Gavril Dejeu; finance minister, Mircea Ciumara; industry and commerce minister, Calin Popescu Tariceanu; reform and privatization minister, Ulm Spineanu. The Democratic Union of Hungarians in Romania is given two portfolios, for national minorities and tourism.

Political developments after the November 1996 presidential and parliamentary elections

23 December 1996: Liberal Party '93 and National Liberal Party–Democratic Convention sign a provisional agreement on re-establishing a National Liberal Party (*EEN*, 1996, vol. 10, no. 25, p. 9).

10 January 1997: Miron Cozma, the coal miners' leader from the Jiu valley, is arrested. (The charges against him so far have been couched in terms of constitutional infringements rather than the breaking of specific laws: *EEN*, 1997, vol. 11, no. 2, p. 6. He was accused of leading riots in 1991, but the charges against him were dropped in June 1998: *The Economist*, 27 June 1998, p. 51.)

17 February 1997: prime minister Victor Ciorbea announces a 'programme of national economic salvation', combining austerity measures with the speeding up of economic reforms (see below for details).

The defence ministers of Romania and Hungary sign an accord on the protection and exchange of military secrets and agree to set up a joint peacekeeping battalion for use with Nato, the UN and OSCE (*Independent*, 18 February 1997, p. 10).

21 February 1997: King Michael has his Romanian citizenship restored.

22 February 1997: at the end of a two-day visit President Chirac of France says that he supports Romania's quest for early membership of Nato.

Valeriu Tabara ('a relative moderate') becomes acting leader of the Romanian National Unity Party, replacing Gheorghe Funar (*EEN*, 1997, vol. 11, no. 4, p. 4).

28 February–5 March 1997: King Michael pays a private visit to Romania.

22 March 1997: Gheorghe Funar is replaced as chairman of the Party of Romanian National Unity by Valeriu Tabara.

2 June 1997: the presidents of Romania and Ukraine sign a friendship treaty, including mutual recognition of existing land frontiers. Sea frontiers will be left to negotiations to be completed by 1999. ('Romania finally recognized Ukrainian sovereignty over lands in Bessarabia and Bukovina ruled by Romania between 1919 and 1940, and taken over by Stalin under the Molotov–Ribbentrop Pact ... One important dispute ... remains outstanding: the delimitation of economic zones in the Black Sea, in a region with possible reserves of oil and gas. However, both sides have pledged to resolve the issue within two years, or failing this, to accept the judgement of the International Court at the Hague': Anatol Lieven: *FT*, Survey, 25 June 1997, p. iv.)

25 June 1997: moderates from the Social Democracy Party of Romania, led by Teodor Melescanu, form a new party called Alliance for Romania (*EEN*, 1997, vol. 11, no. 13, p. 7).

8 July 1997: Nato's secretary-general Javier Solana Madriaga:

> Today heads of state and government have agreed to invite the Czech Republic, Hungary and Poland to begin accession talks with Nato ... We affirm that Nato remains open to new members ... We will review the process at our next meeting in 1999. With regard to aspiring members, we recognize with great interest and take account of the positive developments toward democracy and the rule of law in a number of south-eastern European countries, especially Romania and Slovenia.

(A majority of the sixteen Nato countries, led by France, supported the inclusion of Romania and Slovenia in the first wave of invitations. But the USA was adamant that only three countries would be invited to become members of Nato in the first wave.)

11 July 1997: President Clinton visits Bucharest and describes Romania as one of the 'strongest candidates' for the second wave of invitations provided it keeps to the path of reform. 'The door to Nato is open … Stay the course and Romania will cross that milestone.' (President Richard Nixon visited Romania in August 1969 and President Gerald Ford visited Romania in August 1975.)

16 July 1997: the European Commission recommends that Estonia, Cyprus, the Czech Republic, Hungary, Poland and Slovenia open negotiations in early 1998 for entry to the EU. (The invitations were formally approved at an EU summit on 13 December 1997, formal negotiations for membership beginning on 31 March 1998. Slovakia, Latvia, Lithuania, Bulgaria and Romania were to be given special EU aid to help them meet the conditions necessary for membership negotiations to begin.)

18 October 1997: the government has decided to open the files of the Securitate (the former communist secret police). Under the law passed by the previous government the files were closed for thirty years. The new law will allow citizens immediate access to their own files and to those of public figures, from the president to local councillors (Anatol Lieven, *FT*, 20 October 1997, p. 2).

The government has also decided to reduce the official privileges for so-called 'revolutionaries' ('fighters with special merit') who took part in the overthrow of Ceausescu in 1989, more than 30,000 people being granted tax exemptions, a free hectare of land, free housing, preferential access to office space, and free public transport passes. The new government believes that many received the privileges simply because they supported Iliescu (or bribed officials to get them) and that only those wounded or imprisoned in the uprising and close relatives of those killed will receive tax exemptions. (Anatol Lieven, *FT*, 20 October 1997, p. 2; *Telegraph*, 22 October 1997, p. 15.) (As a result of protests, the government agreed not to amend the law on privileges until all those on the official lists were checked to see if they had genuinely taken part in the revolution: *FT*, 31 October 1997, p. 3.)

2 December 1997: eight new cabinet members are announced (*EEN*, 1997, vol. 11, no. 23, p. 8). 'The cabinet reshuffle announced on 2 December was prompted largely by the failure of privatization policy, due partly to wrangling within the governing coalition … The sense of urgency premier Victor Ciorbea injected into privatization when he took office has evaporated' (p. 4). 'The unimpressive economic performance so far under Ciorbea's government has had little effect on politics – so far' (p. 6).

> The unions have criticized social policies and the way restructuring is being carried out. But demonstrations have for the most part been poorly attended, while golden handshakes have blunted resistance to closures … Industrial restructuring has usually only happened under multilateral pressure, producing some botched last-minute decisions on closures … restructuring [is] not far advanced … The state ownership fund … is now

> close to reaching an ambitious target of fifty enterprises a week. In the first nine months of 1997 1,120 firms were privatized … Restructuring has started … But problems remain. There has been little progress on broader restructuring – witness the slow rise of unemployment – and less in formulating regional policies. Most of the privatized firms have been small … Sales of big companies … are still rare. Few doubt the current government's reform will. But questions are starting to be asked about its competence.
>
> (Business Central Europe 1997: 39–40)

23 December 1997: foreign minister Adrian Severin resigns after an investigation failed to support his allegations that local politicians and journalists had worked as spies for foreign governments.

2 January 1998: prime minister Ciorbea announces that King Michael and his family will be allowed permanent residence in Romania (*EEN*, 1998, vol. 11, no. 25, p. 8).

3 January 1998: President Constantinescu states that during his term of office he will not sanction a return to the monarchy (*EEN*, 1998, vol. 11, no. 25, p. 8).

14 January 1998: the Social Democrats withdraw their support for prime minister Ciorbea and call for talks to form a new coalition government. But Adrian Severin says that the Social Democrats will remain within the coalition in a 'caretaker capacity'. ('The decision … amounted to an ultimatum to Mr Ciorbea to step down to pave the way for a government more intent on proceeding with market reforms': *IHT*, 15 January 1998, p. 5. 'The Democratic Party's dissatisfaction with the government's poor record on economic reform is well-founded': *EEN*, 1998, vol. 12, no. 1, p. 5.)

15 January 1998: the National Peasants reject Ciorbea's offer to resign (*FT*, 16 January 1998, p. 2).

> The present clash is not about different approaches to economic reform: it is rather personal rivalries that mean that this basic agreement is being overwhelmed … The political crisis began at the end of last month when the PD [Democratic Party] demanded the replacement of the prime minister, Victor Ciorbea, after the removal of two PD ministers. The foreign minister, Adrian Severin, was forced to resign after failing to substantiate allegations that senior politicians were foreign agents, while the transport minister, Traian Basescu, was sacked for publicly criticizing Mr Ciorbea … Feuding between the parties has helped delay several key reforms, from the restructuring of the oil industry to the redistribution of agricultural land. One reason for this has been the deeply entrenched clientilism of Romanian politics, with politicians acting on behalf of opposing business and industrial interests. But the most important reason for the present split is hostility derived from the past … Reflecting this past is the [Peasants'] Party stand on the restitution of agricultural land to its former owners, something which the PD opposes … The Civic Alliance has been pressing for a much more rigorous approach to the communist past, including the opening of secret

> police files and the barring from politics of people found to have been Securitate officers or informers – which the PD also opposes. The leadership of the PD, though believers in the free market, is mostly drawn from younger members of the former communist elite … Mr Roman's supporters regard themselves as progressive technocrats, and look down on the Peasants as backward-looking, romantic, inexperienced and incompetent. The peasants for their part see the PD as corrupt former communist apparatchiks who jumped ship from the Ceausescu dictatorship at the last possible moment.
>
> (Anatol Lieven, *FT*, 27 January 1998, p. 3)

'The suspicion is that Mr Roman wants to block reform because it would damage his cronies in business and finance' (*Business Central Europe*, February 1998, p. 7).

> Slow reform, say the Social Democrats. They think themselves superior to the Peasants, and reckon they could run the country better. But the party also has many friends in business and banking whose income streams are threatened by Mr Ciorbea's planned farm reforms and bank privatizations.
>
> (p. 17)

29 January 1998: the Democratic Party withdraws its remaining ministers, including the defence minister, from the cabinet (*EEN*, 1998, vol. 12, no. 2, p. 8).

6 February 1998: the ruling coalition parties, including the Democratic Party, sign a new co-operation agreement. The Democratic Party no longer insists on the replacement of prime minister Ciorbea (*EEN*, 1998, vol. 12, no. 2, pp. 1, 8).

26 February 1998: healthcare workers end a two-week strike. They have been awarded a 30 per cent increase in wages (*FT*, 27 February 1998, p. 2).

28 February 1998: the Civic Alliance Party (led by Nicolae Manulescu) and the National Liberal Party (led by Mircea Ionescu-Quintus) announce a merger under a new name, the National Liberal Alliance (*EEN*, 1998, vol. 12, no. 4, p. 6).

1 March 1998: Gheorghe Funar, former leader of the Romanian Party for National Unity (PUNR), sets up his own party (Romanian Party for National Unity–Funar) 'after a long and heated argument with the far more moderate PUNR leader Valeriu Tabara' (*EEN*, 1998, vol. 12, no. 4, pp. 6, 10).

6 March 1998: the Liberal Party and the National Liberal Party–Campaneanu establish a merged Liberal Federation (*EEN*, 1998, vol. 12, no. 4, p. 10).

29 March 1998: the National Liberal Party calls on the prime minister to resign (*FT*, 30 March 1998, p. 2).

30 March 1998: prime minister Ciorbea submits his resignation to the president. Interior minister Gavril Dejeu becomes acting prime minister.

15 April 1998: parliament approves a new cabinet under the new prime minister Radu Vasile (deputy chairman of the National Peasants'

Party–Christian Democratic Party) (*EEN*, 1998, vol. 12, no. 5, p. 5). He was sworn in by the president the following day.

3 September 1998: the Democratic Party of Hungarians in Romania withdraws support for the governing coalition following the parliamentary cultural committee's rejection of the idea of establishing a Hungarian-language university (*EEN*, 1998, vol. 12, no. 10, p. 9).

23 September 1998: finance minister Daniel Daianu is replaced by Decebal Traian Remes (Liberal Party) after the Liberal Party withdrew its backing. Daianu is an independent who was nominated by the Liberal Party when he was appointed in December 1997. The Liberal Party advocates lower taxes, a policy which Daianu disagrees with owing to the growing budget deficit (*FT*, 24 September 1998, p. 3).

> At the heart of the coalition's problems has been the ideological conflict between the centre-right National Peasants' Party and the more liberal, technocratic Democratic Party … The Peasants' Party is the largest member of the government and the mainstay of the Democratic Convention … Perhaps the coalition's greatest political problem, however, is the split within the Peasants' Party, which contains paternalistic, conservative and nationalist elements as well as more pragmatic politicians like Radu Vasile, the prime minister. The conservative wing is in large part responsible for the difficult relations with the other governing parties. It is associated with Victor Ciorbea – the former prime minister who was forced out of office in the spring by the Democratic Party. It has uncompromising views on, for example, the need for full property restitution and is also the most resistant to granting ethnic Hungarians all the education rights they demand.
>
> (Virginia Marsh, *FT*, Survey, 28 September 1998, p. ii)

> At issue has been whether to increase the amount of land returned to pre-communist owners to up to 50 ha, as demanded by the National Peasants' Party, the largest member of the coalition, or to stick with the 10 ha granted under previous legislation, the option preferred by the smaller Democratic Party … Midway through their four-year term, the parties have, according to Dinu Gavrilescu, agriculture minister, finally come up with a compromise, allowing for the return of up to 50 ha where possible and providing for financial compensation if not. Mr Gavrilescu says he hopes the government will accept a draft law to this effect shortly … A significant minority is still without full property titles.
>
> (p. iv)

3 October 1998: the Democratic Union of Hungarians in Romania decides not to leave the coalition government formally provided the government approves the setting up of a Hungarian-language university and the full implementation of minority rights (*EEN*, 1998, vol. 12, no. 11, p. 5).

19 October 1998:

> Sorin Dimitru [privatization minister] quit following widespread criticism of delays in privatization ... Mr Dimitru is leaving office less than a month after the departure of Daniel Daianu, the former finance minister. While the two ministers were criticized by the government for failing to implement reforms, their departures rob Romania of two well-known public advocates of reforms. Both have blamed other ministers and bureaucrats for their lack of progress. Mr Dimitru said yesterday [19 October] he had received no support for privatization from the government, parliament or political parties. His agency privatized 825 companies by the end of August compared with a target for the year of 1,600.
>
> (*FT*, 20 October 1998, p. 3)

> Mr Daianu, who belongs to no political party, was fired as finance minister ostensibly because he failed to increase tax collection ... In the end he went primarily because he put too many noses out of joint by refusing to sign off on a $1.5 billion order for ninety-six [US] helicopters. And his call for tax hikes and spending cuts did nothing for his popularity either. Nor was popularity the strong point of privatization minister Sorin Dimitru, who was under pressure to increase the pace of Romania's slow but steady sell-offs. He jumped before he was pushed ... In essence Mr Dimitru and the cabinet disagreed over the speed of sell-offs ... The government is banking on lucrative telecoms and bank sales to keep the state budget in check.
>
> (*Business Central Europe*, November 1998, pp. 45–6)

16 November 1998: the nationalist Greater Romania Party and the National Unity Party of Romania merge under the leadership of Cluj mayor Gheorghe Funar (*EEN*, 1998, vol. 12, no. 13, p. 6).

27 November 1998: the agriculture minister is replaced (*EEN*, 1998, vol. 12, no. 13, p. 6).

4 January 1999: the start of a strike by coal miners in the Jiu valley. (On 18 December 1998 the government announced the planned closure of twenty-nine coal mines: *EEN*, 1999, vol. 12, no. 14, p. 7.)

15 January 1999: a district court rules the strike to be illegal (*EEN*, 1999, vol. 12, no. 14, p. 7).

18 January 1999:

> Police helicopters sprayed tear gas and dropped smoke bombs yesterday [18 January] on thousands [an estimated 10,000] of striking miners as they marched towards the capital Bucharest to protest at low wages and possible redundancies. Radu Vasile, the prime minister, appealed to the miners to return home, promising to talk to them personally ... Organized rallies and demonstrations by miners in Bucharest were banned after violent riots there by miners in 1990 ... Miron Cozma, the militant leader of the coal miners'

trade union who was briefly jailed for his part in the 1990 Bucharest riots, ordered the miners to march on Bucharest after the government refused to increase their pay by 35 per cent or to stop planned pit closures ... Coal miners in the Jiu valley began their two-week strike after two pits were closed.

(*FT*, 19 January 1999, p. 2)

19 January 1999:

The Romanian government said yesterday [19 January] it was considering deploying troops to stop some 20,000 striking workers from marching to Bucharest. The move came after riot police failed to stall the advance of 10,000 miners amid signs that the industrial unrest was spreading. Police fired tear gas and miners hurled rocks in a series of battles ... Miners from the Jiu valley coal region ... were joined yesterday by miners from the Oltenia coalfields ... and workers from other regions and industries ... An estimated 70,000 people may lose their jobs if government plans to close or restructure forty-nine loss-making state-owned companies are carried out. Another 70,000 workers in the steel industry are set to lose their jobs as part of a five-year plan to restructure the steel sector.

(*FT*, 20 January 1999, p. 3)

'A court last week declared the strike illegal' (*FT*, 20 January 1999, p. 13).

Coalminers ... want a pay rise of more than a third and the reopening of two mines closed last year ... The miners have some formidable allies, including ex-communists and nationalists ... Miron Cozma ... is an ally of Vadim Tudor, who leads the xenophobic and protectionist Greater Romania Party. Its support, according to opinion polls, has leapt from 4 per cent in the last few months to more than 16 per cent. Mr Tudor ... is calling for a general strike.

(*The Economist*, 23 January 1999, p. 44)

21 January 1999: the miners clash violently with police and break through barricades. The interior minister resigns owing to his inability to halt the march on Bucharest.

22 January 1999:

After hours of talks in a central Romanian monastery the government said Friday [22 January] that it had reached a deal with striking coal miners ... 'Neither the miners nor the government won,' Mr Vasile said. 'Only the country won, because there will be peace.' He did not give details of the deal, saying they would be ironed out in Bucharest in the coming weeks. He said the proposal 'went in the direction of the miners' claims' but would not become final until a plan to reduce production costs in the mines was completed. One miner said they had secured a 30 per cent wage increase. The miners were demanding a wage increase of 35 per cent and large severance payments for workers let go. The government said it could not afford the demands and argued that miners already earned double the average salary … even though the mines are losing money … The miners' march had raised fears of a repeat of the 1990–91 protests in Bucharest that turned violent and sparked the fall of the government of Petre Roman.

(*IHT*, 23 January 1999, p. 2)

The latest accord … would keep unprofitable and heavily subsidized mines open for at least five years and provide raises to the miners … The agreement, which has not been detailed, apparently makes pay increases contingent on a five-year plan to turn round the performance of the mining industry in the Jiu valley … In thirty days mine managers and unions must present a plan to cut losses 20 per cent annually for five years, government officials said.

(*IHT*, 25 January 1999, p. 5)

Romania's government … [agreed] to raise [miners'] pay by 30 per cent and reopen two pits closed last year … Yesterday's deal was struck after four hours of talks between Radu Vasile, the prime minister, and Miron Cozma, the militant miners' leader, in an orthodox monastery outside the town of Rimnicu Vilcea. 170 kilometres north-west of Bucharest … The negotiations followed President Emil Constantinescu's pledge to declare a state of emergency … if the miners did not return to their Jiu valley coal region, 370 kilometres north-west of Bucharest … The move … is a potentially devastating setback to the government's flagging efforts to push through market-orientated reforms – including the planned closure of 140 loss-making coal mines, forty-nine loss-making state enterprises and a five-year plan to restructure the steel industry.

(*FT*, 23 January 1999, p. 3)

15 February 1999:

Romania's supreme court sentenced Miron Cozma, the militant miners' leader, to eighteen years in jail on Monday [15 February] over offences in 1991 when he spearheaded a march that brought down the government … The union chief … was also convicted of illegal possession of arms and undermining state authority. Mr Cozma had been jailed for eighteen months over leading a miners' march in 1991, which turned violent and led to the collapse of the government of then-prime minister Petre Roman. He was released in June 1998. Mr Cozma was kicked out of the far-right Romania Mare Party after the 18–22 January aborted march on the Romanian capital.

(*IHT*, 16 February 1999, p. 6)

> Romanian television reported last night that he [Cozma] had gone into hiding ... In reaching its decision the supreme court reversed the ruling of a lower court which last year [1998] reduced the charges against Mr Cozma to public order violations ... Mr Cozma cannot appeal against the supreme court's sentence because of the nature of the charge of undermining the authority of the state ... In 1990 and 1991 he led coalminers on violent rampages through Bucharest which left several people dead. During the events of 1991 ... miners invaded parliament, set government buildings on fire and forced Petre Roman, who was then prime minister, out of office ... Mr Cozma's influence may also be dented by the suspension from parliament of Vadim Tudor, one of his chief political allies and the leader of the extreme nationalist Greater Romania Party. Mr Tudor was suspended for making allegations about the private life of President Emil Constantinescu.
>
> (*FT*, 16 February 1999, p. 2)

'Cozma ... was convicted of illegally possessing firearms, undermining state authority and jeopardizing railway traffic ... He spent a year in detention awaiting trial but was released in July 1998' (*Guardian*, 16 February 1999, p. 12).

16 February 1999: 'An estimated 4,000 Romanian coal miners yesterday [16 February] set off for Bucharest' (*FT*, 17 February 1999, p. 2).

'A day after he was sentenced ... Miron Cozma led his followers on a defiant march Tuesday [16 February] toward the capital ... Three thousand coal miners massed earlier ... Most of the coal mines in the western Jiu valley were closed Tuesday' (*IHT*, 17 February 1999, p. 5).

17 February 1999:

> [Miron Cozma] was arrested Wednesday [17 February] after clashes between paramilitary police units and miners that left one miner dead and dozens injured. More than 500 arrests were reported. The arrest of Miron Cozma came as he and about 2,000 miners headed towards Bucharest.
>
> (*IHT*, 18 February 1999, p. 7)

19 April 1999: former prime minister Victor Ciorbea forms a new party, called the National Christian Democratic Alliance, in opposition to the ruling National Peasant Christian Democratic Party (*EEN*, 1999, vol. 12, no. 16, p. 10, and no. 19, p. 3).

7–9 May 1999: Pope John Paul II visits Romania.

'John Paul's trip was the first by a Roman pontiff to a mainly Orthodox country since the Eastern church definitively broke away from Rome in the Great Schism of 1054' (*IHT*, 10 May 1999, p. 6).

> Despite his wish to visit the concentration of Catholics in Transylvania and Moldova, the Pope will be confined to Bucharest ... The Orthodox church, which 80 per cent of Romanians follow, is at loggerheads with the 300,000-strong eastern rite Catholics who are seeking the return of more than 2,000

> churches seized by the communists in 1948. The churches were given to the Orthodox church and people forced to convert. Eastern rite Catholics, who broke away from the Orthodox faith in the seventeenth century, still worship according to Orthodox-style rites, but see the Pope as their spiritual leader. In Transylvania, home to the majority of the country's Catholics, the property dispute has led to pitched battles.
>
> (*Guardian*, 6 May 1999, p. 15)

16 July 1999: two former communist generals were sentenced to fifteen years in prison for murder during protests in Timisoara in December 1989 (*Independent*, 17 July 1999, p. 15).

13 October 1999: the European Commission recommends that EU leaders at the December 1999 meeting in Helsinki allow Bulgaria, Latvia, Lithuania, Malta, Romania and Slovakia to begin accession negotiations in 2000.

The 'principle of differentiation' for entry date will apply to each of the twelve candidates, reflecting differing states of readiness for EU entry. A 'fully flexible, multi-speed accession process' is envisaged. 'Each country will be able to proceed on merit, including the possibility for those which join the negotiations from 2000 to catch up with the others.' The European Commission thinks that existing EU members should undertake internal reforms by the end of 2002: 'Whether the first accessions can take place as from 1 January 2003 will then depend entirely on the speed with which the applicant countries can make progress on meeting the criteria.'

'Romania has a long way to go' in economic terms. Romania's position is 'very worrying'. In order to begin negotiations Romania must take steps to deal with its weak economic and budgetary position and act to improve the lot of 100,000 children in child-care institutions.

(*FT*, 14 October 1999, pp. 1, 10; *IHT*, 14 October 1999, p. 5; *Guardian*, 14 October 1999, p. 14; *Independent*, 14 October 1999, p. 18; *The Times*, 14 October 1999, p. 21; *Telegraph*, 14 October 1999, p. 20.)

(For further details, see the Hungary entry for 10 December 1999.)

14 December 1999: prime minister Radu Vasile is dismissed by the president. (Radu Vasile is also deputy chairman of the National Peasants' Party–Christian Democratic Party: *EEN*, 1998, vol. 12, no. 5, p. 5.)

> President Emil Constantinescu dismissed prime minister Radu Vasile early Tuesday [14 December], claiming he was unable to carry out his duties. The move came after seven cabinet ministers from Mr Vasile's own Peasant Party resigned … Alexandru Athanasiu, labour and welfare minister, was named interim prime minister.
>
> (*IHT*, 15 December 1999, p. 4)

'[The prime minister] was charged with incompetence and failing to revive the economy' (*Guardian*, 15 December 1999, p. 17).

> Mr Constantinescu is acting with the support of the Christian Democrats, the dominant partner in the four-party coalition, which yesterday [14 December] suspended Mr Vasile from party offices … [The party decided] to ban him from running for jobs in the leadership of the party over the next two years. However, Mr Vasile said the president's action was unconstitutional as a prime minister could be sacked only through parliament. 'The presidency has breached the constitution. I consider myself the prime minister' … Ion Iliescu, leader of the main leftist opposition party, the ex-communist PDSR, also declared the president's move unconstitutional.
>
> (*FT*, 15 December 1999, p. 10)

Radu Vasile: 'I very firmly declare that the presidency has breached the constitution. I consider myself the prime minister. I will present this abuse to the Senate.'

> Last night, however, Mr Vasile appeared to waver over his decision to fight his dismissal … In one interview last night Mr Vasile … [said] 'Personally I am not going to contest this decision. I have had enough of these Byzantine affairs' … Mr Iliescu said Mr Constantinescu had 'clearly violated the constitution'. His Social Democrats would withdraw from both chambers of parliament until the president cancelled the dismissal decrees.
>
> (*Telegraph*, 15 December 1999, p. 13)

Radu Vasile went on to establish a 'Popular Group' parliamentary faction within the National Peasants' Party–Christian Democrats with over thirty MPs. He was expelled from the party on 27 December. 'Vasile's demise was probably sealed by the violent demonstration by workers of the Brasov truck plant on 8 November' (*EEN*, 2000, vol. 12, no. 21, p. 8). There was also a violent trade union demonstration in Iasi on 23 November, the start of a national rail strike on 6 December and student unrest (p. 6).

16 December 1999: the president nominates Mugur Isarescu, the governor of the central bank, as prime minister.

> Since then [1989] the West has done little but watch as post-communist Romania stagnated, mired in appalling poverty and systemic corruption. This inaction was possible because, unlike some of its Balkan neighbours, Romania remained basically stable – no civil war or genocide to trigger international concern … Last month [November 1999] a startling public opinion poll showed that a majority of Romanians believed that 'life was better under Ceausescu' and two-thirds thought the country was 'headed in the wrong direction'. One tangible benefit of life under the dictator had been the guarantee of a job. That is gone. Living standards are falling, unemployment is rampant, and a third of the population lives in poverty … During their less repressive experience under communism, Poles developed an autonomous civil society and Hungarians a thriving alternative economy.

> Romanians never had that chance ... Gauged by the sheer amount of social, political and economic change, Romanians have done more, not less, than, say, Czechs ... This month [December 1999] Romania performed what amounts to a miracle in its part of the world: it survived a constitutional crisis, salvaged democracy, got an impressive new prime minister, and presented the United States and Western Europe with another chance to do some good ... They must not wait. A society can hold on only so long in the grip of misery and isolation ... The new prime minister is the perfect candidate to manage Western aid: Mugur Isarescu, head of the Romanian National Bank since 1990. Mr Isarescu ... has single-handedly built the credibility of the central bank, kept it out of partisan politics and used its resources to create the building blocks of a market economy while supporting Romanian culture and arts ... Without his integrity and expertise at the monetary helm, the country would have defaulted long ago. The fact that he is in office at all is a credit to Romania's political resilience. This month President Emil Constantinescu, confronting popular anger over crime, corruption and deteriorating living standards, fired prime minister Radu Vasile. But someone had apparently forgotten to tell Mr Constantinescu that presidents are not allowed to fire prime ministers under the Romanian constitution. Mr Vasile refused to step down. The opposition walked out of parliament. But the situation never descended into violence. The crisis was defused – with Mr Vasile agreeing to return to a leadership post with the Peasant Party – when Mr Constantinescu named the respected, politically neutral Mr Isarescu as prime minister.
>
> (Daniel Nelson, *IHT*, 28 December 1999, p. 8)

According to an opinion poll published in early June 1999, more than 60 per cent of Romanians believed that living standards were better under communism. About 66 per cent were worried that the country was moving in the wrong direction, with three-quarters dissatisfied with living standards. Around 85 per cent were still in favour of a market economy, although 88 per cent believed that the market benefits only high-ranking officials (*Transition*, 1999, vol. 10, no. 3, p. 33). 'In a recent survey 61 per cent said they were better off under the Ceausescu regime. Four-fifths said they were unhappy with their lives' (*Telegraph*, 22 December 1999, p. 11).

21 December 1999: the tenth anniversary of the collapse of the Ceausescu regime is a very quiet affair.

28 January 2000: ten parliamentary deputies resign from the ruling National Peasants' Party to join former premier Radu Vasile's new Romanian People's Party (*EEN*, 2000, vol. 12, no. 22, p. 5). 'Radu Vasile, having left the PNT–CD [National Peasants' Party–Christian Democrats], has formed his new Romanian People's Party with the support of at least a dozen PNT–CD MPs' (p. 3).

30 January 2000: waste products containing large quantities of cyanide escape from a gold mine in northern Romania (Transylvania) and enter the River Szamos. In turn the overspill pollutes the River Tisza, which forms the boundary between Romania and Ukraine before flowing through Hungary and then meeting the Danube in Serbia. Large-scale environmental damage brought four compensation claims. (Other cases of toxic spillages were reported later on.)

28 May 2000: the National Investment Fund (the largest private investment fund) fails to make payments. Violent protests follow (*EEN*, 2000, vol. 12, no. 23, p. 10).

4 June 2000:

> Ion Iliescu's Party of Social Democracy was the clear victor in the local elections on 4 June … even stealing control of right-leaning Bucharest for the first time since communism collapsed a decade ago. The results confirm what the opinion polls have been saying: more than half of Romanians think the country is heading in the wrong direction and barely a fifth say life is getting better … Less than 40 per cent of the electorate even bothered to turn out and nearly half, according to one poll, have no idea which way they will vote in the presidential and parliamentary elections due this November … Run-off elections for mayor take place on 18 June … Mr Iliescu … wants Romania to join the EU and Nato … The IMF has at last signed a delayed loan for about $500 million.
>
> (*The Economist*, 10 June 2000, p. 57)

12 July 2000: the Christian Democratic National Peasants' Party, the main party in the current ruling Democratic Convention government, forms an electoral alliance with the Union of Right-Wing Forces (*EEN*, 2000, vol. 12, no. 24, p. 6).

17 July 2000: President Emil Constantinescu announces that he will not run for a second term of office in November 2000.

'In a televised speech Mr Constantinescu said his decision had been prompted by setbacks in his attempts to fight what he called a Mafia-type system of "official corruption, with links to high-ranking state institutions"' (*IHT*, 18 July 2000, p. 7).

2 August 2000: two nationalist parties, the Romanian National Unity Party and the small Romanian National Party, agree to form a new 'National Alliance' (*EEN*, 2000, vol. 12, no. 24, p. 6).

19 August 2000: former premier Victor Ciorbea's small National Christian Democratic Alliance joins the Romanian Democratic Convention (*EEN*, 2000, vol. 12, no. 24, p. 6).

8 November 2000: the EU reports that Romania lies last in terms of membership prospects.

The EU's report on Romania (*Progress Towards Accession*, 8 November 2000, pp. 87–9):

> The government has shown a political commitment to addressing the problems of institutionalized children and progress has been made … In the case of the treatment of Roma, the continued high levels of discrimination are a

> serious concern ... Further progress still needs to be made with regard to demilitarization of the police and other bodies subordinated to the ministry of interior ... Little progress has been made in reducing levels of corruption ... There has been little progress in developing administrative capacity ... Romania cannot be regarded as a functioning market economy and is not able to cope with competitive pressure and market forces within the Union in the medium term. It has not substantially improved its future economic prospects ... The fragile macroeconomic environment, the uncertain legal and institutional framework and the uneven commitment to reforms continue to hinder economic development. Many institutions required to ensure the functioning of a market economy either do not exist or are too weak to be effective. Insufficient reforms and a growing black market economy have undermined progress made on macroeconomic stabilization. The absence of a sound and well-functioning financial system hampers economic activity. A very large part of the enterprise sector has yet to start restructuring or is still in the process of doing so. Investment has continued to fall, delaying the required modernization of the supply side of the economy ... In the case of agriculture a major structural reform of the sector is needed.

(For further details, see the entry in the chapter on Hungary.)

The general and presidential elections of 26 November 2000

There was a marked swing to both the left and the right and away from the centre.

The results of the presidential election were as follows: Ion Iliescu (Party of Social Democracy), 37 per cent; Corneliu Vadim Tudor (the leader of the extreme right-wing Greater Romania Party), 28.47 per cent; Theodor Stolojan (National Liberal Party), 12 per cent; Mugur Isarescu (independent), 9 per cent; Gyorgy Frunda (Hungarian Democratic Union), 6 per cent; Petre Roman, 3 per cent.

In the presidential election the centrist candidates split their vote.

The run-off for the presidential election was held on 10 December 2000. The turnout was 57.51 per cent. Iliescu won comfortably with 66.94 per cent of the vote compared with Tudor's 33.06 per cent.

> Mr Tudor, a former Ceausescu court poet, has been playing politics on the far right throughout the 1990s, espousing both xenophobic and nationalist messages. In this election he moderated his tone and portrayed himself as a nationalist determined to fight corruption, red tape and mismanagement.
>
> (Stefan Wagstyl, *FT*, 29 November 2000, p. 10)

> Mr Tudor has made racist speeches, lashing Jews, Gypsies and Hungarians, drawing on outdated fears that neighbouring Hungary plans to annex the ethnically mixed region of Transylvania. Mr Tudor gained notoriety in 1998 for saying Romania needs to be governed 'from the barrel of a gun'. Recently he said: 'Romania is caught between anarchy and the Mafia. I will liquidate the Mafia so fast that they won't even have time to glance at their watches to let them know that Romania is ruled by an iron fist' … Recently Mr Tudor has toned down his racist attacks.
>
> (Marcus Tanner, *Independent*, 29 November 2000, p. 15)

> Many young Romanians know nothing of Mr Tudor's past as the 'court poet' in the Ceausescu regime and are not concerned about his desire to recover bits of Romania lost since 1918. They have not read his magazines, which refer to 'dirty Jews', 'fascist Hungarians' and 'criminal Gypsies' and have published lists of his enemies and their addresses just as vengeful miners he has stirred up are marching on Bucharest. Rather, they have seen him on television in the last few weeks, when he stuck to his 'liquidate the Mafia' message and promised 500,000 jobs by reviving Romanian factories whose products he says the Third World is still clamouring for.
>
> (Donald McNeil, *IHT*, 29 November 2000, p. 6)

'Mr Tudor promises a tough law-and-order policy and the return of cash "by Christmas" to savers hurt by a string of bank failures … He blames privatization for much of the corruption he denounces' (*The Economist*, 2 December 2000, p. 60).

> The November 2000 presidential and parliamentary elections wholly swept away the administration of the Democratic Convention of Romania … [which] came to power in 1996 led by the National Peasant Party of Romania … The PDSR [Social Democracy Party of Romania] won 36.5 per cent of the parliamentary vote … The Greater Romania Party won … 20 per cent … The Democratic Party did poorly … [with] 7 per cent … The National Party of Romania … failed to win a single seat in parliament [Andrei Marga becoming the new party leader after the election] … The National Liberal Party … last summer [2000] from the Democratic Convention of Romania and their traditional affinity with the National Peasant Party of Romania … The liberals then got into parliament … After the elections [Valeriu] Stoica … saw himself elected the new party leader.
>
> (*EEN*, 2001, vol. 13, no. 3, pp. 1–4)

> The PDSR's [Party of Social Democracy's] policy plans are difficult to fathom. It backed a cross-party, medium-term economic programme earlier this year [2000] that envisages further reform, including prudent budgets, deregulation and privatization. But Mr Iliescu has muddied the water by threatening to reverse some recent privatizations, including the largest –

> Romtelecom. He has also pledged more social support for the poor, including $100 million for winter fuel bills.
>
> (*FT*, 24 November 2000, p. 12)

'Iliescu has been hinting at some possible renationalizations' (*The Economist*, 2 December 2000, p. 60). 'The Social Democracy Party of Romania denounced the irregularities and the fraudulent privatizations allegedly orchestrated by Radu Sirbu, the then head of the state property fund' (*EEN*, 2001, vol. 13, no. 3, p. 3).

'The medium-term economic programme [was] agreed between the government and the opposition in spring 2000. Covering the period to 2004, it provides for a consolidated budget of 3 per cent of GDP' (Business Central Europe 2000: 39).

There were 483 seats in parliament. The Greater Romania Party won 121 of them, the second highest number of seats after the Social Democracy Party of Romania. The latter's Adrian Nastase became prime minister.

'The Greater Romania Party … won around a quarter of the seats in both chambers of parliament. One has already gone independent' (*Business Central Europe*, February 2001, p. 38).

> The Party of Social Democracy is now firmly in power … The party's deputies occupy almost half the seats in both chambers of parliament … It did not need to form a coalition with the Liberals (PNL) … Instead it formed a minority government by striking a co-operation deal with the ethnic Hungarians and the PNL … The deal buys Mr Nastase's cabinet the two parties' support for a year … Within a month the government introduced fiscal breaks for small and medium-sized enterprises, and passed a much-needed property restitution bill [restitution law: p. 13] … which will give back some of the property seized by the communists … The cabinet's economic plans are virtually unchanged from the previous government's medium-term development programme. But the tax breaks for small companies are new and with the budget deficit for 2001 already likely to reach 4 per cent of GDP, the IMF's 3 per cent limit won't be met.
>
> (*Business Central Europe*, February 2001, p. 37)

> [The] government under premier Adrian Nastase, though technically a minority government, appears to have a workable understanding with the ethnic Hungarian Party of Democratic Hungarians in Romania as well as the Liberal Party and the Democratic Party … [The Party of Social Democracy] is obliged to uphold minority rights as a condition of EU accession talks in the future, and has thus accordingly agreed to increase Hungarian language education and the use of Hungarian in public administration where the Hungarian minority is 20 per cent or more of the local population.
>
> (*EEN*, 2001, vol. 13, no. 2, p. 3)

'After a couple of weeks in power civil servants were dismissed *en masse* and party [Social Democracy Party of Romania] faithful appointed in their places' (*EEN*, 2001, vol. 13, no. 3, p. 2).

> The new prime minister, Adrian Nastase … has begun negotiations on a social stability pact with the main trade unions and business associations … The government is planning to create some jobs quickly by building roads, dams and housing … The government is planning to cut corporate taxes and bureaucratic requirements, reduce inflation to less than 25 per cent and hold the budget deficit at 3 to 4 per cent of GDP. It hopes to make a deal with the IMF by mid-May, unfreezing credits suspended last fall [2000].
>
> (Steven Erlanger, *IHT*, 12 February 2001, p. 4)

February 2001:

> Romania's new government has signed a social pact with the unions … a comprehensive deal with the country's unions and employers … A pact was signed in February, setting out the principles that the unions, employers and government agree to abide by. The idea is that it will provide a stable framework, so that negotiations rather than strikes will be used to solve industrial disputes … The unions … have agreed that wage rises should be linked to output and to corporate profitability.
>
> (*Business Central Europe*, April 2001, p. 50)

15 March 2001:

> The EU agreed Thursday [15 March] to lift visa requirements for Bulgaria … EU justice and interior ministers also agreed conditionally to lift the visa requirements for Romania … pending further progress on tackling the problem of illegal immigration. Bulgarians will no longer need a visa to visit one or more EU member nations for a period of up to three months.
>
> (*IHT*, 16 March 2001, p. 4)

1 June 2001: a statue of Marshal Ion Antonescu is unveiled in Bucharest (*IHT*, 2 June 2001, p. 4).

16 June 2001: 'The Social Democracy Party of Romania merges with the small Romanian Social Democratic Party and adopts the name of Social Democratic Party, under the chairmanship of premier Adrian Nastase' (*EEN*, 2001, vol. 13, no. 5, p. 7).

'The opposition parties are wholly moribund, particularly following the ousting of Petre Roman as leader of the Democratic Party … Very recently there have been mass defections from the Democratic Party to Nastase's Social Democratic Party' (*EEN*, 2001, vol. 13, no. 5, p. 4).

27 June 2001:

> Seven governments ... yesterday signed an agreement aimed at liberalizing trade in at least 90 per cent of goods trade between them. The move by Albania, Bosnia-Hercegovina, Bulgaria, Croatia, Romania, Macedonia and Yugoslavia marks the latest stage in efforts, under the EU's Stability Pact for South-Eastern Europe, to enhance stability in the region through economic growth. Moldova is expected to join the arrangement shortly.
>
> (*FT*, 28 June 2001, p. 8)

THE ECONOMY

Planning quickly started to disintegrate, the State Planning Commission being abolished in January 1990. But in the absence of replacement market structures the situation initially became rather chaotic.

Soon after the fall of Ceausescu the financial situation deteriorated quickly as pay increased and working hours were reduced. Independent trade unions played a part in this. Controls on the movement of labour were abolished in 1990 and free collective bargaining was introduced the following year. A wage inflation tax was introduced and austerity measures taken to try to reduce inflation.

As regards aid, Western governments penalized Romania initially because a socialist government had been chosen by the electorate. Romania began to borrow again in January 1990 as relations with the IMF improved. A stand-by agreement was signed in May 1992 and in August the IMF praised Romania for meeting its monetary and fiscal targets. But on 23 July 1993 Romania failed to reach agreement with the IMF on a new stand-by loan due to the lack of success in the battle against inflation. It was not until 9 December 1993 that an austerity package was agreed with the IMF. In January 1994 parliament passed an IMF memorandum of understanding and the IMF formally approved the package on 11 May (the loan being worth $720 million). Agreement was reached, among other things, to float the leu, reduce the budget deficit to 3.5 per cent of GDP, reduce the trade deficit and to speed up privatization and restructuring (Deutsche Bank, *Focus: Eastern Europe*, 1994, no. 114, p. 3). On 6 April 1994 parliament approved a budget deficit target for the year of 3.5 per cent of GDP. The 1995 budget was approved on 1 March 1995. In line with IMF guidelines, the target budget deficit was 2.7 per cent of GDP and the target inflation rate was 29 per cent. 'The Romanian leu has been stable against the dollar for the past year, thanks to a tough stabilization programme backed by the International Monetary Fund' (Alfred Moses, *IHT*, 17 March 1995, p. 8).

An accord was signed on 6 May 1993 on the eve of a threatened general strike. There were strikes by steel workers in May and rail workers in June. In August there were serious strikes by coal miners in the Jiu valley and by train drivers, but a tough approach by the government resulted in these ending with moderate pay awards. On 18 November 1993 large numbers of workers demonstrated against the government and its economic policies and further demonstrations and strikes followed, e.g. a one-day strike by an estimated 2 million workers on 28 February 1994. There were also worker demonstrations in Bucharest between 14 and 16 June 1994. Trade unions wanted improved pay and social security payments, but also (perhaps surprisingly) a faster pace of economic reform. In December 1994 there were strikes by steel workers, coal miners and oil workers. In March 1995 workers protested in Bucharest at a government decision to limit public sector wage increases, while energy workers went on strike 3–5 June 1995. The five largest unions threatened large-scale strikes (starting 4 June) unless the government agreed to higher wages and to amend a government decree which penalized state enterprises offering salaries over a certain level without corresponding increases in productivity (*EEN*, 25 May 1995, vol. 9, no. 11, p. 5). (The largest trade unions are CNSLR–Fratia, claiming 3.7 million members, and Alfa Cartel, claiming 1.2 million members. According to Chrystia Freeland, the combined membership may be as high as 5.5 million out of a total workforce of 10.5 million; the two trade unions favour market reform: *FT*, Survey, 3 May 1994, p. 30.)

(See the entries in the politics section above, beginning on 4 January 1999, which deal with later strikes and the arrest of the coal miners' leader Miron Cozma.)

Enterprise debts have, in effect, been continuously written off by means of credit infusions (Ronnas 1996: 25). A bankruptcy law was not passed by the Chamber of Deputies until 21 March 1995.

> Romania's nascent financial sector has reached a critical stage. Confidence has been eroded by trouble at several banks and mutual funds, the interbank foreign exchange market has all but ceased to function, while confidence in capital markets has been hit by sagging prices and low turnover on the recently opened Bucharest stock exchange.
>
> (Virginia Marsh, *FT*, Survey, 9 July 1996, p. ii)

'The monetarization of large fiscal deficits in the run-up to general elections in … Romania pushed up year-end inflation to … 57 per cent' (EBRD 1997a: 9). 'Credit policies loosened considerably in 1996 as subsidization of the agriculture and energy sectors through directed credits and the financing of part of the budget deficit by the national bank accelerated in the second half of the year.' Restructuring of the large state banks is a priority of the new government. Elimination of the system of directed credits has been announced (p. 32).

There were some price increases in July 1990, e.g. for petrol, luxury goods and newspapers. But the proposed price reform of 1 January 1991 was postponed until 1 April (although a maximum price increase of 125 per cent was laid down for most basic commodities, and political disturbances led to a temporary freeze on the prices of basic goods and services in October). Half of the prices in the consumer goods basket were freed in November 1990 (EBRD 1994:

33). By mid-1991 about 80 per cent of prices were free (Demekas and Khan 1991: 17–19). The remaining subsidies on basic consumer goods were removed in May 1992 and most of the remaining consumer subsidies ended on 1 May 1993. The large rise in prices (e.g. a four-fold increase in the price of bread) led to trade union pressure for wage increases. Price liberalization in 1993 saw consumer subsidies phased out, mark-up limits eliminated (in June) and the number of consumer goods under direct price control fall to five (EBRD 1994: 33). By the middle of 1995 the share of administrative prices for consumer goods and services had fallen to 3 per cent. By the autumn of 1996 the prices for oil and other energy products remained subject to state control, as did a few agricultural products (EBRD 1996b: 168). On 7 April 1994 the government substantially raised the prices of petrol, natural gas, electricity (42 per cent) and thermic energy. On 22 August 1996 the prices of fifty-four goods and services (such as petrol, bread, milk and public transport) were frozen until the end of 1996. Pensions were to be increased from 1 October 1996 (Virginia Marsh, *FT*, 29 August 1996, p. 2; *Baltic Times*, 29 August–4 September 1996, p. 7).

It took until the autumn of 1996 for Romania to shake off the dominance of personalities and parties with roots in the communist past. President Iliescu and the Social Democracy Party of Romania (formerly the Democratic National Salvation Front) lost the November 1996 presidential and parliamentary elections respectively, largely because of economic factors. (This is not to underestimate the importance of factors such as corruption.) The inconsistency of reform measures can be judged by the fact that on 17 February 1997 prime minister Ciorbea felt obliged to make the following announcement:

> We have prepared a comprehensive programme of economic reforms, with the goal of stabilizing the economy and launching the structural reforms necessary for growth … We inherited a budget deficit (including implicit subsidies) of 13 per cent of gross domestic product from the previous government. Our programmes for 1997 will be to eliminate hidden subsidies and cut the total deficit to roughly one-third last year's level, to 4.5 per cent of GDP. To achieve this we will cut agricultural subsidies, end most price controls, eliminate tax breaks and substantially reduce the public sector … At the same time we will put in place programmes of social support to see people through these difficult times.
>
> (*FT*, 18 February 1997, p. 20)

In February 1997 subsidies were withdrawn from fuel, electricity, public transport and telecommunications (*Transition*, 1997, vol. 8, no. 2, p. 26). Price controls were removed on basic commodities such as milk, meat, bread and oil (*Business Central Europe*, May 1997, p. 20). The monthly inflation rate rose to 16.2 per cent in January 1997, 18.8 per cent in February 1997 and 30.7 per cent in March 1997, before falling to 6.9 per cent in April 1997 and 4.7 per cent in May 1997. On 1 May 1997 the price of gas and heating was increased five-fold, putting it on a par with international levels (*FT*, 10 May 1997, p. 2). The leu fell from around 4,000 to the US dollar at the end of 1996 to a low of around 9,000 before stabilizing at just over 7,000 to the US dollar (*FT*, Survey, 25 June 1997, p. iii.) On 17 April 1997 parliament passed an austerity programme. There was to be a reduction in the budget deficit (excluding implicit/hidden subsidies) from 5.7 per cent of GDP in 1996 to 4.5 per cent in 1997. Any of the ten major loss-making state enterprises (accounting for some 7.5 per cent of total commercial losses) or any of the twenty listed state animal farms that failed to be sold would be wound up (*FT*, 18 April 1997, p. 2). As of April 1997 basically all controlled prices had been liberalized, with the exception of electricity and heat, public services, transport and mail (Deutsche Morgan Grenfell, *Focus: Eastern Europe*, 11 June 1997, p. 31). The government planned to put 75 per cent of the economy into private hands within two years and to amend the foreign investment laws by May 1997 (involving tax breaks, the purchase of land and the repatriation of profits) (*Business Central Europe*, April 1997, p. 15). The state ownership fund is now under the control of the cabinet instead of parliament (*The Economist*, 3 May 1997, p. 36). On 23 April the IMF agreed a stand-by loan of $430 million, $86.2 million immediately and the remainder in four quarterly instalments conditional on meeting or at least working towards such goals as inflation of 2 per cent a month in the second half of 1997 (*FT*, 24 April 1997, p. 3). The World Bank has agreed to loans worth $530 million. An anti-corruption committee has been set up (*The Economist*, 3 May 1997, p. 36). The government told the IMF that it would adjust the budget by reallocating resources. More funds would be allotted to the social sector (including health, education and social benefits). Employees laid off as a result of restructuring would be eligible for compensation of up to twelve months' wages (Deutsche Morgan Grenfell, *EEN*, 5 September 1997, pp. 38–41). On 7 August 1997 prime minister Ciorbea announced the immediate closure of seventeen large state enterprises, including engineering enterprises, food-processing enterprises and three (out of eleven) oil refineries. (One enterprise was reprieved when it paid off much of its debt: *The Economist*, 23 August 1997, p. 28. The list has been whittled down from seventeen to twelve: *Business Central Europe*, March 1998, p. 28.)

In August 1999 the IMF approved a $547 million stand-by credit facility (agreed in April 1999). Romania had to 'work vigorously towards obtaining' $450 million in private sector financing by 15 October 1999, when the IMF would consider releasing a second tranche of the loan (*FT*, 18 August 1999, p. 2). 'The current $547 million package, agreed in the summer [of 1999], has been stalled, with disbursement already behind schedule' (*FT*, 23 December 1999, p. 7). 'A stalled $547 million loan package … was agreed last summer [1999], of which only $73 million has been disbursed' (*FT*, 3 February 2000, p. 9).

> The IMF has delayed for two months a decision granting a new assistance programme for Romania … The new programme was planned to replace an existing $540 million stand-by credit awarded last year [1999]. Romania

> has only been permitted to draw $71 million of their credit after failing to meet conditions set by the IMF.
>
> (*FT*, 29 March 2000, p. 10)

> The Romanian government has committed itself to stringent austerity measures and strict monitoring of spending in a preliminary agreement with the IMF for an extension of a $540 million stand-by loan. So far it has received just $73 million from the IMF. One of the most contentious parts of the memorandum is a decision to increase gas and electricity prices by 20 per cent and reduce the workforce by 20,000. Arrears to three public utilities (Petrom, the national oil company, Romgaz and Conel, the state's gas and electricity companies) will be also reduced by 15 per cent by the end of the year. These companies' biggest debtors are local authorities and other state-owned enterprises. The government will try again to privatize Petrom by offering a controlling stake in the company.
>
> (*FT*, 6 May 2000, p. 8)

'Last month [June 2000] the IMF extended a $540 million stand-by loan for Romania until next February [2001]' (*FT*, 17 July 2000, p. 8).

'The IMF has at last signed a delayed loan for about $500 million' (*The Economist*, 10 June 2000, p. 57).

> The IMF has agreed to release $116 million to Romania. The funds represent part of a $535 million stand-by credit originally approved last August [1999]. Romania had drawn only $71 million of the available funds when the funds were halted, following a run on the country's largest bank (Banca Commerciala Romana), the closure of investment fund Fondul National de Investii, and the decision by Banca Populara Romana to suspend payments to depositors. The release of the funds was sanctioned only after the IMF received commitments from the government that state spending would be reduced and salaries pegged and tied to performance.
>
> (*Transition*, 2000, vol. 11, nos 3–4, p. 25)

A three-year, $2.4 billion aid package was unveiled by the EU in November 1999 (Business Central Europe 1999: 36).

Privatization

The law governing the private sector was relaxed in March 1990 to allow four categories of ownership: small enterprises employing up to twenty people; co-operatives of up to ten; family businesses; and self-employment. This law was subsequently abrogated and the employment ceilings removed.

In 1989 the private sector accounted for only 5 per cent of GDP (Deutsche Bank, *Focus: Eastern Europe*, 1994, no. 100. p. 30). Frydman *et al.* (1993: 230) provide figures showing the share of the various sectors in terms of employment at the end of 1991: state, 65.1 per cent; private, 34.9 per cent (private companies, 6.9 per cent; individual and co-operative farmers, 23.1 per cent; non-agricultural co-operatives, 4.9 per cent).

The importance of the private sector varies between sectors. In the first half of 1995 its share of value added was only 12 per cent for industry, compared with 46 per cent for services, 50 per cent for construction and 69 per cent for domestic trade. In 1996 the private sector share was estimated at 24 per cent of agricultural output and 75 per cent in trade and services (EBRD 1994: 10, 1995b: 11, 1996b: 53, 167, and 1997b: 14, 192).

Rough estimates in mid-year of the private sector as a percentage of GDP are provided by the EBRD: 1990, 15 per cent; 1991, 25 per cent; 1992, 25 per cent; 1993, 35 per cent; 1994, 40 per cent; 1995, 45 per cent; 1996, 55 per cent; 1997, 60 per cent; 1998, 60 per cent; 1999, 60 per cent; 2000, 60 per cent (EBRD 1999b: 24, 256, and 2000b: 14, 200).

In February 1997 prime minister Ciorbea talked of the grey economy representing 40 per cent of GDP. According to the chief of the intelligence and security service, the black economy represents 35 to 38 per cent of GDP (*EEN*, 11 April 1997, vol. 11, no. 7, p. 4). 'The black economy now accounts for 40 per cent of GDP – and by some estimates, 70 per cent of that black market is made up of illegal booze companies' (*Business Central Europe*, March 2000, p. 42).

A privatization bill was passed in late July 1990. This provided for the following:

1. State control of 20 per cent of enterprises (these 'strategic' state-owned so-called 'autonomous entities' included mines, the post, railways, armaments and energy);
2. Eighty per cent state enterprises to be converted into joint stock 'commercial enterprises' before privatization;
3. Thirty per cent of the value of the capital of these joint stock companies to be distributed to adult residents for free in the form of vouchers exchangeable for shares (voucher distribution scheduled to start in the first quarter of 1991 and the sale of shares to begin in the last quarter);
4. A probable 30 per cent of the shares of a particular enterprise to be offered to its employees in exchange for cash or vouchers;
5. A block of shares to be reserved for foreigners.

Further legislation was introduced in August 1991, with the following provisions:

1. Five 'private ownership funds' to be set up and to receive 30 per cent of the shares of each of the commercialized enterprises for free distribution in turn to adult citizens (each citizen to receive a certificate of ownership in each of these funds and the fund shares to be tradable);
2. The remaining 70 per cent of the shares of each of the roughly 6,000 commercialized enterprises to be held in a state ownership fund, with the privatization process supposedly spread over a seven-year period and

proceeding via a number of channels (including auctions, direct sell-offs, and sales to foreigners; of the 70 per cent, 10 per cent to be sold to employees of enterprises at a 10 per cent discount).

But implementation of the programme was slow:

1 Fifteen enterprises had been privatized by the end of 1992 (United Nations Economic Commission for Europe 1993: 223).
2 In 1993 only 220 small enterprises were sold off, compared with a target of 800–1,000 (*FT*, 31 December 1993, p. 2). In 1993 only 250 mainly small enterprises were sold off (management or employee buy-outs being the main methods of privatization during the year) (*FT*, Survey, 3 May 1994, p. 30). Romania has sold off about 900 mainly small state enterprises under the 1991 scheme, with most purchased by management and employee groups (*FT*, 22 March 1995, p. 3).
3 About 270 small enterprises were privatized under the privatization programme in 1993 and another 250 during the first four months of 1994, mostly by management–employee buy-outs (p. 32). By the end of 1994, 891 enterprises had been privatized, primarily through management–employee buy-outs (EBRD 1995a: 62). By mid-1995 more than 1,100 enterprises had been privatized, primarily through management–employee buy-outs (EBRD 1995b: 53). By March 1996 more than 1,500 enterprises had been privatized, primarily through management–employee buy-outs (EBRD 1996b: 167). By the end of 1996 only 45 per cent of all enterprises scheduled for privatization had been privatized. During the first eight months of 1997, privatization accelerated. A further 1,100 enterprises were privatized (140 of these being medium-sized or large), bringing the total proportion of enterprises privatized to around 60 per cent (EBRD 1997b: 192).
4 Only some 700 enterprises, out of a total of 6,700, have been privatized so far (President Iliescu, *Guardian*, 5 November 1994, p. 39).
5 Only 900 of the 6,000 state enterprises slated for privatization under the existing law have been sold, mainly through management–employee buy-outs; only about a dozen of them have been large enterprises employing over 2,000 workers (*Business Central Europe*, May 1995, p. 18).

A new privatization law was passed by parliament on 21 March 1995. Romanians would be able to purchase state assets using 'certificates of ownership' distributed to individuals in 1992 and higher-value coupons which were to be distributed. The new law envisaged the eventual sale through various means of 3,000 enterprises (down from 6,000 in the preceding law). A total of 1,500 enterprises were to be sold in 1995 (EBRD 1995a: 62). The privatization framework foresaw the sale through various means of about 3,900 large and medium-sized enterprises. (In mid-August 1995 the government published a list of 3,907 enterprises it hoped to sell: *Transition*, 1995, vol. 6, nos 9–10, p. 20.) The stages were as follows: distribution of coupons (August–September 1995);

subscription for shares in enterprises on offer (15 September to 15 December 1995); the exchange of certificates of ownership (distributed to the population in 1992) and coupons (carrying much greater purchasing power than certificates of ownership) for shares (15 December 1995 to 31 March 1996). Up to 60 per cent of the ownership in an individual enterprise may be sold for coupons and certificates of ownership, with the remaining at least 40 per cent to be sold for cash (EBRD 1995b: 53). Between 60 per cent and 70 per cent of the shares in 3,900 enterprises were to be transferred to the population under the scheme (except in selected enterprises in which a majority stake was to be offered to strategic investors). The remaining shares were to be sold for cash. The deadline for subscription was moved to the end of March 1996. By the end of February 1996, 27 per cent of the 17 million recipients of coupons had subscribed to shares (EBRD 1996a: 10). In September 1996 the Senate approved a bill on the transformation of five ownership funds into investment funds (EBRD 1996b: 167). Only 14 per cent of vouchers were exchanged against shares in the private ownership funds, which were converted to private investment funds in November 1996 (EBRD 1997b: 192).

The programme aimed to sell off, within twelve months of its launch, some 3,900 enterprises for a combination of cash and free privatization coupons distributed to all Romanians. Up to 60 per cent of the equity of most enterprises could be exchanged for coupons with the remainder to be offered to local or foreign investors for cash, mainly at auctions. The state ownership fund set aside 554 enterprises in which a 51 per cent stake was to be reserved for strategic investors. It also intended to sell the cash portion of about fifty, mainly large, enterprises by way of a public offering rather than auction (*FT*, 11 December 1995, p. 27). The state ownership fund began cash auctions in December 1995 (*FT*, Survey, 9 July 1996, p. ii).

Some 3,000 enterprises were to be sold off by the end of 1996 (Business Central Europe 1995: 40).

Apart from the price bid by the prospective investor, decisive criteria were to be proof of sales markets and commitments with regard to employment, environment protection and investment plans. Non-residents were to be permitted to acquire up to 51 per cent of the capital of the enterprises on sale. The eighty-four large state enterprises known as 'autonomous bodies of national interest' (*regies autonomes*, operating, for example, in the oil industry, coal mining, power generation, postal services and telecommunications) were to be converted into commercial companies and then partially privatized (Deutsche Bank, *Focus: Eastern Europe*, 1995, no. 141, p. 6).

The government was forced to extend the subscription period for its ambitious mass privatization programme because of poor public response. Officials said that only 7 per cent of the nearly 18 million Romanians eligible to participate had subscribed by the middle of December 1995. Romanians had been given three months from October 1995 to use free coupons to bid for shares in nearly 4,000 enterprises or to place their coupons in one of the five state-run mutual funds. But parliament extended the final date for bids for enterprises from the end of December 1995 to the end of March 1996 (with the deadline for participation in one of the five funds being the end of April 1996). The government refused to allow securities houses to pool coupons and bid on behalf of clients (*FT*, 20 December 1995, p. 2). Stakes in only five of the nine enterprises offered in the first cash auction in December 1995 found buyers, and the remaining four were to go to a third round of bidding on 23 January 1996. Thirty-nine out of 554 enterprises in which majority stakes had been set aside for strategic investors had been sold by the end of 1995. On 23 January 1996 minority stakes in fifty-one enterprises were to be auctioned off to foreign and domestic investors (23 January 1996, p. 3). On 6 March 1996 there was an international offering of majority stakes (maximum 51 per cent) in thirteen selected enterprises (*IHT*, 7 March 1996, p. 13).

> Under the mass privatization programme, launched in 1995, people were given vouchers to invest in privatizing companies or in Private Ownership Funds (POFs). In the end less than a third of all Romanians opted for the funds. That left most privatized companies in the hands of private individuals. Just before it was thrown out of office in 1996 the government awarded shares in each of the five funds to some 9 million Romanians … The mass privatization scheme was at the bottom of the new government's priorities. It turned them into private companies, but has only now got around to listing them, giving shareholders their first legal opportunity to sell up … Romania's five private investment companies are awaiting their debut on the Bucharest bourse. That will mark the end of mass privatization … Individual shareholders are barred from acquiring more than a paltry 0.1 per cent in each of the funds. That makes it hard for shareholders to swap their stakes and almost impossible for the big international funds to buy in … Fund managers … [will not find it easy] to restructure companies … because they do not actually control many companies … Romania has all but collapsed because it ignored the need for deep restructuring. At worst, programmes like this could ensure that the problems drag on for years
>
> (*Business Central Europe*, October 1999, p. 33)

A list of enterprises to be sold in 1997 was published on 15 February 1997. Nearly seventy enterprises were listed, including the national electricity and railway utilities, oil refineries, farming machine enterprises, and the state radio and television networks (*IHT*, 17 February 1997, p. 15).

In February 1997 prime minister Ciorbea was reported as saying that:

> Romania is still burdened with a large state sector which controls three-fifths of the economy and remains inefficient and unreformed. We intend to privatize rapidly as much of this sector as possible, by auctioning enterprises for cash and vouchers. During 1997 we will auction about fifty enterprises a

> week, liquidate chronic loss-making enterprises and begin restructuring and privatization of leading banks.
>
> (*FT*, 18 February 1997, p. 20)

The government intended to sell 2,750 enterprises by the end of May. Prime minister Ciorbea said that the government would aim to have transferred 69 per cent of enterprises into private hands by the end of 1997 (*FT*, 18 February 1997, p. 20).

In February 1997 the government declared its intention to include seven large *regies autonomes* ('autonomous bodies of national interest') and state farms in the privatization programme (EBRD 1997a: 32). At the start of 1996 over 75 per cent of the total book value of companies allocated to the state ownership fund was still state-owned. The reform programme of early 1997 gave greater decision-making power to the fund, shifting focus to direct sales. More recently increasing emphasis has been placed on IPOs and sales to foreign strategic investors. But 'the pace of privatization remained very slow'. The state ownership fund still maintains a portfolio of 5,500 enterprises to be privatized.

> Little progress has been made in the restructuring of loss-making state-owned enterprises, including the *regies autonomes*. Plans for closing some of the biggest loss-makers – agreed with the IMF and the World Bank in 1997 – have not been realized. However, a rationalization programme was implemented successfully in the mining sector. In addition, the government pressured the *regies autonomes* to develop reorganizational plans. One such plan, for the national oil company Petrom, was submitted in May 1998.
>
> (EBRD 1998b: 184)

> Large-scale privatization has received a new impetus since the last quarter of 1998 … by recent sales to strategic investors of large stakes in the telecommunications operator Romtelecom, the Romanian Development Bank and the oil refinery Petromidia, as well as the agreement to sell the automobile manufacturer Dacia to Renault … The control of approximately 650 large companies remains the responsibility of state ownership fund (SOF) headquarters. Of these between 200 and 300 companies are expected to be offered to foreign investors, while loss-making ones will be liquidated according to proposals submitted to an inter-ministerial committee. While significant restructuring of large enterprises, especially in the steel, metallurgical and other heavy industries, has yet to take place, the SOF has announced the start of liquidation procedures for forty-nine large loss-making companies. The objective is to reduce overall losses in the economy from these enterprises by 30 per cent.
>
> (EBRD 1999a: 42)

Large privatization has gained pace since the last quarter of 1998 (see below) (EBRD 1999b: 254). Large-scale privatization has been proceeding slowly. Only two large sales involving foreign investors were completed in 1999 – the car-maker Dacia and the Romanian PostaBank. A new privatization law, adopted in June 1999, provides for the sale through investment banks of some of the country's largest assets, including Tarom (the national airline), Sidex (a steel company) and Petrom (an oil company) (EBRD 2000a: 72).

> While there was some progress in privatization in 1999, the pace remains slow ... The cumulative total of privatized enterprises at the end of 1999 stood at 35 per cent SOF [state ownership fund] capital ... Despite lower enterprise losses, key structural problems remain ... The government continues to channel money into some of the largest loss-making firms through the toleration of tax arrears and cross-subsidization by the SOF. Enterprise arrears are growing. Arrears to the government have continued to grow ... Domestic arrears to the three major utilities increased by 20 per cent in real terms during the first half of 2000.
>
> (EBRD 2000b: 198–9)

> Large-scale privatization has been slow in Romania and was frozen before the presidential and parliamentary elections of November 2000. As a result, none of the sixty-three commercial enterprises scheduled for privatization as part of the World Bank's PSAL–I programme was sold last year [2000]. In January 2001 the new government dissolved the state ownership fund, set up a new authority for the privatization and administration of state assets [a restructuring fund that will help enterprises prepare for privatization: p. 28] and transferred the responsibility for selling state shares in large utilities and public companies to the appropriate ministries ... The privatization of the energy sector, which includes measures to revitalize the mining sector, is a priority for the new government.
>
> (EBRD 2001: 82)

By the year 2000, 80 per cent of GDP was to be generated in the private sector, compared with slightly over 50 per cent in 1996 (Deutsche Morgan Grenfell, *Focus: Eastern Europe*, 11 June 1997, p. 33). By the end of September 1997, 1,163 enterprises had been privatized, almost all of them small. 'Little progress was made in liquidating or privatizing the large companies.' The government has devolved responsibility for smaller enterprises to the regional level (Deutsche Bank Research, *Emerging Europe Weekly*, 12 June 1998, p. 1). 'The political difficulties at the beginning of the year have thrown the timetable for privatization off track and the goal for 1988 will mostly likely not be met' (p. 2).

The stock exchange opened for trading on 20 November 1995 (*FT*, 10 November 1995, p. 3).

A new law on property restitution was passed by parliament in June 1995, granting rights to former owners of around 250,000 residential properties. But the law was overruled by the constitutional court (EBRD 1995b: 54). On 26 November 1995 the president signed into law a restitution bill which settled ownership rights on some 200,000 properties. Former owners were given the right to claim back one home, provided they still lived in it, or to receive compensation of up to 50 million leu (Virginia Marsh, *FT*, 27 November 1995, p. 3).

On 25 August 1999 parliament passed a property restitution law covering property expropriated after 6 March 1945 (*EEN*, 1999, vol. 12, no. 20, p. 4).

Further developments in privatization

November 1998:

> OTE, the partly privatized Greek telecoms operator, plans to finance the $675 million acquisition of Rom Telecom of Romania through an international bond to be issued early next year [1999] … OTE last week beat Telecom Italia, the only other bidder, to buy 35 per cent of Rom Telecom … The Greek operator will take over management and will have voting rights over a further 16 per cent of Rom Telecom's equity.
>
> (*FT*, 13 November 1998, p. 29)

14 December 1998: it is announced that 51 per cent of the Romanian Bank for Development (the fourth largest bank) has been sold to a French bank (*IHT*, 15 December 1998, p. 16). This is the first state bank to be privatized (EBRD 1999b: 254).

25 January 1999: it is announced that a 65 per cent stake in Romania's largest oil refinery (Petromidia) has been sold to a Turkish company (*IHT*, 26 January 1999, p. 13).

In early 1999 Automobile Dacia was sold (EBRD 1999b: 254).

> The acquisition of car-maker Dacia by France's Renault was achieved only by granting some unique tax breaks. And at the IMF's insistence similar perks had to be withdrawn from existing investors and denied new ones. That scuppered the sale of the Petromidia refinery, with Turkey's Akmaya pulling out when tax breaks were cancelled.
>
> (Business Central Europe 1999: 36)

April 1999: a 45 per cent stake in BancPost was sold to a US/Portuguese consortium (*IHT*, Survey, 26 October 1999, p. 19).

(In May 1999 Bancorex, the second largest state bank, was put under administration. The transfer of bad loans to the asset recovery agency was completed by July 1999, when the bank's licence was withdrawn. The remainder of the bank was merged with Banca Commerciala Romana: EBRD 1999b: 255. 'The Romanian Development Bank was privatized early in the year [1999], while the troubled Bancorex foreign trade bank was folded into the Romanian Commercial bank in July': Business Central Europe 1999: 36.)

16 May 1999: the Romanian government has announced an accelerated privatization programme. The first wave of sixty-four large and medium-sized state companies represents about 14 per cent of GDP. The list is headed by the national airline Tarom, the giant Sidex steel works of Galati and two aluminium companies. The government intends to select investment banks by the end of June 1999 with the first invitations to tender published at the beginning of August 1999, and the first sale contracts concluded at the end of September 1999.

> Romania will place no restrictions on the size of stakes available for investors, nor any limitations on future staffing levels in the privatized companies. The new privatization law allows for companies to be sold at market value, rather than at a minimum price linked to the book value, a condition that has thwarted numerous deals in the past. In another change, rather than channelling all sales through the state ownership fund, the individual ministries which own many of the companies will oversee the sales.
> (*FT*, 17 May 1999, p. 3)

June 1999:

> The privatization process … has significantly accelerated its pace over the last year … Major deals … include the carmaker Dacia Automobile Pitesti to Renault of France in June … Last year's partial privatization of Romtelecom, the national phone operator, was the first step in the enormous task of restructuring and privatizing Romania's *regies autonomes*, or public utilities monopolies owned by the state [state-owned monopolies in the public utilities or resources sectors]. Next in line for changes in ownership and administration are the power distribution, oil and gas, transportation, tobacco, postal services and water distribution public utilities … The privatization show will feature the country's biggest companies, all of them operating in the energy sector: the power company Conel; the oil company Petrom; and the natural gas company Romgaz … Petrom is Romania's largest company and accounts for roughly 10 per cent of the economy … The first stage, a boost in capital negotiated directly with a strategic investor, will later be followed by an initial public offering … The state ownership fund (SOF) … has decentralized the privatization process in order to increase speed and transparency. Small and medium-sized enterprises were transferred to the regional branches of SOF and their sale should be completed by mid-2000. The SOF's central office in Bucharest has the tougher job of privatizing some 500 large state-run companies. One of its major successes was the sale of Dacia … the SOF has decided to hire investment banks as private intermediaries to sell off a selected group of sixty-four companies, which includes the national air carrier Tarom, the country's and Eastern Europe's biggest steel mill (Sidex), and the aluminium smelters Alro and Alpro … The privatization of Tarom is scheduled to be completed by March 2000 … So far two-thirds of the SOF's portfolio in

> terms of the number of companies and more than half in terms of share capital have been privatized. The SOF privatization offer this year [1999] includes 3,600 companies ... The methods of privatization range from auctions and direct negotiations with what the fund defines as 'strategic investors' to tenders on the local over-the-counter market, Rasdaq, and public offers on the Bucharest stock exchange. The SOF is scheduled to be dismantled in mid-2000, so its major privatization target should be achieved by then.
>
> (*IHT*, Survey, 26 October 1999, pp. 18–20)

The new privatization law, approved by parliament in June 1999, provides for the use of investment banks as sales agents, eliminates minimum sales prices linked to book value (thereby allowing sale at market value) and contains provisions for debt workouts. The new law also contains provisions giving minority shareholders the right to more information and control. 'These provisions aim to reduce the power of enterprise insiders, who have gained effective control of privatized enterprises in the majority of cases' (EBRD 1999b: 254–5).

'[In 1999] several indebted firms, including the Galati shipyard, were sold cheaply to reputable investors which are promising to inject some much needed investment' (Business Central Europe 1999: 37).

> One of the biggest problems is corruption, with a recent poll finding that, on average, businessmen spend 4 per cent of their earnings on bribes. Certainly, there is widespread suspicion about the antics of the state ownership fund, whose privatization decisions have sometimes been eccentric. The latest scandal concerns the sale of a relatively profitable company, Automatica, to a Greek company for just $600,000. In 1997 Sweden's ABB signed a contract to buy the same firm for $5.2 million, plus $3.5 million in investment. That contract was mysteriously cancelled and ABB did not bid again this year. While profitable companies are given away, loss-making giants like the Petromidia oil refinery do not even make the priority shortlist for privatization.
>
> (*Business Central Europe*, March 2000, p. 43)

August 2000:

> Romania's agriculture minister ignored advice from ABN Amro Corporate Finance, as independent privatization consultants for the sale of the state tobacco company, that recommended the business should be sold to an international consortium, according to a confidential analysis by the Dutch bank. The ministry is being sued by the consortium after its offer was rejected and Socieatea Nationala Tutunul Romanesc was sold to the Romanian company InterAgro, which is headed by Ioan Niculae, a former officer in the Securitate, the communist-era secret police ... The Bucharest appeal court ordered the cancellation of the privatization and the

> agriculture ministry has appealed against this decision to the supreme court, which is due to announce its ruling on 28 September.
>
> (*FT*, 14 August 2000, p. 6)

'Romania's supreme court has annulled a government decision to sell the state tobacco company [Socieatea Nationala Tutunul Romanesc] to a local company, InterAgro, following objections raised by an international consortium' (*FT*, 26 October 2000, p. 8).

'Scandals have accompanied nearly every [privatization] deal, leading to a spate of sales being investigated or cancelled' (Business Central Europe 2000: 40). 'Romania has cancelled several sales' (p. 53).

February 2001: 'Romania's new left-wing government launched the privatization of seventeen key companies' (*Business Central Europe*, March 2001, p. 12).

> When he became the new privatization supremo [Ovidiu] Musetescu formally declared himself a convert to the merits of privatization, but on the basis of an unusual definition of privatization. According to Musetescu, and later to new regulations, state property may now be privatized only if the new owner keeps the workforce intact, allows state intervention in decision-making and accepts that his corporate management is periodically assessed and approved by the government. At the same time Musetescu expressed a firm preference for Romanian capital as the new preferred preference of state industry. The so-called 'home capital' which the PDSR [Social Democracy Party of Romania] is so much in favour of is actually known in the press under a completely different name – the 'cardboard billionaires' – a name which designates the group of Romanian oligarchs, powerful former Securitate and Communist Party officials who creamed off the state's assets in the early 1990s. There is little to choose between the Russian oligarchs and their Romanian counterparts.
>
> (*EEN*, 2001, vol. 13, no. 3, p. 3)

'Privatized companies [are] usually being allocated to local apparatchiki masquerading as bona fide investors. Foreign investors are blocked from acquiring controlling interests in companies considered to be of strategic national value' (*EEN*, 2001, vol. 13, no. 5, p. 4).

16 April 2001:

> The Romanian government has announced the privatization of Banca Agricola, the first big sell-off by the newly-elected former communist administration. The bank has been bought in a $52 million deal by a consortium Raiffeisen Zentralbank, the Austrian Bank, and the Romanian–American Enterprise Fund. The consortium will pay $15 million to the Romanian government for a 98 per cent stake and inject $32 million for working capital. Banca Agricola had been used by successive governments to subsidize agriculture by giving farmers soft loans. Last year [2000]

the government put $150 million into the bank to cover losses ... The government ... [is to pay] around $30 million to cover the bank's losses for this year ... The government has also announced it is entering the final stage of the privatization of Sidex, the huge steel-making plant in eastern Romania.

(*FT*, 17 April 2001, p. 8)

Foreign trade

In February 1990 state and private enterprises were declared free to engage in foreign trade on their own. Most licensing requirements for exports and imports were eliminated in May 1992, leaving very few quantitative restrictions on imports (e.g. on arms and drugs). There are no duties on exports, although there are some export quotas (such as for certain raw materials and drugs, and, on occasion, agricultural products). Export licensing requirements have been reduced since June 1993. The tariff treatment of imports is fairly liberal (EBRD 1994: 33, 109). There are no duties on exports and the tariff treatment of non-agricultural imports is fairly liberal. But very high tariffs (on average about 110 per cent) remain in place for most agricultural products. In August 1996 a national oil company was established to unify oil import and export trading strategies and to keep control over the associated foreign currency transactions (EBRD 1996b: 168). All quantitative restrictions on exports were eliminated by 1998 and replaced with licensing requirements for monitoring purposes. However, a temporary surcharge of 6 per cent was introduced at the end of 1998. The rate has been reduced to 4 per cent and is scheduled to be eliminated by the end of 1999. In March 1999 Romania signed a declaration with Bulgaria and Turkey to establish free trade in industrial goods by 2002 (EBRD 1999b: 254).

Between 1990 and 1994 agricultural exports were prohibited in order to ensure that domestic demand could be met. But in 1995 permission was given to export certain quotas of farm produce (Deutsche Bank, *Focus: Eastern Europe*, 1995, no. 142, p. 2).

A series of devaluations of the Romanian currency (the leu, or lei) led to internal convertibility being announced in November 1991. A floating exchange rate regime was introduced on 8 April 1994, with the exchange rate determined on daily auctions. The leu is virtually fully convertible for the purpose of foreign trade transactions, but there are controls on capital account transactions (EBRD 1994: 33, 109). At the beginning of 1996, in an attempt to control the downward tendency of the leu, the authorities started to impose tight restrictions on enterprises' access to foreign currency and on the foreign currency operations of commercial banks. In March 1996 only four banks were permitted to participate in the interbank market for foreign exchange. None of the four were foreign banks and only one was private. In August 1996 new surrender requirements were announced for more than a hundred enterprises. These requirements have since been given a liberal interpretation but the decree remains in place (EBRD

1996b: 168). In mid-July 1996 an energy crisis led to the introduction of stringent foreign exchange controls (*FT*, 13 August 1996, p. 2). The government was 'trying to contain inflation by fixing the dollar exchange rate, so lowering the cost of dollar-denominated energy imports' (*Business Central Europe*, October 1996, p. 70).

The foreign exchange regime was liberalized on 18 February 1997 and both foreign and domestic banks were allowed to operate on the market (*FT*, 18 February 1997, p. 3). In February 1997 the restrictions on the foreign exchange market were removed by relicensing twenty-four banks that had applied for access to the interbank market (EBRD 1997a: 32). In February 1997 prime minister Ciorbea stated that:

> To promote trade and integration with Europe, we have ended controls on the foreign exchange needed for trade purposes, and we have allowed the lei to float freely in the exchange markets. We will also end the cumbersome system of export licensing and import quotas, and we will sharply reduce tariffs and other forms of protection.
>
> (*FT*, 18 February 1997, p. 20)

After unifying the exchange rate in early 1997, Romania introduced full current account convertibility in March 1998. The foreign exchange and Treasury bill markets were liberalized, but some restrictions remain on capital account transactions (EBRD 1998b: 184). While there are practically no restrictions on capital inflows, outflows by residents require prior approval of the central bank. Repatriation of earnings on direct and portfolio investments are guaranteed (EBRD 1999b: 254).

An association agreement with the EU was signed on 1 February 1993 (coming fully into effect on 1 February 1995), while a December 1992 trade agreement with EFTA was planned to be made effective as of 1 May 1993. The USA granted MFN status on 13 October 1993. On 12 April 1997 Romania became a member of the Central European Trade Agreement (effective 1 July 1997), joining the Czech Republic, Hungary, Poland, Slovakia and Slovenia. In 1994 more than half of exports went to EU and EFTA countries (Deutsche Bank, *Focus: Eastern Europe*, 1995, no. 129, p. 5). In 1994 the EU accounted for 47.1 per cent of exports (39.3 per cent in 1993) and 50.3 per cent of imports (42.1 per cent in 1993) (DIW, *Economic Bulletin*, 1995, vol. 32, no. 7, p. 18).

Foreign direct investment

Western direct investment is now welcomed, but early obstacles included the inability of foreigners to own land (except in the case where Romanian enterprises had majority foreign ownership and where the Romanian partners contributed the land as their share). According to *Business Europa* (August–September 1993, p. 10), an amendment rejected by parliament in late June 1993 would have allowed foreign companies participating in joint ventures with local firms or with Romanian subsidiaries to own real estate. The reluctance to allow foreign ownership of land may have been partly due to the fear of Hungarians buying up land in Transylvania, home to most of Romania's Hungarian minority (Mark Milner, *Guardian*, 24 July 1993, p. 35). Foreigners could lease but not own land (EBRD 1996b: 169).

> One important hurdle to foreign investment has been removed with the approval recently of a law allowing foreigners to own land. The single clause reads 'Commercial companies with partial or total foreign capital registered as legal Romanian entities may acquire, for their duration, right of ownership and all other title to land necessary for their activities.' Whether there is a substantial clash with the Romanian constitution, which forbids foreign ownership of land, is a little unclear.
>
> (*EEN*, 27 February 1997, vol. 11, no. 4, p. 4)

Net direct foreign investment was −$18 million in 1990, $37 million in 1991, $73 million in 1992, $87 million in 1993, $341 million in 1994 and $417 million in 1995 (United Nations Economic Commission for Europe 1996: 149). Direct foreign investment amounted to only $140 million in the period 1990–3 (EBRD 1994: 123). (See Table 6.2 for the annual figures for net direct foreign investment.)

'Even the big foreign investors seem to have had enough. South Korea's Daewoo is reconsidering its position in Romania after promised tax breaks were withdrawn' (*Business Central Europe*, March 2000, p. 42).

> The World Bank has said further loans to Romania will be made only on condition that the government does not discriminate against or give special concessions to individual foreign investors. The move follows the introduction of tax breaks and other exemptions for Renault, which last year [1999] bought 51 per cent of the state-owned Dacia plant, and the almost simultaneous removal of concessions for Daewoo two years before their agreement concerning the purchase of the Automobile Craiova factory was due to expire … As part of an initial $156 million investment in 1994 Daewoo was granted a seven-year tax concession on profits and did not have to pay VAT on components and machinery. Last year, with two years to run on the agreement, the Romanian government cancelled the concessions. Three weeks earlier a law was passed giving a concession to Renault as part of a $216 million investment in Dacia. The deal saw Renault receive a five-year tax exemption on profits and a three-year postponement on VAT payments. It also does not have to pay customs duties on some imported machinery.
>
> (*FT*, 14 April 2000, p. 12)

Table 6.2 Romania: selected economic indicators 1990–2000

Economic indicator	*1990*	*1991*	*1992*	*1993*	*1994*	*1995*	*1996*	*1997*	*1998*	*1999*	*2000 (estimate)*
Rate of growth of GDP (%)	-5.6	-12.9	-8.8	1.5	3.9	7.1	3.9	-6.1	-5.4	-3.2	1.6
Rate of growth of industrial output (%)	-23.7	-22.8	-21.9	1.3	3.3	9.5	9.8	-5.6	-17.3	-8.8	8.2
Rate of growth of agricultural output (%)	-2.9	0.8	-13.3	12.9	0.2	4.5	1.3	3.4	-7.6	5.5	-15.8
Inflation rate (consumer, %)	5.1	170.2	210.4	256.1	136.7	32.3	38.8	154.8	59.1	45.8	45.7
Budget surplus or deficit (% GDP)[a]	1.2	0.6	-4.6	-0.4	-2.2	-2.5	-3.9	-4.6	-5.0	-3.5	-3.7
Unemployment rate (end of year, %)[b]	0.0	3.1	8.2	10.4	10.1	8.2	6.6	8.9	10.3	11.8	10.5
Balance of payments (current account, $ billion)	-1.650	-1.370	-1.564	-1.174	-0.428	-1.774	-2.584	-2.137	-2.917	-1.308	-1.500
Foreign direct investment (net, $ billion)	-0.018	0.037	0.073	0.087	0.341	0.417	0.415	1.267	2.079	1.070	1.000
Population (million)			22.8	22.8	22.7	22.7	22.6	22.6	22.5	22.5	22.3

Sources: Various issues of European Bank for Reconstruction and Development, *Transition Report*; United Nations Economic Commission for Europe, *Economic Survey of Europe*; United Nations, *World Economic and Social Survey*; IMF, *World Economic Outlook*.

Notes:

[a] General government balance (EBRD)

[b] Registered unemployment

Agriculture

In agriculture one of the first steps was to scrap the systematization programme (on 26 December 1989). Various restrictions were placed on food exports to improve the domestic supply. A land law was passed in February 1991, some 80 per cent of arable land being eligible for return to former owners or their heirs (*EEN*, 'Romania', 20 August 1991, p. 4). Others eligible for land include members who have worked in co-operatives for at least three years. The land received from the state was limited to a maximum of 10 ha, although up to 100 ha was allowed through purchase or inheritance.

> In Romania, Hungary and former Czechoslovakia current land restitution is (explicitly) not based on the 1945 ownership situation, but the ownership strongly influenced by the post-World War II (between 1945 and 1949) land reforms implemented by a government dominated by the Communist Party … The Czech government decided to use the February 1948 date as the basis for restitution. Similarly, Hungary took 1948 and Romania took 1947 as their reference dates … Collective farmland is [thus] restituted to former owners, but state farmland is privatized through different procedures. A reason is the difference in legal ownership: state farms operated mainly on land legally owned by the state. In some cases that farmland was state-owned before 1940; in other cases it was nationalized after the war (taken from foreigners or from the church).
>
> (Swinnen 1999: 642–3)

'Foreign former landowners have not been restituted land' (p. 646).

> In Romania two thirds of the state farmland is in 'new' areas, i.e. land that was created for agricultural use under the communist regime by land improvements and drainage investments in the Danube Valley. This land is not privatized yet … in contrast to the rest of Romania's farmland.
>
> (p. 652)

Co-operatives were dissolved in 1991, while state farms have been transformed into state commercial companies (Frydman *et al.* 1993: 231).

The private sector quickly came to dominate Romanian agriculture. Over 80 per cent of the area farmed had been privatized by the end of 1992 (United Nations Economic Commission for Europe 1993: 223). The ministry of agriculture says that over 90 per cent of land due to be given back is in private hands (*Business Central Europe*, July–August 1994, p. 15). About 80 per cent of agricultural land has been restored to its former owners and their heirs (*EEN*, 10 August 1995, vol. 9, no. 16, p. 5). Over 80 per cent of agricultural output is produced by the private sector (agriculture employs 40 per cent of the workforce) (*EEN*, Country Survey, 15 December 1995, p. 4). About 85 per cent of agricultural land is now private, employing 35 per cent of the active workforce and accounting for 25 per cent of GDP. The 700-odd state farms account for about

12 per cent of agricultural land and roughly the same percentage of output (*EEN*, 31 May 1996, vol. 10, no. 11, pp. 4–5). In 1995 the private sector accounted for 89 per cent of the value-added in agriculture. The privatization of state farms has proceeded relatively slowly, especially since the government has decided to preserve them as unified production units (EBRD 1996b: 167). On 29 March 1994 parliament approved a law introducing a tax on individual land ownership, specifically a tax on estimates of production from the land (implemented on 1 July 1994); agricultural companies such as state farms would continue to pay tax on profits (p. 3). In 1995 state farms and companies accounted for only 13 per cent of agricultural production (*FT*, 11 July 1996, p. 31).

Chrystia Freeland described the initial situation in agriculture after 1989 as an anarchic free-for-all, formalized by the 1991 land reform. The sale of newly privatized rural properties was banned for ten years, but larger farms were being created through leasing. Peasants accounted for 45 per cent of the population (*FT*, Survey, 3 May 1994, p. 32). A number of problems still afflict agriculture:

1 The small size of many farms. Nearly 80 per cent of arable land has been split into too small parcels: a recent survey shows that a quarter of all landholders have a hectare or less of land, 38 per cent have 1–3 ha and 20 per cent have 3–5 ha (Deutsche Bank, *Focus: Eastern Europe*, 17 June 1993, no. 81, pp. 4, 13). Ronnas (1996: 30) cites a 1992 survey which puts the average holding at 2.5 ha. Most farmland has been returned but the average amount is just 2.2 ha, often split into three or four parcels of land (*FT*, 11 July 1996, p. 31). The average farm size is a little over 3 ha; 60 per cent of all farms are 3 ha or less (*EEN*, 25 August 1997, vol. 11, no. 16, p. 5). Private farms are extremely small, with an average size of under 3 ha (*IHT*, Survey, 26 October 1999, p. 21).

2 The delay in granting farmers full title to their land. As deeds of ownership were not handed out in time the farmers were virtually unable to raise credit for the purchase of inputs (Deutsche Bank, *Focus: Eastern Europe*, 17 June 1993, no. 81, p. 4). Only around 5 per cent of new landowners have received full title to their land (*Business Central Europe*, November 1993, p. 15). Fewer than a fifth of farmers have received full titles to the property returned to them (although the private sector now accounts for around 80 per cent of agricultural output) (*FT*, 2 February 1994, p. 2). Although most agricultural land is now worked by private farmers, only 15 per cent of the 5.1 million private landowners have received full titles (*FT*, 30 March 1994, p. 3). Farmers' groups claim that by mid-June 1994 only 24 per cent of landowners had received full legal title to their property (*Business Central Europe*, July–August 1994, p. 15). Around 60 per cent of farmers are still in possession of only provisional property deeds (DIW, *Economic Bulletin*, July 1995, vol. 32, no. 7, p. 22). At least 65 per cent of the so-called 'owners' have not yet received definitive title deeds (*EEN*, 10 August 1995, vol. 9, no. 16, p. 5). Fewer than 50 per cent of definitive property title deeds have been

issued to the estimated 6 million landowners under the terms of the 1991 law (*EEN*, Country Survey, 15 December 1995, p. 4). By the end of 1996 only 65 per cent of definitive title deeds had been issued (*EEN*, 1997, vol. 11, no. 16, p. 5). More than 90 per cent of the new landowners have received 'temporary property certificates' (EBRD 1995b: 54). Only around 65 per cent of titles have been handed out so far but almost all have received preliminary papers (*FT*, 11 July 1996, p. 31). 'A significant minority is still without full property titles' (*FT*, Survey, 28 September 1998, p. iv).

Amendments to the land laws mean that land can now be used as collateral for bank loans (*Business Central Europe*, July–August 1997, p. 40).

3 Romania has found itself with a large number of small farms but without the infrastructure necessary to support them. Of the countries of Eastern Europe only Romania has seen the widespread formation of new co-operative arrangements. New private farmers have been encouraged to join associations. These are loosely organized 'family associations' and more formally structured associations that are legally registered (Cochrane 1993: 851–3). An important advantage of associations is input supply, especially machinery services for mechanized grain farming (Brooks and Meurs 1994: 28–30). There are 6.5 million landowners (a quarter of the population). Many of them are not actually farmers and quite a number have joined together in 3,500 legally constituted associations which now control about 20 per cent of arable land. Landowners who do not have definitive title to their land (40 per cent of the total) and who are not members of associations cannot obtain bank loans because they have no security to offer (*EEN*, 31 May 1996, vol. 10, no. 11, pp. 4–5).

4 'This year's wheat harvest of 3.3 million tonnes is the lowest since WWII … The 1.1 billion lei of credit for the 1995 planting season was not released until last spring, by which time a further 1.1 billion lei credit line had to be made available. About 75 per cent of the credits go to the state agricultural farms despite the fact that state farms account for only 10 per cent of farming land. Private farms are refusing to sell cereals to the National Agency for Agricultural Produce because the offered price does not cover production costs. Only the state farms and the relatively small number of private farmers and companies who have taken out state-subsidized loans and who are consequently obliged to sell part of their output to the state are now delivering to the agency. (There are 627 state farms accounting for 1.3 million ha, 4,000 agricultural companies accounting for 1.8 million ha, 13,800 family farms accounting for 1.5 million ha, and 3.5 million private farmers accounting for 8.4 million ha.)' (*EEN*, 1996, vol. 10, no. 17, p. 4).

Almost 85 per cent of arable land is now in the hands of private farmers.

> Fierce political disputes have raged over whether to restore, privatize, rent or lease the remaining land – managed by 517 state-owned cereal farms – and decisions have been repeatedly postponed. The negative impact of these

farms is far greater than the area of land they take up would suggest. One of the most harmful effects they have had is in distorting the agricultural credit system, since these farms are willing to borrow at any rate. Until recently reforms have been very slow in all areas relating to farming, other than land reform. The grain trade, for example, has been seized by heirs of the centralized, monopolistic structures that dominated communist-era agriculture. Their influence and the lack of a properly functioning land market have taken their toll on Romanian agriculture ... [Private farms] lack appropriate machinery and working capital.

(*IHT*, Survey, 26 October 1999, p. 21)

According to a survey in *The Times*, the government has split up Romcereal, which controlled the prices, storage and distribution of many agricultural products, into more than forty regional entities (29 August 1996, p. 17). The greater part of agricultural equipment has remained in the hands of state farms. The government intends to privatize, break up or liquidate these.

One of the most difficult inheritances from communism has been the system of centralized and monopolized collection and marketing. Breaking this up without disrupting the whole agricultural process is proving extremely difficult. The old collection monopoly, Romcereal, has been divided up into forty-one joint stock companies, which the government plans to privatize by the end of 1998.

(Anatol Lieven, *FT*, Survey, 25 June 1997, p. ii)

The lack of reform is also reflected in the fact that the former state monopoly Romcereal was not divided into forty-one district companies and a national grain agency until 1996. Although the national grain agency was itself divided in 1997 to create further competition, the district storage companies still operate a monopoly and account for the bulk of grain storage.

The privatization of state grain silos would aid the development of competition and improved services to private farmers. However, this has not been pursued by the Romanian government ... The government silos tend to charge farmers rent for grain storage rather than the Western practice of buying grain.

(Davis and Gaburici 1998: 44–5)

On 16 September 1997 the Senate amended the 1991 law on land restitution without specifying how much land could be restored to former owners. Parliament would decide the limits on restituted land by 31 March 1998. Under the 1991 law a maximum of 10 ha of farmland and 1 ha of forestland could be restituted per family (*Transition*, 1997, vol. 8, no. 5, p. 24).

> After months of wrangling the Romanian government hopes to agree soon on a new formula for the restitution of agricultural land … The agriculture minister believes the country's multi-party coalition will now accept legislation allowing the return of up to 50 ha of land per former owner and providing for financial compensation where this was not possible.
>
> (*FT*, 9 September 1998, p. 48)

The 10 January 2000 law permits property restitution of up to 50 ha of arable land and 10 ha of woodland (*EEN*, 2000, vol. 12, no. 22, p. 3).

On 9 November 1999 the upper house passed a bill granting the return of some farmland seized during the communist era. The bill provided for the restitution to the original owners of as much as 50 ha of farmland confiscated in the 1950s. A commission of parliament is expected to mediate issues related to the restitution of forest land that was confiscated, which was also voted on (*IHT*, 10 November 1999, p. 6). Families whose land cannot be returned will receive compensation (*The Times*, 10 November 1999, p. 18).

In 1996 the private sector share in agricultural output was estimated at 87 per cent. Some 83 per cent of all agricultural land is in private hands. Livestock farming has been largely excluded from privatization. There are still large state production units, especially in livestock farming. By mid-1997 eleven large livestock farms had been liquidated (EBRD 1997b: 193). 'Until 1997 the sector [agriculture] was characterized by strong state intervention and a non-functioning land market. Since April 1998 a new law has facilitated the transfer of agricultural land by accelerating restitution and clarifying ownership rights' (EBRD 1998b: 184).

Private ownership now accounts for 72 per cent of total farmland (*FT*, Survey, 28 September 1998, p. iv).

> Structural reforms have advanced at a quicker pace in agriculture than in the rest of the economy … Import taxes have been cut to a maximum of 45 per cent – down from levels that in some cases reached 300 per cent … Almost all 115 large, state-owned pig and poultry farms – most of which were in poor financial shape – have been either privatized or liquidated. The former state monopoly in charge of storing and treating grain was dismantled into some sixty regional units; most of them have been privatized. Agricultural service providers and seed farms have also been privatized or liquidated … [The agriculture minister] is bullish about the privatization of the state-owned cereal farms by the end of the year [1999] … The powers that be seem to be reaching agreement on the issue of ownership rights of land and forests. Chances are that this issue – debated for almost a decade – will be solved before the end of the year.
>
> (*IHT*, Survey, 26 October 1999, p. 21)

> A radical alteration of the structure of property in Romanian agriculture will begin in the coming weeks, following the passage of two new laws, one

> concerning the privatization of state-owned farms and another the restitution of land and forests confiscated by the communists. Agricultural land in Romania will be 92 per cent private.
>
> (p. 19)

'Last year [2000] less than a quarter of the 737 state-owned farms slated for privatization were actually sold' (*Business Central Europe*, April 2001, p. 33).

> [Since 1989] the co-operative farms have been completely transformed into either 'agricultural societies' (ASs), 'farmers' associations' (FAs) or individual farms. 'Agricultural societies' are legal entities that employ both members and non-member workers. 'Farmers' associations' are managed by their members but have no legal status. Land used by co-operatives was partly distributed among co-operative members and partly restituted to former owners, mostly rural households. Many other co-operative farm assets were subject to 'spontaneous privatization' when many co-operatives were spontaneously broken up by members in 1991. In contrast, privatization of state farms has been lagging behind and by 1997 was still largely incomplete … In 1992 around 1.5 million households, out of 5.3 million that benefited from land restitution or distribution, had decided to allocate at least part of their resources to one of approximately 4,000 ASs or 11,500 FAs. By 1997 the number of ASs had fallen to 3,875. They had an average size of 451 ha and occupied 11.8 per cent of total agricultural land. FAs increased in number up to 12,089 in 1997. They were smaller compared to ASs (on average 103 ha) and occupied 8.4 per cent of total agricultural land.
>
> (Rizov *et al.* 2001: 1261)

In 1997 individual farms accounted for 58.6 per cent of total agricultural land, commercial companies (former state farms) for 12.0 per cent and other institutions (land belonging to agricultural research networks and local councils being included here) for 9.2 per cent (p. 1260).

Economic performance

GDP growth turned positive as early as 1993 but output once again fell sharply in three successive years (1997 to 1999). (See Table 6.2.) 'Romania remained mired in a recession, with GDP falling by 3.2 per cent in 1999' (EBRD 2000a: 5). Positive growth was recorded in 2000. In 2000 GDP was an estimated 76 per cent of the 1989 level (EBRD 2001: 15). Romania has never experienced anywhere near hyperinflation but progress on the inflation front has nevertheless been slow. In 1997 the rate rose to 154.8 per cent and was not far off 50 per cent even in 2000.

'Romania has the highest proportion of people in Europe below the official poverty line, outside the former Soviet Union. Some 40 per cent of its 22 million inhabitants can barely afford to feed themselves, according to the World Bank' (*FT*, 9 February 2001, p. 8).

'Eleven years of inconsistent reforms ... have left around 40 per cent of Romanians below the poverty line' (*Business Central Europe*, February 2001, p. 38).

On 17 April 1996 Romania opened its first nuclear plant and the only one in the former Eastern bloc built with Western (Canadian) technology. Romania imports around half its primary energy requirements. The nuclear reactor was to meet around 8 per cent of electricity demand eventually and was planned to begin supplying the national grid later in 1996. The plant is to have five reactors in total and the second one (40 per cent completed) was planned to be operational around the year 2000. Work on the plant started in 1979 and was scheduled for completion in the 1980s. But work was halted in 1990 and restarted in 1991 (*FT*, 17 April 1996, p. 5).

7 Slovakia

POLITICS

The ethnic Hungarian minority and Slovakia's relations with Hungary

On the international front the controversy over the Gabcikovo Dam on the Danube continues to sour relations with Hungary. (The dam is also in an area of Slovakia where Hungarians predominate.) Hungary and Czechoslovakia had jointly signed an agreement in 1977, but Hungary stopped work on the scheme in 1989 after a powerful campaign by environmentalists and formally withdrew in May 1992. On 24 October 1992 the Slovak government (the Czechs wanted a delay) went ahead with the plan to divert water from the Danube as part of the hydro-electric power scheme. Hungary complained that the diversion also violated the international border. The EC intervened and a temporary deal was made regarding work on the power plant and the amount of water diverted. In April 1993 Hungary agreed to refer the dispute to the International Court of Justice at The Hague. The verdict was delivered on 25 September 1997.

> The court has concluded that both parties committed internationally wrongful acts … Hungary and Slovakia must negotiate in good faith … and must take all the necessary measures to achieve the objectives of the 1977 treaty … The issue of compensation could satisfactorily be resolved in the framework of an overall settlement, if each of the parties were to renounce or cancel all financial claims.

The court ruled that both countries should operate the dam jointly (with Hungary paying part of the building and operating costs) and take environmental considerations into account. (The dam accounts for around 10 per cent of Slovakia's electricity generation: *FT*, 26 September 1997, p. 2.) On 6 February 1998 Hungary announced that it was to build a new dam to support Slovakia's Gabcikovo. But on 3 September 1998 the Slovak government announced that it had decided to return the dispute to the International Court of Justice at The Hague. Slovakia claimed that Hungary was not complying with the court's verdict (*EEN*, 1998, vol. 12, no. 10, p. 9). The new government in Hungary appeared to have ruled out building a complementary dam (*FT*, 4 September 1998, p. 2).

On 8 January 1994 the leaders of the Hungarian minority met at Komarno. Before the meeting there had been speculation that there might be calls for a self-governing province, but the actual declaration was very moderate. The government's proposed revamping of regional boundaries was strongly opposed, since the Hungarians would be in a minority in all cases. Instead, the Komarno declaration suggested maintaining a Hungarian majority in areas where historically this has been the case. The eight-point programme included a call for broad autonomy at local government level and in cultural affairs.

In August 1993 a ban was imposed on the use of Hungarian on road signs. On 3 June 1994 a draft law allowing bilingual roadsigns for villages with over 20 per cent Hungarian population was defeated in parliament by one vote. Those voting against were not only Slovak nationalists, but also ethnic Hungarian MPs objecting to the exclusion of villages bearing the names of Slovak heroes. The roadsigns bill was finally passed on 8 July 1994, with 76 for, 49 against and 6 abstentions.

In August 1993 a ban was imposed on the use of non-Slovak Christian names on official documents. In mid-May 1994 a law was passed allowing Hungarian women to use their names on official documents without adding the Slovak '-ova' ending.

On 19 March 1995 Slovakia and Hungary signed, as part of the European Stability Pact, an agreement guaranteeing borders and minority rights. (The Basic Treaty was ratified by the Hungarian parliament in the summer of 1995 and by the Slovak parliament on 26 March 1996.)

On 22 April 1995 around 6,000 ethnic Hungarians held a rally in Komarno. The protest was led by teachers protesting against the Slovak government's plan to introduce bilingual education at schools in ethnic Hungarian areas, i.e. Slovak-language education in ethnic Hungarian schools would become compulsory (*EEN*, 1995, vol. 9, no. 9, p. 4). On 15 November 1995 parliament passed a new language law (signed by the president on 28 November). Slovak was to be the only official language. (On 27 September 1996 the Slovak language was officially designated (by a majority of one vote) as the only language permissible in parliament: *EEN*, 1996, vol. 10, no. 20, p. 9. In October 1996 parliament approved an amendment to the law on higher education, reinstating the powers the education ministry had prior to 1989. This and other measures taken by the government led to mass protests. The biggest demonstration was held in Bratislava on 14 November, under the banner 'Let us save Slovakia': *EEN*, 1996, vol. 10, no. 24, p. 3.)

On 22 March 1996 parliament approved the redrawing of internal boundaries to give eight regions and eighty districts (to take effect as of 1 July 1996). According to *EEN* (1996, vol. 10, no. 7, p. 8), this would dilute the ethnic Hungarian vote, since Slovaks would outnumber Hungarians in every region despite the concentration of the 600,000 Hungarians in the southern regions bordering Hungary.

On 26 February 1997 ethnic Hungarians resigned from the Council for Ethnic Minorities on the grounds that the ruling coalition parties had outvoted the minority representatives on all substantive issues (*EEN*, 1997, vol. 11, no. 5, p. 7).

In June 1997 the education ministry cancelled bilingual certificates in schools where Hungarian is the language of instruction on the grounds that the state language law had been contravened. The government replaced the bilingual certificates with ones issued only in the Slovak language (*EEN*, 1997, vol. 11, no. 24, pp. 1–2).

On 2 September 1997 Meciar publicly suggested that ethnic Hungarians might be transferred voluntarily to Hungary. On 20 September Hungary, as a protest, cancelled a scheduled meeting between the Hungarian and Slovak foreign ministers (*EEN*, 1997, vol. 11, no. 18, p. 7). Meciar suggested that Slovakia and Hungary should swap ethnic minorities (*Business Central Europe*, October 1997, p. 17). In August 1997 he had suggested to Hungarian prime minister Gyula Horn that the swap take place but this was not revealed at the time. Horn rejected the idea. On 1 October 1997 Meciar said that minorities living on the border interfered with the 'territorial integrity of Slovakia'. 'We do not want a repeat of the game of 1938–9,' he said, referring to the time when Hungary gained territory at the expense of Czechoslovakia (Jane Perlez, *IHT*, 13 October 1997, p. 6).

> Hungary accuses Slovakia's government … of failing to honour a 1995 friendship treaty. Hungary is annoyed by Slovakia's failure to pass laws that would grant the 570,000 Hungarians who live in Slovakia – about 11 per cent of the population – the right to use their mother tongue for official business. On the contrary, the Slovak education ministry this year banned the writing of school reports in Hungarian.
>
> (*The Economist*, 13 September 1997, p. 52)

At Hungarian Co-existence's congress, held on 13 June 1998, the party (led by Miklos Duray) voted in favour of merging with the new Hungarian Coalition composed of the Hungarian Civic Party and the Hungarian Christian Democratic Movement. At Hungarian Coalition's inaugural congress, held on 21 June, Bela Bugar was elected chairman and Miklos Duray was elected deputy chairman (*EEN*, 1998, vol. 12, no. 7, p. 9).

On 10 July 1999 parliament approved a bill allowing for the limited use of minority languages in affairs of state (i.e. Hungarian, principally). President Rudolf Schuster signed the law on 20 July (*EEN*, 1999, vol. 12, vol. 19, pp. 4–5).

On 24 August 1999 President Rudolf Schuster said that he would not call referendums on a language law and privatization since neither met constitutional guidelines for plebiscites. In July 1999 he had been given a petition with nearly 447,000 signatures seeking referendums on whether to rescind a law giving the half-million ethnic Hungarian Slovaks expanded use of their language in official dealings. The petition also called for a separate referendum calling for a ban on the privatization of state enterprises (*IHT*, 25 August 1999, p. 6).

A Hungarian consulate opened on 18 August 2000 in Kosice (*EEN*, 2000, vol. 12, no. 24, p. 6).

'Parliament passes [on 23 February 2001] constitutional amendments (administrative reform, minority rights etc.) as a prerequisite for EU accession negotiations' (*EEN*, 2001, vol. 13, no. 3, p. 5).

> A constitutional amendment passed last month [February] ... paves the way for regional reform and hence for Slovakia's EU membership ... The amendment is almost as important as the actual passing of Slovakia's constitution, back in 1992. It lays the framework for devolving power to some twelve to fourteen new regions ... It was a huge achievement for the splintered government to get it past parliament ... Constitutional changes require a two-thirds majority ... Controversial concessions [were made] to the Hungarian Coalition Party, a junior coalition party. Under the old regional scheme established in 1996, Slovak Hungarians were in the majority in just two of seventy-nine regions. Now they will form 40 per cent of the population in a far larger region around the southern town of Komarno.
>
> (*Business Central Europe*, March 2001, pp. 40–1)

Gypsies (Roma)

'Today nearly 10 per cent of Slovakia's 5 million people are Roma, yet they are largely excluded from the mainstream of normal life' (Steven Erlanger, *IHT*, 3 April 2000, p. 6).

> The last published census of 1991 suggests that officially they make up 1.6 per cent of the population, but this figure is thought to underestimate the population substantially. Simply put Roma were so scared of discrimination they marked themselves as Slovak ... The ministry of development and minority affairs ... puts a more realistic figure at around 8 per cent ... Education is one of the key focuses of the government. They have started a 'zero year' programme so that Roma children can go to pre-school for a year and learn basic Slovak, hygiene and socialization.
>
> (Lucy Smy, *FT*, Survey, 4 July 2001, p. ii)

The general election of 30 September–1 October 1994

Eighteen parties competed for the 150 seats on a proportional representation basis via party lists (with a 5 per cent threshold). The turnout was 74.6 per cent. Seven parties made it to parliament.

The Movement for a Democratic Slovakia won a surprisingly high percentage of the vote. (See Table 7.1.) Meciar's campaign platform, however, was entirely predictable, stressing nationalism and promising a slower transition and improved economic conditions (such as more jobs, lower prices and increased pensions). Meciar spoke against the current voucher privatization programme, alleging that control of state assets would go to 'anonymous persons' and that foreign capital might 'buy out' the country. Instead he favoured existing management and workers and giving Slovaks first refusal on sales. (He also wished to prevent the privatization of utilities and the defence sector: Deutsche Bank, *Focus: Eastern Europe*, 1994, no. 120, p. 5.)

Table 7.1 Slovakia: the general election of 30 September–1 October 1994

Party	*Seats*	*% vote*[a]
Movement for a Democratic Slovakia	61	34.96
Common Choice	18	10.41
Hungarian Coalition	17	10.18
Christian Democratic Movement	17	10.08
Democratic Union of Slovakia	15	8.57
Association of Slovak Workers	13	7.34
Slovak National Party	9	5.40
Total	150	

Note:
[a] There is a 5 per cent threshold for parliamentary representation

Common Choice won a surprisingly small percentage of the vote.

The main parties were as follows:

Movement for a Democratic Slovakia: led by Vladimir Meciar.

Common Choice: a coalition of four left-wing parties, the foremost being Peter Weiss's Party of the Democratic Left (the others were the Social Democratic Party of Slovakia, the Green Party and the Slovak Farmers' Party).

Christian Democratic Movement: led by Jan Carnogursky.

Democratic Union of Slovakia (Deus): led by Jozef Moravcik.

National Democratic Party: led by Ludovit Cernak.

Association of Slovak Workers: led by Jan Luptak. Communist.

Slovak National Party: led by Jan Slota. Extreme nationalist.

Alliance of Democrats: led by Milan Knazko.

Hungarian Coalition: a coalition of three ethnic Hungarian parties (the Hungarian Christian Democrats, the Hungarian Civic Party and Co-existence; Co-existence is led by Miklos Duray).

Political developments after the 1994 general election

4 November 1994: Meciar supporters become chairmen of parliamentary committees and win key positions in the areas of privatization (chairman of the

National Property Fund), state radio and television (heads of councils) and the intelligence service.

Prime minister Jozef Moravcik tenders his resignation, but agrees to head a caretaker government until a new one is formed.

18–19 November 1994: in local elections the Movement for a Democratic Slovakia wins 22.8 per cent of the vote.

11 December 1994: a coalition government is formed, with the Movement for a Democratic Slovakia contributing twelve ministers, the Association of Slovak Workers four and the Slovak National Party two.

13 December 1994: Meciar becomes prime minister for the third time. The ministers include the following: economics, Jan Ducky; finance, Sergei Kozlik; privatization, Peter Bisak (Association of Slovak Workers, a party generally anti-privatization); defence, Jan Sitek (Slovak National Party); education, Eva Slavkovska (Slovak National Party).

1 February 1995: the EU association agreement comes fully into effect.

19 March 1995: Slovakia and Hungary sign, as part of the European Stability Pact, an agreement guaranteeing borders and minority rights.

In March 1995 Slovakia granted visa-free travel rights to Russian citizens (Business Central Europe 1995: 9). According to *The Economist* (Survey, 18 November 1995, p. 21), allowing Russians to visit Slovakia without visas represents 'the only such arrangement in the old Eastern bloc'.

25 October 1995: four EU ambassadors in Bratislava relay their 'serious concerns' about the future of democracy in Slovakia. Their sentiments are echoed by the US ambassador. (A resolution of the European parliament expressed 'grave concern' at policies which 'show insufficient respect for democracy, human and minority rights and the rule of law': *The Economist*, 2 December 1995, p. 45.)

26 March 1996: parliament ratifies the Law on the Protection of the Republic by 77 votes to 57. Slovak citizens could face two years' imprisonment if found guilty of 'disseminating false information abroad damaging to the interests of the republic'. Organizers of 'subversive' public rallies could also face jail sentences, i.e. those judged to be subverting the constitutional system, territorial integrity or defence capability of the country.

(But President Kovac refused to sign the law and sent it back to parliament for reconsideration. The president described the law as 'undemocratic and disturbing'. He argued that it contradicted the constitution and European agreements on human rights and it would prejudice the country's bid to join the EU: *Guardian*, 12 April 1996, p. 13. The new draft omitted a clause that would have made spreading false information abroad punishable. This was passed by parliament on 17 December 1996 by 66 votes to 5, with 6 abstentions. Members of all opposition parties had walked out in protest before the vote was taken: *IHT*, 18 December 1996, p. 5.)

April 1996: the leader of the Party of the Democratic Left, Peter Weiss, is replaced by Jozef Migas (*EEN*, 2 May 1996, vol. 10, no. 9, p. 9).

June 1996: the Law on Foundations is approved by parliament. The registration of foundations is the preserve of the interior ministry rather than independent courts, the government is empowered to regulate the internal administration of foundations and every foundation has to place 100,000 crowns (about $3,300) in a bank deposit within six months of registering (*EEN*, 1996, vol. 10, no. 24, p. 2).

1 July 1996: the four existing regions are replaced by eight new ones centred on the largest cities. These are divided into a total of seventy-nine districts.

> To strengthen the party's hand ... many key offices in the new district and regional governments will be filled by appointees rather than elected officials. Education and planning, for example, will be in the hands of officials put in place by the government, with HZDS appointees naturally filling the bulk of these jobs ... The prime minister boasts that HZDS appeals across ethnic and class lines, but its performance at elections disproves this claim. Its power base is central Slovakia, and it has little support in either Bratislava or Kosice, the two largest cities, or in the south.
>
> (Vincent Boland, *FT*, Survey, 23 October 1996, p. ii)

27 August 1996: economics minister Jan Ducky is replaced by Karol Cesnak (the director of the state electricity company), foreign minister Juraj Schenk is replaced by Pavel Hamzik (ambassador to Germany) and interior minister Milan Hudek is replaced by Gustav Krajci.

27 September 1996: the Slovak language is officially designated (by a majority of one vote) as the only language permissible in parliament (*EEN*, 1996, vol. 10, no. 20, p. 9).

October 1996: parliament approves an amendment to the law on higher education, reinstating the powers the education ministry had prior to 1989. This and other measures taken by the government has led to mass protests. The biggest demonstration was held in Bratislava on 14 November, under the banner 'Let us save Slovakia' (*EEN*, 1996, vol. 10, no. 24, p. 3).

December 1996: President Kovac accuses Meciar's government of 'violence, physical liquidation, setting off bombs, making threats, spreading fear, causing the moral decay of our public life, corrupting and criminalizing all sorts of state organs as well as political life, misusing police and prosecutors, controlling the state media and manipulating public opinion'. This statement followed an incident in December in which the house of Frantisek Gaulieder, who was unhurt, was bombed. Gaulieder, a founding member of the Movement for a Democratic Slovakia, had just resigned from the party on the grounds that it was 'striving to seize power in order to dominate society at the whim of Meciar'. A former policeman, Robert Remias, was killed in spring 1996. He had been a contact for journalists investigating the kidnapping, in 1995, of the president's son (who was found in Austria). Kovac accused the secret police of the abduction. 'Police investigations of both the kidnapping of Mr Kovac's son and the death of the policeman have, no less predictably, fizzled out' (*The Economist*, 21 December 1996, p. 44).

13 January 1997: a new civil rights group called Charter 97 is formed (*EEN*, 1997, vol. 11, no. 2, p. 10).

8 April 1997: Slovakia recalls its ambassador to Prague for consultations. (Meciar called off his planned meeting in Prague with Czech prime minister Klaus after Czech president Havel had called on Nato to clarify its decisions over new members so that 'it is clearly understood that nobody was being discriminated against, as Mr Meciar thinks with his customary paranoia': *IHT*, 14 April 1997, p. 7.)

28 April 1997: the Slovak ambassador to the Czech Republic returns to his post.

28–30 April 1997: Russian prime minister Chernomyrdin pays a visit.

23–4 May 1997: a referendum on Nato membership and the election of the president is declared invalid by the independent referendum commission (which refers the issue to the courts).

There were three questions on Nato membership: (1) 'Are you in favour of Slovakia's membership of Nato?' (2) 'Are you in favour of the siting of nuclear weapons in Slovakia?' (3) 'Are you in favour of [foreign] military bases on Slovak territory?' (Note that Nato does not make the last two conditions for membership.) But it was the government's attempt to remove the fourth question that caused the trouble, namely the direct election of the president by popular vote. ('Are you in favour of the direct election of the president of Slovakia in accordance with the attached draft law?' At present the president has to be elected by at least 60 per cent of members of parliament or else the prime minister assumes the powers of the president.) On 14 May the constitutional court had ruled against the government's request. On 23 May the electoral commission declared that only ballot slips with four questions were valid. Some polling stations had no ballot slips at all. The turnout was only 9.53 per cent (compared with the minimum 50 per cent required).

26 May 1997: the foreign minister resigns as a protest against the government's actions over the referendum.

24 June 1997: the Blue Coalition electoral alliance is formed by the Christian Democratic Movement, the Democratic Union, the Democratic Party, the Hungarian Coalition (comprising the three Hungarian parties), the Social Democratic Party of Slovakia and the Green Party (*EEN*, 1997, vol. 11, no. 13, pp. 7–8). The Blue Coalition has become more formally known as the Slovak Democratic Coalition (*EEN*, 1997, vol. 11, no. 15, pp. 5–6). The coalition has five leaders but one spokesman.

8 July 1997: the Czech Republic (but not Slovakia) is invited 'to begin accession talks with Nato'.

16 July 1997: the European Commission recommends that the Czech Republic (but not Slovakia) opens negotiations in early 1998 for entry to the EU.

> The Commission concludes that Slovakia does not fulfil in a satisfying manner the political conditions set by the European Council in Copenhagen

> because of the instability of Slovakia's institutions, their lack of rootedness in political life and the shortcomings in the functioning of its democracy.

('Slovakia ... has been singled out from the ten applicants from East Europe for EU membership as the only one to have failed to satisfy the political criteria rather than the economic conditions for membership': *FT*, Survey, 28 October 1997, p. 19. Slovakia, Latvia, Lithuania, Bulgaria and Romania were to be given special EU aid to help them meet the conditions necessary for membership negotiations to begin.)

3 September 1997: Meciar announces that the presidential election is to be brought forward from February 1998 to December 1997 (*EEN*, 1997, vol. 11, no. 17, p. 8).

30 September 1997: the governing coalition parties refuse an opposition request that Frantisek Gaulieder be reinstated as an MP (*EEN*, 1997, vol. 11, no. 19, p. 7). Parliament votes to ignore a constitutional court ruling ordering the reinstatement of elected member Frantisek Gaulieder (*IHT*, 7 October 1997, p. 5). (See entry for December 1996.)

6 October 1997: the EU presidency issues a statement: 'The European Union expresses regret at the Slovak parliament's decision of 30 September.'

3 December 1997: Meciar announces that regular press conferences on cabinet proceedings are henceforth cancelled (*EEN*, 1997, vol. 11, no. 23, p. 8).

29 January 1998: not one of the three presidential candidates receives the requisite minimum (ninety) of the 150 seats in parliament. The incumbent president, Michal Kovac (whose term ends on 2 March) did not run for a second term. Augustin Kurek (bus driver and independent) does not receive enough votes to proceed to the second round of voting on 6 February. Stefan Markus (supported by the Slovak Democratic Coalition and the ethnic Hungarian parties) and Juraj Hrasko (nominated by the Party of the Democratic Left) advance to the second round.

Meciar supported none of the candidates and did not enter his own candidate. The constitution dictates that in the absence of a president most powers devolve to the prime minister. The role of the president is largely non-executive but includes signing bills into law and appointing the cabinet. No change of government can take place without presidential approval (*Guardian*, 30 January 1998, p. 16; *IHT*, 29 January 1998, p. 7). Meciar's coalition is one seat short of the required three-fifths majority needed in parliament (*IHT*, 29 January 1998, p. 7).

> Of the four [powers] that do not pass to the government – and thus to Mr Meciar – only two matter: the power to sign into law acts of parliament, and the power to recall and appoint a new government. Mr Meciar's men say the first is irrelevant. In the three months before Mr Kovac's election in 1993 laws were enacted without complaint; and the constitutional court could recall the government, but only with parliament's approval.
>
> (*The Economist*, 7 February 1998, p. 50)

6 February 1998: parliament fails for a second time to elect a new president.

19 February 1998: President Kovac announces a rerun on 19 April of a referendum on changing the method of selecting a new president to a direct vote of the people. The announcement came after the constitutional court's ruling that the government had acted unlawfully in May 1997 (*IHT*, 21 February 1998, p. 2).

2 March 1998: President Kovac's term of office expires.

3 March 1998: the government cancels the 19 April referendum on the selection of the president and on Nato membership (*IHT*, 4 March 1998, p. 7).

The government abrogates ex-President Kovac's decision to hold a referendum on Nato and direct presidential elections on 19 April. Meciar issues an amnesty for those subject to criminal proceedings in relation to the obstruction of the May 1997 referendum and to those involved in the abduction of Kovac's son in 1995 (*EEN*, 1998, vol. 12, no. 4, p. 10).

Meciar uses his newly assumed powers to stop an investigation of the interior minister, who aborted a 1997 referendum on joining Nato and holding direct presidential elections. Meciar also halts an investigation into the 1995 kidnapping of Kovac's son (*FT*, 11 March 1998, p. 2).

5 March 1998: parliament again fails to elect a new president.

10 March 1998: the Slovak Democratic Coalition formally registers as a political party (*EEN*, 1998, vol. 12, no. 4, p. 10).

1 April 1998: Mikulas Dzurinda is officially appointed chairman of the Slovak Democratic Coalition alliance (*EEN*, 1998, vol. 12, no. 5, p. 6).

16 April 1998: parliament again fails to elect a new president.

19 April 1998: Sturovo, a town (70 per cent ethnic Hungarian but with a Slovak mayor) near the border with Hungary, holds a referendum despite threats of legal action by the government. Nearly half the voters take part and an overwhelming majority votes in favour of Nato membership and direct election of the president (*IHT*, 21 April 1998, p. 7).

30 April 1998: parliament again fails to elect a new president.

20 May 1998: parliament approves amendments to the electoral law. All electoral coalitions will have to win 5 per cent of the vote for every party they contain, rather than a total of 10 per cent as at present for coalitions of three or more parties. Other amendments strengthen the role of the state in running the election and make scrutiny of the electoral lists more difficult (*FT*, 22 May 1998, p. 2).

An amendment to the electoral law will limit political coverage to party broadcasts on the state-run television and radio stations and appears to restrict non-state broadcasters to reporting election events in news bulletins or face fines (*FT*, 28 May 1998, p. 3). Private broadcasters are forbidden to run party advertisements from thirty days before the vote. They are banned from 'election campaigning' (*FT*, 8 September 1998, p. 2).

As a result of the electoral law the five parties in the Slovak Democratic Convention decided to merge into a separate party under the Slovak Democratic Convention banner, with a single list of candidates. Mikulas Dzurinda was elected chairman on 4 July. The Hungarians decided to bring the three ethnic Hungarian parties together in the Party of the Hungarian Coalition. Rudolf Schuster leads the Party of Civic Understanding, formed in spring 1998 (*EEN*, 1998, vol. 12, no. 8, pp. 1–2).

The new law bans election campaigning in the private media (*Business Central Europe*, July–August 1998, p. 19).

29 May 1998: parliament again fails (at its seventh attempt) to elect a new president.

8 June 1998: Austria reacts angrily to Slovakia's decision to start up the first reactor at the controversial Mochovce nuclear power plant (*IHT*, 9 June 1998, p. 5).

9 July 1998: parliament again fails to elect a president.

14 July 1998: parliament passes a constitutional amendment allowing for the parliamentary chairman to accept the resignation of the government after elections in the absence of a president (*EEN*, 1998, vol. 12, no. 9, p. 5).

4 August 1998: Meciar signs a law giving powers to the parliamentary chairman to accept the resignation of the government after parliamentary elections (*EEN*, 1998, vol. 12, no. 10, p. 9).

The general election of 25–6 September 1998

The parties competed for the 150 seats on a proportional representation basis via party lists (with a 5 per cent threshold). The turnout was 84.22 per cent.

OSCE declared that the election had been carried out 'in an apparently correct and acceptable manner' with no serious incidents (*FT*, 28 September 1998, p. 3). But there had been concern expressed during the election campaign, e.g. media bias in favour of the government. 'A particularly unattractive side of the HZDS [Movement for a Democratic Slovakia] campaign was its exploitation of the state-owned Slovak TV, which systematically attacked opposition parties' (*EEN*, 1998, vol. 12, no. 11, p. 3).

The parties were as follows (with the share of the vote and the number of seats gained in brackets):

Movement for a Democratic Slovakia: (27 per cent; 43). Led by Vladimir Meciar.

Slovak National Party: (9.07 per cent; 14). Led by Jan Slota. Extreme nationalist.

Association of Slovak Workers: (1.3 per cent; no seats). Led by Jan Luptak. Communist.

Slovak Democratic Coalition: (26.33 per cent; 42). Led by Mikulas Dzurinda. Centre-right.

Party of the Democratic Left: (14.66 per cent; 23). Led by Jozef Migas.

Party of Civic Understanding: (8.01 per cent; 13). Centre-left. Led by Rudolf Schuster. The party was set up in 1998 (*The Economist*, 3 October 1998, p. 63).

Hungarian Coalition: (9.12 per cent; 15). A coalition of three ethnic Hungarian parties (the Hungarian Christian Democrats, the Hungarian Civic Party and Co-existence; Co-existence is led by Miklos Duray).

Communist Party of Slovakia: (2.79 per cent; no seats).

Political developments after the September 1998 general election

27 September 1998: a referendum on prohibiting the privatization of six energy utilities is declared invalid as only 44 per cent instead of the minimum 50 per cent of the electorate voted (*FT*, 28 September 1998, p. 3).

29 September 1998: as the largest single party, the Movement for a Democratic Slovakia is given the first chance to try to form a government.

30 September 1990: Meciar concedes defeat and announces that he will not try to form or be a member of a new government and that he may even resign as an MP (*FT*, 2 October 1998, p. 2).

29 October 1998: the new government convenes, comprising the Slovak Democratic Coalition, the Party of the Democratic Left, the Party of Civic Understanding and the Hungarian Coalition.

The deputy prime minister in overall charge of economics is Ivan Miklos, while the economics minister is Ludovit Cernak.

Meciar resigns his parliamentary seat.

A minister for minorities and human rights is appointed. Pal Csaky is an ethnic Hungarian (*The Economist*, 7 November 1998, p. 50).

30 October 1998: Mikulas Dzurinda becomes prime minister.

24 November 1998: Christian Democratic Party leader Jan Carnogursky votes against the government's policy statement. The party is the largest component of the Slovak Democratic Coalition (*EEN*, 1998, vol. 12, no. 13, p. 8).

11 January 1999: Jan Ducky is assassinated. A close associate of Meciar, he was economy minister from December 1994 to August 1996 and head of the national gas utility from April 1997 to November 1998. 'Slovak press reports recently indicated that he was involved in a number of suspicious business deals' (*The Times*, 13 January 1999, p. 10). 'He had been accused of embezzlement on a grand scale while head of the Slovak gas authority' (*The Economist*, 16 January 1999, p. 46).

14 January 1999: 'The new government moved Thursday to end an embarrassing constitutional impasse, pushing through parliament a vote to allow the president to be elected directly by the people' (*IHT*, 15 January 1999, p. 5).

18 March 1999: parliament passes a law on the direct election of the president.

9 April 1999: former intelligence service director and Movement for a Democratic Slovakia leader Ivan Lexa has parliamentary immunity from prosecution withdrawn. On 15 April parliament voted in favour of his detention (*EEN*, 1999, vol. 12, no. 16, p. 11).

Meciar announces his candidacy for the presidency (*FT*, 10 April 1999, p. 3).

11 May 1999: former president Michal Kovac withdraws from the presidential race in favour of Rudolf Schuster.

15 May 1999: the first round of the presidential election takes place. The turnout is 73.89 per cent. Rudolf Schuster wins 47.38 per cent of the vote. He is the centre-left mayor of Kosice, chairman of the Party of Civic Understanding and candidate of the Slovak Democratic Coalition. Vladimir Meciar receives

37.24 per cent of the vote. The candidate in third place (Magda Vasaryova, a former actress) receives only 6.6 per cent of the vote. The second round of voting will take place on 29 May.

29 May 1999: the second round of the presidential election takes place. The turnout is 75 per cent. Rudolf Schuster wins with 57.2 per cent of the vote to Vladimir Meciar's 42.8 per cent.

25 September 1999: the Slovak National Party chairman Jan Slota is voted out of office at the party congress. On 2 October he was replaced by his deputy Anna Malikova (*EEN*, 1999 vol. 12, no. 20, p. 5).

13 October 1999: the European Commission recommends that EU leaders at the December 1999 meeting in Helsinki allow Bulgaria, Latvia, Lithuania, Malta, Romania and Slovakia to begin accession negotiations in 2000.

The 'principle of differentiation' for entry date will apply to each of the twelve candidates, reflecting differing states of readiness for EU entry. A 'fully flexible, multi-speed accession process' is envisaged. 'Each country will be able to proceed on merit, including the possibility for those which join the negotiations from 2000 to catch up with the others.' The European Commission thinks that existing EU members should undertake internal reforms by the end of 2002: 'Whether the first accessions can take place as from 1 January 2003 will then depend entirely on the speed with which the applicant countries can make progress on meeting the criteria.'

Slovakia has made strong progress on political reform since the change of government in September 1998. Slovakia has a good chance of catching up with the group led by Hungary. It should meet the market economy criterion in 2000 and the competitive criterion in the medium term. Slovakia could become a functioning market economy in 2000 if it pushes ahead with promised reforms.

(*FT*, 14 October 1999, pp. 1, 10; *IHT*, 14 October 1999, p. 5; *Guardian*, 14 October 1999, p. 14; *Independent*, 14 October 1999, p. 18; *The Times*, 14 October 1999, p. 21; *Telegraph*, 14 October 1999, p. 20.)

(For further details, see the Hungary entry for 10 December 1999.)

14 October 1999: economy minister Ludovit Cernak announces his resignation. He was replaced on 20 October by Lubomir Harach (*EEN*, 1999 vol. 12, no. 20, p. 5).

20 October 1999: the president and vice-president of the national property fund are dismissed after a parliamentary vote (*EEN*, 1999 vol. 12, no. 20, p. 5).

17 January 2000: prime minister Mikulas Dzurinda leaves the Slovak Democratic Coalition and sets up the Slovak Democratic and Christian Union. Several senior ministers follow him. But the governing coalition survives (*FT*, 18 January 2000, p. 6; *Business Central Europe*, March 2000, p. 44).

> After losing a bitter battle with Mr Carnogursky and the other party leaders to turn the SDK into a united counterweight to Mr Meciar's HZDS and give himself a real platform, Mr Dzurinda founded his own SDKU party this year … Former government supporters have gravitated to the new Smer (Direction) party established by Robert Fico in December [1999], which …

is likely to hold the balance of power in the next parliament. Mr Fico, thirty-five, was once the rising star of the SDL but has since reinvented himself by focusing on populist issues, such as rising crime, the Roma (Gypsies) and unemployment.

(*FT*, Survey, 25 May 2000, p. 15)

19 February 2000: Democratic Union leader and foreign minister Eduard Kukan switches allegiance to premier Mikulas Dzurinda's new party (*EEN*, 2000, vol. 12, no. 22, p. 6).

27 March 2000: Ivan Miklos (deputy prime minister):

There is broad consensus about this [a policy in favour of joining Nato]. Even Mr Meciar's party ... has recently declared it is now in favour. Within the government there is no doubt. A small country like Slovakia cannot be isolated. Nato membership is also crucial to economic recovery, in that it reinforces stability.

(*IHT*, 28 March 2000, p. 2)

'A recent [18 March 2000] HZDS party congress embraced Nato and the EU much more enthusiastically than ever before' (*FT*, Survey, 25 May 2000, p. 15).

20 April 2000:

The Slovak authorities ended a three-week standoff with ... Vladimir Meciar on Thursday morning [20 April] as masked commandos blew open the back door of his home and then arrested him on charges of abusing his power for allegedly paying illegal bonuses to cabinet officials while in office ... Mr Meciar was questioned ... in connection with the 1995 kidnapping of the son of Slovakia's then president, Michal Kovac. He was released at midday after being charged with abuse of power and fraud while in office, offences carrying potential prison terms of three to ten years. He was also fined 10,000 crowns ($225) for refusing to answer police questions about the kidnapping. Mr Meciar was the final witness in the state's case against Ivan Lexa, a close aide who ran the secret services and is charged with orchestrating Mr Kovac's kidnapping.

(*IHT*, 21 April 2000, p. 8)

'The siege began on 26 March when ... [Meciar] locked himself into his villa ... He was refusing to appear at the trial of an aide accused of kidnapping' (*Telegraph*, 21 April 2000, p. 14).

Vladimir Meciar ... was charged with abuse of power and fraud. The charges ... relate to allegations that he illegally paid bonuses worth 13.9 million crowns to cabinet members while prime minister. Mr Meciar was later released and fined 10,000 crowns for refusing to answer questions about the charges and those against Ivan Lexa ... The former prime

> minister had holed himself up in his house to resist attempts by prosecutors to question him about the operation of the secret service during his administration, in particular allegations that it organized the kidnapping of the president's son in 1995. Mr Meciar argues that the investigation is politically motivated and unconstitutional, as he awarded all those involved an amnesty before leaving office in 1998.
>
> (*FT*, 22 April 2000, p. 6)

> Mr Meciar was … charged with abuse of power and the illegal payment of bonuses to his ministers, amounting to more than $300,000 … In March 1998 Mr Meciar ordered an amnesty for all those responsible for the kidnapping, but the case was reopened when the opposition won power.
>
> (*Guardian*, 21 April 2000, p. 18)

> Slovakia's chief prosecutor dropped charges of fraud against former premier Vladimir Meciar, saying there were no laws against the controversial bonuses Mr Meciar paid to his ministers during his tenure. But Mr Meciar could still face charges of abuse of power.
>
> (*Business Central Europe*, June 2000, pp. 14–15)

22 May 2000: Slovakia and the Czech Republic announce a formal end to their property dispute. (The Czech Republic and Slovakia reached agreement on 24 November 1999 on long-standing property disputes, including cross-border stakes in major banks: *IHT*, 25 November 1999, p. 7.)

28 July 2000: the OECD agrees to ask Slovakia to join, making it the thirtieth member. 'Membership was blocked in June [2000] as France demanded clear guarantees that Slovakia would heed its obligations towards the EU regarding television and radio broadcasting rules' (*FT*, 29 July 2000, p. 8).

26 August 2000: the small Democratic Union party decides to merge with premier Mikulas Dzurinda's Slovak Christian and Democratic Union (*EEN*, 2000, vol. 12, no. 25, p. 5).

'The inaugural congress … [of the] Slovak Democratic and Christian Union … took place a week after the [11 November 2000] referendum' (*Business Central Europe*, December 2000–January 2001, p. 44).

8 November 2000: the latest EU report recognizes the progress that Slovakia has made but highlights the areas still causing concern.

The EU's report on Slovakia (*Progress Towards Accession*, 8 November 2000, pp. 81–2):

> Slovakia has further advanced in the consolidation of its democratic system and in the normal functioning of its institutions. However, the speed of the reform process has lost some of its momentum due, in part, to dissension within the ruling coalition … Continued efforts are needed to ensure the independence of the judiciary. Progress was achieved in the fight against crime and corruption, mainly in formulating a government policy and trans-

> posing international obligations. The translation of good intentions and well thought-out concepts into specific actions should not be delayed … Tangible improvement of the situation of the Roma minority in particular by implementing specific measures … has not been achieved to a large extent … Priority should be given to effective implementation of the legal framework and to administrative capacity … Slovakia can be regarded as a functioning market economy and should be able to cope with competitive pressure and market forces within the Union in the medium term, provided that the structural reform agenda is fully implemented and broadened to include remaining reforms. Macroeconomic stability has presently been restored through measures to reduce the fiscal and external deficits. The legislative framework for business activity is now largely in place. Price distortions are being eliminated and the privatization of utilities has started. The authorities are making good progress in the restructuring and privatization of the state-owned banks.

(For further details, see the entry for Hungary.)
11 November 2000:

> In Slovakia's referendum on early elections … only 20 per cent of the electorate turned out to vote, well short of the 50 per cent needed to make the referendum stick … The referendum had been initiated by … the Movement for a Democratic Slovakia. It collected over 700,000 signatures last summer.
>
> (*Business Central Europe*, December 2000–January 2001, p. 44)

23 February 2001: 'Parliament passes constitutional amendments (administrative reform, minority rights etc.) as a prerequisite for EU accession negotiations' (*EEN*, 2001, vol. 13, no. 3, p. 5).

> A constitutional amendment passed last month [February] … paves the way for regional reform and hence for Slovakia's EU membership … The amendment is almost as important as the actual passing of Slovakia's constitution, back in 1992. It lays the framework for devolving power to some twelve to fourteen new regions … It was a huge achievement for the splintered government to get it passed by parliament … Constitutional changes require a two-thirds majority … Controversial concessions [were made] to the Hungarian Coalition Party, a junior coalition party. Under the old regional scheme established in 1996, Slovak Hungarians were in the majority in just two of seventy-nine regions. Now they will form 40 per cent of the population in a far larger region around the southern town of Komarno.
>
> (*Business Central Europe*, March 2001, pp. 40–1)

6 April 2001: 'The European Commission suspends financial aid on the grounds of alleged corruption in the Slovak administration' (*EEN*, 2001, vol. 13, no. 5, p. 7).

26 April 2001:

> The European Commission yesterday [26 April] suspended the signing of new aid contracts with Slovakia after a top government official was dismissed for alleged corruption … Roland Toth, head of the foreign assistance department in the government office, was dismissed last month [March] … The Commission has suspended new EU tenders and contracts pending the results of the inquiry.
>
> (*FT*, 27 April 2001, p. 10)

'Roland Toth, head of Slovakia's department of foreign assistance, is now under criminal investigation for fraud by the Slovak authorities' (*Telegraph*, 27 April 2001, p. 16).

14 May 2001: 'The ruling coalition leaders discuss without success a formula for resolving their differences over proposed reform of the country's administrative districts' (*EEN*, 2001, vol. 13, no. 5, p. 7).

June 2001:

> The coalition now looks likely to survive until the [September 2002] election … The coalition has an enormous task ahead of it to rebuild its popularity, which has been buffeted by economic austerity, infighting, corruption allegations and its failure to convict any of the fraudsters of the Meciar era … Economic reform has hurt the government's support … Opinion polls show that only the SDKU [of Mikulas Dzurinda], Christian Democrats and Hungarians would currently pass the 5 per cent threshold to enter parliament. One recent opinion poll even put the SDKU in fifth place with only 9 per cent, compared to 26 per cent for Mr Meciar's HZDS … The coalition parties hope that the economic recovery will increase their support but ministers admit they will probably need Robert Fico's Smer (Direction) Party in order to form a majority government … Mr Fico … who broke with the Democratic Left in 1999 … is running at a stable 18 per cent in opinion polls … His populist policies on crime – supporting the death penalty and forcing prisoners to pay for their upkeep – and on Gypsies – restricting their access to social benefits – have attracted some of the disenchanted voters who would have gone over to the HZDS … Robert Fico [is] an inexperienced but pragmatic young populist [thirty-six years of age].
>
> (Robert Anderson, *FT*, Survey, 4 July 2001, p. i)

> The ruling Slovak Democratic Coalition and its constituent parties continue to fall in opinion polls. Corruption, nepotism and unemployment of nearly 20 per cent threaten to give former premier Vladimir Meciar and his Movement for a Democratic Slovakia (HZDS) a good chance in the 2002 parliamentary elections … Meciar is at present in a strong position, helped

> by dissatisfaction with the economy ... and the government's chronic inability to agree on institutional reforms ... The balance of power, as things now stand, will be held by Robert Fico's Smer Party, which is at 18 to 19 per cent in opinion polls ... The revived Slovak National Party is now on 7.5 per cent in the opinion polls thanks to the more dynamic leadership of Anna Malikova ... Mikulas Dzurinda's Slovak Democratic and Christian Union (SDKU) is on 13 per cent, the Party of the Hungarian Coalition is on 10 per cent ... [and] the Christian Democrats are hovering at just over the 5 per cent parliamentary threshold figure.
>
> (*EEN*, 2001, vol. 13, no. 5, p. 5)

'Polls consistently show the HZDS party ... in the lead with around 30 per cent ... The HZDS is likely to remain the strongest party for years to come – if only because it is the only one with a grass-roots organization' (*Business Central Europe*, July–August 2001, p. 41).

THE ECONOMY

The Meciar government had a surprisingly good record on macroeconomic stabilization and GDP growth, although its unemployment record is far inferior to that of the Czech Republic and relations with the IMF were not always smooth. (See Table 7.2.)

On 20 February 1993 the IMF broke off discussions, saying that the government was in disarray and that the fund was unable to gather even the most basic economic data (*IHT*, 24 March 1993, p. 13). Slovak officials protested that Slovakia was 'not a banana republic' (*EEN*, 2 March 1993, vol. 7, no. 5, p. 4). The IMF returned in May after the government had passed laws on bankruptcy, privatization and income taxation (*Business Central Europe*, June 1993, p. 18). In mid-June the IMF agreed to a loan of $90 million under the 'systemic transformation facility' (with the option of a further $90 million in six months) in return for commitments such as keeping the budget deficit to 5 per cent of GDP at most and holding inflation at 1 per cent per month (*Business Central Europe*, July–August 1993, p. 45; *IHT*, 10 July 1993, p. 11; *EEN*, 20 July 1993, vol. 7, no. 15, p. 6; Deutsche Bank, *Focus: Eastern Europe*, 1993, no. 82, p. 7).

On 24 February 1995 the government resolved the budget proposals for 1995. The budget deficit was to be a maximum 3 per cent of GDP, with a target inflation rate for the year of 10 per cent (Deutsche Bank, *Focus: Eastern Europe*, 28 February 1995, no. 126, p. 13). Parliament endorsed the budget in early March 1995. The central government deficit (i.e. excluding social insurance, local budgets and extra-budgetary funds) was to be a maximum 3 per cent of GDP (Deutsche Bank, *Focus: Eastern Europe*, 1995, no. 127, p. 6).

An austerity package was introduced at the end of May 1999. The measures included raising fees for public services, rises in VAT and excise tax, price deregulation and a 7 per cent import surcharge on some 80 per cent of the goods

Table 7.2 Slovakia: selected economic indicators 1990–2000

Economic indicator	*1990*	*1991*	*1992*	*1993*	*1994*	*1995*	*1996*	*1997*	*1998*	*1999*	*2000 (estimate)*
Rate of growth of GDP (%)	-2.5	-14.6	-6.5	-3.7	4.9	6.7	6.2	6.2	4.1	1.9	2.2
Rate of growth of industrial output (%)	-4.0	-25.4	-9.6	-5.4	6.8	8.3	2.5	1.7	3.4	-3.4	9.1
Rate of growth of agricultural output (%)	-7.2	-7.4	-21.7	-8.1	4.8	2.3	2.0	-1.0	-5.9	1.0	-2.0
Inflation rate (consumer, %)	10.8	61.2	10.0	23.2	13.4	9.9	5.8	6.1	6.7	10.6	12.0
Budget surplus or deficit (% GDP)[a]	0.1	-2.0	-11.9	-6.0	-1.5	0.4	-1.3	-5.2	-5.0	-3.6	-3.5
Unemployment rate (end of year, %)	1.6	11.8	10.4	14.4	14.6	13.1	12.8	12.5	15.6	19.2	17.9
Balance of payments (current account, $ billion)	-1.100	0.400	0.200	-0.601	0.665	0.391	-2.098	-1.952	-2.059	-1.083	-0.680
Foreign direct investment (net, $ billion)	0.018	0.082	0.100	0.107	0.236	0.194	0.199	0.084	0.374	0.701	1.500
Population (million)			5.3	5.3	5.3	5.4	5.4	5.4	5.4	5.4	5.4

Sources: Various issues of European Bank for Reconstruction and Development, *Transition Report*; United Nations Economic Commission for Europe, *Economic Survey of Europe*; United Nations, *World Economic and Social Survey*; IMF, *World Economic Outlook*.

Note:

[a] General government balance: includes the state, municipalities and extrabudgetary funds; excludes privatization revenues (EBRD)

entering the country (*Business Central Europe*, July–August 1999, p. 34). On 31 May the government imposed an immediate 7 per cent import surcharge, although there was a promise to reduce it to 5 per cent at the end of 1999, to 3 per cent by July 2000 and to abolish it at the beginning of 2001. The austerity package increased the lower rate of VAT from 6 per cent to 10 per cent and raised a range of regulated prices by up to 70 per cent (*FT*, 2 June 1999, p. 3).

A tax on 'excessive' increases was imposed during 1991, with agreement from unions, to regulate the rise in real wages. The taxes expired at the end of 1992. Remaining selective controls on wages were abolished in late 1994. Wages policy is currently determined via collective bargaining between the government, employers and trade unions. The number of enterprises declared bankrupt has been small (EBRD 1997b: 199). The new law on wage regulation, which stipulates a cap on wage increases, has been amended to cover smaller enterprises (EBRD 1998a: 41). At the end of 1997 a comprehensive wage regulation scheme was introduced for both public and private enterprises. The scheme limits wage growth in firms to between 6 per cent and 12 per cent, depending on performance (EBRD 1998b: 188). The government has annulled the wage regulation introduced in 1997 that limited the wage growth of public and private firms. But austerity measures have included a public sector wage freeze (EBRD 1999b: 262).

A law on the 'revitalization of enterprises' went into force in mid-1997. Eligible enterprises were to receive state aid in the form of tax deferrals and debt forgiveness, conditional on criteria related to employment, social and regional development, as well as exports. These enterprises were also to be exempt from bankruptcy proceedings (EBRD 1997b: 199).

> The virtual absence of bankruptcy continues to inhibit the exit of unprofitable firms and to weaken financial discipline. Inter-enterprise arrears amounted to 18 per cent of GDP in 1997, roughly unchanged from 1996. An amendment to the bankruptcy law became effective in February 1998 to facilitate proceedings. However, 'strategic' enterprises and enterprises under the new 'revitalization' programme remain excluded. The 1997 law on revitalization induced over 1,000 companies to apply for tax and debt relief, further weakening market discipline. Recently the size of the programme has been scaled back significantly.
>
> (EBRD 1998b: 189)

The new government has reversed a number of controversial policies, including the 'revitalization act' (supporting companies through state aid, tax deferrals and debt relief) and the new wage regulation (EBRD 1999a: 26).

Under the recently introduced 'enterprise revitalization' law, struggling enterprises based in areas of high unemployment can apply for government debt write-offs and deferrals on tax, excise duty and social security payments (*FT*, 2 September 1997, p. 2; *Business Central Europe*, October 1997, p. 20). The government has recently passed laws to regulate wages in private as well as state enterprises (p. 20).

The only remaining significant price controls pertain to utility charges, rents and public services. In addition mark-ups are closely regulated in the energy sector (EBRD 1994: 37). In November 1995 parliament approved a law (effective 1 April 1996) allowing the ministry of finance to regulate the prices of certain goods and services in the domestic market, including gas and electricity (EBRD 1996b: 173). The new government has substantially raised a number of regulated prices, e.g. utility and transport tariffs were raised drastically in 1999 (EBRD 1999b: 262–3). 'The government has sharply increased utility prices in the last eighteen months following several years of little or no adjustments ... However, local energy prices are still well below cost-recovery levels' (EBRD 2000b: 206). 'Significant [energy] tariff increases have occurred recently' (EBRD 2001: 29).

Privatization

According to official figures, the private sector as a whole accounted for around 20 per cent of national income in 1992 (United Nations Economic Commission for Europe 1993: 215). In 1993 it seemed that more than one-third of GDP was produced in the private sector (United Nations, *World Economic and Social Survey*, 1994, p. 35). The private sector now generates 35–40 per cent of GDP (*Business Central Europe*, February 1994, p. 19). In the first half of 1993 the private sector accounted for 36.9 per cent of GDP, 18.1 per cent of industrial output, 51.2 per cent of construction and 83.8 per cent of trade receipts (*Business Europa*, February–March 1994, p. 20). The non-state sector now has a 58 per cent share of industrial output (*Business Europa*, April–May 1995, p. 40). According to the Statistical Office, the private sector accounted for about 40 per cent of GDP in mid-1994 (*Transition*, 1994, vol. 5, no. 6, p. 22). The shadow economy was estimated to have amounted to 12 per cent of GDP in 1996, compared with about 13 per cent in 1993 and 1994 (EBRD 1997b: 198).

Rough estimates in mid-year of the private sector as a percentage of GDP are provided by the EBRD: 1990, 10 per cent; 1991, 15 per cent; 1992, 30 per cent; 1993, 45 per cent; 1994, 55 per cent; 1995, 60 per cent; 1996, 70 per cent; 1997, 75 per cent; 1998, 75 per cent; 1999, 75 per cent; 2000, 75 per cent (EBRD 1999b: 24, 264, and 2000b: 14, 208).

The second round of large privatization was set to begin in mid-1993 (involving 514 enterprises), but the start was rescheduled for early 1994 and then 5 September 1994 (when the voucher booklets were to start being distributed). Vouchers were to play only a 'residual' or 'supplementary' role, with the bulk of shares sold to Slovaks or foreigners via auctions, tenders or the stock exchange. The number of enterprises on the list was not easy to determine and the whole process got caught up in campaigning for the general election (fixed for 30 September–1 October 1994).

On 11 August 1994 President Kovak called a referendum for 22 October on whether Slovak citizens buying state property in the privatization programme should have to disclose the source of their funds. But the referendum attracted only a 20 per cent turnout instead of the minimum necessary 51 per cent.

On 4 November 1994 parliament voted to cancel all privatization contracts involving (around fifty) direct sales to Slovak investors signed since 6 September, but on 25 May 1995 the constitutional court pronounced that: 'Parliament now has six months to redraft the law to make it conform with the Slovak constitution. Otherwise it will be annulled' (*FT*, 26 May 1995, p. 3).

The second round of coupon privatization was then set to begin on 15 December 1994, but the planned start was later postponed to 1 July 1995. The sell-off theoretically included 549 enterprises. In July 1995 a voucher sale was to put up equity in some 200 enterprises. No more than 46 per cent in any one of these enterprises was to be sold via vouchers, with the average size of the stake being 25 per cent. The remaining assets earmarked for sale were to be divested gradually by way of direct sale, most being sold on easy terms to enterprise managers, trade unions and employees. The government intended to keep 'strategic' enterprises such as energy utilities, arms manufacturers and big financial institutions under its firm control. Foreigners were to get a chance to invest primarily through joint ventures (*The Economist*, 6 May 1995, p. 99).

But in June 1995 the government unexpectedly announced a new programme, scheduled to begin on 1 July. Vouchers were to be replaced by five-year state bonds. The bonds could be used for the following purposes: held until 31 December 2000 and cashed in for 10,000 crowns plus the accumulated interest; sold for cash; sold to those who use bonds to buy shares in enterprises being privatized; exchanged for shares in enterprises; additional health and pension insurance; part-payment for apartments and/or health insurance.

The remaining equity was to be gradually divested by way of direct sales and auctions, with preference given to management buy-outs on easy terms (*Business Central Europe*, July–August 1995, p. 15). Most of the assets to be privatized in the new programme were to be by means of direct sales, including management and employee buy-outs. The law relating to state interests identified over twenty enterprises which were not to be privatized (mainly in gas and electricity generation, telecommunications, armaments and agriculture). It also listed a further forty enterprises (some of which had already been partially privatized) which were defined as 'strategically important' (mainly in mining, chemicals, construction, engineering and the agricultural sectors). The state was to retain ownership in these and enjoy special voting rights (EBRD 1995b: 57). The direct sale of assets is proceeding apace, primarily to management and/or employees via management buy-outs. Many of these assets have been sold for an initial down-payment of 10 to 20 per cent of the book value, with subsequent loan instalments to be written off if the new owners make investments up to an equivalent amount in the company (EBRD 1996a: 10). Since the cancellation of the voucher scheme privatization has continued via direct sales, including management and employee buy-outs, with a preference given to existing management. An estimated number of over 600 privatization proposals were submitted by

March 1996 under the 'second wave' and two-thirds of these enterprises had been privatized by mid-1996. The intention was to sell the remainder (many of which are in the agricultural sector) by the end of 1996. The law relating to state interests lists twenty-nine enterprises which will not be privatized (mainly in gas and electricity generation, telecommunications, armaments and agriculture). It also lists a further forty-five enterprises, some of which have already been partially privatized and which are defined as 'strategically important' (mainly in mining, chemicals, construction, engineering and the agricultural sectors). Under the amendment the state would retain ownership either via a shareholding in excess of a third of the total number of shares or through a 'golden share' (thus enjoying special voting rights). But in April 1996 the constitutional court declared that the 'golden share' was unconstitutional on the grounds that it violated the rights of other shareholders (EBRD 1996b: 172). Many sales have been to existing management, who have the opportunity to buy assets on favourable terms. In November 1996 the constitutional court ruled that the government rather than the national property fund is responsible for direct sales of state property. The intention was to complete the mass privatization programme in 1997 (EBRD 1997a: 33). The style of privatization has remained controversial. In February 1998, 8 per cent of the shares of a large petrochemical company were sold for half the market price to a hitherto unknown company. In addition to an often very favourable sales price, new owners can offset their payments to the National Property Fund against investments (EBRD 1998a: 41). 'After abandoning the second wave of mass voucher privatization in 1995, privatization has continued via direct sales – usually to former management or domestic holding companies. As foreigners have been virtually excluded from the privatization process, they have played little role in the development of corporate governance.' After further sales in 1998 the large privatization programme is nearing completion. But the national property fund and other ministries still manage enterprises excluded from the privatization process. These account for about 30 per cent of the book value of all productive state assets and include utilities, the postal service, telecoms, railways, some agricultural enterprises, as well as the savings bank and the main insurance company.

> In February 1998 around 8 per cent of Slovnaft, the large petroleum company, whose shares are actively traded on the stock exchange, was sold for half the market price to a previously unknown company. In another surprise move the national property fund sold 74 per cent of the large aluminium producer ZSNP in July 1998 to a newly founded holding company whose ownership was uncertain. The average price for all direct sales completed in 1997 was only 18 per cent of the average book value. New owners have also been able to reduce their subsequent instalments by undertaking investments in the privatized company.
>
> (EBRD 1998b: 188–9)

The 1995 law excluding certain 'strategic' enterprises (mostly infrastructure companies and major financial institutions) from the privatization process was cancelled in June 1999 and replaced by a new law on large privatization (EBRD 1999b: 262).

> Progress in enterprise restructuring has been hampered by weak corporate governance and by an ineffective bankruptcy system … The September 1999 law on privatization has facilitated the sale of state shares in strategic enterprises. These include majority stakes in the dominant telecommunications operator and large banks, and minority stakes in the energy sector companies.
>
> (EBRD 2000a: 76)

'The privatization of large-scale enterprise has been reinvigorated. However, the pace of industrial restructuring and liquidations needs to be accelerated … Despite some recent progress industrial restructuring remains slow' (EBRD 2000b: 206). 'The main focus is now on selling state shares in the banking sector and large infrastructure enterprises, such as those in the telecommunications and energy sectors' (EBRD 2001: 28). 'With progress in privatization well advanced, the remaining state-owned companies are concentrated in the banking and energy sectors … Privatization in the banking sector has proceeded further in recent months' (p. 86).

Originally privatization was to have been completed by the summer of 1996. But the expected completion date was extended to between the end of 1996 and mid-1997. The privatization of three major banks and one insurance company was postponed until 31 March 1997. It was reported that the remaining shares held by the National Property Fund were then to be offered to industrial companies. It was said that of the 375 privatizations in 1995 in only three to five cases did the companies go to foreign investors (Deutsche Bank, *Focus: Eastern Europe*, 1996, no. 159, pp. 5–6).

Under the 1995 Strategic Companies Act the Meciar government obliged the state to keep a majority stake in the forty listed enterprises. There has been disagreement within the new coalition government as to which enterprises were to be excluded from the list.

> Last month [September 1999] … the Party of the Democratic Left reluctantly agreed to redefine what it considered to be 'strategic' companies. A new bill was hurried through parliament … binding the government to retain control of only 'natural' monopolies … That means that the government will maintain majority stakes in the electricity generator and grid company Slovenska Elektrarne (as well as three regional distributors), the gas distribution monopoly Slovensky Plynarensky Priemysel, and Transpetrol, the crude oil distributor. It must also keep 100 per cent stakes in the post office and state railways … The legislative block is lifted on the state savings bank Slovenska Sporitelna, the country's main insurer Slovenska Pojistovna and the fixed-line telecoms monopoly, Slovak Telecom.

> Here, ceding a majority stake will now be decided on a case-by-case basis by the authorities ... A large minority stake in Slovak Telecom was already slated for auction by the end of the year [1999].
>
> (*Business Central Europe*, October 1999, p. 42)

The way in which the second wave of privatization was conducted has aroused considerable controversy:

1 It is claimed that the new privatization programme shifted the balance in favour of a narrow group of owner/managers.

> Assets are often sold at knock-down prices and buyers have ten years to pay for them. If the enterprise is important enough a controversial and ambiguous law on strategic enterprises enables the state to retain a golden share that allows it to wield influence long after the stake has been sold.
>
> (*EEN*, 1996, vol. 10, no. 5, p. 9)

Critics argue that 'assets are sold only to those deemed loyal to Mr Meciar's all-embracing Movement for a Democratic Slovakia. Scores of company bosses have been replaced this year by allies of the government prior to the sales' (*ibid.*).

> The current drive by the HZDS [Movement for a Democratic Slovakia] to implement a new wave of pseudo privatization in which employers of each privatized enterprise will be eligible to control 34 per cent of the enterprise, together with Meciar's crash drive to privatize banks (by handing them largely to the HZDS cabal), is compounding Meciar's internationally poor reputation. Opposition attempts to restrict HZDS privatization policy by appealing to the constitutional court ... are unlikely to be upheld.
>
> (*EEN*, 1996, vol. 10, no. 5, p. 9)

Voucher privatization has been replaced by

> a promissory method which benefits only a small group within the state elite. State factories are being sold to managers and HZDS cronies at knockdown rates – which can be paid in small long-term instalments. It will create a large stratum of politically loyal entrepreneurs – precisely what Meciar wants. This could best be described as a corrupted plutocracy.
>
> (*EEN*, 1996, vol. 10, no. 8, pp. 5–6)

'The government's privatization policy discriminates against most existing managements, which tend to support the SDL [Party of the Democratic Left]' (p. 8). 'The government continues to its profoundly corrupt practice of "privatizing" state industry by giving it at concessionary prices exclusively to HZDS lackeys and supporters of the ruling parties' (*EEN*, 21 December 1997, vol. 11, no. 24, p. 2).

2 'The announcement that VSZ, a steel maker, has taken control of Slovakia's largest insurance company shows just how little markets matter. The share issue that enabled VSZ to replace the government as the biggest shareholder in Slovenska Pojistovna is the latest in a long line of pacts that have handed control of Slovak companies to cronies of Vladimir Meciar, the prime minister ... This is the steel maker's second venture into finance. Back in 1996 it took over IRB, Slovakia's third-largest bank, despite central bank opposition and a law banning it from owning more than a minority stake. Then it used friendly companies to cobble together a controlling stake surreptitiously. Its method this time was to suggest that Pojistovna should have a capital increase ... IRB lent firms linked to VSZ at least 200 million korunas ($5.9 million) that has not been repaid, helping to send IRB into state administration last year [1997] ... The government used the insurer to bail IRB out ... By buying control of Pojistovna, VSZ thus regains control of a bank it helped to ruin ... Over half of Slovakia's sixty most profitable companies have been sold during Mr Meciar's tenure, in most cases to friends of the ruling party and often at bargain prices. Many of these purchases were financed by state-owned banks. The banks were also used to prop up ailing state companies. As a result of all this the banking system is bust' (*The Economist*, 29 August 1998, p. 76).

> There is no minority shareholder protection to speak of – helpful if you are selling listed companies for a fraction of their value – and no transparency. Last year [1997], for example, a Czech company lost control of a privatized Slovak chemicals plant it had bought in 1994, when shares were stolen from the securities registry and resold to Slovak investors.
>
> (p. 79)

> In apparent violation of the law – and commercial sense – the National Property Fund, which manages state assets, connived with VSZ, an HZDS [Movement for a Democratic Slovakia]-friendly steel giant, to dilute the state's majority stake in Slovenska Pojistovna, the country's dominant insurer. That left VSZ and its allies in control.
>
> (*Business Central Europe*, September 1998, p. 52)

3 On 13 July 1995 parliament approved legislation restricting the powers of investment funds (*EEN*, 1995, vol. 9, no. 15, p. 8). There has been 'a major crackdown on the investment funds ... A new law bars them from exercising corporate governance in companies they control' (*Business Central Europe*, September 1995, p. 58).

4 'Earlier this year, faced with a court action that could have bankrupted Slovenske Telekomunikacie, legislation was passed making all state companies exempt from bankruptcy' (*FT*, Survey, 23 October 1996, p. iv).

5 Slovakia has carried out a controversial management buy-out scheme 'whereby companies were sold to their managers for a knock-down price but with stringent performance criteria attached' (*Business Central Europe*, July–August 1997, p. 50). 'Meciar ... sold off the state's assets cheap to his friends, who raised much of the money through loans from state banks ... Many buyers ignored their investment pledges' (*Business Central Europe*, March 1999, p. 36).

> Gas storage firm Nafta Gbely was a litmus test for the government's handling of the Meciar legacy. It was the clearest case of the previous government's abuse of the privatization process – and one that this government was determined should be dealt with by the courts. That is now changed. Under an outline agreement reached last month [March 1999] owner Druha Obchodna would surrender 41 per cent of the firm without any payment. In return it would keep 5 per cent and some unfinished gas storage tanks. The criminal proceedings would be dropped. Yet for many Slovaks the sale of Nafta Gbely three years ago discredited both the Meciar administration and the entire privatization process. A 46 per cent stake was sold to Druha Obchodna ... the stake was worth at least six times more. Later it transpired that Druha Obchodna was owned by Vladimir Poor, a senior official in Meciar's party. Other senior politicians are thought to be joint owners ... The outline deal with Mr Poor would allow the government to sell what amounts to a controlling stake.
>
> (*Business Central Europe*, April 1999, pp. 26, 28)

6 The privatization process continues to be criticized for a lack of transparency. In June 1997 a 15 per cent stake in the petrochemical company Slovnaft was sold to the management for 20 per cent of the market price (EBRD 1997b: 198).

> In February 1998 around 8 per cent of Slovnaft, the large petroleum company, whose shares are actively traded on the stock exchange, was sold for half the market price to a previously unknown company. In another surprise move the national property fund sold 74 per cent of the large aluminium producer ZSNP in July 1998 to a newly founded holding company whose ownership was uncertain. The average price for all direct sales completed in 1997 was only 18 per cent of the average book value. New owners have also been able to reduce their subsequent instalments by undertaking investments in the privatized company.
>
> (EBRD 1998b: 188)

Past privatizations are being reviewed by the national property fund, targeting companies whose initial privatization involved illegalities or whose owners have not paid their instalments to the fund in full.

> An early case was the oil and gas storage company, Nafta Gbely, which had been privatized for a fraction of its market price in 1996. The new government has now declared the privatization invalid and a 46 per cent stake is to return to state hands.
>
> (EBRD 1999b: 262)

But all is not doom and gloom as regards restructuring. Simeon Djankov and Gerhard Pohl (*Transition*, 1997, vol. 8, no. 3, p. 33) summarize the results of their analysis of twenty-one enterprises for the period 1991–6:

> Large industrial firms in Slovakia have restructured more rapidly than expected, even those regarded as 'non-viable' only a few years ago … Privatization to insiders, through management–employee buy-outs, did not hamper restructuring because the new owners (old managers) invested heavily in new technology, laid off a substantial part of the workforce, sought foreign partnerships, and were prepared to sell controlling stakes to outsiders for fresh financial resources.

Share trading on the Bratislava stock exchange began on 1 July 1993.

Further developments in privatization

Hungarian oil and gas company MOL has agreed to buy a strategic 36 per cent stake in the Slovak oil company Slovnaft and intends to raise its holding to 50 per cent (*Business Central Europe*, May 2000, p. 15). In April 2000 a significant share in the Slovnaft refinery was sold to MOL. 'This represents the first large acquisition within the region without the direct involvement of investors from a non-transition country' (EBRD 2000a: 76). 'In April 2000 the Hungarian oil and gas company MOL acquired one-third of an oil refinery, Slovnaft, including the right to increase its stake to above 50 per cent after two years. This is the largest single foreign investment in the country to date, as well as the biggest cross-border deal in the region' (EBRD 2000b: 206).

> The new government investigated Mr Meciar's privatization procedures and a number of assets have been renationalized, such as a 10 per cent stake in Slovnaft, the oil company. But most entrepreneurs linked to the Meciar administration have held on to their wealth.
>
> (*FT*, Survey, 25 May 2000, p. 16)

'The government has … [called] a halt to the renationalization of some of the previous government's dubious sell-offs' (p. 17).

Deutsche Telekom has announced the purchase of a 51 per cent stake in Slovenske Telekomunikacie, the national telephone company (*IHT*, 8 July 2000, p. 11). 'Deutsche Telekom became the new owner of Slovak Telecom, paying Euro 1 billion for a 51 per cent stake. It is the largest Slovak privatization to date' (*Business Central Europe*, September 2000, p. 14). 'A majority stake in Slovak Telecom, the monopoly telecommunications company, was sold to Deutsche Telekom in July' (EBRD 2000b: 207). 'The Slovak government sold 87 per cent of state savings bank Slovenska Sporitelna to Austria's Erste Bank [in December 2000: p. 42] … Germany's RWE Gas gathered a 40 per cent stake in Slovakia's gas storage company Nafta' (*Business Central Europe*, February 2001, pp. 12–13).

'Restructuring of VSZ, a large steel mill, which defaulted on its foreign debt in late 1998, was advanced through the sell-off of its core assets to US steel in September 2000' (EBRD 2000b: 206).

> Foreign investors are starting to revive some of the companies Mr Meciar's allies destroyed. Take steel-maker VSZ, which was driven to bankruptcy by its Meciar-friendly managers. Revived under the control of its creditors, it was finally sold to US Steel in November 2000 in a $1 billion deal. VSZ was once Slovakia's biggest exporter.
>
> (Business Central Europe 2000: 29)

Foreign trade

Foreign trade has been substantially liberalized, but there are still some quantitative restrictions and licensing.

Full convertibility on the trade account was introduced in 1991 (OECD, *Economic Outlook*, June 1996, p. 104).

There is convertibility as regards current account transactions for enterprises, but there are still some restrictions on the capital account (EBRD 1994: 37, 109). Further steps have been taken to liberalize international capital flows. In December 1997 the short-term Treasury bill market was opened to foreign investors. In April 1998 limits on foreign exchange purchases by Slovak subjects were lifted and short-term capital flows liberalized (EBRD 1998b: 188).

Full current account convertibility for both individuals and enterprises was introduced on 1 October 1995 (in line with Article 8 of the IMF statutes). Some restrictions on the capital account remain, including limits of foreign lending by Slovak entities and purchases of real estate by non-residents. The exchange rate is pegged to a basket in which the DM has a weight of 60 per cent and the US dollar a weight of 40 per cent. The national bank widened the fluctuation band around the central parity for the Slovak crown from plus or minus 1.5 per cent to plus or minus 3 per cent at the beginning of 1996, plus or minus 5 per cent in July 1996 and then plus or minus 7 per cent at the beginning of 1997 (EBRD

1996b: 173, and 1997a: 33; Deutsche Bank, *Focus: Eastern Europe*, 1996, no. 150, p. 10, and no. 159, p. 4).

> While the central bank has thus far been able to alter the crown's exchange rate by small steps of 0.1 per cent per day, it may now make full use of the entire fluctuation band, if necessary. This will make exchange rate speculation considerably more risky.
>
> (Deutsche Bank, *Focus: Eastern Europe*, 1996, no. 160, p. 10)

'The Slovak crown was effectively devalued by around 6 per cent last night [1 October 1988] as the central bank was forced by mounting speculation to abandon its fixed exchange regime' (*FT*, 2 October 1998, p. 2).

> Slovakia's central bank spent nearly $1 billion – close to a quarter of its official foreign exchange reserves – in the past two months in its unsuccessful attempt to protect the currency. The bank was forced to abandon its fixed exchange rate system late on Thursday [1 October] in the face of mounting speculation. Yesterday [2 October] the crown fell against the DM and the US dollar ... on the first day of a new floating exchange rate regime. Official reserves peaked at $3.8 billion in July, but had fallen to $2.9 billion by 1 October. The bank said it was not prepared to allow reserves to fall further and chose to float the currency, abandoning the system of fixing the value of the Slovak crown within a fluctuation band against a basket of currencies.
>
> (*FT*, 3 October 1998, p. 2)

Export licences are required only for certain natural resources. A 10 per cent surcharge on all imports of consumer goods and foodstuffs was introduced in March 1994. The government was to reduce the surcharge to 7.5 per cent on 1 July 1996 and to abolish it at the beginning of 1997.

In the late summer of 1997, a 7 per cent import surcharge was imposed on the bulk of imports (*Business Central Europe*, October 1997, pp. 19–20). Partly as a result of a persistent current account deficit, the government introduced a range of protectionist measures in the spring of 1997. These included an import deposit scheme which forced importers to deposit 20 per cent of the imported value for 180 days in an interest-free account. But the measure was replaced by the reintroduction of a 7 per cent import surcharge – which had been reduced to zero in January 1997. It applied to some 80 per cent of imports. The import surcharge was to be gradually reduced and eliminated in January 1999 (EBRD 1997b: 199). The 7 per cent surcharge, introduced in mid-1997, was phased out by October 1998 (EBRD 1998b: 188). The government has reintroduced a 7 per cent import surcharge, applicable to about three-quarters of imports. The surcharge is seen as a short-term stabilization measure and is to be gradually phased out by January 2001 (EBRD 1999b: 262). 'The import surcharge was lowered to 5 per cent in January 2000 and to 3 per cent in July as planned. The import surcharge is to be abolished at the end of 2000' (EBRD 2000b: 206).

In 1993 the EU accounted for 34.2 per cent of foreign trade (*FT*, Survey, 16 December 1994, p. I). The association agreement with the EU went fully into effect on 1 February 1995.

Foreign direct investment

Slovakia has been far less successful than the Czech Republic in attracting direct foreign investment, despite the fact that some tax and other incentives continue to be offered. Austria accounted for 23.8 per cent of the foreign investment attracted in 1993, Germany 21.1 per cent, the USA 12.8 per cent and the Czech Republic 10.9 per cent (*Business Central Europe*, April 1994, p. 42). Net direct foreign investment was $18 million in 1990, $82 million in 1991, $100 million in 1992, $134 million in 1993, $170 million in 1994 and $157 million in 1995 (the 1993 and 1994 figures excluding flows between Slovakia and the Czech Republic) (United Nations Economic Commission for Europe 1996: 149). (See Table 7.2 for EBRD figures for annual volumes of net direct foreign investment.)

Slovakia does not offer incentives for foreign investment. But the economy ministry has announced that it might introduce tax holidays for foreign investors (*Business Central Europe*, November 1997, p. 26). Tax incentives have been introduced for foreign investors. Manufacturers will be eligible for tax reductions if certain investment and production targets are reached (*Business Central Europe*, June 1998, p. 25). In 1998 the Tesla semi-conductor plant was declared bankrupt. The US company Motorola agreed to buy the firm.

> The Americans managed to squeeze a ten-year tax holiday out of the former Meciar government – the first ever such incentive. The new government hopes to build on that success by offering similar incentives to anyone investing over $5 million. It will also set up free-trade zones and more tax write-offs for research and development.
>
> (*Business Central Europe*, April 1999, p. 66)

In March 1999 the government announced a package of tax incentives to boost foreign investment, including a five-year tax holiday and zero VAT and import duties on imported machinery (p. 12).

> The Social Democratic Party favours targeting resources to where they are needed most, making sure that workers remain the cornerstone of policy. That is why it has insisted that incentives for foreign investors be heavily weighted in favour of high unemployment areas.
>
> (p. 46)

The government is considering whether actively to encourage foreign investment, possibly through tax incentives (EBRD 1997b: 199). In July 1998 the government introduced corporate income tax relief for the first five years for investments exceeding $30 million, subject to conditions regarding investment and output growth (EBRD 1998b: 189). Since April 1999 greenfield foreign direct investment above Euro 5 million and exporting at least 60 per cent of output has been eligible for a five-year corporate income tax holiday, duty-free imports of capital goods, and VAT and property tax exemptions (EBRD 1999b: 263).

> In the middle of 2000 the incentives were further strengthened by extending tax holidays from five to ten years and eliminating some requirements, such as exporting at least 60 per cent of production and producing goods that were previously not manufactured in the Slovak Republic.
>
> (EBRD 2000b: 207)

On 10 May 2000 the government approved a draft law on incentives for foreign investors and helping poorer regions. A 10 per cent tax break will be available depending on the amount invested and its location. Varying subsidies per new job created will be paid. Parliamentary approval is needed (*Transition*, 2000, vol. 11, no. 2, p. 39).

The government has unveiled new incentives for foreign investors, including an extension of tax breaks from five to ten years and government subsidies for job creation (*Business Central Europe*, June 2000, p. 14). 'Tax holidays of up to ten years [are available], while the basic [corporation] tax rate has dropped from 40 per cent to 29 per cent. From January 2001 such incentives apply to local companies too' (Business Central Europe 2000: 29).

> After years of being a black spot for FDI in Central Europe, Slovakia last year [2000] attracted $2 billion, more than the entire amount received since … 1993 … VW accounts for 16 per cent of exports … In May [2001], after prolonged discussions with the EU, the government agreed to revamp the incentives. Once they are approved by parliament, they should take effect from September [2001]. The new incentives – which the EU insisted should not apply to the rich Bratislava region – increase the tax holiday to ten years … and grant subsidies for job creation and retraining, and allow zero import duty on some machinery. The investment requirements have been lowered … The government has also dropped requirements to export more than 60 per cent of production and reinvest any tax savings.
>
> (*FT*, Survey, 4 July 2001, p. iii)

Agriculture

Private farms still play a negligible role, with an average size of less than 1 ha (*Business Central Europe*, September 1993, p. 25).

'In formerly collectivized Central Europe … the majority response of landowners [after restitution] was to rent their land to the larger units that emerged from the transformation process, whether it was the transformed co-operative or a new successor company' (Swain 1999: 1205). 'Most people … rejected the idea of farming their newly acquired land themselves and rented it back to either the co-operative or one of its successor companies' (p. 1216).

> In Slovakia, as in the Czech Republic, the co-operatives continued to be important, only more so … During transformation 98 per cent of co-operatives opted to retain the co-operative form, and in 1994 co-operatives continued to farm 69.9 per cent ofp agricultural land. Other corporate bodies farmed 4.6 per cent of agricultural land, and private individual farms only 5.2 per cent. Of the latter some 76 per cent of private farms were under 10 ha, and around 2 per cent were over 100 ha.
>
> (p. 1212)

'The Meciar government agreed to restitute former church land in the Slovak Republic in exchange for political support for his minority government during a political crisis in 1993' (Swinnen 1999: 651).

Economic performance

Macroeconomic performance has been relatively good compared with Slovakia's political record. But restructuring was neglected, with substantial state support for ailing enterprises, under the Meciar administrations.

GDP growth turned positive as early as 1994. (See Table 7.2.) GDP regained its 1989 level in 1999 (EBRD 2000b: 65, and 2001a: 15). The annual inflation rate reached a peak of only 61.2 per cent in 1991. The inflation rate moved into single figures in 1995 but in 1999 and 2000 the rate was in double figures.

Part II

General issues

8 General issues in the transition from command to market economies

'BIG BANG'/'SHOCK THERAPY' VERSUS GRADUALISM

In late 1989 the world witnessed the stunning and unexpected collapse of communism in Eastern Europe. The Soviet president, Mikhail Gorbachev, was unwilling to use force to preserve Soviet control over the East European Comecon countries. Indeed, towards the end of 1991 the Soviet Union itself ceased to exist. Gorbachev did not intend this to happen but, again, he did not try to preserve it by force.

Not surprisingly, the question of how to handle the transition from 'communism' to 'capitalism' has led to immense controversy and problems. There is even controversy about how unique the economic process is. Sachs, for example, argues that the conversion of a socialist into a capitalist economy is

> In many ways ... a well-trodden path ... Although parts of the transformation represent uncharted territory (such as massive privatization of industry), many other aspects of Eastern Europe's reform tasks are quite familiar. Many other countries that were once cut off from the rest of the world by inward-looking, authoritarian regimes have successfully opened up and become integrated into the global mainstream.
>
> (Sachs 1994: 2–3)

Sachs surely understates, to a marked degree, the differences in jettisoning a command economy. But while there are major areas of dispute as to how to handle the economic transition, it may be argued that the virulence of the debate often hides substantial areas of agreement.

Only the main aspects of the theoretical debate can be given here, while the ways in which the transition has actually been tackled are best dealt with in the country chapters. There are two broad approaches to transition, 'big bang'/'shock therapy' and 'gradualism', although even definitions are not as clear as one might wish for. Thus 'large' privatization is a relatively lengthy process even in the former, while China's 'gradualism' includes relatively rapid agricultural reform. Vietnam has clearly been influenced by China, but the bundle of reforms in 1989–91 has a 'big bang'/'shock therapy' look about it.

'Big bang'/'shock therapy'

'Big bang'/'shock therapy' is a programme of rapid and comprehensive market transformation (comprising a package of interdependent measures) coupled with macroeconomic stabilization where necessary. First, a word about terms. The terms 'big bang' and 'shock therapy' are often used interchangeably, while the term 'shock therapy' is more often than not used in a broad sense to cover both (1) severe austerity measures and (2) a rapid and comprehensive change in the economic system. But at times the term has been used in a narrower sense, referring only to (1). For example, the claim that in 1993 Russia had not undertaken 'shock therapy' makes sense only if definition (1) is employed. It would be preferable to reserve 'shock therapy' for (1) and 'big bang' for (2), but current usage renders the composite term 'big bang'/'shock therapy' more appropriate. The measures constituting 'big bang'/'shock therapy' are as follows:

1 *Liberalization.* This includes the end of central planning and the freeing of prices in the context of a liberal international trade regime, i.e. a rapid progression to a market economy. Rapid *current* account convertibility of the currency is recommended. (The Asian/Russian financial crisis bolstered the arguments against undue haste in dismantling controls on the capital account.)
2 *Privatization.* The rapid expansion of the private sector through deregulation (i.e. freedom of entry into sectors of the economy by new enterprises) and the privatization of state enterprises is recommended. It is acknowledged that 'large' privatization will take longer than 'small' privatization. (The details of the various schemes proposed for privatization are dealt with below.) In the meantime the remaining state enterprises will need to be disciplined by measures such as demonopolization, exposure to domestic and foreign competition and the ending of 'soft budget constraints'. (Where soft budget constraints operate inefficient enterprises are bailed out by the government through such means as direct budget subsidies, soft credits from state banks and tax concessions – including write-offs.)
3 *Stabilization.* Macroeconomic stabilization is needed in order to bring inflation under control and generate confidence in domestic money. Severe austerity measures are necessary in cases of chronic inflationary pressures. If repressed inflation exists a 'big bang' liberalization of prices will transform this into open inflation, i.e. if a 'monetary overhang' exists these forced savings will be eroded in real terms.

Macroeconomic stabilization, however, does not mean zero inflation and various empirical studies have tackled this question. Fischer *et al.* (1996) analyse data on the experience of growth and stabilization in twenty-six transition countries for the period 1989–94. 'The evidence discussed in this paper strongly suggests that growth requires stabilization and that stabilization leads to growth. Moreover, it appears that for growth to begin annual inflation should be less than 50 per cent' (p. 47). 'Evidence from a wide range of market economies shows that once annual inflation rises above a threshold level of around 40 per cent, growth deteriorates dramatically' (World Bank 1996: 22). Sachs defines 'relatively low' inflation rates as, for example, 30 per cent a year (1997: 248).

Proponents such as Jeffrey Sachs (1994) also recommend a 'social safety net' (especially an unemployment compensation scheme) and see the need for a generous international aid (and trade) policy.

There are various arguments supporting 'big bang'/'shock therapy':

1. It is argued that the various measures are interdependent, e.g. price liberalization is feasible even with uncompetitive market structures if there is simultaneous foreign trade liberalization, foreign companies thus providing the competition. (The details of price liberalization are dealt with below.)
2. 'Big bang'/'shock therapy' provides unambiguous signals of intent as to the direction of reform.
3. The bureaucracy is bypassed and the rapid reduction of state regulations helps deter corruption and crime.
4. Vested interests in shrinking sectors (which attempt to delay reform) are outweighed by new vested interests in favour of reform.
5. Governments can make use of a brief political 'honeymoon period' after being elected to undertake rapid, comprehensive and often painful measures. This 'window of opportunity' is to be used to ensure that the reform process becomes irreversible, i.e. the farther the process of reform proceeds the more unfeasible it becomes to return to the old system.

The advocates of 'big bang'/'shock therapy' also argue that they have been vindicated by actual developments in the transitional countries of Eastern Europe and the former Soviet Union. Frequent mention is made of the fact that Poland (which, in 1990, was the first to start rapid and comprehensive change) was the first to return to positive growth (in 1992) and the first to regain its 1989 level of national output (in 1996). Thus Sachs (1996a: 128) argues that 'The first lesson of the first five years is that rapid systemic transformation can work. It is possible to introduce the institutions of a market economy within five years and to reestablish economic growth.'

Major advocates of 'big bang'/'shock therapy' include Jeffrey Sachs, Anders Åslund and Leszek Balcerowicz. Leszek Balcerowicz was Poland's finance minister (1989–92) and implemented the first actual 'big bang'/'shock therapy'. (He was reappointed as Poland's finance minister on 31 October 1997 but was replaced on 8 June 2000.)

'Big bang' price liberalization versus gradual price reform

In the former 'communist' countries most prices were determined by the state. There is a debate about (1) whether economies in transition should free most prices at once (typical exceptions including energy prices and housing rents) as part of a programme of rapid and comprehensive economic reform and macroeconomic stabilization, or (2) whether to allow the market to determine prices only gradually over time.

Among the arguments in favour of rapid price liberalization are the following:

1 The need to make use of the political 'honeymoon' period to make painful economic decisions.
2 Market-determined prices lead to a more efficient allocation of resources.
3 Queues and forced substitution of goods are eliminated when price controls are ended. Confidence is restored in the currency. The benefits of the elimination of queues include more leisure time and greater incentives to work (since money income can command control over goods and services). There is the argument that the welfare costs of monopoly are less than those of queues. Controls over prices and the consequent shortages encourage corruption and 'rent-seeking' (the seeking of favours, such as subsidies, from the government).
4 Repressed inflationary pressures are eased as any 'monetary overhang' (forced savings) is eroded. Although the release of most price controls leads to an immediate increase in open inflation, macroeconomic stabilization policies will gradually bring down the rate of increase in the general price level.
5 The liberalization of foreign trade, including rapid current account convertibility, is emphasized. 'International competition would provide the competition in the internal market that … firms themselves would not provide at the start. If free trade could be introduced, prices could be liberalized' (Sachs 1994: 50). Likewise, Balcerowicz (1994: 28) recommends that 'a comprehensive price liberalization should be complemented by comprehensive liberalization of foreign trade'. It is thus not only inadvisable but not even necessary to wait until privatization and competitive domestic conditions are created. (The existence of a healthy private sector at the start of the transition would, of course, enhance the supply response. Thus Poland was in a better position than Russia to engage in 'big bang' price liberalization.)
6 'Big bang' price rises will lead to dishoarding and increased supply, while demand will be reduced (thus encouraging a subsequent fall in prices). With staged price increases supplies will be withheld from the market in anticipation of future price rises, while consumers try to speed up their purchases.
7 Woo (1994: 278–9) argues that the common consequence of partial price reform is that the state is obliged to accede to requests for subsidies from loss-making firms that have their output prices controlled. There is little incentive for such firms to increase their efficiency because it is hard for the government to determine whether the losses are due to price controls or to mismanagement and misappropriation. Similarly, Balcerowicz believes that slow price liberalization would prolong the existence of distorted prices. Thus the performance of enterprises cannot be judged reliably and the soft

budget constraint is likely to persist as loss-makers are able to blame distorted prices.

Among the arguments in favour of gradual price reform are the following:

1 The communist legacy was a structure of industry dominated by large state-owned enterprises. Releasing most prices in these circumstances would not lead to the sort of elastic supply responses assumed by 'big bang' advocates, while monopoly profits on a large scale would be made. Monopoly price rises would increase inflationary pressures. Thus prices are best released gradually, in line with privatization (defined broadly to include the creation of new firms) and the creation of more competitive conditions through demonopolization and regulation of remaining monopolies. Tsang (1996: 190) forcibly argues against a sudden freeing of prices:

> The price elasticity of supply is so low that the inflation rate will shoot up to unprecedented levels, seriously derailing production and generating extreme impacts on income distribution and people's livelihood ... The monopolists in the CPEs [centrally planned economies] may simply get abnormal profits ... The non-monopolists will not be able to cope with the huge rises in production costs and will probably suffer huge losses ... Together, these phenomena may generate a serious situation of stagflation, which not only threatens the short-term prospects of reform, but also the long-term growth potential of the economy.

(Note the arguments against the rapid liberalization of foreign trade below.)

2 If macroeconomic stabilization measures are not successfully taken the price rises could set off a price–wage spiral. McKinnon (1994: 462) argues that 'the big bang argument for total price decontrol is flawed if the important actors bidding for scarce resources have soft budget constraints'. Indeed, 'until budget constraints are hardened, uncontrolled bidding by state enterprises will cause the producer price to increase indefinitely'. (Russia in 1992 may be cited as an example.)

3 There is the danger of social unrest as the real value of savings is rapidly eroded by large price rises. This danger is enhanced if increases in money wages and pensions are not kept in line with price rises as macroeconomic stabilization measures are implemented.

4 Foreign aid may be inadequate and/or not synchronized with the ending of price controls.

5 China has shown that gradual price reform is compatible with an impressive economic performance. Hussain and Stern (1994: 7) argue that one lesson of the Chinese experience is that

market transactions can flourish even under a heavily distorted price structure and in particular economic sectors, whilst others remain closed. Once established they themselves can become a powerful force for a rationalization of prices. Experience with market transactions enhances the capacity of agents to adapt to changes in relative prices.

Gradualism

The advocates of 'gradualism' criticize various aspects of 'big bang'/'shock therapy':

1 There are doubts about the feasibility of achieving so much so quickly (although the precise time scale involved is another debate in itself). The proponents of 'big bang'/'shock therapy', it is argued, are generally too optimistic about the time needed to adjust, e.g. the time needed for appropriate institutions (political, legal and economic), attitudes and behaviour to develop (including informal codes of behaviour such as 'gentlemen's agreements'). There is, for example, a vital need for an efficient and honest legal system to enforce contracts and property rights. (This is dealt with in detail below, in the section on seeking a compromise.)
2 The cost of making a mistake in a rapid and comprehensive programme is likely to be large. With a more gradual approach the cost of smaller errors can be contained and corrective action taken more quickly. This may encourage a more positive reaction to the whole reform process among the population. A modest but successful start to the reforms would also boost political support. (China prior to 1978 had a history of huge, albeit left-wing, mistakes.)
3 The wisdom of attempting 'big bang'/'shock therapy' is questioned because severe strains could be put on society. There is the danger that democracy and markets could become associated in many people's eyes with intolerable hardship for too long a period of time, exacerbated by growing inequalities in income and wealth (often earned in shady or downright criminal ways in the 'Wild East' stage of transition). It is argued that proponents were generally too optimistic about the prospective costs of transition, including falling output and living standards and increasing open unemployment. The sharp decline in investment associated with austerity measures actually hinders the adjustment process. It is also argued that Western advisers advocate policies of rapid market liberalization which even their own governments would find unacceptable, including foreign trade. (The problems and time dimension of West European integration, including the movement towards a single currency, is often quoted as a comparison.) As much as possible should be done to ease the transition for the 'losers', e.g. the provision of Western aid and as generous a system of training and unemployment benefit as possible. (Unemployment in Eastern Europe has especially affected groups like the

young, the unskilled and women and areas such as those dependent on declining heavy industries.)

(It is generally recognized that the officially recorded falls in output and real wages in the early years of transition may have been exaggerated. For example, inadequate account is taken of the rapidly growing private sector – especially that operating in the black economy, the improving quality and usefulness of goods, and the increasing availability of goods as shortages diminish. Some economists advocate the use of electricity consumption as a better indicator of the decline in economic activity, this generally giving a more optimistic picture. There is also a separate debate about the relative importance of the causes of output decline, such as deflationary policies, the change of economic system, the collapse of Comecon trade, the price-raising behaviour of state enterprises and recession in the West in the early 1990s.)

4 A liberal foreign trade policy (e.g. low tariffs) could have severe adverse effects on domestic producers, especially if there is a fixed exchange rate regime, i.e. too early and radical an opening to foreign competition could decimate generally relatively inefficient domestic industry in transitional economies.

5 Tsang (1996) stresses the problems arising from the difficulty of asset valuation and from the inheritance of 'implicit contracts' from the socialist era: low wages in return for housing subsidies (p. 186); 'the implicit rights of many citizens to the previously state-owned property and assets' (p. 185); 'the worker's implicit rights to the state enterprises' (p. 187). The neglect of such contracts would 'lead to unfair and counter-productive outcomes' (p. 185).

6 A subdivision of gradualism is the 'evolutionary' school typified by the views of Peter Murrell (1993: 113). 'Big bang' advocates like Lipton and Sachs, he claims, do not

> examine existing institutional structures and how to change them to reach the goal [the creation of a Western-type economic system], but rather focus on ways, the methods, and the strategies to replace these structures entirely … There is complete disdain for all that exists … History, society, and the economics of present institutions are all minor issues in choosing a reform programme … Given the existing structures are a problem, society must be side-stepped in the reform process.

Evolutionists like Murrell advocate a gradual phasing out of the old institutional framework, e.g. the private sector should be actively encouraged to grow as opposed to 'forced' privatization (p. 119). He argues that an understanding of the success of capitalism requires primary emphasis to be placed on mechanisms that produce growth and change as opposed to equilibrium processes. In Schumpeterian fashion he thus focuses on the role played by innovation rather than on allocative efficiency. The evolutionary approach stresses 'the existence of rigidities in organizational behaviour and the importance of entry and exit processes to the dynamism of capitalism' (Murrell 1992b: 52). Hence, during the transition privatization should be given a lower priority than policies encouraging the growth of new private firms (pp. 36, 46). Murrell also argues that some of the existing structures could be used. Thus 'during the transition there might be a case for direct controls on state enterprises to promote macroeconomic stability, rather than relying upon solely market-based measures' (p. 47).

7 The example of China since 1978 shows the virtues of gradualism.

But while there is general agreement that the sort of 'tinkering around' indulged in by most of the communist countries was largely a dead end, China's overall economic success since 1978 has led to a considerable debate about whether the transitional countries of Eastern Europe and the former Soviet Union should adopt (or rather should have adopted) China's model. Woo goes so far as to say that 'gradual reform in China was not the optimal reform for China' (1994: 306). But sceptics, recognizing China's economic successes, generally put forward the following arguments against its relevance in Eastern Europe and the former Soviet Union:

1 China's position in 1978 was generally more favourable in terms of inflation, foreign debt and trade with the West. Initial circumstances in countries can vary and thus policy responses may have to differ.
2 The critical aspect in which China differed was the structure of the economy. The World Bank (1996: 21) points out that in 1978, 71 per cent of the workforce were employed in agriculture and only 15 per cent in industry (the respective figures for 1994 being 58 per cent and 18 per cent). By way of contrast, the respective 1990 figures for Russia were 13 per cent and 42 per cent.

   Sachs and Woo (1994: 103–43) argue that rapid growth in China was possible because the large agricultural sector contained vast surplus labour and did not enjoy subsidies. This labour fuelled the rapidly growing new industries in the non-state sector, while the reallocation of labour allowed all groups to gain. In Eastern Europe and the former Soviet Union the much larger state sector has impeded the necessary structural adjustments. Gradualism would not work because curtailing subsidies would produce losers who would use their power to resist this adjustment. Gradualism would not result in sufficient productivity gains to overcome the losses. Layard (*Economics of Transition*, 1993, vol. 1, no. 3, p. 358) argues that Russia has a huge industrial sector which must be improved; it is no good simply to rely on entry by new firms. Others, too, point to the necessity of restructuring and privatizing the large industrial sectors in Eastern Europe and the former Soviet Union. China has been able to continue subsidizing its industrial sector because it is relatively small.

3 Even Nolan (1996), a strong defender of the Chinese model, admits that 'careful study of China's reform path would have been relevant to devising a reform strategy for the country in the late 1980s. It is not much relevant to Russia's current situation' (p. 248).

> The fundamental cause of the Soviet collapse lies in the destruction of the nation state and the state administrative apparatus under Gorbachev ... To be successful an economic reform strategy requires political stability and effective government ... Once the state apparatus had collapsed the range of options for any successor government was greatly reduced.
>
> (pp. 242–3)

'Without a coherent, effective state apparatus ... it was impossible to follow an "East Asian" approach to the transition' (p. 244). (There are, of course, objections to a one-party state in itself.)

4 For China's township–village enterprises to work there is need for a culture in which decisions can be made in the absence of conventional property rights. 'The key missing element [in conventional property rights theory] is the ability of a group to solve conflicts internally, without explicit rules, laws, rights, procedures and so forth' (Weitzman and Xu 1993: 28).

5 China was able to tap the vast capital and entrepreneurial resources of ethnic Chinese in other countries. (This source of capital was adversely affected by the Asian financial crisis, which began in July 1997.)

The quest for compromise

Since everybody agrees that not 'everything' can be done 'at once', the question of the correct 'sequencing' of reforms comes to the fore. Sequencing explores the merits and demerits of various sequences or orders in which reforms can be introduced. Economists are at odds over issues such as the following: whether price liberalization should precede or accompany/follow demonopolization/privatization; whether the restructuring of the typically very large enterprises (e.g. breaking them up) should precede or follow privatization; when to liberalize the financial system.

Another sequencing problem is how quickly to liberalize the foreign trade sector. Those advocating gradual change argue that too early and radical an opening to foreign competition could decimate generally relatively inefficient domestic industry in transitional economies. The Asian financial crisis started in July 1997 with a speculative attack on the currency of Thailand and then spread to other emerging markets. Russia started to be affected in October 1997 and May 1998 was a bad month. But disaster struck on 17 August 1998 when Russia was forced to devalue the rouble and default on its domestic debt. The Asian/Russian financial crisis bolstered the arguments against undue haste in dismantling controls on the capital account. 'Because implementation of the necessary structural and macroeconomic measures requires time to become effective governments should explore market-based means of containing the volatility of short-term capital flows while significant vulnerability remains' (EBRD 1998b: vi–vii).

There is increasing recognition that the institutional basis of a market economy takes a long time to put in place.

> Some aspects of a market economy can and have been created quickly in transition economies, in particular through market liberalization and privatization. However, developing the institutions and business practices required for a well-functioning market economy takes much longer ... Developing the capacity of the state to regulate effectively, as well as to provide other institutional arrangements required in a market economy, demands a radical reorientation of governance away from the direct control of economic activity to an effective supporting role. This reorientation inevitably takes time since it depends on the development of the necessary skills and practices. As the example of regulation shows, much remains to be done in transition economies in building this new role for the state.
>
> (EBRD 1998b: iv)

> [During 1998] market-oriented reforms have generally been slow and inconsistent throughout the region ... Policy reversals have become more common, partly in response to economic crisis. This imbalance has continued to widen between the earlier successes of privatization and liberalization and the more difficult structural and institutional challenges of the next phase of transition. These challenges include corporate governance and enterprise restructuring, financial sector reforms, infrastructure reform, and fiscal and social reforms ... The challenges of the next phase ... require a substantial and constructive role of the state at a time when its capacity is still underdeveloped and subject to capture by powerful economic interests ... Reversals in macroeconomic stabilization as the transition progresses point to the fragile foundations in many countries for sustained growth and stability. Large and persistent fiscal imbalances, particularly in the CIS, reflect underlying structural weaknesses, including soft budget constraints for loss-making enterprises, an opaque and distorted tax system, and inefficient tax administration. As a result the tax base is small (and shrinking), the burden on those enterprises still paying taxes is excessive and evasion is widespread ... The financial systems of the transition economies remain underdeveloped, burdened by the legacies of central planning and the structural and macroeconomic upheavals early in the transition. When compared with those of market economies at comparable levels of development, the banking systems of transition economies appear relatively stunted, particularly in lending to the private sector. At the same time their securities markets are even more severely underdeveloped. In other words, the finan-

cial sectors of transition economies are both small and heavily bank-based, a holdover from central planning's monobank system.

(pp. vi–vii)

'Experience has demonstrated that the process of transition from the command to the market economy is complex, difficult and lengthy' (EBRD 1999b: 4). 'The evidence now shows clearly that the central lesson of transition is that markets will not function well without supporting institutions, a state that carries through its basic responsibilities and a healthy civil society' (p. 5).

> Some aspects of a market economy can and have been created quickly, in particular through liberalization and privatization. However, developing the institutions and behaviour required for well-functioning markets and private enterprise takes much longer. The promotion of effective institutions, such as government structures, laws and regulations and the sound behaviour of governments, enterprises and financial institutions, lies at the heart of the challenge of transition as it enters the next decade.
>
> (p. iv)

> Building institutions that support markets and private enterprise remains a fundamental challenge of transition, but establishing the appropriate laws and regulations is not sufficient. They must be embodied in the social norms, practices and behaviours of both government and the private sector – institutions that need social capital and social foundations.
>
> (p. 9)

'Social capital may be defined in terms of voluntary compliance with established laws, trust, co-operative behaviour and basic codes of conduct' (p. 5). 'In the more advanced countries rapid liberalization and sustained macroeconomic stabilization have laid the basis for gradual institutional change' (p. vi). 'Countries that have achieved sustained progress in liberalization, macroeconomic stabilization, small-scale privatization and openness to foreign trade and investment have also advanced steadily in the development of market institutions' (p. 38).

The World Bank's conclusion is interesting. 'Gradual, partial reforms were not an option for most … countries' of Eastern Europe and the former Soviet Union (World Bank 1996: 23).

> Differences between countries are very important, both in setting the feasible range of policy choice and in determining the response to reforms. Which works best, rapid or gradual reform? This question has no single or simple answer … Nevertheless, for the bulk of these economies [the coun-

> tries of the former Soviet Union and Central and Eastern Europe] the answer is now clear: faster and more consistent reform is better.
>
> (p. 143)

> A country's starting circumstances, both economic and political, greatly affect the range of reform policies and outcomes open to it. Within this range, however, the clear lesson of the past few years' reforms is that, regardless of the starting point, decisive and consistent reform pays off.
>
> (p. 9)

'In every case [including China and Vietnam] what matters is the breadth of the policy reforms attempted and the consistency with which they are maintained' (p. 21). 'Consistent policies, combining liberalization of markets, trade and new business entry with reasonable price stability, can achieve a great deal – even in countries lacking clear property rights and strong market institutions' (p. 142).

The question essentially revolves around how much can or should be attempted at the 'same' time. Scepticism about the wisdom and feasibility of a 'big bang' solution must be countered by awareness that doing next to nothing brings about economic catastrophe. (In the early years of Ukrainian independence there was hyperinflation and collapsing output at the same time, hence the term 'Ukrainianization'.) Consequently, there may be merit in the idea of (1) a 'critical mass' of co-ordinated measures on a sufficient scale to provide an irreversible and ongoing momentum to the reform process, and (2) a credible programme for which a democratically elected government must seek and maintain popular approval (as stressed by the United Nations Economic Commission for Europe: 1993: 9). Choosing the appropriate blend and scale of measures best suited to individual countries is a political art rather than an economic 'science'. The initial circumstances vary between countries, such as the severity of macroeconomic disequilibrium, the size of the private sector, the extent of the previous reforms, the burden of foreign debt and the availability of aid.

The debate seems to boil down to what is politically and economically feasible. As Clague (1992: 15) points out, the difference between the 'big bang' and evolutionary approaches 'lies primarily in judgements about what is politically feasible'. In similar fashion, Åslund (1994: 37) has concluded that 'the interesting limitation [on swift and comprehensive change] is what is practically and politically possible, and nothing else'. Portes (1994: 1180) usefully adds:

> The range of sensible strategies is limited and there may be little margin for choice. Some elements of stabilization and liberalization make sense only when done simultaneously. The range observed across countries is in fact surprisingly limited and mainly a function of initial conditions.

Rhetoric has often concealed considerable agreement in a new area of economics where clear definitions are frequently hard to come by. Many of the alleged protagonists would probably agree that as much as possible should be done as quickly as possible, but the problem is that this begs all sorts of questions.

THE PRIVATIZATION OF INDUSTRIAL ENTERPRISES

The special problems facing transitional economies in privatizing industrial enterprises

It is 'large' privatization that is emphasized here, namely the privatization of medium-sized and large enterprises. 'Small' privatization (of shops and restaurants, for example) presents far fewer difficulties and has typically been rapid in transitional economies. There is also much less resistance socially to small privatization, for the benefits in terms of much needed improvements in the quantity and quality of consumer goods are quickly apparent.

The sheer scale of state ownership in the former socialist ('communist') economies makes the issue of privatization a vital one. The communist legacy also included the following: one of generally inefficient enterprises (which were often social units as well, providing benefits such as health care); managers working in a non-competitive environment and often chosen for political loyalty rather than expertise; and monopolistic structures of industry.

Property rights include the right to use an asset, to enjoy any income generated by the asset and to sell the asset. Such rights give an incentive to use property efficiently. State ownership (and 'social ownership', as in the former Yugoslavia) has the potential for property abuse ('everybody's property is nobody's property'). This is especially the case where, as in command economies, a 'soft budget constraint' operates, i.e. where inefficient enterprises are kept in operation by governments unwilling to see unemployment and closures on a large scale. Support includes direct budget subsidies, soft credit from state banks and tax concessions (even write-offs). (Note that 'commercialization' or 'corporatization', which helps clarify property rights, involves the conversion of state enterprises into joint stock companies free of ministerial control. The state owns the shares at first but these can be sold later. The issue of whether to restructure enterprises before or after privatization is not considered here.)

The important (and academically non-controversial) question of encouraging new private firms is not considered here. But lifting constraints such as those on employment can be done very quickly.

> Research shows start-up firms [greenfield activity] are overwhelmingly most efficient and superior to even the best privatized firms … An equally important conclusion is how the presence of start-up firms contributes to the appropriate competitive environment and puts pressure on newly privatized firms of all types to achieve comparable efficiency.
>
> (Havrylyshyn and McGettigan 1999: 10)

Poland has shown that a relatively slow process of large privatization can still bring benefits when state industrial enterprises are made to face 'hard budget constraints' (i.e. no automatic bail-outs by the state) and competition from domestic and foreign companies. Measures such as anti-monopoly (anti-trust) policy, an open trade policy and an open investment policy, coupled with appropriate management incentives for state enterprises, 'may result in a set of conditions where the speed of implementing privatization is no longer crucial' (Rausser 1992: 326, 328).

> The backdrop against which privatization efforts have taken place is important. And what is known about supportive market environments suggests that four elements are essential: macroeconomic stability, hard budget constraints, competitive markets and adequate property rights.
>
> (Havrylyshyn and McGettigan 1999: 11)

'Investigation shows that Polish managers of state firms performed well because they expected privatization and hoped their achievements would assure their survival when it came' (p. 5).

Thus even those who see virtue in state ownership in certain sectors of the economy are aware of the importance of competition wherever possible and regulation otherwise. There is the problem of the degree of privatization. The question of whether to privatize state companies, especially in the case of 'natural monopolies' (such as water supply, telecommunications and electricity generation and distribution) is, of course, an important issue even in Western countries.

The potential for abuse is massive. Thus there is need for an honest, democratic and hence accountable state to control the process of privatization (and for an efficient and honest legal system to enforce contracts and property rights). Otherwise state assets may be taken over in ways which vary in their degree of legality and which benefit only certain sections of society. 'Spontaneous' privatization essentially means that managers and other members of the *nomenklatura* get their hands on state property at below market prices. 'Those entrusted with state assets take possession of them in one way or another or initiate arrangements for their disposal to private agents.' Earlier forms of uncontrolled or 'wild' spontaneous privatization in Eastern Europe involved 'a more or less sophisticated theft from the state or society as a whole', such as obtaining shares or guaranteed jobs in the new companies (United Nations Economic Commission for Europe 1992: 231). Frydman *et al.* (1993: 34) distinguish between 'illegal' and 'quiet' forms of spontaneous privatization. The latter involves no formal illegality, but relies on acts which do not provide the open, public and competitive sales of state property.

A word may be in order at this point on two systems of corporate finance and control:

1 The UK and USA model of relatively powerful stock markets has advantages, such as the threat of takeovers disciplining managers to act in the best interests of shareholders. But the model has been criticized on grounds such as the danger of 'short-termism' (investments bringing long-term benefits are avoided because of the possible initial dip in profits) and the possible lack of effective corporate control in the event of relatively dispersed ownership. In transitional economies stock markets are young or even non-existent. The absence of effective regulation of stock markets can lead to the sort of problems experienced by the Czech Republic (such as the defrauding of shareholders).

2 The German and Japanese model involves banks becoming long-term suppliers of finance to companies. The role of banks is extended to ownership and control and there is little second-hand trading on secondary markets. The arguments in favour include stronger corporate control and longer-term commitments to enterprises. Arguments against include the lack of suitable banks in transitional economies. The weaknesses of this system have been exposed by the Asian financial crisis which began in July 1997, e.g. banks providing loans on the basis of cronyism and patronage rather than profitability.

The methods of privatization

There are a variety of methods of privatization, although in reality privatization programmes are mixtures (packages) of some sort or another. The varying emphases in these mixed programmes reflect political as well as economic circumstances. As is seen below, Russia's weak central (federal) government claimed that it needed to 'buy off' a powerful managerial lobby (in a society sceptical about the value of privatization), while the former Czechoslovakia had a strong central government (which was not faced by severe inflationary pressures, and therefore had less need to raise revenue for budgetary purposes). Although burdened by a large *per capita* foreign debt, Hungary has not sought debt-forgiveness. Hence revenue raised from sales has been particularly important. The director of the Slovenian privatization agency has said that 'the political conditions here would make it impossible to do it all through the state like in Germany, because all managers here believe they already own the companies' (Patrick Blum, *FT*, Survey, 12 April 1994, p. 32).

The sale of state-owned industrial enterprises to 'outsiders'

The 'outsiders' may be domestic or foreign. There are a variety of ways of selling assets, e.g. auctions, tenders (which involve factors additional to price, such as investment and employment commitments) and public share offerings. Sales may target 'strategic' investors who buy whole enterprises or at least a sufficient number of shares to exercise strong corporate control.

Among the advantages of sales are the following:

1 Funds are made available both for enterprises to invest and for governments typically having difficulty in raising tax revenue. Even if some of the funds include 'dirty money' (ill-gotten gains) it may be considered preferable to use such funds productively rather than to use them illegally (perhaps in ways that subvert the democratic process).
2 'Strategic owners' may bring a package of benefits such as superior management, new technology, marketing skills and access to fresh capital.

Among the disadvantages of sales are the following:

1 Savings are typically low in transitional economies, especially when a 'big bang' price liberalization has drastically reduced the real value of both voluntary savings and forced savings ('monetary overhang'). In addition, stock markets are in their infancy in the early stages of transition.
2 Many citizens are too poor to participate. If the general public suspect (rightly or wrongly) that the process involves 'dirty money' or is corruptly carried out, the very notion of privatization may be brought into disrepute. There are also problems if citizens feel that foreigners are gaining control of assets cheaply, especially if such assets are considered 'vital' or 'strategic'.
3 Slow privatization owing to the difficulties of valuing enterprises and negotiating deals on a case-by-case basis.
4 Brada (1996: 71) highlights the possible drawbacks of tenders, using the example of German reunification.

> The use of investment and employment guarantees by the Treuhand [privatization agency] is a two-edged sword. It ensures that the new owners will not strip and liquidate their new holdings; however, it also ensures that firms remain in the same line of activity, which slows the process of needed structural change.

Management–employee buy-outs

Existing managers and employees are referred to as 'insiders' and may be allowed to use vouchers and/or cash to purchase all or a controlling portion of shares in 'their' enterprises, perhaps on relatively favourable terms. With management–employee buy-outs, shares of an enterprise are thus sold or given to some combination of managers and other employees. Straight management buy-outs are possible at one extreme.

Among the advantages of management–employee buy-outs are the following:

1 More rapid privatization is likely when powerful vested interests have an incentive not to thwart the process. The need to 'buy off' these 'insiders' (especially existing managers) in a situation where the central government is relatively weak was used as a reason for the privileges given 'insiders' in the first phase of Russian privatization (which ended in mid-1994). Workers'

councils were powerful in post-communist Poland and in the successor countries of the former Yugoslavia.

2 'Insiders' have better access to information about the worth of an enterprise than 'outsiders'.

3 'Insiders' now own all or a majority of the shares of their enterprise and this provides an incentive to be more efficient and to be more concerned with the long-run health of their enterprise. (Many actual privatization schemes have made provision for at least a small proportion of shares to go to 'insiders' for incentive purposes.)

Among the disadvantages of management–employee buy-outs are the following:

1 The rest of society does not directly benefit from this form of privatization and the gains to various groups of 'insiders' vary enormously, depending on the financial situation of their particular enterprise. 'Insiders' themselves put 'all their eggs in one basket'. Political patronage may be involved in the choice of managers (and even workers) prior to privatization.

2 Any special privileges to 'insiders' are at the expense of government revenue.

3 The problem of disciplining existing management.

4 Outsider investors (especially foreigners) may be deterred by additional factors, such as the temptation for 'insiders' to stress wages and salaries over reinvestment.

5 'The method of privatization seems to matter a great deal in a way not foreseen earlier: some forms of insider-dominated privatization may generate oligopolistic vested interests that will work against the establishment of an open, competitive environment, and against providing a level playing field for start-up entrepreneurial activity. With government privileges added (most commonly in the form of tax exemptions) the result is a continuation of a soft budget and a distorted allocation of resources toward the less efficient and the politically favoured' (Havrylyshyn and McGettigan 1999: 8–9).

Frydman *et al.* (1999) have undertaken an econometric analysis of state and privatized manufacturing firms in the Czech Republic, Hungary and Poland based on a survey conducted in the autumn of 1994. Performance measures involved the growth of revenue, employment, labour productivity and costs per unit of output.

> Our findings show that in the context of Central Europe, privatization has no beneficial effect on any performance measure in the case of firms controlled by insider owners (managers or employees), and that it has a very pronounced effect on firms with outsider owners … While the effect of privatization on revenue performance is very pronounced for certain types

> of owners, there is no significant effect of any type of ownership change on cost reduction.
>
> (pp. 1154–5)

'In the context of the transition economies of Central Europe … privatization is effective in enhancing revenue and productivity performance of firms that come to be controlled by outsiders, but produces no significant effect in firms controlled by insiders' (pp. 1186–7).

Mass (voucher) privatization

In a programme of mass privatization citizens (all or those deemed eligible, by age, for example) are allocated (equally or with account taken of such things as length of employment) vouchers for free or at nominal cost. These vouchers may or may not be tradable for cash. But vouchers can be exchanged directly for shares in enterprises to be privatized, in private investment funds which then buy shares in enterprises, or in (perhaps temporary) government-created (but not run) investment funds that own shares in enterprises. This 'top-down' approach is more feasible in a country where the central government is strong (as in the former Czechoslovakia).

Among the advantages of mass privatization are the following:

1. 'Fairness' (distributional equity).
2. Speed. ('Fairness' and speed help make market-orientated reforms irreversible by benefiting society as a whole.) Enterprises may be valued via a number of rounds in which vouchers are bid for shares, as in the former Czechoslovakia.
3. Operates in the absence of large savings.
4. 'Voucher-based mass privatization auctions … have, in theory, the lowest potential for severe corruption in their implementation' (Kaufmann and Siegelbaum 1997: 433).

> Where privatization implementation is the focus, the following were emphasized: speed, the level of administrative discretion employed, transparency and access to information, and whether or not the programme is administered by a government agency differing from the one which previously owned the assets in question. Applying these factors to the most common methods of privatization generally points to voucher-based mass privatization and liquidation [in which insolvent enterprises are disassembled and systematically sold off as individual assets: p. 428] as the least corruption-prone implementation methods.
>
> (p. 455)

Among the disadvantages of mass privatization are the following:

1 Little or no revenue is raised in situations where governments in transitional economies often have great difficulty in raising sufficient tax revenue to balance the budget. Financing budget deficits by printing money can lead to inflation.
2 Enterprises being privatized are not provided with capital for investment purposes.
3 Free gifts are not valued so highly.
4 If vouchers are tradable for money, poorer citizens may be tempted to sell quickly and cheaply to others better informed of the value of assets being privatized.
5 Shares may be sold quickly by poorer and ill-informed sections of the community, thus depressing share prices. If stock exchanges are absent or poorly developed there is a 'liquidity' problem. (In Russia, for example, shares were often snapped up on the cheap by those 'in the know', leading to individuals quickly exercising control over valuable assets. Pressure was also sometimes put on workers to sell against their will.)
6 The issue of vouchers may be inflationary, e.g. through wealth effects.
7 A great problem arises if vouchers are directly exchanged for shares. Existing managers remain at their posts when vouchers are exchanged. There is widely dispersed ownership and thus an absence of corporate control of management. (It is the separation of ownership and management in large enterprises that creates the need for external monitoring, an example of the so-called 'principal-agent' problem.) This is where investment funds have a role to play by gaining control of sufficient shares (by means of deposited or purchased vouchers) to pressurize managers to act in the interest of shareholders, replacing them altogether if necessary by others who would do so. Managers can be disciplined or replaced by direct intervention or indirectly through the sale of shares. ('Holding companies' exercise direct control through representation on company boards, power being gained through ownership of all or a large proportion of the shares of each enterprise. 'Mutual funds' [known as 'unit trusts' in the UK], on the other hand, own enough shares to influence events by buying and selling them.)

But there remains the question of 'who controls the controllers', especially in situations where regulatory regimes are weak, investment funds are powerful and information is unevenly available. The state may be tempted to manipulate investment funds, especially when they are owned by banks which are still majority-owned by the state (as was the case, for example, in the Czech Republic). In the Czech Republic critics pointed to a lack of restructuring of enterprises and the tendency of banks to lend to enterprises controlled by their investment funds rather than lending funds for more profitable activities. The lack of regulation of stock markets led to mass abuse. For example, 'tunnelling' involves investment fund managers defrauding shareholders by selling shares cheaply to 'dummy' companies (owned by the managers themselves or their cronies) which then resell the shares at a profit.

> The adverse effects of privatizations leading to asset stripping, rather than wealth creation in the presence of inadequate corporate governance (in the context of the Czech Republic often referred to as 'tunnelling'), is corroborated in research showing that privatizations in those economies in transition and without strong corporate governance do not lead to faster growth.
>
> (James Wolfensohn and Joseph Stiglitz, *FT*, 22 September 1999, p. 22; James Wolfensohn is president of the World Bank and Joseph Stiglitz is the World Bank's chief economist and senior vice-president.)

> We use the term 'tunnelling', coined originally to characterize the expropriation of minority shareholders in the Czech Republic (as in removing assets through an underground tunnel), to describe the transfer of assets and profits out of firms for the benefit of those who control them.
>
> (Johnson *et al.* 2000: 22)

Restitution

Property may be returned in physical form ('natural' restitution) to former owners or their heirs. Because of the problems associated with physical restitution there may be financial compensation or compensation in the form of vouchers exchangeable for shares in enterprises to be privatized. (Note that as a rule restitution has typically been much more important in agriculture and housing than in industry.)

Among the advantages of restitution are the following:

1 Rectifying the injustices ('unfairness') of former widespread acts of confiscation or compensation below market-determined levels. This also helps signify a complete break with the past and thus a commitment to irreversible market-orientated reforms. (German reunification is a special case of rectifying the wrongs of the past; see below.)
2 The recreation of a strong propertied middle class, thus stimulating entrepreneurship.

Among the disadvantages of restitution are the following:

1 No revenue is raised.
2 The immense difficulties of proving claims to property, especially over long periods of time and when assets have been destroyed, reconstructed or incorporated into other assets. Putting a value on financial compensation is difficult at the best of times, but exceedingly so in poorly developed property markets. Uncertainty of ownership and long delays in sorting out these problems can be highly detrimental to economic activity in general and

investment in particular. Such problems, for example, forced reunified Germany substantially to amend legislation which initially emphasized physical restitution (see below). (Note the traumatic effects on those currently living in or using premises reverting to the original owners.)

3 Those receiving restituted property may not have experience of business and there may be delays in selling or even renting in poorly developed property markets. Old rent control and tenant protection laws may still be in operation.
4 The enrichment of certain sections of society (and perhaps even people who have by now gained foreign nationality) at a time when many others are feeling the pain of economic transition may breed a great deal of resentment.
5 There is the argument that the process of restitution is necessarily selective, and therefore an unsatisfactory way of achieving justice retroactively (Havrylyshyn and McGettigan 1999: 7).

Privatization in East Germany after German reunification: a case study

German reunification has been covered in the two previous volumes, but it may be worthwhile exploring the lessons of privatization in East Germany since physical restitution was the main initial approach. This is unusual in transitional economies outside agriculture and housing.

The Treuhandanstalt (THA) was set up in March 1990, but privatization only became its prime function after German Economic and Monetary Union. (It was also set up to deal with restructuring, liquidation and credit guarantees to provide temporary protection to enterprises.) The THA was wound up at the end of 1994 (a year later than planned), although it was succeeded by a number of public-sector institutions to clear up unfinished business, e.g. to sell remaining saveable enterprises and to monitor investment and job commitments. (There has been some disquiet about the extent to which commitments have been kept.)

All told, 40 per cent of EG's surface area and around 50 per cent of its workforce became the THA's responsibility. The THA was placed in charge of the administration of two-thirds of the forested area, almost 30 per cent of agricultural land and non-agricultural land accounting for almost a quarter of EG's surface area. It was responsible for state farms and forests and the agricultural and forestry land used by co-operatives and individuals.

Its first task was to keep the 8,000 'large' enterprises (those with more than 250 employees) employing around 4 million people. (The combines were split up, hence the larger number of enterprises actually privatized.) (A former chairman, Detlev Rohwedder, was assassinated by the Red Army faction on 1 April 1991. He was replaced by Birgit Breuel. The Red Army faction finally disbanded in April 1998.)

Privatization was slow to begin with and then became very rapid. The smaller enterprises nationalized in 1972 quickly started being returned to their former owners.

The main initial approach to (and major problem with) privatization was *physical restitution*. (This seemed the politically correct thing to do upon reunification.)

Physical restitution only applies to the period after 1949. Land and property seized between 1945 and 1949 could not be reclaimed by former owners or their heirs because of the reunification treaties agreed with the Soviet Union, although Gorbachev has apparently cast some doubt on this (some limited compensation later became available). Property was to be returned 'as far as this is possible taking into account the social and economic realities that have developed over the last forty years'. (This meant, for example, that domestic tenants would be able to see their present contracts through and that buildings which had been converted for 'general and commercial use' or for communal use or firms which became part of larger units would not be affected. Financial compensation would thus be an alternative.)

The problem with physical restitution is that it takes a long time to sort out claims. In the meantime economic activity, such as domestic and foreign investment, is adversely affected. (Property rights are unclear.) This led to major changes in the legislation. Above all, tenders were put out not only in terms of price but also in terms of investment and employment programmes. A former owner would at least have to match the best offer in terms of these investment and employment programmes to secure the property. Otherwise financial compensation would be given. (The new policy also covered the Nazi seizures of property 1933–45.)

The THA also attempted to seek a greater variety of privatization methods:

1 Management buy-outs.
2 The 'management KG'. These are holding companies run by experienced outside managers who rehabilitate and eventually sell enterprises placed in their care. The THA provides financial support.
3 After the spring of 1991 a greater effort was made to involve foreigners.

(Note also that in 1991 it became THA policy to retain the industrial 'cores' of areas heavily dependent on large enterprises.)

Dyck (1997) defends the chosen method of privatization, involving rapid privatization rather than state-led restructuring, reliance on sales rather than giveaways or vouchers, and the sale of most eastern enterprises to established western firms (p. 565).

> The key to successful restructuring of large firms … is the ability of owners to select able managers to restructure their enterprises' (p. 566). 'If the government pursues a policy of continued public ownership and attempts to hire western managers to install in eastern firms, it acts as an uninformed owner … uninformed owners, such as the government and citizens of eastern countries, hire managers of below-average ability … Western

owners can utilize their inside information on managerial ability and make an internal transfer of management from their western to their eastern operations.

(p. 567)

'The positive message of the paper is that privatization programmes that allow for management change and are open to foreign purchasers can improve firm performance' (p. 592). West German firms bought most eastern facilities, accounting for three-quarters of privatization transactions, with 5.9 per cent of sales to foreign buyers (although often West German affiliates of multinational companies) and 20 per cent of sales to East Germans (p. 570). (About 10 per cent of former GDR state property has been sold to foreigners: Birgit Breuel, *Moscow News*, 10–16 June 1994, p. 9.)

But various criticisms have been made of THA privatization:

1 Sales revenues have been well short of target. This is partly because of early over-optimism about the value of enterprises but also to factors such as the speed of the sales process, which depressed prices.

2 Wolfgang Münchau:

> [The THA] has been a great disappointment. Industrial output in the former East Germany has plummeted. The mechanism suffered massive fraud, estimated at DM 3 billion. West German industrialists have frequently abused the Treuhand mechanism in order to close down East German competitors, even if these companies might otherwise have been viable.
>
> (*The Times*, 22 December 1992, p. 19)

'Companies have been auctioned off to the highest bidders with utter disregard for industrial consequences. Whole industries have disappeared' (*The Times*, 12 January 1993, p. 25). (The THA maintains that West German companies have not in fact closed down EG companies in order to prevent competition. But Judy Dempsey believes that in the early days WG companies bought the cream of EG enterprises to keep out foreign competition. They also bought enterprises for the real estate and then closed them down: *FT*, Survey, 25 October 1993, p. x. 'Eastern Germany is full of tales of West Germans who took over companies in the east only to strip their assets and shut them down': *IHT*, 13 November 1999, p. 9.) (According to a report by a parliamentary committee, economic crime linked to reunification cost the state some DM 3 billion to DM 10 billion. It was admitted that this was probably an underestimate. The THA and its successors were particular sources of economic crime: *FT*, 17 June 1998, p. 2.)

3 Priewe (1993: 341–6) criticizes the stress on rapid privatization rather than restructuring. He argues that in numerous cases enterprises have been sold to West German investors, often to market-dominating companies, although

they would have been independently viable immediately or after restructuring. Thus many opportunities for revitalizing competition in a united Germany have been missed.

4 'A conspicuous feature of swift privatization was that the large majority of East German firms (some three-quarters) was taken over by existing West German companies. Thus the East German firms became "subsidiaries" of firms having their headquarters in the western part of the country. It is also worth emphasizing that the size distribution of companies is more dominated by small and medium-sized enterprises than in West Germany … Not only are subsidiaries more exposed to the risk of closure in times of economic crisis, but they often tend to buy fewer inputs in the regional markets than indigenous firms. The dominance of such plants also has repercussions on the skill structure of jobs. Upper managerial, technical and R&D staff will, in general, tend to remain in headquarters and the overall regional demand for labour will accordingly be biased towards less skilled workers' (United Nations Economic Commission for Europe 1997: 32–3).

5 Some 20 per cent of all buyers have seemingly been unable or unwilling to meet their contractual obligations.

> The use of investment and employment guarantees by the Treuhand is a two-edged sword. It ensures that the new owners will not strip and liquidate their new holdings; however, it also ensures that firms remain in the same line of activity, which slows the process of needed structural change.
>
> (Brada 1996: 71)

6 Berlin's DIW recommended that all THA enterprises (with the exception of those being liquidated) should have received adequate equity capital plus a supplement to compensate them for their difficult initial situation. This would have guaranteed their survival for a limited period (they would have been financially autonomous, e.g. made their own investment decisions). There would have been no arbitrary subsidization. The firms that failed to seize the opportunity offered them would have been liquidated.

7 Sinn (1992: 166–7) recommended a 'participation model' (social compact) in which the THA kept stakes in enterprises (preferably minority ones) without voting rights. The THA should have distributed its shares to the population, at least a third to the employees of the privatized firms. In return the employees would have had to accept a union wage 'freeze' (in the sense of keeping the gap between wages in EG and WG constant for a certain number of years).

8 'The whole economy is in private hands, but over the past few years the state has stepped in to stop over 150 large privatized companies from going bankrupt. And despite massive investment in new plant and infrastructure,

half of East German companies are still in the red, productivity is far below West German levels and unemployment is still a massive 18 per cent' (*Business Central Europe*, November 1999, p. 16).

Postscript

Hungary

> The liberalization of the Hungarian forint on 16 June marked the beginning of a new monetary regime that includes the substantial widening of the National Bank of Hungary's intervention band to 15 per cent above and below central parity (from 2.25 per cent), the adoption of explicit inflation targets and the abandonment of the crawling peg system effective from 1 October.
>
> (*The Economist*, Hungarian Economic Review, 29 September 2001, p. 94)

Poland

19 September 2001:

> Poland's Social Democratic Party … took the unusual step of unveiling top appointments to its shadow cabinet yesterday [19 September]. Marek Belka, an economist with US training, will assume the post of finance minister and deputy prime minister responsible for economic policy if the SLD democratic left alliance forms Poland's next government … Mr Belka has been preparing a financial rescue plan, details of which he will present today [20 September] … Opinion polls give [the alliance] 47 per cent to 50 per cent support … Marek Pol, head of the SLD's smaller partner, the Union of Labour, will hold a second deputy prime minister spot and head a new infrastructure ministry. Financial analysts applauded the appointment of Mr Belka, who had said he would serve in the next government only if given broad powers over Poland's ailing economy. Past finance ministers have foundered on a lack of political support … Wlodzimierz Cimoszewicz, who served as prime minister in 1996–7, is the SLD's candidate for foreign minister. Jerzy Szmajdzinski … would become defence minister.
>
> (*FT*, 20 September 2001, p. 11)

20 September 2001:

> An opinion poll published yesterday [20 September] showed a last-minute slip in support for the opposition Social Democrats … [The] poll gave the Democratic Left Alliance, or SLD, and its electoral partner, the Union of Labour, 43 per cent support, compared with 47 per cent to 50 per cent in previous polls … Yesterday Marek Belka … gave details of a 'rescue plan for the Polish economy' the party will implement if it forms a government. Mr Belka said he would seek to pay existing state arrears before undertaking an overhaul of state finances aimed at restoring 5 per cent economic growth within two years. To boost revenues he said he would seek to raise value-added tax and introduce a tax on income from bank interest and sales of securities … To cut spending Mr Belka said he was considering a 'menu' of options … He upheld the current government's deficit target of … 5 per cent of GDP as an 'absolute upper limit'.
>
> (*FT*, 21 September 2001, p. 16)

21 September 2001: 'An opinion poll yesterday [21 September] gave [the ex-communists] 48 per cent' (*Telegraph*, 22 September 2001, p. 23).

23 September 2001: a general election is held for the 460 seats in the Sejm. There is an 8 per cent threshold for coalitions. The turnout was 46 per cent.

The results in order of seats were as follows:

1 The Democratic Left Alliance and the Union of Labour: 41.04 per cent of the vote and 216 seats (i.e. fewer than half the seats in the Sejm).

The leader of the SLD is Leszek Miller. 'Leszek Miller … [is] an electrician by training, who rose up through the old Communist Party. He took part in the "roundtable" talks with Solidarity that led to the elections in 1989' (*IHT*, 22 September 2001, p. 5). 'Leszek Miller … became an electrician in a linen factory … joined the Polish United Workers' Party in 1969 and … became a Politburo member in 1989' (*Guardian*, 24 September 2001, p. 14).

2 Civic Platform: 12.7 per cent of the vote and sixty-five seats.

'Civic Platform … pledges a low flat-rate income tax and war on red tape' (*The Economist*, 18 August 2001, p. 33).

'Civic Platform … was created at the start of the year … Combining economic liberalism and social conservatism it is drawing defectors from Freedom Union' (*IHT*, 3 September 2001, p. 4).

3 Samoobrona (Self-Defence): 10.2 per cent of the vote and fifty-three seats. 'Samoobrona … [is a] Eurosceptic fringe … a radical farmers' union … [which] is headed by Andrzej Lepper, a former boxer and opponent of globalization who has faced criminal charges in the past for his statements and protests' (*FT*, 24 September 2001, p. 14).

> A populist party that opposes EU membership … [it campaigned on a] radical-agrarian platform … Andrzej Lepper [24 September]: 'We will do everything possible to make Poland stop serving as a market for the EU's agricultural surpluses. If things do not change be warned that in Poland there will be a social explosion and Samoobrona will lead it' … He has led dozens of aggressive and sometimes violent protests since founding Samoobrona in 1992.
>
> (*FT*, 25 September 2001, p. 12)

> Andrzej Lepper and his xenophobic Samoobrona (Self-Defence) Party won a good tenth of the vote. He says he might reluctantly support Poland's entry to the EU, but only if he gained concessions that he is unlikely to get … [He] adroitly used television to tell small farmers and former collective farm workers that the crooked *nouveaux riches* of Warsaw had bled the country dry and that joining the EU, in its present form, would be death to Poland's countryside and those who lived in it.
>
> (*The Economist*, 29 September 2001, p. 43)

4 Law and Justice Party: 9.5 per cent of the vote and forty-four seats.

'A conservative party formed by defectors from the defeated ruling Solidarity camp' (*FT*, 27 September 2001, p. 12).

> Law and Justice … inveighs against corruption and organized crime. It is run by a pair of twins, Lech and Jaroslaw Kaczynski. Lech was the current government's most popular minister (for justice), until Mr Busek recently fired him for insubordination. Jaroslaw is the former leader of Centre Alliance, a now defunct party devoted to 'decommunization'.
>
> (*The Economist*, 18 August 2001, p. 33)

'[A party] of the hard right that few pundits had hitherto taken seriously … [It has] demanded the return of the death penalty and inveighed against corruption' (*The Economist*, 29 September 2001, p. 43).

> To the right of Civic Platform is Law and Justice, a group created by twin brothers, Lech and Jaroslaw Kaczynski. Lech Kaczynski was a popular justice minister in the Solidarity government until he was dismissed … after a dispute between his ministry and the intelligence service.
>
> (*IHT*, 3 September 2001, p. 4)

5 Polish Peasants' Party: 9 per cent of the vote and forty-two seats. 'The Polish Peasants' Party wants [EU] membership only if it brings big farm subsidies' (*FT*, 25 September 2001, p. 18). 'The Polish Peasants' Party … is not

excluding a new coalition. But its leader, Jaroslaw Kalinowski, is setting tough conditions on economic policy, including the introduction of a controversial import tax and a law limiting the powers of Poland's central bank' (*FT*, 27 September 2001, p. 12).

6 League of Polish Families: 7.9 per cent of the vote and thirty-eight seats.

> The populist and nationalist League of Polish Families is a vocal opponent of the reformed communist and liberal governments that have ruled Poland since 1989 and it campaigned under the slogan 'Let Poland be Poland' ... [It is a] Eurosceptic fringe party.
>
> (*FT*, 24 September 2001, p. 14)

> A populist party that opposes EU membership ... [it] includes some members who favour EU accession, but, as a group, it wants annulment of Poland's trade-liberalizing association agreement with the EU. Formed for expediency just two months before elections, it groups far-right politicians, including several close to Radio Maryja, an ultra-nationalist Catholic radio station.
>
> (*FT*, 25 September 2001, p. 12)

> [A party] of the hard right that few pundits had hitherto taken seriously ... Often antisemitic, it is backed by the ultra-nationalist wing of the Roman Catholic Church, whose Radio Maryja is said to have 4 million listeners. The league has damned the EU as a 'civilization of death' for what it takes to be the EU's views on abortion and euthanasia.
>
> (*The Economist*, 29 September 2001, p. 43)

7 The German minority has two seats in the Sejm.

Solidarity Electoral Action of the Right gained no seats in the Sejm because it won only 5.6 per cent of the vote. Adam Michnik (editor of *Gazeta Wyborcza*): '[Solidarity] was a huge coalition of all kinds of anti-communist forces. The moment that communism fell the movement began to fall apart. It lost its raison d'être, because it was a movement against dictatorship' (*IHT*, 22 September 2001, p. 5).

Freedom Union also gained no seats in the Sejm, winning only 3 per cent of the vote.

In the Senate the Democratic Left Alliance won seventy-five of the hundred seats (*IHT*, 24 September 2001, p. 7).

28 September 2001:

> Poland reacted angrily yesterday [28 September] to a survey which found that 40 per cent of the adult working population, or 6 million people, would like to live and work in another European country. Government leaders

strongly criticised the study by the consultants PricewatersCoopers as unreliable and damaging to Poland's bid to join the EU because it could add to worries in some countries of a flood of migrant labour … Despite the findings sociologists say that many people are reluctant to move even within the country to improve their living standards, let alone seek their fortune abroad.

(*FT*, 29 September 2001, p. 21)

5 October 2001:

Leaders of the Democratic Left Alliance and the Polish Peasants' Party took three days to reach a broad agreement … to form a leftwing coalition government pledged to rescue leaky public finances and get EU entry talks back on track … [The agreement] should be rubber-stamped by their party executives today [6 October].

(*FT*, 6 October 2001, p. 10)

6–8 October 2001:

The Democratic Left Alliance [SLD] … and the Union of Labour are expected to sign an agreement to form a government today [8 October] … with the Polish Peasants' Party … They will hold a combined majority of 258 out of 460 seats in the Sejm … The pro-business Civic Platform … rejected a coalition with the SLD … The Polish Peasants' Party … is internally divided over whether to join a government. It accepted the SLD's offer on Saturday [6 October] only after hours of discussion … [Its leader] Jaroslaw Kanilowski … said that remaining state-owned banks slated for privatization 'should remain Polish' and that the central bank should broaden its inflation-cutting mandate to include 'fighting unemployment' … Mr Kalinowski also said the coalition would not increase … taxes such as value-added tax, a rise in which would hit farmers. Marek Belka, finance minister-designate, has supported the measure as part of an economic rescue plan aimed at averting a massive budget deficit.

(*FT*, 8 October 2001, p. 16)

9 October 2001: the coalition partners issue a statement which includes the following: 'The coalition expects the Monetary Policy Council to co-operate more actively in achieving our goals and to take on more responsibility for the country's economic growth' (*IHT*, 10 October 2001, p. 6).

14 October 2001: 'Bronislaw Geremek, a former foreign minister and party chairman, and secretary-general Miroslaw Czech … resigned Sunday [14 October] after … Freedom Union … failed to win any parliamentary seats' (*IHT*, 15 October 2001, p. 6).

16 October 2001:

> Prosecutors began reading the indictment, which under Polish law marks the formal start of a trial … [against] Wojciech Jaruzelski over the 1970 shootings of protesting shipyard workers … [He is] charged with ordering the military to fire on shipyard workers protesting price increases in the Baltic coast cities of Gdynia, Gdansk, Szczecin and Elblag on 17 December 1970. At least forty-four people were killed.
>
> (*IHT*, 17 October 2001, p. 6)

19 October 2001: 'Leszek Miller … was sworn in Friday [19 October] as Poland's prime minister' (*IHT*, 20 October 2001, p. 10).

20 October 2001:

> Poland's new government has resolved to reduce current-year spending, freeze ministers' and top bureaucrats' wages and streamline the apparatus handling its EU accession bid … [The] cabinet froze salaries of top functionaries in the government and central administration for at least a year … The government will also block 8.5 billion zlotys in planned budget spending this year … [and the finance ministry confirmed it] had downgraded its GDP growth for this year to 1.5 per cent, compared with an earlier 2.3 per cent estimate … Mr Miller will head the European integration committee … [and] promised to bring Poland into the EU as quickly as possible.
>
> (*FT*, 22 October 2001, p. 12)

25 October 2001:

> Poland's two top security chiefs … the head of the state protection office, which controls all state security operations … and chief of the military intelligence service … resigned Thursday [25 October] and sharply criticised plans … to reorganize the intelligence services and put them under civilian control … [The former] said he had tried to warn that the reorganization could undermine the intelligence services and their ability to help the United States and other Nato allies combat terrorism.
>
> (*IHT*, 26 October 2001, p. 4)

(On 11 September 2001 there were terrorist attacks in New York and Washington.)

> Prime minister Leszek Miller … promised that his government would stabilize public finances within 100 days, complete EU accession negotiations on schedule next year [2002] and join the EU in an expected first expansion wave in 2004 … [He] outlined a programme pledging leaner government, economic revival and acceleration of Poland's snagged EU talks. By the

> second half of November, he said, his cabinet would present a draft budget capping … the deficit at … 5 per cent of GDP … [He said] 'Our goal is to overcome the crisis and lead the economy on to a path of growth. But first we have to save the country from bankruptcy' … The government will introduce a package of laws to help small and middle-sized companies, he said, and unveil a long-term economic plan next year … Mr Miller said his government would not compromise the independence of Poland's central bank.
>
> (*FT*, 26 October 2001, p. 10)

('With unemployment approaching 20 per cent reform of the labour market has become essential. Until now the left and right have always joined forces to block big changes in the strict labour code. This was negotiated in the early 1990s … Polish workers are overprotected, which makes them expensive to hire': *The Economist*, Survey on Poland, 27 October 2001, p. 11. 'State-owned mines, steel mills and factories remain a disproportionate problem: although most of Poland's GDP comes from the private sector, three-quarters of its tangible assets are in state hands. Most of these are deep in debt and bleeding money. Only one in ten communist-era enterprises are turning a profit. And many are still an environmental liability … The previous government forced some restructuring on the sickest sectors, but they will have to shrink much further before they become viable': p. 12.)

Romania

> Romania is having a better year than its citizens dared hope … The new social democratic government … has provided some much-needed political stability, and progress on EU accession has picked up remarkably … The EU, which last year [2000] branded Romania as the worst performer among accession candidates, is expected to deliver a more positive assessment in its annual report next month [November] … Mircea Geoana, the foreign minister … [is] serving as this year's chairman-in-office of OSCE.
>
> (*FT*, Survey, 3 October 2001, p. i)

> The economy is growing at its fastest rate since 1995 … The government [is] forecasting 5 per cent growth in GDP [in 2001] and a further 5 per cent next year [2002] … Excessive public sector pay increases have kept Romanian inflation rates among Europe's highest – 41 per cent last year [2000] … Inflation has fallen, but is still running at nearly 30 per cent, fuelled … by public sector pay … The government's answer is a tough public sector financial plan, including wage curbs, plus wide-ranging reform in a programme agreed in outline with the IMF.
>
> (*FT*, Survey, 3 October 2001, p. i)

'The fund has agreed a $380 million eighteen-month loan programme … subject to final approval from the IMF board' (p. iii).

'Adrian Nastase, the prime minister … has already virtually completed the privatization of Sidex, the country's largest steelworks and biggest loss-making industrial plant' (*FT*, Survey, 3 October 2001, p. i). 'Barring accidents, Ispat International, the UK-based steel group, will complete the takeover of Sidex … at the end of the month' (p. iii). 'About half the [banking] sector's assets are in private hands. The sale of BCR … Banca Commerciale Romana, the big state-owned bank … planned for next year [2002] would take the level above 80 per cent' (p. ii).

> Ovidiu Musetescu, privatization minister … has also seen an overhaul of the privatization process, with the replacement of the former SOF agency with a new unit called Apaps, the privatization authority. However, as before, the privatization unit will control about half the state's industrial assets. Individual ministries will continue to be responsible for key sectors, including telecommunications, transport and energy.
>
> (p. iii)

'Foreign companies … still find business conditions difficult and complain of red tape, corruption and administrative inconsistency, especially in taxation. The government has promised to address these issues' (*FT*, Survey, 3 October 2001, p. i).

> The government … has established a Department for Relations with Foreign Investors, a one-stop shop for investors with more than $10 million … a first point of contact for new investors … The government has also simplified the tax system … [One advantage is the] lack of serious organized crime.
>
> (p. ii)

> In February 2001 the government signed a one-year pact with the main trade unions in which the unions promised not to undertake industrial action in return for social protection measures, including a pledge to raise real wages by 4.0 per cent to 4.5 per cent and the minimum wage by 10 per cent in 2001 and to cut unemployment to less than 10 per cent from its current 11 per cent. In June 2001 the government and the central bank launched an anti-inflationary programme based on exchange rate targets and focussed on more restrictive income policies (particularly for utilities and state enterprises), faster privatization and tighter monetary and foreign exchange policies … Nastase argues that … the budget deficit needs to be at least 3.5 per cent of GDP for the time being, to stem the potential for industrial unrest to completely derail reforms.
>
> (*Transition*, 2001, vol. 12, no. 33, p. 22)

Bibliography

Periodicals and journals

CDSP	*Current Digest of the Soviet Press* (since 5 February 1992, *Post-Soviet*)
EEN	*Eastern Europe* (formerly *Eastern Europe Newsletter*)
EBRD	European Bank for Reconstruction and Development
EIU	Economist Intelligence Unit
FEER	*Far Eastern Economic Review*
FT	*Financial Times*
IHT	*International Herald Tribune*

Books and journals

Aghion, P. and Blanchard, O. (1994) *On the Speed of Transition in Central Europe*, Oxford: Nuffield College Oxford, Discussion Paper no. 87.

Akerlof, G., Rose, A., Yellen, J. and Hessenius, H. (1991) 'East Germany in from the cold; the economic aftermath of currency union', *Brookings Papers on Economic Activity*, no. 1.

Allsopp, C. and Kierzkowski, H. (1997) 'The assessment: economics of transition in Eastern and Central Europe', *Oxford Review of Economic Policy*, vol. 13, no. 2.

Ash, T. (1992) *Agricultural Reform in Central and Eastern Europe*, Edinburgh: Heriot-Watt University, Discussion Paper in Economics no. 14.

——(1993) 'Agriculture in the former centrally-planned economies in transition', *Economics of Transition*, vol. 1, no. 4.

Åslund, A. (1994) 'Lessons of the first four years of systemic change in Eastern Europe', *Journal of Comparative Economics*, vol. 19, no. 1.

——(1996) 'Introduction: the Balkan transformation in perspective', in I. Jeffries (ed.) *Problems of Economic and Political Transformation in the Balkans*, London: Pinter.

Åslund, A. and Sjöberg, Ö. (1991) *Privatization and Transition to Market Economies in Albania*, Stockholm: Stockholm Institute of Soviet and East European Economics, Working Paper no. 27.

Åslund, A., Boone, P. and Johnson, S. (1996) 'How to stabilize: lessons from post-communist countries', *Brookings Papers on Economic Activity*, no. 1.

Balcerowicz, L. (1989) 'Polish economic reform, 1981–88: an overview', in Economic Commission for Europe, *Economic Reform in the European Centrally Planned Economies*, New York: United Nations, Economic Studies no. 1.

——(1993) 'Transition to market economy: Central and East European countries in comparative perspective', *British Review of Economic Issues*, vol. 15, no. 37.

——(1994) 'Common fallacies in the debate on the transition to a market economy', *Economic Policy*, no. 19 (Supplement).

Balcerowicz, L., Blaszczyk, B. and Dabrowski, M. (1997) 'The Polish way to the market economy 1989–1995', in W. Woo, S. Parker and J. Sachs (eds) *Economies in Transition: Comparing Asia and Eastern Europe*, London: MIT Press.

Baldwin, R., Francois, J. and Portes, R. (1997) 'The costs and benefits of eastern enlargement: the impact on the EU and central Europe', *Economic Policy*, no. 24.

Bartholdy, K. (1993) 'Statistical review', *Economics of Transition*, vol. 1, no. 1.

Bartholdy, K. and Szegvari, I. (1993) 'Statistical review', *Economics of Transition*, vol. 1, no. 2.

Begg, D. (1991) 'Economic reform in Czechoslovakia: should we believe in Santa Klaus?', *Economic Policy*, no. 13 (October).

Begg, D. and Portes, R. (1993a) 'Enterprise debt and economic transformation', *Economics of Transition*, vol. 1, no. 1.

——(1993b) 'East Germany since reunification: wage subsidies remain a better way', *Economics of Transition*, vol. 1, no. 4.

Berg, A. and Sachs, J. (1992) 'Structural adjustment and international trade in Eastern Europe: the case of Poland', *Economic Policy*, no. 14.

Berliner, J. (1976) *The Innovation Decision in Soviet Industry*, Cambridge, Mass.: MIT Press.

Bideleux, R. and Jeffries, I. (1998) *A History of Eastern Europe: Crisis and Change*, London: Routledge.

Birman, I. (1978) 'From the achieved level', *Soviet Studies*, vol. XXXI, no. 2.

Blanchard, O. (1994) 'Transition in Poland', *Economic Journal*, vol. 104, no. 426.

Blanchard, O. and Layard, R. (1990) *Economic Change in Poland*, London: Centre for Research into Communist Economies (New Series 1, July).

Blanchard, O., Dornbusch, R., Krugman, P., Layard, R. and Summers, L. (1991) *Reform in Eastern Europe*, Cambridge, Mass.: MIT Press.

Blaszczyk, B. and Dabrowski, M. (1993) *The Privatization Process in Poland 1989–1992*, London: Centre for Research into Communist Economies.

Blazyca, G. (1980a) 'An assessment of Polish economic development in the 1970s', *European Economic Review*, vol. 14.

——(1980b) 'Industrial structure and the economic problems of industry in a centrally planned economy: the Polish case', *Journal of Industrial Economics*, March.

——(1982) 'The degeneration of central planning in Poland', in J. Woodall (ed.) *Policy and Politics in Contemporary Poland: Reform and Crisis*, London: Pinter.

——(1985) 'The Polish economy under martial law: a dissenting view', *Soviet Studies*, vol. 37, no. 3.

——(1986) *Poland to the 1990s: Retreat or Reform?*, London: EIU.

——(1987) 'The new round of economic reform in Eastern Europe', *National Westminster Review*, November.

——(1991) *Poland's Next Five Years: The Dash for Capitalism*, London: EIU.

——(1992) 'Poland', in I. Jeffries (ed.) *Industrial Reform in Socialist Countries: From Restructuring to Revolution*, Aldershot: Edward Elgar.

Blazyca, G. and Rapacki, R. (1996) 'Continuity and change in Polish economic policy: the impact of the 1993 election', *Europe–Asia Studies*, vol. 48, no. 1.

Bleaney, M. (1988) *Do Socialist Economies Work? The Soviet and East European Experience*, Oxford: Blackwell.

Blejer, M., Mecagni, M., Sahay, R., Hides, R., Johnston, B., Nagy, P. and Pepper, R. (1992) *Albania: From Isolation Toward Reform*, Washington, DC: IMF, Occasional Paper no. 98.

Bogetic, Z. (1993) 'The role of employee ownership in privatization of state enterprises in Eastern and Central Europe', *Europe–Asia Studies*, vol. 45, no. 3.

Bogetic, Z. and Fox, L. (1993) 'Incomes policy during stabilization: a review and lessons from Bulgaria and Romania', *Comparative Economic Studies*, vol. XXXV, no. 1.

Boltho, A., Carlin, W. and Scaramozzino, P. (1997) 'Will East Germany become a new *Mezzogiorno?*', *Journal of Comparative Economics*, vol. 24, no. 3.

Bolton, P. (1995) 'Privatization and the separation of ownership and control: lessons from Chinese enterprise reform', *Economics of Transition*, vol. 3, no. 1.

Bolton, P. and Roland, G. (1992) 'Privatization policies in Central and Eastern Europe', *Economic Policy*, no. 15.

Bonin, J. and Leven, B. (1996) 'Polish bank consolidation and foreign competition: creating a market-oriented banking sector', *Journal of Comparative Economics*, vol. 23, no. 1.

Borensztein, E. and Kumar, M. (1991) 'Proposals for privatization in Eastern Europe', *IMF Staff Papers*, vol. 38, no. 2.

Borensztein, E., Demekas, D. and Ostry, J. (1993) 'An empirical analysis of the output decline in three Eastern European countries', *IMF Staff Papers*, vol. 40, no. 1.

Boycko, M. (1991) 'Price decontrol: the microeconomic case for the "big bang" approach', *Oxford Review of Economic Policy*, vol. 7, no. 4.

Boycko, M., Shleifer, A. and Vishny, R. (1994) 'Voucher privatization', *Journal of Financial Economics*, vol. 35, no. 2.

——(1996) 'A theory of privatization', *Economic Journal*, vol. 106, no. 435.

Brada, J. (1993) 'The transformation from communism to capitalism: how far? how fast?', *Post-Soviet Affairs*, vol. 9, no. 2.

——(1996) 'Privatization is transition – or is it?', *Journal of Economic Perspectives*, vol. 10, no. 2.

Brada, J. and King, A. (1992) 'Is there a J-curve for the economic transition from socialism to capitalism?', *Economics of Planning*, vol. 25, no. 1.

——(1993) 'Is private farming more efficient than socialized agriculture?', *Economica*, vol. 60, no. 237.

Brom, K. and Orenstein, M. (1994) 'The privatized sector in the Czech Republic: government and bank control in a transitional economy', *Europe–Asia Studies*, vol. 46, no. 6.

Brooks, K. and Meurs, M. (1994) 'Romanian land reform, 1991–93', *Comparative Economic Studies*, vol. XXXVI, no. 2.

Brooks, K., Guash, L., Braverman, A. and Csaki, C. (1991) 'Agriculture and the transition to the market', *Journal of Economic Perspectives*, vol. 5, no. 4.

Bruno, M. (1993a) 'Stabilization and the macroeconomics of transition – how different is Eastern Europe?', *Economics of Transition*, vol. 1, no. 1.

——(1993b) *Crisis, Stabilization and Economic Reform: Therapy by Consensus*, Oxford: Clarendon Press.

Brus, W. (1993) 'Marketization and democratization: the Sino-Soviet divergence', *Cambridge Journal of Economics*, vol. 17, no. 4.

Burda, M. (1993) 'Unemployment, labour markets and structural change in Eastern Europe', *Economic Policy*, no. 16.

Business Central Europe (1995) *The Annual*, London: The Economist Group.

——(1997) *The Annual: 1997–98*, London: The Economist Group.

——(1998) *The Annual: 1998–99*, London: The Economist Group.

——(1999) *The Annual: 2000*, London: The Economist Group.

——(2000) *The Annual: 2001*, London: The Economist Group.

Calvo, G. and Coricelli, F. (1993) 'Output collapse in Eastern Europe', *IMF Staff Papers*, vol. 40, no. 1.

Calvo, G. and Frenkel, J. (1991a) 'From centrally planned to market economy', *IMF Staff Papers*, vol. 38, no. 2.

——(1991b) 'Credit markets, credibility, and economic transformation', *Journal of Economic Perspectives*, vol. 5, no. 4.

Capek, A. and Sazama, G. (1993) 'Czech and Slovak economic relations', *Europe–Asia Studies*, vol. 45, no. 2.

Carlin, W. and Mayer, C. (1992) 'Restructuring enterprises in Eastern Europe', *Economic Policy*, no. 15.

Carlin, W. and Soskice, D. (1997) 'Shocks to the system: the German political economy under stress', *National Institute Economic Review*, no. 159 (January).

Cepl, V. (1991) 'A note on the restitution of property in post-communist Czechoslovakia', *Journal of Communist Studies*, vol. 7, no. 3.

Charemza, W. (1992) 'Market failure and stagflation: some aspects of privatization in Poland', *Economics of Planning*, vol. 25, no. 1.

Clague, C. (1992) 'Introduction: the journey to a market economy', in C. Clague and G. Rausser (eds) *The Emergence of Market Economies in Eastern Europe*, Oxford: Blackwell.

Clague, C. and Rausser, G. (eds) (1992) *The Emergence of Market Economies in Eastern Europe*, Oxford: Blackwell.

Cnossen, S. (1992) 'Key questions in considering a value-added tax for Central and Eastern European countries', *IMF Staff Papers*, vol. 39, no. 2.

Cochrane, N. (1993) 'Central European agrarian reforms in a historical perspective', *American Journal of Agricultural Economics*, vol. 75, no. 3.

Collier, I. and Siebert, H. (1991) 'The economic integration of post-Wall Germany', *American Economic Review*, Papers and Proceedings, May.

Corbett, J. and Mayer, C. (1991) 'Financial reform in Eastern Europe: progress with the wrong model', *Oxford Review of Economic Policy*, vol. 7, no. 4.

Crampton, R. (1994) *Eastern Europe in the Twentieth Century*, London: Routledge.

Cungu, A. and Swinnen, J. (1999) 'Albania's radical agrarian reform', *Economic Development and Cultural Change*, vol. 47, no. 3.

Davis, J. and Gaburici, A. (1998) *The Economic Activity of Private Farms in Romania during Transition: Just How Competitive Are They?*, Edinburgh: Heriot-Watt University, CERT Discussion Paper no. 98/7.

Demekas, D. and Khan, M. (1991) *The Romanian Reform Programme*, Washington, DC: IMF, Occasional Paper no. 89.

Demougin, D. and Sinn, H.-W. (1994) 'Privatization, risk-taking and the communist firm', *Journal of Public Economics*, vol. 55, no. 2.

Dewatripont, M. and Roland, G. (1995) 'The design of reform packages under uncertainty', *American Economic Review*, vol. 85, no. 5.

Dobozi, I. and Pohl, G. (1995) 'Real output decline in transition economies: forget GDP, try power consumption data', *Transition*, vol. 6, nos 1–2.

Dyck, I. (1997) 'Privatization in Eastern Germany: management selection and economic transition', *American Economic Review*, vol. 87, no. 4.

East, R. (1992) *Revolutions in Eastern Europe*, London: Pinter.

Eastwood, R. and Durski, A. (1993) *Financial Reform in Poland: Some Parallels with Chilean Experience 1973–83*, Brighton: University of Sussex, Discussion Paper no. 3/93.
Eberstadt, N. (1994a) 'Demographic shocks after communism: Eastern Germany, 1989–93', *Population and Development Review*, vol. 20, no. 1.
——(1994b) 'Demographic shocks in Eastern Germany, 1989–93', *Europe–Asia Studies*, vol. 46, no. 3.
EBRD (1994) *Transition Report*, London: European Bank for Reconstruction and Development.
——(1995a) *Transition Report Update* (April), London: European Bank for Reconstruction and Development.
——(1995b) *Transition Report*, London: European Bank for Reconstruction and Development.
——(1996a) *Transition Report Update* (April), London: European Bank for Reconstruction and Development.
——(1996b) *Transition Report*, London: European Bank for Reconstruction and Development.
——(1997a) *Transition Report Update* (April), London: European Bank for Reconstruction and Development.
——(1997b) *Transition Report*, London: European Bank for Reconstruction and Development.
——(1998a) *Transition Report Update* (April), London: European Bank for Reconstruction and Development.
——(1998b) *Transition Report*, London: European Bank for Reconstruction and Development.
——(1999a) *Transition Report Update* (April), London: European Bank for Reconstruction and Development.
——(1999b) *Transition Report*, London: European Bank for Reconstruction and Development.
——(2000a) *Transition Report Update* (May), London: European Bank for Reconstruction and Development.
——(2000b) *Transition Report*, London: European Bank for Reconstruction and Development.
——(2001) *Transition Report Update* (April), London: European Bank for Reconstruction and Development.
Economic Commission for Europe (1989) *Economic Reform in the European Centrally Planned Economies*, New York: United Nations, Economic Studies no. 1.
Economist survey (1990) 'The new Germany', 30 June.
——(1991) 'Business in Eastern Europe', 21 September.
——(1992) 'Germany', 23 May.
——(1993) 'Eastern Europe', 13 March.
——(1994a) 'Poland', 16 April.
——(1994b) 'Germany', 21 May.
——(1995) 'Central Europe', 18 November.
——(1996) 'Germany', 9 November.
——(1997) 'Business in Eastern Europe', 22 November.
——(1998) 'The Balkans', 24 January.
Eichengreen, B. and Uzan, M. (1992) 'The Marshall Plan: economic effects and implications for Eastern Europe and the former USSR', *Economic Policy*, no. 14.
Ellman, M. (1979) *Socialist Planning*, London: Cambridge University Press.

——(1993) 'General aspects of transition', in M. Ellman, E. Gaidar and G. Kolodko, *Economic Transition in Eastern Europe*, edited P. Admiraal, Oxford: Blackwell.

——(1997) 'The political economy of transition', *Oxford Review of Economic Policy*, vol. 13, no. 2.

Ellman, M., Gaidar, E. and Kolodko, G. (1993) *Economic Transition in Eastern Europe*, edited P. Admiraal, Oxford: Blackwell.

Estrin, S. and Richet, X. (1993) 'Industrial restructuring and microeconomic adjustment in Poland: a cross-sectional approach', *Comparative Economic Studies*, vol. XXXV, no. 4.

Fan, Q. and Schaffer, M. (1994) 'Government financial transfers and enterprise adjustments in Russia, with comparisons to Central and Eastern Europe', *Economics of Transition*, vol. 2, no. 2.

Financial Times (various surveys) Albania: 21 July 1994; 2 October 1995; 19 February 1997; 23 February 2000.

——Bulgaria: 7 December 1984; 27 October 1988; 17 May 1991; 5 May 1993; 13 October 1994; 21 October 1997; 8 March 1999.

——Central and Eastern Europe: 8 May 1998; 10 November 1999; 24 October 2000; 2 July 2001.

——Czechoslovakia: 23 October 1985; 8 November 1991.

——Czech Republic: 11 January 1993; 24 March 1993; 19 December 1994; 2 June 1995; 22 November 1995; 26 April 1996; 6 December 1996; 14 May 1997; 1 December 1997; 14 May 1998; 19 January 1999; 26 September 2000.

——Eastern Europe: 4 February 1991.

——Germany: 29 October 1990; 10 April 1991; 28 October 1991; 26 October 1992; 25 October 1993; 4 May 1994 (restructuring of Eastern Germany); 21 November 1994; 23 October 1995; 21 October 1996; 13 October 1998 (Eastern Germany); 10 November 1998; 5 February 1999; 1 June 1999; 22 May 2000.

——Hungary: 11 September 1987; 17 September 1990; 30 October 1991; 29 October 1992; 17 November 1993; 11 November 1994; 21 November 1995; 16 December 1996; 9 December 1997; 7 December 1998; 9 December 1999; 22 November 2000.

——IMF: World Economy and Finance: 24 September 1993.

——Poland: 25 May 1989; 20 November 1990; 2 May 1991; 28 April 1992; 17 June 1993; 18 March 1994; 28 March 1995; 29 September 1995; 27 March 1996; 30 October 1996; 26 March 1997; 25 March 1998; 27 October 1998; 30 March 1999; 17 April 2000; 25 June 2001.

——Privatization in Eastern Europe: 3 July 1992.

——Romania: 3 May 1994; 25 May 1995; 9 July 1996; 25 June 1997; 28 September 1998.

——Slovakia: 2 November 1993; 16 December 1994; 20 December 1995; 23 October 1996; 28 October 1997; 25 May 2000; 4 July 2001.

Fischer, S. (1992) 'Privatization in East European transformation', in C. Clague and G. Rausser (eds) *The Emergence of Market Economies in Eastern Europe*, Oxford: Blackwell.

Fischer, S. and Gelb, A. (1991) 'The process of socialist economic transformation', *Journal of Economic Perspectives*, vol. 5, no. 4.

Fischer, S. and Sahay, R. (2000) 'Taking stock', *Finance and Development*, vol. 37, no. 3.

Fischer, S., Sahay, R. and Vegh, C. (1996) 'Stabilization and growth in transition economies: the early experience', *Journal of Economic Perspectives*, vol. 10, no. 2.

Fry, M. and Nuti, D. (1992) 'Monetary and exchange-rate policies during Eastern Europe's transition: some lessons from further east', *Oxford Review of Economic Policy*, vol. 8, no. 1.

Frydman, R. and Rapaczynski, A. (1993) 'Insiders and the state: overview of responses to agency problems in East European privatization', *Economics of Transition*, vol. 1, no. 1.

Frydman, R., Rapaczynski, A., Earle, J. *et al.* (1993) *The Privatization Process in Central Europe*, London: Central European University Press.

Frydman, R., Gray, C. Hessel, M., and Rapaczynski, A. (1999) 'When does privatization work? The impact of private ownership on corporate performance in the transition countries', *Quarterly Journal of Economics*, vol. CXIV, no. 4.

Ghosh, A., Gulde, A.-M. and Wolf, H. (2000) 'Currency boards: more than a quick fix?', *Economic Policy*, October.

Glaeser, E. and Scheinkman, J. (1996) 'The transition to free markets: where to begin privatization', *Journal of Comparative Economics*, vol. 22, no. 1.

Gomulka, S., Yong-Chool Ha and Cae-One Kim (eds) (1989) *Economic Reforms in the Socialist World*, London: Macmillan.

Gora, M. (1991) 'Shock therapy for the Polish labour market', *International Labour Review*, vol. 130, no. 2.

Gregory, P. and Stuart, R. (1990) *Soviet Economic Structure and Performance*, 4th edn, New York: Harper & Row (2nd edn 1981 and 3rd edn 1986).

——(1994) *Soviet and Post-Soviet Economic Structure and Performance*, 5th edn, New York: HarperCollins.

Grosfeld, I. and Hare, P. (1991) 'Privatization in Hungary, Poland and Czechoslovakia', *European Economy: The Path of Reform in Central and Eastern Europe*, Special Edition no. 2, Brussels: Commission of the European Communities.

Gulde, A.-M. (1999) 'The role of the currency board in Bulgaria's stabilization', *Finance and Development*, September.

Hare, P. (1990a) 'Creating market economies: Eastern Europe in the 1990s', *The Economic Review*, vol. 7, no. 5.

——(1990b) 'From central planning to market economy: some microeconomic issues', *Economic Journal*, vol. 100, no. 401.

——(1991) 'Eastern Europe: the transition to a market economy', *The Royal Bank of Scotland Review*, no. 169 (March).

——(1992) 'Hungary', in I. Jeffries (ed.) *Industrial Reform in Socialist Countries: From Restructuring to Revolution*, Aldershot: Edward Elgar.

——(1993) 'Competitiveness and restructuring: issues for Eastern Europe', *British Review of Economic Issues*, vol. 15, no. 37.

Hare, P. and Revesz, T. (1992) 'Hungary's transition to the market: the case against a "big-bang"', *Economic Policy*, no. 14.

Havrylyshyn, O. and McGettigan, D. (1999) *Privatization in Transition Countries: Lessons of the First Decade*, Washington, DC: IMF, Economic Issues no. 18.

Havrylyshyn, O. and Odling-Smee, J. (2000) 'Political economy of stalled reforms', *Finance and Development*, vol. 37, no. 3.

Heady, C., Rajah, N. and Smith, S. (1994) 'Tax reform and economic transition in the Czech Republic', *Fiscal Studies*, vol. 15, no. 1.

Herd, G. (1998) 'Regional meltdown?', *The World Today*, vol. 54, no. 10.

Hewer, U. (1997) 'Czech enterprises seeking true owners', *Transition*, vol. 8, no. 3.

Hewett, E. (1988) *Reforming the Soviet Economy: Equality versus Efficiency*, Washington, DC: Brookings Institution.

Hexter, D. (1993) 'The bad debt problem in Eastern Europe', *Economics of Transition*, vol. 1, no. 1.

Hingorani, A., Lehn, K. and Makhija, A. (1997) 'Investor behaviour in mass privatization: the case of the Czech voucher scheme', *Journal of Financial Economics*, vol. 44, no. 3.

Holzman, F. (1976) *International Trade under Communism*, New York: Basic Books.

——(1987) *The Economics of Soviet Bloc Trade and Finance*, Boulder and London: Westview Press.

Holzman, R. (1992) 'Tax reform in countries in transition', *Public Finance*, vol. 47, Supplement.

Hrncir, M. (1993) *Economic Recovery and Foreign Exchange Regime: The Case of the Czech Republic*, Cambridge: University of Cambridge, Discussion Paper on Economic Transition DPET 9301.

Hughes, G. and Hare, P. (1991) 'Competitiveness and industrial restructuring in Czechoslovakia, Hungary and Poland', *European Economy: The Path of Reform in Central and Eastern Europe*, Special Edition no. 2, Brussels: Commission of the European Communities.

——(1992) 'Industrial policy and restructuring in Eastern Europe', *Oxford Review of Economic Policy*, vol. 8, no. 1.

——(1994) 'The international competitiveness of industries in Bulgaria, Czechoslovakia Hungary and Poland', *Oxford Economic Papers*, vol. 46, no. 2.

Hughes, M. (1993) 'Eastern pain and Western promise: the reaction of Western governments to the economic plight of the "New Eastern Europe" ', *International Relations*, vol. XI, no. 6.

Hughes Hallet, A. and Ma, Y. (1993) 'East Germany, West Germany, and their Mezzogiorno problem: a parable for European economic integration', *Economic Journal*, vol. 103, no. 417.

——(1994) 'Real adjustment in a union of incompletely converged economies: an example from East and West Germany', *European Economic Review*, vol. 38, no. 9.

Hume, I. and Pinto, B. (1993) 'Prejudice and fact in Poland's industrial transformation', *Finance and Development*, vol. 30, no. 2.

Husain, A. and Sahay, R. (1992) 'Does sequencing of privatization matter in reforming planned economies', *IMF Staff Papers*, vol. 39, no. 4.

Hussain, A. and Stern, N. (1994) *Economic Transition on the Other Side of the Wall: China*, London: LSE, CP no. 29.

Ickes, B. and Slemrod, J. (1992) 'Tax implementation issues in the transition from a planned economy', *Public Finance*, Supplement to vol. 47.

Inotai, A. (1994) 'Transforming the East: Western illusions and strategies', *The Hungarian Quarterly*, vol. 35, no. 133.

International Herald Tribune (various surveys) Central and Eastern Europe: 30 June 1999.

——Czech Republic: 25 June 1994; 26 June 1995; 25 April 1996; 3 June 1997; 28 May 1998.

——East–West Trade: 6 June 1989.

——Germany: 10 April 1991; 16 December 1992; 23 April 1993; 15 December 1993; 1 March 1994; 7 December 1994 (Germany: the New States); 15 December 1994; 3 April 1995; 22 April 1996.

——Hungary: 12 June 1985; 4 March 1991; 7 October 1993; 19 April 1994; 5 December 1994; 11 December 1995; 11 March 1996; 5 June 1997; 12 December 1997; 4 June 1998; 22 June 1999.

——Poland: 6 May 1994; 24 June 1995; 17 October 1996; 13 June 1997; 27 May 1998.

——Romania: 28 October 1997; 26 October 1999.

Jackman, R. (1994) 'Economic policy and employment in the transition economies of Central and Eastern Europe: what have we learned?', *International Labour Review*, vol. 133, no. 3.

Jackson, M. (ed.) (1991) 'Privatization in Central Europe', *Eastern European Economics*, vol. 30, no. 1.

Jarvis, C. (2000a) 'The rise and fall of Albania's pyramid schemes', *Finance and Development*, vol. 37, no. 1.

——(2000b) 'The rise and fall of the pyramid schemes in Albania', *IMF Staff Papers*, vol. 47, no. 1.

Jeffries, I. (ed.) (1981) *The Industrial Enterprise in Eastern Europe*, New York: Praeger.

——(1990) *A Guide to the Socialist Economies*, London: Routledge.

——(1992a) 'The impact of reunification on the East German economy', in J. Osmond (ed.) *German Reunification: A Reference Guide and Commentary*, London: Longman.

——(ed.) (1992b) *Industrial Reform in Socialist Countries: From Restructuring to Revolution*, Aldershot: Edward Elgar.

——(1993) *Socialist Economies and the Transition to the Market: A Guide*, London: Routledge.

——(1996a) *A Guide to the Economies in Transition*, London: Routledge.

——(ed.) (1996b) *Problems of Economic and Political Transformation in the Balkans*, London: Pinter.

——(2001a) *Economies in Transition: A Guide to China, Cuba, Mongolia, North Korea and Vietnam at the Turn of the Twenty-First Century*, London: Routledge.

——(2001b) 'Good governance and the first decade of transition: an overview', in W. Hoen (ed.) *Good Governance in Central and Eastern Europe: The Puzzle of Capitalism by Design*, Cheltenham: Edward Elgar.

Jeffries, I., Melzer, M. (eds) and Breuning, E. (advisory ed.) (1987) *The East German Economy*, London: Croom Helm.

Jenkins, G. (1992) 'Privatization and pension reform in transition economies', *Public Finance*, vol. 47, Supplement.

Johnson, S., La Porta, R., Lopez-de-Silanes, F. and Scheifer, A. (2000) 'Tunnelling', *American Economic Review*, Papers and Proceedings, May.

Jones, D. (1991) 'The Bulgarian labour market in transition', *International Labour Review*, vol. 130, no. 2.

——(1992) 'The transformation of labor unions in Eastern Europe: the case of Bulgaria', *Industrial and Labor Relations Review*, vol. 45, no. 3.

Jones, D. and Meurs, M. (1991a) 'On the entry of new firms in socialist economies: evidence from Bulgaria', *Soviet Studies*, vol. 43, no. 2.

——(1991b) 'Worker participation and worker self-management in Bulgaria', *Comparative Economic Studies*, vol. XXXIII, no. 4.

Jürgens, U., Klinzing, L. and Turner, L. (1993) 'The transformation of industrial relations in Eastern Germany', *Industrial and Labour Relations Review*, vol. 46, no. 2.

Kaminski, B., Wang, Z. and Winters, A. (1996) 'Export performance in transition economies', *Economic Policy*, no. 23.

Kaser, M. (2001) *Albania*, London: EIU.

Kaser, M. and Allsopp, C. (1992) 'The assessment: macroeconomic transition in Eastern Europe, 1989–91', *Oxford Review of Economic Policy*, vol. 8, no. 1.

Katsenelinboigen, A. (1977) 'Coloured markets in the Soviet Union', *Soviet Studies*, vol. 29, no. 1.

Kaufmann, D. and Siegelbaum, P. (1997) 'Privatization and corruption in transition economies', *Journal of International Affairs*, vol. 50, no. 2.

Kennedy, R. (1997) 'A tale of two economies: economic and restructuring in post-socialist Poland', *World Developments*, vol. 25, no. 6.

Kenway, P. and Klvacova, E. (1996) 'The web of cross-ownership among Czech financial intermediaries: an assessment', *Europe–Asia Studies*, vol. 48, no. 5.

Kiss, Y. (1992) 'Privatization in Hungary: two years later', *Soviet Studies*, vol. 44, no. 6.

——(1993) 'Lost illusions? Defence industry conversion in Czechoslovakia, 1989–92', *Europe–Asia Studies*, vol. 45, no. 6.

Klaus, V. (1992a) 'Policy dilemmas of Eastern European reforms: notes of an insider', in A. Prindle (ed.) *Banking and Finance in Eastern Europe*, London: Woodhead-Faulkner.

——(1992b) 'Transition: an insider's view', *Problems of Communism*, January–April.

Kolodko, G. (1993a) 'Recession and growth during transition to a market economy', in M. Ellman, E. Gaidar and G. Kolodko (eds) *Economic Transition in Eastern Europe*, edited P. Admiraal, Oxford: Blackwell.

——(1993b) 'From recession to growth in post-communist economies: expectations versus reality', *Communist and Post-Communist Studies*, vol. 26, no. 2.

——(1993c) 'Perverse effects of fiscal adjustment in transition economies', *Economics of Transition*, vol. 1, no. 3.

Kornai, J. (1990a) *The Road to a Free Economy*, New York: W.W. Norton.

——(1990b) 'Comment', *Brookings Papers on Economic Activity*, no. 1.

——(1992a) *The Socialist System: The Political Economy of Communism*, Oxford: Oxford University Press.

——(1992b) 'The postsocialist transition and the state: reflections in the light of Hungarian fiscal problems', *American Economic Review*, Papers and Proceedings, May.

Koslowski, R. (1992) 'Market institutions, East European reform, and economic theory', *Journal of Economic Issues*, vol. XXVI, no. 3.

Koves, A. (1992) *Central and East European Economies in Transition: The International Dimension*, Boulder: Westview Press.

Kozminski, A. (1992) 'Transition from planned to market economy: Hungary and Poland compared', *Studies in Comparative Communism*, vol. XXV, no. 4.

Kramer, H. (1993) 'The European Community's response to the "new Eastern Europe" ', *Journal of Common Market Studies*, vol. 31, no. 2.

Kupka, M. (1992) 'Transformation of ownership in Czechoslovakia', *Soviet Studies*, vol. 44, no. 2.

Laban, R. and Wolf, H. (1993) 'Large-scale privatization in transition economies', *American Economic Review*, vol. 83, no. 5.

Landesmann, M. (1993) *Industrial Policy and the Transition in East-Central Europe*, Cambridge: University of Cambridge, Discussion Paper on Economic Transition DPET 9204.

Lansbury, M., Pain, N. and Smidkova, K. (1996) 'Foreign direct investment in Central Europe since 1990: an econometric study', *National Institute Economic Review*, no. 156.

Lavigne, M. (2000) 'The years of transition: a review article', *Communist and Post-Communist Studies*, vol. 33, no. 4.

Lerman, Z. (1999) 'Land reform and farm restructuring: what has been accomplished to date?', *American Economic Review*, Papers and Proceedings, May.

Levine, R. and Scott, D. (1993) 'Old debt and new beginnings: a policy choice in transitional socialist economies', *World Development*, vol. 21, no. 3.

Lipton, D. and Sachs, J. (1990a) 'Creating a market in Eastern Europe: the case of Poland', *Brookings Papers on Economic Activity*, no. 1.

——(1990b) 'Privatization in Eastern Europe: the case of Poland', *Brookings Papers on Economic Activity*, no. 2.

Lomax, B. (1999) 'The 1998 elections in Hungary: third time lucky for the Young Democrats', *Communist Studies and Transition Politics*, vol. 15, no. 2.
Lorinc, H. (1992) 'Foreign debt, debt management and implications for Hungary's development', *Soviet Studies*, vol. 44, no. 6.
Losch, D. (1990) 'The post-war transformation of West Germany's economy: a model for the GDR?', *Intereconomics*, vol. 25, no. 2.
Lueschen, L. (1994) 'Collective farms in transition in the former German Democratic Republic', *Comparative Economic Studies*, vol. XXXVI, no. 2.
Maciaszek-Roberts, B. (1993a) 'Transition in Eastern Europe: does the sequence of privatization matter?', *Journal of International Development*, vol. 5, no. 2.
——(1993b) 'The sequence of privatization: the case of Poland', *British Review of Economic Issues*, vol. 15, no. 37.
——(1995) *Output Decline in Eastern Europe: A Comparison of Explanations for Poland*, Leicester: University of Leicester, Discussion Paper no. 95/1.
McKinnon, R. (1992a) 'Taxation, money, and credit in a liberalizing socialist economy', *Economics of Planning*, vol. 25, no. 1.
——(1992b) 'Taxation, money and credit in a liberalizing socialist economy', in C. Clague and G. Rausser (eds) *The Emergence of Market Economies in Eastern Europe*, Oxford: Blackwell.
——(1994) 'Financial growth and macroeconomic stability in China, 1978–92: implications for Russia and other transitional economies', *Journal of Comparative Economics*, vol. 18, no. 3.
Messerlin, P. (1993) 'The EC and Central Europe: the missed rendez-vous of 1992?', *Economics of Transition*, vol. 1, no. 1.
Metcalf, G. and Ambrus-Lakatos, L. (1992) 'The optimal rate of privatization in a dynamic economy', *Public Finance*, vol. 47, Supplement.
Milanovic, B. (1992) 'Poland's quest for economic stabilization, 1988–91: interaction of political economy and economics', *Soviet Studies*, vol. 44, no. 3.
Mizsei, K. (1992) 'Privatization in Eastern Europe: a comparative study of Poland and Hungary', *Soviet Studies*, vol. 44, no. 2.
Mladek, J. and Hashi, I. (1993) 'Voucher privatization, investment funds and corporate governance in Czechoslovakia', *British Review of Economic Issues*, vol. 15, no. 37.
Mroz, B. (1991) 'Poland's economy in transition to private ownership', *Soviet Studies*, vol. 43, no. 4.
Mullineux, A. (1992a) *Banks, Privatization and Restructuring in Poland*, Birmingham: University of Birmingham, Discussion Paper IFGWP–92–02.
——(1992b) *Privatization in the UK and Germany: Lessons for Central and Eastern Europe*, Birmingham: University of Birmingham, Discussion Paper IFGWP–92–01.
Mullineux, A. and Belka, M. (1993) *Hardening Micro Budget Constraints: Bank Behaviour and Corporate Governance in Poland*, Birmingham: University of Birmingham, Discussion Paper IFGWP–93–08.
Murrell, P. (1990) *The Nature of Socialist Economies: Lessons from Eastern European Foreign Trade*, Princeton, NJ: Princeton University Press.
——(1992a) 'Evolutionary and radical approaches to economic reform', *Economics of Planning*, vol. 25, no. 1.
——(1992b) 'Evolution in economics and in the economic reform of the centrally planned economies', in C. Clague and G. Rausser (eds) *The Emergence of Market Economies in Eastern Europe*, Oxford: Blackwell.

——(1993) 'What is shock therapy? What did it do in Poland and Russia?', *Post-Soviet Affairs*, vol. 9, no. 2.

Nellis, J. (1999) 'Time to rethink privatization in transition economies?', *Finance and Development*, vol. 36, no. 2.

Nelson, G. (1993) 'Agricultural policy reform in Eastern Europe', *American Journal of Agricultural Economics*, vol. 75, no. 3.

Neuber, A. (1993) 'Towards a political economy of transition in Eastern Europe', *Journal of International Development*, vol. 5, no. 5.

Nolan, P. (1992) *Transforming Stalinist Systems: China's Reforms in the Light of Russian and East European Experience*, Cambridge; University of Cambridge, Discussion Paper on Economic Transition DPET 9203.

——(1996) 'China's rise, Russia's fall', *Journal of Peasant Studies*, vol. 24, nos 1 and 2.

Nove, A. (1961) *The Soviet Economy*, London: Allen & Unwin.

——(1981) 'The Soviet industrial enterprise', in I. Jeffries (ed.) *The Industrial Enterprise in Eastern Europe*, New York: Praeger.

——(1986) *The Soviet Economic System*, 3rd edn, London: Allen & Unwin.

——(1994) 'A gap in transition models? A comment on Gomulka', *Europe–Asia Studies*, vol. 46, no. 5.

Nuti, D. (2000) 'The Polish zloty, 1990–99: success and underperformance', *American Economic Review*, Papers and Proceedings, May.

OECD (1992) *Bulgaria: An Economic Assessment*, Geneva: OECD.

Osmond, J. (ed.) (1992) *German Reunification: A Reference Guide and Commentary*, London: Longman.

Pashko, G. (1991) 'The Albanian economy at the beginning of the 1990s', in Ö. Sjöberg and M. Wyzan (eds) *Economic Change in the Balkan States: Albania, Bulgaria, Romania and Yugoslavia*, London: Pinter.

——(1993) 'Obstacles to economic reform in Albania', *Europe–Asia Studies*, vol. 45, no. 5.

——(1996) 'Problems of the transition in Albania, 1990–94' in I. Jeffries (ed.) *Problems of Economic and Political Transformation in the Balkans*, London: Pinter.

Petrovic, P., Bogetic, Z. and Vujosevic, Z. (1999) 'The Yugoslav hyperinflation of 1992–94: causes, dynamics and money supply process', *Journal of Comparative Economics*, vol. 27, no. 2.

Pinto, B., Belka, M. and Krajewski, S. (1993) 'Transforming state enterprises in Poland: evidence of adjustment by manufacturing firms', *Brookings Papers on Economic Activity*, no. 1.

Pohl, G., Anderson, R., Claessens, S. and Djankov, S. (1997) 'Findings of a survey: leaders and laggers', *Transition*, vol. 8, no. 3.

Portes, R. (1994) 'Transformation traps', *Economic Journal*, vol. 104, no. 426.

Poznanski, K. (1992a) 'Privatization of the Polish economy: problems of transition', *Soviet Studies*, vol. 44, no. 4.

——(ed.) (1992b) *Constructing Capitalism: The Reemergence of Civil Society and Liberal Economy*, Boulder: Westview Press.

Priewe, J. (1993) 'Privatization of the industrial sector: the function and activity of the Treuhandanstalt', *Cambridge Journal of Economics*, vol. 17, no. 3.

Rausser, G. (1992) 'Lessons for emerging market economies in Eastern Europe', in C. Clague and G. Rausser (eds) *The Emergence of Market Economies in Eastern Europe*, Oxford: Blackwell.

Rausser, G. and Johnson, S. (1993) 'State–market–civil institutions: the case of Eastern Europe and the Soviet republics', *World Development*, vol. 21, no. 4.

Rizov, M., Gavrilescu, D., Gow, H., Mathijs, E. and Swinnen, J. (2001) 'Transition and enterprise restructuring: the development of individual farming in Romania', *World Development*, vol. 29, no. 7.

Roberts, B. (1996) *Transition in Poland and Shifts in Sectoral Composition of Demand*, Leicester: University of Leicester, Discussion Paper no. 96/2.

Roberts, E. (1999) 'Trouble ahead', *The World Today*, vol. 55, no. 12.

Roesler, J. (1994) 'Privatization in Eastern Germany: experience with the Treuhand', *Europe–Asia Studies*, vol. 46, no. 3.

Roland, G. (1994a) 'The role of political constraints in transition economies', *Economics of Transition*, vol. 2, no. 1.

——(1994b) 'On the speed and sequencing of privatization and restructuring', *Economic Journal*, vol. 104, no. 426.

Roland, G. and Verdier, T. (1994) 'Privatization in Eastern Europe: irreversibility and critical mass effects', *Journal of Public Economics*, vol. 54, no. 2.

Rollo, J. and Smith, A. (1992) *The Political Economy of Central Europe Trade with the European Community: Why So Sensitive?*, London: Royal Institute of International Affairs.

——(1993) 'The political economy of Eastern European trade with the European Community', *Economic Policy*, no. 16.

Rollo, J. with Batt, J., Granville, B. and Malcolm, N. (1990) *The New Eastern Europe: Western Responses*, London: Royal Institute of International Affairs (Chatham House Papers).

Ronnas, P. (1996) 'Romania: transition to underdevelopment', in I. Jeffries (ed.) *Problems of Economic and Political Transformation in the Balkans*, London: Pinter.

Rosati, D. (1992) 'The CMEA demise, trade restructuring, and trade destruction in Central and Eastern Europe', *Oxford Review of Economic Policy*, vol. 8, no. 1.

——(1994) 'Output declines during the transition from plan to market: a consideration', *Economics of Transition*, vol. 2, no. 4.

Rybczynski, T. (1991) 'The sequencing of reform', *Oxford Review of Economic Policy*, vol. 7, no. 4.

Sachs, J. (1992) 'The economic transformation of Eastern Europe: the case of Poland', *Economics of Planning*, vol. 25, no. 1.

——(1994) *Poland's Jump to the Market Economy*, Cambridge, Mass.: MIT Press.

——(1995) 'Consolidating capitalism', *Foreign Policy*, no. 98.

——(1996a) 'The transition at mid-decade', *American Economic Review*, Papers and Proceedings (May).

——(1996b) 'Economic transition and the exchange rate regime', *American Economic Review*, Papers and Proceedings (May).

——(1997) 'An overview of stabilization issues facing economies in transition', in W. Woo, S. Parker and J. Sachs (eds) *Economies in Transition: Comparing Asia and Eastern Europe*, London: MIT Press.

Sachs, J. and Lipton, D. (1990) 'Poland's economic reform', *Foreign Affairs*, vol. 69, no. 3.

Sachs, J. and Woo, W. (1994) 'Structural factors in the economic reforms of China, Eastern Europe and the former Soviet Union', *Economic Policy*, no. 18.

——(1996) 'China's transition experience reexamined', *Transition*, vol. 7, nos 3–4.

Schmiedling, H. (1993) 'From plan to market: on the nature of the transformation crisis', *Weltwirtschaftliches Archiv*, vol. 129, no. 2.

Schnytzer, A. (1992) 'Albania: the purge of Stalinist economic ideology' in I. Jeffries (ed.) *Industrial Reform in Socialist Countries: From Restructuring to Revolution*, Aldershot: Edward Elgar.

Schroeder, G. (1982) 'Soviet economic reform decrees: more steps on the treadmill', US Congress, Joint Economic Committee, Washington, DC: Government Printing Office.

——(1986) *The System versus Progress: Soviet Economic Problems*, London: Centre for Research into Communist Economies.

——(1988a) 'Organisations and hierarchies: the perennial search for solutions', in S. Linz and W. Moskoff (eds) *Reorganization and Reform in the Soviet Union*, Armonk, NY, and London: M.E. Sharpe.

——(1988b) 'Property rights issues in economic reforms in socialist countries', *Studies in Comparative Communism*, vol. XXI, no. 2.

——(1992) 'The Soviet industrial enterprise in the 1980s', in I. Jeffries (ed.) *Industrial Reform in Socialist Countries: From Restructuring to Revolution*, Aldershot: Edward Elgar.

Schwartz, G. and Lopes, P. (1993) 'Privatization: expectations, trade-offs and results', *Finance and Development*, vol. 30, no. 2.

Scott, N. (1992) 'The implications of the transition for foreign trade and investment', *Oxford Review of Economic Policy*, vol. 8, no. 1.

Shleifer, A. (1997) 'Government in transition', *European Economic Review*, vol. 41, nos 3–5.

Siebert, H. (1991a) *German Unification: The Economics of Transition*, Kiel: Kiel Institute of World Economics, Working Paper no. 468.

——(1991b) 'German unification: the economics of transition', *Economic Policy*, no. 13 (October).

Silberman, J., Weiss, C. and Dutz, M. (1994) 'Jump-starting ex-communist economies: a leaf from the Marshall Plan', *Foreign Affairs*, vol. 75, no. 1.

Sinn, H.-W. (1992) 'Privatization in East Germany', *Public Finance*, vol. 47, Supplement.

Sjöberg, Ö. (1989) *The Agrarian Sector in Albania during the 1980s: A Changing Regional Focus*, Stockholm: Economic Research Institute of the Stockholm School of Economics, Research Report no. 4.

——(1990) *The Albanian Economy in the 1980s: The Nature of a Low-Performing System*, Stockholm: Economic Research Institute of the Stockholm School of Economics, Working Paper no. 10.

——(1991a) 'The Albanian economy in the 1980s: coping with a centralised system', in Ö. Sjöberg and M. Wyzan (eds) *Economic Change in the Balkan States: Albania, Bulgaria, Romania and Yugoslavia*, London: Pinter.

——(1991b) *Rural Change and Development in Albania*, Boulder: Westview Press.

——(1996) 'The regional effects of economic transformation in Albania: towards an assessment', in I. Jeffries (ed.) *Problems of Economic and Political Transformation in the Balkans*, London: Pinter.

Sjöberg, Ö. and Wyzan, M. (eds) (1991) *Economic Change in the Balkan States: Albania, Bulgaria, Romania and Yugoslavia*, London: Pinter.

Slay, B. (2000) 'The Polish economic transition: outcome and lessons', *Communist and Post-Communist Studies*, vol. 33, no. 1.

Smith, A.H. (1992) 'The Romanian enterprise', in I. Jeffries (ed.) *Industrial Reform in Socialist Countries: From Restructuring to Revolution*, Aldershot: Edward Elgar.

Sorm, V. and Terrell, K. (2000) 'Sectoral restructuring and labour mobility: a comparative look at the Czech Republic', *Journal of Comparative Economics*, vol. 28, no. 3.

Summers, L. (1992) 'The next decade in Central and Eastern Europe', in C. Clague and G. Rausser (eds) *The Emergence of Market Economies in Eastern Europe*, Oxford: Blackwell.

Summers, M. (1992) 'Privatization by coupon in Czechoslovakia', *Economic Affairs*, vol. 12, no. 3.

Swain, N. (1999) 'Agricultural restitution and co-operative transformation in the Czech Republic, Hungary and Slovakia', *Europe–Asia Studies*, vol. 51, no. 7.

Swinnen, J. (1999) 'The political economy of land reform choices in Central and Eastern Europe', *Economics of Transition*, vol. 7, no. 3.

Tsang, S. (1996) 'Against "big bang" in economic transition: normative and positive arguments', *Cambridge Journal of Economics*, vol. 20, no. 2.

United Nations (1993) *World Economic Survey 1993*, New York: United Nations.

United Nations Economic Commission for Europe (1992) *Economic Survey of Europe in 1991–92*, New York: United Nations.

——(1993) *Economic Survey of Europe in 1992–93*, New York: United Nations.

——(1994) *Economic Survey of Europe in 1993–94*, New York: United Nations.

——(1995) *Economic Survey of Europe in 1994–95*, New York: United Nations.

——(1996) *Economic Survey of Europe in 1995–96*, New York: United Nations.

——(1997) *Economic Survey of Europe in 1996–97*, New York: United Nations.

——(1998a) *Economic Survey of Europe 1998*, No. 1, New York: United Nations.

——(1998b) *Economic Survey of Europe 1998*, No. 2, New York: United Nations.

——(1998c) *Economic Survey of Europe 1998*, No. 3, New York: United Nations. (Subsequent issues are not specifically quoted from, but data are used.)

Van Brabant, J. (1993) 'Lessons from the wholesale transformations in the East', *Comparative Economic Studies*, vol. XXXV, no. 4.

——(1994) 'Trade, integration and transformation in Eastern Europe', *Journal of International Affairs*, vol. 48, no. 1.

Vincentz, V. (1991) *Privatization in Eastern Germany: Principles and Practice*, Munich: Eastern Europe Institute, Working Paper no. 146.

Wallace, W. and Clarke, R. (1986) *Comecon, Trade and the West*, London: Pinter.

Weitzman, M. (1993) 'Economic transition: can theory help?', *European Economic Review*, vol. 37, nos 2/3.

Weitzman, M. and Xu, C. (1993) *Chinese Township–Village Enterprises as Vaguely Defined Co-operatives*, London: LSE, CP no. 26.

——(1994) 'Chinese township–village enterprises as vaguely defined co-operatives', *Journal of Comparative Economics*, vol. 18, no. 2.

Williamson, J. (1993) 'Why did output fall in Eastern Europe?', in L. Somogyi (ed.) *The Political Economy of the Transition Process in Eastern Europe*, Aldershot: Edward Elgar.

Woo, W. (1994) 'The art of reforming centrally planned economies: comparing China, Poland and Russia', *Journal of Comparative Economics*, vol. 18, no. 3.

——(1997) 'Improving the performance of enterprises in transition', in W. Woo, S. Parker and J. Sachs (eds) *Economies in Transition: Comparing Asia and Eastern Europe*, London: MIT Press.

Woo, W., Parker, S. and Sachs, J. (eds) (1997) *Economies in Transition: Comparing Asia and Eastern Europe*, London: MIT Press.

World Bank (1996) *World Development Report: From Plan to Market*, New York: Oxford University Press.

Wyzan, M. (1991) 'The Bulgarian economy in the immediate post-Zhivkov era', in Ö. Sjöberg and M. Wyzan (eds) *Economic Change in the Balkan States: Albania, Bulgaria, Romania and Yugoslavia*, London: Pinter.

——(1992) 'Bulgaria: shock therapy followed by steep recession', *Radio Free Europe/Radio Liberty Research Report*, vol. 1, no. 45.

——(1996) 'Economic change in Bulgaria since the fall of communism', in I. Jeffries (ed.) *Problems of Economic and Political Transformation in the Balkans*, London: Pinter.

——(1998) 'The political economy of Bulgaria's peculiar post-communist business cycle', *Comparative Economic Studies*, vol. XXXX, no. 1.

Zizmond, E. (1993) 'Slovenia – one year of independence', *Europe–Asia Studies*, vol. 45, no. 5.

Zukowski, R. (1993) 'Stabilization and recession in a transitional economy: the case of Poland', *World Development*, vol. 21, no. 7.

Index

abortion law (Poland) 243, 248
acquis communautaire 214
Aghion, P. and Blanchard, O. 282
Ahmeti, V. 6, 71
Albiniak, M. 246
Alia, R. 5–6, 70, 88, 93, 100
Allmucaj, V. 83–4
Anderson, R. 165, 187–8, 192
Andrews, E. 195
Antall, J. 202
antisemitism and Jewish affairs (Poland) 241–3, 250–5, 261, 266–7
Antonescu, I. 321
Article 8 (IMF) 32, 34, 38, 62, 150, 196, 283, 376
Asian/Russian financial crisis 63, 384, 391–2, 397
Åslund, A. 13, 101, 114, 385, 394
Athanasiu, A. 46, 314

Babiuc, V. 304
Balcerowicz, L. 36–7, 246–7, 252, 258–60, 263, 269, 276, 385–6
Balcerowicz, L., Blaszczyk, B. and Dabrowski, M. 273, 286, 293
Baleta, A. 75
bankruptcy 102, 136–7, 156, 179, 182, 195, 224, 270, 276, 323, 367, 374
Barber, L. 248
Bartha, F. 206, 225
Bartholdy, K. 224
Basescu, T.
Bauc, J. 260, 268
Bekesi, L. 204–6
Belka, M. 243, 246
Benes, E. 189
Berisha, S. 4–7, 9–13, 67–101
Berov, L. 19, 143
Bielecki, J. 278–9
big bang price liberalization 384–8
big bang/shock therapy 13, 34, 37, 101, 268–9, 383–95
Bisak, P. 353
Biserov, K. 124–5
black market (shadow or grey economy) 225, 389, 327, 368
Blanchard, O. 270, 282, 285
Blazyca, G. 270, 284
Blejer, M. *et al.* 14, 104
Blinken, D. and Moses, A. 298–9
Blue Coalition (Romania) 355
Blum, P. 397
Bobinski, C. 279–80
Bobosikova, J. 175
Bod, P. 206
Bogetic, Z. and Hillman, A. 29, 147
Bokros, L. 206, 222
Boland, V. 354
Bonin, J. and Leven, B. 286
Bonner, R. 107
Borenzstein, E., Demekas, D. and Ostry, J. 133, 135
Borger, J. 28, 83, 146
Boris III 127
Boross, P. 203
Boyes, R. 211
Boyko, M.
Brada, J. 398, 406
Brady bonds 26, 274
Breuel, B. 403, 405
Bridge, A. 188
Brokaj, S. 92
Brom, K. and Orenstein, M. 179–80, 185
Brooks, K. and Meurs, M. 343
Brozi, Z. 72
Bufi, Y. 6, 92
Bugaj, R. 246–7
Bugar, B. 350

Bulatovic, M. 71
Buzek, J. 36, 247–8, 254, 258–9, 263, 267–8
Buzkova, P. 158

Cami, F. 70
Campeanescu, R. 303
capital controls 384, 392
capital privatization (Poland) 282
Carcani, A. 70, 100
cardboard billionaires 336
Caritas (Charity, Romania) 297
Carnogursky, J. 352, 359–60
Ceausescu, Nicolae 46–8, 300, 306, 308, 315–16, 318
Ceausescu, Nicu 302
CEFTA (Central European Free Trade Association) 150, 230
Ceka, N. 11, 75, 92–3, 95
Cela, A. 73
Cernak, L. 352, 358, 360
Cesnak, K. 354
Charter 97 157, 355
China as an economic model 383, 390–1
Chikan, A. 212, 214, 230
Churchill, W. 168, 213, 254
Cimoszewicz, W. 240, 242, 244
Ciorbea, V. 43–5, 51, 54, 304–9, 313, 317, 324, 330–1
CIS (Commonwealth of Independent States) 25, 141, 392
Ciumara, M. 304
civil society 303
Clague, C. 394
Clinton, W. (Bill) 49, 123, 157, 244, 306
Cochrane, N. 343
Cody, E. 7, 67
Cohen, R. 162, 251
Comecon 22, 133, 270, 232, 383, 389
commercialization (corporatization) 278, 395
concordat between the Vatican and Poland 248
Constantinescu, E. 41–3, 46–8, 51, 299, 302–4, 307, 313–17
Copenhagen criteria 214
Coposcu, C. 301
corporate finance and control 396–7
corporate goverance 27, 144
Council of Europe 157, 298
Cozma, M. 48–9, 304, 310–13, 323
crawling peg exchange rate regime 34, 231, 270–1
critical mass 394
Csarky, P. 239
Csurka, I. 202–3, 212
Cunescu, S. 43, 301–2
Cungu, A. and Swinnen, J. 16, 110
currency board 25, 140–1, 150, 155
Czarnecki, R. 247–8

Daianu, D. 46, 309–10
Darollari, G. 76
Davis, J. and Gaburici, A. 344
Dejeu, G. 45, 304, 308
Demekas, D. and Khan, M. 324
Dempsey, J. 405
Demsky, G. 218
Denton, N. 203, 234, 236
deregulation 384
Dianconescu, I. 301
differentiation *see* principle of differentiation
Dimitru, S. 46, 310
dirty money 398
Djankov, S. and Pohl, G. 375
Dlouhy, V. 158, 184
Dmitrov, F. 19, 21, 116, 120
Dobrev, N. 119–21
Dochia, A. 300
Dogan, A. 116–17, 122, 130
Dokle, N. 75
Dossiers (Law on, Albania) 72
Ducky, J. 353–4, 359
Dunai, I. 206–7
Duray, M. 350, 352, 358
Dyck, I. 404
Dzurinda, M. 60–1, 357–64

Eastwood, R. and Durski, A. 286
EFTA 232
Ellman, M. 274
emancipation of the *nomenklatura* 278
enfranchisement bill (Poland) 39, 260, 290–1
Erlanger, S. 174
Estrin, S. and Richet, X. 285
EU (membership negotiations) 21–2, 31, 33–4, 36, 49–50, 59–60, 122–4, 163, 169, 203, 208, 213–22, 244, 257–8, 262, 306–7, 314–18, 355–6, 360–4
European Stability Pact 206, 349, 353
evolutionary theory 389
Expo '96 205

Fico, R. 360–1, 364–5

Fieldorf, A. 256
Finn, P. 216, 259
Fino, B. 87, 89, 92, 95
Fischer, S. 164
Fischer, S., Sahay, R. and Vegh, C. 384
flood bonds 187
Fodor, G. 204–5, 211
Foundations (Law of) (Slovakia) 353–4
Freeland, C. 323, 342
friendship treaty between Romania and Ukraine 305
friendship and co-operation treaty between Albania and Greece 5, 70
friendship and co-operation treaty between Romania and the Federal Republic of Yugoslavia 301
Frunda, G. 302–3, 318
Frydman, R., Rapaczynski, A. and Earle, J. 151, 224–5, 396, 399, 326, 341
Funar, G. 297–9, 302–3, 305, 308

Gabcikovo Dam dispute 33, 60, 208, 348
Ganchev, G. 116, 118, 122
Gaulieder, F. 354, 356
Gavrilescu, D. 45, 309
Gegs 19, 83, 113
Genocide (Law on Communist Genocide, Albania) 72, 76–7, 90, 93
Geremek, B. 247, 258, 263, 268
German minority (Romania) 300
Getchev, R. 116
Ghosh, A., Gulde, A.-M. and Wolf, H. 25, 141
Gierek, E. 268
Gjinushi, S. 11, 72, 75, 85, 92
Glemp, J. 250, 267
gminas (Poland) 253
Godo, S. 76
golden share(s) 34, 22, 370
Goncz, A. 206, 216
Gorbachev, M. 168, 213, 254, 383, 391
Gozhita, A. 89
Grabowski, B. 259
gradualism 383–95
Grebenicek, M. 159, 166
Greek ethnic minority (Albania) 4–5, 68–9
Green, P. 165, 181
greenfield activity (start-up firms) 395
greenfield foreign investment 230
Gregr, M. 167, 177–8, 191–3
Gronkiewicz-Waltz, H. 240, 263, 269
Grosz, K. 206
group of 13 (Bulgaria) 29, 147, 147
Grulich, V. 167
Gulde, A.-M. 24–5, 139, 141
Gypsies (Roma) 50, 60, 157, 169–70, 217–20, 297, 319, 351, 363

Hajdari, A. 11, 93–4
Hajek, J. 157
Hamzik, P. 354
Hansen, J. 114
Harach, L. 360
Harley, M. 235
hard budget constraint 38, 63, 284–5, 396
Havel, J. 178
Havel, V. 30, 156–7, 162–8, 171–6, 183
Havrylyshyn, O. 25, 141, 285
Havrylyshyn, O. and McGettigen, D. 38, 395–6, 403
Hazaparu, D. 302
Hewer, U. 181
hidden privatization *see nomenklatura* privatization
Hingorani, A., Lehn, K. and Makhija, A. (CR) 180
Hodac, J. 173–6
holding companies 401
Holocaust 207, 250, 255
honeymoon period 385–6
Hope, K. 153
Horn, G. 204–5, 213, 222, 226–7, 233, 299, 350
Horthy, M. 202
Hoxha, A. 71
Hoxha, E. 70, 84
Hoxha, N. 70, 77
Hrasko, J. 356
Hudek, M. 354
Hungarian ethnic minority 50, 60, 205, 220–1, 297–300, 348–51, 357, 363
Hussain, A. and Stern, N. 387
hyperinflation 22, 51, 155, 269

Ijdelea, E. 300–1
Iliescu, I. 40–2, 47, 50, 298, 302, 304, 315, 317–20, 324, 328
Illyria 68
Imami, A. 75, 85
implicit contracts 389
Indzhova, R. 19
insiders 398–9
Ionescu-Qintas, M. 308
iron curtain 168, 213, 254
Isarescu, M. 47–8, 315–16, 318
isolation programme (Bulgaria) 24, 138–9

Ivanov, D. 125

Jagielinski, R. 244
Janiszewski, J. 247
Janosz, Z. 251
Jarai, Z. 212, 219
Jaruzelski, W. 241, 265
Jarvis, C. 7, 9, 78–81
Jeffries, I. 158, 206
Jewish property (Czech Republic and Poland) 188, 243
Jiu valley 48, 304, 311–12, 322
Johnson, S. *et al.* 184, 402
Jotev, P. 123

Kacmarek, W. 243
Kaczurba, J. 256
Kaczynski, L. 266
Kadria, S. 83
Kakakula, P. 75
Kalinowski, J. 243, 247
Kalvoda, J. 158, 161
Kamela-Sowinska, A. 293
Kaminska, T. 247
Kamm, H. 114
Kasal, J. 168
Kaser, M. 13, 19, 97, 103, 108, 113
Kaufmann, D. and Siegelbaum, P. 400
Kavan, J. 167
Keay, J. 230
Keleti, G. 205
Kennedy, R. 285
Kenway, P. and Klvacova, E. 185
Kieres, L. 261
Kiss, Y. 226
Kiszczak, C. 265
Klaus, V. 30–1, 156, 158–60, 162–8, 170–1, 173–5, 196, 201, 355
Klosi, F. 96
Knazko, M. 352
Kohl, H. 31, 162
Kolodko, G. 242–3
Komolowski, L. 247
Koron, J. 240
Kosovo crisis 4, 11, 14, 22, 93–4, 98, 105, 113–14, 141, 155
Kostov, D. 117
Kostov, I. 19, 21, 29, 116, 121–30, 132, 148, 150
Kovac, M. 353–4, 356–7, 359, 361, 368
Kovac, R. 60
Kovacs, L. 205, 212
Kovacs, M. 206
Kowolok, S. 246
Kozlik, S. 353
Kozloduy nuclear power station 27, 143–4
Krajci, G. 354
Krzaklewski, M. 245–6, 248, 263, 291
Kuehnl, K. 178
Kukan, E. 61, 361
Kuncze, G. 203, 205, 208
Kurek, A. 356
Kwasniewski, A. 36–7, 40, 240–1, 244, 248–9, 354, 260–2, 264–6, 275–6, 290, 292–3

Lansbury, M., Pain, N. and Smidkova, K. 197, 234, 295
Lansky, J. 167
Layard, R. 390
Leka I 71, 90
Lerman, Z. 200
Leszek, S. 207
Lexa, I. 359, 361
liberalization (theory) 384
Lieven, A. 44, 305–6, 308, 344
Lipton, D. 389
liquidation 23, 138, 226, 278, 281–2, 284
liquidation programme (Bulgaria) 24, 138–9
Lizner, J. 157
Lleshi, H. 73
Lobkowicz, M. 164
Lomax, B. 211
London Club (of commercial bank creditors) 22, 135
Lotz, K. 205
Lukanov, A. 20, 118
Luptak, J. 352, 358
lustracja 256–7
lustration 123
Lux, J. 158, 164, 168

McKinnon, R. 387
McNeil, D. 319
Madl, F. 216
mafiaisation 146
Majko, P. 12, 96
Malaj, A. 92
Malikova, A. 360, 365
management KG 404
Mania, H. 266
Manulescu, N. 301, 303, 308
Marazov, I. 117–18
Marga, A. 319
Markov, G. 118

Markus, S. 356
Marsh, V. 29–30, 42–3, 45, 147, 151–2, 207, 304, 309, 323, 333
Matolcsi, G. 214
Martonyi, J. 212
Marvanova, H. 178
Maxim (Patriarch) (Bulgaria) 132
Mazowiecki, T. 278
Meciar, V. 59–61, 350–62, 365, 371–5, 380
Medgyessy, P. 207
Mehta, I. 8, 75, 82, 96, 99
Meidani, R. 11–12, 95–6
Meksi, A. 6–7, 96
Melescanu, T. 206, 305
Melo, V. 11, 76, 92
Mertlik, P. 167–8, 177–8, 191
Michael (King) 126, 300, 305, 307
Migas, J. 353, 358
Mikhailova, E. 130
Mikke, K. 246
Miklos, I. 61, 359–61
Milczanowski, A. 240
Miller, L. 248, 252, 255
Milner, M. 152, 339
Milo, P. 73, 92
Mladek, J, 178
Mochovce nuclear power station (Slovakia) 358
Mohara, T. 302–3
Molotov–Ribbentrop Pact 305
monetary overhang 384, 386
Moravcik, J. 352–3
Mortimer, E. 203
Moser, A. 21, 121
Moses, A. 322
Mroziewicz, R. 256
Mulak, J. 246
Mullineux, A. and Belka, M. 281
Münchau, W. 405
Munich agreement of 1938
Murrell, P. 389–90
Musetescu, O. 336
mutual funds 401
Myftiu, M. 73

Nagy, S. 204
Nano, F. 5–6, 11–12, 70, 72, 75–6, 85, 88, 91–6
Nastase, A. 42, 300, 302, 304, 320–1
National Wealth Management Funds (Poland) 38, 279–80
Nato expansion 31, 34, 37, 49, 59, 124, 163, 165, 168, 208, 213, 244, 254, 305–6, 355
natural monopolies 396
Negritoiu, M. 300
Nellis, J. 182, 285
Nelson, D. 48, 316
Nice Treaty (December 2000) 34, 218–19, 221–2
Nixon, R. 49, 306
Nolan, P. 391
nomenklatura 28, 146, 247, 278, 396
nomenklatura (hidden) privatization 28, 146–7
nuclear power station (Romania) 347
Nuti, M. 270

Odling-Smee, J. 25, 141
Olechowski, A. 262–4
Oleksy, J. 240–1, 246, 248, 262
oligarchs 336
Olszewski, J. 246, 252, 279
Onyszkiewicz, J. 247
Operation Alba (Sunrise) 11, 90
Orban, V. 33, 202, 204, 208–12, 216, 221
Ottoway, D. 156
outsiders 397

Pal, L. 205–6
Paris Club (of sovereign/country creditors) 22, 133, 135
participation model 406
Partnership for Peace 157, 301
Parvanov, G. 119, 121–3
Pashko, G. 5–6, 75, 101–2, 107
Pashkovski, S. 20, 117–18
Paskalev, K. 131
Passy, S. 132
Patriciu, D. 303
Paunescu, A. 302–3
Pawlak, W. 240, 246–7, 279
Pehe, J. 174
Pellumbi, P. 75–6
Perlez, J. 75, 87, 18, 184, 242, 350
Pettifer, J. 118, 147
Peto, I. 203, 207
Phare 37, 248
Pick, O. 179
Pietrewicz, M. 242
Pilip, I. 163–4
Pinter, S. 212
Pinto, B., Belka, M. and Krajewski, S. 284
Pirinski, G. 117–18
Piskovski, P. 263–4

Pithart, P. 161
Plazynski, M. 263–4
Pohl, G. *et al.* 185
Pollo, G. 12, 96–7
Pomfret, J. 28, 146
Pop de Popa, I. 303
Pope John Paul II 70–1, 157, 244, 250, 255, 313–14
popiwek 269
Popov, D. 133
Portes, R. 180, 394
powiats (Poland) 253
Prague Spring 167–8
Priewe, J. 405
principal-agent problem 401
principle of differentiation (EU) 21, 50, 59, 123, 169, 213, 257, 314, 360
private ownership funds (Romania) 53, 327, 330
privatization *see the relevant sections of individual chapters and summaries*
employee buy-outs 398–400, 404; mass (voucher) 400–2; restitution 402–4; sales 397–8
privatization (German reunification) 403–7
privatization terms: insider 398–400; investment funds 401; large 383–4, 395; management–property rights (theory) 395; small 384, 395
Protection of the Republic (Law of, Slovakia) 353
pyramid schemes 7–10, 77–85, 91–2, 96, 297

Quad Coalition 173, 177–8
Quesku, P. 69
queues (theory) 386

Radio Maryja (Poland) 249–50
Ramizi, Z. 73
Rapacki, R. 270
Rapid Reaction Force 219
Rausser, G. 396
reconciliation agreement between the Czech Republic and Germany 161–2
reconciliation and friendship treaty between Hungary and Romania 207, 298
Red Army faction 403
regies autonomes (autonomous bodies of national interest, Romania) 54–5, 327, 329, 331, 334
Remes, D. 309
Remias, R. 354
rent-seeking 396
repressed inflation 384
revitalization of enterprises (Slovakia) 367
revitalization programme (Czech Republic) 32, 191–3
Rizov, M. *et al.* 59, 346
Robinson, A. 29, 118, 147–8, 152, 235
Rohwedder, D. 403
Roma *see* Gypsies
Roman, P. 40–2, 44, 49, 300–3, 308, 312–13, 318, 321
Ronnas, P. 342
Ruli, G. 6, 71
Ruml, J. 163, 170
Rusnok, J. 178
Russian financial crisis *see* Asian/Russian financial crisis

Sachs, J. 269, 274, 383–6, 389–90
Safov, S. 21, 121
Sarkander, J. 157
Schenk, J. 354
Schism (1054) 313
Schnytzer, A. 101
Schröder, G. 162
Schuster, R. 60, 350, 358–60
Schwartz, A. 183
securitate 300, 336
Sedivy, J. 164
sejmiks 253
Selami, E. 7, 72
Selfo, H. 76
self-privatization 226
sequencing 391
Severin, A. 44, 304, 307
shadow economy *see* black market
Shehu, T. 91
Shik (Albania) 88–9
shock therapy *see* big bang/shock therapy
Shuleva, L. 131
Shyti, A. 90
Sigurimi 72
Simeon II 22, 117, 121–132
simplified privatization 227
Sinn, H.-W. 406
Sitek, J. 353
Sjöberg, Ö. 13, 101, 114
Skalicky, J. 163–5
Sladek, M. 159, 164–6
Slavkovska, E. 353
Slomka, A. 246, 250
Slota, J. 352, 358, 360

Smith, H. 87
Smy, L. 351
social capital 393
social ownership 395
social pact (Bulgaria) 136
social safety net 385
social stability pact (Romania) 321
Sofiyansky, S. 21, 24, 121, 139
soft budget constraint 384, 386–7, 395
Solana, J. 49, 305
Sorm, V. and Terrell, K. 186
Spidla, V. 178
Spineanu, U. 304
Spolar, C. 84, 209, 243
spontaneous privatization 225, 346, 396
Stability Pact *see* European Stability Pact
Stability Pact for South-Eastern Europe (Bulgaria) 100, 130, 322
stabilization (theory) 384–5
stabilization fund 270
stagflation 387
State Planning Commission (Romania) 322
Status Law 220
Steinhoff, J. 247
Stepan, M. 157
Stephen (King) 215
Stiglitz, J. 183–4, 402
Stoica, I. 297, 319
Stolojan, T. 41–2, 318
Stoyanov, P. 19–21, 117–21, 124, 129, 131
strategic investors (owners) 397–8
Strategy for Poland 269
Suchman, J. 206–7
Suchocka, H. 247
Sudeten Germans 31, 157, 161–2, 189, 200
Suranyi, G. 206, 219
Surdu, V. 303
Surjan, L. 203
Svoboda, C. 167, 169, 173, 177
Swain, N. 200, 236, 380
Swartzberg, T. 184
Swiatkowski Cannon, L. 282
Swinnen, J. 16, 57, 110, 152, 200, 237, 278, 341
Switon, K. 250–1, 255
Sylvester II (Pope) 215
Szabo, J. 207, 212
Szmajdinski, A. 245

Tabara, V. 299, 305, 308
Tanner, M. 319
Tariceanu, C. 304
Temelin nuclear power station 172
Teplik, T. 162
Teta, P. 95
'Thank you, now leave' movement 31–2, 170
Thurmer, G. 204
Toekes, L. 299
Tomaszewski, J. 247, 256–7, 266
Tomov, A. 121
Torgyan, J. 203, 209, 212, 219–20
Toscik affair 207, 211, 225
Tosks 83
Tosovsky, J. 31, 164, 167, 171–2
Toth, R. 364
township–village enterprises 391
trade unions 119–20, 204
Traynor, I. 166
Treuhandanstalt 398, 403–6
Troev, T. 152–3
Tsang, S. 387. 389
Tsochev, K. 117
Tsonev, Y. 124
Tudor, V. 51, 302–3, 311, 313, 318–19
Tuma, Z. 173
tunnelling 183–4, 401–2
Tusk, D. 263–4

Ukrainianization 394

Vacaroiu, N. 42, 301
Varga, L. 219
Vasaryova, M. 360
Vasile, R. 45–8, 308–12, 314–16
Vasilev, N. 129, 131, 133
Velchev, M. 129, 131–3
velvet revolution 156
Verdet, I. 303
Verheugen, G. 214
Vetchy, V. 167
Videnov, Z. 19, 23, 116–17, 138
Vlach, J. 158
Voiculescu, D. 303
voivodships (Poland) 249, 253

Wagner, J. 161–3
Wagstyl, S. (CR, P, R) 165, 254, 276, 318
Walesa, L. 36–7, 240–1, 248, 252, 260–1, 280
Warsaw Pact (1955) 167
Wasacz, E. 247
Wasilewska-Trenkner, H. 268
Weiss, P. 352–3
Weitzman, M. and Xu, C. 391

Wienert, H. 226
wild spontaneous privatization 396
Wolfensohn, J. 184, 402
Wolinska-Brus, H. 255
Woo, W. 396, 390
workers' councils (Poland) 38
WTO (World Trade Organization) 13, 103, 115
Wyzan, M. 26, 159, 142–3

Xhuveli, L. 11, 92

Yeltsin, B. 167

Zantovsky, M. 162–3
Zieleniec, J. 163
Zeman, M. 31–2, 158–60, 162, 166–70, 173–4, 178, 189, 193
Zhelev, Z. 19–20, 117–19, 153
Zhivkov, T. 122
Zhulali, S. 93
Zielinski, L. 246
Zogaj, P. 75
Zog (King) 71, 90
zunk (bad loan) bonds 23, 26–7, 136–7, 144
Zwack, P. 202